Opel Astra
Service and Repair Manual

Steve Rendle

(3156/1832 - 384 - 9AC6)

Models covered

Opel Astra models with petrol engines, including special/limited editions
Saloon, Hatchback, Estate and Van

1389 cc, 1598 cc, 1796 cc & 1998 cc (SOHC and DOHC)

Covers major mechanical features of 1993-on Convertible
Does not cover Diesel engine models
For information on 1992 Convertible, see manual no. 3196

© J H Haynes & Co. Ltd. 1999

A book in the **Haynes Service and Repair Manual Series**

ISBN **978 1 78521 331 1**

British Library Cataloguing in Publication Data
A catalogue record for this book is available from the British Library.

J H Haynes & Co. Ltd.
Haynes North America, Inc

www.haynes.com

Contents

LIVING WITH YOUR VAUXHALL ASTRA

ROUTINE MAINTENANCE

Routine Maintenance and Servicing

Contents

REPAIRS AND OVERHAUL

Engine and Associated Systems

Transmission

Brakes and Suspension

Body Equipment

Wiring Diagrams

REFERENCE

Index

The Astra covered by this manual was first introduced to the European market in Autumn 1991, and was discontinued in February 1998. Although mechanically there is a fundamental similarity to the previous Astra/Belmont/Kadett models, the later version is much improved and refined in all respects. This manual covers models fitted with petrol engines, but other models in the range were available with diesel engines.

Five petrol engines were available in the Astra range, although not all of the engines were available in all markets. The engines available were 1.4, 1.6, 1.8 and 2.0 litre single overhead camshaft (SOHC) versions, and 1.4, 1.6, 1.8 and 2.0 litre double overhead camshaft (DOHC) versions. All of the engines use fuel injection, and are fitted with a range of emission control systems, with the exception of a 1.4 litre carburettor engine available in certain markets. All the engines are of a well-proven design and, provided regular maintenance is carried out, are unlikely to give trouble.

The Astra was available in 4-door Saloon, 3- and 5-door Hatchback, Estate and Van bodystyles (although the GSi model was only available in Hatchback form), with a wide range of fittings and interior trim depending on the model specification.

Fully-independent front suspension is fitted, with the components attached to a subframe assembly; the rear suspension is semi-independent, with a torsion beam and trailing arms.

A five-speed manual gearbox is fitted as standard to all models, and four-speed electronically-controlled automatic transmission is available as an option on certain models.

A wide range of standard and optional equipment is available within the Astra range to suit most tastes, including an anti-lock braking system.

For the home mechanic, the Astra is a straightforward vehicle to maintain, and most of the items requiring frequent attention are easily accessible.

Astra GSi 16V

Astra LS Estate

The Vauxhall Astra Team

Haynes manuals are produced by dedicated and enthusiastic people working in close co-operation. The team responsible for the creation of this book included:

Author	Steve Rendle
Sub-editor	Sophie Yar
Editor & Page Make-up	Steve Churchill
Workshop manager	Paul Buckland
Photo Scans	Steve Tanswell John Martin
Cover illustration & Line Art	Roger Healing

We hope the book will help you to get the maximum enjoyment from your car. By carrying out routine maintenance as described you will ensure your car's reliability and preserve its resale value.

Your Vauxhall Astra Manual

The aim of this manual is to help you get the best value from your vehicle. It can do so in several ways. It can help you decide what work must be done (even should you choose to get it done by a garage). It will also provide information on routine maintenance and servicing, and give a logical course of action and diagnosis when random faults occur. However, it is hoped that you will use the manual by tackling the work yourself. On simpler jobs it may even be quicker than booking the car into a garage and going there twice, to leave and collect it. Perhaps most important, a lot of money can be saved by avoiding the costs a garage must charge to cover its labour and overheads.

The manual has drawings and descriptions to show the function of the various components so that their layout can be understood. Tasks are described and photographed in a clear step-by-step sequence.

Acknowledgements

Thanks are due to Champion Spark Plug who supplied the illustrations showing spark plug conditions. Certain illustrations are the copyright of Vauxhall Motors Ltd, and are used with their permission. Thanks are also due to Draper Tools Limited, who provided some of the workshop tools, and to all those people at Sparkford who helped in the production of this manual.

We take great pride in the accuracy of information given in this manual, but vehicle manufacturers make alterations and design changes during the production run of a particular vehicle of which they do not inform us. No liability can be accepted by the authors or publishers for loss, damage or injury caused by any errors in, or omissions from, the information given.

Working on your car can be dangerous. This page shows just some of the potential risks and hazards, with the aim of creating a safety-conscious attitude.

General hazards

Scalding

• Don't remove the radiator or expansion tank cap while the engine is hot.
• Engine oil, automatic transmission fluid or power steering fluid may also be dangerously hot if the engine has recently been running.

Burning

• Beware of burns from the exhaust system and from any part of the engine. Brake discs and drums can also be extremely hot immediately after use.

Crushing

• When working under or near a raised vehicle, always supplement the jack with axle stands, or use drive-on ramps. *Never venture under a car which is only supported by a jack.*

• Take care if loosening or tightening high-torque nuts when the vehicle is on stands. Initial loosening and final tightening should be done with the wheels on the ground.

Fire

• Fuel is highly flammable; fuel vapour is explosive.
• Don't let fuel spill onto a hot engine.
• Do not smoke or allow naked lights (including pilot lights) anywhere near a vehicle being worked on. Also beware of creating sparks (electrically or by use of tools).
• Fuel vapour is heavier than air, so don't work on the fuel system with the vehicle over an inspection pit.
• Another cause of fire is an electrical overload or short-circuit. Take care when repairing or modifying the vehicle wiring.
• Keep a fire extinguisher handy, of a type suitable for use on fuel and electrical fires.

Electric shock

• Ignition HT voltage can be dangerous, especially to people with heart problems or a pacemaker. Don't work on or near the ignition system with the engine running or the ignition switched on.

• Mains voltage is also dangerous. Make sure that any mains-operated equipment is correctly earthed. Mains power points should be protected by a residual current device (RCD) circuit breaker.

Fume or gas intoxication

• Exhaust fumes are poisonous; they often contain carbon monoxide, which is rapidly fatal if inhaled. Never run the engine in a confined space such as a garage with the doors shut.
• Fuel vapour is also poisonous, as are the vapours from some cleaning solvents and paint thinners.

Poisonous or irritant substances

• Avoid skin contact with battery acid and with any fuel, fluid or lubricant, especially antifreeze, brake hydraulic fluid and Diesel fuel. Don't syphon them by mouth. If such a substance is swallowed or gets into the eyes, seek medical advice.
• Prolonged contact with used engine oil can cause skin cancer. Wear gloves or use a barrier cream if necessary. Change out of oil-soaked clothes and do not keep oily rags in your pocket.
• Air conditioning refrigerant forms a poisonous gas if exposed to a naked flame (including a cigarette). It can also cause skin burns on contact.

Asbestos

• Asbestos dust can cause cancer if inhaled or swallowed. Asbestos may be found in gaskets and in brake and clutch linings. When dealing with such components it is safest to assume that they contain asbestos.

Special hazards

Hydrofluoric acid

• This extremely corrosive acid is formed when certain types of synthetic rubber, found in some O-rings, oil seals, fuel hoses etc, are exposed to temperatures above 400°C. The rubber changes into a charred or sticky substance containing the acid. *Once formed, the acid remains dangerous for years. If it gets onto the skin, it may be necessary to amputate the limb concerned.*
• When dealing with a vehicle which has suffered a fire, or with components salvaged from such a vehicle, wear protective gloves and discard them after use.

The battery

• Batteries contain sulphuric acid, which attacks clothing, eyes and skin. Take care when topping-up or carrying the battery.
• The hydrogen gas given off by the battery is highly explosive. Never cause a spark or allow a naked light nearby. Be careful when connecting and disconnecting battery chargers or jump leads.

Air bags

• Air bags can cause injury if they go off accidentally. Take care when removing the steering wheel and/or facia. Special storage instructions may apply.

Diesel injection equipment

• Diesel injection pumps supply fuel at very high pressure. Take care when working on the fuel injectors and fuel pipes.

⚠ *Warning: Never expose the hands, face or any other part of the body to injector spray; the fuel can penetrate the skin with potentially fatal results.*

Remember...

DO

• Do use eye protection when using power tools, and when working under the vehicle.

• Do wear gloves or use barrier cream to protect your hands when necessary.

• Do get someone to check periodically that all is well when working alone on the vehicle.

• Do keep loose clothing and long hair well out of the way of moving mechanical parts.

• Do remove rings, wristwatch etc, before working on the vehicle – especially the electrical system.

• Do ensure that any lifting or jacking equipment has a safe working load rating adequate for the job.

DON'T

• Don't attempt to lift a heavy component which may be beyond your capability – get assistance.

• Don't rush to finish a job, or take unverified short cuts.

• Don't use ill-fitting tools which may slip and cause injury.

• Don't leave tools or parts lying around where someone can trip over them. Mop up oil and fuel spills at once.

• Don't allow children or pets to play in or near a vehicle being worked on.

The following pages are intended to help in dealing with common roadside emergencies and breakdowns. You will find more detailed fault finding information at the back of the manual, and repair information in the main chapters.

If your car won't start and the starter motor doesn't turn

- ☐ If it's a model with automatic transmission, make sure the selector is in 'P' or 'N'.
- ☐ Open the bonnet and make sure that the battery terminals are clean and tight.
- ☐ Switch on the headlights and try to start the engine. If the headlights go very dim when you're trying to start, the battery is probably flat. Get out of trouble by jump starting (see next page) using a friend's car.

If your car won't start even though the starter motor turns as normal

- ☐ Is there fuel in the tank?
- ☐ Is there moisture on electrical components under the bonnet? Switch off the ignition, then wipe off any obvious dampness with a dry cloth. Spray a water-repellent aerosol product (WD-40 or equivalent) on ignition and fuel system electrical connectors like those shown in the photos. Pay special attention to the ignition coil wiring connector and HT leads.

A Check the condition and security of the battery connections.

B Check that the spark plug HT leads are securely connected by pushing them onto the ignition coil or DIS module (as applicable).

C Check that the spark plug HT leads are securely connected by pushing them onto the spark plugs.

Check that electrical connections are secure (with the ignition switched off) and spray them with a water dispersant spray like WD40 if you suspect a problem due to damp

D Check that the engine wiring harness connectors are secure (fuel injection model shown).

E Check that the fuel injector wiring is secure (where applicable – CFi model shown).

Jump starting

When jump-starting a car using a booster battery, observe the following precautions:

✔ Before connecting the booster battery, make sure that the ignition is switched off.

✔ Ensure that all electrical equipment (lights, heater, wipers, etc) is switched off.

✔ Take note of any special precautions printed on the battery case.

✔ Make sure that the booster battery is the same voltage as the discharged one in the vehicle.

✔ If the battery is being jump-started from the battery in another vehicle, the two vehicles MUST NOT TOUCH each other.

✔ Make sure that the transmission is in neutral (or PARK, in the case of automatic transmission).

1 Connect one end of the red jump lead to the positive (+) terminal of the flat battery

2 Connect the other end of the red lead to the positive (+) terminal of the booster battery.

3 Connect one end of the black jump lead to the negative (-) terminal of the booster battery

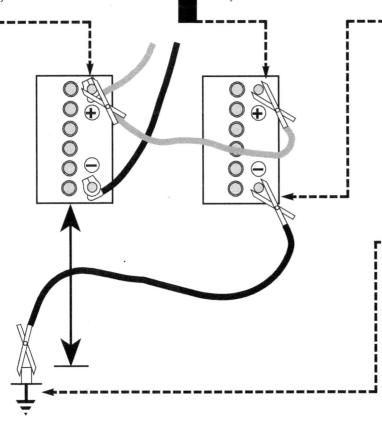

4 Connect the other end of the black jump lead to a bolt or bracket on the engine block, well away from the battery, on the vehicle to be started.

5 Make sure that the jump leads will not come into contact with the fan, drive-belts or other moving parts of the engine.

6 Start the engine using the booster battery and run it at idle speed. Switch on the lights, rear window demister and heater blower motor, then disconnect the jump leads in the reverse order of connection. Turn off the lights etc.

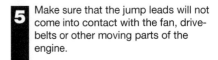

Wheel changing

Some of the details shown here will vary according to model. However, the basic principles apply to all vehicles.

 Warning: Do not change a wheel in a situation where you risk being hit by another vehicle. On busy roads, try to stop in a lay-by or a gateway. Be wary of passing traffic while changing the wheel - it is easy to become distracted by the job in hand.

Preparation

☐ When a puncture occurs, stop as soon as it is safe to do so.
☐ Park on firm level ground, if possible, and well out of the way of other traffic.
☐ Use hazard warning lights if necessary.

☐ If you have one, use a warning triangle to alert other drivers of your presence.
☐ Apply the handbrake and engage first or reverse gear (or Park on models with automatic transmission).

☐ Chock the wheel diagonally opposite the one being removed – a couple of large stones will do for this.
☐ If the ground is soft, use a flat piece of wood to spread the load under the jack.

Changing the wheel

1 Clear the boot area, and remove the carpet and spare wheel cover.

2 Remove the tool holder and unscrew the spare wheel clamp.

3 For safety, place the spare wheel under the car near the jacking point.

4 Remove the wheel trim (where fitted) and slacken each wheel bolt by half a turn.

5 Raise the jack whilst locating below the jacking point (ensure that the jack is on firm ground and located under the car correctly).

6 Turn the handle clockwise until the wheel is raised clear of the ground. Remove the bolts and lift the wheel clear.

7 Position the spare wheel and fit the bolts. Hand-tighten with the wheel brace and lower the car to the ground. Tighten the wheel bolts in the sequence shown, fit the wheel trim and secure the punctured wheel in the boot.

Finally...

☐ Remove the wheel chocks.

☐ Stow the jack and tools in the correct locations in the car.

☐ Check the tyre pressure on the wheel just fitted. If it low, or if you don't have a pressure gauge with you, drive slowly to the nearest garage and inflate the tyre to the correct pressure. Have the damaged tyre or wheel repaired or replaced, as soon as possible.

☐ Have the damaged tyre or wheel repaired as soon as possible.

Identifying leaks

Puddles on the garage floor or drive, or obvious wetness under the bonnet or underneath the car, suggest a leak that needs investigating. It can sometimes be difficult to decide where the leak is coming from, especially if the engine bay is very dirty already. Leaking oil or fluid can also be blown rearwards by the passage of air under the car, giving a false impression of where the problem lies.

 Warning: Most automotive oils and fluids are poisonous. Wash them off skin, and change out of contaminated clothing, without delay.

 The smell of a fluid leaking from the car may provide a clue to what's leaking. Some fluids are distinctively coloured. It may help to clean the car carefully and to park it over some clean paper overnight as an aid to locating the source of the leak.
Remember that some leaks may only occur while the engine is running.

Sump oil

Engine oil may leak from the drain plug...

Oil from filter

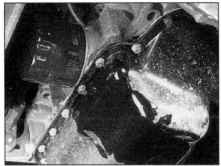

...or from the base of the oil filter.

Gearbox oil

Gearbox oil can leak from the seals at the inboard ends of the driveshafts.

Antifreeze

Leaking antifreeze often leaves a crystalline deposit like this.

Brake fluid

A leak occurring at a wheel is almost certainly brake fluid.

Power steering fluid

Power steering fluid may leak from the pipe connectors on the steering rack.

Towing

When all else fails, you may find yourself having to get a tow home – or of course you may be helping somebody else. Long-distance recovery should only be done by a garage or breakdown service. For shorter distances, DIY towing using another car is easy enough, but observe the following points:

☐ Use a proper tow-rope – they are not expensive. The vehicle being towed must display an 'ON TOW' sign in its rear window.
☐ Always turn the ignition key to the 'on' position when the vehicle is being towed, so that the steering lock is released, and that the

direction indicator and brake lights will work.
☐ Only attach the tow-rope to the towing eyes provided.
☐ Before being towed, release the handbrake and select neutral on the transmission.
☐ Note that greater-than-usual pedal pressure will be required to operate the brakes, since the vacuum servo unit is only operational with the engine running.
☐ On models with power steering, greater-than-usual steering effort will also be required.
☐ The driver of the car being towed must keep the tow-rope taut at all times to avoid snatching.

☐ Make sure that both drivers know the route before setting off.
☐ Only drive at moderate speeds and keep the distance towed to a minimum. Drive smoothly and allow plenty of time for slowing down at junctions.
☐ Never tow automatic transmission model backwards. If the transmission appears to be in working order, the vehicle can be towed for a maximum distance of 62 miles (100 km), at no more than 50 mph (80 km/h). The vehicle can be towed greater distances with the front wheel raised

Introduction

There are some very simple checks which need only take a few minutes to carry out, but which could save you a lot of inconvenience and expense.

These "Weekly checks" require no great skill or special tools, and the small amount of time they take to perform could prove to be very well spent, for example;

☐ Keeping an eye on tyre condition and pressures, will not only help to stop them wearing out prematurely, but could also save your life.

☐ Many breakdowns are caused by electrical problems. Battery-related faults are particularly common, and a quick check on a regular basis will often prevent the majority of these.

☐ If your car develops a brake fluid leak, the first time you might know about it is when your brakes don't work properly. Checking the level regularly will give advance warning of this kind of problem.

☐ If the oil or coolant levels run low, the cost of repairing any engine damage will be far greater than fixing the leak, for example.

Underbonnet check points

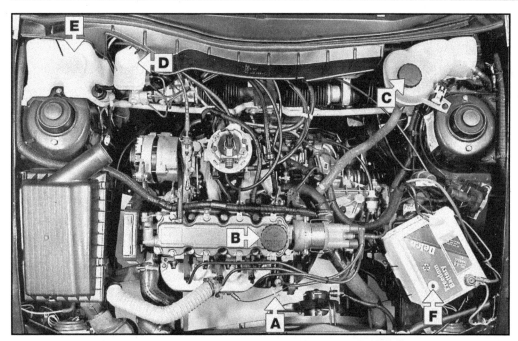

◀ **1.4 litre SOHC (C14NZ engine) model**

A *Engine oil level dipstick*
B *Engine oil filler cap*
C *Coolant expansion tank*
D *Brake fluid reservoir*
E *Washer fluid reservoir*
F *Battery*

◀ **1.6 litre SOHC (C16SE engine) model**

A *Engine oil level dipstick*
B *Engine oil filler cap*
C *Coolant expansion tank*
D *Brake fluid reservoir*
E *Washer fluid reservoir*
F *Battery*

Underbonnet check points

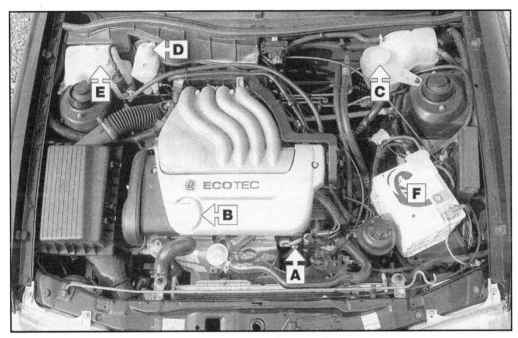

◀ 1.6 litre DOHC (X16XEL engine) model

A *Engine oil level dipstick*

B *Engine oil filler cap*

C *Coolant expansion tank*

D *Brake fluid reservoir*

E *Washer fluid reservoir*

F *Battery*

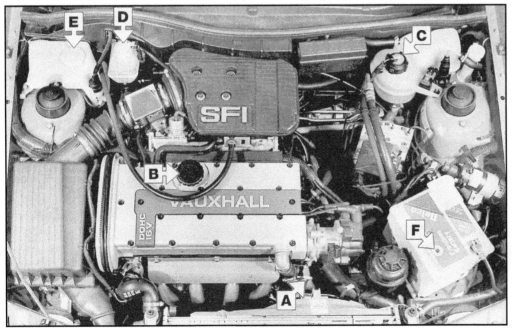

◀ 1.6 litre DOHC (C20XE engine) model

A *Engine oil level dipstick*

B *Engine oil filler cap*

C *Coolant expansion tank*

D *Brake fluid reservoir*

E *Washer fluid reservoir*

F *Battery*

Engine oil level

Before you start

✔ Make sure that your car is on level ground.
✔ Check the oil level before the car is driven, or at least 5 minutes after the engine has been switched off.

 If the oil is checked immediately after driving the vehicle, some of the oil will remain in the upper engine components, resulting in an inaccurate reading on the dipstick!

The correct oil

Modern engines place great demands on their oil. It is very important that the correct oil for your car is used (See "Lubricants and Fluids" on page 0•17).

Car Care

● If you have to add oil frequently, you should check whether you have any oil leaks. Place some clean paper under the car overnight, and check for stains in the morning. If there are no leaks, the engine may be burning oil *(see "Fault Finding")*.

● Always maintain the level between the upper and lower dipstick marks (see photo 3). If the level is too low severe engine damage may occur. Oil seal failure may result if the engine is overfilled by adding too much oil.

1 The dipstick top is often brightly coloured for easy identification (see *"Underbonnet check points"* on pages 0•10 and 0•11 for exact location). Withdraw the dipstick.

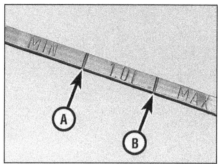

3 Note the level on the end of the dipstick, which should be between the upper (B) and lower (A) mark.

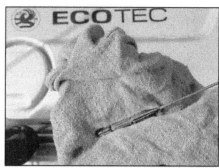

2 Using a clean rag or paper towel, wipe all oil from the dipstick. Insert the clean dipstick into the tube as far as it will go, then withdraw it again.

4 Oil is added through the filler cap. Unscrew the cap and top-up the level. A funnel may help to reduce spillage. Add the oil slowly, checking the level on the dipstick frequently. Avoid overfilling (see *"Car care"*).

Coolant level

 Warning: DO NOT attempt to remove the expansion tank pressure cap when the engine is hot, as there is a very great risk of scalding. Do not leave open containers of coolant about, as it is poisonous.

Car Care

● With a sealed-type cooling system, adding coolant should not be necessary on a regular basis. If frequent topping-up is required, it is likely there is a leak. Check the radiator, all hoses and joint faces for signs of staining or wetness, and rectify as necessary.

● It is important that antifreeze is used in the cooling system all year round, not just during the winter months. Don't top-up with water alone, as the antifreeze will become too diluted.

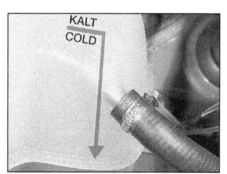

1 The coolant level varies with the temperature of the engine. When the engine is cold, the coolant level should be near the "COLD" (or "KALT") mark.

2 If topping-up is necessary, wait until the engine is **cold**. Slowly unscrew the cap to release any pressure present in the cooling system, and remove the cap.

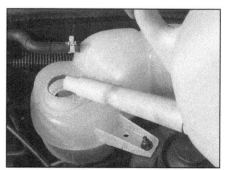

3 Add a mixture of water and antifreeze to the expansion tank until the coolant level is halfway between the level marks.

Brake fluid level

Warning:
● Brake fluid can harm your eyes and damage painted surfaces, so use extreme caution when handling and pouring it.
● Do not use fluid that has been standing open for some time, as it absorbs moisture from the air, which can cause a dangerous loss of braking effectiveness.

HAYNES HiNT
• Make sure that your car is on level ground.

• The fluid level in the reservoir will drop slightly as the brake pads wear down, but the fluid level must never be allowed to drop below the "MIN" mark.

Safety First!
● If the reservoir requires repeated topping-up this is an indication of a fluid leak somewhere in the system, which should be investigated immediately.

● If a leak is suspected, the car should not be driven until the braking system has been checked. Never take any risks where brakes are concerned.

1 The "MIN" and "MAX" marks are indicated on the reservoir. The fluid level must be kept between the marks at all times.

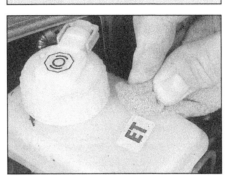

2 If topping-up is necessary, first wipe clean the area around the filler cap to prevent dirt entering the hydraulic system. Unscrew the reservoir cap.

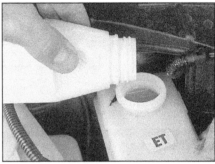

3 Carefully add fluid, taking care not to spill it onto the surrounding components. Use only the specified fluid; mixing different types can cause damage to the system. On completion, securely refit the cap and wipe away any spilt fluid.

Power steering fluid level

Before you start:
✔ Park the vehicle on level ground.
✔ Set the steering wheel straight-ahead.
✔ The engine should be turned off.

HAYNES HiNT
For the check to be accurate, the steering must not be turned once the engine has been stopped.

Safety First!
● The need for frequent topping-up indicates a leak, which should be investigated immediately.

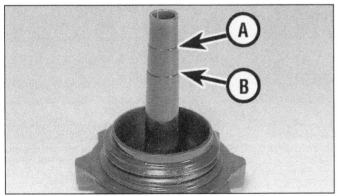

1 The reservoir is located at the front left-hand side of the engine compartment, next to the battery. The power steering fluid level is checked with a dipstick attached to the reservoir filler cap. Unscrew the filler cap from the top of the reservoir, and wipe all the fluid from the end with a clean rag or paper towel. Refit the reservoir cap, then remove it once more. Note the fluid level on the dipstick. When the engine is cold, the fluid level should be up to the lower mark on the dipstick (A). When the engine is at normal operating temperature, the fluid level should be up to the upper mark on the dipstick (B).

2 Top-up with the specified type of fluid if necessary, and securely refit the reservoir cap on completion.

Tyre condition and pressure

It is very important that tyres are in good condition, and at the correct pressure - having a tyre failure at any speed is highly dangerous. Tyre wear is influenced by driving style - harsh braking and acceleration, or fast cornering, will all produce more rapid tyre wear. As a general rule, the front tyres wear out faster than the rears. Interchanging the tyres from front to rear ("rotating" the tyres) may result in more even wear. However, if this is completely effective, you may have the expense of replacing all four tyres at once!

Remove any nails or stones embedded in the tread before they penetrate the tyre to cause deflation. If removal of a nail does reveal that the tyre has been punctured, refit the nail so that its point of penetration is marked. Then immediately change the wheel, and have the tyre repaired by a tyre dealer.

Regularly check the tyres for damage in the form of cuts or bulges, especially in the sidewalls. Periodically remove the wheels, and clean any dirt or mud from the inside and outside surfaces. Examine the wheel rims for signs of rusting, corrosion or other damage. Light alloy wheels are easily damaged by "kerbing" whilst parking; steel wheels may also become dented or buckled. A new wheel is very often the only way to overcome severe damage.

New tyres should be balanced when they are fitted, but it may become necessary to re-balance them as they wear, or if the balance weights fitted to the wheel rim should fall off. Unbalanced tyres will wear more quickly, as will the steering and suspension components. Wheel imbalance is normally signified by vibration, particularly at a certain speed (typically around 50 mph). If this vibration is felt only through the steering, then it is likely that just the front wheels need balancing. If, however, the vibration is felt through the whole car, the rear wheels could be out of balance. Wheel balancing should be carried out by a tyre dealer or garage.

1 *Tread Depth - visual check*
The original tyres have tread wear safety bands (B), which will appear when the tread depth reaches approximately 1.6 mm. The band positions are indicated by a triangular mark on the tyre sidewall (A).

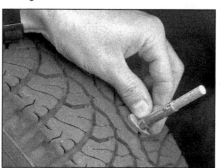

2 *Tread Depth - manual check*
Alternatively, tread wear can be monitored with a simple, inexpensive device known as a tread depth indicator gauge.

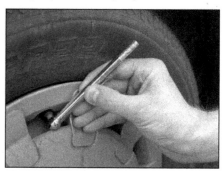

3 *Tyre Pressure Check*
Check the tyre pressures regularly with the tyres cold. Do not adjust the tyre pressures immediately after the vehicle has been used, or an inaccurate setting will result. Tyre pressures are shown on page 0•17.

Tyre tread wear patterns

Shoulder Wear

Underinflation (wear on both sides)
Under-inflation will cause overheating of the tyre, because the tyre will flex too much, and the tread will not sit correctly on the road surface. This will cause a loss of grip and excessive wear, not to mention the danger of sudden tyre failure due to heat build-up.
Check and adjust pressures
Incorrect wheel camber (wear on one side)
Repair or renew suspension parts
Hard cornering
Reduce speed!

Centre Wear

Overinflation
Over-inflation will cause rapid wear of the centre part of the tyre tread, coupled with reduced grip, harsher ride, and the danger of shock damage occurring in the tyre casing.
Check and adjust pressures

If you sometimes have to inflate your car's tyres to the higher pressures specified for maximum load or sustained high speed, don't forget to reduce the pressures to normal afterwards.

Uneven Wear

Front tyres may wear unevenly as a result of wheel misalignment. Most tyre dealers and garages can check and adjust the wheel alignment (or "tracking") for a modest charge.
Incorrect camber or castor
Repair or renew suspension parts
Malfunctioning suspension
Repair or renew suspension parts
Unbalanced wheel
Balance tyres
Incorrect toe setting
Adjust front wheel alignment
Note: *The feathered edge of the tread which typifies toe wear is best checked by feel.*

Battery

Caution: Before carrying out any work on the vehicle battery, read the precautions given in "Safety first" at the start of this manual.

✔ Make sure that the battery tray is in good condition, and that the clamp is tight. Corrosion on the tray, retaining clamp and the battery itself can be removed with a solution of water and baking soda. Thoroughly rinse all cleaned areas with water. Any metal parts damaged by corrosion should be covered with a zinc-based primer, then painted.

✔ Periodically (approximately every three months), check the charge condition of the battery as described in Chapter 5A.

✔ If the battery is flat, and you need to jump start your vehicle, see **Roadside Repairs**.

1 The battery is located at the front left-hand corner of the engine compartment.

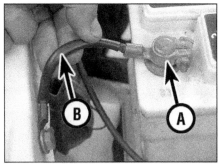

2 Check the tightness of battery clamps (A) to ensure good electrical connections. You should not be able to move them. Also check each cable (B) for cracks and frayed conductors.

HAYNES HiNT

Battery corrosion can be kept to a minimum by applying a layer of petroleum jelly to the clamps and terminals after they are reconnected.

3 If corrosion (white, fluffy deposits) is evident, remove the cables from the battery terminals, clean them with a small wire brush, then refit them. Automotive stores sell a tool for cleaning the battery post . . .

4 . . . as well as the battery cable clamps

Electrical systems

✔ Check all external lights and the horn. Refer to the appropriate Sections of Chapter 12 for details if any of the circuits are found to be inoperative.

✔ Visually check all accessible wiring connectors, harnesses and retaining clips for security, and for signs of chafing or damage.

HAYNES HiNT *If you need to check your brake lights and indicators unaided, back up to a wall or garage door and operate the lights. The reflected light should show if they are working properly.*

1 If a single indicator light, brake light or headlight has failed, it is likely that a bulb has blown and will need to be replaced. Refer to Chapter 12 for details. If both brake lights have failed, it is possible that the brake light switch operated by the brake pedal has failed. Refer to Chapter 9 for details.

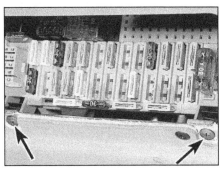

2 If more than one indicator light or tail light has failed it is likely that either a fuse has blown or that there is a fault in the circuit (see Chapter 12). The main fuses are in the fusebox under the lower driver's side of the facia. For access to the fuses, pull off the fusebox cover. The circuits protected by fuses are marked on a sticker on the fusebox cover.

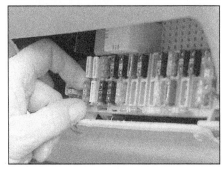

3 To replace a blown fuse, remove it, where applicable, using the plastic tool provided. Fit a new fuse of the same rating, available from car accessory shops. It is important that you find the reason that the fuse blew (see *"Electrical fault finding"* in Chapter 12).

Screen washer fluid level

Screenwash additives not only keep the winscreen clean during foul weather, they also prevent the washer system freezing in cold weather - which is when you are likely to need it most. Don't top up using plain water as the screenwash will become too diluted, and will freeze during cold weather. *On no account use coolant antifreeze in the washer system - this could discolour or damage paintwork.*

1 The screenwash fluid reservoir is located at the rear right-hand corner of the engine compartment.

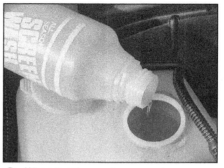

2 When topping-up the reservoir, a screen-wash additive should be added in the quantities recommended on the bottle.

Wiper blades

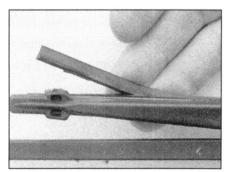

1 Check the condition of the wiper blades; if they are cracked or show any signs of deterioration, or if the glass swept area is smeared, renew them. For maximum clarity of vision, wiper blades should be renewed annually, as a matter of course.

2 To remove a windscreen wiper blade, pull the arm fully away from the screen until it locks. Swivel the blade through 90°, press the locking tab with your fingers, and slide the blade out of the hooked end of the arm.

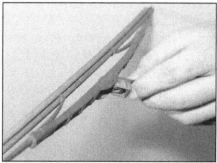

3 Where applicable, don't forget to check the tailgate wiper blade as well. To remove the blade, depress the retaining tab and slide the blade out of the hooked end of the arm.

Lubricants and fluids

Engine	Multigrade engine oil, viscosity SAE 10W/40, 15W/40, 15W/50, or 20W/50, to API SH or SJ *(Duckhams QXR Premium Petrol Engine Oil, or Duckhams Hypergrade Petrol Engine Oil)*
Cooling system	Ethylene glycol-based antifreeze *(Duckhams Antifreeze and Summer Coolant)*
Manual transmission	Gear oil, viscosity SAE 80 EP *(Duckhams Hypoid Gear Oil 80W GL-4)*
Automatic transmission	Dexron II type ATF *(Duckhams ATF Autotrans III)*
Braking system	Hydraulic fluid to SAE J1703F or DOT 4 *(Duckhams Universal Brake and Clutch Fluid)*
Power steering reservoir	Dexron II type ATF *(Duckhams ATF Autotrans III)*

Choosing your engine oil

Engines need oil, not only to lubricate moving parts and minimise wear, but also to maximise power output and to improve fuel economy. By introducing a simplified and improved range of engine oils, Duckhams has taken away the confusion and made it easier for you to choose the right oil for your engine.

HOW ENGINE OIL WORKS

• *Beating friction*

Without oil, the moving surfaces inside your engine will rub together, heat up and melt, quickly causing the engine to seize. Engine oil creates a film which separates these moving parts, preventing wear and heat build-up.

• *Cooling hot-spots*

Temperatures inside the engine can exceed 1000° C. The engine oil circulates and acts as a coolant, transferring heat from the hot-spots to the sump.

• *Cleaning the engine internally*

Good quality engine oils clean the inside of your engine, collecting and dispersing combustion deposits and controlling them until they are trapped by the oil filter or flushed out at oil change.

OIL CARE - FOLLOW THE CODE

To handle and dispose of used engine oil safely, always:

OIL CARE
0800 66 33 66

- *Avoid skin contact with used engine oil. Repeated or prolonged contact can be harmful.*
- *Dispose of used oil and empty packs in a responsible manner in an authorised disposal site. Call 0800 663366 to find the one nearest to you. Never tip oil down drains or onto the ground.*

DUCKHAMS ENGINE OILS

For the driver who demands a premium quality oil for complete reassurance, we recommend synthetic formula **Duckhams QXR Premium Engine Oils.**
For the driver who requires a straight-forward quality engine oil, we recommend **Duckhams Hypergrade Engine Oils.**

For further information and advice, call the Duckhams UK Helpline on 0800 212988.

Tyre pressures (cold)

	Front	Rear
Saloon and Convertible:		
1.4 and 1.6 litre SOHC engines	2.0 bars (29 psi)	1.7 bars (24 psi)
1.6 and 1.8 litre SOHC engines	2.2 bars (32 psi)	1.9 bars (27 psi)
1.8 DOHC engine and all 2.0 litre engines	2.4 bars (35 psi)	2.1 bars (30 psi)
Estate and Van:		
1.4 litre engine and 1.6 litre engines (except C 16 SE)	2.0 bars (29 psi)	1.8 bars (26 psi)
C 16 SE engines and 1.8 litre SOHC engines	2.2 bars (32 psi)	2.0 bars (29 psi)
1.8 DOHC engine and all 2.0 litre engines	2.2 bars (35 psi)	2.0 bars (29 psi)

Note: *The pressures quoted are for a normal load (up to 3 passengers). For full load pressures, consult your handbook or a Vauxhall/Opel dealer.*

Note: *Pressures given here are a guide only, and apply to original-equipment tyres – the recommended pressures may vary if any other make or type of tyre is fitted; check with the vehicle handbook, or the tyre manufacturer or supplier for latest recommendations.*

Notes

Chapter 1
Routine maintenance and servicing

Contents

Degrees of difficulty

Easy, suitable for novice with little experience	**Fairly easy,** suitable for beginner with some experience	**Fairly difficult,** suitable for competent DIY mechanic	**Difficult,** suitable for experienced DIY mechanic	**Very difficult,** suitable for expert DIY or professional

Lubricants and fluids . . . . Refer to end of *"Weekly Checks"* on page 0•17

Capacities

Engine oil
Capacity (including filter):
1.4 and 1.6 litre engines	3.5 litres
1.8 and 2.0 litre engines (except engines with two-piece sump)	4.5 litres
Engines with two-piece sump	5.0 litres
Difference between MAX and MIN dipstick marks (all models)	1.0 litre

Cooling system

	Manual transmission	Automatic transmission
All 1.4 litre engines	5.8 litres	5.7 litres
1.6 litre SOHC engines	5.6 litres	5.5 litres (except C 16 SE engines)
		6.3 litres (C 16 SE engines)
1.6 litre DOHC engines	6.0 litres	5.9 litres
1.8 litre engines	6.9 litres	N/A
2.0 litre SOHC engines	6.5 litres	N/A
2.0 litre DOHC engines	6.9 litres	N/A

Fuel tank
Saloon and Hatchback models	52.0 litres
Estate and Van models	50.0 litres

Manual transmission*
F10 and F13	1.6 litres
F15	1.8 litres
F16, F18, F18+ and F20	1.9 litres

Automatic transmission**

	Drain and refill	From dry
AF13	3.0 to 3.5 litres (approx.)	5.0 litres (approx.)
AF20	3.0 to 3.5 litres (approx.)	7.0 litres (approx.)

Power steering fluid reservoir . . . . 1.0 litre

Washer reservoirs
Windscreen and tailgate	2.3 litres
Headlamp (if fitted)	5.0 litres

*See Chapter 7A Specifications for details of transmission codes
**See Chapter 7B Specifications for details of transmission codes

Cooling system

Antifreeze mixtures (antifreeze to specification GME L 6)	Antifreeze	Water
Protection to –10°C	20%	80%
Protection to –20°C	34%	66%
Protection to –30°C	44%	56%
Protection to –40°C	52%	48%

Note: *Refer to antifreeze manufacturer for latest recommendations.*

Fuel system

Idle speed
Note: *Idle speed adjustment is not possible on models with fuel injection. Details shown for information only. For further details refer to Chapter 4A or 4B, as applicable.*

14 NV engines	900 to 950 rpm
14 SE engines	820 to 980 rpm
C 14 NZ and X 14 NZ engines	830 to 990 rpm
X 14 XE engines:	
Manual transmission models	820 to 980 rpm
Automatic transmission models	720 to 880 rpm
C 14 SE engines	820 to 980 rpm
C 16 NZ engines	830 to 990 rpm
C 16 SE engines	820 to 980 rpm
X 16 SZ and X 16 SZR engines:	
Manual transmission models	770 to 930 rpm
Automatic transmission models	750 to 910 rpm
X 16 XE and X 16 XEL engines	770 to 930 rpm
C 18 NZ:	
Manual transmission models	820 to 980 rpm
Automatic saloon models	750 to 910 rpm
Automatic estate models	650 to 810 rpm
1.8 and 2.0 litre DOHC engines	670 to 1030 rpm

Fuel system (continued)

Idle mixture CO content
Carburettor models . . . . 0.5% or less
Fuel injection engines (all models) . . . . 0.3% or less

Ignition system

Ignition timing (stroboscopic, at idle speed, with vacuum hose disconnected):
Carburettor engines . . . . 5° BTDC
Fuel-injection engines . . . . Controlled by electronic control unit – no adjustment possible

Spark plugs	Type	Electrode gap
14 NV, C 14 NZ, C 14 SE and 14 SE engines:		
16 mm across plug flats	Bosch FR 91 X	Not adjustable
21 mm across plug flats	Bosch WR 8 D+	0.8 mm
X 14 NZ engines	Bosch FR 78 X	Not adjustable
X 14 XE engines	Bosch FLR 8 LD+U	1.0 mm
C 16 SE, X 16 SZ and X 16 SZR engines	Bosch FR 91 X	Not adjustable
C 16 NZ engines:		
16 mm across plug flats	Bosch FR 91 X	Not adjustable
21 mm across plug flats	Bosch WR 8 D+	0.8 mm
X 16 XEL engines	Bosch FLR 8 LD+U	1.0 mm
C 18 NZ engines:		
16 mm across plug flats	Bosch FR 91 X	Not adjustable
21 mm across plug flats	Bosch WR 8 D+	0.8 mm
C 18 XE, C 18 XEL and X 18 XE engines	Bosch FLR 8 LD+U	1.0 mm
C 20 NE engines:		
16 mm across plug flats	Bosch FR 91 X	Not adjustable
21 mm across plug flats	Bosch WR 8 D+	0.8 mm
C 20 XE and X 20 XEV engines	Bosch FLR 8 LD+U	1.0 mm

Clutch

Clutch pedal travel
Right-hand-drive models . . . . 134 to 141 mm
Left-hand -drive models . . . . 125 to 132 mm

Braking system

Minimum front brake pad lining thickness (including backing plate)
All models . . . . 7.0 mm

Minimum rear brake pad lining thickness (including backing plate)
All models . . . . 7.0 mm

Minimum rear brake shoe lining thickness
All models . . . . 0.5 mm above rivet heads

Suspension and steering

Power steering pump drivebelt deflection
All models . . . . 10.0 mm

Electrical system

Alternator drivebelt deflection
All models . . . . 10.0 mm

Torque wrench settings	Nm	lbf ft
Alternator mounting nuts and bolts:		
Alternator to bracket (M8)	30	22
Alternator to bracket (M10)	40	29
Engine oil drain plug	55	41
Power steering pump mounting bolts – 1.8 and 2.0 litre engine models:		
Bolts 'A' and 'C' (see illustration 17.19)	25	18
Bolts 'B' (see illustration 17.19)	40	30
Roadwheel bolts	110	81
Spark plugs	25	18

The maintenance intervals in this manual are provided with the assumption that you, not the dealer, will be carrying out the work. These are the minimum maintenance intervals recommended by the manufacturer for vehicles driven daily. If you wish to keep your vehicle in peak condition at all times, you may wish to perform some of these procedures more often. We encourage frequent maintenance, because it enhances the efficiency, performance and resale value of your vehicle.

If the vehicle is driven in dusty areas, used to tow a trailer, or driven frequently at slow speeds (idling in traffic) or on short journeys, more frequent maintenance intervals are recommended. Opel recommend that the service intervals are halved for vehicles that are used under these conditions.

When the vehicle is new, it should be serviced by a factory-authorised dealer service department, to preserve the factory warranty.

Every 250 miles (400 km) or weekly
☐ Refer to *"Weekly checks"*

Every 9000 miles (15 000 km) or 12 months - whichever comes first
☐ Renew the engine oil and oil filter (Section 3).
☐ Check all hoses and other components for fluid leaks (Section 4).
☐ Check the steering and suspension components (Section 5).
☐ Check the condition of the driveshaft rubber gaiters (Section 6).
☐ Check the automatic transmission fluid level (where applicable) (Section 7).
☐ Check the radiator for blockage (e.g. dead insects) and clean as necessary (Section 8).
☐ Check and adjust the idle speed and mixture (if applicable) (Section 9).
☐ Check the exhaust system for corrosion, leaks and security (Section 10).
☐ Check all wiring for condition and security (Section 11).
☐ Check and adjust the ignition timing (where applicable) (Section 12).
☐ Renew the brake fluid (Section 13).
☐ Check the brake pad friction material for wear (Section 14).
☐ Check the handbrake linkage (Section 15).
☐ Check the rear brake pressure-regulating valve adjustment (Estate and Van models) (Section 16)
☐ Check the auxiliary drivebelt(s)(Section 17).
☐ Check the rear suspension level control system height, if fitted (Section 18).
☐ Check the condition of the bodywork (Section 19).
☐ Lubricate all locks and hinges (Section 20).
☐ Check the headlamp alignment (Section 21).
☐ Renew the pollen filter (Section 22)
☐ Replace the battery in the door lock key (if applicable) (Section 23).
☐ Carry out a road test (Section 24).
Note: *Vauxhall/Opel specify that an Exhaust Emissions Test should be carried out at least annually. However, this requires special equipment, and is performed as part of the MOT test.*

Every 18 000 miles (30 000 km) or 2 years - whichever comes first
In addition to the items in the 9000 mile (15 000 km) service, carry out the following:
☐ Renew the coolant (Section 25).
☐ Renew the air cleaner element (Section 26).
☐ Renew the fuel filter (Section 27).
☐ Renew the spark plugs (SOHC engines) (Section 28).
☐ Check the condition of the distributor cap (where applicable) and HT leads (Section 29).
☐ Check the clutch cable adjustment (Section 30).
☐ Check the manual transmission oil level (Section 31).
☐ Check the operation of the automatic transmission (Section 32).
☐ Check the rear brake shoes for wear – where applicable (Section 33).
☐ Check the condition and operation of the seat belts (Section 34).

Every 36 000 miles (60 000 km) or 4 years - whichever comes first
In addition to the items in the 9000 mile (15 000 km) service, and 18 000 mile (30 000 km) service, carry out the following:
☐ Renew the timing belt (Section 35)*.
☐ Renew the spark plugs (DOHC models only) (Section 36).
☐ Renew the automatic transmission fluid (Section 37)**.
* **Note:** *Vauxhall/Opel recommend the following timing belt renewal intervals:*
  a) *Models up to 1995 – every 4 years or 36 000 miles, whichever comes first.*
  b) *Models from 1995 to 1997 – every 4 years or 40 000 miles, whichever comes first.*
  c) *Models from 1997 – every 8 years or 80 000 miles, whichever comes first.*
It is up to the individual owner to decide on when to renew the timing belt, but it is strongly recommended that the interval of every 4 years or 36 000 miles is applied to all models, bearing in mind the possible consequences of timing belt failure. On 'Ecotec' type engines (see Chapter 2B 'Specifications'), it is strongly recommended that the timing belt tensioner and idler pulleys are also renewed whenever the timing belt is renewed.
** **Note:** *The manufacturers specify that fluid renewal is only required at the recommended intervals if the vehicle is used for heavy-duty work (e.g. taxi work, caravan/trailer towing, mostly short-distance, stop-start city driving). No renewal intervals are specified for vehicles under normal usage conditions. It is up to the individual owner to decide whether to renew the transmission fluid.*

Underbonnet view (airbox removed) of a 1.4 litre SOHC (C 14 NZ engine) model

1 VIN plate
2 Air cleaner casing
3 Suspension strut top cover
4 Washer fluid reservoir
5 Brake fluid reservoir
6 Alternator
7 Throttle cable
8 Tie-rods
9 Fuel injection unit
10 Coolant expansion tank
11 Clutch cable
12 Ignition coil
13 Battery positive lead
14 Battery negative lead
15 Battery condition indicator
16 Distributor
17 Radiator
18 Cooling fan motor
19 Engine oil level dipstick
20 Engine oil filler cap
21 Oxygen sensor
22 Air cleaner hot air tube

Underbonnet view of a 1.6 litre SOHC (C 16 SE engine) model

1 VIN plate
2 Air cleaner casing
3 Suspension strut top cover
4 Washer fluid reservoir
5 Brake fluid reservoir
6 Throttle body
7 Inlet manifold
8 Tie-rods
9 Throttle cable
10 Coolant expansion tank
11 Clutch cable
12 Battery positive lead
13 Battery negative lead
14 Battery condition indicator
15 Power steering fluid
    reservoir
16 Ignition coil
17 Radiator
18 Cooling fan motor
19 Engine oil level dipstick
20 Engine oil filler cap
21 Fuel injectors
22 Fuel rail

Underbonnet view of a 1.6 litre DOHC (X 16 XEL engine) models

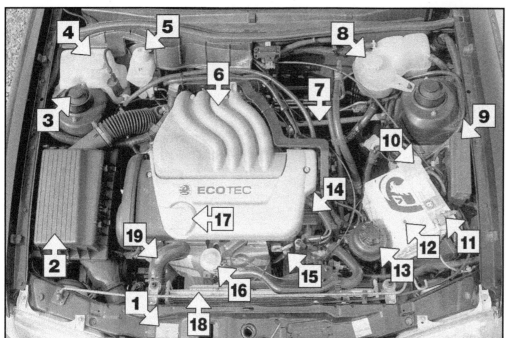

1　VIN plate
2　Air cleaner casing
3　Suspension strut top cover
4　Washer fluid reservoir
5　Brake fluid reservoir
6　inlet manifold
7　Tie-rod
8　Coolant expansion tank
9　Fuse/relay box
10　Battery positive lead
11　Battery negative lead
12　Battery condition indicator
13　Power steering fluid reservoir
14　DIS module
15　Engine oil level dipstick
16　Secondary air injection combination valve
17　Engine oil filler cap
18　Radiator
19　Radiator top hose

Underbonnet view of a 2.0 litre DOHC (C 20 XE engine) model

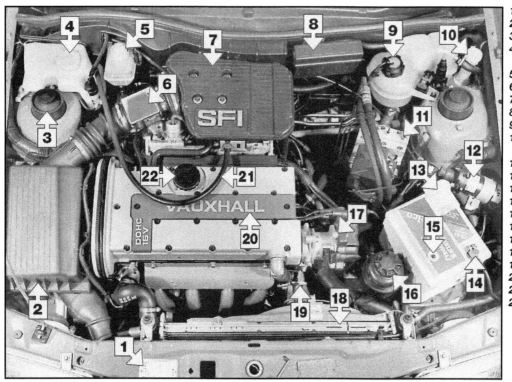

1　VIN plate
2　Air cleaner casing
3　Suspension strut top cover
4　Windscreen/tailgate washer fluid reservoir
5　Brake fluid reservoir
6　Air mass meter
7　Airbox
8　Fuse/relay box
9　Coolant expansion tank
10　Headlight washer fluid reservoir
11　ABS hydraulic modulator
12　Ignition coil
13　Battery positive lead
14　Battery negative lead
15　Battery condition indicator
16　Power steering fluid reservoir
17　Distributor
18　Radiator
19　Engine oil level dipstick
20　Spark plug cover
21　Throttle cable
22　Engine oil filler cap

Front underbody view of a 1.6 litre SOHC (C 16 SE engine) model

1 Brake caliper
2 Anti-roll bar securing nut
3 Suspension lower arm
4 Catalytic converter
5 Subframe
6 Power steering fluid cooler pipes
7 Oil filter
8 Clutch cover plate
9 Differential cover plate
10 Engine oil drain plug
11 Driveshaft
12 Rear engine/transmission mounting-to-subframe nuts
13 Exhaust sprung joint

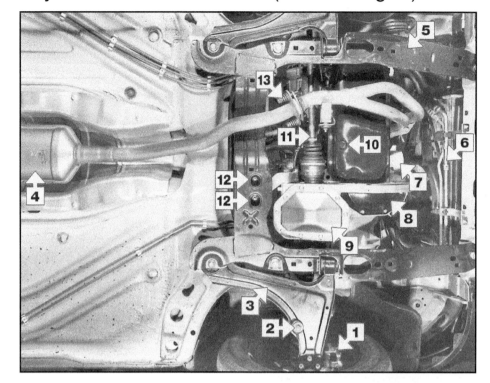

Rear underbody view

1 Shock absorber
2 Exhaust expansion box
3 Fuel tank filler pipe
4 Torsion beam
5 Fuel filter
6 Fuel tank
7 Fuel tank securing straps
8 Handbrake cable
9 Coil spring
10 Trailing arm

Maintenance procedures

1 General information

This Chapter is designed to help the home mechanic maintain his/her vehicle for safety, economy, long life and peak performance.

The Chapter contains a master maintenance schedule, followed by Sections dealing specifically with each task in the schedule. Visual checks, adjustments, component renewal and other helpful items are included. Refer to the accompanying illustrations of the engine compartment and the underside of the vehicle for the locations of the various components.

Servicing your vehicle according to the mileage/time maintenance schedule and the following Sections will provide a planned maintenance programme, which should result in a long and reliable service life. This is a comprehensive plan, so maintaining some items but not others at the specified service intervals, will not produce the same results.

As you service your vehicle, you will discover that many of the procedures can - and should - be grouped together, because of the particular procedure being performed, or because of the proximity of two otherwise-unrelated components to one another. For example, if the vehicle is raised for any reason, the exhaust can be inspected at the same time as the suspension and steering components.

The first step in this maintenance programme is to prepare yourself before the actual work begins. Read through all the Sections relevant to the work to be carried out, then make a list and gather all the parts and tools required. If a problem is come across, seek advice from a parts specialist, or a dealers service department.

2 Regular maintenance

If, from the time the vehicle is new, routine maintenance schedule is followed closely, frequent checks made of fluid levels and high-wear items, as recommended, the engine will be kept in relatively good running condition. The need for additional work will be minimised.

It is possible that there will be times when the engine is running poorly due to the lack of regular maintenance. This is even more likely if a used vehicle, which has not received regular and frequent maintenance checks, is purchased. In such cases, additional work may need to be carried out, outside of the regular maintenance intervals.

If engine wear is suspected, a compression test (refer to Chapter 2A or 2B) will provide valuable information regarding the overall performance of the main internal components. Such a test can be used as a basis to decide on the extent of the work to be carried out. If, for example, a compression test indicates serious internal engine wear, conventional maintenance as described in this Chapter will not greatly improve the performance of the engine. It may also prove a waste of time and money, unless extensive overhaul work is carried out first.

The following series of operations are those most often required to improve the performance of a generally poor-running engine:

Primary operations

a) Clean, inspect and test the battery (See "Weekly Checks")
b) Check all the engine related fluids (See "Weekly Checks")
c) Check the condition and tension of the auxiliary drivebelt (Section 17).
d) Renew the spark plugs (Section 28 or 36, as appropriate).
e) Inspect the distributor cap and rotor arm (where applicable) and HT leads (Section 29).
f) Check the condition of the air filter, and renew if necessary (Section 26).
g) Renew the fuel filter (Section 27).
h) Check the condition of all hoses, and check for fluid leaks (Section 4).
i) Check the idle speed and mixture settings, where applicable (Section 9).

If the above operations do not prove fully effective, carry out the following secondary operations:

Secondary operations

All items listed under "Primary operations", plus the following:
a) Check the charging system (Chapter 5A).
b) Check the ignition system (Chapter 5B).
c) Check the fuel system (Chapter 4A or 4B).
d) Renew the distributor cap and rotor arm – where applicable (Section 29).
e) Renew the ignition HT leads (Section 29).

Every 9000 miles (15 000 km) or 12 months

3 Engine oil and filter renewal

Note: *Always buy a sump plug washer (and plug, if possible) when buying an oil filter.*

1 Frequent oil and filter changes are the most important preventative maintenance procedures which can be undertaken by the DIY owner. As engine oil ages, it becomes diluted and contaminated, which leads to premature engine wear.
2 Before starting this procedure, gather together all the necessary tools and materials. Also make sure that you have plenty of clean rags and newspapers handy, to mop up any spills. Ideally, the engine oil should be warm, as it will drain more easily, and more built-up sludge will be removed with it. Take care not to touch the exhaust or any other hot parts of the engine when working under the vehicle. To avoid any possibility of scalding, and to protect yourself from possible skin irritants and other harmful contaminants in used engine oils, it is advisable to wear gloves when carrying out this work.
3 Access to the underside of the vehicle will be greatly improved if it can be raised on a lift, driven onto ramps, or jacked up and supported on axle stands (see "*Jacking and vehicle support*"). Whichever method is chosen, make sure that the vehicle remains level, or if it is at an angle, that the drain plug is at the lowest point. The drain plug is located in the rear face of the sump.
4 Where applicable, release the securing clips, and remove the access hatch from the engine undershield for access to the oil drain plug **(see illustration).**
5 Remove the oil filler cap from the camshaft cover (twist it through a quarter turn anti-clockwise and withdraw it).

3.4 Removing the engine undershield - DOHC models

3.7a Loosening the oil drain plug - SOHC models

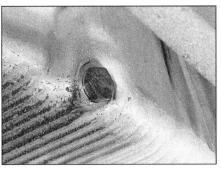

3.7b Engine oil drain plug - DOHC models

3.11 Removing the access hatch for access to the oil filter - DOHC models

6 Place a container beneath the oil drain plug at the rear of the sump.

7 Using a spanner, or preferably a socket and bar, slacken the drain plug about half a turn **(see illustrations)**. Remove the plug completely. If possible, try to keep the plug pressed into the sump while unscrewing it by hand the last couple of turns.

As the drain plug releases from the threads, move it away quickly so the stream of oil, running out of the sump, goes into the container not up your sleeve!

8 Allow ten to fifteen minutes for the oil to drain completely. It may be necessary to move the container as the oil flow slows to a trickle.

9 After all the oil has drained, wipe the drain plug and the sealing washer with a clean rag. Examine the condition of the sump plug and renew it if it shows signs of wear, especially rounding of the corners. Clean the area around the drain plug opening and refit the plug complete with the new washer. Tighten the plug securely, preferably to the specified torque using a torque wrench.

10 The oil filter is located at the front left-hand side of the engine on 1.4 and 1.6 litre engines, or on the right-hand end of the engine on 1.8 and 2.0 litre engines. On 1.8 and 2.0 litre models, improved access to the oil filter can be obtained by jacking up the front of the vehicle (if not already done) and removing the right-hand roadwheel.

11 Where applicable, release the securing clips, and remove the access hatch to the

right-hand side of the engine for access to the oil filter **(see illustration)**.

12 Move the container into position under the oil filter.

13 Use an oil filter removal tool to slacken the filter initially, then unscrew it by hand the rest of the way **(see illustrations)**. Empty the oil from the old filter into the container.

14 Use a clean rag to remove all oil, dirt and sludge from the filter sealing area on the engine. Check the old filter to make sure that the rubber sealing ring has not stuck to the engine. If it has, carefully remove it.

15 Apply a light coating of clean engine oil to the sealing ring on the new filter, then screw the filter into position on the engine. Tighten the filter firmly by hand only – **do not** use any tools.

16 Remove the old oil and all tools from under the vehicle then, where applicable, lower the vehicle to the ground.

17 Fill the engine through the filler hole in the camshaft cover, using the correct grade and type of oil (see *'Lubricants and fluids'*). Pour in half the specified quantity of oil first, then wait a few minutes for the oil to drain into the sump. Continue to add oil a small quantity at a time until the level is up to the lower mark on the dipstick. Adding approximately a further 1.0 litre will bring the level up to the upper mark on the dipstick.

18 Start the engine and run it for a few minutes, while checking for leaks around the oil filter seal and the sump drain plug. Note that there may be a delay of a few seconds before the low oil pressure warning light goes out when the engine is first started. The oil circulates through the new oil filter and the

engine oil galleries before the pressure builds up.

19 Where applicable, refit the access hatches to the engine undershield after checking for oil leaks.

20 Stop the engine and wait a few minutes for the oil to settle in the sump again. With the new oil circulated and the filter now completely full, recheck the level on the dipstick and add more oil as necessary.

21 Dispose of the old engine oil safely; do not pour it down a drain.

4 Hose and fluid leak check

1 Visually inspect the engine joint faces, gaskets and seals for any signs of water or oil leaks. Pay particular attention to the areas around the camshaft cover, cylinder head, oil filter and sump joint faces. Remember that, over a period of time, some very slight seepage from these areas is to be expected - what you are really looking for is any indication of a serious leak. Should a leak be found, renew the offending gasket or oil seal by referring to the appropriate Chapters in this manual.

2 Also check the security and condition of all the engine related pipes and hoses. Ensure that all cable ties or securing clips are in place, and in good condition. Clips that are broken or missing can lead to chafing of the hoses, pipes or wiring, which could cause more serious problems in the future.

3.13a Using an oil filter removal tool to slacken the filter - SOHC models

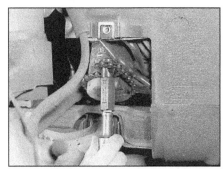

3.13b Using an oil filter removal tool to slacken the filter - DOHC models

3 Carefully check the radiator hoses and heater hoses along their entire length. Renew any hose that is cracked, swollen or deteriorated. Cracks will show up better if the hose is squeezed. Pay close attention to the clips that secure the hoses to the cooling system components. Hose clips can pinch and puncture hoses, resulting in cooling system leaks. It is always beneficial to renew hose clips whenever possible.

4 Inspect all the cooling system components (hoses, joint faces, etc.) for leaks.

A leak in the cooling system will usually show up as white or rust coloured deposits on the area adjoining the leak.

5 Where any problems are found on system components, renew the component or gasket with reference to Chapter 3.

6 Where applicable, inspect the automatic transmission fluid cooler hoses for leaks or deterioration.

7 With the vehicle raised, inspect the petrol tank and filler neck for punctures, cracks and other damage. The connection between the filler neck and tank is especially critical. Sometimes a rubber filler neck or connecting hose will leak due to loose retaining clamps or deteriorated rubber.

8 Carefully check all rubber hoses and metal fuel lines leading away from the petrol tank. Check for loose connections, deteriorated hoses, crimped lines, and other damage. Pay particular attention to the vent pipes and hoses, which often loop up around the filler neck and can become blocked or crimped. Follow the lines to the front of the vehicle, carefully inspecting them all the way. Renew damaged sections as necessary.

5.4 Checking the front wheel hub for wear

9 From within the engine compartment, check the security of all fuel hose attachments and pipe unions, and inspect the fuel hoses and vacuum hoses for kinks, chafing and deterioration.

10 Where applicable, check the condition of the power steering fluid hoses and pipes.

11 Check all brake pipes and hoses, including those running under the vehicle floor, for damage, deterioration and leaks.

5 Steering and suspension check

Front suspension and steering check

1 Raise the front of the vehicle, and securely support it on axle stands (see "*Jacking and vehicle support*").

2 Visually inspect the balljoint dust covers and the steering rack-and-pinion gaiters for splits, chafing or deterioration. Any wear of these components will cause loss of lubricant, together with dirt and water entry, resulting in rapid deterioration of the balljoints or steering gear.

3 On vehicles with power steering, check the fluid hoses for chafing or deterioration, and the pipe and hose unions for fluid leaks. Also check for signs of fluid leakage under pressure from the steering gear rubber gaiters, which would indicate failed fluid seals within the steering gear.

4 Grasp the roadwheel at the 12 o'clock and 6 o'clock positions, and try to rock it **(see illustration)**. Very slight free play may be felt, but if the movement is appreciable, further investigation is necessary to determine the source. Continue rocking the wheel while an assistant depresses the footbrake. If the movement is now eliminated or significantly reduced, it is likely that the hub bearings are at fault. If the free play is still evident with the footbrake depressed, then there is wear in the suspension joints or mountings.

5 Now grasp the wheel at the 9 o'clock and 3 o'clock positions, and try to rock it as before. Any movement felt now may again be caused by wear in the hub bearings or the steering tie-rod balljoints. If the inner or outer balljoint is worn, the visual movement will be obvious.

6 Using a large screwdriver or flat bar, check for wear in the suspension mounting bushes by levering between the relevant suspension component and its attachment point. Some movement is to be expected as the mountings are made of rubber, but excessive wear should be obvious. Also check the condition of any visible rubber bushes, looking for splits, cracks or contamination of the rubber.

7 Inspect the front suspension lower arms for distortion or damage – see Chapter 10.

8 With the car standing on its wheels, have an assistant turn the steering wheel back and forth about an eighth of a turn each way.

There should be very little, if any, lost movement between the steering wheel and roadwheels. If this is not the case, closely observe the joints and mountings previously described, but in addition, check the steering column universal joints for wear, and the rack-and-pinion steering gear itself.

Rear suspension check

9 Chock the front wheels, then jack up the rear of the vehicle and support securely on axle stands (see "*Jacking and vehicle support*").

10 Working as described previously for the front suspension, check the rear hub bearings, the suspension bushes and the shock absorber mountings for wear.

Suspension strut/ shock absorber check

Note: *Suspension struts/shock absorbers should always be renewed in pairs on the same axle.*

11 Check for any signs of fluid leakage around the suspension strut/shock absorber body, or from the rubber gaiter around the piston rod. Should any fluid be noticed, the suspension strut/shock absorber is defective internally, and should be renewed.

12 The efficiency of the suspension strut/shock absorber may be checked by bouncing the vehicle at each corner. The body will return to its normal position and stop after being depressed. If it rises and returns on a rebound, the suspension strut/shock absorber is probably suspect. Examine also the suspension strut/shock absorber upper and lower mountings for any signs of wear.

6 Driveshaft gaiter check

1 With the vehicle raised and securely supported on stands (see "*Jacking and vehicle support*"), turn the steering onto full lock, then slowly rotate the roadwheel. Inspect the condition of the outer constant velocity (CV) joint rubber gaiters, squeezing the gaiters to open out the folds **(see illustration)**. Check for signs of cracking, splits or deterioration of the

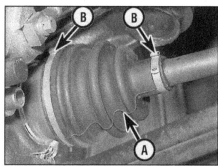

6.1 Check the condition of the driveshaft joint gaiters

A Gaiter   B Retaining clips

rubber, which may allow the grease to escape, and lead to water and grit entry into the joint. Also check the security and condition of the retaining clips. Repeat these checks on the inner CV joints. If any damage or deterioration is found, the gaiters should be renewed as described in Chapter 8.

2 At the same time, check the general condition of the CV joints themselves by first holding the driveshaft and attempting to rotate the wheel. Repeat this check by holding the inner joint and attempting to rotate the driveshaft. Any appreciable movement indicates wear in the joints, wear in the driveshaft splines, or a loose driveshaft retaining nut.

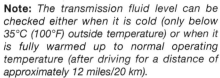

7 Automatic transmission fluid level check

Note: *The transmission fluid level can be checked either when it is cold (only below 35°C (100°F) outside temperature) or when it is fully warmed up to normal operating temperature (after driving for a distance of approximately 12 miles/20 km).*

⚠ **Warning: Be careful to keep loose clothing, long hair, etc., well clear of hot or moving components when working under the bonnet**

Transmission cold

1 Park the vehicle on level ground and apply the handbrake firmly. With the engine running at no more than idle speed and your foot firmly on the brake pedal, move the selector lever through all positions, ending in position "P". Allow the engine to idle for one minute, then check the level within two minutes.

2 With the engine still idling and position "P" still selected, open the bonnet and withdraw the transmission dipstick from the filler tube located in the front of the transmission casing, at the left-hand end of the engine **(see illustration)**.

3 Note the condition of the fluid (see below), then wipe clean the dipstick using a clean, non-fluffy rag, insert it fully back into the tube and withdraw it again.

4 The level should be up to the "MAX" mark on the "+20°C" side of the dipstick **(see illustration)**.

5 If topping-up is required, switch off the ignition and add only good quality fluid of the specified type through the filler tube. If significant amounts of fluid are being lost (carefully note the amounts being added, and how often), check the transmission for leaks and either repair the fault or take the vehicle to a Vauxhall/Opel dealer for attention.

6 When the level is correct, ensure that the dipstick is pressed firmly into the filler tube.

Transmission fully warmed up

7 Work exactly as described above, but take the level reading from the "+ 80°C" side of the dipstick. In this case, the level must be between the dipstick "MAX" and "MIN" marks.

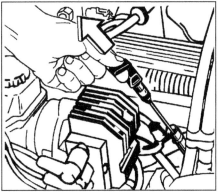

7.2 Withdrawing the automatic transmission fluid level dipstick

Checking the condition of the fluid

8 Whenever the fluid level is checked, examine the condition of the fluid and compare its colour, smell and texture with that of new fluid.

9 If the fluid is dark, almost black, and smells burnt, it is possible that the transmission friction material is worn or disintegrating. The vehicle should be taken to a Vauxhall/Opel dealer or automatic transmission specialist for immediate attention.

10 If the fluid is milky, this is due to the presence of emulsified droplets of water. This may be caused either by condensation after a prolonged period of short journeys or by the entry of water through the dipstick/filler tube or breather. If the fluid does not revert to its normal appearance after a long journey it must be renewed or advice should be sought from a Vauxhall/Opel dealer or automatic transmission specialist.

11 If the fluid is varnish-like (i.e. light to dark brown and tacky) it has oxidised due to overheating or to over- or under-filling. If renewal of the fluid does not cure the problem, the vehicle should be taken to a Vauxhall/Opel dealer or automatic transmission specialist for immediate attention.

12 If at any time on checking the fluid level or on draining the fluid, particles of dirt, metal chips or other foreign matter are found in the fluid, the vehicle must be taken to a

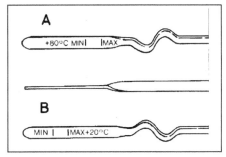

7.4 Automatic transmission fluid level dipstick markings

A Markings for fluid at operating temperature
B Markings for cold fluid

Vauxhall/Opel dealer or automatic transmission specialist for immediate attention. It may be necessary to strip, clean and reassemble at least the valve body, if not the complete transmission, to rectify any fault.

8 Radiator inspection and cleaning

1 Inspect radiator for leaks or corrosion, especially around the outlet or inlet connectors.

2 Clean the radiator fins with a soft brush or compressed air – take care, the radiator fins are easily damaged, and are sharp. Remove any debris, like dead insects or leaves.

3 If leaks are visible, renew the radiator. Refer to Chapter 3, if necessary.

9 Idle speed and mixture adjustment

⚠ **Warning: Certain procedures in this Section require the removal of fuel lines and connections, which may result in some fuel spillage. Before carrying out any operation on the fuel system, refer to the precautions given in 'Safety first!' at the beginning of this manual, and follow them implicitly. Petrol is a highly dangerous and volatile liquid, and the precautions necessary when handling it cannot be overstressed.**

Note: *Certain adjustment points in the fuel system are protected by tamperproof caps, plugs or seals. In some territories, it is an offence to drive a vehicle with broken or missing tamperproof seals. Before disturbing a tamperproof seal check that no local or national laws will be broken by doing so, and fit a new tamperproof seal after adjustment is complete, where required by law. Do not break tamperproof seals on an engine that is still under warranty. To carry out the adjustments, an accurate tachometer and an exhaust gas analyser (CO meter) will be required.*

Carburettor models

1 In order to check the idle speed and mixture adjustment, the following conditions must be met.

a) *The engine must be at normal operating temperature.*
b) *All electrical consumers (cooling fan, heater blower, headlights, etc.) must be switched off.*
c) *The ignition timing and spark plug gaps must be correctly adjusted – see Sections 12, and 28 or 36.*
d) *The throttle cable free play must be correctly adjusted – see Chapter 4A.*
e) *The air intake components must be free from leaks, and the air cleaner filter element must be clean.*

9.3 Carburettor idle speed adjustment (throttle stop) screw (arrowed)

f) The fast idle speed adjustment screw must not touch the fast idle cam during the procedure.

2 Connect a tachometer and an exhaust gas analyser to the vehicle in accordance with the manufacturer's instructions.

3 Start the engine and run it an 2000 rpm for approximately 30 seconds, then allow it to idle. If the idle speed is outside the specified limits, adjust by means of the throttle stop screw **(see illustration)**.

4 When the idle speed is correct, check the CO level in the exhaust gas. If it is outside the specified limits, adjust by means of the idle mixture adjustment screw **(see illustration)**. Turn the screw in very small increments until the CO level is correct.

5 With the idle mixture correct, readjust the idle speed if necessary.

6 If the cooling fan cuts in during the adjustment procedure, stop the adjustments and continue when the cooling fan stops.

7 When both idle speed and mixture are correctly set, stop the engine and disconnect the test equipment.

8 Fit new tamperproof seals to the adjustment screws, where this is required by law.

Fuel injection models

9 On all fuel injection engines, the idle speed and mixture are controlled by the electronic control unit (ECU), and no adjustment is possible. If any problems are suspected, the vehicle should be taken to a Vauxhall/Opel dealer who will have the necessary specialist test equipment to carry out system checks and fault diagnosis. Refer to Chapter 4B for further details of the fuel injection systems.

9.4 Tamperproof plug (arrowed) covering carburettor idle mixture adjustment screw

10 Exhaust system check

1 With the engine cold (at least half an hour after the vehicle has been driven), check the complete exhaust system from the engine to the end of the tailpipe. The exhaust system is most easily checked with the vehicle raised so that the exhaust components are readily visible and accessible.

2 Check the exhaust pipes and connections for evidence of leaks, severe corrosion and damage. Make sure that all brackets and mountings are in good condition and tight. Leakage at any of the joints or in other parts of the system will usually show up as a black sooty stain in the vicinity of the leak.

3 Rattles and other noises can often be traced to the exhaust system, especially the brackets and mountings. Try to move the pipes and silencers. If the components are able to come into contact with the body or suspension parts, secure the system with new mountings or if possible, separate the joints and twist the pipes as necessary to provide additional clearance.

11 Wiring check

1 Check all wiring in both the engine compartment and under the car.

2 Ensure that all wiring clips or clamps are secure.

3 Pay particular attention to wiring near components that get hot, i.e. exhaust systems.

4 Make sure that electrical connections are secure and undamaged.

12 Ignition timing check

⚠ *Warning: Voltages produced by an electronic ignition system are considerably higher than those produced by conventional ignition systems. Extreme care must be taken when working on the system with the ignition switched on. Persons with surgically implanted cardiac pacemaker devices should keep away from the ignition circuits, components and test equipment.*

Carburettor engines

Note: *A tachometer and a timing light will be required during this procedure.*

Check

1 Start the engine and run it until it reaches normal operating temperature, then switch off.

2 Disconnect the vacuum pipe from the distributor vacuum unit.

3 Connect a tachometer and a stroboscopic timing light to the engine, in accordance with the equipment manufacturer's instructions. Note that the timing light should be connected to No 1 cylinder HT circuit (No 1 cylinder is nearest the timing belt end of the engine).

4 Start the engine, and check that the idle speed is between 700 and 1000 rpm.

5 Point the timing light at the timing pointer on the rear timing belt cover, and check that the pointer is aligned with the upper notch in the crankshaft pulley, representing 5° BTDC. There are two notches on the pulley representing 5° and 10° BTDC **(see illustration)**.

Adjustment

6 If the notches and the pointer are not aligned as previously described, loosen the distributor clamp nut and turn the distributor body slightly in the required direction to align the notches and pointer.

7 Tighten the distributor clamp nut, and check that the notches and pointer are still aligned.

8 Stop the engine and disconnect the timing light and the tachometer, then reconnect the vacuum pipe to the distributor vacuum diaphragm unit.

Fuel injection engines

9 No adjustment of the ignition timing is possible on fuel injection engines, as the adjustment is carried out automatically by the electronic control unit.

10 If a fault is suspected, the ignition timing can be checked by a Vauxhall/Opel dealer, using dedicated test equipment.

13 Brake fluid renewal

1 The procedure is similar to that for the bleeding of the hydraulic system as described in Chapter 9, except that the brake fluid reservoir should be emptied by syphoning, using a (clean) old battery hydrometer or similar before starting, and allowance should be made for the old fluid to be expelled from the circuit when bleeding each section of the circuit.

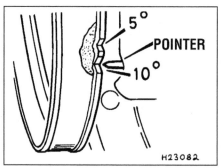

12.5 Timing marks on crankshaft pulley – carburettor engine

14 Brake pad check

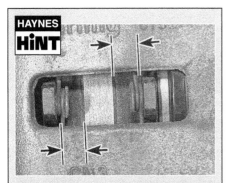

For a quick check, the thickness of the friction material on each brake pad can be measured through the aperture in the caliper

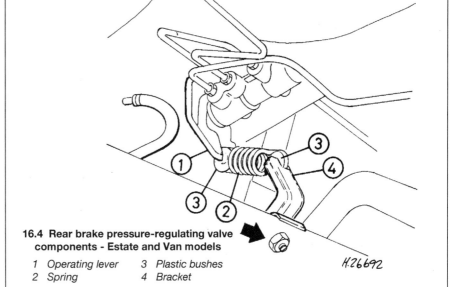

16.4 Rear brake pressure-regulating valve components - Estate and Van models

1 Operating lever	3 Plastic bushes
2 Spring	4 Bracket

H.26692

1 Jack up the front or rear of the vehicle (as applicable) and support securely on axle stands (see *"Jacking and vehicle support"*), then remove the roadwheels.
2 For a quick check, the thickness of friction material remaining on each pad can be measured through the slot in the front of the caliper body. If the friction material on any pad is worn to the specified minimum thickness or less, all four pads must be renewed (see Chapter 9).
3 For a comprehensive check, the brake pads should be removed and cleaned. This will allow the operation of the caliper to be checked, and the condition of the brake disc itself to be fully examined on both sides.

15 Handbrake linkage check

1 With the vehicle raised, check the operation of the handbrake and lubricate the linkages. Refer to Chapter 9, for further details.

16 Rear brake pressure-regulating valve check (Estate and Van models)

Check

1 To check the adjustment of the valve, the vehicle must be unladen (i.e. there should be no luggage or passengers in the vehicle) and the fuel tank should be a maximum of half-full. On models fitted with manual rear suspension level control, check that the system is pressurised to a minimum of 0.8 bars (see Section 18).
2 The vehicle must be standing on its wheels.
3 To check the operation of the valve, fully

depress the brake pedal, then quickly release it.
4 The valve operating lever **(see illustration)** should move. If the lever does not move, the valve is faulty, and should be renewed.

Adjustment

5 To adjust the valve, ensure that the valve operating lever is resting against its stop - if necessary, press the operating lever up to its stop, towards the front of the vehicle. The ends of the spring should lie in the plastic bushes in the valve operating lever and the bracket on the rear suspension torsion beam, and the spring should be free of play, and free from tension.
6 If necessary, loosen the nut securing the spring bracket to the rear suspension torsion beam, and move the bracket backwards or forwards as necessary until the spring is free of play and free from tension. Tighten the bracket securing nut on completion of adjustment.

17 Auxiliary drivebelt(s) check

Check

1 Due to their function and material makeup, drivebelts are prone to failure after a long period of time and should therefore be inspected regularly.
2 With the engine stopped, inspect the full length of the drivebelt(s) for cracks and separation of the belt plies. It will be necessary to turn the engine (using a spanner or socket and bar on the crankshaft pulley bolt) in order to move the belt from the pulleys so that the belt can be inspected thoroughly.

Twist the belt(s) between the pulleys so that both sides can be viewed. Also check for fraying, and glazing which gives the belt a shiny appearance. Check the pulleys for nicks, cracks, distortion and corrosion.
3 Check the tension of the belt(s) as described later in this Section.
4 If a belt shows signs of wear or damage, the belt must be renewed.

Alternator V-belt

Adjustment

5 Correct tensioning of the alternator drivebelt will ensure that it has a long life. Beware, however, of overtightening, as this can cause excessive wear in the alternator.
6 On 1.4 and 1.6 litre SOHC engine models with power steering, the alternator drivebelt also drives the power steering pump.
7 Disconnect the air intake trunking from the air cleaner, and the airbox or the throttle body, as applicable, and remove it for improved access.
8 Although special tools are available for measuring the belt tension, a good approximation can be achieved if the belt is tensioned so that there is approximately 13.0 mm of free movement under firm thumb pressure at the mid-point of the longest run between the pulleys. If in doubt, err on the slack side, as an excessively tight belt may cause damage to the alternator.
9 If adjustment is required, loosen the alternator upper and lower mounting nuts and bolts, and with the mounting bolts just holding the unit firm, lever the alternator away from the engine using a wooden lever at the mounting bracket until the correct tension is achieved, then tighten the mounting nuts and bolts. On no account lever at the free end of the alternator, as serious internal damage could be caused to the alternator.

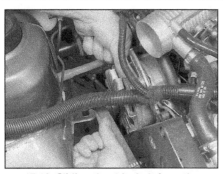

17.12 Sliding the drivebelt from the alternator pulley - C 16 SE engine with power steering

Renewal

10 To remove the belt on 1.8 and 2.0 litre engine models, first remove the power steering drivebelt as described later in this Section.

11 Disconnect the air intake trunking from the air cleaner and the airbox or the throttle body, as applicable, and remove it for improved access. Loosen the alternator upper and lower mounting nuts and bolts sufficiently to allow the alternator to pivot towards the engine.

12 Slide the belt from the pulleys **(see illustration)**.

13 Fit the new belt around the pulleys, and take up the slack in the belt by swinging the alternator away from the engine and lightly tightening the mounting nuts and bolts.

17.20 Adjusting the length of the power steering pump threaded rod - 1.8 and 2.0 litre SOHC models

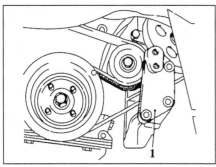

17.29 Remove the engine mounting bracket (1) – DOHC engines

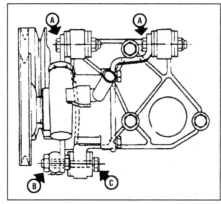

17.19 Mounting and adjuster bolts (arrowed) must be loosened to adjust power steering pump drivebelt tension - 1.8 and 2.0 litre SOHC engines

For A, B and C see 'Torque wrench settings'

14 Tension the drivebelt as described previously in this Section, and recheck the tension after a few hundred miles.

15 On 1.8 and 2.0 litre engine models, refit and tension the power steering pump drivebelt as described later in this Section.

Power steering pump V-belt

16 On 1.4 and 1.6 litre engines models, the power steering pump is driven by the alternator drivebelt (described previously in this Section).

17 On 1.8 and 2.0 litre engine models, proceed as follows.

18 Although special tools are available for measuring the drivebelt tension, a good approximation can be achieved if the belt is tensioned so that there is about 10.0 mm of free movement under firm thumb pressure at the mid-point of the belt run between the pulleys. If in doubt, err on the slack side, as an excessively-tight belt may cause damage to the pump.

19 If adjustment is required, or if the belt is to be renewed, slacken the mounting and adjuster bolts **(see illustration)**.

20 Slacken the adjuster nuts, and adjust the length of the threaded rod in order to tension

or remove the belt as desired **(see illustration)**.

21 Where applicable, fit the new belt around the pulleys, then tension the belt as described previously.

22 Tighten the adjuster nuts and tighten the adjuster and mounting bolt to the specified torque on completion.

23 If a new drivebelt has been fitted, recheck the tension after a few hundred miles.

Ribbed belt

24 Models with a ribbed belt are fitted with an automatic belt tensioner.

25 On models with an intake air temperature sensor, first disconnect the battery negative lead, then disconnect the sensor wiring plug.

26 Disconnect the air intake trunking from the air cleaner and the airbox or the throttle body, as applicable, and remove it for improved access. On some models, it may be necessary to remove the complete air cleaner assembly as described in Chapter 4B.

27 If necessary for improved access, remove the cover from the top of the camshaft cover.

28 If desired, to improve access to the crankshaft pulley, raise the front of the vehicle, and remove the right-hand roadwheel. Remove the access panel from the wheel arch liner, or remove the complete wheel arch liner, as desired.

29 Remove the right-hand engine mounting and bracket, as described in Chapter 2A **(see illustration)**.

30 Note the routing of the belt around the various pulleys, and if the belt is to be re-used, mark the running direction of the belt.

31 Using a suitable spanner or socket fitted to the tensioner pulley centre bolt, lever the tensioner away from the belt until there is sufficient slack to enable the belt to be slipped off the pulleys. Carefully release the tensioner pulley until it is against its stop, then remove the belt from the vehicle.

32 To refit, manoeuvre the belt into position, routing it correctly around the pulleys **(see illustrations)**. If the original belt is being refitted, use the marks made prior to removal to ensure that the belt is fitted the correct way round.

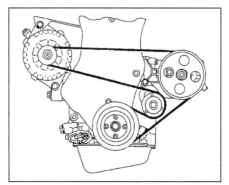

17.32a Ribbed auxiliary drivebelt shown correctly routed – 1.8 and 2.0 litre DOHC engines

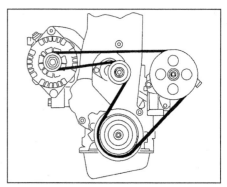

17.32b Ribbed auxiliary drivebelt shown correctly routed – 1.4 and 1.6 litre SOHC engines

33 Lever the tensioner roller back against its spring, and seat the belt on the pulleys. Ensure that the belt is centrally located on all pulleys, then slowly release the tensioner pulley until the belt is correctly tensioned. **Do not** allow the tensioner to spring back and stress the belt.
34 Refit the right-hand engine mounting bracket as described in Chapter 2A, Section 17.
35 Further refitting is a reversal of removal.

18 Rear suspension level control system check

1 The rear suspension level control system pressure is checked using a tyre pressure gauge on the inflation valve located in the rear right-hand side of the luggage compartment floor. The check should be carried out with the vehicle unladen.
2 Remove the cap from the valve, and check that the system pressure is 0.8 bars (11.6 lbf/in^2). The pressure must never be allowed to drop below this value, even with the vehicle unladen. Adjust if necessary using a tyre pump.

19 Bodywork condition check

Bodywork damage/ corrosion check

1 Once the car has been washed and all tar spots and other surface blemishes have been cleaned off, carefully check all paintwork, looking closely for chips and scratches. Pay particular attention to the vulnerable areas such as the front panels (bonnet and spoiler), and around the wheel arches.
2 If a chip or light scratch is found which is recent and still free from rust, it can be touched-up using the appropriate touch-up stick. Any more serious damage or rusted stone chips, can be repaired as described in Chapter 11, but if damage or corrosion is to severe that a panel must be renewed, seek professional advice as soon as possible.
3 Always check that the door ventilation opening drain holes and pipes are completely clear, so that the water can drain out.

Underbody corrosion protection check

4 The wax-based underbody protective coating should be inspected annually, preferably just prior to Winter, when the underbody should be washed down as thoroughly as possible without disturbing the protective coating. Any damage to the coating should be repaired using a wax-based sealer. If any of the body panels are disturbed for repair or renewal, do not forget to replace the coating and to inject wax into door panels, sills and box sections, to maintain the level of protection provided by the vehicle manufacturer.

20 Lock and hinge lubrication

1 Lubricate the hinges of the bonnet, doors and tailgate or boot lid (as applicable) with a light general purpose oil. Similarly, lubricate all latches, locks and lock strikers. At the same time, check the security and operation of all the locks, adjusting them if necessary (see Chapter 11).
2 Lightly lubricate the bonnet release mechanism and cable with a suitable grease.

21 Headlamp alignment check

Refer to Chapter 12 for details.

22 Pollen filter renewal

Removal

1 Open the bonnet, and remove the windscreen cowl panels, as described in Chapter 11.
2 Release the securing clips at the front of the now-exposed pollen filter, and carefully lift the filter from its housing **(see illustration)**.

Refitting

3 Fit the new filter using a reversal of the removal procedure, ensuring that the windscreen cowl panels are correctly located on the scuttle.

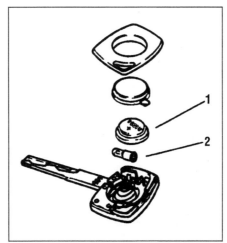

23.3 Replacing the battery in the door key

1 Battery (note, positive '+' side up)
2 Bulb

22.2 Lifting the pollen filter from its housing

23 Door lock key battery renewal

1 Carefully prise open the outer cover from the key. Take care not to lose any of the internal components, as they are loose.
2 Remove the battery and discard it safely.
3 Place the new battery, "+" side up **(see illustration)**. Check the operation of the key. If the bulb does not light obtain a replacement.
4 Replace the outer cover.

24 Road test

Instruments and electrical equipment

1 Check the operation of all instruments and electrical equipment.
2 Make sure that all instruments read correctly, and switch on all electrical equipment in turn to check that it functions properly.

Steering and suspension

3 Check for any abnormalities in the steering, suspension, handling or road "feel".
4 Drive the vehicle, and check that there are no unusual vibrations or noises.
5 Check that the steering feels positive, with no excessive "sloppiness", or roughness, and check for any suspension noises when cornering, or when driving over bumps.

Drivetrain

6 Check the performance of the engine, clutch, transmission and driveshafts.
7 Turn the radio/cassette off and listen for any unusual noises from the engine, clutch and transmission.
8 Make sure that the engine runs smoothly when idling, and that there is no hesitation when accelerating.
9 Check that , where applicable, the clutch action is smooth and progressive, that the drive is taken up smoothly, and that the pedal travel is not excessive. Also listen for any noises when the clutch pedal is depressed.

10 On manual transmission models, check that all gears can be engaged smoothly, without noise, and that the gear lever action is not abnormally vague or "notchy".

11 On automatic transmission models, make sure that all gearchanges occur smoothly without snatching, and without an increase in engine speed between changes. Check that all gear positions can be selected with the vehicle at rest. If any problems are found, they should be referred to a Vauxhall/Opel dealer.

12 Listen for a metallic clicking sound from the front of the vehicle, as the vehicle is driven slowly in a circle with the steering on full lock. Carry out this check in both directions. If a clicking noise is heard, this indicates wear in a driveshaft joint, in which case, the complete driveshaft must be renewed (see Chapter 8).

Every 18 000 miles (30 000 km) or 2 years

25 Coolant renewal

Draining

⚠️ *Warning: Wait until the engine is cold before starting this procedure. Do not allow antifreeze to come in contact with your skin, or with the painted surfaces of the vehicle. Rinse off spills immediately with plenty of water. Never leave antifreeze lying around in an open container, or in a puddle in the driveway or on the garage floor. Children and pets are attracted by its sweet smell, but antifreeze can be fatal if ingested.*

1 To drain the cooling system, carefully remove the expansion tank filler cap.

2 Where applicable, remove the engine undershield, with reference to Chapter 11, Section 25.

3 Position a container beneath the radiator bottom hose connection. Then slacken the hose clip and ease the hose from the radiator stub. If the hose joint has not been disturbed for some time, it may be necessary to twist the hose to break the joint. Allow the coolant to drain into the container.

4 As no cylinder block drain plug is fitted, and the radiator bottom hose may be situated above the bottom of the radiator, the system cannot be drained completely. Care should therefore be taken when refilling the system to maintain antifreeze strength.

5 If the coolant has been drained for a reason other than renewal, then provided it is clean and less than two years old, it can be re-used. Vauxhall/Opel do not specify renewal intervals for the coolant installed in the system when the vehicle is new, so renewal is up to the discretion of the owner.

Flushing

6 If coolant renewal has been neglected, or if the antifreeze mixture has become diluted, then in time, the cooling system may gradually lose efficiency, as the coolant passages become restricted due to rust, scale deposits, and other sediment. The cooling system efficiency can be restored by flushing the system clean.

7 The radiator should be flushed independently of the engine, to avoid unnecessary contamination.

8 To flush the radiator, disconnect the top hose at the radiator. Disconnect the bottom hose. Then insert a garden hose into the radiator top inlet. Direct a flow of clean water through the radiator and continue flushing until clean water emerges from the radiator bottom outlet. If after a reasonable period, the water still does not run clear, the radiator can be flushed with a flushing solution. Available at all good motorist outlets. It is important that the cleaning agent manufacturer's instructions are followed carefully. If the contamination is particularly bad, insert the hose in the radiator bottom outlet, and flush the radiator in reverse ('reverse-flushing').

9 To flush the engine, proceed as follows, according to model.

1.4 and 1.6 litre models

10 Remove the thermostat as described in Chapter 3, then temporarily refit the thermostat cover.

11 With the radiator top and bottom hoses disconnected from the radiator, insert a hose into the radiator bottom hose. Direct a clean flow of water through the engine, and continue flushing until clean water emerges from the radiator top hose.

12 On completion of flushing, refit the thermostat, with reference to Chapter 3 and reconnect the hoses.

1.8 and 2.0 litre models

13 Remove the thermostat and cover assembly, as described in Chapter 3.

14 With the radiator bottom hose disconnected from the radiator, insert a hose into the radiator bottom hose. Direct a flow of clean water through the engine and continue flushing until clean water emerges from the thermostat housing. It is advisable to place a sheet of plastic under the thermostat housing to deflect water away from the engine and surrounding components during the flushing process.

15 On completion of flushing, refit the thermostat and cover assembly, reconnect the hoses and remove the plastic sheet.

Refilling

Note: *On DOHC engine models, suitable sealant will be required to coat the threads of the bleed screw on refitting.*

16 Before attempting to fill the cooling system, make sure that all hoses and clips are in good condition, and that the clips are tight. Antifreeze must be used all year round, to prevent corrosion of the alloy engine components.

17 On 1.4 and 1.6 litre SOHC engine models, disconnect the wire and unscrew the coolant temperature sender from the inlet manifold. On DOHC engine models, remove the bleed screw from the thermostat housing cover (**see illustrations**).

18 Remove the expansion tank cap, and fill the system by slowly pouring the coolant into the expansion tank to prevent airlocks from forming.

19 If the coolant is being renewed, begin by pouring in a couple of litres of water, followed by the correct quantity of antifreeze, then top-up with more water.

20 On 1.4 and 1.6 litre SOHC engine models, refit the coolant temperature sender when coolant free of air bubbles emerges from the orifice in the manifold. Similarly, on DOHC engine models refit the bleed screw when coolant free of air bubbles emerges from the orifice in the thermostat housing cover (coat the threads of the bleed screw with suitable sealing compound).

25.17a Bleeding the cooling system by removing the temperature sender unit – 1.6 litre SOHC (C 16 SE) engine

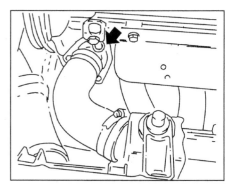

25.17b Location of bleed screw – 2.0 litre DOHC (C 20 XE) engine

21 Top-up the coolant level to the 'KALT' (or 'COLD') mark on the expansion tank, then refit the expansion tank cap.

22 Start the engine and run it until it reaches normal operating temperature, then stop the engine and allow it to cool.

23 Check for leaks, particularly around disturbed components. Check the coolant level in the expansion tank, and top-up if necessary. Note that the system must be cold before an accurate level is indicated in the expansion tank. if the expansion tank cap is removed while the engine is still warm, cover the cap with a thick cloth and unscrew the cap slowly to gradually relieve the system pressure (a hissing sound will normally be heard). Wait until any pressure remaining in the system is released, then continue to turn the cap until it can be removed.

24 Where applicable, refit the engine undershield on completion.

Antifreeze mixture

25 The antifreeze should always be renewed at the specified intervals. This is necessary not only to maintain the antifreeze properties, but also to prevent corrosion which would otherwise occur as the corrosion inhibitors become progressively less effective.

26 Always use an ethylene-glycol based antifreeze which is suitable for use in mixed-metal cooling systems. The quantity of antifreeze and levels of protection are given in the Specifications.

27 Before adding antifreeze, the cooling system should be completely drained, preferably flushed, and all hoses checked for condition and security.

28 After filling with antifreeze, a label should be attached to the expansion tank, stating the type and concentration of antifreeze used, and the date installed. Any subsequent topping-up should be made with the same type and concentration of antifreeze.

29 Do not use engine antifreeze in the wind-screen/tailgate washer system, as it will cause damage to the vehicle paintwork. A screen-wash additive should be added to the washer system in the quantities stated on the bottle.

26 Air cleaner element renewal

1 The air cleaner assembly is located at the front right-hand side of the engine compartment.

2 Release the clips securing the cover to the air cleaner casing, then lift the cover sufficiently to remove the element **(see illustrations)**.

3 Wipe clean the inside surfaces of the cover and the main casing, and check that there is no foreign matter visible in the inlet duct.

4 Fit the new element, noting that the rubber locating flange should be uppermost, then refit the air cleaner cover and secure with the clips.

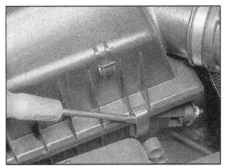

26.2a Release the clips securing the cover to the air cleaner casing . . .

27 Fuel filter renewal

⚠️ *Warning: Before carrying out the following operation, refer to the precautions given in "Safety first!" at the beginning of this manual, and follow them implicitly. Petrol is a highly dangerous and volatile liquid, and the precautions necessary when handling it cannot be overstressed.*

Carburettor models

1 The fuel filter is located in the carburettor fuel inlet pipe.

2 Disconnect the trunking from the air cleaner, then disconnect the vacuum pipe and breather hose from the airbox. Extract the three securing screws and lift off the airbox, complete with air trunking.

3 Place a wad of rag under the fuel inlet pipe at the carburettor to catch any fuel that may be spilled during the procedure.

4 Disconnect the fuel inlet hose from the carburettor. Be prepared for fuel spillage, and clamp or plug the end of the hose to reduce unnecessary fuel loss. Take adequate fire precautions.

5 To remove the filter, carefully screw an M3 bolt approximately 5.0 mm into the end of the filter, and pull on the bolt to withdraw the filter from the end of the inlet pipe **(see illustration)**.

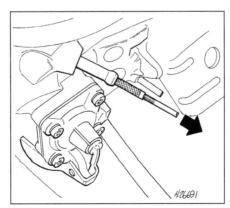

27.5 Removing the fuel filter from the carburettor fuel inlet pipe

26.2b . . . then lift the cover sufficiently to remove the element

6 Push the new filter into the inlet pipe, ensuring that it engages securely, then reconnect the fuel inlet hose, and refit the airbox.

Fuel injection models

7 The fuel filter is located on a bracket attached to the right-hand side of the fuel tank **(see illustration)**.

8 Clamp the fuel hoses at either end of the filter to minimise fuel loss when the hoses are disconnected, then place a container beneath the filter to catch the fuel that will be released.

9 Disconnect the fuel hoses from the filter. Be prepared for fuel spillage, and take adequate fire precautions.

10 Note the orientation of the filter (note the orientation of any flow direction markings that may appear on the filter body), then unscrew the clamp bolt, and withdraw the filter from its bracket. Note that the filter will still contain some petrol, which should be drained safely into a container. Dispose of the old filter safely.

11 Position the new filter in the retaining strap, ensuring that it is orientated correctly (make sure that the flow direction arrow(s) are correctly orientated, where applicable), then tighten the retaining strap screw to secure the filter.

12 Reconnect the hoses to the filter.

13 Run the engine and check for leaks on completion. If leakage is evident, stop the engine immediately, and rectify the problem without delay.

27.7 Fuel filter location – fuel injection model

28.3 Removing a spark plug - SOHC models

28.9a Measuring a spark plug electrode gap using a feeler gauge

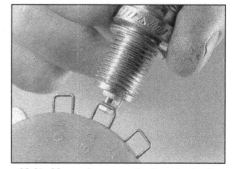

28.9b Measuring a spark plug electrode gap using a wire gauge

28 Spark plug renewal (SOHC engines)

1 The correct functioning of the spark plugs is vital for the correct running and efficiency of the engine. It is essential that the plugs fitted are appropriate for the engine. If the engine is in good condition, the spark plugs should not need attention between scheduled service intervals. Spark plug cleaning is rarely necessary and should not be attempted unless specialised equipment is available, as damage can easily be caused to the firing ends.

2 Identify each HT lead for position so that the leads can be refitted to their correct cylinders. Then disconnect the leads from the plugs by pulling on the connectors, not the leads.

3 Clean the area around each spark plug using a small paintbrush, then using a plug spanner (preferably with a rubber insert), unscrew and remove the plugs **(see illustration)**. Cover the spark plug holes with a clean rag to prevent the ingress of any foreign matter.

4 The condition of the spark plugs will tell much about the overall condition of the engine.

5 If the insulator nose of the spark plug is clean and white, with no deposits, this is a sign of a weak mixture, or too hot a plug. A hot plug transfers heat away from the electrode slowly and a cold plug transfers heat away quickly.

28.9c Adjusting a spark plug electrode gap using a special tool

6 If the tip and insulator nose is covered with hard black-looking deposits, then this is indicative that the mixture is too rich. Should the plug be black and oily, then it is likely that the engine is fairly worn, as well as the mixture being too rich.

7 If the insulator nose is covered with light tan to greyish brown deposits, then the mixture is correct, and it is likely that the engine is in good condition.

8 The spark plug gap is of considerable importance, because if it is either too large or too small, the size of the spark and its efficiency will be seriously impaired. The spark plug gap should be set to the figure given in the Specifications, where applicable.

9 To set it, where possible, measure the gap with a feeler gauge and then bend open, or close, the outer plug electrode until the correct gap is achieved. The centre electrode should never be bent, as this may crack the insulation and cause plug failure, if nothing worse **(see illustrations)**.

10 Before fitting new spark plugs check that their threaded connector sleeves are tight.

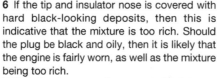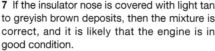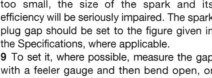

It is very often difficult to insert spark plugs into their holes without cross-threading them. To avoid this, fit a short length of 8 mm (internal diameter), rubber hose over the end of the spark plug. The flexible hose acts as a universal joint to help align the plug correctly. Should the plug begin to cross-thread, the hose will slip on the spark plug, preventing damage to the thread in the cylinder head.

11 Screw in the plugs by hand, then tighten them to the specified torque. Do not exceed the torque figure.

12 Push the HT leads firmly onto the spark plugs, ensuring that they are connected to their correct cylinders.

29 Distributor cap, rotor arm and HT lead check

 Warning: Voltages produced by an electronic engine management system are considerably higher than those produced by conventional systems. Extreme care must be taken when working on the system with the ignition switched on. Persons with surgically-implanted cardiac pacemaker devices should keep well clear of the ignition circuits, components and test equipment.

 Number the HT leads before removal to ensure correct refitting.

1 To check the HT leads, proceed as follows.

2 On DOHC engine models, unscrew the two securing bolts, and withdraw the spark plug cover from the camshaft cover for access to the spark plug cover for access to the spark plug HT leads.

3 Ensure that the leads are numbered before removing them to avoid confusion when refitting. Working on each HT lead in turn, pull the end of the lead from the spark plug by gripping the end connector, not the lead, otherwise the lead connection may be fractured.

4 Check the inside of the connector for signs of corrosion, which will look like a white crusty powder. Push the connector back onto the spark plug, ensuring that it is a tight fit on the plug. If it is not, remove the lead again, and use pliers to carefully crimp the metal terminal inside the connector until it fits securely on the end of the spark plug.

5 Using a clean rag, wipe the entire length of the lead to remove any built-up dirt and

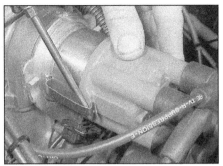

29.8 Releasing a distributor cap securing clip

30.1a Measure the distance from the centre of the top edge of the pedal to the lowest point of the steering wheel . . .

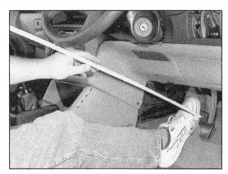

30.1b . . . then fully depress the pedal and repeat the measurement

grease. Once the lead is clean, check for burns, cracks and other damage. Do not bend the lead excessively, or pull the lead lengthwise – the conductor inside might break.

6 Disconnect the other end of the lead from the distributor cap, or coil, as applicable. Again, pull only on the connector. Check for corrosion and a tight fit, as described previously. Refit the lead securely on completion.

7 Check the remaining HT leads one at a time, in the same way, including the lead from the distributor cap to the coil, where applicable.

8 On models fitted with a distributor, loosen the securing screws, or release the securing clips, as applicable, and remove the distributor cap **(see illustration)**. Wipe the cap clean inside and out, and carefully inspect it for signs of cracks, 'tracking' (indicated by thin black lines running between the contacts) and worn, corroded, burnt or loose contacts. Check that the carbon brush in the centre of the cap is not worn, that it moves freely, and stands proud of the surface of the cap. Renew the cap if any faults are found. When fitting a new cap, remove the HT leads from the old cap one at a time, and fit them to the new cap in the exact same location – do not simultaneously remove all the leads, as it is easy to fit the leads in the wrong order, resulting in the wrong cylinder firing order.

9 Where applicable, remove the rotor arm, noting that on certain models the rotor arm is secured by screws. Examine the rotor arm for corrosion, cracks or other damage. If the metal portion of the rotor arm is badly burnt or loose, renew the rotor arm. If slightly burnt or

corroded, it may be cleaned with a fine file.
10 Note that it is common practise to renew the distributor cap and rotor arm whenever new HT leads are fitted.

30 Clutch cable adjustment

1 Working inside the vehicle, ensure that the clutch pedal is in its normal rest position, then measure the distance from the centre of the top edge of the pedal to the lowest point of the steering wheel. Fully depress the pedal, and repeat the measurement **(see illustrations)**. The measurements can be taken using a strip of wood or metal, as the important figure is the *difference* between the two measurements, i.e. the movement (stroke) of the pedal.

2 The difference between the two measurements must be as given in the Specifications. If not, adjust the clutch cable as follows to achieve the specified pedal movement.

3 Working in the engine compartment, remove the clip from the threaded rod at the clutch release arm on the transmission, then turn the threaded rod as required, using a spanner on the flats provided **(see illustration)**. Turn the rod clockwise to increase pedal movement, or anti-clockwise to decrease pedal movement. Recheck the pedal movement, and then refit the clip to the threaded rod on completion.

4 On a vehicle in which the clutch has

covered a high mileage, it may no longer be possible to adjust the cable to achieve the specified pedal movement, and this indicates that the clutch friction disc requires renewal.
Caution: Note that when correctly adjusted, the clutch pedal will rest slightly higher than the brake pedal – it is incorrect for the two pedals to be in alignment. If the pedals are aligned, the cable requires adjustment. Note also that there should be no play in the clutch pedal.
5 Check also, the condition of the cable. Inspect the cable strands for fraying, and ensure that the cable is correctly routed, to avoid chafing against surrounding components. Renew the cable, as described in Chapter 6, if excessive wear or damage is evident.

31 Manual transmission oil level check

Note: *On models built after 1994 the manufacturers state that it is no longer necessary to check the transmission oil level.*
1 Ensure that the vehicle is on level ground. Where applicable, remove the engine undershield as described in Chapter 11, Section 25.
2 Unscrew the transmission oil level plug, which is located in the rear left of the differential housing, or the rear right of the differential housing, depending on transmission type **(see illustrations)**. The oil level should be up to the bottom of the level plug orifice.

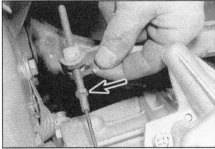

30.3 Removing the clip from the clutch cable threaded rod. Threaded rod adjuster flats arrowed

31.2a Removing the transmission oil level plug - F13 type transmission

31.2b Transmission oil level plug (arrowed) - F16 type transmission (viewed from below, with driveshaft removed)

31.3a Unscrew the breather/filler plug . . .

31.3b . . . and top-up with the specified grade of oil

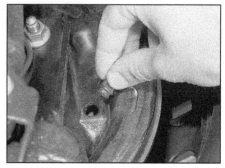

33.2 Removing the sealing grommet from the inspection hole in the rear brake backplate

3 If necessary, top up the oil level through the breather/filler orifice in the gear selector cover. Unscrew the breather/filler plug, and top up with the specified grade of oil, until oil just begins to run from the level plug orifice. Refit the level plug and the breather/filler plug on completion **(see illustrations)**.

4 Renewal of the transmission oil is not specified by the manufacturers, and no drain plug is provided. If necessary, renew the oil as a precaution. The oil may be drained by removing the differential cover plate. Use a new gasket when refitting the cover plate. Fill the transmission through the breather/filler orifice, as described previously in this Section.

5 Periodically inspect the transmission for oil leaks, and check the gear selector linkage components for wear and smooth operation.

6 Where applicable, refit the engine undershield.

32 Automatic transmission operation check

1 Carry out a thorough road test, ensuring that all gearchanges occur smoothly, without snatching and with no increase in engine speed between changes.

2 Check the operation of the kickdown. Check that all gear positions can be engaged at the appropriate movement of the selector lever and with the vehicle at rest, check that the operation of the parking pawl in position "P" prevents it from being moved. Ensure that the starter motor will work only with the selector lever in positions "P" or "N", and that the reversing lamps light only when position "R" is selected.

3 The manufacturer's schedule calls for a regular check of the electrical control system using the special Vauxhall/Opel test equipment - owners will have to have this check carried out by a Vauxhall/Opel dealer.

4 Periodically inspect the transmission casing, checking all joint surfaces and seals for signs of fluid leaks. If any are found, the fault must be rectified immediately.

5 Check also that the transmission breather hose (under the battery mounting bracket) is clear and not blocked, kinked or twisted.

33 Rear brake shoe check

Note: *On models fitted with rear brake pads, the handbrake operates brake shoes which are located inside the rear brake discs.*

1 Chock the front wheels, then jack up the rear of the vehicle and support it securely on axle stands (see *"Jacking and vehicle support"*).

2 For a quick check, the thickness of friction material remaining on one of the brake shoes can be observed through the hole in the brake backplate which is exposed by prising out the sealing grommet **(see illustration)**. A torch or inspection light will probably be required to help observation. If the friction material on any shoe is worn down to the specified minimum thickness or less, all four shoes must be renewed.

3 For a comprehensive check, the brake drum should be removed and cleaned. This will allow the wheel cylinders to be checked, and the condition of the brake drum itself to be fully examined (see Chapter 9).

34 Seat belt check

1 Carefully examine the seat belt webbing for cuts or any signs of serious fraying or deterioration. If the seat belt is of the retractable type, pull the belt all the way out, and examine the full extent of the webbing.

2 The seat belts are designed to lock up during a sudden stop or impact, yet allow free movement during normal driving. Fasten and unfasten the belt, ensuring that the locking mechanism holds securely and releases properly when intended. Check also that the retracting mechanism operates correctly when the belt is released.

Every 36 000 miles (60 000 km) or 4 years

35 Timing belt renewal

Note: *If the timing belt is to be renewed on 'Ecotec' type engines (see Chapter 2B 'Specifications'), it is strongly recommended that the timing belt tensioner and idler pulleys are also renewed, as described in Chapter 2B.*

1 To minimise risk of major damage to the engine, the timing belt (or cambelt, as it is sometimes called), should be renewed at regular intervals. If the timing belt breaks when the engine is running, serious and expensive engine damage can result.

2 The manufacturer's recommend renewal intervals of 40 000 miles (60 000 km), or 4 years, whichever comes first. The belt should be renewed if there is the slightest doubt about its condition, or if you have bought a vehicle with an unclear service history.

3 Details of timing belt renewal are given in Chapter 2A or 2B, as applicable.

36 Spark plug renewal (DOHC engines)

1 This procedure is basically similar to that given in Section 28 for SOHC engines, however on DOHC engines, a spark plug cover must be removed from the camshaft cover for access to the spark plugs.

2 A special tool (Vauxhall/Opel No. KM-836) is available to safely and easily pull the HT

leads from the plugs. If the special tool is not available, take care not to strain the lead connectors, as internal damage to the lead may occur. Take great care when removing and refitting spark plugs on these engines. Hairline cracks in the ceramic section of the plug can cause occasional or complete ignition failure (which may cause damage to the catalytic converter).

3 A special adapter tool (Vauxhall/Opel No. KM-194-B), with a 3 part conical sliding element is available, to reduce the risk of plug damage **(see illustration)**.

4 After renewing the spark plugs with reference to Section 28, refit the plug cover.

37 Automatic transmission fluid renewal

Note: *The manufacturers specify that fluid renewal is only required at the recommended intervals if the vehicle is used for heavy-duty work (e.g. taxi work, caravan/trailer towing, mostly short-distance, stop-start city driving). No renewal intervals are specified for vehicles under normal usage conditions. It is up to the individual owner to decide whether to renew the transmission fluid.*

1 This operation is much more efficient if the vehicle is first taken on a journey of sufficient length to warm the engine/transmission up to normal operating temperature.

Caution: If the procedure is to be carried out on a hot transmission unit, take care not to burn yourself on the hot exhaust or the transmission/engine unit.

2 Park the vehicle on level ground, switch off the ignition and apply the handbrake firmly. Alternatively, to improve access, jack up the front and rear of the vehicle and support it securely on axle stands, ensuring that the vehicle is level (see *"Jacking and vehicle support"*). Where necessary, undo the retaining bolts and remove the undercover from beneath the engine/transmission unit.

3 Wipe clean the area around the transmission fluid drain plug, and place a suitable container beneath the drain plug to collect the transmission fluid **(see illustration)**.

4 Slowly slacken and remove the drain plug, and allow the transmission oil to drain in to the container.

5 Allow the fluid to drain completely into the

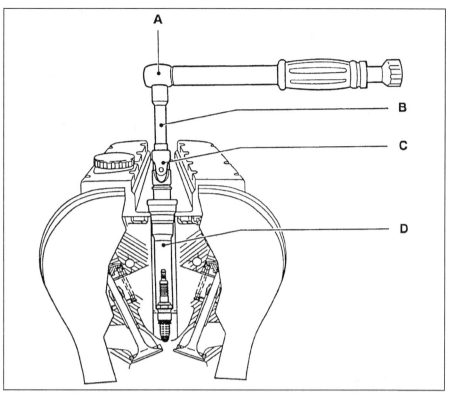

36.3 Removing spark plugs using special adapter (DOHC models)

A *Torque wrench*
B *Extension*
C *Joint*
D *Special adaptor (P/N KM-194-B)*

container. If the fluid is hot, take precautions against scalding. Remove all traces of dirt and fluid from the drain plug.

6 Once the fluid has finished draining, refit and tighten the drain plug.

7 The transmission is refilled via the transmission fluid level dipstick tube. Remove the dipstick (see Section 7), then pour in the specified quantity of the correct type of transmission fluid (see Specifications).

8 Refit the dipstick and check the transmission fluid level as described in Section 7. If necessary, top up the fluid level.

9 Where applicable, lower the vehicle to the ground.

10 Take the vehicle on a short journey so that the new fluid is distributed fully around the transmission components.

11 On return, park the vehicle on level ground and re-check the transmission fluid level as described in Section 7.

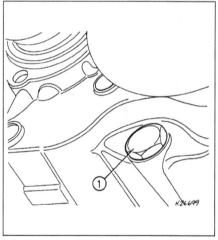

37.3 Automatic transmission fluid drain plug (1)

Chapter 2 Part A:
SOHC engine in-car repair procedures

Contents

Degrees of difficulty

Easy, suitable for novice with little experience		Fairly easy, suitable for beginner with some experience		Fairly difficult, suitable for competent DIY mechanic		Difficult, suitable for experienced DIY mechanic		Very difficult, suitable for expert DIY or professional	

Specifications

General

Engine type . . . . Four-cylinder, in-line, water-cooled. Single overhead camshaft, belt-driven, acting on hydraulic tappets

Manufacturer's engine codes:
Note: *The code can be found on the cylinder block, in front of the clutch housing.*

14 NV	1.4 litre carburettor
14 SE	1.4 litre Multi-point fuel injection (MPi)
C 14 NZ	1.4 litre + catalytic converter (cat) + Central fuel injection (CFi)
X 14 NZ	1.4 litre + cat + CFi
C 14 SE	1.4 litre + cat + MPi
C 16 NZ	1.6 litre + cat + CFi
C 16 SE	1.6 litre + cat + MPi
X 16 SZ	1.6 litre + cat + CFi
X 16 SZR	1.6 litre + cat + CFi
C 18 NZ	1.8 litre + cat + CFi
C 20 NE	2.0 litre + cat + MPi

Capacity:

	Bore	Stroke
1.4 litre engines (1389 cc)	77.6 mm	73.4 mm
1.6 litre engines (1598 cc)	79.0 mm	81.5 mm
1.8 litre engines (1796 cc)	84.8 mm	79.5 mm
2.0 litre engines (1998 cc)	86.0 mm	86.0 mm

Firing order . . . . 1 - 3 - 4 - 2 (No 1 cylinder at timing belt end)
Direction of crankshaft rotation . . . . Clockwise (viewed from timing belt end of engine)
Compression ratio:

14 NV, C 14 NZ and X 14 NZ	9.4 : 1
14 SE	9.8 : 1
C 14 SE and X 16 SZ	10.0 : 1
C 16 NZ, C 18 NZ and C 20 NE	9.2 : 1
X 16 SZR	9.6 : 1
C 16 SE	9.8 : 1

General (continued)

Maximum power:

14 NV	55 kW at 5800 rpm
14 SE	60 kW at 5600 rpm
C 14 NZ and X 14 NZ	44 kW at 5200 rpm
C 14 SE	60 kW at 5800 rpm
C 16 NZ and X 16 SZR	55 kW at 5200 rpm
C 16 SE	74 kW at 5800 rpm
X 16 SZ	52 kW at 5000 rpm
C 18 NZ	66 kW at 5400 rpm
C 20 NE	85 kW at 5400 rpm

Maximum torque:

14 NV	110 Nm at 3000 rpm
14 SE	115 Nm at 3400 rpm
C 14 NZ and X 14 NZ	103 Nm at 2800 rpm
C 14 SE	113 Nm at 3400 rpm
C 16 NZ	125 Nm at 2800 rpm
C 16 SE	135 Nm at 3400 rpm
X 16 SZ	128 Nm at 2800 rpm
X 16 SZR	128 Nm at 2600 rpm
C 18 NZ	145 Nm at 3000 rpm
C 20 NE	170 Nm at 2600 rpm

Compression pressures

Standard	12 to 15 bar (172 to 217 psi)
Maximum difference between any two cylinders	1 bar (15 psi)

Timing belt

Tension using special tool KM-510-A (1.8 and 2.0 engines) – see Section 7:

New belt, cold	4.5
New belt, warm	7.5
Used belt, cold	2.5
Used belt, warm	7.0

Camshaft

Endfloat	0.09 to 0.21 mm
Maximum permissible radial run-out	0.040 mm

Lubrication system

Oil pump type	Gear type, driven directly from crankshaft
Minimum permissible oil pressure at idle speed, with engine at operating temperature (oil temperature of at least 80°C)	1.5 bar (22 psi)
Oil pump clearances:	
Inner-to-outer gear teeth clearance (backlash)	0.10 to 0.20 mm
Gear-to-housing clearance (endfloat):	
1.4 and 1.6 litre engines	0.08 to 0.15 mm
1.8 and 2.0 litre engines	0.03 to 0.10 mm

Torque wrench settings

Note: Use new bolts where marked with an asterisk (*).

The torque settings stated are only applicable to latest specification cylinder head bolts, available from Vauxhall. Earlier type or alternative make, head bolts may require different torques. Consult your supplier.

	Nm	lbf ft
Camshaft cover bolts	8	6
Camshaft sprocket bolt	45	33
Camshaft thrustplate bolts	8	6
Camshaft housing end cover bolts	8	6
Connecting rod big-end bearing cap bolt:*		
1.4 and 1.6 litre engines:		
Stage 1	25	18
Stage 2	Angle tighten by a further 30°	
1.8 and 2.0 litre engines:		
Stage 1	35	25
Stage 2	Angle tighten by a further 45°	
Stage 3	Angle tighten by a further 15°	
Coolant pump bolts:		
M6 (1.4 and 1.6 litre engines)	8	6
M8 (1.8 and 2.0 litre engines)	25	18

Torque wrench settings (continued)

	Nm	lbf ft
Crankshaft pulley/crankshaft sprocket bolt (1.4 and 1.6 litre engines):*		
Models with V-belt	55	41
Models with ribbed belt:		
M10 bolt:		
Stage 1	55	41
Stage 2	Angle-tighten a further 45°	
Stage 3	Angle-tighten a further 15°	
M12 bolt:		
Stage 1	95	70
Stage 2	Angle-tighten a further 45°	
Stage 3	Angle-tighten a further 15°	
Crankshaft sprocket bolt (1.8 and 2.0 litre engines):*		
Stage 1	130	96
Stage 2	Angle-tighten a further 45°	
Crankshaft pulley-to-sprocket bolts (1.8 and 2.0 litre engines)	55	41
Crankshaft sensor mounting bracket bolt	6	4
Cylinder head bolts:*		
1.4 and 1.6 litre engines:		
Stage 1	25	18
Stage 2	Angle tighten by a further 60°	
Stage 3	Angle tighten by a further 60°	
Stage 4	Angle tighten by a further 60°	
1.8 and 2.0 litre engines:		
Stage 1	25	18
Stage 2	Angle tighten by a further 90°	
Stage 3	Angle tighten by a further 90°	
Stage 4	Angle tighten by a further 90°	
Driveplate bolts	60	44
Engine/transmission mounting bolts:		
Front left-hand mounting:		
Mounting-to-body bolts	65	47
Mounting-to-bracket bolts	60	44
Front right-hand mounting:		
Mounting-to-body bolts*	65	47
Mounting-to-bracket bolts	35	25
Rear mounting:		
Mounting-to-bracket bolts	45	33
Mounting-to-subframe bolts	40	30
Engine-to-transmission unit bolts:		
M8 bolts	20	15
M10 bolts	40	30
M12 bolts	60	44
Flywheel bolts:*		
1.4 and 1.6 litre engines:		
Stage 1	35	25
Stage 2	Angle tighten by a further 30°	
Stage 3	Angle tighten by a further 15°	
1.8 and 2.0 litre engines:		
Stage 1	65	47
Stage 2	Angle tighten by a further 30°	
Stage 3	Angle tighten by a further 15°	
Flywheel/driveplate lower cover plate bolts	8	6
Main bearing cap bolts:*		
Stage 1	50	37
Stage 2	Angle-tighten a further 45°	
Stage 3	Angle-tighten a further 15°	
Oil pump:		
Retaining bolts	6	4
Pump cover screws	6	4
Oil pressure relief valve bolt	30	22
Oil pick-up pipe-to-oil pump bolts	8	6
Sump bolts (use thread-locking compound):		
1.4 and 1.6 litre engines	8	6
1.8 and 2.0 litre engines	10	7
Sump drain plug	55	41
Timing belt tensioner bolt	20	15

1 General information

How to use this Chapter

1 This Part of Chapter 2 is devoted to in-car repair procedures for the single overhead camshaft (SOHC) engines. All procedures concerning engine removal and refitting, and engine block/cylinder head overhaul can be found in Chapter 2C.

2 Most of the operations included in this Part are based on the assumption that the engine is still installed in the car. Therefore, if this information is being used during a complete engine overhaul, with the engine already removed, many of the steps included here will not apply.

Engine description

3 The engine is a single overhead camshaft, four-cylinder, in-line unit, mounted transversely at the front of the car, with the clutch and transmission on its left-hand end.

4 The crankshaft runs in five shell-type main bearings, and the centre bearing incorporates thrust bearing shells to control crankshaft endfloat.

5 The connecting rods are attached to the crankshaft by horizontally split shell-type big-end bearings, and to the pistons by interference-fit gudgeon pins. The aluminium alloy pistons are of the slipper type, and are fitted with three piston rings, two compression rings and a scraper-type oil control ring.

6 The camshaft runs directly in the camshaft housing, which is mounted on top of the cylinder head. The camshaft is driven by the crankshaft via a toothed rubber timing belt (which also drives the coolant pump). The camshaft operates each valve via a follower. Each follower pivots on a hydraulic self-adjusting valve lifter (tappet) which automatically adjust the valve clearances.

7 Lubrication is by pressure-feed from a gear-type oil pump, which is mounted on the timing belt end of the crankshaft. It draws oil through a strainer located in the sump, and then forces it through an externally-mounted

2.4 Compression tester fitted to No 1 spark plug hole

full-flow cartridge-type filter. The oil flows into galleries in the cylinder block/crankcase, cylinder head and camshaft housing, from where it is distributed to the crankshaft (main bearings) and camshaft. The big-end bearings are supplied with oil via internal drillings in the crankshaft, while the camshaft bearings also receive a pressurised supply. The camshaft lobes and valves are lubricated by splash, as are all other engine components.

8 A semi-closed crankcase ventilation system is employed; crankcase fumes are drawn from the cylinder head cover, and passed via a hose to the inlet manifold.

Repair operations possible with the engine in the vehicle

9 The following operations can be carried out without having to remove the engine from the vehicle:

  a) Removal and refitting of the cylinder head.
  b) Removal and refitting of the timing belt and sprockets.
  c) Renewal of the camshaft oil seals.
  d) Removal and refitting of the camshaft housing and camshaft.
  e) Removal and refitting of the sump.
  f) Removal and refitting of the connecting rods and pistons*.
  g) Removal and refitting of the oil pump.
  h) Renewal of the crankshaft oil seals.
  i) Renewal of the engine mountings.
  j) Removal and refitting of the flywheel/driveplate.

* Although the operation marked with an asterisk can be carried out with the engine in the vehicle after removal of the sump, it is better for the engine to be removed, in the interests of cleanliness and improved access. For this reason, the procedure is described in Chapter 2C.

2 Compression test - description and interpretation

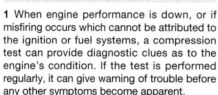

1 When engine performance is down, or if misfiring occurs which cannot be attributed to the ignition or fuel systems, a compression test can provide diagnostic clues as to the engine's condition. If the test is performed regularly, it can give warning of trouble before any other symptoms become apparent.

2 The engine must be fully warmed-up to normal operating temperature, the battery must be fully charged, and the spark plugs must be removed (see Chapter 1). The aid of an assistant will also be required.

3 Disable the ignition system by disconnecting the wiring connector from the ignition coil or DIS module (see Chapter 5B) and, on fuel injection models, the fuel system by removing the fuel pump relay from the engine compartment relay box (see Chapter 4B).

4 Fit a compression tester to the number 1 cylinder spark plug hole. The type of tester

which screws into the plug thread is to be preferred (see illustration).

5 Have the assistant hold the throttle wide open and crank the engine on the starter motor; after one or two revolutions, the compression pressure should build up to a maximum figure, and then stabilise. Record the highest reading obtained.

6 Repeat the test on the remaining cylinders, recording the pressure in each.

7 All cylinders should produce very similar pressures; any difference greater than that specified indicates the existence of a fault. Note that the compression should build up quickly in a healthy engine. Low compression on the first stroke, followed by gradually-increasing pressure on successive strokes, indicates worn piston rings. A low compression reading on the first stroke, which does not build up during successive strokes, indicates leaking valves or a blown head gasket (a cracked head could also be the cause). Deposits on the undersides of the valve heads can also cause low compression.

8 If the pressure in any cylinder is reduced to the specified minimum or less, carry out the following test to isolate the cause. Introduce a teaspoonful of clean oil into that cylinder through its spark plug hole, and repeat the test.

9 If the addition of oil temporarily improves the compression pressure, this indicates that bore or piston wear is responsible for the pressure loss. No improvement suggests that leaking or burnt valves, or a blown head gasket, may be to blame.

10 A low reading from two adjacent cylinders is almost certainly due to the head gasket having blown between them; the presence of coolant in the engine oil will confirm this.

11 If one cylinder is about 20 per cent lower than the others, and the engine has a slightly rough idle, a worn camshaft lobe could be the cause.

12 If the compression reading is unusually high, the combustion chambers are probably coated with carbon deposits. If this is the case, the cylinder head should be removed and decarbonised.

13 On completion of the test, refit the spark plugs (see Chapter 1), refit the fuel pump relay (where applicable), and reconnect the wiring connector to the ignition coil or DIS module.

3 Top dead centre (TDC) for No 1 piston - locating

1 Top Dead Centre (TDC) is the highest point that each piston reaches in its travel up and down its cylinder bore, as the crankshaft rotates. While each piston reaches TDC both at the top of the compression stroke and again at the top of the exhaust stroke, for the purpose of timing the engine, TDC refers to the position of No 1 piston at the top of its compression stroke.

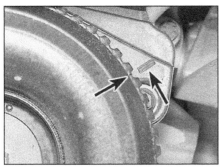

3.6a TDC pointer on timing belt cover aligned with timing notch in crankshaft sensor wheel (arrowed) – 1.6 litre fuel injection engine

3.6b TDC pointer on timing belt cover aligned with timing notch in crankshaft pulley (arrowed) – 2.0 litre fuel injection engine

3.6c Timing mark on camshaft sprocket aligned with notch in timing belt rear cover (arrowed) – 1.6 litre fuel injection engine

2 Number 1 piston (and cylinder) is at the timing belt end of the engine, and its TDC position is located as follows. Note that the crankshaft rotates clockwise when viewed from the timing belt end of the engine.
3 Disconnect the battery negative lead. If necessary, remove all the spark plugs as described in Chapter 1 to enable the crankshaft to be turned more easily.
4 To gain access to the camshaft sprocket timing mark, remove the timing belt upper cover as described in Section 6.
5 Using a socket and extension bar on the crankshaft pulley bolt, turn the crankshaft to bring No 1 piston to TDC as follows.

All engines except 1.4 litre carburettor engine

6 The pointer on the timing belt cover must be aligned with the notch in the crankshaft pulley, or the timing mark on the crankshaft sensor wheel, as applicable, and the timing mark on the camshaft sprocket must be aligned with the notch in the top of the timing belt rear cover **(see illustrations)**.
7 Note that there is also a timing mark on the crankshaft sprocket (visible with the crankshaft pulley/sensor wheel removed). When No 1 piston is positioned at TDC, the mark on the crankshaft sprocket should be aligned with the corresponding mark at the bottom of the oil pump flange – ie, the mark on the sprocket should be pointing vertically downwards.

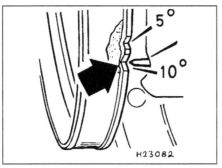

3.8 Crankshaft pulley 10°BTDC notch aligned with pointer on rear timing belt cover – 1.4 litre carburettor engine

1.4 litre carburettor engines

8 The pointer on the rear timing belt cover must be aligned with the 10°BTDC notch in the crankshaft pulley, and the timing mark on the camshaft sprocket must be aligned with the notch in the top of the rear timing belt cover **(see illustration)**. Note that when the timing marks are aligned as described, although No 1 piston is positioned at 10°BTDC, this is acceptable for all the tasks in this manual requiring No 1 piston to be positioned at TDC.
9 Note that there is also a timing mark on the crankshaft sprocket (visible with the crankshaft pulley/sensor wheel removed). When No 1 piston is positioned at TDC, the mark on the crank-shaft sprocket should be aligned with the corresponding mark at the bottom of the oil pump flange or timing belt rear cover (as

3.9 Timing mark on crankshaft sprocket aligned with mark at bottom of timing belt rear cover – 1.6 litre engine

applicable) – ie, the mark on the sprocket should be pointing vertically downwards **(see illustration)**.

4 Camshaft cover - removal and refitting

Removal

Note: *A new gasket will almost certainly be required on refitting.*
1 Release the retaining clip(s) and disconnect the breather hose(s) from the camshaft cover **(see illustrations)**.
2 Slacken and remove the retaining bolts, noting the correct fitted location of any clips or brackets retained by the bolts **(see illustration)**.

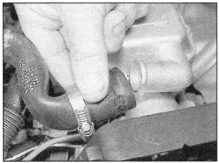

4.1a Disconnect the breather hoses . . .

4.1b . . . from the camshaft cover - 1.6 litre engine

4.2 Note the positions of any brackets and clips (arrowed) secured by the camshaft cover bolts – 1.6 litre engine

4.3 Lifting the camshaft cover from the cylinder head

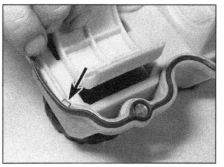

4.5 Tag (arrowed) on gasket engages with notch in camshaft cover – 1.6 litre engine

5.4 Removing the crankshaft pulley bolt and washer – 1.6 litre engine

3 Lift the camshaft cover from the camshaft housing **(see illustration)**. If the cover is stuck, do not lever between the cover and camshaft housing mating surfaces - if necessary, gently tap the cover sideways to free it. Recover the gasket; if it shows signs of damage or deterioration it must be renewed.

Refitting

4 Prior to refitting, examine the inside of the cover for a build-up of oil sludge or any other contamination, and if necessary clean the cover with paraffin, or a water-soluble solvent. Examine the condition of the crankcase ventilation filter inside the camshaft cover, and clean as described for the inside of the cover if clogging is evident (on some engines, if desired, the filter can be removed from the cover, after removing the securing bolts). Dry the cover thoroughly before refitting.

5 Ensure that the cover is clean and dry and seat the gasket in the cover recess, then refit the cover to the camshaft housing, ensuring that the gasket remains correctly seated **(see illustration)**.

6 Refit the retaining bolts, ensuring that all relevant clips/brackets are correctly positioned, and tighten the bolts to the specified torque, working in a diagonal sequence.

7 Reconnect the breather hose(s) and secure with the retaining clip(s).

5.5 Refit the crankshaft pulley, aligning the cut-out with the raised notch on the crankshaft sprocket (arrowed) – 1.6 litre engine

5 Crankshaft pulley - removal and refitting

1.4 and 1.6 litre engines

Note: *A new pulley retaining bolt will be required on refitting.*

Removal

1 Apply the handbrake, then jack up the front of the vehicle and support it on axle stands (see *"Jacking and vehicle support"*). Remove the right-hand roadwheel.

2 Remove the auxiliary drivebelt(s) as described in Chapter 1. Prior to removal, mark the direction of rotation on the belt(s) to ensure that the belt is refitted the same way round.

3 Slacken the crankshaft pulley retaining bolt. To prevent crankshaft rotation on manual transmission models, have an assistant select top gear and apply the brakes firmly. On automatic transmission models prevent rotation by removing one of the torque converter retaining bolts and bolting the driveplate to the transmission housing using a metal bar, spacers and suitable bolts (see Chapter 7B). If the engine is removed from the vehicle it will be necessary to lock the flywheel/driveplate (see Section 15).

4 Unscrew the retaining bolt and washer and remove the crankshaft pulley from the end of the crankshaft, taking care not to damage the crankshaft sensor, where applicable **(see illustration)**.

Refitting

5 Refit the crankshaft pulley, aligning the pulley cut-out with the raised notch on the timing belt sprocket, then fit the washer and new retaining bolt **(see illustration)**.

6 Prevent the crankshaft from turning by the method used on removal, and tighten the pulley retaining bolt to the specified torque, in the specified stages, where applicable. On engines which require the bolt to be angle-tightened, it is recommended that an angle-measuring gauge is used during the final stages of the tightening, to ensure accuracy **(see illustration)**. If a gauge is not available, use white paint to make alignment marks between the bolt head and pulley prior to

tightening; the marks can then be used to check that the bolt has been rotated through the correct angle.

7 Refit the auxiliary drivebelt as described in Chapter 1 using the mark made prior to removal to ensure that the belt is fitted the correct way around.

8 Refit the roadwheel then lower the vehicle to the ground and tighten the wheel bolts to the specified torque.

1.8 and 2.0 litre engines

Removal

9 Proceed as described in paragraphs 1 and 2.

10 Slacken the four bolts securing the pulley to the crankshaft sprocket, using a suitable Allen key or hexagon bit, then remove the pulley. To prevent the crankshaft from turning, use a suitable female Torx socket on the crankshaft pulley bolt, or alternatively, use one of the methods described in paragraph 3.

11 Unscrew the retaining bolts and remove the crankshaft pulley from the end of the crankshaft, taking care not to damage the crankshaft sensor, where applicable.

Refitting

12 Refit the crankshaft pulley, aligning the pulley cut-out with the raised notch on the timing belt sprocket, then fit the retaining bolts.

13 Prevent the crankshaft from turning by the method used on removal, and tighten the pulley retaining bolts to the specified torque.

14 Proceed as described in paragraphs 7 and 8.

5.6 Tighten the pulley retaining bolt to the specified torque in the specified stages – 1.6 litre engine

6.3a Unscrew the retaining screws (arrowed) . . .

6.3b . . . and withdraw the timing belt upper cover – 1.6 litre engine

6.7 Timing belt lower cover retaining bolts (arrowed) – 1.6 litre engine

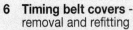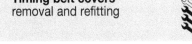

6 Timing belt covers - removal and refitting

1.4 and 1.6 litre engines

Upper cover - removal

1 For improved access, remove the air cleaner housing as described in Chapter 4A or 4B.

2 Remove the auxiliary drivebelt(s) as described in Chapter 1. Prior to removal, mark the direction of rotation on the belt to ensure that the belt is fitted the same way around on refitting. Note that on carburettor and single-point fuel injection engines, it may be necessary to remove the power steering pump (see Chapter 10) if the timing belt it to be removed.

3 Unscrew the retaining screws, then unclip the timing belt upper cover and remove it from the engine **(see illustrations)**.

Upper cover - refitting

4 Refitting is the reverse of removal, but refit and tension the auxiliary drivebelt(s) as described in Chapter 1, observing the direction marking made before removal.

Lower cover - removal

5 Remove the crankshaft pulley, as described in Section 5.

6 Where applicable, unclip the crankshaft sensor wiring from the timing belt lower cover.

7 Unscrew the retaining screws and remove the lower cover from the engine **(see illustration)**. Note that on some models it may be necessary to remove the upper cover as

described previously in this Section before the lower cover can be removed.

Lower cover - refitting

8 Refitting is the reverse of removal, but refit the crankshaft pulley as described in Section 5.

Rear cover - removal

9 Remove the outer covers as described previously in this Section, noting that on some models it may be necessary to remove the power steering pump (see Chapter 10) to enable the timing belt to be removed.

10 Remove the timing belt as described in Section 7.

11 Remove the camshaft and crankshaft sprockets, and the timing belt tensioner, as described in Section 8.

12 Unscrew and remove the bolts securing the rear cover to the camshaft housing and the cylinder block, then withdraw the rear cover. Where applicable, unclip the crankshaft sensor wiring from the rear of the cover **(see illustrations)**.

Rear cover - refitting

13 Refitting is the reverse of removal, bearing in mind the following points.
a) *Refit the camshaft and crankshaft sprockets, and the timing belt tensioner, as described in Section 8.*
b) *Refit and tension the timing belt as described in Section 7.*
c) *Refit the outer timing belt covers as described previously in this Section.*
d) *Where applicable, refit the power steering pump and bleed the fluid circuit as described in Chapter 10.*

1.8 and 2.0 litre engines

Upper cover - removal

14 Proceed as described in paragraphs 1 and 2.

15 Where applicable, disconnect the wiring from the temperature gauge sender.

16 Release the securing clips, and remove the upper timing belt cover.

Upper cover - refitting

17 Refitting is the reverse of removal, but refit and tension the auxiliary drivebelt(s) as described in Chapter 1, observing the direction marking made before removal.

Lower (coolant pump) cover - removal

18 Remove the upper timing belt cover as described previously in this Section, then unclip the lower cover from the coolant pump.

Lower (coolant pump) cover - refitting

19 Refitting is the reverse of removal, but refit and tension the auxiliary drivebelt(s) as described in Chapter 1, observing the direction marking made before removal.

Rear cover - removal

20 Remove the outer timing belt covers as described previously in this Section.

21 Remove the timing belt as described in Section 7.

22 Remove the timing belt sprockets as described in Section 8.

Where applicable, disconnect the wiring plug from the crankshaft sensor, and unclip the wiring from the rear belt cover.

23 Unscrew the securing bolts and remove the rear cover, manipulating it from the smaller rear cover on the coolant pump.

24 If desired, the smaller rear belt cover can be removed from the coolant pump, after unscrewing the securing bolt, by rotating it to disengage it from the retaining flange on the pump.

Rear cover - refitting

25 Refitting is a reversal of removal, bearing in mind the following points.
a) *Refit the camshaft and crankshaft sprockets, and the timing belt tensioner, as described in Section 8.*
b) *Refit and tension the timing belt as described in Section 7.*
c) *Refit the outer timing belt covers as described previously in this Section.*

6.12a Slacken and remove the retaining bolts and remove the timing belt rear cover – 1.6 litre engine

6.12b Crankshaft sensor wiring clipped to rear of timing belt rear cover – 1.6 litre engine

7.5a Insert a tool (such as a punch) into the hole (arrowed) in the tensioner arm . . .

7 Timing belt - removal and refitting

Note: *The timing belt must be removed and refitted with the engine cold.*

1.4 and 1.6 litre engines

Removal

1 Remove the timing belt upper cover as described in Section 6.

2 Position No 1 cylinder at TDC on its compression stroke as described in Section 3.

3 Remove the crankshaft pulley as described in Section 5.

4 Unbolt the timing belt lower cover and remove it from the engine (see Section 6).

5 Insert a suitable tool (such as a pin punch) into the hole in the timing belt tensioner arm, then lever the arm clockwise to its stop, and

7.7a Slacken the coolant pump bolts . . .

7.7b . . . and relieve the timing belt tension by rotating the pump with a suitable adapter

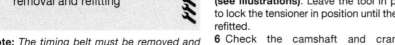

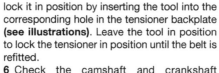

7.5b . . . then lever the arm clockwise and lock the tensioner in position by locating the tool in the backplate hole

lock it in position by inserting the tool into the corresponding hole in the tensioner backplate **(see illustrations)**. Leave the tool in position to lock the tensioner in position until the belt is refitted.

6 Check the camshaft and crankshaft sprocket timing marks are correctly aligned with the marks on the belt rear cover and oil pump flange.

7 Slacken the coolant pump retaining bolts then, using an open-ended spanner, carefully rotate the pump anti-clockwise to relieve the tension in the timing belt. Adapters to fit the pump are available from most tool shops (Vauxhall/Opel tool KM-421-A or equivalent) and allow the pump to be easily turned using a ratchet or extension bar **(see illustrations)**.

8 Slide the timing belt from its sprockets and remove it from the engine **(see illustration)**. If the belt is to be re-used, use white paint or similar to mark the direction of rotation on the belt. **Do not** rotate the crankshaft until the timing belt has been refitted.

9 Check the timing belt carefully for any signs of uneven wear, splitting or oil contamination, and renew it if there is the slightest doubt about its condition. If the engine is undergoing an overhaul and is approaching the manufacturers' specified interval for belt renewal (see Chapter 1) renew the belt as a matter of course, regardless of its apparent condition. If signs of oil contamination are found, trace the source of the oil leak and rectify it, then wash down the engine timing belt area and all related components to remove all traces of oil.

7.8 Slip the timing belt off from the sprockets and remove it from the engine

Refitting

10 On reassembly, thoroughly clean the timing belt sprockets then check that the camshaft sprocket timing mark is still correctly aligned with the cover cut-out and the crankshaft sprocket mark is still aligned with the mark on the oil pump flange (see Section 3).

11 Fit the timing belt over the crankshaft and camshaft sprockets, ensuring that the belt front run is taut (ie, all slack is on the tensioner pulley side of the belt), then fit the belt over the coolant pump sprocket and tensioner pulley. Do not twist the belt sharply while refitting it. Ensure that the belt teeth are correctly seated centrally in the sprockets, and that the timing marks remain in alignment. If a used belt is being refitted, ensure that the running direction mark made on removal points in the normal direction of rotation.

12 Carefully remove the punch from the timing belt tensioner to release the tensioner spring.

13 Check that the sprocket timing marks are still correctly aligned. If adjustment is necessary, lock the tensioner in position again, then disengage the belt from the sprockets and make any necessary adjustments.

14 If the marks are still correctly positioned, tension the timing belt by rotating the coolant pump whilst observing the movement of the tensioner arm. Turn the pump clockwise, so that the tensioner arm is fully over against its stop, without exerting any excess strain on the belt, then tighten the coolant pump retaining bolts.

15 Temporarily refit the crankshaft pulley bolt, then rotate the crankshaft smoothly through two complete turns (720°) in the normal direction of rotation to settle the timing belt in position.

16 Check that both the camshaft and crankshaft sprocket timing marks are still aligned (see Section 3), then slacken the coolant pump bolts. Adjust the pump so that the tensioner arm pointer is aligned with the centre of the 'V'-shaped cut-out on the tensioner backplate, then tighten the coolant pump bolts to the specified torque **(see illustration)**. Rotate the crankshaft smoothly

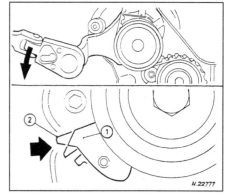

7.16 Rotate the coolant pump until the tensioner arm pointer (1) is correctly aligned with the cut-out (2) on the backplate

through another two complete turns in the normal direction of rotation, to bring the sprocket timing marks back into alignment. Check that the tensioner arm pointer is still aligned with the centre of the cut-out in the backplate.

17 If the tensioner arm pointer is not correctly aligned with the centre of the cut-out, repeat the procedure in paragraph 16.

18 Once the tensioner arm and cut-out remain correctly aligned, ensure that the coolant pump bolts are tightened to the specified torque, then refit the timing belt covers and crankshaft pulley as described in Sections 5 and 6.

1.8 and 2.0 litre engines up to 1993

Note: *The tension of a new belt must be adjusted with the engine cold. The tension of a used belt must be checked with the engine at normal operating temperature. The manufacturers specify the use of a special gauge, Vauxhall/Opel tool KM-510-A, for checking the timing belt tension. If access to a gauge cannot be obtained. it is strongly recommended that the vehicle is taken to a Vauxhall/Opel dealer to have the belt tension checked at the earliest opportunity.*

Removal

19 Proceed as described previously for 1.4 and 1.6 litre engines, in paragraphs 1 to 9, but ignore paragraph 5.

Refitting - using Vauxhall/Opel tool KM-510-A

20 On reassembly, thoroughly clean the timing belt sprockets then check that the camshaft sprocket timing mark is still correctly aligned with the cover cut-out and the crankshaft sprocket mark is still aligned with the mark on the oil pump flange.

21 Fit the timing belt over the crankshaft and camshaft sprockets, ensuring that the belt front run is taut (ie, all slack is on the coolant pump side of the belt), then fit the belt over the coolant pump sprocket. Do not twist the belt sharply while refitting it. Ensure that the belt teeth are correctly seated centrally in the sprockets, and that the timing marks remain in alignment. If a used belt is being refitted, ensure that the running direction mark made on removal points in the normal direction of rotation.

22 Read the instructions supplied with the gauge (Vauxhall/Opel tool KM-510-A) before proceeding.

23 Place the locked gauge at the centre of the belt run between the coolant pump and the camshaft gear. The gauge should locate on the timing belt as shown **(see illustration)**.

24 Slowly release the operating lever on the gauge, then lightly tap the gauge two or three times and note the reading on the scale **(see illustration)**.

25 If the reading is not as specified, loosen the three coolant pump securing bolts, using an Allen key or hexagon bit (if not already done)

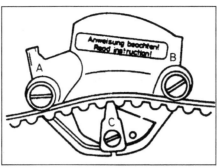

7.23 Tension gauge KM-510-A correctly positioned on timing belt. Belt must pass through points A, B and C – 1.8 and 2.0 litre engines up to 1993

and rotate the coolant pump in the required direction to achieve the necessary reading on the gauge. Rotate the pump clockwise to increase the belt tension, or anti-clockwise to decrease the tension.

26 Lightly tighten the coolant pump securing bolts sufficiently to prevent the pump from moving.

27 Remove the tensioning gauge and turn the crankshaft through one complete revolution clockwise.

28 Re-check the belt tension as described in paragraphs 23 and 24.

29 If the tension is not as specified, repeat paragraphs 25 to 28 inclusive until the required reading is obtained.

30 On completion of adjustment, remove the checking gauge and tighten the coolant pump bolts to the specified torque.

31 Refit the timing belt covers and crankshaft pulley as described in Sections 5 and 6.

Refitting - without Vauxhall/Opel tool KM-510-A (temporary adjustment)

32 Proceed as described in paragraphs 20 and 21.

33 If the special gauge (Vauxhall/Opel tool KM-510-A) is not available, the timing belt tension can be checked approximately by twisting the belt between the thumb and forefinger, at the centre of the run between the coolant pump and the camshaft gear. It should be just possible to twist the belt

through 90° using moderate pressure **(see illustration)**.

34 If adjustment is necessary, continue as described previously for adjustment using the special gauge (i.e., adjust the tension by moving the coolant pump), but have the belt tension checked by a Vauxhall/Opel dealer at the earliest opportunity.

35 If in doubt, err on the tight side when adjusting the tension, as if the belt is too slack it may jump on the sprockets, which could result in serious engine damage.

36 Ensure that the coolant pump bolts are tightened to the specified torque, then refit the timing belt covers and crankshaft pulley as described in Sections 5 and 6.

1.8 and 2.0 litre engines from 1993

Removal

37 Proceed as described previously for 1.4 and 1.6 litre engines, in paragraphs 1 to 4.

38 Slacken the timing belt tensioner securing bolt slightly then, insert a suitable Allen key or hexagon bit into the hole provided in the tensioner arm, and turn the tensioner arm clockwise until the tensioner pointer is at its left stop. Tighten the tensioner securing bolt.

39 Slide the timing belt from its sprockets and remove it from the engine. If the belt is to be re-used, use white paint or similar to mark the direction of rotation on the belt. **Do not** rotate the crankshaft until the timing belt has been refitted.

40 Check the timing belt carefully for any signs of uneven wear, splitting or oil contamination, and renew it if there is the slightest doubt about its condition. If the engine is undergoing an overhaul and is approaching the manufacturers' specified interval for belt renewal (see Chapter 1) renew the belt as a matter of course, regardless of its apparent condition. If signs of oil contamination are found, trace the source of the oil leak and rectify it, then wash down the engine timing belt area and all related components to remove all traces of oil.

Refitting

41 On reassembly, thoroughly clean the timing belt sprockets then check that the

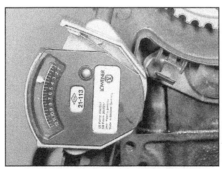

7.24 Note the reading on the scale of the tension gauge – 1.8 and 2.0 litre engines up to 1993

7.33 Checking the timing belt tension by twisting the belt through 90° between thumb and forefinger – 2.0 litre engine

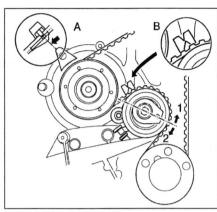

**7.42 Timing belt tensioning details –
1.8 and 2.0 litre engines from 1993**

A *Alignment lugs on coolant pump and
cylinder block*
B *Tensioner pointer aligned with notch in
tensioner bracket*
1 *Move the tensioner arm anti-clockwise
to tension the belt*
2 *Move the tensioner arm clockwise to
release the belt tension*

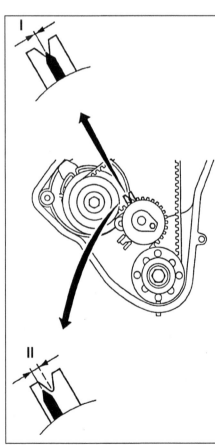

**7.48 Timing belt adjustment for new
and used timing belts –
1.8 and 2.0 litre engines from 1993**

I *Tensioner pointer alignment for new belts*
II *Tensioner pointer alignment for used belts
(approx 4.0 mm to the left of centre)*

camshaft sprocket timing mark is still
correctly aligned with the cover cut-out and
the crankshaft sprocket mark is still aligned
with the mark on the oil pump flange (see
Section 3).
42 Check that the coolant pump is correctly
positioned by checking that the lug on the
coolant pump flange is aligned with the
corresponding lug on the cylinder block. If this
is not the case, slacken the coolant pump
retaining bolts slightly, and move the pump
until the lugs are aligned **(see illustration)**.
Tighten the coolant pump bolts to the
specified torque on completion.
43 Fit the timing belt over the crankshaft and
camshaft sprockets, ensuring that the belt
front run is taut (ie, all slack is on the tensioner
pulley side of the belt), then fit the belt over
the coolant pump sprocket and tensioner
pulley. Do not twist the belt sharply while
refitting it. Ensure that the belt teeth are
correctly seated centrally in the sprockets,
and that the timing marks remain in alignment.
If a used belt is being refitted, ensure that the
running direction mark made on removal
points in the normal direction of rotation.
44 Slacken the tensioner securing bolt and
move the tensioner arm anti-clockwise, until
the tensioner pointer lies at its stop, without
exerting excess pressure on the timing belt.
Tighten the tensioner securing bolt to hold the
tensioner in this position.
45 Check that the sprocket timing marks are
still correctly aligned. If adjustment is
necessary, release the tensioner again, then
disengage the belt from the sprockets and
make any necessary adjustments.
46 Using a socket on the crankshaft
pulley/sprocket bolt (as applicable), rotate the
crankshaft smoothly through two complete
turns (720°) in the normal direction of rotation
to settle the timing belt in position.
47 Check that both the camshaft and
crankshaft sprocket timing marks are still
aligned (see Section 3), then slacken the
tensioner bolt again.
48 If a new timing belt is being fitted, adjust
the tensioner (turn it clockwise) so that the
pointer is aligned with the centre of the 'V'-
shaped cut-out on the tensioner backplate
(see illustration). Hold the tensioner in the
correct position and tighten its retaining bolt
to the specified torque. Rotate the crankshaft
smoothly through another two complete turns
in the normal direction of rotation, to bring the
sprocket timing marks back into alignment.
Check that the tensioner pointer is still aligned
with the centre of the backplate cut-out.
49 If the original belt is being refitted, adjust
the tensioner (turn it clockwise) so that the
pointer is positioned 4 mm to the left of the
centre of the 'V'-shaped cut-out on the
tensioner backplate (see illustration 7.48).
Hold the tensioner in the correct position and
tighten its retaining bolt to the specified
torque. Rotate the crankshaft smoothly
through another two complete turns in the
normal direction of rotation, to bring the

sprocket timing marks back into alignment.
Check that the tensioner pointer is still
correctly positioned in relation to the centre of
the backplate cut-out.
50 If the tensioner pointer is not correctly
positioned in relation to the backplate cut-out,
repeat the procedure in paragraph 48 (new
belt) or 49 (original belt), as applicable.
51 Once the tensioner pointer and cut-out
remain correctly aligned, refit the timing belt
covers and crankshaft pulley as described in
Sections 5 and 6.

8 Timing belt tensioner and sprockets - removal and refitting

Camshaft sprocket

Removal

1 Remove the timing belt as described in
Section 7.
2 The camshaft must be prevented from
turning as the sprocket bolt is unscrewed, and
this can be achieved in one of two ways as
follows.
a) *Make up a sprocket-holding tool using
two lengths of steel strip (one long, the
other short), and three nuts and bolts; one
nut and bolt forms the pivot of a forked
tool, with the remaining two nuts and
bolts at the tips of the 'forks' to engage
with the sprocket spokes as shown **(see
illustration)**.*
b) *Remove the camshaft cover as described
in Section 4 and hold the camshaft with
an open-ended spanner on the flats
provided between Nos 3 and 4 cam
lobes.*
3 Unscrew the retaining bolt and washer and
remove the sprocket from the end of the
camshaft.

Refitting

4 Prior to refitting check the camshaft front oil
seal for signs of damage or leakage, if
necessary, renewing it as described in
Section 9.
5 Refit the sprocket to the end of the
camshaft, aligning the hole in the sprocket

**8.2 Using a home-made sprocket holding
tool to retain the camshaft sprocket whilst
the bolt is slackened**

8.5 Refit the camshaft sprocket making sure the locating pin (1) engages with the sprocket hole (2)

8.6 Using an open-ended spanner to hold the camshaft whilst the sprocket retaining bolt is tightened

8.10 Refit the crankshaft sprocket making sure its timing mark is facing outwards

with the camshaft locating pin, then refit the retaining bolt and washer (see illustration).

6 Tighten the sprocket retaining bolt to the specified torque, whilst preventing rotation using the method employed on removal (see illustration).

7 Refit the timing belt as described in Section 7 then, where applicable, refit the camshaft cover as described in Section 4.

Crankshaft sprocket – 1.4 and 1.6 litre engines

Removal

8 Remove the timing belt as described in Section 7.

9 Slide the sprocket from the end of the crankshaft, noting which way around it is fitted. Where applicable, recover the Woodruff key from the end of the crankshaft.

8.14a Remove the crankshaft sprocket . . .

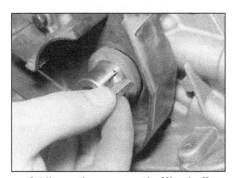

8.14b . . . then remove the Woodruff key . . .

Refitting

10 Where applicable, refit the Woodruff key to the end of the crankshaft, then slide the sprocket into position, making sure its timing mark is facing outwards (see illustration).

11 Refit the timing belt as described in Section 7.

Crankshaft sprocket – 1.8 and 2.0 litre engines

Note: A suitable puller may be required to remove the sprocket. A new sprocket bolt should be used on refitting.

Removal

12 Remove the timing belt as described in Section 7.

13 Slacken the crankshaft sprocket retaining bolt. Do not allow the crankshaft to turn, as the timing belt has been removed, and there may be a danger of piston-to-valve contact on some engines if the crankshaft it turned. To prevent crankshaft rotation on manual transmission models, have an assistant select top gear and apply the brakes firmly. On automatic transmission models prevent rotation by removing one of the torque converter retaining bolts and bolting the driveplate to the transmission housing using a metal bar, spacers and suitable bolts (see Chapter 7B). If the engine is removed from the vehicle it will be necessary to lock the flywheel/driveplate (see Section 15).

8.14c . . . and the thrust washer – 1.8 and 2.0 litre engines

14 Remove the sprocket bolt and washer, then remove the sprocket from the end of the crankshaft, using a suitable puller if necessary. Where applicable, recover the Woodruff key and the thrust washer from the end of the crankshaft (see illustrations).

Refitting

15 Where applicable, refit the thrust washer and the Woodruff key to the end of the crankshaft, then refit the crankshaft sprocket.

16 Fit a new sprocket securing bolt, ensuring that the washer is in place under the bolt head, and tighten the bolt to the specified torque in the two stages given in the Specifications. Prevent the crankshaft from turning using the method employed on removal.

17 Refit the timing belt as described in Section 7.

Tensioner assembly

Removal

18 Remove the timing belt as described in Section 7.

19 Slacken and remove the retaining bolt and remove the tensioner assembly from the engine (see illustration).

Refitting

20 Fit the tensioner to the engine. On 1.4 and 1.6 litre engines, make sure that the positioning lug on the tensioner backplate is

8.19 Slacken and remove the retaining bolt and remove the timing belt tensioner assembly

8.20 On refitting ensure the tensioner backplate lug (1) is correctly located in the oil pump housing hole (2) – 1.4 and 1.6 litre engines

correctly located in the oil pump housing hole **(see illustration)**. On 1.8 and 2.0 litre engines, make sure that the positioning lug on the tensioner backplate is correctly located between the two guide lugs on the oil pump.

21 Ensure that the tensioner is correctly seated, then refit the retaining bolt, and on all models except 1.8 and 2.0 litre models from 1993, tighten it to the specified torque.

22 Refit the timing belt as described in Section 7.

9 Camshaft oil seal - renewal

Front oil seal

1 Remove the camshaft sprocket as described in Section 8.

2 Carefully punch or drill two small holes opposite each other in the oil seal. Screw a self-tapping screw into each, and pull on the screws with pliers to extract the seal **(see illustration)**.

3 Clean the seal housing, and polish off any burrs or raised edges which may have caused the seal to fail in the first place.

4 Lubricate the lips of the new seal with clean engine oil, and press it into position using a suitable tubular drift (such as a socket) which bears only on the hard outer edge of the seal **(see illustration)**. Take care not to damage

9.2 Removing the camshaft oil seal

the seal lips during fitting; note that the seal lips should face inwards.

5 Refit the camshaft sprocket as described in Section 8.

Rear oil seal - 1.4 and 1.6 litre engines

6 Remove the distributor, or DIS module, as applicable, from the end of the camshaft housing, as described in Chapter 5B.

7 On models with a distributor, the camshaft rear oil seal takes the form of an O-ring on the rear of the distributor body. Prise off the old O-ring using a screwdriver **(see illustration)**, then fit the new O-ring and refit the distributor as described in Chapter 5B.

8 On models with DIS, the camshaft rear oil seal takes the form of an O-ring on the rear of the DIS module mounting plate. Unscrew the DIS module mounting plate securing bolts and withdraw the plate from the end of the camshaft housing **(see illustration)**. Prise off the old O-ring using a screwdriver, then fit the new O-ring and refit the DIS module mounting plate. Refit the DIS module to the mounting plate, with reference to Chapter 5B if necessary.

Rear oil seal – 1.8 and 2.0 litre engines

9 Remove the distributor components, as described in Chapter 5B.

10 Prise the seal from the camshaft housing **(see illustration)**.

11 Clean the oil seal seat with a wooden or plastic scraper.

9.4 Fitting a new camshaft oil seal

12 Grease the lips of the new seal and drive it into position until it is flush with the end of the camshaft housing, using a socket or tube. Take care not to damage the seal lips during fitting.

13 Refit the distributor components as described in Chapter 5B.

10 Camshaft housing and camshaft - removal, inspection and refitting

Note: *The camshaft oil seal(s) should be renewed on refitting.*

Removal

Using Vauxhall/Opel service tool (tool no. MKM 891)

Caution: Prior to fitting the special tool, rotate the crankshaft 90° past the TDC position (see Section 3). This will position the pistons approximately mid-way in the bores and prevent the valves contacting them when the tool is fitted.

1 If access to the special service tool can be gained, the camshaft can be removed from the engine without disturbing the camshaft housing, as follows.

a) *Once the camshaft cover and timing belt have been removed (see Sections 4 and 7), the tool is fitted to the top of the camshaft housing, and depresses the cam followers.*

b) *Once the timing belt sprocket (see Section 8), fuel pump (carburettor engines) and the distributor or DIS module*

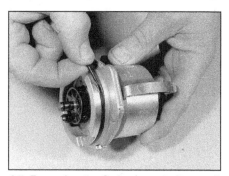

9.7 Removing the O-ring/camshaft rear oil seal from the rear of the distributor

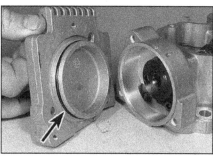

9.8 Removing the DIS module mounting plate for access to the O-ring/camshaft rear oil seal

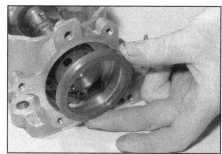

9.10 Removing the camshaft rear oil seal – 2.0 litre engine (shown with camshaft housing removed from engine)

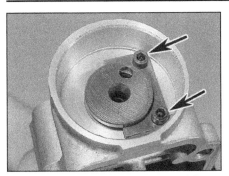

10.8 Unscrew the thrustplate securing bolts (arrowed) . . .

10.9 . . . and withdraw the thrustplate

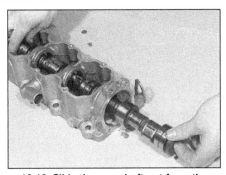

10.10 Slide the camshaft out from the housing

mounting bracket have been removed, and the thrustplate has been unbolted (see paragraphs 4 to 9), the camshaft can be withdrawn from the transmission (left-hand) end of the housing.

Without Vauxhall/Opel service tool

Note: *Assuming that the special service tool is not available, the camshaft housing must be removed. Since the cylinder head bolts must be removed (the cylinder head bolts secure both the cylinder head and the camshaft housing), it is strongly recommended that a new cylinder head gasket is fitted. If the gasket is not renewed, and it 'blows' on reassembly, the cylinder head will have to be removed in order to renew the gasket, and another new set of cylinder head bolts will have to be obtained for refitting. You have been warned!*

2 Removal and refitting of the camshaft housing is described in Section 12, along with cylinder head removal and refitting. If it is decided not to disturb the cylinder head, the relevant paragraphs referring specifically to cylinder head removal and refitting can be ignored, and it is strongly recommended that the cylinder head is clamped to the cylinder block using four head bolts and some spacers, to reduce the possibility of the seal between the head and the block being broken.

3 With the camshaft housing removed, proceed as follows.

4 On carburettor engines, remove the fuel pump as described in Chapter 4A.

5 Remove the distributor, distributor components, or DIS module (as applicable) from

the end of the housing, with reference to Chapter 5B.

6 On models with DIS, unscrew the securing bolts and remove the DIS module mounting plate from the end of the camshaft housing.

7 On 1.8 and 2.0 litre engines, prise out the camshaft rear oil seal.

8 Working at the distributor/DIS module end of the camshaft, unscrew the two camshaft thrustplate securing bolts, using an Allen key or hexagon bit **(see illustration)**.

9 Withdraw the thrustplate, noting which way round it is fitted **(see illustration)**.

10 Carefully withdraw the camshaft from the distributor/DIS module end of the housing, taking care not to damage the bearing journals **(see illustration)**.

Inspection

11 With the camshaft removed, examine the bearings in the camshaft housing for signs of obvious wear or pitting. If evident, a new camshaft housing will probably be required. Also check that the oil supply holes in the camshaft housing are free from obstructions **(see illustration)**.

12 The camshaft itself should show no marks or scoring on the journal or cam lobe surfaces. If evident, renew the camshaft. Note that if the camshaft is renewed, all the rocker arms should also be renewed.

13 Check the camshaft thrustplate for signs of wear or grooves and renew if evident.

Refitting

14 It is advisable to renew the camshaft front oil seal as a matter of course if the camshaft

has been removed. Prise out the old seal using a screwdriver and tap in the new seal until it is flush with the housing, using a socket or tube.

15 Begin refitting by liberally oiling the oil seal lip, and the bearings in the housing.

16 Carefully insert the camshaft into the housing from the distributor/DIS module end, taking care to avoid damage to the bearings.

17 Refit the thrustplate, ensuring that it is fitted the correct way round (as noted before removal), and tighten the securing bolts to the specified torque. Check the camshaft endfloat by inserting a feeler gauge between the thrustplate and the camshaft end flange. If the endfloat exceeds that specified, renew the thrustplate **(see illustrations)**.

18 On 1.8 and 2.0 litre engines, fit a new camshaft rear oil seal to the housing, using a socket or tube. The oil seal should be flush with the end of the camshaft housing.

19 On models with DIS, examine the condition of the O-ring on the rear of the DIS module mounting plate and renew it if necessary, then refit the DIS module mounting plate.

20 Refit the distributor, distributor components or DIS module, as applicable, as described in Chapter 5B. Where applicable, check the condition of the O-ring on the rear of the distributor, and renew if necessary.

21 On carburettor engines, refit the fuel pump as described in Chapter 4A.

22 Where applicable, remove the bolts and spacers clamping the cylinder head to the block.

23 Refit the camshaft housing, as described in Section 12.

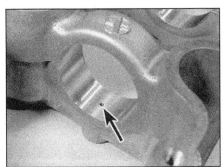

10.11 Check the oil supply holes (arrowed) in the camshaft housing for obstructions

10.17a Tightening a camshaft thrustplate securing bolt

10.17b Checking the camshaft endfloat using a feeler gauge

11.11a Remove each follower . . .

11.11b . . . thrust pad . . .

11.11c . . . and hydraulic tappet from the cylinder head

24 If a new camshaft has been fitted, it is important to observe the following running-in schedule (unless otherwise specified by the manufacturer – consult a Vauxhall/Opel dealer, or the camshaft manufacturer for latest recommendations) immediately after initially starting the engine:

a) *One minute at 2000 rpm.*
b) *One minute at 1500 rpm.*
c) *One minute at 3000 rpm.*
d) *One minute at 2000 rpm.*

25 Change the engine oil (but not the filter, unless due in any case) approximately 600 miles (1000 km) after fitting a new camshaft.

11 Camshaft followers and hydraulic tappets - removal, inspection and refitting

Using Vauxhall/Opel service tool (tool no. KM-565)

Removal

1 If access to the special tool (KM-565) or a suitable equivalent can be gained, the cam followers and tappets can be removed as follows, without disturbing the camshaft.
2 Firmly apply the handbrake then jack up the front of the vehicle and support it on axle stands (see "*Jacking and vehicle support*"). Remove the right-hand front roadwheel.
3 Remove the camshaft cover as described in Section 4.
4 Using a socket and extension bar on the crankshaft pulley/sprocket bolt, rotate the crankshaft in the normal direction of rotation until the camshaft lobe of the first follower/tappet to be removed is pointing vertically upwards.
5 Fit the service tool to the top of the camshaft housing, making sure that the tool end is correctly engaged with the top of the valve. Screw the tool stud into one of the housing bolt holes until the valve is sufficiently depressed to allow the follower to be slid out from underneath the camshaft. The hydraulic tappet can then also be removed, as can the thrust pad from the top of the valve. Inspect the components (see paragraphs 10 and 11) and renew if worn or damaged.

Inspection

6 Refer to paragraphs 12 to 15.

Refitting

7 Lubricate the tappet and follower with clean engine oil, then slide the tappet into its bore in the cylinder head. Similarly, where applicable, refit the thrust pad to the top of the valve. Manoeuvre the follower into position, ensuring that it is correctly engaged with the tappet and the thrust pad, then carefully remove the service tool.
8 Repeat the operation on the remaining followers and tappets.

Without Vauxhall/Opel service tool

Removal

9 If the special service tool is not available, it will be necessary to remove the camshaft housing to allow the followers and tappets to be removed (see Section 10, paragraph 2).
10 With the camshaft housing removed, obtain eight small, clean plastic containers, and number them 1 to 8; alternatively, divide a larger container into eight compartments.
11 Lift out each follower, thrust pad and hydraulic tappet in turn from the cylinder head, and place them in their respective container or compartment, so that they can be refitted in their original locations. Do not interchange the components, or the rate of wear will be much-increased **(see illustrations)**.

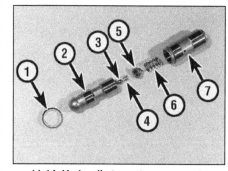

11.14 Hydraulic tappet components

1 *Collar*
2 *Plunger*
3 *Ball*
4 *Small spring*
5 *Plunger cap*
6 *Large spring*
7 *Cylinder*

Inspection

12 Check the follower and thrust pad faces (the areas that contact the valve lifters and valve stems) for pits, wear, score-marks or any indication that the surface-hardening has worn through. Check the follower camshaft contact faces in the same manner. Clean the oil hole in the top of each follower using a length of wire. Renew any followers or thrust pads which appear suspect.
13 Check the hydraulic tappet bores in the cylinder head for wear. If excessive wear is evident, the cylinder head must be renewed. Also check the tappet oil holes in the cylinder head for obstructions.
14 On models that have covered a high mileage, or for which the service history (particularly oil changes) is suspect, it is possible for the hydraulic tappets to suffer internal contamination, which in extreme cases may result in increased engine top-end noise and wear. To minimise the possibility of problems, on high mileage engines, it is advisable to dismantle and clean the hydraulic tappets whenever the cylinder head is overhauled. No spare parts are available for the tappets, and if any of the individual components are unserviceable, the complete tappet assembly must be renewed **(see illustration)**.
15 To dismantle and clean a hydraulic tappet, proceed as follows:
a) *Carefully pull the collar from the top of the tappet cylinder. It should be possible to remove the collar by hand - if a tool is used, take care not to distort the collar.*
b) *Withdraw the plunger from the cylinder and remove the spring.*
c) *Using a small screwdriver, carefully prise the cap from the base of the plunger. Remove the spring and ball from under the cap, taking care not to lose them as the cap is removed.*
d) *Carefully clean all the components using paraffin or a solvent, paying particular attention to the machined surfaces of the cylinder (internal surfaces) and piston (external surfaces). Thoroughly dry all the components using a lint-free cloth. Carefully examine the springs for damage or distortion - the complete tappet must be renewed if the springs are not in perfect condition.*

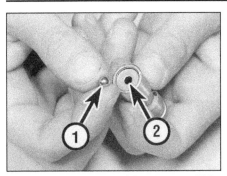

11.15a Locate the ball (1) on its seat (2) in the base of the plunger

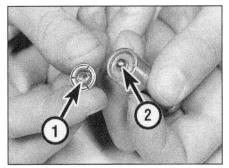

11.15b Spring (1) located in plunger cap, and ball (2) located on seat in plunger

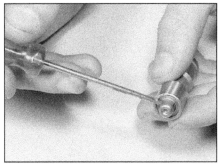

11.15c Locate the cap flange in the plunger groove

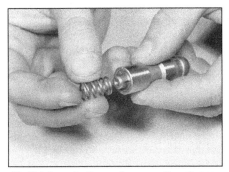

11.15d Locate the spring over the plunger cap . . .

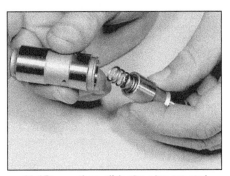

11.15e . . . then slide the plunger and spring assembly into the cylinder

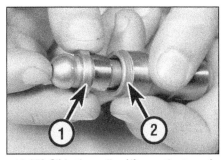

11.15f Slide the collar (1) over the top of the plunger, and engage with the groove (2) in the cylinder

e) *Lubricate the components sparingly with clean engine oil of the correct grade, then reassemble as follows.*

f) *Invert the plunger and locate the ball on its seat in the base of the plunger (see illustration).*

g) *Locate the smaller spring on its seat in the plunger cap, then carefully refit the cap and spring, ensuring that the spring locates on the ball. Carefully press around the flange of the cap, using a small screwdriver if necessary, until the flange is securely located in the groove in the base of the plunger (see illustrations).*

h) *Locate the larger spring over the plunger cap, ensuring that the spring is correctly seated and slide the plunger and spring assembly into the cylinder (see illustrations).*

i) *Slide the collar over the top of the plunger and carefully compress the plunger by hand, until the collar can be pushed down to engage securely with the groove in the cylinder (see illustration).*

Refitting

16 Lubricate the hydraulic tappets and their cylinder head bores with clean engine oil. Refit the tappets to the cylinder head, making sure that they are fitted in their original locations.

17 Refit the thrust pads in their original locations.

18 Lubricate the followers with clean engine oil. Fit each follower in its original location, making sure that it engages correctly with both the tappet and thrust pad.

19 On completion, refit the camshaft housing (see Section 12).

12 Cylinder head - removal and refitting

Removal

Note: *The engine must be cold when removing the cylinder head. New cylinder head bolts and a new cylinder head gasket must be used on refitting.*

1 On fuel injection models, depressurise the fuel system as described in Chapter 4B.

2 Disconnect the battery negative lead.

3 Drain the cooling system, and remove the spark plugs as described in Chapter 1.

4 Remove the timing belt as described in Section 7.

5 Remove the inlet and exhaust manifolds as described in Chapter 4A or 4B. If no work is to be carried out on the cylinder head, the head can be removed complete with manifolds once the following operations have been carried out.

a) *Disconnect the various wiring connectors from the carburettor or throttle body (as applicable), manifold and associated components, and free the wiring harness(es) from the inlet manifold.*

b) *Disconnect the fuel hoses from the carburettor or throttle body (as applicable), and fuel pump (carburettor models), and the various vacuum and*

coolant hoses from the inlet manifold.

c) *Unbolt the inlet manifold support bracket and the alternator upper bracket.*

d) *Disconnect the accelerator cable from the carburettor or throttle body (as applicable).*

e) *Unbolt the exhaust front pipe from manifold and, where applicable, disconnect the oxygen sensor wiring connector.*

f) *On carburettor models, disconnect the hot air hose from the shroud on the exhaust manifold.*

6 Remove the camshaft cover as described in Section 4.

7 Remove the camshaft sprocket as described in Section 8.

8 Unscrew the bolts securing the timing belt rear cover to the camshaft housing.

9 Disconnect the wiring connectors from the following components, as applicable **(see illustrations)**:

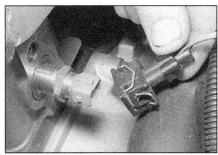

12.9a Disconnecting the coolant temperature sender wiring plug – 1.6 litre engine

12.9b Unbolting a wiring harness earth wire from the camshaft housing – 1.6 litre engine

12.10 Disconnecting the breather hose from the camshaft housing – 1.6 litre engine

12.11 Unscrewing a crankcase breather tube bracket bolt – 2.0 litre engine

a) *Distributor or DIS module (as applicable) – see Chapter 5B.*
b) *Coolant temperature sender unit – see Chapter 3.*
c) *Evaporative emission control purge valve – see Chapter 4C.*
d) *Wiring harness earth wire(s) on camshaft housing.*

Free the wiring from its retaining clips, noting its routing, and position the wiring clear of the cylinder head.

10 Where applicable, release the securing clip and disconnect the breather hose from the camshaft housing **(see illustration)**.

11 Where applicable, unscrew the bolts securing the crankcase breather tube bracket to the end of the cylinder head **(see illustration)**.

12 Slacken the retaining clip(s) and disconnect the coolant hose(s) from the thermostat housing **(see illustration)**.

13 Make a final check to ensure that all relevant hoses, pipes and wires, etc, have been disconnected.

14 Working in the **reverse** of the tightening sequence **(see illustration 12.32a)**, progressively slacken the cylinder head bolts by a third of a turn at a time until all bolts can be unscrewed by hand. Remove each bolt in turn, along with its washer.

15 Lift the camshaft housing from the cylinder head **(see illustration)**. If necessary, tap the housing gently with a soft-faced mallet to free it from the cylinder head, but **do not** lever at the mating faces. Note the fitted positions

of the two locating dowels, and remove them for safe keeping if they are loose.

16 Lift the cylinder head from the cylinder block, taking care not to dislodge the cam followers or thrust pads **(see illustration)**. If necessary, tap the cylinder head gently with a soft-faced mallet to free it from the block, but **do not** lever at the mating faces. Note the fitted positions of the two locating dowels, and remove them for safe keeping if they are loose.

17 Recover the cylinder head gasket, and discard it.

Preparation for refitting

18 The mating faces of the cylinder head and block must be perfectly clean before refitting the head. Use a scraper to remove all traces of gasket and carbon, and also clean the tops of the pistons. Take particular care with the aluminium surfaces, as the soft metal is damaged easily. Also, make sure that debris is not allowed to enter the oil and water channels - this is particularly important for the oil circuit, as carbon could block the oil supply to the camshaft or crankshaft bearings. Using adhesive tape and paper, seal the water, oil and bolt holes in the cylinder block. To prevent carbon entering the gap between the pistons and bores, smear a little grease in the gap. After cleaning the piston, rotate the crankshaft so that the piston moves down the bore, then wipe out the grease and carbon with a cloth rag. Clean the other piston crowns in the same way.

19 Check the block and head for nicks, deep scratches and other damage. If slight, they may be removed carefully with a file. More serious damage may be repaired by machining, but this is a specialist job.

20 If warpage of the cylinder head is suspected, use a straight-edge to check it for distortion. Refer to Chapter 2C if necessary.

21 Ensure that the cylinder head bolt holes in the crankcase are clean and free of oil. Syringe or soak up any oil left in the bolt holes. This is most important in order that the correct bolt tightening torque can be applied, and to prevent the possibility of the block being cracked by hydraulic pressure when the bolts are tightened.

22 Renew the cylinder head bolts regardless of their apparent condition.

Refitting

23 Position number 1 piston at TDC, and wipe clean the mating faces of the cylinder head and block.

24 Ensure that the two locating dowels are in position at each end of the cylinder block/crankcase surface.

25 Fit the new cylinder head gasket to the block, making sure that it is fitted the correct way up, with the 'OBEN/TOP' mark uppermost **(see illustrations)**.

26 Carefully refit the cylinder head, locating it on the dowels.

27 Ensure that the mating surfaces of the cylinder head and camshaft housing are clean and dry. Check that the camshaft is still

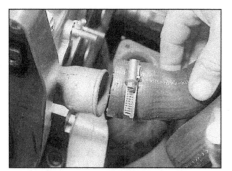

12.12 Disconnecting the coolant hose from the thermostat housing – 1.6 litre engine

12.15 Lifting the camshaft housing from the cylinder head – 1.6 litre engine

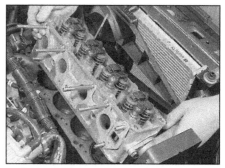

12.16 Lifting the cylinder head from the cylinder block – 1.6 litre engine

12.25a Fit the new gasket to the cylinder block, engaging it with the locating dowels (arrowed) . . .

12.25b . . . making sure its OBEN/TOP marking is uppermost

12.28 Apply sealant to the cylinder head upper mating surface then refit the camshaft housing

12.31 Fit the washers to the new cylinder head bolts and screw the bolts into position

correctly positioned by temporarily fitting the camshaft sprocket and checking that the sprocket timing mark is still pointing vertically upwards.

28 Apply a bead of suitable sealant (Vauxhall/Opel part no. 90094714, or equivalent) to the camshaft housing mating surface on the cylinder head (see illustration).

29 Ensure the two locating dowels are in position then lubricate the camshaft followers with clean engine oil.

30 Carefully lower the camshaft housing assembly into position on the cylinder head, locating it on the dowels.

31 Fit the washers to the **new** cylinder head bolts, then carefully insert them into position (**do not drop** the bolts into position), tightening them finger-tight only at this stage (see illustration).

32 Working progressively and in the sequence shown, first tighten all the cylinder head bolts to the stage 1 torque setting (see illustrations).

33 Once all bolts have been tightened to the stage 1 torque, again working in the sequence shown, tighten each bolt through its specified stage 2 angle, using a socket and extension bar. It is recommended that an angle-measuring gauge is used during this stage of the tightening procedure, to ensure accuracy (see illustration).

34 Again working in the specified sequence, tighten all bolts through the specified stage 3 angle.

35 Finally, again working in the specified sequence, tighten all bolts through the specified stage 4 angle.

36 Refit the bolts securing the timing belt rear cover to the camshaft housing and tighten them securely.

37 Refit the camshaft sprocket as described in Section 8, then fit the timing belt as described in Section 7.

38 Refit the camshaft cover as described in Section 4.

39 Reconnect the wiring connectors to the cylinder head components, ensuring all wiring is correctly routed, and secure it in position with the necessary clips.

40 Reconnect the coolant hose(s) to the thermostat housing and securely tighten the retaining clip(s).

41 Where applicable, refit the bolts securing the crankcase breather tube bracket to the end of the cylinder head.

42 Where applicable, reconnect the breather hose to the camshaft housing and secure with the clip.

43 Refit/reconnect (as applicable) the manifolds as described in Chapter 4A or 4B.

44 Refit the roadwheel, then lower the vehicle to the ground and tighten the wheel bolts to the specified torque.

45 Make a final check to ensure that all pipes and hoses are correctly reconnected and routed, then refill the cooling system and refit the spark plugs as described in Chapter 1.

46 Reconnect the battery, then start the engine and check for signs of leaks.

13 Sump and oil pick-up pipe - removal and refitting

Note: *A new sump gasket and sump baffle gasket (1.8 and 2.0 litre engines) must be used on refitting. Sealant (Vauxhall/Opel part no. 90485251, or equivalent) will be required to coat the cylinder block face (see text) and thread-locking compound will be required to coat the sump securing bolt threads. If the oil pick-up pipe is removed, a new O-ring should be used on refitting.*

Removal

1 Disconnect the battery negative lead.

2 Drain the engine oil, with reference to Chapter 1 if necessary, then refit and tighten the drain plug to the specified torque.

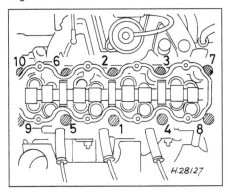

12.32a Cylinder head bolt tightening sequence

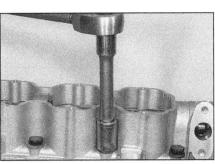

12.32b Working in the specified sequence, tighten the cylinder head bolts to the specified stage 1 torque setting . . .

12.33 . . . and then through the various specified angles (see text)

13.6 Removing the engine-to-transmission blanking plate

13.7 Withdrawing the sump

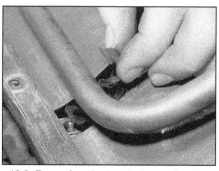

13.9 Removing the bracket securing the oil pick-up pipe to the cylinder block – 2.0 litre engine

3 Apply the handbrake, then jack up the front of the vehicle and support securely on axle stands (see "*Jacking and vehicle support*").

4 Remove the front section of the exhaust system as described in Chapter 4C.

5 Where applicable, disconnect the wiring from the oil level sensor mounted in the sump.

6 Unscrew the securing bolts and remove the engine-to-transmission blanking plate from the bellhousing **(see illustration)**.

7 Unscrew the securing bolts and withdraw the sump **(see illustration)**. If necessary, tap the sump with a soft-faced mallet to free it from the cylinder block. **Do not** lever between the sump and cylinder block mating faces. On 1.8 and 2.0 litre engines, the sump baffle will probably be pulled away from the cylinder block with the sump, but cannot be removed

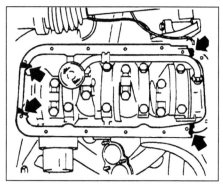

13.12a Apply sealant to the oil pump and rear main bearing cap joints (arrowed) before the sump is refitted

until the bracket securing the oil pick-up pipe has been removed.

8 Remove the gasket.

9 On 1.8 and 2.0 litre engines, to remove the sump baffle, unbolt the bracket securing the oil pick-up pipe to the cylinder block **(see illustration)**. The baffle can then be manipulated over the oil pick-up pipe. Remove the sump baffle gasket.

10 The oil pick-up pipe can be removed by unscrewing the single bolt securing the support bracket to the cylinder block (if not already done) and the two bolts securing the end of the pipe to the oil pump. Remove the O-ring.

Refitting

11 Clean all traces of old gasket from the mating faces of the cylinder block, sump baffle (where applicable) and sump.

12 Begin refitting by applying sealant (Vauxhall/Opel part no. 90485251, or equivalent) to the joints between the oil pump and cylinder block and the rear main bearing cap and cylinder block **(see illustrations)**.

13 On 1.8 and 2.0 litre engines, fit a new sump baffle gasket, if necessary applying a little sealing compound to hold it in place. Offer the sump baffle up to the cylinder block, manipulating it over the oil pick-up pipe where applicable. Locate the remaining gasket on the sump baffle, but do not use sealing compound.

14 If the oil pick-up pipe has been removed, refit it to the oil pump using a new O-ring **(see illustrations)**.

15 Where applicable, refit the bracket securing the oil pick-up pipe to the cylinder block, ensuring that it passes through the relevant hole in the sump baffle on 1.8 and 2.0 litre engines.

16 Coat the sump securing bolts with thread-locking compound, then refit the sump and tighten the securing bolts to the specified torque.

17 Further refitting is a reversal of removal, but refit the front section of the exhaust system with reference to Chapter 4C and on completion, refill the engine with oil as described in Chapter 1.

14 Oil pump - removal, overhaul and refitting

Removal

Note: *The pressure relief valve can be removed with the pump in position on the engine. A new oil pump gasket and a new crankshaft front oil seal will be required on refitting.*

1 Remove the timing belt as described in Section 7.

2 Remove the timing belt sprockets and the tensioner as described in Section 8.

3 Unbolt the timing belt rear cover from the camshaft housing and cylinder block and remove it from the engine. Where applicable, unclip the crankshaft sensor wiring from the rear of the cover.

13.12b Applying sealing compound to the joint between the oil pump and the cylinder block – 2.0 litre engine

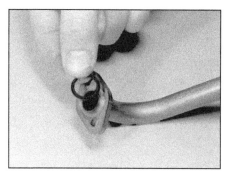

13.14a Fit a new O-ring to the oil pick-up . . .

13.14b . . . and refit the pick-up pipe to the oil pump – 1.6 litre engine

14.8 Undo the retaining screws and remove the oil pump cover

14.10 Lift the inner and outer gears (arrowed) out from the pump housing

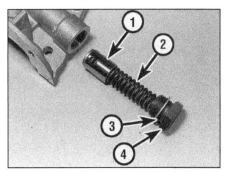

14.11 Oil pressure relief valve components

1 Plunger   *3 Sealing washer*
2 Spring   *4 Valve bolt*

4 Remove the sump and oil pump pick-up pipe as described in Section 13.

5 Disconnect the wiring connector from the oil pressure switch.

6 Where applicable, unbolt the crankshaft sensor mounting bracket and position it clear of the oil pump.

7 Slacken and remove the retaining bolts then slide the oil pump housing assembly off of the end of the crankshaft, taking great care not to lose the locating dowels. Remove the housing gasket and discard it.

Overhaul

Note: *A new pressure relief valve bolt sealing washer will be required on reassembly, and thread-locking compound will be required to coat the threads of the oil pump cover screws.*

8 Undo the retaining screws and lift off the pump cover from the rear of the housing (see illustration). The screws may be very tight, in which case it may be necessary to use an impact driver to remove them.

9 Using a suitable marker pen, mark the surface of both the pump inner and outer gears; the marks can then be used to ensure that the rotors are refitted the correct way around.

10 Lift the inner and outer gears from the pump housing (see illustration).

11 Unscrew the oil pressure relief valve bolt from the front of the housing and withdraw the spring and plunger from the housing, noting which way around the plunger is fitted (see illustration). Remove the sealing washer from the valve bolt.

14.15 Fitting a new crankshaft oil seal to the oil pump housing

14.13a Using a feeler blade to check gear clearance

12 Clean the components, and carefully examine the gears, pump body and relief valve plunger for any signs of scoring or wear. Renew any component which shows signs of wear or damage; if the gears or pump housing are worn or marked, then the complete pump assembly should be renewed.

13 If the components appear serviceable, measure the clearance between the inner gear and outer gear using feeler blades. Also measure the gear endfloat, and check the flatness of the end cover (see illustrations). If the any of the clearances exceed the specified tolerances, the pump must be renewed.

14 If the pump components are in satis-factory condition, reassemble the components in the reverse order of removal, noting the following:

a) *Ensure that both gears are fitted the correct way round, as noted before removal.*

b) *Fit a new sealing washer to the pressure relief valve bolt, and tighten the bolt to the specified torque.*

c) *Remove all traces of locking compound from the cover screws. Apply a drop of fresh locking compound to each screw and tighten the screws to the specified torque.*

d) *On completion, before refitting, prime the oil pump by filling it with clean engine oil whilst rotating the inner gear.*

Refitting

15 Prior to refitting, carefully lever out the crankshaft oil seal using a flat-bladed screwdriver. Fit a new oil seal, ensuring its

14.13b Using a straight-edge and feeler blade to measure gear endfloat

sealing lip is facing inwards, and press it squarely into the housing using a tubular drift which bears only on the hard outer edge of the seal (see illustration). Press the seal into position so that it is flush with the housing and lubricate the oil seal lip with clean engine oil.

16 Ensure that the mating surfaces of the oil pump and cylinder block are clean and dry and that the locating dowels are in position.

17 Fit a new gasket to the cylinder block.

18 Carefully manoeuvre the oil pump into position and engage the inner gear with the flats on the crankshaft (see illustration). Take care not to damage the oil seal lip on the front of the crankshaft. Locate the pump on the dowels.

19 Refit the pump housing retaining bolts in their original locations and tighten them to the specified torque.

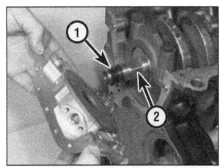

14.18 On refitting take care not to damage the oil seal on the crankshaft lip (1) and engage the inner gear with the crankshaft flats (2)

15.2 Lock the flywheel/driveplate ring gear with a tool similar to that shown

15.8a On manual transmission models, tighten the flywheel bolts to the specified stage 1 torque setting . . .

15.8b . . . then tighten them through the specified stage 2 and 3 angles

20 Where applicable, refit the crankshaft sensor bracket to the pump housing and tighten its mounting bolt to the specified torque.
21 Reconnect the oil pressure sensor wiring connector.
22 Refit the oil pump pick-up pipe and sump as described in Section 13.
23 Refit the rear timing belt cover to the engine, tightening its retaining bolts securely.
24 Refit the timing belt sprockets and tensioner as described in Section 8, then refit the timing belt as described in Section 7.
25 On completion refill the engine with clean oil as described in Chapter 1.

15 Flywheel/driveplate - removal, inspection and refitting

Flywheel - manual transmission models

Note: *New flywheel retaining bolts will be required on refitting.*

Removal

1 Remove the transmission as described in Chapter 7A, then remove the clutch assembly as described in Chapter 6.
2 Prevent the flywheel from turning by locking the ring gear teeth with a similar arrangement to that shown **(see illustration)**. Alternatively, bolt a strap between the flywheel and the cylinder block/crankcase. Make alignment marks between the flywheel and crankshaft using paint or a suitable marker pen.
3 Slacken and remove the retaining bolts and remove the flywheel. Do not drop it, as it is very heavy!

Inspection

4 Examine the flywheel for scoring of the clutch face. If the clutch face is scored, the flywheel may be surface-ground, but renewal is preferable. Check for wear or chipping of the ring gear teeth. Renewal of the ring gear is also possible, but is not a task for the home mechanic; renewal requires the new ring gear to be heated (up to 180° to 230°C) to allow it to be fitted.

5 If there is any doubt about the condition of the flywheel, seek the advice of a Vauxhall/Opel dealer or engine reconditioning specialist. They will be able to advise whether reconditioning or renewal is the best option.

Refitting

6 Clean the mating surfaces of the flywheel and crankshaft.
7 Offer up the flywheel and fit the new retaining bolts. If the original flywheel is being refitted, align the marks made prior to removal.
8 Lock the flywheel by the method used on removal, and tighten the retaining bolts to the specified stage 1 torque setting, then angle-tighten the bolts through the specified stage 2 angle, using a socket and extension bar, and finally through the specified stage 3 angle. It is recommended that an angle-measuring gauge is used during the final stages of tightening, to ensure accuracy **(see illustrations)**. If a gauge is not available, use white paint to make alignment marks between the bolt head and flywheel prior to tightening; the marks can then be used to check that the bolt has been rotated through the correct angle.
9 Refit the clutch as described in Chapter 6, then remove the locking tool from the flywheel, and refit the transmission as described in Chapter 7A.

Driveplate - automatic transmission models

Note: *Thread-locking compound will be required to coat the threads of the driveplate retaining bolts on refitting.*

Removal

10 Remove the transmission as described in Chapter 7B, then remove the driveplate as described in paragraphs 2 and 3, noting that there is a retaining plate fitted between the retaining bolts and driveplate.

Inspection

11 Carefully examine the driveplate and ring gear teeth for signs of wear or damage and check the driveplate surface for any signs of cracks.
12 If there is any doubt about the condition of the driveplate, seek the advice of a Vauxhall/

Opel dealer or engine reconditioning specialist. They will be able to advise whether reconditioning or renewal is the best option.

Refitting

13 Clean the mating surfaces of the driveplate and crankshaft, and remove all traces of locking compound from the driveplate retaining bolt threads.
14 Apply a drop of locking compound to each of the retaining bolt threads, then offer up the driveplate. If the original driveplate is being refitted align the marks made prior to removal.
15 Refit the retaining plate and screw in the retaining bolts.
16 Lock the driveplate using the method employed on removal then, working in a diagonal sequence, evenly and progressively tighten the retaining bolts to the specified torque.
17 Remove the locking tool and refit the transmission as described in Chapter 7B.

16 Crankshaft oil seals - renewal

Timing belt end (right-hand) oil seal

1 Remove the crankshaft sprocket as described in Section 8. Ensure that, where applicable, the Woodruff key is removed from the end of the crankshaft.
2 On 1.8 and 2.0 litre engines, remove the rear timing belt cover with reference to Section 6.
3 Carefully punch or drill two small holes opposite each other in the oil seal. Screw a self-tapping screw into each hole, and pull on the screws with pliers to extract the seal **(see illustration)**.
Caution: Great care must be taken to avoid damage to the oil pump.
4 Clean the oil seal housing and polish off any burrs or raised edges which may have caused the seal to fail in the first place.
5 Lubricate the lips of the new seal with clean engine oil and ease it into position over the end of the crankshaft, with the seal lips facing

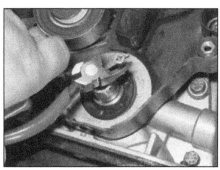

16.3 Removing the crankshaft front oil seal

16.5 Fitting a new crankshaft front oil seal

inwards. Press the seal squarely into position until it is flush with the housing. If necessary, a suitable tubular drift, such as a socket, which bears only on the hard outer edge of the seal, can be used to tap the seal into position **(see illustration)**. Take great care not to damage the seal lips during fitting.

6 On 1.8 and 2.0 litre engines, refit the rear timing belt cover, with reference to Section 6.

7 Wash off any traces of oil, then refit the crankshaft sprocket as described in Section 8.

Flywheel/driveplate end (left-hand) oil seal

8 Remove the flywheel/driveplate as described in Section 15.

9 Renew the seal as described in paragraphs 3 to 5.

10 Refit the flywheel/driveplate as described in Section 15.

17 Engine/transmission mountings -
inspection and renewal

Inspection

1 If improved access is required, raise the front of the vehicle and support it securely on axle stands (see "Jacking and vehicle"

support"). Where necessary, undo the retaining bolts and remove the engine undershield.

2 Check the mounting rubber to see if it is cracked, hardened or separated from the metal at any point; renew the mounting if any such damage or deterioration is evident.

3 Check that all the mounting fasteners are securely tightened; use a torque wrench to check if possible.

4 Using a large screwdriver or a pry bar, check for wear in the mounting by carefully levering against it to check for free play; where this is not possible, enlist the aid of an assistant to move the engine/transmission unit back and forth, or from side-to-side, while you watch the mounting. While some free play is to be expected even from new components, excessive wear should be obvious. If excessive free play is found, check first that the fasteners are correctly secured, then if necessary renew any worn components as described in the following paragraphs.

Renewal

Right-hand mounting

Note: *Suitable thread-locking compound will be required to coat the threads of the mounting-to-body bolts on refitting.*

5 If not already done, apply the handbrake,

then raise the front of the vehicle and support securely on axle stands (see "Jacking and vehicle support").

6 Attach lifting tackle to the engine lifting brackets on the cylinder head and support the weight of the engine.

7 Working under the vehicle, unbolt the engine mounting bracket from the cylinder block and unbolt the mounting from the body, then withdraw the bracket/mounting assembly **(see illustration)**.

8 Unbolt the mounting from the bracket.

9 Fit the new mounting to the bracket and tighten the securing bolts to the specified torque.

10 Refit the mounting bracket to the cylinder block and tighten the securing bolts to the specified torque.

11 Coat the threads of the mounting-to-body bolts with thread-locking compound, then refit them and tighten to the specified torque.

12 Disconnect the lifting tackle and hoist from the engine.

13 Lower the vehicle to the ground.

Left-hand mounting

Note: *The manufacturers recommend that new mounting-to-body bolts are used on refitting.*

14 Proceed as described in paragraphs 5 and 6.

15 Working under the vehicle, unbolt the engine/transmission mounting bracket from the transmission and unbolt the mounting from the body, then withdraw the bracket/mounting assembly **(see illustration)**.

16 Unbolt the mounting from the bracket.

17 Fit the new mounting to the bracket and tighten the securing bolts to the specified torque.

18 Before refitting the bracket/mounting assembly, check that the original bolts that secured the mounting to the body rotate freely in their threaded bores in the body. If necessary, recut the threaded bores using an M10 x 1.25 mm tap.

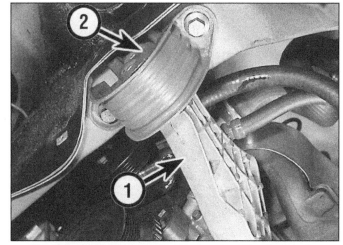

17.7 Right-hand engine mounting bracket (1) and mounting block (2) – 1.6 litre engine (viewed from underneath)

17.15 Left-hand engine/transmission mounting bracket (1) and mounting block (2) – 1.6 litre engine (viewed from underneath)

17.23a Rear engine mounting block-to-front subframe nuts (arrowed) – viewed from underneath

17.23b Rear engine mounting bracket (arrowed) – 1.6 litre engine (viewed from underneath)

19 Refit the mounting bracket to the transmission and tighten the securing bolts to the specified torque.

20 Fit **new** mounting-to-body bolts and tighten them to the specified torque.

21 Disconnect the lifting tackle and hoist from the engine. Lower the vehicle to the ground.

Rear mounting

22 Proceed as described in paragraphs 5 and 6.

23 Working under the vehicle, unbolt the mounting from the front subframe and the mounting bracket and withdraw the mounting **(see illustrations)**.

24 Fit the new mounting to the subframe and mounting bracket and tighten the securing bolts and nuts to the specified torque.

25 Disconnect the lifting tackle and hoist from the engine. Lower the vehicle to the ground.

Chapter 2 Part B:
DOHC engine in-car repair procedures

Contents

Degrees of difficulty

Easy, suitable for novice with little experience		Fairly easy, suitable for beginner with some experience		Fairly difficult, suitable for competent DIY mechanic		Difficult, suitable for experienced DIY mechanic		Very difficult, suitable for expert DIY or professional	

Specifications

General

Engine type	Four-cylinder, in-line, water-cooled. Double overhead camshaft, belt-driven, acting on hydraulic tappets

Manufacturer's engine codes:

Note: *The code can be found on the cylinder block, in front of the clutch housing.*

X 14 XE ('Ecotec')	1.4 litre + catalytic converter + Multi-point fuel injection (MPi)
X 16 XEL ('Ecotec')	1.6 litre + cat + MPi
C 18 XE	1.8 litre + cat + MPi
C 18 XEL ('Ecotec')	1.8 litre + cat + MPi
X 18 XE ('Ecotec')	1.8 litre + cat + MPi
C 20 XE	2.0 litre + cat + MPi
X 20 XEV ('Ecotec')	2.0 litre + cat + MPi

Capacity:	Bore	Stroke
1.4 litre engines (1389 cc)	77.6 mm	73.4 mm
1.6 litre engines (1598 cc)	79.0 mm	81.5 mm
1.8 litre engines (1796 cc)	81.6 mm	86.0 mm
2.0 litre engines (1998 cc)	86.0 mm	86.0 mm

Compression ratio:	
X 14 XE and X 16 XEL	10.5 : 1
C 18 XE, C 18 XEL and X 18 XE	10.8 : 1
C 20 XE	10.5 : 1
X 20 XEV	10.8 : 1

Maximum power:	
X 14 XE	66 kW at 6000 rpm
X 16 XEL	74 kW at 6200 rpm
C 18 XE	92 kW at 5600 rpm
C 18 XEL and X 18 XE	85 kW at 5400 rpm
C 20 XE	110 kW at 6000 rpm
X 20 XEV	100 kW at 5400 rpm

Maximum torque:	
X 14 XE	125 Nm at 4000 rpm
X 16 XEL	148 Nm at 3500 rpm
C 18 XE	168 Nm at 4800 rpm
C 18 XEL	168 Nm at 4000 rpm
X 18 XE	170 Nm at 3600 rpm
C 20 XE	196 Nm at 4600 rpm
X 20 XEV	185 Nm at 4000 rpm

Firing order	1 - 3 - 4 - 2 (No 1 cylinder at timing belt end)
Direction of crankshaft rotation	Clockwise (viewed from timing belt end of engine)

Compression pressures
Standard . . . .   12 to 15 bar (172 to 217 psi)
Maximum difference between any two cylinders . . . .   1 bar (15 psi)

Camshaft
Endfloat . . . .   0.04 to 0.15 mm
Maximum permissible radial run-out . . . .   0.040 mm

Lubrication system
Oil pump type . . . .   Gear-type, driven directly from crankshaft
Minimum permissible oil pressure at idle speed, with engine at operating
   temperature (oil temperature of at least 80°C) . . . .   1.5 bar (22 psi)
Oil pump clearances:
   Inner-to-outer gear teeth clearance . . . .   0.10 to 0.20 mm
   Gear endfloat:
      1.4 and 1.6 litre engines . . . .   0.08 to 0.15 mm
      1.8 and 2.0 litre engines . . . .   0.03 to 0.10 mm

Torque wrench settings
Note: *Use new bolts where marked with an asterisk (*).*

1.4 and 1.6 litre engines

	Nm	lbf ft
Camshaft bearing cap bolts	8	6
Camshaft cover bolts	8	6
Camshaft sprocket bolt:*		
Stage 1	50	37
Stage 2	Angle-tighten a further 60°	
Stage 3	Angle-tighten a further 15°	
Connecting rod big-end bearing cap bolt:*		
Stage 1	25	18
Stage 2	Angle-tighten a further 30°	
Crankshaft pulley bolt:*		
Stage 1	95	70
Stage 2	Angle-tighten a further 30°	
Stage 3	Angle-tighten a further 15°	
Crankshaft sensor mounting bracket bolt	8	6
Cylinder head bolts:		
Stage 1	25	18
Stage 2	Angle-tighten a further 90°	
Stage 3	Angle-tighten a further 90°	
Stage 4	Angle-tighten a further 90°	
Stage 5	Angle-tighten a further 45°	
Driveplate bolts	60	44
Engine/transmission mounting bolts:		
Front left-hand mounting:		
Mounting-to-body bolts	65	47
Mounting-to-bracket bolts	60	44
Front right-hand mounting:		
Mounting-to-body bolts*	65	47
Mounting-to-bracket bolts	35	25
Rear mounting:		
Mounting-to-bracket bolts	45	33
Mounting-to-subframe bolts	40	30
Engine-to-transmission unit bolts:		
M8 bolts	20	15
M10 bolts	40	30
M12 bolts	60	44
Flywheel bolts:*		
Stage 1	35	26
Stage 2	Angle-tighten a further 30°	
Stage 3	Angle-tighten a further 15°	
Main bearing cap bolts:*		
Stage 1	50	37
Stage 2	Angle-tighten a further 45°	
Stage 3	Angle-tighten a further 15°	
Oil pump:		
Retaining bolts	6	4
Pump cover screws	6	4
Oil pressure relief valve bolt	30	22

Torque wrench settings (continued)

1.4 and 1.6 litre engines (continued)

	Nm	lbf ft
Oil pick-up pipe bolts	8	6
Sump bolts:		
Sump to cylinder block/oil pump bolts	15	11
Sump flange-to-transmission bolts	20	15
Sump drain plug	45	33
Timing belt cover bolts:		
Upper and lower covers	4	3
Rear cover	6	4
Timing belt idler pulley bolt	25	18
Timing belt tensioner bolt	20	15

Torque wrench settings

1.8 and 2.0 litre engines

	Nm	lbf ft
Camshaft bearing cap bolts:		
All except C 20 XE engines	8	6
C 20 XE engines:		
M8 bolts	20	15
M6 bolts	10	7
Camshaft cover bolts	8	6
Camshaft sprocket bolt:*		
Stage 1	50	37
Stage 2	Angle-tighten a further 60°	
Stage 3	Angle-tighten a further 15°	
Connecting rod big-end bearing cap bolt:*		
Stage 1	35	25
Stage 2	Angle-tighten a further 45°	
Stage 3	Angle-tighten a further 15°	
Crankshaft pulley bolts	20	15
Crankshaft sprocket bolt:*		
Stage 1	130	96
Stage 2	Angle-tighten a further 40 to 50°	
Cylinder head bolts:*		
Stage 1	25	18
Stage 2	Angle-tighten a further 90°	
Stage 3	Angle-tighten a further 90°	
Stage 4	Angle-tighten a further 90°	
Driveplate bolts*	60	44
Engine/transmission mounting bolts:		
Front left-hand mounting:		
Mounting-to-body bolts	65	47
Mounting-to-bracket bolts	60	44
Front right-hand mounting:		
Mounting-to-body bolts*	65	47
Mounting-to-bracket bolts	35	25
Rear mounting:		
Mounting-to-bracket bolts	45	33
Mounting-to-subframe bolts	40	30
Engine-to-transmission unit bolts:		
M8 bolts	20	15
M10 bolts	40	30
M12 bolts	60	44
Flywheel bolts:*		
Stage 1	65	47
Stage 2	Angle-tighten a further 30°	
Stage 3	Angle-tighten a further 15°	
Main bearing cap bolts:		
Stage 1	50	37
Stage 2	Angle-tighten a further 45°	
Stage 3	Angle-tighten a further 15°	
Main bearing ladder casting bolts	20	15
Oil pump:		
Retaining bolts	6	4
Pump cover screws	6	4
Oil pressure relief valve bolt	30	22

Torque wrench settings (continued)

	Nm	lbf ft
1.8 and 2.0 litre engines (continued)		
Oil pick-up pipe bolts:		
Pick-up pipe-to-oil pump bolts	8	6
Pick-up pipe-to-cylinder block bolt	6	4
Sump bolts:		
One-piece sump:		
Sump-to-cylinder block bolts	15	11
Sump drain plug	45	33
Two-piece sump:		
Sump lower section-to-upper section bolts:		
Stage 1	8	6
Stage 2	Angle-tighten a further 30°	
Sump upper section-to-cylinder block bolts	15	11
Sump upper section-to-transmission bolts	20	15
Sump drain plug	10	7
Sump baffle plate bolts	20	15
Timing belt idler pulley bolt:		
Pre-1993 2.0 litre engines:		
Stage 1	25	18
Stage 2	Angle-tighten a further 45°	
Stage 3	Angle-tighten a further 15°	
Engines from 1993	25	18
Timing belt idler pulley bracket bolt (models from 1993)	25	18
Timing belt tensioner bolt:		
Pre-1993 2.0 litre engines:		
Stage 1	25	18
Stage 2	Angle-tighten a further 45°	
Stage 3	Angle-tighten a further 15°	
Engines from 1993	25	18

---

1 General information

How to use this Chapter

1 This Part of Chapter 2 is devoted to in-car repair procedures for the double overhead camshaft (DOHC) engines. All procedures concerning engine removal and refitting, and engine block/cylinder head overhaul can be found in Chapter 2C.

2 Most of the operations included in this Part are based on the assumption that the engine is still installed in the car. Therefore, if this information is being used during a complete engine overhaul, with the engine already removed, many of the steps included here will not apply.

Engine description

3 The engine is a double overhead camshaft, four-cylinder, in-line unit, mounted transversely at the front of the car, with the clutch and transmission on its left-hand end.

4 The crankshaft runs in five shell-type main bearings, and the centre bearing incorporates thrust bearing shells to control crankshaft endfloat.

5 The connecting rods are attached to the crankshaft by horizontally split shell-type big-

end bearings. The connecting rods are attached to the pistons by interference-fit gudgeon pins on all except C 20 XE engines, and by fully-floating gudgeon pins (secured by circlips) on C 20 XE engines. The aluminium alloy pistons are of the slipper type, and are fitted with three piston rings, comprising two compression rings and a scraper-type oil control ring.

6 The camshafts run directly in the cylinder head, and are driven by the crankshaft via a toothed rubber timing belt (which also drives the coolant pump). The camshafts operate each valve via a follower. Each follower incorporates a hydraulic self-adjusting valve which automatically adjusts the valve clearance.

7 Lubrication is by pressure-feed from a gear-type oil pump, which is mounted on the timing belt end of the crankshaft. It draws oil through a strainer located in the sump, and then forces it through an externally mounted full-flow cartridge-type filter. The oil flows into galleries in the cylinder block/crankcase and cylinder head, from where it is distributed to the crankshaft (main bearings) and camshafts. The big-end bearings are supplied with oil via internal drillings in the crankshaft, while the camshaft bearings also receive a pressurised supply. The camshaft lobes and valves are lubricated by splash, as are all other engine components.

8 A semi-closed crankcase ventilation system is employed; crankcase fumes are drawn from the cylinder head cover, and passed via a hose to the inlet manifold.

Repair operations possible with the engine in the vehicle

9 The following operations can be carried out without having to remove the engine from the vehicle.

a) Removal and refitting of the cylinder head.
b) Removal and refitting of the timing belt and sprockets.
c) Renewal of the camshaft oil seals.
d) Removal and refitting of the camshafts and followers.
e) Removal and refitting of the sump.
f) Removal and refitting of the connecting rods and pistons*.
g) Removal and refitting of the oil pump.
h) Renewal of the crankshaft oil seals.
i) Renewal of the engine mountings.
j) Removal and refitting of the flywheel/driveplate.

* Although the operation marked with an asterisk can be carried out with the engine in the vehicle after removal of the sump, it is better for the engine to be removed, in the interests of cleanliness and improved access. For this reason, the procedure is described in Chapter 2C.

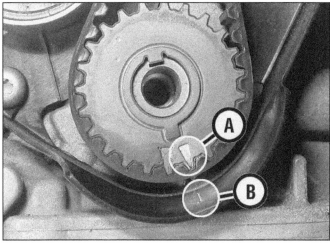

3.5 Align the camshaft sprocket timing marks (A) with the cylinder head upper surface (B) as shown to position No 1 cylinder at TDC on its compression stroke - 1.6 litre engines

3.6 Crankshaft sprocket (A) and belt cover (B) timing marks - 1.6 litre engine

2 Compression test - description and interpretation

Refer to Chapter 2A, Section 2.

3 Top dead centre (TDC) for No 1 piston - locating

1 Top Dead Centre (TDC) is the highest point that each piston reaches in its travel up and down its cylinder bore, as the crankshaft rotates. While each piston reaches TDC both at the top of the compression stroke and again at the top of the exhaust stroke, for the purpose of timing the engine, TDC refers to the position of No 1 piston at the top of its compression stroke.
2 Number 1 piston (and cylinder) is at the timing belt end of the engine, and its TDC position is located as follows. Note that the crankshaft rotates clockwise when viewed from the timing belt end of the engine.
3 Disconnect the battery negative lead. If necessary, remove all the spark plugs as described in Chapter 1 to enable the crankshaft to be turned more easily.

1.4 and 1.6 litre engines

4 To gain access to the camshaft sprocket timing marks, remove the timing belt upper cover as described in Section 6.
5 Using a socket and extension bar on the crankshaft pulley bolt, rotate the crankshaft until the timing marks on the camshaft sprockets are facing towards each and are both correctly aligned with the cylinder head upper surface. With the camshaft sprocket marks correctly positioned, the notch on the crankshaft pulley rim should align with the mark on the timing belt lower cover (**see illustration**). The engine is now positioned with No 1 piston at TDC on its compression stroke.

6 Note that there is also a timing mark on the crankshaft sprocket (visible with the crankshaft pulley/sensor wheel removed). When No 1

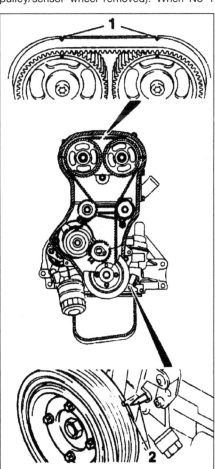

3.8 Align the camshaft sprocket timing marks with the marks (1) on the cylinder head cover, and the crankshaft pulley notch with the pointer (2) to position No 1 cylinder at TDC on its compression stroke - 1.8 and 2.0 litre engines

piston is positioned at TDC, the mark on the crankshaft sprocket should be aligned with the corresponding mark at the bottom of the oil pump flange or timing belt rear cover, as applicable (**see illustration**).

1.8 and 2.0 litre models

7 To gain access to the camshaft sprocket timing marks, remove the timing belt outer cover as described in Section 6.
8 Using a socket and extension bar on the crankshaft sprocket bolt, rotate the crankshaft until the timing marks on the camshaft sprockets are both pointing vertically upwards, and are correctly aligned with the timing marks on the camshaft cover. With the camshaft sprocket marks correctly positioned, the notch on the crankshaft pulley rim should be aligned with the pointer on the rear timing belt cover (**see illustration**). The engine is now positioned with No 1 piston at TDC on its compression stroke.
9 Note that there is also a timing mark on the crankshaft sprocket (visible with the crankshaft pulley/sensor wheel removed). When No 1 piston is positioned at TDC, the mark on the crankshaft sprocket should be aligned with the corresponding mark at the bottom of the oil pump flange – ie, the mark on the sprocket should be pointing vertically downwards.

4 Camshaft cover - removal and refitting

1.4 and 1.6 litre engines

Note: *Suitable sealing compound will be required when refitting the camshaft cover – see text.*

Removal

1 On 1.6 litre engines, remove the upper section of the inlet manifold as described in Chapter 4A or 4B.

2 Unscrew the two securing screws and withdraw the engine/spark plug cover (see illustration). If necessary, mark the spark plug HT leads for position (to avoid confusion when refitting), then disconnect them from the plugs and unclip them from the camshaft cover.

3 Release the retaining clips and disconnect the breather hoses from the camshaft cover (see illustration).

4 Evenly and progressively slacken and remove the camshaft cover retaining bolts (see illustration).

5 Lift the camshaft cover away from the cylinder head and recover the cover seals, and the sealing rings which are fitted to each of the retaining bolt locations (see illustration). Examine the seals and sealing rings for signs of wear or damage and renew if necessary.

Refitting

6 Ensure that the cover and cylinder head surfaces are clean and dry, then fit the camshaft cover seals securely to the cover grooves. Fit the sealing rings to the recesses around each retaining bolt location, holding them in position with a smear of grease (see illustrations).

7 Apply sealing compound to the edges of the inlet and exhaust camshaft bearing cap locations at the timing belt end of the engine, and to the semi-circular cut-outs at the transmission end of the cylinder head.

8 Carefully manoeuvre the camshaft cover into position, taking great care to ensure all the sealing rings remain correctly seated. Refit the cover retaining bolts and tighten the retaining

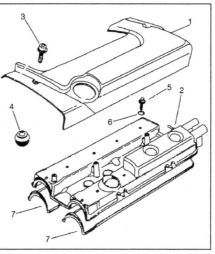

4.2 Engine/spark plug cover and camshaft cover – 1.4 and 1.6 litre engines

1 Engine/spark plug cover	4 Bushes
2 Camshaft cover	5 Camshaft cover bolts
3 Engine/spark plug cover securing bolts	6 Washers
	7 Gaskets

bolts to the specified torque, working in a spiral pattern from the centre outwards.

9 Reconnect the breather hoses, securing them in position with the retaining clips.

10 Reconnect the HT leads to the spark plugs, ensuring that they are correctly connected as noted before removal. Clip the HT leads into position in the camshaft cover,

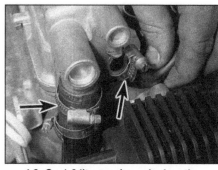

4.3 On 1.6 litre engines slacken the retaining clips and disconnect the breather hoses (arrowed) from the left-hand end of the camshaft cover

then refit the engine/spark plug cover and tighten the securing screws.

11 On 1.6 litre engines, refit the inlet manifold upper section as described in Chapter 4B.

1.8 and 2.0 litre engines

Removal

12 On C 20 XE engines, remove the outer timing belt cover as described in Section 6.

13 Slacken the retaining clips and disconnect the breather hoses from the rear of the cover (see illustration).

14 Unscrew the two securing screws and withdraw the spark plug cover (see illustration). If necessary, mark the spark plug HT leads for position (to avoid confusion when refitting), then disconnect them from the plugs and unclip them from the camshaft cover.

4.4 Unscrew the retaining bolts . . .

4.5 . . . and lift the camshaft cover away from the engine – 1.6 litre engine

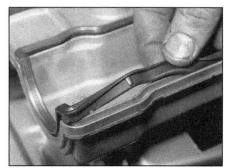

4.6a Ensure the seals are correctly seated in the cover recesses . . .

4.6b . . . and fit the sealing rings to the recess around each retaining bolt hole – 1.6 litre engine

4.13 On 1.8 and 2.0 litre engines release the retaining clips and disconnect the breather hoses (arrowed) from the rear of the cover

4.14 Withdrawing the spark plug cover – 2.0 litre engine

15 Where applicable, disconnect the camshaft sensor wiring connector and unclip the wiring from the camshaft cover.

16 Evenly and progressively slacken and remove the camshaft cover retaining bolts **(see illustration)**.

17 Lift the camshaft cover away from the cylinder head and recover the cover seal(s) and the sealing rings which are fitted to each of the retaining bolt holes. Examine the seal(s) and sealing rings for signs of wear or damage and renew if necessary.

Refitting

18 Ensure that the cover and cylinder head surfaces are clean and dry, then fit the camshaft cover seal(s) securely to the cover grooves. Where applicable, fit the sealing rings to the recesses around each retaining bolt location, holding them in position with a smear of grease.

19 Carefully manoeuvre the camshaft cover into position, taking great care to ensure that all the sealing rings remain correctly seated (where applicable). Refit the cover retaining bolts and tighten the retaining bolts to the specified torque, working in a spiral pattern from the centre outwards.

20 Where applicable, reconnect the camshaft sensor wiring connector and clip the wiring into position on the camshaft cover.

21 Reconnect the breather hoses, securing them in position with the retaining clips.

22 Reconnect the HT leads to the spark plugs, ensuring that they are correctly connected as noted before removal. Clip the HT leads into position in the camshaft cover, then refit the spark plug cover and tighten the securing screws.

23 On C 20 XE engines, refit the outer timing belt cover.

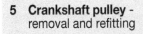

5 Crankshaft pulley - removal and refitting

1.4 and 1.6 litre engines

Note: *A new pulley retaining bolt will be required on refitting.*

Removal

1 Apply the handbrake, then jack up the front of the car and support it on axle stands (see *"Jacking and vehicle support"*). Remove the right-hand roadwheel.

2 Remove the auxiliary drivebelt as described in Chapter 1. Prior to removal, mark the direction of rotation of the belt to ensure that the belt is refitted the same way round.

3 Slacken the crankshaft pulley retaining bolt. To prevent crankshaft rotation on manual transmission models, have an assistant select top gear and apply the brakes firmly. On automatic transmission models prevent rotation by removing one of the torque converter retaining bolts and bolting the driveplate to the transmission housing using a

---

4.16 Removing a camshaft cover retaining bolt – 2.0 litre engine

metal bar, spacers and suitable bolts (see Chapter 7B). If the engine is removed from the vehicle it will be necessary to lock the flywheel/driveplate (see Section 14).

4 Unscrew the retaining bolt and washer and remove the crankshaft pulley from the end of the crankshaft, taking care not to damage the crankshaft sensor, where applicable.

Refitting

5 Refit the crankshaft pulley, aligning the pulley cut-out with the raised notch on the timing belt sprocket, then fit the washer and **new** retaining bolt.

6 Lock the crankshaft using the method used on removal, and tighten the pulley retaining bolt to the specified stage 1 torque setting, then angle-tighten the bolt through the specified stage 2 angle, using a socket and extension bar, and finally through the specified stage 3 angle. It is recommended that an angle-measuring gauge is used during the final stages of the tightening, to ensure accuracy. If a gauge is not available, use white paint to make alignment marks between the bolt head and pulley prior to tightening; the marks can then be used to check that the bolt has been rotated through the correct angle.

7 Refit the auxiliary drivebelt as described in Chapter 1 using the mark made prior to removal to ensure the belt is fitted the correct way round.

8 Refit the roadwheel then lower the car to the ground and tighten the wheel bolts to the specified torque (see Chapter 10 Specifications).

6.2 Removing the timing belt upper cover - 1.6 litre engine

1.8 and 2.0 litre engines

Removal

9 Carry out the operations described in paragraphs 1 and 2.

10 Using a socket and extension bar on the crankshaft sprocket bolt, turn the crankshaft until the timing notch on the pulley rim is correctly aligned with the pointer on the rear timing belt cover (see Section 3).

11 Slacken and remove the small retaining bolts securing the pulley to the crankshaft sprocket, then remove the pulley from the engine. If necessary, prevent crankshaft rotation by holding the sprocket retaining bolt with a suitable socket.

Refitting

12 Check that the crankshaft sprocket mark is still aligned with the mark on the oil pump flange (see Section 3), then manoeuvre the crankshaft pulley into position. Align the notch on the pulley rim with the pointer on the rear timing belt cover, then seat the pulley on the sprocket and tighten its retaining bolts to the specified torque. If necessary, counterhold the crankshaft using a suitable socket on the sprocket bolt.

13 Proceed as described in paragraphs 7 and 8.

---

6 Timing belt covers - removal and refitting

1.4 and 1.6 litre engines

Upper cover

1 Remove the air cleaner housing as described in Chapter 4A or 4B.

2 Unscrew the retaining screws, then unclip the upper cover from the rear cover and remove it from the engine compartment **(see illustration)**.

3 Refitting is the reverse of removal, tightening the retaining bolts securely.

Lower cover

4 Remove the upper cover as described in paragraphs 1 and 2.

5 Remove the crankshaft pulley as described in Section 5.

6 Unscrew the retaining bolts, then unclip the cover from the rear cover and manoeuvre it out of position **(see illustrations overleaf)**.

7 Refitting is the reverse of removal, tightening the cover bolts securely. Refit the crankshaft pulley as described in Section 5.

Rear cover

8 Remove the timing belt as described in Section 7.

9 Remove the camshaft sprockets, crankshaft sprocket, and timing belt tensioner, and the idler pulley from the inlet manifold side of the engine, as described in Section 8.

6.6a Timing belt lower cover upper retaining bolt (arrowed) . . .

6.6b . . . and lower retaining bolt (arrowed) - 1.6 litre engine

6.10 Timing belt rear cover retaining bolt locations - 1.6 litre engine (shown with timing belt and sprockets still fitted)

6.14a On 1.8 and 2.0 litre engines unscrew the timing belt cover retaining bolts . . .

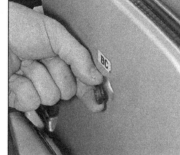

6.14b . . . and recover the rubber spacers

6.15 On refitting ensure the seal is correctly fitted to the outer cover

10 Unscrew the retaining bolts and remove the rear timing belt cover from the engine (see illustration).

11 Refitting is the reverse of removal, tightening the cover bolts securely. Refit the sprockets and the tensioner and idler pulleys as described in Section 8, and refit the timing belt as described in Section 7.

1.8 and 2.0 litre engines

Outer cover

12 Remove the air cleaner housing as described in Chapter 4A or 4B.

13 Remove the auxiliary drivebelt(s) as described in Chapter 1. Prior to removal, mark the direction of rotation on the belt(s) to ensure that the belt is refitted the same way round.

14 Slacken and remove the retaining bolts, along with their washers and rubber spacers, and remove the cover from the engine, along with its seal (see illustrations).

15 Refitting is the reverse of removal, ensure that the cover seal is correctly fitted (see illustration). Refit the auxiliary drivebelt(s) as described in Chapter 1, using the mark(s) made prior to removal to ensure that the belt(s) is/are fitted the correct way round.

Rear cover

16 Remove the timing belt as described in Section 7.

17 Remove the camshaft sprockets, crankshaft sprocket, timing belt tensioner idler pulley(s) and, on models from 1993, the idler pulley bracket, as described in Section 8.

18 Where applicable, unbolt the camshaft sensor from the cylinder head.

19 Unscrew the retaining bolts and remove the rear cover from the engine (see illustrations).

20 Refitting is the reverse of removal, tightening all bolts securely. Refit the sprockets, tensioner pulley, idler pulley(s) and idler pulley bracket (where applicable), as described in Section 8. Refit the timing belt as described in Section 7.

7 Timing belt - removal, refitting and adjustment

Note: *The timing belt must be removed and refitted with the engine cold. If the timing belt is to be renewed on 'Ecotec' type engines (see 'Specifications'), it is strongly recommended that the timing belt tensioner and idler pulleys are also renewed, as described in Section 8.*

1.4 and 1.6 litre engines

Removal

1 Position No 1 cylinder at TDC on its compression stroke as described in Section 3.

2 Remove the crankshaft pulley as described in Section 5.

3 Unbolt the timing belt lower cover and remove it from the engine (see Section 6).

4 Check that the camshaft sprocket timing marks are correctly aligned with the cylinder head surface and the crankshaft sprocket timing mark is aligned with the mark on the oil pump flange. Unscrew the two bolts securing the camshaft sensor to the cylinder head and position it clear of the engine (see illustrations).

6.19a Timing belt rear cover upper fixings – pre-1993 2.0 litre engine

1 Cover screw upper stud
2 Rear belt cover upper securing bolts

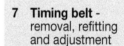

6.19b Timing belt rear cover lower right-hand securing bolt (arrowed) – pre-1993 2.0 litre engine

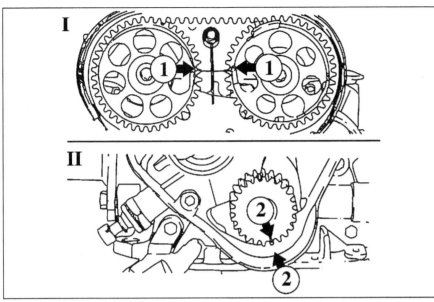

7.4b On 1.6 litre engines unbolt the camshaft sensor and position it clear of the timing belt

7.4a Camshaft and crankshaft sprocket timing marks - 1.6 litre engine

I Camshaft sprocket timing marks aligned with the cylinder head upper surface (1)
II Crankshaft sprocket timing mark aligned with mark on oil pump housing (2)

5 Slacken the timing belt tensioner bolt. Using an Allen key, rotate the tensioner arm clockwise to its stop, to relieve the tension in the timing belt, hold it in position and securely tighten the retaining bolt **(see illustration)**.

6 Slide the timing belt off from its sprockets and remove it from the engine **(see illustration)**. If the belt is to be re-used, use white paint or similar to mark the direction of rotation on the belt. **Do not** rotate the crankshaft or camshafts until the timing belt has been refitted.

7 Check the timing belt carefully for any signs of uneven wear, splitting or oil contamination, and renew it if there is the slightest doubt about its condition. If the engine is undergoing an overhaul and is approaching the manufacturer's specified interval for belt renewal (see Chapter 1), renew the belt as a matter of course, regardless of its apparent condition. If signs of oil contamination are found, trace the source of the oil leak and rectify it, then wash down the engine timing belt area and all related components to remove all traces of oil.

Refitting

8 Before refitting the belt, thoroughly clean the timing belt sprockets and tensioner/idler pulleys.

9 Check that the camshaft sprocket timing marks are still correctly aligned with the cylinder head surface, and that the crankshaft sprocket mark is still aligned with the mark on the oil pump flange (see Section 3). Also check that the edge of the coolant pump flange is aligned with the mark on the cylinder block **(see illustration)**.

10 Fit the timing belt over the crankshaft and camshaft sprockets and around the idler pulleys, ensuring that the belt front run is taut (ie, all slack is on the tensioner side of the belt),

7.5 Slacken the timing belt tensioner bolt (1) and rotate the tensioner clockwise using an Allen key in the arm cut-out (2)

then fit the belt over the coolant pump sprocket and tensioner pulley. Do not twist the belt sharply while refitting it. Ensure that the belt teeth are correctly seated centrally in the sprockets, and that the timing marks remain in alignment. If a used belt is being refitted, ensure that the arrow mark made on removal points in the normal direction of rotation.

11 Slacken the timing belt tensioner bolt to release the tensioner spring. Rotate the tensioner arm anti-clockwise until the tensioner pointer is fully over against its stop, without exerting any excess strain on the belt. Hold the tensioner in position and securely tighten its retaining bolt **(see illustration)**.

7.6 Removing the timing belt

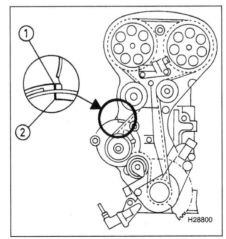

7.9 Coolant pump alignment marks – 1.4 and 1.6 litre engines

1 Mark on cylinder block
2 Edge of coolant pump flange

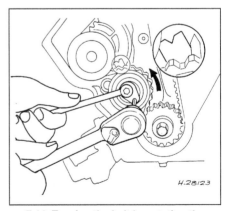

7.11 Tension the belt by rotating the tensioner arm fully anti-clockwise until the pointer is positioned as shown

7.15 If a new belt is being fitted, position the tensioner so that the pointer is aligned with the backplate cut-out

12 Check that the sprocket timing marks are still correctly aligned. If adjustment is necessary, release the tensioner again, then disengage the belt from the sprockets and make any necessary adjustments.

13 Using a socket on the crankshaft pulley bolt, rotate the crankshaft smoothly through two complete turns (720°) in the normal direction of rotation to settle the timing belt in position.

14 Check that both the camshaft and crankshaft sprocket timing marks are correctly aligned with the upper edge of the cylinder head and the timing mark on the rear belt cover respectively, then slacken the tensioner bolt again.

15 If a new timing belt is being fitted, adjust the tensioner so that the pointer is aligned with the centre of the "V"-shaped cut-out on the backplate **(see illustration)**. Hold the tensioner in the correct position and tighten its retaining bolt to the specified torque. Rotate the crankshaft smoothly through another two complete turns in the normal direction of rotation, to bring the sprocket timing marks back into alignment. Check that the tensioner pointer is still aligned with the centre of the backplate cut-out.

16 If the original belt is being refitted, adjust the tensioner so that the pointer is positioned 4 mm to the left of the centre of the "V"-shaped cut-out on the backplate **(see illustration)**. Hold the tensioner in the correct position and tighten its retaining bolt to the

specified torque. Rotate the crankshaft smoothly through another two complete turns in the normal direction of rotation, to bring the sprocket timing marks back into alignment. Check that the tensioner pointer is still correctly positioned in relation to the backplate cut-out.

17 If the tensioner pointer is not correctly positioned in relation to the backplate cut-out, repeat the procedure in paragraph 15 (new belt) or 16 (original belt) (as applicable).

18 Once the tensioner pointer and backplate cut-out remain correctly aligned, refit the timing belt covers and crankshaft pulley as described in Sections 5 and 6. Refit the camshaft sensor to the cylinder head, and tighten its retaining bolts to the specified torque (see Chapter 4B), prior to refitting the upper cover.

Pre-1993 1.8 and 2.0 litre engines

Removal

19 Proceed as described in paragraphs 1 and 2.

20 Remove the outer timing belt cover as described in Section 6.

21 Check that the timing marks are still aligned with the marks on the camshaft cover, then remove the timing belt as follows **(see illustration)**.

22 Slacken the timing belt tensioner bolt, then slide the timing belt off from its sprockets and remove it from the engine **(see illustration)**. If the belt is to be re-used, use white paint or similar to mark the direction of rotation on the belt. **Do not** rotate the crankshaft or camshafts until the timing belt has been refitted.

23 Proceed as described in paragraph 7.

Refitting

24 Remove the timing belt tensioner pulley bolt, then fit a new bolt, but do not fully tighten it at this stage.

25 Before refitting the belt, thoroughly clean the timing belt sprockets and tensioner/idler pulleys.

26 Check that the camshaft sprockets timing marks are still correctly aligned with the marks

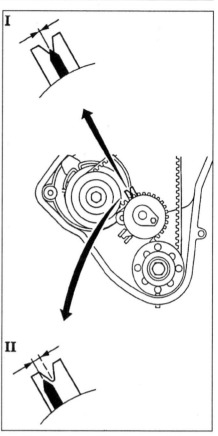

7.16 Timing belt tensioner pointer positions

I Location if a new belt is being fitted
II Location if the original belt is being re-used (pointer should be 4 mm to the left of the backplate cut-out

on the camshaft cover, then temporarily refit the crankshaft pulley and check that the timing mark on the crankshaft pulley is still aligned with the pointer on the rear timing belt cover (see Section 3) **(see illustration)**.

27 Fit the timing belt over the crankshaft and camshaft sprockets and around the idler pulley, ensuring that the belt front run is taut (ie, all slack is on the tensioner side of the belt), then fit the belt over the coolant pump

7.21 On 1.8 and 2.0 litre engines ensure the camshaft sprocket marks are correctly aligned with the marks on the camshaft cover (arrowed)

7.22 Slackening the timing belt tensioner bolt – pre-1993 2.0 litre engine

7.26 Timing pointer on rear timing belt cover aligned with notch in crankshaft pulley (arrowed) – pre-1993 2.0 litre engine

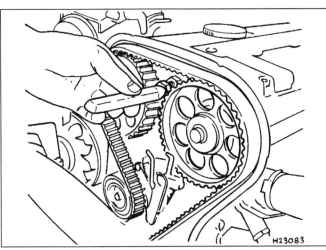

7.31 Working anti-clockwise from the TDC mark on the exhaust camshaft sprocket, mark the eighth tooth on the sprocket – pre-1993 2.0 litre engine

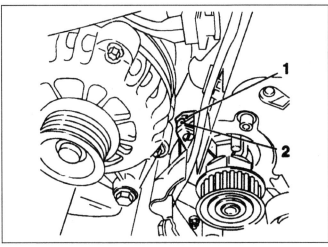

7.46 The lug (1) on the coolant pump should be aligned with the lug (2) on the cylinder block - 1.8 and 2.0 litre engines from 1993-on

sprocket and tensioner pulley. Do not twist the belt sharply while refitting it. Ensure that the belt teeth are correctly seated centrally in the sprockets, and that the timing marks remain in alignment. If a used belt is being refitted, ensure that the arrow mark made on removal points in the normal direction of rotation.

28 Refit the crankshaft pulley, and tighten the securing bolts to the specified torque. Do not allow the crankshaft to turn as the bolts are tightened.

29 Check that the timing marks are still aligned as described previously, then adjust the timing belt tension as follows.

Adjustment using Vauxhall/Opel tool KM-666

Note: *The manufacturers specify the use of a special adjustment wrench, Vauxhall/Opel tool KM-666 for adjusting the timing belt tension. If access to this tool cannot be obtained, an approximate adjustment can be achieved using the method described in paragraph 37 onwards; however it is emphasised that the vehicle should be taken to a Vauxhall/Opel dealer at the earliest opportunity to have the tension checked using the special tool. Do not drive the vehicle over any long distance until the belt tension has been checked using the special tool. No checking of "fitted" (in-use) timing belt adjustment is specified, and the following adjustment procedure applies only to a newly-fitted belt. The adjustment must be carried out with the engine cold.*

30 Fit the special tool KM-666 to the belt tensioner pulley mounting plate in accordance with the tool manufacturer's instructions.

31 Working anti-clockwise from the TDC mark on the exhaust camshaft sprocket, mark the eighth tooth on the sprocket **(see illustration)**.

32 Using a socket or spanner on the crankshaft sprocket bolt, turn the crankshaft slowly and evenly clockwise through two complete turns. Continue to turn the crankshaft until the reference mark made in

paragraph 31 is aligned with the timing notch on the cylinder head cover.

33 Tighten the **new** tensioner pulley bolt to the specified torque in the three stages given in the Specifications.

34 Remove special tool KM-666.

35 Turn the crankshaft clockwise until the TDC marks on the camshaft sprockets are aligned with the timing notches in the cylinder head cover, and check that the TDC mark on the crankshaft pulley is aligned with the pointer on the rear timing belt cover.

36 Refit the outer timing belt cover as described in Section 6.

Approximate adjustment

Note: *Refer to the note at the beginning of the previous sub-Section before proceeding.*

37 Have an assistant press the tensioner pulley against the belt until the belt can just be twisted through 45°, using moderate pressure with the thumb and forefinger, on the longest belt run between the exhaust camshaft sprocket and the belt idler pulley.

38 Have the assistant hold the tensioner pulley in position, then tighten the new tensioner pulley bolt to the specified torque in the three stages given in the Specifications.

39 Turn the crankshaft clockwise through two complete turns, and check that the timing marks still align as described in paragraph 35.

40 Refit the outer timing belt cover as described in Section 6.

1.8 and 2.0 litre engines from 1993-on

Removal

41 Proceed as described in paragraphs 1 and 2.

42 Check that the camshaft sprocket timing marks are correctly aligned with the camshaft cover marks, and the crankshaft sprocket timing mark is aligned with the mark on the oil pump flange (see Section 3).

43 Proceed as described in paragraphs 5 to 7.

Refitting

44 Before refitting the belt, thoroughly clean the timing belt sprockets and tensioner/idler pulleys.

45 Check that the camshaft sprocket timing marks are still correctly aligned with the camshaft cover marks, and the crankshaft sprocket mark is still aligned with the mark on the oil pump flange (see Section 3).

46 Check the position of the coolant pump. The lug on the pump should be aligned with the lug on the cylinder block **(see illustration)**.

47 Proceed as described in paragraphs 10 to 17, but use a socket on the crankshaft sprocket bolt to turn the crankshaft.

48 Once the tensioner pointer and backplate cut-out remain correctly aligned, refit the timing belt cover and crankshaft pulley as described in Sections 5 and 6.

8 Timing belt sprockets, tensioner and idler pulleys - removal and refitting

Camshaft sprockets

Note: *New sprocket retaining bolt(s) will be required on refitting.*

Removal

1 Remove the timing belt as described in Section 7.

2 The relevant camshaft must be prevented from turning as the sprocket bolt is unscrewed, and this can be achieved in one of two ways as follows.

a) Make up a sprocket-holding tool using two lengths of steel strip (one long, the other short), and three nuts and bolts; one nut and bolt forms the pivot of a forked tool, with the remaining two nuts and bolts at the tips of the 'forks' to engage with the sprocket spokes (see illustration 8.2 in Chapter 2A).

8.2 Using an open-ended spanner to retain the camshaft whilst the sprocket retaining bolt is slackened

b) *Remove the camshaft cover as described in Section 4 and hold the camshaft with an open-ended spanner on the flats provided* (see illustration).

3 Unscrew the retaining bolt and washer and remove the sprocket from the end of the camshaft (see illustrations). If the sprocket locating pin is a loose fit in the camshaft end, remove it and store it with the sprocket for safe-keeping.

4 If necessary, remove the remaining sprocket using the same method. On 1.4 and 1.6 litre engines the inlet and exhaust sprockets are different; the exhaust camshaft sprocket can be easily identified by the lugs which activate the camshaft position sensor. On 1.8 and 2.0 litre engines both sprockets are the same.

Refitting

5 Prior to refitting check the oil seal(s) for signs of damage or leakage. If necessary, renew as described in Section 9.

6 Ensure that the locating pin is in position in the camshaft end.

7 On 1.4 and 1.6 litre engines refit the sprocket to the camshaft end, aligning its cut-out with the locating pin, and fit the washer and **new** retaining bolt (see illustration). If both sprockets have been removed, ensure that each sprocket is fitted to the correct camshaft; the exhaust camshaft sprocket can be identified by the lugs on the sprocket outer face which trigger the camshaft position sensor.

8.3a Remove the retaining bolt and washer . . .

8 On 1.8 and 2.0 litre engines both inlet and exhaust camshaft sprockets are the same, but each one is equipped with two locating pin cut-outs. If the sprocket is being fitted to the inlet camshaft, engage the locating pin in the 'IN' cut-out, and if the sprocket is being fitted to the exhaust camshaft engage the locating pin in the 'EX' cut-out (see illustration). Ensure that the camshaft locating pin is engaged in the correct sprocket cut-out, then fit the washer and **new** retaining bolt.

9 On all models, retain the sprocket by the method used on removal, and tighten the pulley retaining bolt to the specified stage 1 torque setting, then angle-tighten the bolt through the specified stage 2 angle, using a socket and extension bar, and finally through the specified stage 3 angle (see illustration). It is recommended that an angle-measuring gauge is used during the final stages of the tightening, to ensure accuracy. If a gauge is not available, use white paint to make alignment marks between the bolt head and pulley prior to tightening; the marks can then be used to check that the bolt has been rotated through the correct angle.

10 Refit the timing belt as described in Section 7, then (where applicable) refit the camshaft cover as described in Section 4.

Crankshaft sprocket - 1.4 and 1.6 litre engines

Removal

11 Remove the timing belt as described in Section 7.

8.3b . . . and the camshaft sprocket – pre-1993 2.0 litre engine

12 Slide the sprocket off from the end of the crankshaft, noting which way around it is fitted.

Refitting

13 Align the sprocket locating key with the crankshaft groove, then slide the sprocket into position, making sure that its timing mark is facing outwards.

14 Refit the timing belt as described in Section 7.

Crankshaft sprocket - 1.8 and 2.0 litre engines

Note: *A new crankshaft sprocket retaining bolt will be required on refitting.*

Removal

15 Remove the timing belt as described in Section 7.

16 Slacken the crankshaft sprocket retaining bolt. To prevent crankshaft rotation on manual transmission models, have an assistant select top gear and apply the brakes firmly. On automatic transmission models prevent rotation by removing one of the torque converter retaining bolts and bolting the driveplate to the transmission housing using a metal bar, spacers and suitable bolts (see Chapter 7B). If the engine is removed from the vehicle it will be necessary to lock the flywheel/driveplate (see Section 14).

17 Unscrew the retaining bolt and washer and remove the crankshaft sprocket from the end of the crankshaft. Where applicable, recover the thrust washer and the Woodruff key from the end of the crankshaft.

8.7 On 1.4 and 1.6 litre engines ensure the camshaft sprocket cut-out (arrowed) is correctly engaged with the locating pin

8.8 On 1.8 and 2.0 litre engines ensure the locating pin is engaged in the correct sprocket hole on refitting (see text)

8.9 Using a spanner to prevent camshaft rotation

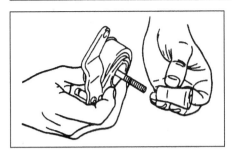

8.28 Tensioner pulley assembly and spacer sleeve – pre-1993 2.0 litre engines

Note that smaller diameter of spacer fits against pulley

Refitting

18 Where applicable, refit the Woodruff key and the thrust washer to the end of the crankshaft.

19 Align the sprocket location key with the crankshaft groove, or align the sprocket groove with the Woodruff key, as applicable, and slide the sprocket into position, ensuring its timing mark is facing outwards. Fit the washer and new retaining bolt.

20 Lock the crankshaft by the method used on removal, and tighten the sprocket retaining bolt to the specified stage 1 torque setting then angle-tighten the bolt through the specified stage 2 angle, using a socket and extension bar. It is recommended that an angle-measuring gauge is used during the final stages of the tightening, to ensure accuracy. If a gauge is not available, use white paint to make alignment marks between the bolt head and sprocket prior to tightening; the marks can then be used to check that the bolt has been rotated through the correct angle.

21 Refit the timing belt as described in Section 7.

Tensioner pulley assembly - all engines except pre-1993 2.0 litre engines

Removal

22 Remove the timing belt as described in Section 7.

23 Slacken and remove the retaining bolt and remove the tensioner pulley assembly from the engine. Where applicable, recover the spacer sleeve from the retaining bolt.

Refitting

24 Fit the tensioner to the engine, making sure that the lug on the backplate is correctly located in the oil pump housing hole. Ensure the tensioner is correctly seated then refit the retaining bolt. Using an Allen key, rotate the tensioner arm clockwise to its stop then securely tighten the retaining bolt.

25 Refit the timing belt as described in Section 7.

Tensioner pulley assembly - pre-1993 2.0 litre engines

Note: *A new tensioner pulley assembly securing bolt will be required on refitting.*

Removal

26 Remove the timing belt as described in Section 7.

27 Slacken and remove the retaining bolt and remove the tensioner pulley and mounting plate from the engine. Note the orientation of the mounting plate to aid refitting. Recover the spacer sleeve from the bolt.

Refitting

28 Refit the mounting plate and tensioner pulley using a new bolt, noting that the spacer sleeve should be fitted with the smaller diameter against the pulley **(see illustration).**

29 Do not fully tighten the bolt until the timing belt has been refitted and tensioned as described in Section 7.

Idler pulleys - all engines except pre-1993 2.0 litre engines

Removal

30 Remove the timing belt as described in Section 7.

31 Slacken and remove the retaining bolt(s) and remove the idler pulley(s) from the engine. On 1.8 and 2.0 litre models, if necessary, unbolt the pulley mounting bracket and remove it from the cylinder block.

Refitting

32 On 1.8 and 2.0 litre models refit the pulley mounting bracket (where removed) to the cylinder block and tighten its retaining bolts to the specified torque.

33 On all models, refit the idler pulley(s) and tighten the retaining bolt(s) to the specified torque.

34 Refit the timing belt as described in Section 7.

Idler pulley – pre-1993 2.0 litre engines

Note: *A new idler pulley securing bolt will be required on refitting.*

Removal

35 Remove the timing belt as described in Section 7.

36 Slacken and remove the retaining bolt and remove the idler pulley from the engine. Recover the spacer sleeve from the bolt.

Refitting

37 Refit the idler pulley using a new bolt, noting that the spacer sleeve should be fitted with the smaller diameter against the pulley.

38 Tighten the new securing bolt to the specified torque in the three stages given in the Specifications.

9 Camshaft oil seals - renewal

Front oil seal

1 Remove the relevant camshaft sprocket as described in Section 8.

9.4a Fitting a camshaft front oil seal – pre-1993 2.0 litre engine shown

2 Carefully punch or drill two small holes opposite each other in the oil seal. Screw a self-tapping screw into each, and pull on the screws with pliers to extract the seal.

3 Clean the seal housing, and polish off any burrs or raised edges which may have caused the seal to fail in the first place.

4 Lubricate the lips of the new seal with clean engine oil, and press it into position using a suitable tubular drift (such as a socket) which bears only on the hard outer edge of the seal **(see illustrations).** Take care not to damage the seal lips during fitting; note that the seal lips should face inwards.

5 Refit the camshaft sprocket as described in Section 8.

Rear oil seal

6 No rear camshaft oil seals are fitted to DOHC engines, although an O-ring is fitted to the rear of the distributor body on 2.0 litre engines up to 1993. To renew the O-ring, remove the distributor as described in Chapter 5B, then prise off the old O-ring using a screwdriver. Fit the new O-ring, and refit the distributor as described in Chapter 5B.

10 Camshafts and followers - removal, inspection and refitting

Removal

1 Remove the timing belt as described in Section 7. Prior to releasing the timing belt

9.4b Fitting a new camshaft oil seal - 1.6 litre engine shown

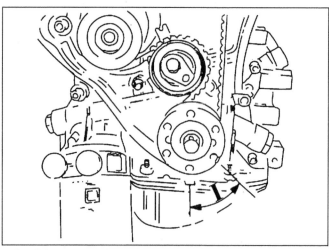

10.1 Prior to removing the timing belt, rotate the crankshaft 60º backwards to ensure the camshafts are correctly positioned - 1.8 and 2.0 litre engine shown

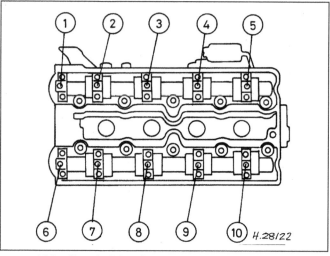

10.3a Camshaft bearing cap numbering sequence - 1.6 litre engine shown

tension and removing the belt, rotate the crankshaft **backwards** by approximately 60° (4 teeth of movement); this will position the camshafts so that the valve spring pressure is evenly exerted along the complete length of the shaft, reducing the risk of the bearing caps being damaged on removal/refitting **(see illustration)**.

2 On early C 20 XE engines, if the exhaust camshaft is to be removed, remove the distributor as described in Chapter 5B. Remove the camshaft sprockets as described in Section 8.

10.3b The identification numbers should be marked on both the bearing caps and the cylinder head (arrowed)

3 Starting on the inlet camshaft, working in a spiral pattern from the outside inwards (the reverse of illustration 10.15), slacken the camshaft bearing cap retaining bolts, or nuts as applicable, by one turn at a time, to relieve the pressure of the valve springs on the bearing caps gradually and evenly. Once the valve spring pressure has been relieved, the bolts (or nuts and washers, where applicable) can be fully unscrewed and removed along with the caps; the bearing caps and the cylinder head locations are numbered (inlet camshaft 1 to 5, exhaust camshaft 6 to 10, or 6 to 11 on early C 20 XE engines) to ensure that the caps are correctly positioned on refitting. Note that on early C 20 XE engines with a distributor, the No 11 (rear exhaust camshaft) bearing cap is secured by four nuts). Take care not to lose the locating dowels (where fitted) **(see illustrations)**.

Caution: If the bearing cap bolts are carelessly slackened, the bearing caps may break. If any bearing cap breaks then the complete cylinder head assembly must be renewed; the bearing caps are matched to the head and are not available separately.

4 Lift the camshaft out of the cylinder head and slide off the oil seal **(see illustration)**.

5 Repeat the operations described in paragraphs 3 and 4 and remove the exhaust camshaft.

6 Obtain sixteen small, clean plastic containers, and label them for identification. Alternatively, divide a larger container into compartments. Lift the followers out from the top of the cylinder head and store each one in its respective fitted position **(see illustration)**.
Note: *Store all the followers the correct way up to prevent the oil draining from the hydraulic valve adjustment mechanisms.*

Inspection

7 Examine the camshaft bearing surfaces and cam lobes for signs of wear ridges and scoring. Renew the camshaft if any of these conditions are apparent. Examine the condition of the bearing surfaces both on the camshaft journals and in the cylinder head. If the head bearing surfaces are worn excessively, the cylinder head will need to be renewed.

8 Support the camshaft end journals on V-blocks, and measure the run-out at the centre journal using a dial gauge. If the run-out exceeds the specified limit, the camshaft should be renewed.

9 Examine the cam follower surfaces which contact the camshaft lobes for wear ridges

10.3c Rear exhaust camshaft bearing cap securing nuts (arrowed) – C 20 XE engines with distributor

10.4 Removing the exhaust camshaft

10.6 Using a rubber sucker to remove a camshaft follower

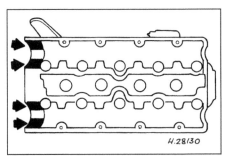

10.13 Apply a smear of sealant to the cylinder head mating surface of the right-hand (No 1 and No 6) bearing caps (arrowed)

10.14 Refit the bearing caps using the identification markings to ensure each one is correctly fitted

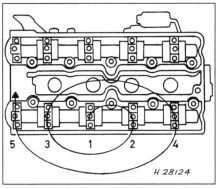

10.15 Camshaft bearing cap tightening sequence (exhaust camshaft shown - inlet the same)

10.16 Working as described in the text, tighten the bearing cap bolts or nuts to the specified torque

and scoring. Check the followers and their bores in the cylinder head for signs of wear or damage. If any follower is thought to be faulty or is visibly worn it should be renewed.

Refitting

10 Lubricate the followers with clean engine oil and carefully insert each one into its original location in the cylinder head.

11 Lubricate the tops of the camshaft followers with molybdenum disulphide paste, then lay the camshafts in position. Ensure that the crankshaft is still positioned as described in paragraph 1. Temporarily refit the sprockets to the camshafts and position each camshaft so that the sprocket timing mark is positioned approximately 4 teeth anti-clockwise from its TDC alignment position (see Section 3).

12 Ensure the mating surfaces of the bearing caps and cylinder head are clean and dry and lubricate the camshaft journals and lobes with clean engine oil.

13 Apply a smear of sealant to the mating surfaces of both the inlet (No 1) and exhaust (No 6) camshaft timing belt end bearing caps **(see illustration)**. On early C 20 XE engines with a distributor, also apply a smear of sealant to the cylinder head mating face of the transmission end exhaust (No 11) bearing cap.

14 Ensure that the locating dowels (where fitted) are in position, then refit the camshaft bearing caps and the retaining bolts, or washers and nuts, as applicable, in their original locations on the cylinder head **(see illustration)**. The caps are numbered (inlet camshaft 1 to 5, exhaust camshaft 6 to 10, or 6 to 11 on early C 20 XE engines) from the timing belt end of the engine, and the corresponding numbers are marked on the cylinder head upper surface. All bearing cap numbers should be the right way up when viewed from the front of the vehicle.

15 Working on the inlet camshaft, tighten the bearing cap bolts or nuts by hand only then, working in a spiral pattern from the centre outwards, tighten the bolts by one turn at a time to gradually apply the pressure of the valve springs on the bearing caps **(see illustration)**. Repeat this sequence until all bearing caps are in contact with the cylinder head then, working in the same sequence,

tighten the camshaft bearing cap bolts or nuts to the specified torque.

Caution: If the bearing cap bolts or nuts (as applicable) are carelessly tightened, the bearing caps may break. If any bearing cap breaks then the complete cylinder head assembly must be renewed; the bearing caps are matched to the head and are not available separately.

16 Tighten the exhaust camshaft bearing cap bolts or nuts as described in paragraph 15 **(see illustration)**.

17 Fit new camshaft front oil seals as described in Section 9.

18 Refit the camshaft sprockets as described in Section 8.

19 Align all the sprocket timing marks to bring the camshafts and crankshaft back to TDC as described in Section 3 (turn each camshaft and the crankshaft four teeth clockwise), then refit the timing belt as described in Section 7.

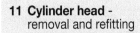

11 Cylinder head - removal and refitting

1.4 and 1.6 litre engines

Note: *The engine must be cold when removing the cylinder head. A new cylinder head gasket and new cylinder head bolts must be used on refitting.*

Removal

1 Depressurise the fuel system as described in Chapter 4A or 4B then disconnect the battery negative lead.

2 Drain the cooling system and remove the spark plugs as described in Chapter 1.

3 Remove the timing belt as described in Section 7. Prior to releasing the timing belt tension and removing the belt, rotate the crankshaft **anti-clockwise** by approximately 60° (4 teeth of movement on the crankshaft sprocket); this will position the camshafts so that the valve spring pressure is evenly exerted along the complete length of the camshafts, reducing the risk of the bearing caps being damaged during the removal and refitting procedure, and reducing the risk of the valves

contacting the pistons **(see illustration)**.

4 Remove the complete inlet manifold as described in Chapter 4A or 4B.

5 Remove the exhaust manifold as described in Chapter 4A or 4B. If no work is to be carried out on the cylinder head, the head can be removed complete with the manifold once the following operations have been carried out.

a) Unbolt the exhaust front pipe from the manifold.

b) Disconnect the oxygen sensor wiring connector.

c) Disconnect the air hose and vacuum hose from the air injection valve.

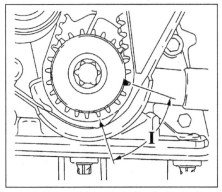

11.3 Prior to removing the timing belt, rotate the crankshaft 60° backwards to ensure the camshafts are correctly positioned - 1.6 litre engine shown

11.13 Remove the cylinder head bolts . . .

11.14 . . . and lift off the cylinder head assembly

11.23 Ensure the head gasket is fitted with its OBEN/TOP marking uppermost

6 Remove the camshaft cover as described in Section 4.

7 Remove the camshaft sprockets and the timing belt idler pulleys as described in Section 8.

8 Unscrew the bolts securing the timing belt rear cover to the cylinder head.

9 Referring to Chapter 10, unbolt the power steering pump and position it clear of the cylinder head.

10 Disconnect the wiring connectors from the DIS module and the coolant temperature sender units on the cylinder head. Free the wiring from its retaining clips, noting its routing, and position it clear of the cylinder head.

11 Release the retaining clips, then disconnect and remove the upper coolant hose linking the cylinder head to the radiator. Release the retaining clip and disconnect the cylinder head coolant hose from the expansion tank.

12 Make a final check to ensure that all relevant hoses, pipes and wires, etc, have been disconnected.

13 Working in the **reverse** of the tightening sequence (see illustration 11.26a), progressively slacken the cylinder head bolts by a third of a turn at a time until all bolts can be unscrewed by hand. Remove each bolt in turn, along with its washer **(see illustration)**.

14 Lift the cylinder head from the cylinder block **(see illustration)**. If necessary, tap the cylinder head gently with a soft-faced mallet to free it from the block, but **do not** lever at the mating faces. Note the fitted positions of the two locating dowels, and remove them for safe keeping if they are loose.

15 Recover the cylinder head gasket, and discard it.

Preparation for refitting

16 The mating faces of the cylinder head and block must be perfectly clean before refitting the head. Use a scraper to remove all traces of gasket and carbon, and also clean the tops of the pistons. Take particular care with the aluminium surfaces, as the soft metal is damaged easily. Also, make sure that debris is not allowed to enter the oil and water channels - this is particularly important for the oil circuit, as carbon could block the oil supply to the camshaft or crankshaft bearings. Using adhesive tape and paper, seal the water, oil and bolt holes in the cylinder block. To prevent carbon entering the gap between the pistons and bores, smear a little grease in the gap. After cleaning the piston, rotate the crankshaft so that the piston moves down the bore, then wipe out the grease and carbon with a cloth rag. Clean the other piston crowns in the same way.

17 Check the block and head for nicks, deep scratches and other damage. If slight, they may be removed carefully with a file. More serious damage may be repaired by machining, but this is a specialist job.

18 If warpage of the cylinder head is suspected, use a straight-edge to check it for distortion. Refer to Chapter 2C if necessary.

19 Ensure that the cylinder head bolt holes in

the crankcase are clean and free of oil. Syringe or soak up any oil left in the bolt holes. This is most important in order that the correct bolt tightening torque can be applied and to prevent the possibility of the block being cracked by hydraulic pressure when the bolts are tightened.

20 Renew the cylinder head bolts regardless of their apparent condition.

Refitting

21 Ensure that the crankshaft is still positioned approximately 60° BTDC (see paragraph 3) and wipe clean the mating faces of the head and block.

22 Ensure that the two locating dowels are in position at each end of the cylinder block/crankcase surface.

23 Fit the new cylinder head gasket to the block, making sure it is fitted the correct way up with its OBEN/TOP mark uppermost **(see illustration)**.

24 Carefully refit the cylinder head, locating it on the dowels.

25 Fit the washers to the **new** cylinder head bolts then carefully insert them into position (**do not drop** the bolts into position), tightening them finger-tight only at this stage **(see illustration)**.

26 Working progressively and in the sequence shown, first tighten all the cylinder head bolts to the stage 1 torque setting **(see illustrations)**.

11.25 Fit the new head bolts tightening them by hand only

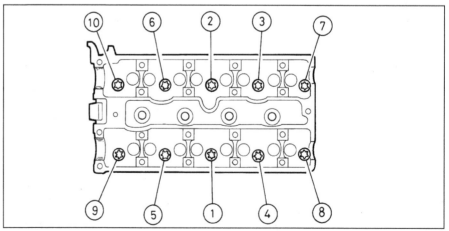

11.26a Cylinder head bolt tightening sequence (1.8 and 2.0 litre engine shown – 1.4 and 1.6 litre engines similar)

11.26b Tighten the cylinder head bolts to the specified stage 1 torque setting . . .

11.27 . . . and then through the various specified angles as described in the text

11.48 Removing the timing belt outer cover upper stud – 2.0 litre engine

27 Once all bolts have been tightened to the stage 1 torque, again working in the sequence shown, tighten each bolt through its specified stage 2 angle, using a socket and extension bar. It is recommended that an angle-measuring gauge is used during this stage of the tightening, to ensure accuracy **(see illustration)**.

28 Working in the specified sequence, tighten all bolts through the specified stage 3 angle.

29 Working again in the specified sequence, tighten all bolts through the specified stage 4 angle.

30 Finally, working in the specified sequence, tighten all bolts through the specified stage 5 angle.

31 Reconnect the coolant hoses, securing them in position with the retaining clips.

32 Reconnect the DIS module and coolant temperature sender wiring connectors, ensuring that the harness is correctly routed and retained by all the necessary clips.

33 Refit the power steering pump, with reference to Chapter 10.

34 Refit the timing belt rear cover retaining bolts and tighten them securely.

35 Refit the camshaft sprockets and idler pulleys as described in Section 8.

36 Align all the sprocket timing marks to bring the camshafts and crankshaft back to TDC, then refit the timing belt as described in Section 7.

37 Refit the camshaft cover and timing belt cover(s) as described in Sections 4 and 6.

38 Refit the inlet manifold, and where applicable the exhaust manifold, as described in Chapter 4A or 4B.

39 If the cylinder head has been removed complete with the exhaust manifold, carry out the following operations with reference to Chapter 4A or 4B.

 a) Reconnect the exhaust front pipe to the manifold.

 b) Reconnect the oxygen sensor wiring connector.

 c) Reconnect the air hose and vacuum hose to the air injection valve.

40 Ensure that all pipes and hoses are securely reconnected, then refill the cooling system and refit the spark plugs as described in Chapter 1.

41 Reconnect the battery, then start the engine and check for signs of leaks.

1.8 and 2.0 litre engines

Note: *The engine must be cold when removing the cylinder head. A new cylinder head gasket and new cylinder head bolts must be used on refitting.*

Removal

42 Proceed as described in paragraphs 1 to 3.

43 Remove the inlet and exhaust manifolds as described in Chapter 4B. If no work is to be carried out on the cylinder head, the head can be removed complete with manifolds once all the hoses/wires etc have been disconnected (see Chapter 4B).

44 Remove the camshaft cover as described in Section 4.

45 Remove the camshaft sprockets as described in Section 8.

46 On all except C 20 XE engines, remove the camshafts as described in Section 10.

47 Unscrew the bolts securing the timing belt rear cover to the cylinder head.

48 Where applicable, unscrew the upper and middle studs for the timing belt outer cover screws. Note that the upper stud simply unscrews from the cylinder head, but the middle stud is secured by a bolt **(see illustration)**.

49 On early C 20 XE engines, remove the distributor cap and HT leads, and disconnect the distributor wiring plug, as described in Chapter 5B.

11.51 Disconnecting the coolant hose from the thermostat housing – 2.0 litre engine

50 Where applicable, unscrew the bolt securing the crankcase breather tube bracket to the end of the cylinder head.

51 Remove the cylinder head as described in paragraphs 11 to 15 **(see illustration)**.

Preparation for refitting

52 Proceed as described in paragraphs 16 to 20.

Refitting

53 Proceed as described in paragraphs 21 to 31 **(see illustration)**.

54 Reconnect the coolant hoses, securing them in position with the retaining clips.

55 Refit the timing belt rear cover retaining bolts and tighten them securely.

56 Where applicable, refit the bolt securing the crankcase breather tube bracket to the end of the cylinder head.

57 On early C 20 XE engines, refit the distributor cap and HT leads, and reconnect the distributor wiring plug.

58 Where applicable, refit the upper and middle studs for the timing belt outer cover screws.

59 Refit the camshaft sprockets as described in Section 8.

60 Carry out the procedures described in paragraphs 36 to 41.

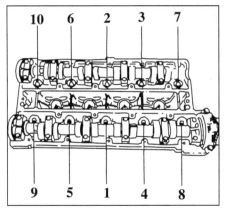

11.53 Cylinder head bolt tightening sequence – C 20 XE engines

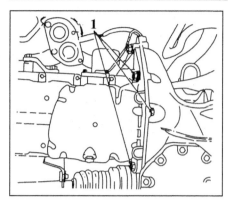

12.6 Sump flange-to-transmission housing bolts – 1.4 and 1.6 litre engines

1 Sump-to-transmission bolts

12 Sump -
removal and refitting

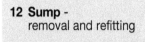

1.4 and 1.6 litre engines

Note: *A new sump gasket will be required on refitting, and suitable sealant will be required to coat the mating surfaces around the oil pump housing and rear main bearing cap joints. Suitable thread-locking compound will be required to coat the sump bolt threads and, where applicable, the oil pump pick up/strainer bolt threads on refitting.*

Removal

1 Disconnect the battery negative lead.
2 Apply the handbrake then jack up the front of the vehicle and support it on axle stands (see *"Jacking and vehicle support"*). Where necessary, undo the retaining screws and remove the undershield from beneath the engine/transmission unit.
3 Drain the engine oil as described in Chapter 1, then fit a new sealing washer and refit the drain plug, tightening it to the specified torque.
4 Remove the exhaust system front pipe as described in Chapter 4B.

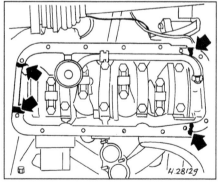

12.13 Apply sealant to the oil pump and rear main bearing cap joints (arrowed) before the sump is refitted – 1.4 and 1.6 litre engines

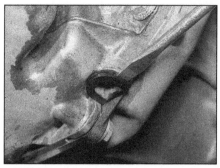

12.7 Remove the rubber plugs from the sump flange to access the remaining sump bolts – 1.4 and 1.6 litre engines

5 Disconnect the wiring connector from the oil level sensor (where fitted).
6 Slacken and remove the bolts securing the sump flange to the transmission housing **(see illustration)**.
7 Remove the rubber plugs from the transmission end of the sump flange to gain access to the sump end retaining bolts **(see illustration)**.
8 Progressively slacken and remove the bolts securing the sump to the base of the cylinder block/oil pump. Break the sump joint by striking the sump with the palm of the hand, then lower the sump away from the engine and withdraw it. Remove the gasket and discard it.
9 While the sump is removed, take the opportunity to check the oil pump pick-up/strainer for signs of clogging or splitting. If necessary, unbolt the pick-up/strainer and remove it from the engine along with its sealing ring. The strainer can then be cleaned easily in solvent or renewed.

Refitting

10 Remove all traces of dirt, oil and gasket from the mating surfaces of the sump and cylinder block, and (where removed) the oil pump pick-up/strainer. Also remove all traces of locking compound from the oil pump pick-up bolts (where removed).
11 Where necessary, position a new sealing ring on top of the oil pump pick-up/strainer and fit the pick up/strainer. Apply locking compound to the threads of the pick up/strainer retaining bolts, then fit the bolts and tighten to the specified torque.
12 Ensure that the sump and cylinder block mating surfaces are clean and dry, and clean all traces of locking compound from the sump bolts.
13 Apply a smear of suitable sealant to the areas of the cylinder block mating surface around the areas of the oil pump housing and rear main bearing cap joints **(see illustration)**.
14 Fit a new gasket to the sump and apply a few drops of locking compound to the threads of the sump-to-cylinder block/oil pump/trans-mission bolts.
15 Offer up the sump, ensuring that the gasket remains correctly positioned, and loosely refit all the retaining bolts. Working out

from the centre in a diagonal sequence, progressively tighten the bolts securing the sump to the cylinder block/oil pump to their specified torque setting.
16 Tighten the bolts securing the sump flange to the transmission housing to their specified torque settings. Refit the rubber plugs to the sump flange cut-outs.
17 Refit the exhaust front pipe, as described in Chapter 4B, and where applicable, reconnect the oil level sender wiring connector.
18 Where applicable, refit the undershield, then lower the vehicle to the ground then fill the engine with fresh oil, with reference to Chapter 1. Reconnect the battery negative lead.

1.8 and 2.0 litre engines with one-piece sump

Removal

19 Proceed as described in paragraphs 1 to 5.
20 Where applicable, unscrew the securing bolts and remove the engine-to-transmission blanking plate from the bellhousing.
21 Unscrew the securing bolts and withdraw the sump. If necessary, strike the sump with the palm of the hand to free it from the cylinder block. **Do not** lever between the sump and cylinder block mating faces. The sump baffle will probably be pulled away from the cylinder block with the sump, but cannot be removed until the oil pump pick-up/strainer has been removed.
22 Remove the gasket, where applicable.
23 To remove the sump baffle, unbolt the bracket(s) securing the oil pump pick-up/strainer to the cylinder block, and unscrew the two bolts securing the pick-up/strainer to the oil pump (recover the O-ring). The baffle can then be removed. Remove the sump baffle gasket. Note that on some engines, the gasket is integral with the baffle.
24 While the sump is removed, take the opportunity to check the oil pump pick-up/strainer for signs of clogging or splitting. Clean the strainer using solvent, or renew if necessary.

Refitting

25 Remove all traces of dirt, oil and gasket from the mating surfaces of the sump, sump baffle and cylinder block (as applicable), and (where removed) the oil pump pick-up/strainer. Also remove all traces of locking compound from the oil pump pick-up bolts (where removed).
26 Ensure that the sump, sump baffle and cylinder block mating faces are clean and dry, and clean all traces of locking compound from the sump bolts.
27 Apply a smear of suitable sealant to the areas of the cylinder block mating surface around the areas of the oil pump housing and rear main bearing cap joints (see illustration 12.13).
28 On models with separate sump and sump baffle gaskets, fit a new sump baffle gasket, then offer the sump baffle into position, and fit

the oil pump pick-up/strainer, using a new sealing ring. Apply locking compound to the threads of the pick-up/strainer retaining bolts, then fit the bolts and tighten to the specified torque.

29 On models where the gasket is integral with the sump baffle, fit a new sump baffle, then refit the oil pump pick-up/strainer as described in the previous paragraph.

30 Offer up the sump, ensuring that the gasket remains correctly positioned, and loosely refit all the retaining bolts. Working out from the centre in a diagonal sequence, progressively tighten the bolts securing the sump to the cylinder block/oil pump to their specified torque setting.

31 Where applicable, refit the engine-to-transmission blanking plate to the bellhousing and tighten the securing bolts.

32 Proceed as described in paragraphs 17 and 18.

1.8 and 2.0 litre engines with two-piece sump – lower section of sump

Removal

33 Proceed as described in paragraphs 1 to 5, but note that there is no need to remove the exhaust system front section unless the upper section of the sump is to be removed.

34 Slacken and remove the bolts securing the lower section of the sump to the upper section, then free the lower section (if necessary break the sump joint by striking the sump with the palm of the hand, or by using a wide-bladed scraper), and remove it along with its gasket **(see illustration)**.

Refitting

35 Ensure that the mating faces of the sump upper and lower sections are clean and dry.

36 Place a new gasket on the top of the sump lower section and offer it up to the upper section. Fit the new sump lower section securing bolts (if the threads of the new securing bolts are not coated with thread-locking compound, coat them with a suitable compound before fitting), then tighten them in a diagonal sequence to the specified torque in the two stages given in the Specifications.

37 Proceed as described in paragraphs 17 and 18.

1.8 and 2.0 litre engines with two-piece sump – upper section of sump

Removal

38 Remove the lower section of the sump as described previously in this Section.

39 If not already done, remove the exhaust system front section as described in Chapter 4B.

40 To improve access, remove the oil filter as described in Chapter 1.

41 Unscrew and remove the bolts securing the upper section of the sump to the transmission.

12.34 If the lower section of the sump is stuck, carefully ease it away using a wide-bladed scraper

42 Progressively unscrew and remove the bolts securing the upper section of the sump to the cylinder block, then lower the sump away from the engine and withdraw it. If necessary, strike the sump with the palm of the hand to free it from the cylinder block. *Do not* lever between the sump and cylinder block mating faces. Remove the gasket.

43 While the sump is removed, take the opportunity to check the oil pump pick-up/strainer for signs of clogging or splitting. If necessary, unbolt the pick-up/strainer and remove it from the engine along with its sealing ring. The strainer can then be cleaned easily in solvent or renewed.

Refitting

44 Proceed as described in paragraphs 10 to 14.

45 Offer up the upper section of the sump, ensuring that the gasket remains correctly positioned, and loosely refit all the retaining bolts. Tighten all the bolts loosely.

46 Tighten the bolts securing the upper section of the sump to the transmission to the specified torque.

47 Tighten the bolts securing the upper section of the sump to the cylinder block and oil pump to the specified torque.

48 Fit a new oil filter, then refit the lower section of the sump as described previously in this Section.

13 Oil pump - removal, overhaul and refitting

Removal

Note: *The pressure relief valve can be removed with pump in position on the engine unit, although on some models it will be necessary to unbolt the mounting bracket assembly from the block to allow the valve to be removed.*

1 Remove the timing belt as described in Section 7.

2 Remove the rear timing belt cover as described in Section 6.

3 Remove the sump and oil pump pick-up/strainer as described in Section 12.

13.8 Undo the retaining screws and remove the oil pump cover

4 Disconnect the wiring connector from the oil pressure switch.

5 Where applicable, unbolt the crankshaft sensor mounting bracket and position it clear of the oil pump.

6 Where applicable, unscrew the union and disconnect the oil cooler pipe from the adapter on the oil pump.

7 Slacken and remove the retaining bolts then slide the oil pump housing assembly off of the end of the crankshaft, taking great care not to lose the locating dowels. Remove the housing gasket and discard it.

Overhaul

8 Undo the retaining screws and lift off the pump cover from the rear of the housing **(see illustration)**.

9 Using a suitable marker pen, mark the surface of both the pump inner and outer gears; the marks can then be used to ensure the gears are refitted the correct way around.

10 Lift out the inner and outer gears from the pump housing **(see illustration)**.

11 Unscrew the oil pressure relief valve bolt from the front of the housing and withdraw the spring and plunger from the housing, noting which way around the plunger is fitted. Remove the sealing washer from the valve bolt **(see illustration overleaf)**.

12 Clean the components, and carefully examine the gears, pump body and relief valve plunger for any signs of scoring or wear. Renew any component which shows signs of wear or damage; if the gears or pump housing are marked then the complete pump assembly should be renewed.

13.10 Lift the inner and outer gears (arrowed) out from the pump housing

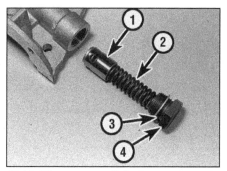

13.11 Oil pressure relief valve components

1	*Plunger*	3	*Sealing washer*
2	*Spring*	4	*Valve bolt*

13 If the components appear serviceable, measure the clearance between the inner and outer gears using feeler blades. Also measure the gear endfloat, and check the flatness of the end cover **(see illustrations)**. If the clearances exceed the specified tolerances, the pump must be renewed.

14 If the pump is satisfactory, reassemble the components in the reverse order of removal, noting the following.

a) *Ensure that both gears are fitted the correct way around.*

b) *Fit a new sealing ring to the pressure relief valve bolt and tighten the bolt to the specified torque.*

c) *Tighten the pump cover screws to the specified torque.*

d) *On completion prime the oil pump by filling it with clean engine oil whilst rotating the inner gear.*

Refitting

15 Prior to refitting, carefully lever out the crankshaft oil seal using a flat-bladed screwdriver. Fit the new oil seal, ensuring its sealing lip is facing inwards, and press it squarely into the housing using a tubular drift which bears only on the hard outer edge of the seal **(see illustration)**. Press the seal into position so that it is flush with the housing and lubricate the oil seal lip with clean engine oil.

16 Ensure that the mating surfaces of the oil pump and cylinder block are clean and dry and that the locating dowels are in position.

17 Fit a new gasket to the cylinder block.

13.15 Fitting a new crankshaft oil seal to the oil pump housing

13.13a Using a feeler blade to check gear clearance

18 Carefully manoeuvre the oil pump into position and engage the inner gear with the crankshaft end **(see illustration)**. Locate the pump on the dowels, taking great care not damage the oil seal lip.

19 Refit the pump housing retaining bolts in their original locations and tighten them to the specified torque.

20 Where applicable, reconnect the oil cooler pipe, and tighten the union nut.

21 Where applicable, refit the crankshaft sensor bracket to the pump housing and tighten its mounting bolt to the specified torque.

22 Reconnect the oil pressure sensor wiring connector.

23 Refit the oil pump pick-up/strainer and sump as described in Section 12.

24 Refit the rear timing belt cover to the engine, and tighten the retaining bolts securely.

25 Refit the timing belt sprockets, idler pulleys and tensioner as described in Section 8, then refit the belt as described in Section 7.

26 On completion, fit a new oil filter and fill the engine with clean oil as described in Chapter 1.

14 Flywheel/driveplate - removal, inspection and refitting

Refer to Chapter 2A, Section 15.

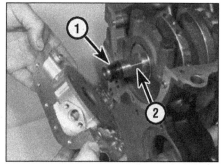

13.18 On refitting take care not to damage the oil seal on the crankshaft lip (1) and engage the inner gear with the crankshaft flats (2)

13.13b Using a straight-edge and feeler blade to measure gear endfloat

15 Crankshaft oil seals - renewal

Timing belt end (right-hand) oil seal

1 Remove the crankshaft sprocket as described in Section 8.

2 Carefully punch or drill two small holes opposite each other in the oil seal. Screw a self-tapping screw into each hole, and pull on the screws with pliers to extract the seal **(see illustration)**.

Caution: Great care must be taken to avoid damage to the oil pump

3 Clean the seal housing and polish off any burrs or raised edges which may have caused the seal to fail in the first place.

4 Lubricate the lips of the new seal with clean engine oil and ease it into position on the end of the shaft. Press the seal squarely into position until it is flush with the housing. If necessary, a suitable tubular drift, such as a socket, which bears only on the hard outer edge of the seal can be used to tap the seal into position **(see illustration)**. Take great care not to damage the seal lips during fitting and ensure that the seal lips face inwards.

5 Wash off any traces of oil, then refit the crankshaft sprocket as described in Section 8.

Flywheel/driveplate end (left-hand) oil seal

6 Remove the flywheel/driveplate as des-

15.2 Removing the crankshaft front oil seal

15.4 Fitting a new crankshaft front oil seal

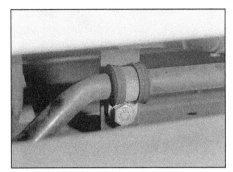

17.3 Oil cooler pipe bracket viewed through front bumper

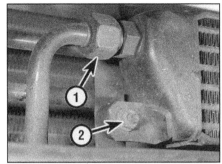

17.4 Oil cooler pipe union (1) and oil cooler securing nuts (2) viewed through front bumper

cribed in Chapter 2A, Section 15.
7 Renew the seal as described in paragraphs 2 to 4 of this Section.
8 Refit the flywheel/driveplate as described in Chapter 2A, Section 15.

16 Engine/transmission mountings -
inspection and renewal

Refer to Chapter 2A, Section 17.

17 Oil cooler -
removal and refitting

Removal

1 To gain sufficient access to enable the oil cooler to be removed, the radiator must be removed, as described in Chapter 3. Alternatively, the front bumper can be removed as described in Chapter 11.
2 With the appropriate components removed for access, unscrew the oil cooler pipe unions

from the oil cooler. Be prepared for oil spillage, and plug the open ends of the pipes, to prevent further oil leakage and dirt entry.
3 If necessary, unbolt the oil cooler pipes from their brackets, to allow sufficient space for the oil cooler to be removed **(see illustration)**.
4 Unscrew the two securing nuts, and remove the oil cooler from its mounting brackets **(see illustration)**.

Refitting

5 Refitting is a reversal of removal, but on completion, check and if necessary top up the engine oil level as described in *"Weekly checks"*.

Notes

Chapter 2 Part C:
Engine removal and overhaul procedures

Contents

Degrees of difficulty

Easy, suitable for novice with little experience	Fairly easy, suitable for beginner with some experience	Fairly difficult, suitable for competent DIY mechanic	Difficult, suitable for experienced DIY mechanic 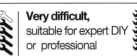	Very difficult, suitable for expert DIY or professional

Specifications

Note: *Where specifications are given as N/A, no information was available at the time of writing. Refer to your Vauxhall/Opel dealer for the latest information available.*

SOHC engines

Cylinder head

Maximum gasket face distortion . . . . 0.05 mm
Cylinder head height:
    1.4 and 1.6 litre engines . . . . 95.90 to 96.10 mm
    1.8 and 2.0 litre engines . . . . 95.75 to 96.25 mm

Valves and guides

Valve guide height in cylinder head:
    1.4 and 1.6 litre engines . . . . 80.85 to 81.25 mm
    1.8 and 2.0 litre engines . . . . 83.25 to 84.05 mm

Valve stem diameter*:	Inlet	Exhaust
Standard (K)	6.998 to 7.012 mm	6.978 to 6.992 mm
1st oversize (0.075 mm - K1)	7.073 to 7.087 mm	7.053 to 7.067 mm
2nd oversize (0.150 mm - K2)	7.148 to 7.162 mm	7.128 to 7.142 mm
3rd oversize (0.250 mm - A)	7.248 to 7.262 mm	7.228 to 7.262 mm

Valve stem runout . . . . Less than 0.03 mm
Valve guide bore diameter*:
    Standard (K) . . . . 7.030 to 7.050 mm
    1st oversize (0.075 mm - K1) . . . . 7.105 to 7.125 mm
    2nd oversize (0.150 mm - K2) . . . . 7.180 to 7.200 mm
    3rd oversize (0.250 mm - A) . . . . 7.280 to 7.300 mm
Stem-to-guide clearance:
    Inlet . . . . 0.018 to 0.052 mm
    Exhaust . . . . 0.038 to 0.072 mm

Valve length:	Production	Service
1.4 litre engines	105.0 mm	104.6 mm
1.6 litre engines	101.5 mm	101.1 mm
1.8 and 2.0 litre engines:		
Inlet	104.2 mm	103.8 mm
Exhaust	104.0 mm	103.6 mm

SOHC engines (continued)

Valves and guides (continued)

Valve stem fitted height:

1.4 and 1.6 litre engines	13.75 to 14.35 mm
1.8 and 2.0 litre engines	17.85 to 18.25 mm

Valve head diameter:

	Inlet	Exhaust
14NV and C 14 NZ engines	33 mm	29 mm
14SE and C 14 SE engines	38 mm	31 mm
1.6 litre engines	38 mm	31 mm
1.8 and 2.0 litre engines	41.8 mm	36.5 mm

*Identification marking in brackets

Cylinder block

Maximum gasket face distortion	0.05 mm

Cylinder bore diameter:

1.4 litre engines:

Standard:

Size group 6	77.555 to 77.565 mm
Size group 7	77.565 to 77.575 mm
Size group 8	77.575 to 77.585 mm
Size group 99	77.585 to 77.595 mm
Size group 00	77.595 to 77.605 mm
Size group 01	77.605 to 77.615 mm
Size group 02	77.615 to 77.625 mm
Size group 07	77.665 to 77.675 mm
Oversize (0.5 mm)	78.065 to 78.075 mm

1.6 litre engines:

Standard:

Size group 5	78.945 to 78.955 mm
Size group 6	78.955 to 78.965 mm
Size group 7	78.965 to 78.975 mm
Size group 8	78.975 to 78.985 mm
Size group 99	78.985 to 78.995 mm
Size group 00	78.995 to 79.005 mm
Size group 01	79.005 to 79.015 mm
Size group 02	79.015 to 79.025 mm
Size group 03	79.025 to 79.035 mm
Size group 04	79.035 to 79.045 mm
Size group 05	79.045 to 79.055 mm
Size group 06	79.055 to 79.065 mm
Size group 07	79.065 to 79.075 mm
Size group 08	79.075 to 79.085 mm
Size group 09	79.085 to 79.095 mm
Oversize (0.5 mm)	79.465 to 79.475 mm

1.8 litre engines:

Standard:

Size group 8	84.775 to 84.785 mm
Size group 99	84.785 to 84.795 mm
Size group 00	84.795 to 84.805 mm
Size group 01	84.805 to 84.815 mm
Size group 02	84.815 to 84.825 mm
Oversize (0.5 mm)	85.265 to 85.275 mm

2.0 litre engines:

Standard:

Size group 8	85.975 to 85.985 mm
Size group 99	85.985 to 85.995 mm
Size group 00	85.995 to 86.005 mm
Size group 01	86.005 to 86.015 mm
Size group 02	86.015 to 86.025 mm
Oversize (0.5 mm)	86.465 to 86.475 mm
Maximum cylinder bore ovality and taper	0.013 mm

Gudgeon pins

	1.4 and 1.6 litre engines	1.8 and 2.0 litre engines
Diameter	18.0 mm	21.0 mm
Length	55.0 mm	61.5 mm
Gudgeon pin-to-piston clearance	0.009 to 0.012 mm	0.011 to 0.014 mm

Connecting rod

Big-end side clearance	0.07 to 0.24 mm

SOHC engines (continued)

Pistons and rings
Piston diameter	Subtract 0.02 mm from corresponding bore diameter size group
Piston-to-bore clearance	0.02 ± 0.01 mm
Piston ring end gaps (fitted in bore):	
Top and second compression rings	0.3 to 0.5 mm
Oil control ring	0.4 to 1.4 mm
Piston ring thickness:	
Top compression ring:	
1.4, 1.8 and 2.0 litre engines	1.5 mm
1.6 litre engines	1.2 mm
Second compression ring	1.5 mm
Oil control ring	3.0 mm
Piston ring-to-groove clearance	N/A

Crankshaft
Endfloat	0.1 to 0.2 mm
Main bearing journal diameter:	
Standard	54.980 to 54.997 mm
1st (0.25 mm - blue) undersize	54.730 to 54.747 mm
2nd (0.50 mm - white) undersize	54.482 to 54.495 mm
Big-end bearing journal (crankpin) diameter:	
Standard	42.971 to 42.987 mm
1st (0.25 mm - blue) undersize	42.721 to 42.737 mm
2nd (0.50 mm - white) undersize	42.471 to 42.487 mm
Journal out-of round	0.04 mm
Journal taper	N/A
Crankshaft runout	Less than 0.03 mm
Main bearing running clearance	0.017 to 0.047 mm
Big-end bearing (crankpin) running clearance	0.019 to 0.071 mm

Torque wrench settings
Refer to Chapter 2A Specifications

1.4 and 1.6 litre DOHC engines

Cylinder head
Maximum gasket face distortion	0.05 mm
Cylinder head height	134.90 to 135.10 mm

Valves and guides
	Inlet	Exhaust
Valve guide height in cylinder head	10.70 to 11.00 mm	
Valve stem diameter*:		
Standard (K)	5.995 to 5.970 mm	5.935 to 5.950 mm
1st oversize (0.075 mm - K1)	6.030 to 6.045 mm	6.010 to 6.025 mm
2nd oversize (0.150 mm - K2)	6.105 to 6.120 mm	6.085 to 6.100 mm
Valve stem runout	Less than 0.03 mm	
Valve guide bore diameter*:		
Standard (K)	6.000 to 6.012 mm	
1st oversize (0.075 mm - K1)	6.075 to 6.090 mm	
2nd oversize (0.150 mm - K2)	6.150 to 6.165 mm	
Stem-to-guide clearance:		
Inlet	0.03 to 0.06 mm	
Exhaust	0.04 to 0.07 mm	
Valve length:		
1.4 litre engines:		
Inlet	101.92 mm	
Exhaust	100.96 mm	
1.6 litre engines:		
Inlet	103.1 mm	
Exhaust	102.2 mm	
Valve head diameter:		
Inlet	31.0 mm	
Exhaust	27.5 mm	

*Identification marking in brackets

1.4 and 1.6 litre DOHC engines (continued)

Cylinder block

Maximum gasket face distortion .... 0.05 mm
Cylinder bore diameter:
  1.4 litre engines:
    Standard:
      Size group 6 .... 77.555 to 77.565 mm
      Size group 7 .... 77.565 to 77.575 mm
      Size group 8 .... 77.575 to 77.585 mm
    Oversize (0.5 mm) .... 78.065 to 78.075 mm
  1.6 litre engines:
    Standard:
      Size group 5 .... 78.945 to 78.955 mm
      Size group 6 .... 78.955 to 78.965 mm
      Size group 7 .... 78.965 to 78.975 mm
      Size group 8 .... 78.975 to 78.985 mm
      Size group 99 .... 78.985 to 78.995 mm
      Size group 00 .... 78.995 to 79.005 mm
      Size group 01 .... 79.005 to 79.015 mm
      Size group 02 .... 79.015 to 79.025 mm
      Size group 03 .... 79.025 to 79.035 mm
      Size group 04 .... 79.035 to 79.045 mm
      Size group 05 .... 79.045 to 79.055 mm
      Size group 06 .... 79.055 to 79.065 mm
      Size group 07 .... 79.065 to 79.075 mm
      Size group 08 .... 79.075 to 79.085 mm
      Size group 09 .... 79.085 to 79.095 mm
      Size group 1 .... 79.095 to 79.105 mm
    Oversize (0.5 mm) .... 79.465 to 79.475 mm
Maximum cylinder bore ovality and taper .... 0.013 mm

Pistons and rings

Piston diameter .... Subtract 0.02 mm from corresponding bore diameter size group
Piston-to-bore clearance .... 0.01 to 0.03 mm
Piston ring end gaps (fitted in bore):
  Top and second compression rings .... 0.3 to 0.5 mm
  Oil control ring .... 0.4 to 1.4 mm
Piston ring thickness:
  Top compression ring:
    1.4 litre engines .... 1.5 mm
    1.6 litre engines .... 1.2 mm
  Second compression ring .... 1.5 mm
  Oil control ring .... 2.5 mm
Piston ring-to-groove clearance .... N/A

Gudgeon pins

Diameter .... 18 mm
Length .... 55 mm
Gudgeon pin-to-piston clearance .... 0.007 to 0.010 mm

Connecting rod

Big-end side clearance .... 0.11 to 0.24 mm

Crankshaft

Endfloat .... 0.1 to 0.2 mm
Main bearing journal diameter:
  Standard .... 54.980 to 54.997 mm
  1st (0.25 mm - blue) undersize .... 54.730 to 54.747 mm
  2nd (0.50 mm - white) undersize .... 54.482 to 54.495 mm
Big-end bearing journal (crankpin) diameter:
  Standard .... 42.971 to 42.987 mm
  1st (0.25 mm - blue) undersize .... 42.721 to 42.737 mm
  2nd (0.50 mm - white) undersize .... 42.471 to 42.487 mm
Journal out-of round .... 0.04 mm
Journal taper .... N/A
Crankshaft runout .... Less than 0.03 mm
Main bearing running clearance .... 0.013 to 0.043 mm
Big-end bearing (crankpin) running clearance .... 0.019 to 0.071 mm

Torque wrench settings

Refer to Chapter 2B Specifications

1.8 and 2.0 litre DOHC engines

Cylinder head

Maximum gasket face distortion .... 0.05 mm
Cylinder head height:
   All except C 20 XE engines .... 134 mm
   C 20 XE engines .... 135.58 to 135.68 mm

Valves and guides

Valve guide height in cylinder head:
   All except C 20 XE engines .... 13.70 to 14.00 mm
   C 20 XE engines .... 10.70 to 11.00 mm

Valve stem diameter*:	Inlet	Exhaust
Standard (K):		
All except C 20 XE engines	5.955 to 5.970 mm	5.945 to 5.960 mm
C 20 XE engines	6.955 to 6.970 mm	6.945 to 6.960 mm
1st oversize (0.075 mm - K1):		
All except C 20 XE engines	6.030 to 6.045 mm	6.020 to 6.035 mm
C 20 XE engines	7.030 to 7.045 mm	7.020 to 7.035 mm
2nd oversize (0.150 mm - K2):		
All except C 20 XE engines	6.105 to 6.120 mm	6.095 to 6.110 mm
C 20 XE engines	7.105 to 7.120 mm	7.095 to 7.110 mm

Valve stem runout .... Less than 0.03 mm
Valve guide bore diameter*:
   Standard (K):
      All except C 20 XE engines .... 6.000 to 6.015 mm
      C 20 XE engines .... 7.000 to 7.015 mm
   1st oversize (0.075 mm - K1):
      All except C 20 XE engines .... 6.075 to 6.090 mm
      C 20 XE engines .... 7.075 to 7.090 mm
   2nd oversize (0.150 mm - K2):
      All except C 20 XE engines .... 6.150 to 6.165 mm
      C 20 XE engines .... 7.150 to 7.165 mm
Stem-to-guide clearance:
   Inlet .... 0.030 to 0.060 mm
   Exhaust .... 0.040 to 0.070 mm

Valve length:	Inlet	Exhaust
Production:		
All except C 20 XE engines	102.1 mm	92.25 mm
C 20 XE engines	105.0 mm	91.8 mm
Service:		
All except C 20 XE engines	101.7 mm	91.8 mm
C 20 XE engines	104.6 mm	104.6 mm
Valve head diameter:		
All except C 20 XE engines	32.0 mm	29.0 mm
C 20 XE engines	33.0 mm	29.0 mm

Identification marking in brackets

Cylinder block

Maximum gasket face distortion .... 0.05 mm

Cylinder bore diameter:	1.8 litre engine	2.0 litre engine
Standard:		
Size group 8	81.575 to 81.585 mm	85.975 to 85.985 mm
Size group 99	81.585 to 81.595 mm	85.985 to 85.995 mm
Size group 00	81.595 to 81.605 mm	85.995 to 86.005 mm
Size group 01	81.605 to 81.615 mm	86.005 to 86.015 mm
Size group 02	81.615 to 81.625 mm	86.015 to 86.025 mm
Oversize (0.5 mm)	82.065 to 82.075 mm	86.465 to 86.475 mm

Maximum cylinder bore ovality and taper .... 0.013 mm

Pistons and rings

Piston diameter .... Subtract 0.02 mm from corresponding bore diameter size group
Piston-to-bore clearance .... 0.01 to 0.03 mm
Piston ring end gaps (fitted in bore):
   Top and second compression rings .... 0.3 to 0.5 mm
   Oil control ring .... 0.4 to 1.4 mm
Piston ring thickness:
   Top and second compression ring .... 1.5 mm
   Oil control ring .... 3.0 mm
Piston ring-to-groove clearance .... N/A

1.8 and 2.0 litre DOHC engines (continued)

Gudgeon pins

Diameter	21 mm
Length	61.5 mm
Gudgeon pin-to-piston clearance	0.011 to 0.013 mm

Connecting rod

Big-end side clearance	0.07 to 0.24 mm

Crankshaft

Endfloat	0.05 to 0.15 mm
Main bearing journal diameter:	
Standard:	
1st size group (white)	57.974 to 57.981 mm
2nd size group (green)	57.981 to 57.988 mm
3rd size group (brown)	57.988 to 57.995 mm
1st (0.25 mm) undersize (green/blue)	57.732 to 57.738 mm
1st (0.25 mm) undersize (brown/blue)	57.738 to 57.745 mm
2nd (0.50 mm) undersize (green/white)	57.482 to 57.488 mm
2nd (0.50 mm) undersize (brown/white)	57.488 to 57.495 mm
Big-end bearing journal (crankpin) diameter:	
Standard	48.970 to 48.988 mm
1st (0.25 mm) undersize (blue)	48.720 to 48.738 mm
2nd (0.50 mm) undersize (white)	48.470 to 48.488 mm
Journal out-of round	0.04 mm
Journal taper	N/A
Crankshaft runout	Less than 0.03 mm
Main bearing running clearance	0.015 to 0.040 mm
Big-end bearing (crankpin) running clearance	0.006 to 0.031 mm

Torque wrench settings

Refer to Chapter 2B Specifications

---

1 General information

Included in this Part of Chapter 2 are details of removing the engine/transmission from the car and general overhaul procedures for the cylinder head, cylinder block and all other engine internal components.

The information given ranges from advice concerning preparation for an overhaul and the purchase of replacement parts, to detailed step-by-step procedures covering removal, inspection, renovation and refitting of engine internal components.

After Section 8, all instructions are based on the assumption that the engine has been removed from the car. For information concerning in-car engine repair, as well as the removal and refitting of those external components necessary for full overhaul, refer to the relevant in-car repair procedure section (Chapter 2A or 2B) of this Chapter and to Section 8. Ignore any preliminary dismantling operations described in the relevant in-car repair sections that are no longer relevant once the engine has been removed from the car.

Apart from torque wrench settings, which are given at the beginning of the relevant in-car repair procedure (Chapter 2A or 2B), all specifications relating to engine overhaul are at the beginning of this Part of Chapter 2.

2 Engine overhaul - general information

It is not always easy to determine when, or if, an engine should be completely overhauled, as a number of factors must be considered.

High mileage is not necessarily an indication that an overhaul is needed, while low mileage does not preclude the need for an overhaul. Frequency of servicing is probably the most important consideration. An engine which has had regular and frequent oil and filter changes, as well as other required maintenance, should give many thousands of miles of reliable service. Conversely, a neglected engine may require an overhaul very early in its life.

Excessive oil consumption is an indication that piston rings, valve seals and/or valve guides are in need of attention. Make sure that oil leaks are not responsible before deciding that the rings and/or guides are worn. Perform a compression test, as described in Part A or Part B of this Chapter (as applicable), to determine the likely cause of the problem.

Check the oil pressure with a gauge fitted in place of the oil pressure switch, and compare it with that specified. If it is extremely low, the main and big-end bearings, and/or the oil pump, are probably worn out.

Loss of power, rough running, knocking or metallic engine noises, excessive valve gear noise, and high fuel consumption may also point to the need for an overhaul, especially if they are all present at the same time. If a complete service does not remedy the situation, major mechanical work is the only solution.

An engine overhaul involves restoring all internal parts to the specification of a new engine. During an overhaul, the pistons and the piston rings are renewed. New main and big-end bearings are generally fitted; if necessary, the crankshaft may be renewed, to restore the journals. The valves are also serviced as well, since they are usually in less-than-perfect condition at this point. While the engine is being overhauled, other components, such as the starter and alternator, can be overhauled as well. The end result should be an as-new engine that will give many trouble-free miles. **Note:** *Critical cooling system components such as the hoses, thermostat and coolant pump should be renewed when an engine is overhauled. The radiator should be checked carefully, to ensure that it is not clogged or leaking. Also, it is a good idea to renew the oil pump whenever the engine is overhauled.*

Before beginning the engine overhaul, read through the entire procedure, to familiarise yourself with the scope and requirements of the job. Overhauling an engine is not difficult if you follow carefully all of the instructions, have the necessary tools and equipment, and pay close attention to all specifications. It can, however, be time-consuming. Plan on the car being off the road for a minimum of two weeks, especially if parts must be taken to an engineering works for repair or reconditioning. Check on the availability of parts and make sure that any necessary special tools and equipment are obtained in advance. Most work can be done with typical hand tools, although a number of precision measuring tools are required for inspecting parts to determine if they must be renewed. Often the engineering works will handle the inspection of parts and offer advice concerning reconditioning and renewal. **Note:** *Always wait until the engine has been completely dismantled, and until all components (especially the cylinder block and the crankshaft) have been inspected, before deciding what service and repair operations must be performed by an engineering works. The condition of these components will be the major factor to consider when determining whether to overhaul the original engine, or to buy a reconditioned unit. Do not, therefore, purchase parts or have overhaul work done on other components until they have been thoroughly inspected.* As a general rule, time is the primary cost of an overhaul, so it does not pay to fit worn or sub-standard parts.

As a final note, to ensure maximum life and minimum trouble from a reconditioned engine, everything must be assembled with care, in a spotlessly-clean environment.

3 Engine removal - methods and precautions

If you have decided that the engine must be removed for overhaul or major repair work, several preliminary steps should be taken.

Locating a suitable place to work is extremely important. Adequate work space, along with storage space for the car, will be needed. If a workshop or garage is not available, at the very least, a flat, level, clean work surface is required.

Cleaning the engine compartment and engine/transmission before beginning the removal procedure will help keep tools clean and organised.

An engine hoist or A-frame will also be necessary. Make sure the equipment is rated in excess of the combined weight of the engine and transmission. Safety is of primary importance, considering the potential hazards involved in lifting the engine/transmission out of the car.

If this is the first time you have removed an engine, an assistant should ideally be available. Advice and aid from someone more experienced would also be helpful. There are many instances when one person cannot simultaneously perform all of the operations required when lifting the engine out of the vehicle.

4.10 Disconnecting the brake servo vacuum hose from the inlet manifold – 1.6 litre SOHC engine

Plan the operation ahead of time. Before starting work, arrange for the hire of or obtain all of the tools and equipment you will need. Some of the equipment necessary to perform engine/transmission removal and installation safely and with relative ease (in addition to an engine hoist) is as follows: a heavy duty trolley jack, complete sets of spanners and sockets as described in the back of this manual, wooden blocks, and plenty of rags and cleaning solvent for mopping up spilled oil, coolant and fuel. If the hoist must be hired, make sure that you arrange for it in advance, and perform all of the operations possible without it beforehand. This will save you money and time.

Plan for the car to be out of use for quite a while. An engineering works will be required to perform some of the work which the do-it-yourselfer cannot accomplish without special equipment. These places often have a busy schedule, so it would be a good idea to consult them before removing the engine, in order to accurately estimate the amount of time required to rebuild or repair components that may need work.

Always be extremely careful when removing and refitting the engine/transmission. Serious injury can result from careless actions. Plan ahead and take your time, and a job of this nature, although major, can be accomplished successfully.

4 Engine - removal and refitting (leaving manual transmission in vehicle)

Removal

1 Disconnect both battery leads and remove the bonnet.
2 Drain the cooling system and remove the radiator as described in Chapter 3.
3 Drain the engine oil as described in Chapter 1 and, on 1.8 and 2.0 litre engines, remove the oil filter.
4 Where applicable, unscrew the unions and disconnect the oil cooler pipes from the engine. Be prepared for oil spillage.
5 On DOHC engines, where applicable, remove the engine cover or spark plug cover from the camshaft cover.

4.12 Disconnecting the MAP sensor vacuum hose from the throttle body – 1.6 litre SOHC engine

6 Remove the air cleaner assembly from the body panel and remove the air inlet trunking and the airbox from the carburettor or throttle body, referring to Chapter 4A or 4B, as applicable.
7 On carburettor models, disconnect the hot air hose from the exhaust manifold hot air shroud and the air cleaner and remove the hose.
8 Remove the alternator as described in Chapter 5A.
9 Remove the power steering pump, if fitted, as described in Chapter 10.
10 Disconnect the brake servo vacuum hose from the inlet manifold **(see illustration)**.
11 Disconnect the throttle cable from the throttle lever and the bracket on the carburettor or inlet manifold, as applicable.
12 Disconnect the vacuum pipe(s) from the carburettor or throttle body (as applicable), noting their locations **(see illustration)**.
13 On DOHC engine models, where applicable, disconnect the vacuum hoses from the air injection switchover valve and the carbon canister purge valve. Where applicable, also disconnect the air and vacuum hoses from the air injection combination valve.
14 Disconnect the coolant hose(s) from the inlet manifold and/or throttle body, as applicable **(see illustration)**.
15 On carburettor engines, disconnect the coolant hoses from the automatic choke housing and disconnect the wiring from the automatic choke heater and the choke pull-down solenoid. Disconnect the airbox vacuum pipe from the carburettor.

4.14 Disconnecting a coolant hose from the throttle body – 1.6 litre SOHC engine

4.19 Disconnecting the coolant hose (arrowed) from the inlet manifold – 1.6 litre SOHC engine

16 On fuel injection models, depressurise the fuel system as described in Chapter 4B. Disconnect the fuel hoses from the fuel pump and vapour separator on carburettor models, or from the fuel injection unit, the pipes on the inlet manifold, or the fuel rail and pressure regulator (as applicable) on fuel injection models. Be prepared for fuel spillage and take adequate fire precautions. Plug or clamp the open ends of the pipes and hoses to prevent dirt ingress and further fuel leakage.

17 On fuel injection models, disconnect all relevant wiring connections and plugs, noting their locations and move the fuel injection wiring harness to one side.

18 Release the securing clips and withdraw the wiring harness from the brackets on the camshaft cover, if applicable.

19 Disconnect the heater coolant hoses from the coolant gallery at the rear of the cylinder block and from the cylinder head or inlet manifold, as applicable **(see illustration)**.

20 Disconnect the wiring from the following components (if not already done). Note that on certain models, a large single plug can be disconnected to separate the engine wiring loom from the main wiring harness (the connector can usually be found clipped to a bracket on the battery tray). This will leave the wiring loom attached to the engine, avoiding the need to remove the plugs and connections from individual components.

a) Starter motor.
b) Distributor/DIS module (as applicable, note HT lead positions).
c) Oil pressure switch.

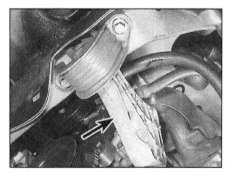

4.31 Right-hand engine mounting bracket

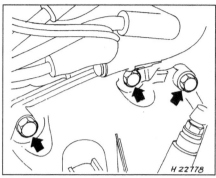

4.22 Three upper engine-to-transmission bolts (arrowed)

d) TDC sensor (if fitted).
e) Oil level sensor (if fitted).
f) Coolant temperature sensor (if fitted).
g) Temperature gauge sender.
h) Knock sensor (if fitted)

21 Make a final check to ensure that all relevant hoses, pipes and wires have been disconnected and that they are positioned clear of the engine.

22 Unscrew and remove the three upper engine-to-transmission bolts accessible from the engine compartment, noting the locations of any brackets that may be secured by the bolts **(see illustration)**.

23 If not already done, apply the handbrake, then jack up the front of the vehicle and support securely on axle stands (see "Jacking and vehicle support").

24 Remove the crankshaft pulley, with reference to Part A (SOHC engines) or Part B (DOHC engines) of this Chapter.

25 Remove the front section of the exhaust system, as described in Chapter 4A or 4B.

26 On models where it is possible to remove the clutch with the engine and transmission in the vehicle, remove the clutch as described in Chapter 6.

27 On models where it is not possible to remove the clutch with the engine and transmission in the vehicle, pull the transmission input shaft from engagement with the splined hub of the clutch friction disc. This procedure is described in Chapter 6, as part of the clutch removal procedure for models where it is possible to remove the clutch with the engine and transmission in the vehicle.

4.33 Lifting the engine from the vehicle – 1.6 litre SOHC engine

28 Unbolt and remove the transmission bellhousing cover plate.

29 Attach a hoist and lifting tackle to the engine lifting brackets on the cylinder head and support the weight of the engine.

30 Support the transmission using a trolley jack with a block of wood to spread the load.

31 Unbolt the right-hand engine mounting from the cylinder block and the body and withdraw the mounting bracket **(see illustration)**.

32 Unscrew and remove the four lower engine-to-transmission bolts (again noting the location of any brackets that may be secured by the bolts), then manipulate the engine as necessary to separate it from the transmission. The transmission locates on dowels in the cylinder block.

33 Carefully raise the hoist and lift the engine from the vehicle, taking care not to damage any of the surrounding components in the engine compartment **(see illustration)**.

34 With the engine removed, the transmission can be supported by placing a length of wood between the bellhousing and the front suspension subframe. Once the wooden support is in place, remove the trolley jack from under the transmission.

Refitting

Note: Thread-locking compound will be required to coat the threads of the right-hand engine mounting-to-body bolts.

35 With the front of the vehicle raised and supported on axle stands (see "Jacking and vehicle support"), support the transmission with a trolley jack and block of wood and remove the previously positioned support from between the transmission bellhousing and the subframe.

36 Support the engine with the hoist and lifting tackle and gently lower the engine into position in the engine compartment.

37 Mate the engine and the transmission together, ensuring that the transmission locates on the dowels in the cylinder block. Refit the three upper engine-to-transmission bolts (ensuring that any brackets noted during removal are in place) do not fully tighten the bolts at this stage.

38 Refit the four lower engine-to-transmission bolts (again ensuring that any brackets noted during removal are in place), but again do not fully tighten them at this stage.

39 Fit the right-hand engine mounting bracket to the cylinder block and tighten its securing bolts to the specified torque.

40 Coat the engine mounting-to-body bolts with thread-locking compound, then manipulate the engine and transmission as necessary to enable the bolts to be fitted. Fit the bolts and tighten them to the specified torque.

41 Tighten all the engine-to-transmission bolts to the specified torque, then disconnect the lifting tackle and hoist from the engine and remove the trolley jack from beneath the transmission.

42 Refit the transmission bellhousing cover plate.

43 Refit the clutch, if applicable and engage the transmission input shaft with the splined hub of the clutch friction disc (as described in Chapter 6).

44 Refit the front section of the exhaust system, as described in Chapter 4A or 4B.

45 Refit the crankshaft pulley, with reference to Part A or Part B of this Chapter, as applicable.

46 Lower the vehicle to the ground.

47 Refit and reconnect all relevant pipes, wires and hoses, etc., using a reversal of the removal procedure described in paragraphs 10 to 20 inclusive.

48 Where applicable, refit the power steering pump, and on 1.8 and 2.0 litre engines tension the pump drivebelt as described in Chapter 1.

49 Refit the alternator and tension the drivebelt, as described in Chapter 1.

50 Refit the air cleaner components, referring to Chapter 4A or 4B if necessary, and on carburettor models, reconnect the hot air hose to the exhaust manifold hot air shroud.

51 Fill the engine with oil, and where applicable fit a new oil filter, as described in Chapter 1.

52 Refit the radiator and refill the cooling system as described in Chapter 3.

53 Refit the bonnet as described in Chapter 11.

54 Reconnect the battery leads.

55 On completion, if applicable, bleed the power steering fluid circuit as described in Chapter 10.

---

5 Engine/manual transmission assembly - removal and refitting

Note: *New bolts must be used to secure the left-hand engine/transmission mounting to the body on refitting and new locking plates must be used on the bolts securing the rear engine/transmission mounting to the transmission. Thread-locking compound will be required to coat the threads of the right-hand engine mounting-to-body bolts. An M10 x 1.25 mm tap may be required during this procedure - refer to the text.*

Removal

1 Proceed as described in Section 4, paragraphs 1 to 20 inclusive.

2 Working in the engine compartment, make alignment marks between the gear selector rod and the clamp sleeve, then loosen the clamp bolt and disconnect the gear selector rod from the clamp sleeve **(see illustration)**.

3 Remove the retaining clip, then slide the clutch cable from the release lever, pushing the release lever back towards the bulkhead if necessary to allow the cable to be disconnected. Pull the cable support from the bracket on the transmission casing, then move the cable to one side out of the way, taking note of its routing.

4 Disconnect the wiring from the reversing light switch, which is located at the front of the transmission casing.

5 Unscrew the securing sleeve and disconnect the speedometer cable from the transmission.

6 Unscrew the retaining nut and disconnect the earth strap from the transmission end-plate.

7 Make a final check to ensure that all relevant pipes, hoses, wires, etc., have been disconnected and that they are positioned clear of the engine and transmission.

8 Proceed as described in Section 4, paragraphs 23 to 25 inclusive.

9 Disconnect the inboard ends of the driveshafts from the differential, referring to the relevant paragraphs of Chapter 8, Section 2. Be prepared for oil spillage as the driveshafts are withdrawn and plug the apertures in the differential, to prevent further loss of oil and dirt ingress. Support the driveshafts by suspending them with wire or string. *Do not* allow them to hand down under their own weight.

10 Attach a hoist and lifting tackle to the engine lifting brackets on the cylinder head and support the weight of the engine.

11 Remove the left-hand engine/transmission mounting completely by unscrewing the two bolts securing the rubber mounting to the vehicle body and the three bolts securing the mounting bracket to the transmission.

12 Unbolt the right-hand engine mounting from the body and from the cylinder block and withdraw the mounting bracket.

13 Working under the vehicle, unscrew and remove the two nuts securing the engine/transmission rear mounting to the front subframe and the three bolts securing the mounting bracket to the transmission, then withdraw the mounting bracket.

14 Carefully swing the engine/transmission assembly across the engine compartment as necessary, to allow the assembly to be lifted vertically from the vehicle by raising the hoist. Take care not to damage any of the surrounding components in the engine compartment.

15 With the engine/transmission assembly removed, support the assembly on blocks of wood positioned on a workbench, or failing that, on a clean area of the workshop floor.

16 Clean away any external dirt using paraffin or a water-soluble solvent and a stiff brush.

17 Unbolt and remove the transmission bellhousing cover plate.

18 Ensure that both engine and transmission are adequately supported, then unscrew and remove the engine-to-transmission bolts, noting the locations of any brackets that may be secured by the bolts.

19 Carefully withdraw the transmission from the engine, ensuring that the weight of the transmission is not allowed to hang on the input shaft while it is engaged with the clutch

friction disc. Note that the transmission locates on dowels positioned in the cylinder block.

Refitting

20 Before starting the refitting operations, check that the two original bolts that secure the left-hand engine/transmission rubber mounting to the vehicle body rotate freely in their threaded bores in the body. If necessary, re-cut the threaded bores using an M10 x 1.25 mm tap.

21 On models where the clutch can be removed and refitted with the engine and transmission in the vehicle, if the clutch has been removed, it will prove easier to refit after the engine/transmission assembly has been refitted to the vehicle.

22 Carefully offer the transmission to the engine until the bellhousing is located on the dowels in the cylinder block, then refit the engine-to-transmission bolts and tighten them to the specified torque. Make sure that any brackets secured by the bolts are correctly positioned as noted before removal. If the clutch is still bolted to the flywheel, ensure that the weight of the transmission is not allowed to hang on the input shaft as it is engaged with the clutch friction disc.

23 If the clutch is in place, refit the transmission bellhousing cover plate.

24 With the front of the vehicle raised and supported on axle stands (see "*Jacking and vehicle support*"), support the engine/transmission assembly with the hoist and lifting tackle, then gently lower it into position in the engine compartment.

25 Working under the vehicle, refit the rear engine/transmission mounting to the transmission, using new locking plates under the bolt heads and tighten the bolts to the specified torque.

26 Fit the two bolts and nuts securing the engine/transmission rear mounting to the front subframe, but do not fully tighten them at this stage.

27 Fit the right-hand engine mounting bracket to the cylinder block and tighten the securing bolts to the specified torque.

28 Coat the right-hand engine mounting-to-body bolts with thread-locking compound, then fit the bolts, but do not fully tighten them at this stage.

5.2 Gear selector rod clamp sleeve (arrowed)

29 Fit the left-hand transmission mounting bracket to the transmission and tighten the securing bolts to the specified torque.
30 Fit new left-hand transmission mounting-to-body bolts and tighten them to the specified torque.
31 Tighten the right-hand engine mounting and the rear engine/transmission mounting-to-front subframe bolts to their specified torques, then remove the lifting tackle and the hoist from the engine.
32 Where applicable, the clutch can now be fitted and/or the transmission input shaft can be pressed into engagement with the splined hub of the clutch friction disc, as described in Chapter 6. Refit the transmission bellhousing cover plate, where applicable.
33 Reconnect the inboard ends of the driveshafts to the differential, with reference to the relevant paragraphs of Chapter 8, Section 2, using new snap-rings.
34 Refit the front section of the exhaust system, as described in Chapter 4A or 4B.
35 Refit the crankshaft pulley, with reference to Part A or Part B of this Chapter, as applicable.
36 Reconnect the transmission earth strap and tighten the securing nut.
37 Lower the vehicle to the ground.
38 Reconnect the speedometer cable to the transmission and tighten the securing sleeve.
39 Reconnect the reversing light switch wiring.
40 Refit the clutch cable to the bracket on the transmission casing, then reconnect the cable to the release lever and adjust the cable as described in Chapter 1. Ensure that the cable is routed as noted during removal.
41 Reconnect the gear selector rod to the clamp sleeve, ensuring that the marks made before disconnection are aligned and tighten the clamp bolt.
42 Proceed as described in Section 4, paragraphs 47 to 52 inclusive.
43 Top-up the transmission oil level, as described in Chapter 1.
44 Refit the bonnet as described in Chapter 11.
45 Reconnect the battery leads.

6 Engine - removal and refitting (leaving automatic transmission in vehicle)

Note: *New torque converter-to-driveplate bolts must be used on refitting and if the original torque converter is being used, an M10 x 1.25 mm tap will be required. Thread-locking compound will be required to coat the threads of the right-hand engine mounting-to-body bolts.*

Removal

1 Proceed as described in Section 4, paragraphs 1 to 20 inclusive.
2 Make a final check to ensure that all relevant hoses, pipes and wires have been disconnected and that they are positioned clear of the engine.

3 Unscrew and remove the three upper engine-to-transmission bolts, accessible from the engine compartment, noting the location of any brackets that may be secured by the bolts.
4 Proceed as described in Section 4, paragraphs 23 to 25 inclusive.
5 Unbolt and remove the transmission bellhousing cover plate.
6 If the original torque converter and driveplate are to be refitted, make alignment marks between the torque converter and the driveplate, to ensure that the components are reassembled in their original positions.
7 Working through the bottom of the bellhousing, unscrew the three torque converter-to-driveplate bolts. It will be necessary to turn the crankshaft using a spanner or socket on the crankshaft pulley or gear bolt (as applicable), to gain access to each bolt in turn through the aperture. Use a screwdriver or a similar tool to jam the driveplate ring gear, preventing the driveplate from rotating as the bolts are loosened. Discard the bolts.
8 Attach a hoist and lifting tackle to the engine lifting brackets on the cylinder head and support the weight of the engine.
9 Support the transmission using a trolley jack with a block of wood to spread the load.
10 Unbolt the right-hand engine mounting from the cylinder block and the body and withdraw the mounting bracket.
11 Unscrew and remove the lower engine-to-transmission bolts, then manipulate the engine as necessary to separate it from the transmission, noting that the transmission locates on dowels in the cylinder block. Ensure that the torque converter is held firmly in place in the transmission casing as the engine and transmission are separated, otherwise it could fall out, resulting in fluid spillage and possible damage. Retain the torque converter while the engine is removed by bolting a strip of metal across the transmission bellhousing end face.
12 Carefully raise the hoist and lift the engine from the vehicle, taking care not to damage any of the surrounding components in the engine compartment.
13 With the engine removed, the transmission can be supported by placing a length of wood between the bellhousing and the front suspension subframe. Once the wooden support is in place, remove the trolley jack from under the transmission.

Refitting

14 With the front of the vehicle raised and supported on axle stands (see *"Jacking and vehicle support"*), support the transmission with a trolley jack and a block of wood. Remove the axle stands from between the transmission bellhousing and the subframe.
15 If the original torque converter is still in place, begin refitting by recutting the torque converter-to-driveplate bolt threads in the torque converter using an M10 x 1.25 mm tap.
16 Support the engine with the hoist and

lifting tackle and gently lower the engine into position in the engine compartment.
17 Where applicable, remove the strip of metal retaining the torque converter in the transmission casing and hold the torque converter in position as the engine is mated to the transmission.
18 Ensure that the transmission locates on the dowels in the cylinder block, then refit the three upper engine-to-transmission bolts (ensuring that any brackets are in place as noted before removal) - do not fully tighten the bolts at this stage.
19 Refit the lower engine-to-transmission bolts (again ensuring that any brackets are in place), but again do not fully tighten them at this stage.
20 Fit the right-hand engine mounting bracket to the cylinder block and tighten its securing bolts to the specified torque.
21 Coat the engine mounting-to-body bolts with thread-locking compound, then manipulate the engine and transmission as necessary to enable the bolts to be fitted. Fit the bolts and tighten them to the specified torque.
22 Tighten all the engine-to-transmission bolts to the specified torque, then disconnect the lifting tackle and hoist from the engine and remove the trolley jack from beneath the transmission.
23 If the original torque converter and driveplate have been refitted, carefully turn the crankshaft to align the marks made before removal before fitting the torque converter-to-driveplate bolts.
24 Fit **new** torque converter-to-driveplate bolts and tighten them to the specified torque. Turn the crankshaft for access to each bolt in turn and prevent the driveplate from turning as during removal.
25 Refit the transmission bellhousing cover plate.
26 Proceed as described in Section 4, paragraphs 44 to 55 inclusive.
27 Check the transmission fluid level and top-up if necessary, as described in Chapter 1.

7 Engine/automatic transmission assembly - removal and refitting

Note: *New torque converter-to-driveplate bolts must be used on refitting. New bolts must be used to secure the left-hand engine/transmission mounting to the body on refitting and new locking plates must be used on the bolts securing the rear engine/transmission mounting to the transmission. Thread-locking compound will be required to coat the threads of the right-hand engine mounting-to-body bolts. An M10 x 1.25 mm tap may be required during this procedure. Refer to the text.*

Removal

1 Proceed as described in Section 4, paragraphs 1 to 20 inclusive.

2 To reduce fluid spillage as the driveshafts are withdrawn from the transmission, drain the transmission fluid as described in Chapter 7B.

3 Unscrew the securing sleeve and disconnect the speedometer cable from the transmission.

4 If not already done, apply the handbrake, then jack up the front of the vehicle and support securely on axle stands (see "*Jacking and vehicle support*").

5 Remove the crankshaft pulley, with reference to Part A (SOHC engines) or Part B (DOHC engines) of this Chapter.

6 Remove the front section of the exhaust system, as described in Chapter 4A or 4B.

7 Disconnect the transmission fluid cooler hoses either at the transmission or at the radiator, noting their routing. Clamp or plug the hoses to minimise fluid loss and dirt ingress.

8 Disconnect the transmission wiring harness connector and unbolt the two wiring harness brackets from the transmission casing.

9 Disconnect the vent hose from the transmission (the vent hose is located below the battery tray), noting its routing.

10 Remove the retaining clamp and the washer and disconnect the selector cable from the actuating lever on the transmission. Move the cable to one side away from the transmission.

11 Make a final check to ensure that all relevant pipes, hoses, wires, etc., have been disconnected and that they are positioned clear of the engine and transmission.

12 Proceed as described in Section 5, paragraphs 9 to 14 inclusive.

13 With the engine/transmission assembly removed, support the assembly on blocks of wood positioned on a workbench, or failing that, on a clean area of the workshop floor.

14 Clean away any external dirt using paraffin or a water-soluble solvent and a stiff brush.

15 Unbolt and remove the transmission bellhousing cover plate.

16 If the original torque converter and driveplate are to be refitted, make alignment marks between the torque converter and the driveplate, to ensure that the components are reassembled in their original positions.

17 Ensure that both the engine and transmission are adequately supported, then working through the bottom of the bellhousing, unscrew the three torque converter-to-driveplate bolts. It will be necessary to turn the crankshaft using a spanner or socket on the crankshaft pulley or gear bolt (as applicable), to gain access to each bolt in turn through the aperture. Use a screwdriver or a similar tool to jam the driveplate ring gear, preventing the driveplate from rotating as the bolts are loosened. Discard the bolts.

18 Unscrew and remove the engine-to-transmission bolts, noting the locations of any brackets that may be secured by the bolts.

19 Carefully pull the engine and transmission apart, ensuring that the torque converter is held firmly in place in the transmission casing, otherwise it could fall out, resulting in fluid spillage and possible damage. It may be necessary to rock the units slightly to separate them. If the transmission is to be left removed for some time, retain the torque converter by bolting a strip of metal across the bellhousing end face.

Refitting

20 If the original torque converter is being refitted, begin refitting by recutting the torque converter-to-driveplate bolt threads in the torque converter using an M10 x 1.25 mm tap.

21 If a new transmission is being fitted, the manufacturers recommend that the radiator fluid cooler passages are flushed clean before the new transmission is installed. Ideally, compressed air should be used (in which case, ensure that adequate safety precautions are taken). Alternatively, the cooler can be flushed with clean automatic transmission fluid until all the old fluid has been expelled and fresh fluid runs clear from the cooler outlet.

22 Check that the two original bolts that secure the left-hand engine/transmission rubber mounting to the vehicle body rotate freely in their threaded bores in the body. If necessary, re-cut the threaded bores using an M10 x 1.25 mm tap.

23 Carefully offer the transmission to the engine until the bellhousing is located on the dowels in the cylinder block (ensure that the torque converter is held firmly in place in the transmission casing as the engine and transmission are connected). Refit the engine-to-transmission bolts and tighten them to the specified torque. Make sure that any brackets secured by the bolts are correctly positioned as noted before removal.

24 If the original torque converter and driveplate are being refitted, carefully turn the crankshaft to align the marks made before removal, before fitting the torque converter-to-driveplate bolts.

25 Fit **new** torque converter-to-driveplate bolts and tighten them to the specified torque. Turn the crankshaft for access to each bolt in turn and prevent the driveplate from turning as during removal.

26 Refit the transmission bellhousing cover plate.

27 Attach the lifting tackle to the engine/transmission assembly, then lower the assembly into the engine compartment and reconnect the mountings as described in Section 5, paragraphs 25 to 31 inclusive.

28 Reconnect the inboard ends of the driveshafts to the differential, with reference to Chapter 8, Section 2, using new snap-rings.

29 Reconnect the transmission vent hose, ensuring that it is routed as noted before removal.

30 Reconnect the selector cable to the actuating lever on the transmission and adjust the cable as described in Chapter 7B.

31 Refit the transmission wiring harness brackets and reconnect the transmission wiring harness connector.

32 Reconnect the transmission fluid cooler hoses, using new sealing washers where applicable and making sure that they are correctly routed.

33 Refit the front section of the exhaust system, as described in Chapter 4A or 4B.

34 Refit the crankshaft pulley, with reference to Part A or Part B of this Chapter, as applicable.

35 Lower the vehicle to the ground.

36 Reconnect the speedometer cable and tighten the securing sleeve.

37 Proceed as described in Section 4, paragraphs 47 to 52 inclusive.

38 Refill the transmission with the correct quantity and type of fluid, through the dipstick tube.

39 Refit the bonnet as described in Chapter 11.

40 Make a final check to ensure that all hoses, pipes and wires have been correctly reconnected.

41 Reconnect the battery leads.

42 On completion, where applicable bleed the power steering fluid circuit as described in Chapter 10 and top-up the automatic transmission fluid level as described in Chapter 1.

8 Engine overhaul - dismantling sequence

1 It is much easier to dismantle and work on the engine if it is mounted on a portable engine stand. These stands can often be hired from a tool hire shop. Before the engine is mounted on a stand, the flywheel/driveplate should be removed, so that the stand bolts can be tightened into the end of the cylinder block.

2 If a stand is not available, it is possible to dismantle the engine with it blocked up on a sturdy workbench, or on the floor. Be extra-careful not to tip or drop the engine when working without a stand.

3 If you are going to obtain a reconditioned engine, all the external components must be removed first, to be transferred to the replacement engine (just as they will if you are doing a complete engine overhaul yourself). These components include the following:

a) *Inlet and exhaust manifolds (Chapter 4A or 4B).*
b) *Alternator/power steering pump/air conditioning compressor bracket(s) (as applicable).*
c) *Coolant pump (Chapter 3).*
d) *Fuel system components (Chapter 4A or 4B).*
e) *Wiring harness and all electrical switches and sensors.*
f) *Oil filter (Chapter 1).*
g) *Flywheel/driveplate (relevant Part of this Chapter).*

Note: *When removing the external components from the engine, pay close attention to details that may be helpful or important*

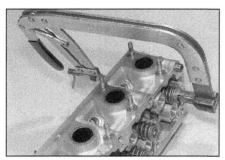

9.3a Valve spring compressor tool fitted to No 1 exhaust valve – 2.0 litre SOHC engine shown

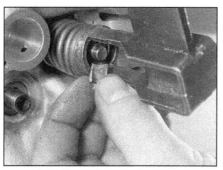

9.3b Removing a split collet – SOHC engine shown

9.3c Lift off the spring retainer . . .

9.3d . . . and the spring – SOHC engine shown

9.3e Extract the valve stem seal . . .

9.3f . . . then slide off the spring seat – SOHC engine shown

during refitting. Note the fitted position of gaskets, seals, spacers, pins, washers, bolts, and other small items.

4 If you are obtaining a 'short' engine (which consists of the engine cylinder block, crankshaft, pistons and connecting rods all assembled), then the cylinder head, sump, oil pump, and timing belt/chains (as applicable) will have to be removed also.

5 If you are planning a complete overhaul, the engine can be dismantled, and the internal components removed, in the order given below, referring to the relevant Part of this Chapter unless otherwise stated.

a) Inlet and exhaust manifolds (Chapter 4A or 4B).
b) Timing belt, sprockets and tensioner.
c) Cylinder head.
d) Flywheel/driveplate.
e) Sump.
f) Oil pump.
g) Piston/connecting rod assemblies.
h) Crankshaft.

6 Before beginning the dismantling and overhaul procedures, make sure that you have all of the correct tools necessary. Refer to the "Tools and working facilities" Section of this manual for further information.

9 Cylinder head - dismantling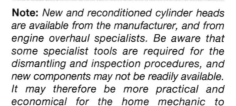

Note: New and reconditioned cylinder heads are available from the manufacturer, and from engine overhaul specialists. Be aware that some specialist tools are required for the dismantling and inspection procedures, and new components may not be readily available. It may therefore be more practical and economical for the home mechanic to purchase a reconditioned head, rather than dismantle, inspect and recondition the original head.

1 On SOHC engines, referring to Part A of this Chapter, remove the cylinder head from the engine then lift the camshaft followers, thrust pads and hydraulic tappets out from the cylinder head.

2 On DOHC engines remove the camshafts and followers as described in Part B of this Chapter, then remove the cylinder head from the engine.

3 Using a valve spring compressor, compress each valve spring in turn until the split collets can be removed. Release the compressor, and lift off the spring retainer and spring. Using a pair of pliers, carefully extract the valve stem seal from the top of the guide then slide off the spring seat **(see illustrations)**.

4 If, when the valve spring compressor is screwed down, the spring retainer refuses to free and expose the split collets, gently tap the top of the tool, directly over the retainer, with a light hammer. This will free the retainer.

5 Withdraw the valve through the combustion chamber. It is essential that each valve is stored together with its collets, retainer, spring, and spring seat. The valves should also be kept in their correct sequence, unless they are so badly worn that they are to be renewed **(see Haynes Hint)**.

10 Cylinder head and valves - cleaning and inspection

1 Thorough cleaning of the cylinder head and valve components, followed by a detailed inspection, will enable you to decide how much valve service work must be carried out during the engine overhaul. **Note:** If the engine has been severely overheated, it is best to assume that the cylinder head is warped - check carefully for signs of this.

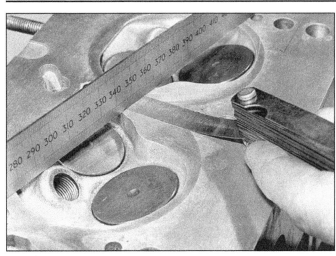

10.6 Checking the cylinder head surface for distortion

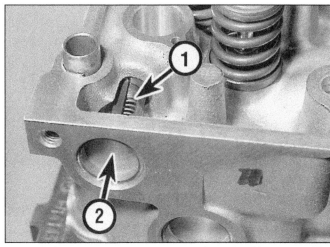

10.11 Cylinder head oil pressure regulating valve (1) and plug (2) –
1.8 and 2.0 litre SOHC engines

Cleaning

2 Scrape away all traces of old gasket material from the cylinder head.
3 Scrape away the carbon from the combustion chambers and ports, then wash the cylinder head thoroughly with paraffin or a suitable solvent.
4 Scrape off any heavy carbon deposits that may have formed on the valves, then use a power-operated wire brush to remove deposits from the valve heads and stems.

Inspection

Note: *Be sure to perform all the following inspection procedures before concluding that the services of a machine shop or engine overhaul specialist are required. Make a list of all items that require attention.*

Cylinder head

5 Inspect the head very carefully for cracks, evidence of coolant leakage, and other damage. If cracks are found, a new cylinder head should be obtained.
6 Use a straight-edge and feeler blade to check that the cylinder head surface is not distorted **(see illustration)**. If it is, it may be possible to resurface it, provided that the cylinder head is not reduced to less than the minimum specified height.
7 Examine the valve seats in each of the combustion chambers. If they are severely pitted, cracked or burned, then they will need to be re-cut by an engine overhaul specialist. If they are only slightly pitted, this can be removed by grinding-in the valve heads and seats with fine valve-grinding compound, as described below.
8 If the valve guides are worn (indicated by a side-to-side motion of the valve, and accompanied by excessive blue smoke in the exhaust when running) new guides must be fitted. Measure the diameter of the existing valve stems (see below) and the bore of the guides, then calculate the clearance and compare the result with the specified value. If

the clearance is not within the specified limits, renew the valves and/or guides as necessary.
9 The renewal of valve guides is best carried out by an engine overhaul specialist. If the work is to be carried out at home, however, use a stepped, double-diameter drift to drive out the worn guide towards the combustion chamber. On fitting the new guide, place it first in a deep-freeze for one hour, then drive it into its cylinder head bore from the camshaft side until it projects the specified amount above the cylinder head surface (where no measurement is given seek the advice of a Vauxhall dealer).
10 If the valve seats are to be re-cut this must be done only after the guides have been renewed.
11 On 1.8 and 2.0 litre SOHC engines, an oil pressure regulating valve is fitted to the oil gallery in the cylinder head **(see illustration)**. This valve can be renewed if it appears to be damaged, or if its operation is suspect. Access is gained via the circular plug covering the end of the valve. The old valve must be crushed, then its remains extracted and a thread (M10) cut in the valve seat to allow removal using a bolt. A new valve and plug can then be driven into position. In view of the intricacies of this operation, it is probably best to have the valve renewed by a Vauxhall/Opel dealer if necessary.

10.12 Renewing the thermostat housing sealing ring –
1.8 and 2.0 litre SOHC engines

12 On 1.8 and 2.0 litre engines, always renew the sealing ring between the cylinder head and the thermostat housing when the head is removed for overhaul **(see illustration)**.

Valves

13 Examine the head of each valve for pitting, burning, cracks and general wear, and check the valve stem for scoring and wear ridges. Rotate the valve, and check for any obvious indication that it is bent. Look for pitting and excessive wear on the tip of each valve stem. Renew any valve that shows any such signs of wear or damage.
14 If the valve appears satisfactory at this stage, measure the valve stem diameter at several points using a micrometer **(see illustration)**. Any significant difference in the readings obtained indicates wear of the valve stem. Should any of these conditions be apparent, the valve(s) must be renewed.
15 If the valves are in satisfactory condition, they should be ground (lapped) into their respective seats, to ensure a smooth gas-tight seal. If the seat is only lightly pitted, or if it has been re-cut, fine grinding compound **only** should be used to produce the required finish. Coarse valve-grinding compound should **not** be used unless a seat is badly burned or deeply pitted; if this is the case, the

10.14 Measuring a valve stem diameter

10.17 Grinding-in a valve seat

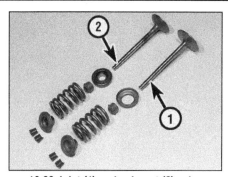
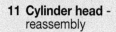

10.22 Inlet (1) and exhaust (2) valve components – SOHC engines

cylinder head and valves should be inspected by an expert to decide whether seat re-cutting, or even the renewal of the valve or seat insert, is required.

16 Valve grinding is carried out as follows. Place the cylinder head upside-down on a bench.

17 Smear a trace of the appropriate grade of valve-grinding compound on the seat face, and press a suction grinding tool onto the valve head. With a semi-rotary action, grind the valve head to its seat, lifting the valve occasionally to redistribute the grinding compound **(see illustration)**. A light spring placed under the valve head will greatly ease this operation.

18 If coarse grinding compound is being used, work only until a dull, matt even surface is produced on both the valve seat and the valve, then wipe off the used compound and repeat the process with fine compound. When

a smooth unbroken ring of light grey matt finish is produced on both the valve and seat, the grinding operation is complete. **Do not** grind in the valves any further than absolutely necessary, or the seat will be sunk into the cylinder head.

19 When all the valves have been ground-in, carefully wash off all traces of grinding compound using paraffin or a suitable solvent before reassembly of the cylinder head.

Valve components

20 Examine the valve springs for signs of damage and discoloration; if possible; also compare the free length of the existing springs with new components.

21 Stand each spring on a flat surface, and check it for squareness. If any of the springs are damaged, distorted or have lost their tension, obtain a complete new set of springs.

22 On certain SOHC engines, each exhaust

valve spring seat incorporates a bearing; the bearing rotates the valve which helps to keep the valve seat clean **(see illustration)**. If any spring seat bearing shows signs of wear or does not rotate smoothly, then the relevant seat should be renewed.

11 Cylinder head - reassembly

1 Lubricate the stems of the valves, and insert them into their original locations **(see illustration)**. If new valves are being fitted, insert them into the locations to which they have been ground.

2 Working on the first valve, refit the spring seat. Dip the new valve stem seal in fresh engine oil, then carefully locate it over the valve and onto the guide. Take care not to damage the seal as it is passed over the valve stem. Use a suitable socket or metal tube to press the seal firmly onto the guide. **Note:** *If genuine Vauxhall/Opel seals are being fitted, use the oil seal protector which is supplied with the seals; the protector fits over the valve stem and prevents the oil seal lip being damaged on the valve* **(see illustrations)**.

3 Locate the spring on the seat and fit the spring retainer **(see illustrations)**.

4 Compress the valve spring, and locate the split collets in the recess in the valve stem **(see illustration)**. Release the compressor, then repeat the procedure on the remaining valves.

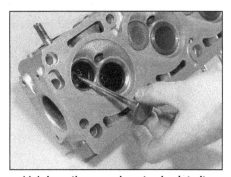

11.1 Inserting an exhaust valve into its guide – SOHC engine shown

11.2a Fitting a valve seat – SOHC engine shown

11.2b Slide the oil seal fitting sleeve down the valve stem, . . .

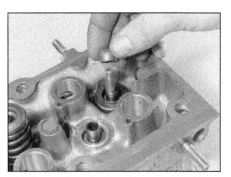

11.2c . . . then fit the valve stem seal, . . .

11.2d . . . and press firmly onto the guide using a socket

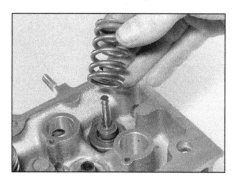

11.3a Locate the spring on the seat, . . .

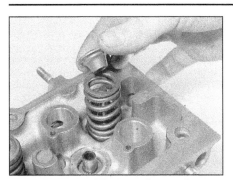

11.3b . . . and fit the spring retainer

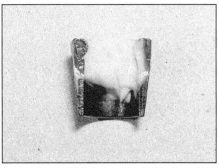

11.4 Use a little grease to hold the split collets in place

5 With all the valves installed, place the cylinder head flat on the bench and, using a hammer and interposed block of wood, tap the end of each valve stem to settle the components.
6 On SOHC engines, working as described in Part A of this Chapter, refit the hydraulic tappets, thrust pads and followers to the head then refit the cylinder head.
7 On DOHC petrol engines, working as described in Part B of this Chapter, refit the cylinder head to the engine and install the followers and camshafts.

12 Piston/connecting rod assembly - removal

Note: *New connecting rod big-end cap bolts will be required on refitting.*
1 On all except 1.8 and 2.0 litre DOHC engines, remove the cylinder head and sump then unbolt the pick-up/strainer from the base of the oil pump. Refer to Part A of this Chapter for information on SOHC engines and Part B for information on DOHC engines.
2 On 1.8 and 2.0 litre DOHC engines, referring to Part B of this Chapter, remove the cylinder head and sump, then unbolt the pick-up/strainer from the base of the oil pump. Where applicable, undo the retaining screws and remove the baffle plate from the base of the cylinder block. Where applicable on later engines, to further improve access, evenly and progressively slacken the retaining bolts and remove the main bearing ladder casting from the base of the cylinder block.

3 On all engines, if there is a pronounced wear ridge at the top of any of the cylinder bores, it may be necessary to remove it with a scraper or ridge reamer, to avoid piston damage during removal. Such a ridge indicates excessive wear of the cylinder bore.
4 Prior to removal, using feeler blades on each piston/connecting rod assembly in turn, measure the connecting rod big-end cap side clearance (between the end faces of the big-end cap and crankshaft web)**(see illustration)**. If the clearance for any rod/cap assembly exceeds the specified maximum, the assembly must be renewed.
5 Using a hammer and centre-punch, paint or similar, mark each connecting rod and its bearing cap with its respective cylinder number on the flat machined surface provided; if the engine has been dismantled before, note carefully any identifying marks made previously **(see illustration)**. Note that No 1 cylinder is at the timing belt end of the engine.
6 Turn the crankshaft to bring pistons 1 and 4 to BDC (bottom dead centre).
7 Unscrew the bolts from No 1 piston big-end bearing cap. Take off the cap and recover the bottom half bearing shell. If the bearing shells are to be re-used, tape the cap and the shell together.
Caution: On some engines, the connecting rod/bearing cap mating surfaces are not machined flat; the big-end bearing caps are 'cracked' off from the rod during production and left unmachined to ensure that the cap and rod mate perfectly. Where this type of connecting rod is fitted, great care must be

taken to ensure that the mating surfaces of the cap and rod are not marked or damaged in anyway. Any damage to the mating surfaces will adversely affect the strength of the connecting rod and could lead to premature failure.
8 Using a hammer handle, push the piston up through the bore, and remove it from the top of the cylinder block. Recover the bearing shell, and tape it to the connecting rod for safe-keeping.
9 Loosely refit the big-end cap to the connecting rod, and secure with the bolts - this will help to keep the components in their correct order.
10 Remove No 4 piston/connecting rod assembly in the same way.
11 Turn the crankshaft through 180° to bring piston Nos 2 and 3 to BDC (bottom dead centre), and remove them in the same way.

13 Crankshaft - removal

Note: *New main bearing cap bolts will be required on refitting.*

All except 1.8 and 2.0 litre DOHC engines

1 Remove the oil pump and flywheel/driveplate. Refer to Part A of this Chapter for information on SOHC engines and Part B for information on DOHC engines.
2 Remove the piston and connecting rod assemblies as described in Section 12. If no work is to be done on the pistons and connecting rods, unbolt the caps and push the pistons far enough up the bores that the connecting rods are positioned clear of the crankshaft journals.
3 Check the crankshaft endfloat as described in Section 16, then proceed as follows.
4 The main bearing caps should be numbered 1 to 5 from the timing belt end of the engine and all identification numbers should be the right way up when read from the inlet manifold side of the cylinder block **(see illustration)**. Note: *On some engines the flywheel/driveplate end (number 5) bearing cap may not be numbered but is easily*

12.4 Checking a connecting rod big-end side clearance

12.5 Big-end bearing cap centre punch identification marks (circled)

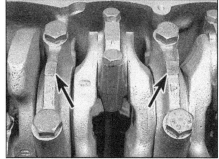

13.4 Main bearing cap identification markings (arrowed) – 1.6 litre SOHC engine

identified anyway. If the bearing caps are not marked, using a hammer and punch or a suitable marker pen, number the caps from 1 to 5 from the timing belt end of the engine and mark each cap to indicate its correct fitted direction to avoid confusion on refitting.

5 Working in a diagonal sequence, evenly and progressively slacken the ten main bearing cap retaining bolts by half a turn at a time until all bolts are loose. Remove all bolts.

6 Carefully remove each cap from the cylinder block, ensuring that the lower main bearing shell remains in position in the cap.

7 Carefully lift out the crankshaft, taking care not to displace the upper main bearing shells **(see illustration)**. Remove the crankshaft rear oil seal and discard it.

8 Recover the upper bearing shells from the cylinder block, and tape them to their respective caps for safe-keeping.

1.8 and 2.0 litre DOHC engines

9 Remove the flywheel/driveplate and the oil pump as described in Part B of the Chapter.

10 Where applicable, undo the retaining screws and remove the baffle plate from the base of the cylinder block.

11 Where applicable, on later engines, evenly and progressively slacken the retaining bolts and remove the main bearing ladder casting from the base of the block.

12 Remove the crankshaft as described in paragraphs 2 to 8.

14 Cylinder block -
cleaning and inspection

Cleaning

1 Remove all external components and electrical switches/sensors from the block. For complete cleaning, the core plugs should ideally be removed. Drill a small hole in the plugs, then insert a self-tapping screw into the hole. Pull out the plugs by pulling on the screw with a pair of grips, or by using a slide hammer.

2 Scrape all traces of gasket from the cylinder block, and from the main bearing casting (where fitted), taking care not to damage the gasket/sealing surfaces.

3 Remove all oil gallery plugs (where fitted). The plugs are usually very tight - they may have to be drilled out, and the holes re-tapped. Use new plugs when the engine is reassembled.

4 If any of the castings are extremely dirty, all should be steam-cleaned.

5 If the block has been steam-cleaned, clean all oil holes and oil galleries one more time. Flush all internal passages with warm water until the water runs clear. Dry thoroughly, and apply a light film of oil to all mating surfaces, to prevent rusting. Also oil the cylinder bores. If you have access to compressed air, use it to speed up the drying process, and to blow out all the oil holes and galleries.

13.7 Lifting the crankshaft from the crankcase

⚠ *Warning: Wear eye protection when using compressed air.*

6 If the castings are not very dirty, you can do an adequate cleaning job with hot (as hot as you can stand), soapy water and a stiff brush. Take plenty of time, and do a thorough job. Regardless of the cleaning method used, be sure to clean all oil holes and galleries very thoroughly, and to dry all components well. Protect the cylinder bores as described above, to prevent rusting.

7 All threaded holes must be clean, to ensure accurate torque readings during reassembly. To clean the threads, run the correct-size tap into each of the holes to remove rust, corrosion, thread sealant or sludge, and to restore damaged threads. If possible, use compressed air to clear the holes of debris produced by this operation. A good alternative is to inject aerosol-applied water-dispersant lubricant into each hole, using the long spout usually supplied. Ensure that the holes are thoroughly dried out on completion.

⚠ *Warning: Wear eye protection when cleaning out these holes in this way.*

8 Apply suitable sealant to the new oil gallery plugs, and insert them into the holes in the block. Tighten them securely.

9 If the engine is not going to be reassembled right away, cover it with a large plastic bag to keep it clean; protect all mating surfaces and the cylinder bores as described previously, to prevent rusting.

Inspection

10 Visually check the castings for cracks and corrosion. Look for stripped threads in the threaded holes. If there has been any history of internal water leakage, it may be worthwhile having an engine overhaul specialist check the cylinder block/crankcase with special equipment. If defects are found, have them repaired if possible, or renew the assembly.

11 Check the bore of each cylinder for scuffing and scoring.

12 Measure the diameter of each cylinder bore at the top (just below the wear ridge), centre and bottom of the bore, both parallel to the crankshaft axis and at right angles to it, so that a total of six measurements are taken.

13 Compare the results with the Specifications at the beginning of this Chapter; if any

measurement exceeds the service limit specified, the cylinder block must be rebored if possible, or renewed and new piston assemblies fitted. Note that there are various size groups of standard bore diameter to allow for manufacturing tolerances; the size group markings are stamped on the cylinder block.

14 If the cylinder bores are badly scuffed or scored, or if they are excessively worn, out-of-round or tapered, or if the piston-to-bore clearance is excessive (see Section 14), the cylinder block must be rebored (if possible) or renewed and new pistons fitted. Oversize (0.5 mm) pistons are available for all engines.

15 If the bores are in reasonably good condition and not worn to the specified limits, then the piston rings should be renewed. If this is the case, the bores should be honed to allow the new rings to bed in correctly and provide the best possible seal. The conventional type of hone has spring-loaded stones, and is used with a power drill. You will also need some paraffin (or honing oil) and rags. The hone should be moved up and down the bore to produce a crosshatch pattern, and plenty of honing oil should be used. Ideally, the crosshatch lines should intersect at approximately a 60° angle. Do not take off more material than is necessary to produce the required finish. If new pistons are being fitted, the piston manufacturers may specify a finish with a different angle, so their instructions should be followed. Do not withdraw the hone from the bore while it is still being turned – stop it first. After honing a bore, wipe out all traces of the honing oil. An engine overhaul specialist will be able to carry out this work at a moderate cost if required.

15 Piston/connecting rod assembly -
inspection

1 Before the inspection process can begin, the piston/connecting rod assemblies must be cleaned, and the original piston rings removed from the pistons.

2 Carefully expand the old rings over the top of the pistons. The use of two or three old feeler blades will be helpful in preventing the rings dropping into empty grooves **(see illustration)**.

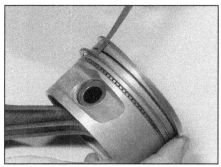

15.2 Using a feeler gauge to aid removal of a piston ring

Be careful not to scratch the piston with the ends of the ring. The rings are brittle, and will snap if they are spread too far. They're also very sharp - protect your hands and fingers. Note that the third (oil control) ring consists of a spacer and two side rails. Always remove the rings from the top of the piston. Keep each set of rings with its piston if the old rings are to be re-used.

3 Scrape away all traces of carbon from the top of the piston. A hand-held wire brush (or a piece of fine emery cloth) can be used, once the majority of the deposits have been scraped away. The piston identification markings should now be visible.

4 Remove the carbon from the ring grooves in the piston, using an old ring. Break the ring in half to do this (be careful not to cut your fingers - piston rings are sharp). Be careful to remove only the carbon deposits - do not remove any metal, and do not nick or scratch the sides of the ring grooves.

5 Once the deposits have been removed, clean the piston/connecting rod assembly with paraffin or a suitable solvent, and dry thoroughly. Make sure that the oil return holes in the ring grooves are clear.

6 If the cylinder bores are not damaged or worn excessively, and if the cylinder block does not need to be rebored (see Section 14), check the pistons as follows.

7 Carefully inspect each piston for cracks around the skirt, around the gudgeon pin holes, and at the piston ring 'lands' (between the ring grooves).

8 Look for scoring and scuffing on the piston skirt, holes in the piston crown, and burned areas at the edge of the crown. If the skirt is scored or scuffed, the engine may have been suffering from overheating, and/or abnormal combustion which caused excessively high operating temperatures. The cooling and lubrication systems should be checked thoroughly. Scorch marks on the sides of the pistons show that blow-by has occurred. A hole in the piston crown, or burned areas at the edge of the piston crown, indicates that abnormal combustion (pre-ignition, knocking, or detonation) has been occurring. If any of the above problems exist, the causes must be investigated and corrected, or the damage will occur again. The causes may include incorrect ignition timing, incorrect air/fuel mixture, or leaks in the inlet air tracts.

9 Corrosion of the piston, in the form of pitting, indicates that coolant has been leaking into the combustion chamber and/or the crankcase. Again, the cause must be corrected, or the problem may persist in the rebuilt engine.

10 Measure the piston diameter at right angles to the gudgeon pin axis; compare the results with the Specifications at the beginning of this Chapter. Note that there are various size groups of standard piston diameter to allow for manufacturing tolerances; the size group markings are stamped on the piston crown.

15.15a Prise out the circlips and push out the gudgeon pins

11 To measure the piston-to-bore clearance, either measure the bore (see Section 14) and piston skirt (as described in the previous paragraph) and subtract the skirt diameter from the bore measurement, or insert each piston into its original bore, then select a feeler gauge blade and slip it into the bore along with the piston. The piston must be aligned exactly in its normal attitude, and the feeler gauge blade must be between the piston and bore, on one of the thrust faces, just up from the bottom of the bore. Divide the measured clearance by two, to provide the clearance when the piston is central in the bore. If the clearance is excessive, a new piston will be required. If the piston binds at the lower end of the bore and is loose towards the top, the bore is tapered. If tight spots are encountered as the piston/feeler gauge blade is rotated in the bore, the bore is out-of-round.

12 Repeat this procedure for the remaining pistons and bores. Any piston which is worn beyond the specified limits must be renewed.

13 Examine each connecting rod carefully for signs of damage, such as cracks around the big-end and small-end bearings. Check that the rod is not bent or distorted. Damage is highly unlikely, unless the engine has been seized or badly overheated. Detailed checking of the connecting rod assembly can only be carried out by a Vauxhall/Opel dealer or engine repair specialist with the necessary equipment.

14 On all except C 20 XE DOHC engines, the gudgeon pins are an interference fit in the connecting rod small-end bearing. Piston and/or connecting rod renewal should be entrusted to a Vauxhall/Opel dealer or engine repair specialist, who will have the necessary tooling to remove and install the gudgeon

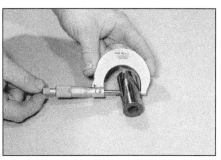

15.15b Measuring the diameter of a gudgeon pin using a micrometer

pins. If new pistons are to be fitted, ensure that the correct size group pistons are fitted to each bore. **Note:** *Vauxhall/Opel state that the piston/connecting rod assemblies should not be disassembled. If any components requires renewal, then the complete assembly must be renewed. Do not fit a new piston to an old connecting rod or vice versa.*

15 On C 20 XE DOHC engines, the gudgeon pins are of the floating type, secured in position by two circlips. On these engines, the pistons and connecting rods can be separated as follows.

a) Using a small flat-bladed screwdriver, prise out the circlips, and push out the gudgeon pin (see illustration). Hand pressure should be sufficient to remove the pin. Identify the piston and rod to ensure correct reassembly. Discard the circlips - new ones must be used on refitting.

b) Examine the gudgeon pin and connecting rod small-end bearing for signs of wear or damage (see illustration). Wear will require the renewal of both the pin and connecting rod.

c) Examine all components, and obtain any new parts from your Vauxhall/Opel dealer. If new pistons are purchased, they will be supplied complete with gudgeon pins and circlips. Circlips can also be purchased individually.

d) Apply a smear of clean engine oil to the gudgeon pin. Slide it into the piston and through the connecting rod small-end. Check that the piston pivots freely on the rod, then secure the gudgeon pin in position with two new circlips, ensuring that each circlip is correctly located in its groove in the piston (see illustrations).

15.15c Slide the gudgeon pin into the piston and connecting rod . . .

15.15d . . . and secure it in position with new circlips

16.2 Check the crankshaft endfloat using a dial gauge . . .

16.3 . . . or a feeler gauge

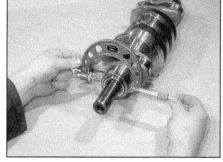

16.10 Using a micrometer to measure a crankshaft main bearing journal diameter

16 Crankshaft - inspection

Checking crankshaft endfloat

1 If the crankshaft endfloat is to be checked, this must be done when the crankshaft is still installed in the cylinder block, but is free to move (see Section 13).

2 Check the endfloat using a dial gauge in contact with the end of the crankshaft. Push the crankshaft fully one way, and then zero the gauge. Push the crankshaft fully the other way, and check the endfloat **(see illustration)**. The result can be compared with the specified amount, and will give an indication as to whether new main thrust bearing shells (No 3 main bearing shells) are required.

3 If a dial gauge is not available, feeler gauges can be used. First push the crankshaft fully towards the flywheel/driveplate end of the engine, then use feeler gauges to measure the gap between the web of the crankpin and the side of thrust bearing shell **(see illustration)**.

Inspection

4 Clean the crankshaft using paraffin or a suitable solvent, and dry it, preferably with compressed air if available. Be sure to clean the oil holes with a pipe cleaner or similar probe, to ensure that they are not obstructed.

> ⚠ **Warning: Wear eye protection when using compressed air.**

17.1 Typical main bearing shell identification markings

5 Check the main and big-end bearing journals for uneven wear, scoring, pitting and cracking.

6 Big-end bearing wear is accompanied by distinct metallic knocking when the engine is running (particularly noticeable when the engine is pulling from low speed) and some loss of oil pressure.

7 Main bearing wear is accompanied by severe engine vibration and rumble - getting progressively worse as engine speed increases - and again by loss of oil pressure.

8 Check the bearing journal for roughness by running a finger lightly over the bearing surface. Any roughness (which will be accompanied by obvious bearing wear) indicates that the crankshaft requires regrinding (where possible) or renewal.

9 Check for burrs around the crankshaft oil holes (the holes are usually chamfered, so burrs should not be a problem unless regrinding has been carried out carelessly). Remove any burrs with a fine file or scraper, and thoroughly clean the oil holes as described previously.

10 Using a micrometer, measure the diameter of the main and big-end bearing journals, and compare the results with the Specifications **(see illustration)**. By measuring the diameter at a number of points around each journal's circumference, you will be able to determine whether or not the journal is out-of-round. Take the measurement at each end of the journal, near the webs, to determine if the journal is tapered. Compare the results obtained with those given in the Specifications.

11 Check the oil seal contact surfaces at each end of the crankshaft for wear and damage. If the seal has worn a deep groove in the surface of the crankshaft, consult an engine overhaul specialist; repair may be possible, but otherwise a new crankshaft will be required.

12 Set the crankshaft up in V-blocks, and position a dial gauge on the top of the crankshaft number 1 main bearing journal. Zero the dial gauge, then slowly rotate the crankshaft through two complete revolutions, noting the journal run-out. Repeat the procedure on the remaining four main bearing journals, so that a run-out measurement is available for all main bearing journals. If the difference between the run-out of any two journals exceeds the

service limit given in the Specifications, the crankshaft must be renewed.

13 Undersize (0.25 mm and 0.50 mm) big-end and main bearing shells are produced by Vauxhall/Opel for all engines. If the crankshaft journals have not already been reground, it may be possible to have the crankshaft reconditioned, and to fit undersize shells.

17 Main and big-end bearings - inspection

1 Even though the main and big-end bearings should be renewed during the engine overhaul, the old bearings should be retained for close examination, as they may reveal valuable information about the condition of the engine **(see illustration)**.

2 Bearing failure can occur due to lack of lubrication, the presence of dirt or other foreign particles, overloading the engine, or corrosion **(see illustration)**. Regardless of the cause of bearing failure, the cause must be corrected (where applicable) before the engine is reassembled, to prevent it from happening again.

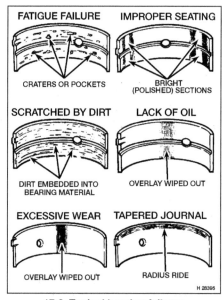

17.2 Typical bearing failures

3 When examining the bearing shells, remove them from the cylinder block, the main bearing caps, the connecting rods and the connecting rod big-end bearing caps. Lay them out on a clean surface in the same general position as their location in the engine. This will enable you to match any bearing problems with the corresponding crankshaft journal.

4 Dirt and other foreign matter gets into the engine in a variety of ways. It may be left in the engine during assembly, or it may pass through filters or the crankcase ventilation system. It may get into the oil, and from there into the bearings. Metal chips from machining operations and normal engine wear are often present. Abrasives are sometimes left in engine components after reconditioning, especially when parts are not thoroughly cleaned using the proper cleaning methods. Whatever the source, these foreign objects often end up embedded in the soft bearing material, and are easily recognised. Large particles will not embed in the bearing, and will score or gouge the bearing and journal. The best prevention for this cause of bearing failure is to clean all parts thoroughly, and keep everything spotlessly-clean during engine assembly. Frequent engine oil and filter changes are also recommended.

5 Lack of lubrication (or lubrication breakdown) has a number of interrelated causes. Excessive heat (which thins the oil), overloading (which squeezes the oil from the bearing face) and oil leakage (from excessive bearing clearances, worn oil pump or high engine speeds) all contribute to lubrication breakdown. Blocked oil passages, which usually are the result of misaligned oil holes in a bearing shell, will also oil-starve a bearing, and destroy it. When lack of lubrication is the cause of bearing failure, the bearing material is wiped or extruded from the steel backing of the bearing. Temperatures may increase to the point where the steel backing turns blue from overheating.

6 Driving habits can have a definite effect on bearing life. Full-throttle, low-speed operation (labouring the engine) puts very high loads on bearings, tending to squeeze out the oil film. These loads cause the bearings to flex, which produces fine cracks in the bearing face (fatigue failure). Eventually, the bearing material will loosen in pieces, and tear away from the steel backing.

7 Short-distance driving leads to corrosion of bearings, because insufficient engine heat is produced to drive off the condensed water and corrosive gases. These products collect in the engine oil, forming acid and sludge. As the oil is carried to the engine bearings, the acid attacks and corrodes the bearing material.

8 Incorrect bearing installation during engine assembly will lead to bearing failure as well. Tight-fitting bearings leave insufficient bearing running clearance, and will result in oil starvation. Dirt or foreign particles trapped behind a bearing shell result in high spots on the bearing, which lead to failure.

9 As mentioned at the beginning of this Section, the bearing shells should be renewed as a matter of course during engine overhaul; to do otherwise is false economy.

18 Engine overhaul - reassembly sequence

1 Before reassembly begins, ensure that all new parts have been obtained, and that all necessary tools are available. Read through the entire procedure to familiarise yourself with the work involved, and to ensure that all items necessary for reassembly of the engine are at hand. In addition to all normal tools and materials, thread-locking compound will be needed. A good quality tube of liquid sealant will also be required for the joint faces that are fitted without gaskets.

2 In order to save time and avoid problems, engine reassembly can be carried out in the following order:
  a) *Crankshaft.*
  b) *Piston/connecting rod assemblies.*
  c) *Oil pump.*
  d) *Sump.*
  e) *Flywheel/driveplate.*
  f) *Cylinder head.*
  g) *Timing belt tensioner and sprockets, and belts.*
  h) *Inlet and exhaust manifolds (Chapter 4A or 4B).*
  i) *Engine external components.*

3 At this stage, all engine components should be absolutely clean and dry, with all faults repaired. The components should be laid out (or in individual containers) on a completely clean work surface.

19 Piston rings - refitting

1 Before fitting new piston rings, the ring end gaps must be checked as follows.

2 Lay out the piston/connecting rod assemblies and the new piston ring sets, so that the ring sets will be matched with the same piston and cylinder during the end gap measurement and subsequent engine reassembly.

3 Insert the top ring into the first cylinder, and push it down the bore using the top of the piston. This will ensure that the ring remains square with the cylinder walls. Push the ring down into the bore until it is positioned 15 to 20 mm down from the top edge of the bore, then withdraw the piston.

4 Measure the end gap using feeler gauges, and compare the measurements with the figures given in the Specifications **(see illustration)**.

5 If the gap is too small (unlikely if genuine Vauxhall/Opel parts are used), it must be enlarged, or the ring ends may contact each

19.4 Measuring a piston ring end gap using a feeler gauge

other during engine operation, causing serious damage. Ideally, new piston rings providing the correct end gap should be fitted. As a last resort, the end gap can be increased by filing the ring ends very carefully with a fine file. Mount the file in a vice with soft jaws, slip the ring over the file with the ends contacting the file face, and slowly move the ring to remove material from the ends. Take care, as piston rings are sharp, and are easily broken.

6 With new piston rings, it is unlikely that the end gap will be too large. If the gaps are too large, check that you have the correct rings for your engine and for the particular cylinder bore size.

7 Repeat the checking procedure for each ring in the first cylinder, and then for the rings in the remaining cylinders. Remember to keep rings, pistons and cylinders matched up.

8 Once the ring end gaps have been checked and if necessary corrected, the rings can be fitted to the pistons.

9 Fit the piston rings using the same technique as for removal. Fit the bottom (oil control) spacer first, then install both the side rails, noting that both the spacer and side rails can be installed either way up.

10 The second and top compression rings are different and can be identified by their cross-sections; the top ring is square whilst the second ring is tapered. Fit the second and top compression rings ensuring that each ring is fitted the correct way up with its identification ('TOP') mark uppermost **(see illustration)**. **Note:** *Always follow any instructions supplied with the new piston ring sets - different manufacturers may specify different procedures.*

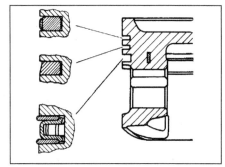

19.10 Sectional view showing correct orientation of piston rings

Do not mix up the top and second compression rings. On some engines the top ring will not have an identification marking and can be fitted either way up.

11 With the piston rings correctly installed, check that each ring is free to rotate easily in its groove. Using feeler blades, check that the ring-to-groove clearance of each ring is within the specified range, then position the ring end gaps as shown **(see illustration)**.

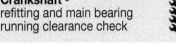

20 Crankshaft -
refitting and main bearing running clearance check

Note: *It is recommended that new main bearing shells are fitted regardless of the condition of the original ones.*

Selection of bearing shells

1 On all engines, although the original bearing shells fitted at the factory may be of various grades, all replacement bearing shells sold are of the same grade. Vauxhall/Opel supply both standard size bearing shells and undersize shells for use when the crankshaft has been reground. The size of shell required can be determined by measuring the crankshaft journals (see Section 16).

Main bearing running clearance check

2 Clean the backs of the bearing shells and the bearing locations in both the cylinder block and the main bearing caps.

20.3a Fitting a main bearing shell to the cylinder block

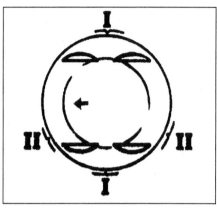

19.11 Piston ring end gap positions

I   Top and second compression rings
II Oil control ring side rails

3 Press the bearing shells into their locations, ensuring that the tab on each shell engages in the notch in the cylinder block or main bearing cap. If the original bearing shells are being used for the check, ensure that they are refitted in their original locations. The clearance can be checked in either of two ways. Note that the central main bearing shells have thrust flanges which control crankshaft endfloat **(see illustrations)**.

4 One method (which will be difficult to achieve without a range of internal micrometers or internal/external expanding calipers) is to refit the main bearing caps to the cylinder block, with bearing shells in place. With the cap retaining bolts correctly tightened (use the original bolts for the check, not the new ones), measure the internal diameter of each assembled pair of bearing shells. If the diameter of each corresponding crankshaft journal is measured and then subtracted from the bearing internal diameter, the result will be the main bearing running clearance.

5 The second (and more accurate) method is to use a product known as Plastigauge. This consists of a fine thread of perfectly round plastic which is compressed between the bearing shell and the journal. When the shell is removed, the plastic is deformed and can be measured with a special card gauge supplied with the kit. The running clearance is determined from this gauge. Plastigauge is

sometimes difficult to obtain but enquiries at one of the larger specialist motor factors should produce the name of a stockist in your area. The procedure for using Plastigauge is as follows.

6 With the main bearing upper shells in place, carefully lay the crankshaft in position. Do not use any lubricant; the crankshaft journals and bearing shells must be perfectly clean and dry.

7 Cut several lengths of the appropriate size Plastigage (they should be slightly shorter than the width of the main bearings) and place one length on each crankshaft journal axis **(see illustration)**.

8 With the main bearing lower shells in position, refit the main bearing caps, using the identification marks to ensure that each one is correctly positioned. Refit the original retaining bolts and tighten them to the specified stage 1 torque and then through the stage 2 and 3 angles (see Specifications). Take care not to disturb the Plastigauge and **do not** rotate the crankshaft at any time during this operation. Evenly and progressively slacken and remove the main bearing cap bolts, then lift off the caps again taking great care not to disturb the Plastigauge or rotate the crankshaft.

9 Compare the width of the crushed Plastigauge on each journal to the scale printed on the Plastigauge envelope, to obtain the main bearing running clearance **(see illustration)**. Compare the clearance measured with that given in the Specifications at the start of this Chapter.

10 If the clearance is significantly different from that expected, the bearing shells may be the wrong size (or excessively worn if the original shells are being re-used). Before deciding that the crankshaft is worn, make sure that no dirt or oil was trapped between the bearing shells and the caps or block when the clearance was measured. If the Plastigauge was wider at one end than at the other, the crankshaft journal may be tapered.

11 Before condemning the components concerned, seek the advice of your Vauxhall/Opel dealer or a suitable engine repair specialist. They will also be able to inform you as to the best course of action, or whether renewal will be necessary.

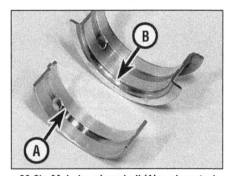

20.3b Main bearing shell (A) and central main bearing shell (B) with thrust flange

20.7 Plastigage in place on crankshaft main bearing journal

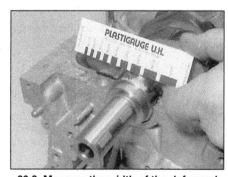

20.9 Measure the width of the deformed Plastigauge using the scale on the card

20.16 Lubricate the main bearing shells with clean engine oil before fitting the crankshaft

20.18 Refitting a main bearing cap

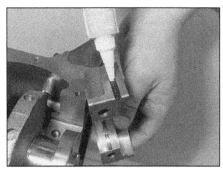

20.19 Fill the side grooves of the flywheel end (No 5) bearing cap with sealant prior to refitting

12 Where necessary, obtain the correct size of bearing shell and repeat the running clearance checking procedure as described above.
13 On completion, carefully scrape away all traces of the Plastigauge material from the crankshaft and bearing shells using a fingernail or other object which is unlikely to score the bearing surfaces.

Final crankshaft refitting

All except 1.8 and 2.0 litre DOHC engines

14 Carefully lift the crankshaft out of the cylinder block.
15 Place the bearing shells in their locations as described above in paragraphs 2 and 3. If new shells are being fitted, ensure that all traces of the protective grease are cleaned off using paraffin. Wipe dry the shells and caps with a lint-free cloth.
16 Lubricate the upper shells with clean engine oil, then lower the crankshaft into position **(see illustration)**.
17 Ensure that the crankshaft is correctly seated, then check the endfloat as described in Section 16.
18 Ensure that the bearing shells are correctly located in the caps, and refit the caps Nos 2 to 4 to the cylinder block **(see illustration)**. Ensure that the caps are fitted in their correct locations (No 1 cap fits at the timing belt end), and are fitted the correct way round so that all the numbers are the correct way up when read from the inlet manifold side of the cylinder block.

19 Fill the side grooves of the timing belt end (No 1 - where applicable, not all engines have grooves in No 1 main bearing cap) and flywheel end (No 5) bearing caps with sealing compound (Vauxhall/Opel recommend the use of sealant, Part No. 90485251, available from your Vauxhall/Opel dealer) **(see illustration)**. Fit the bearing caps to the engine, ensuring that they are fitted the correct way round. Ensure that No 1 bearing cap is exactly flush with the end face of the cylinder block.
20 Apply a smear of clean engine to oil to the threads and underneath the heads of the new main bearing cap bolts. Fit the bolts, tightening them all by hand **(see illustration)**.
21 Working in a diagonal sequence from the centre outwards, tighten the main bearing cap bolts to the specified Stage 1 torque setting **(see illustration)**.
22 Once all bolts are tightened to the specified Stage 1 torque, go round again and tighten all bolts through the specified Stage 2 angle, then go round once more and tighten all bolts through the specified Stage 3 angle. It is recommended that an angle-measuring gauge is used during the final stages of the tightening, to ensure accuracy **(see illustration)**. If a gauge is not available, use white paint to make alignment marks between the bolt head and cap prior to tightening; the marks can then be used to check that the bolt has been rotated through the correct angle.
23 Once all the bolts have been tightened, inject more sealant down the grooves in the No 1 (where applicable) and No 5 bearing

caps until sealant is seen to be escaping through the joints. Once you are sure the cap grooves are full of sealant, wipe off all excess sealant using a clean cloth.
24 Check that the crankshaft is free to rotate smoothly; if excessive pressure is required to turn the crankshaft, investigate the cause before proceeding further.
25 Refit/reconnect the piston connecting rod assemblies to the crankshaft as described in Section 21.
26 Referring to Part A (SOHC engine) or Part B (DOHC engine) of this Chapter, fit a new flywheel end crankshaft oil seal, then refit the flywheel/ driveplate, oil pump, cylinder head, timing belt sprocket(s) and fit a new timing belt.

1.8 and 2.0 litre DOHC engines

27 Refit the crankshaft as described in paragraphs 14 to 25.
28 On engines fitted with a main bearing ladder, ensure that the bearing cap and the main bearing ladder casting surfaces are clean and dry, then refit the casting to the engine. Refit the retaining bolts and tighten them to the specified torque, working in a diagonal sequence from the centre outwards.
29 Where applicable, refit the baffle plate to the base of the cylinder block assembly and tighten its retaining bolts to the specified torque.
30 Working as described Part B of this Chapter, fit a new flywheel end crankshaft oil seal, then refit the flywheel/driveplate, oil pump, cylinder head, timing belt sprocket(s) and a new timing belt.

20.20 Lubricate the threads of the new main bearing cap bolts, . . .

20.21 . . . then tighten the bolts to the specified Stage 1 torque setting, . . .

20.22 . . . and then through the specified Stages 2 and 3 angles

21.3 Fit the bearing shells, making sure that their tabs are correctly located in the connecting rod/cap groove (arrowed)

21.9a The arrow marking on the piston crown must point towards the timing belt end of the engine

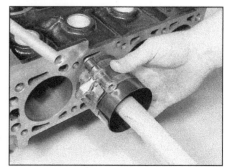

21.9b Tapping a piston into its bore

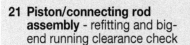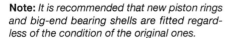

21 Piston/connecting rod assembly - refitting and big-end running clearance check

Note: *It is recommended that new piston rings and big-end bearing shells are fitted regardless of the condition of the original ones.*

Selection of bearing shells

1 On all engines, although the original bearing shells fitted at the factory maybe of various grades, all replacement bearing shells sold are of the same grade. Vauxhall/Opel supply both standard size bearing shells and undersize shells for use when the crankshaft has been reground. The size of shell required can be determined by measuring the crankshaft journals (see Section 16).

Big-end bearing running clearance check

2 Clean the backs of the bearing shells and the bearing locations in both the connecting rods and bearing caps.
3 Press the bearing shells into their locations, ensuring that the tab on each shell engages in the notch in the connecting rod and cap **(see illustration)**. If the original bearing shells are being used for the check ensure they are refitted in their original locations. The clearance can be checked in either of two ways.
4 One method is to refit the big-end bearing cap to the connecting rod, with bearing shells

in place. With the cap retaining bolts (use the original bolts for the check) correctly tightened, use an internal micrometer or vernier caliper to measure the internal diameter of each assembled pair of bearing shells. If the diameter of each corresponding crankshaft journal is measured and then subtracted from the bearing internal diameter, the result will be the big-end bearing running clearance.
5 The second method is to use Plastigauge as described in Section 20, paragraphs 5 to 13. Place a strand of Plastigauge on each (cleaned) crankpin journal and refit the (clean) piston/connecting rod assemblies, shells and big-end bearing caps. Tighten the bolts correctly taking care not to disturb the Plastigauge. Dismantle the assemblies without rotating the crankshaft and use the scale printed on the Plastigauge envelope to obtain the big-end bearing running clearance. On completion of the measurement, carefully scrape off all traces of Plastigauge from the journal and shells using a fingernail or other object which will not score the components.

Final piston/connecting rod assembly refitting

6 Ensure that the bearing shells are correctly refitted as described previously in paragraphs 2 and 3. If new shells are being fitted, ensure that all traces of the protective grease are cleaned off using paraffin. Wipe dry the shells and connecting rods with a lint-free cloth.
7 Lubricate the bores, the pistons and the piston rings, then lay out each piston/

connecting rod assembly in its respective position.
8 Starting with assembly No 1, make sure that the piston rings are still spaced as described in Section 19, then clamp them in position with a piston ring compressor.
9 Insert the piston/connecting rod assembly into the top of cylinder No 1, ensuring that the arrow marking on the piston crown is pointing towards the timing belt end of the engine. Using a block of wood or hammer handle against the piston crown, tap the assembly into the cylinder until the piston crown is flush with the top of the cylinder **(see illustrations)**.
10 Taking care not to mark the cylinder bore, liberally lubricate the crankpin and both bearing shells, then pull the piston/connecting rod assembly down the bore and onto the crankpin and refit the big-end bearing cap using the previously made markings to ensure that it is fitted the correct way round (the lug on the bearing cap base should be facing the flywheel/driveplate end of the engine). Screw in the new retaining bolts **(see illustration)**.
11 On 1.4 and 1.6 litre engines, tighten both bearing cap bolts to the specified Stage 1 torque setting and then tighten them through the specified Stage 2 angle. It is recommended that an angle-measuring gauge is used to ensure accuracy **(see illustrations)**. If a gauge is not available, use white paint to make alignment marks between the bolt head and cap prior to tightening; the marks can then be used to check that the bolt has been rotated through the correct angle.

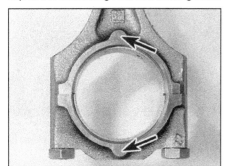

21.10 Refit the bearing cap to the connecting rod making sure that its lug (arrowed) is facing the flywheel/driveplate end of the engine

21.11a Tighten the big-end bearing cap bolts to the specified torque, . . .

21.11b . . . then through the specified angle

12 On 1.8 and 2.0 litre engines, tighten both bearing cap bolts to the specified Stage 1 torque setting then tighten them through the specified Stage 2 angle, and finally through the specified Stage 3 angle. It is recommended that an angle-measuring gauge is used during the final stages of the tightening, to ensure accuracy. If a gauge is not available, use white paint to make alignment marks between the bolt head and cap prior to tightening; the marks can then be used to check that the bolt has been rotated through the correct angle.

13 Refit the remaining three piston and connecting rod assemblies in the same way.

14 Rotate the crankshaft, and check that it turns freely, with no signs of binding or tight spots.

15 On 1.8 and 2.0 litre DOHC engines, where applicable, ensure that the bearing cap and main bearing ladder casting surfaces are clean and dry. Refit the casting to the engine and tighten its retaining bolts to the specified torque, working in a diagonal sequence from the centre outwards. Refit the baffle plate to the base of the cylinder block and tighten its retaining bolts to the specified torque.

16 On all engines, refit the oil pump strainer, sump and the cylinder head as described in Part A (SOHC engines) or Part B (DOHC engines) of this Chapter.

22 Engine -
initial start up after overhaul

1 With the engine refitted in the vehicle, double-check the engine oil and coolant levels (see "Weekly checks"). Make a final check to ensure that everything has been reconnected, and that there are no tools or rags left in the engine compartment.

2 Disable the ignition system by disconnecting the coil LT lead or wiring plug, or disconnecting the wiring connector from the ignition DIS module, as applicable, and on models with fuel injection, disable the fuel system by removing the fuel pump relay from the engine compartment relay box (see Chapter 4A). Turn the engine on the starter until the oil pressure warning light goes out then stop and reconnect the wiring connector and refit the relay.

3 Start the engine as normal, noting that this may take a little longer than usual, due to the fuel system components having been disturbed.

4 While the engine is idling, check for fuel, water and oil leaks. Don't be alarmed if there are some odd smells and smoke from parts getting hot and burning off oil deposits.

5 Assuming all is well, keep the engine idling until hot water is felt circulating through the radiator top hose, then switch off the engine.

6 Allow the engine to cool, then recheck the oil and coolant levels as described in "Weekly Checks", and top-up as necessary.

7 If new pistons, rings or crankshaft bearings have been fitted, the engine must be treated as new, and run-in for the first 500 miles (800 km). Do not operate the engine at full-throttle, or allow it to labour at low engine speeds in any gear. It is recommended that the engine oil and filter are changed at the end of this period.

Chapter 3
Cooling, heating and air conditioning systems

Contents

Degrees of difficulty

Easy, suitable for novice with little experience	Fairly easy, suitable for beginner with some experience	Fairly difficult, suitable for competent DIY mechanic	Difficult, suitable for experienced DIY mechanic	Very difficult, suitable for expert DIY or professional 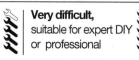

Specifications

Thermostat
Type . . . . Wax
Start-to-open temperature (all models) . . . . 92°C
Fully-open temperature (all models) . . . . 107°C

Electric cooling fan
Switches on at (all models) . . . . 100°C
Switches off at . . . . 95°C

Torque wrench settings	Nm	lbf ft
Coolant flange to cylinder head:		
1.4 and 1.6 litre DOHC engines	25	18
1.8 and 2.0 litre DOHC engines:		
M8 bolts	20	15
M10 bolts	30	22
Coolant outlet to thermostat housing	8	6
Coolant pump to cylinder block:		
1.4 and 1.6 litre engines (M6 bolts)	8	6
1.8 and 2.0 litre engines (M8 bolts)	25	18
Oil pipes to radiator (where applicable)	22	16
Thermostat housing to cylinder head		
1.4 and 1.6 litre SOHC engines	10	7
1.4 and 1.6 litre DOHC engines	20	15
1.8 and 2.0 litre engines	15	11

1 General information and precautions

General information

Engine cooling is achieved using a pump-assisted system, in which the coolant is pressurised. The system consists of a radiator, a coolant pump driven by the engine timing belt, an electric cooling fan, a thermostat, an expansion tank, and connecting hoses.

The system works in the following way. Cold coolant from one side of the radiator, which is mounted at the front of the engine compartment, passes to the coolant pump, which forces the coolant through the coolant passages in the cylinder block and cylinder head. The coolant absorbs heat from the engine, and then returns to the radiator via the heater system. As the coolant flows across the radiator, it is cooled, and the cycle is repeated.

Air flows through the radiator, to cool the radiator as a result of the vehicle's forward motion. However, if the coolant temperature exceeds a given figure, a temperature-sensitive switch in the radiator switches on the electric cooling fan, to increase the airflow through the radiator. The fan only operates when necessary, with a consequent reduction in noise and energy consumption.

To reduce the time taken for the engine to warm up when starting from cold, the thermostat, located in the cylinder head outlet, prevents coolant flowing to the radiator until the temperature has risen sufficiently. Instead, the outflow from the cylinder head bypasses the radiator and is redirected around the engine. When the temperature reaches a given figure, the thermostat opens, to allow coolant to flow to the radiator. The thermostat is operated by the expansion of a temperature-sensitive wax capsule.

An expansion tank is incorporated in the system, to allow for coolant expansion. The system is topped-up through a filler cap on the expansion tank.

On models fitted with automatic transmission, the radiator incorporates a heat exchanger to cool the automatic transmission fluid.

2.3 Disconnecting the radiator top hose

Precautions

⚠️ *Warning: Do not attempt to remove the expansion tank filler cap or disturb any part of the cooling system while the engine is hot, as there is a high risk of scalding. If the expansion tank filler cap must be removed before the engine and radiator have fully cooled (even though this is NOT recommended) the pressure in the cooling system must first be relieved. Cover the cap with a thick layer of cloth, to avoid scalding, and slowly unscrew the filler cap until a hissing sound can be heard. When the hissing has stopped, indicating that the pressure has reduced, slowly unscrew the filler cap until it can be removed; if more hissing sounds are heard, wait until they have stopped before unscrewing the cap completely. At all times keep well away from the filler cap opening.*

⚠️ *Warning: Do not allow antifreeze to come into contact with skin or painted surfaces of the vehicle. Rinse off immediately with plenty of water. Never leave antifreeze lying around in an open container or in a puddle on the driveway or garage floor. Children and pets are attracted by its sweet smell, but antifreeze can be fatal if ingested.*

⚠️ *Warning: If the engine is hot, the electric cooling fan may start rotating even if the engine is not running, so be careful to keep hands, hair and loose clothing well clear when working in the engine compartment.*

2 Cooling system hoses – disconnection and renewal

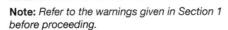

Note: *Refer to the warnings given in Section 1 before proceeding.*

Disconnection

1 If the checks described in Chapter 1 reveal a faulty hose, it must be renewed as follows.

2 First drain the cooling system (see Chapter 1). If the coolant is not due for renewal, it may be re-used if it is collected in a clean container.

3 To disconnect a hose, use a screwdriver to slacken the clips, then move them along the hose, clear of the relevant inlet/outlet. Carefully work the hose free **(see illustration)**. While the hoses can be removed with relative ease when new, or when hot, **do not** attempt to disconnect any part of the system while it is still hot.

4 Note that the radiator inlet and outlet stubs are fragile; do not use excessive force when attempting to remove the hoses. If a hose proves to be difficult to remove, try to release it by rotating the ends on the relevant inlet/outlet before attempting to free it. If all else fails, cut the hose with a sharp knife, then

slit it so that it can be peeled off in two pieces. Although this may prove expensive if the hose is otherwise undamaged, it is preferable to buying a new radiator.

Renewal

5 When fitting a hose, first slide the clips onto the hose, then work the hose into position. If clamp type clips were originally fitted, it is a good idea to replace them with screw type clips when refitting the hose. If the hose is stiff, use a little soapy water as a lubricant, or soften the hose by soaking it in hot water.

6 Work the hose into position, checking that it is correctly routed, then slide each clip along the hose until it passes over the flared end of the relevant inlet/outlet, before tightening the clip securely.

7 Refill the cooling system with reference to Chapter 1.

8 Check thoroughly for leaks as soon as possible after disturbing any part of the cooling system.

3 Radiator – removal, inspection and refitting

Note: *Refer to the warnings given in Section 1 before proceeding. Minor leaks from the radiator can be cured without removing the radiator, using a liquid-based sealant, available from all good car accessory shops. Where applicable, new sealing rings must be used when reconnecting the automatic transmission fluid cooler hoses.*

Removal

1 The radiator can be removed complete with the cooling fan and shroud if there is no need to disturb the fan. The fan and its shroud can be removed from the radiator with reference to Section 6.

2 Disconnect the battery negative lead.

3 Drain the cooling system as described in Chapter 1.

4 Where applicable, disconnect the wiring plugs from the cooling fan and the cooling fan switch mounted in the bottom right-hand side of the radiator.

5 On DOHC engines, where applicable, remove the secondary air injection air hose, and the combination valve and switchover valve bracket.

6 Disconnect the top hose from the radiator.

7 On models with automatic transmission, clamp the transmission fluid cooler hoses. Then disconnect them from the cooler in the side of the radiator. Be prepared for fluid spillage, and plug the open ends of the cooler and hoses immediately, to minimise fluid loss and prevent dirt ingress.

8 Unscrew the two top radiator mounting bracket securing bolts, and lift the brackets from the radiator rubber mountings **(see illustration)**.

3.8 Removing a top radiator mounting bracket

9 Lift the radiator to disengage the lower securing lugs, and withdraw it from the vehicle **(see illustration)**.

Inspection

10 If the radiator has been removed due to suspected blockage, reverse flush it as described in Chapter 1. Clean dirt and debris from the radiator fins, using an air line (in which case, wear eye protection) or a soft brush. Be careful, as the fins are easily damaged, and are sharp.
11 If necessary, a radiator specialist can perform a 'flow test' on the radiator, to establish whether an internal blockage exists.
12 A leaking radiator must be referred to a specialist for permanent repair. Do not attempt to weld or solder a leaking radiator, as damage to the plastic components may result.
13 In an emergency, minor leaks from the radiator can be cured by using a radiator sealant in accordance with its manufacturer's instructions with the radiator *in situ*.
14 If the radiator is to be sent for repair or renewed, remove all hoses and the cooling fan switch.
15 Inspect the condition of the radiator mounting rubbers, and renew them if necessary **(see illustration)**.

Refitting

16 Refitting is a reversal of removal, bearing in mind the following points.
17 Ensure that the radiator rubber mountings are in good condition and renew if necessary, and ensure that the lower securing lugs engage correctly as the radiator is refitted.

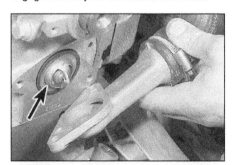

5.3 Lifting off the thermostat housing to expose the thermostat (arrowed) – 1.6 litre SOHC engine

3.9 Withdrawing the radiator

18 Where applicable, use new sealing rings when reconnecting the automatic transmission fluid cooler hoses, and on completion check and if necessary top-up the fluid level as described in *"Weekly checks"*.
19 Refill the cooling system as described in Chapter 1.

4 Expansion tank - removal and refitting

Note: *Refer to the warnings given in Section 1 before proceeding.*

Removal

1 Where applicable, disconnect the battery negative lead, and disconnect the coolant level sensor wiring plug from the expansion tank filler cap.
2 Unscrew the two securing nuts, and lift the expansion tank clear of the body for access to the two coolant hose connections.
3 Where applicable, unclip the octane coding plug assembly from the side of the expansion tank.
4 Disconnect the hose from the side of the tank, then clamp or plug the hose, and suspend it as high as possible above the height of the engine to prevent coolant loss.
5 Position a container beneath the tank, then disconnect the bottom hose and allow the contents of the tank to drain into the container. Clamp or plug the bottom hose, then suspend the hose as high as possible above the engine to prevent coolant loss.

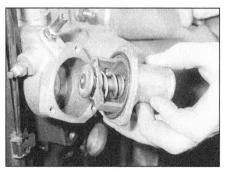

5.10a Withdraw the thermostat cover complete with the thermostat . . .

3.15 Radiator mounting rubber (arrowed) in lower body panel

6 Withdraw the expansion tank from the engine compartment.

Refitting

7 Refitting is a reversal of removal, but on completion, check and if necessary top-up the coolant level, as described in *"Weekly checks"*. The coolant drained from the expansion tank during removal can be re-used, provided that it has not been contaminated.

5 Thermostat - removal, testing and refitting

Removal

1.4, 1.6 litre SOHC engine models

1 Partially drain the cooling system with reference to Chapter 1.
2 Remove the rear timing belt cover as described in Chapter 2A.
3 Unscrew and remove the two thermostat housing securing bolts, and lift off the thermostat housing **(see illustration)**.
4 Disconnect the coolant hose from the thermostat housing, and remove the housing.
5 Withdraw the thermostat from the cylinder head, noting that coolant may be released from the radiator bottom outlet as the thermostat is withdrawn, even though the cooling system has been partially drained.
6 Remove the sealing ring from the edge of the thermostat.
7 The thermostat can be tested, as described later in this Section.

1.8 and 2.0 litre SOHC engine models and all DOHC engine models

8 Partially drain the cooling system with reference to Chapter 1.
9 Disconnect the radiator top hose from the thermostat cover.
10 Unscrew and remove the three thermostat cover securing bolts, and withdraw the cover complete with the thermostat. Recover the O-ring **(see illustrations)**.
11 The thermostat can be tested as described later in this Section.

5.10b ... and recover the O-ring – 2.0 litre SOHC engine

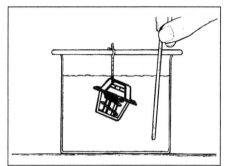

5.14a Testing the thermostat opening temperature

5.14b View of thermostat showing opening temperature markings

12 If it is necessary to renew the thermostat, the complete cover and thermostat must be renewed as an assembly, as the two components are not available separately.

Testing

13 A rough test of the thermostat may be made by suspending it with a piece of string in a container full of water. Heat the water to bring it to the boil - the thermostat must open by the time the water boils. If not, renew it.
14 If a thermometer is available, the precise opening temperature of the thermostat may be determined, and compared with the figures given in the Specifications. The opening temperature is also marked on the thermostat **(see illustrations)**.
15 A thermostat which fails to close as the water cools must also be renewed.

Refitting

16 Refitting is a reversal of removal, but use a new sealing ring, and bear in mind the following points.
17 Ensure that the lugs on the thermostat engage with the corresponding cut-outs in the cylinder head.
18 Where applicable, refit the rear timing belt cover as described in Chapter 2A.
19 Refill the cooling system with reference to Chapter 1.

6 Cooling fan -
testing, removal and refitting

Testing

1 The cooling fan is supplied with current via the ignition switch and fuse 11 (which may be mounted in the fusebox, or under the fusebox, depending on model, see Chapter 12). The circuit is completed by the cooling fan thermostatic switch, which is mounted in the lower right-hand side of the radiator **(see illustration)**.
2 If the fan does not appear to work, run the engine until normal operating temperature is reached, then allow it to idle. If the fan does not cut in within a few minutes, switch off the ignition and disconnect the wiring plug from the cooling fan switch. Bridge the two contacts in the wiring plug using a length of spare wire, and switch on the ignition. If the fan now operates, the switch is probably faulty and should be renewed.

3 If the fan still fails to operate, check that full battery voltage is available at the brown and white wire terminal of the switch; if not, then there is a fault in the feed wire to the switch (possibly due to a fault in the fan motor, or a blown fuse). If there is no problem with the feed, check that there is continuity between the switch brown wire terminal and a good earth point on the body; if not, then the earth connection is faulty and must be re-made.
4 If the switch and the wiring are in good condition, the fault must lie in the motor itself. The motor can be checked by disconnecting it from the wiring loom, and connecting a 12-volt supply directly to it. If the motor is faulty, it must be renewed, as no spares are available.

Removal

5 Disconnect the battery negative lead.
6 Disconnect the wiring from the cooling fan **(see illustration)**.
7 Unscrew the two fan shroud securing bolts, then tilt the assembly back slightly towards the engine, and withdraw it upwards away from the radiator **(see illustrations)**.
8 To separate the fan motor from the shroud, unscrew the three securing nuts.
9 No spare parts are available for the motor, and if the unit is faulty, it must be renewed.

Refitting

10 Refitting is a reversal of removal, but ensure that the left-hand lower end of the fan shroud locates correctly in the clip on the radiator **(see illustration)**.

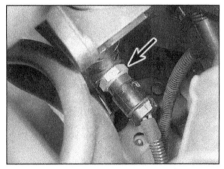

6.1 Cooling fan thermostatic switch (arrowed)

6.6 Disconnecting the cooling fan wiring plug

6.7a Cooling fan shroud securing bolt (arrowed) – 2.0 litre DOHC engine

6.7b Withdrawing the cooling fan shroud assembly – 1.6 litre SOHC engine

6.10 Ensure that the left-hand lower end of the fan shroud locates correctly in the clip on the radiator

11 On completion, start the engine and run it until it reaches normal operating temperature, then continue to run the engine and check that the cooling fan cuts in and functions correctly.

7 Cooling system electrical switches and sensors – testing, removal and refitting

Cooling fan thermostatic switch

Testing

1 Testing of the switch is described in Section 6, as part of the cooling fan test procedure.

Removal

2 The switch is located in the lower right-hand side of the radiator. The engine and radiator should be cold before removing the switch.

3 Either partially drain the cooling system (as described in Chapter 1) to just below the level of the switch, or have ready a plug which can be used to plug the switch aperture in the radiator while the switch is removed. If a plug is used, take great care not to damage the radiator, and do not use anything which will allow foreign matter to enter the radiator.

4 Disconnect the battery negative lead.

5 Disconnect the wiring plug from the switch.

6 Carefully unscrew the switch from the radiator, and recover the sealing ring.

Refitting

7 Refitting is a reversal of removal, but use a new sealing ring, and refill the cooling system as described in Chapter 1.

8 On completion, start the engine and run it until it reaches normal operating temperature, then continue to run the engine and check that the cooling fan cuts in and functions correctly.

Coolant temperature gauge sender

Note: *Sealant will be required to coat the sender threads when refitting.*

Testing

9 The coolant temperature gauge, mounted in the instrument panel, is fed with a stabilised voltage supply from the instrument panel feed (via the ignition switch and a fuse), and its earth is controlled by the sender.

10 The sender is screwed into either the inlet manifold, the thermostat housing or the coolant flange, depending on model (see illustrations). The sender contains a thermistor, which consists of an electronic component whose electrical resistance decreases at a pre-determined rate as its temperature rises. When the coolant is cold, the sender resistance is high, current flow through the gauge is reduced, and the gauge needle points towards the blue (cold) end of the scale. If the sender is faulty, it must be renewed.

11 If the gauge develops a fault, first check the other instruments. If they do not work at all, check the instrument panel electrical feed. If the readings are erratic, there may be a fault in the voltage stabiliser, which will need replacing (see Chapter 12). If the fault lies in the temperature gauge alone, check it as follows.

12 If the gauge needle remains at the 'cold' end of the scale, disconnect the sender wire and earth it to the cylinder head. If the needle then deflects when the ignition is switched on, the sender unit is faulty and should be renewed. If the needle still does not move, remove the instrument panel (Chapter 12) and check the continuity of the brown/white wire between the sender unit and the gauge and the feed to the gauge unit. If continuity is shown, and the fault still exists, then the gauge is faulty and should be replaced.

13 If the gauge needle remains at the 'hot' end of the scale, disconnect the sender wire. If the needle then returns to the 'cold' end of

the scale when the ignition is switched on, the sender unit is faulty and should be renewed. If the needle still does not move, check the remainder of the circuit as described previously.

Removal

14 Partially drain the cooling system, as described in Chapter 1, to minimise coolant spillage.

15 Disconnect the battery negative lead.

16 Disconnect the wiring from the switch, then unscrew the switch from its location.

Refitting

17 Refitting is a reversal of removal, bearing in mind the following points.

18 Coat the threads of the sender with sealant before fitting.

19 Top-up the cooling system as described in "Weekly checks".

20 On completion, start the engine and check the operation of the temperature gauge. Also check for coolant leaks.

Engine coolant temperature sensor

21 Refer to Chapter 4B.

Coolant level sensor

Testing

22 On models fitted with a coolant level sensor, the sensor is located in the coolant expansion tank, and is an integral part of the expansion tank cap.

23 To test the sensor, with the engine cold, slowly unscrew the expansion tank cap to relieve any pressure in the cooling system.

24 Fully unscrew the cap, and carefully withdraw it, complete with the sensor.

25 Hold the cap/sensor assembly vertically, clear of the coolant in the expansion tank, taking care not to strain the wiring, then have an assistant switch on the ignition (do not start the engine).

26 Have your assistant observe the check control panel on the dashboard, which should indicate 'Coolant level'.

27 Switch off the ignition, and refit the cap/sensor assembly, then switch on the ignition again, and check that the check control panel does not indicate a problem.

7.10a Coolant temperature gauge sender (arrowed) – 1.6 litre SOHC engine

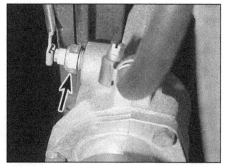

7.10b Coolant temperature gauge sender location (arrowed) – 2.0 litre SOHC engine

7.10c Coolant temperature gauge sender location (arrowed) – 2.0 litre DOHC engine

8.6 Withdrawing the coolant pump (O-ring arrowed) – 1.6 litre SOHC engine

28 If the sensor does not operate as described, check the wiring for obvious signs of damage.

29 If the wiring appears to be intact, further fault diagnosis must be entrusted to a Vauxhall/Opel dealer. Note that if the sensor is renewed, the cap and sensor must be renewed as an assembly.

Removal

30 The engine must be cold before attempting to remove the expansion tank cap.

31 Disconnect the battery negative lead.

32 Disconnect the wiring from the terminals on top of the expansion tank cap.

33 Slowly unscrew the expansion tank cap to relieve any pressure in the cooling system, then withdraw the cap/sensor assembly.

34 Note that the sensor is an integral part of the cap, and the two cannot be separated.

Refitting

35 Refitting is a reversal of removal.

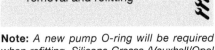

8 Coolant pump - removal and refitting

Note: *A new pump O-ring will be required when refitting. Silicone Grease (Vauxhall/Opel P/N 90167353, or equivalent) will be required to coat the pump mounting face in the cylinder block.*

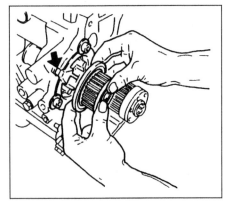

8.11a Lugs (arrowed) on coolant pump and cylinder block must be aligned – 2.0 litre DOHC engine

Removal

1 Drain the cooling system as described in Chapter 1.

2 Remove the timing belt as described in Chapter 2A (SOHC engines) or 2B (DOHC engines).

3 Where necessary, to gain access to the water pump, remove the timing belt rear cover, and where applicable the timing belt tensioner as described in Chapter 2A (SOHC engines) or 2B (DOHC engines).

4 On 1.8 and 2.0 litre SOHC engines, where applicable, unscrew and remove the bolt securing the smaller timing belt rear cover on the coolant pump to the cylinder block.

5 Unscrew and remove the three coolant pump securing bolts.

6 Withdraw the coolant pump from the cylinder block, and recover the O-ring **(see illustration)**. It may be necessary to tap the pump lightly with a soft-faced hammer to free it from the cylinder block.

7 No overhaul of the pump is possible, and if faulty, the unit must be renewed.

8 On 1.8 and 2.0 litre SOHC engines, if desired, the smaller rear timing belt cover can be removed from the pump by rotating the cover to release it from the flange on the pump.

Refitting

9 If the original pump is being refitted, ensure that the sealing surfaces are clean. Where applicable, on 1.8 and 2.0 litre SOHC engines, refit the smaller rear timing belt cover to the pump.

10 Smear the pump mounting face in the cylinder block with a Silicone Grease (Vauxhall/Opel P/N 90167353, or equivalent).

11 Fit the pump using a new O-ring. On 1.8 and 2.0 litre SOHC engines from 1993, and all 1.8 and 2.0 litre DOHC engines, make sure that the lug on the coolant pump flange is aligned with the corresponding lug on the cylinder block **(see illustrations)**. On 1.4 and 1.6 litre DOHC engines make sure that the edge of the coolant pump flange is aligned with the mark on the cylinder block.

12 Refit the pump securing bolts, and on all except 1.4 and 1.6 litre SOHC engines, and 1.8 and 2.0 litre SOHC engines up to 1993, tighten the bolts to the specified torque. On 1.4 and 1.6 litre SOHC engines, and 1.8 and 2.0 litre SOHC engines up to 1993, do not fully tighten the pump securing bolts until the timing belt has been refitted and tensioned as described in Chapter 2A.

13 On 1.8 and 2.0 litre SOHC engines, where applicable, refit and tighten the bolt securing the smaller rear timing belt cover on the coolant pump to the cylinder block.

14 Where applicable, refit the timing belt rear cover and the timing belt tensioner, as described in Chapter 2A (SOHC engines) or 2B (DOHC engines).

15 Refit and tension the timing belt as described in Chapter 2A (SOHC engines) or 2B (DOHC engines).

16 On completion, refill the cooling system as described in Chapter 1.

9 Heating and ventilation system - general

1 The heating/ventilation system consists of a pollen filter, a three (or four), speed blower motor (housed in the engine compartment), face-level vents in the centre and at each end of the facia, and air ducts to the front and rear footwells **(see illustrations)**. During 1994 models were fitted with additional side vents to improve ventilation of the side windows.

2 The control unit is located in the facia, and the controls operate flap valves to deflect and mix the air flowing through the various parts of the heating/ventilation system. The flap valves are contained in the air distribution housing, which acts as a central distribution unit, passing air to the various ducts and vents.

3 Cold air enters the system through the grille at the rear of the engine compartment, and passes through the pollen filter. If required, the airflow is boosted by the blower, and then flows through the various ducts, according to the settings of the controls. Stale air is expelled through ducts behind the rear bumper. If warm air is required, the cold air is passed over the heater matrix, which is heated by the engine coolant.

4 A recirculation switch enables the outside air supply to be closed off, while the air inside the vehicle is recirculated. This can be useful to prevent unpleasant odours entering from outside the vehicle, but should only be used briefly, as the recirculated air inside the vehicle will soon deteriorate.

5 Certain models may be fitted with heated front seats. The heat is produced by electrically-heated mats in the seat and backrest cushions. The temperature is regulated automatically by a thermostat, and cannot be adjusted.

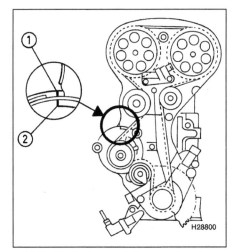

8.11b Coolant pump alignment marks – 1.4 and 1.6 litre DOHC engines

1 Mark on cylinder block
2 Edge of coolant pump flange

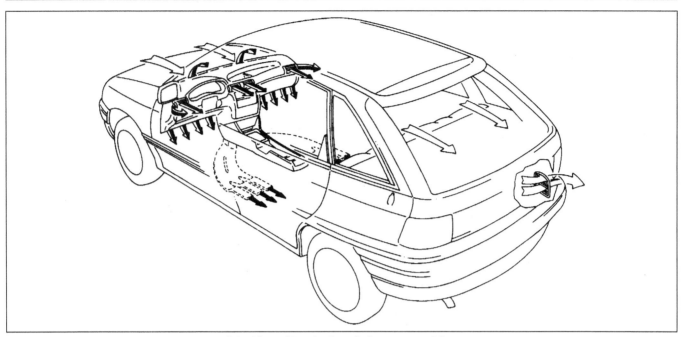

9.1a View of heating/ventilation system airflow

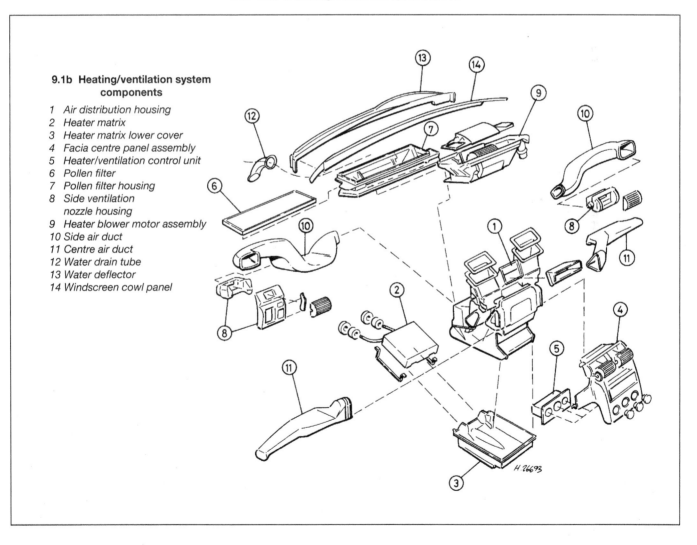

9.1b Heating/ventilation system components

1   Air distribution housing
2   Heater matrix
3   Heater matrix lower cover
4   Facia centre panel assembly
5   Heater/ventilation control unit
6   Pollen filter
7   Pollen filter housing
8   Side ventilation
    nozzle housing
9   Heater blower motor assembly
10 Side air duct
11 Centre air duct
12 Water drain tube
13 Water deflector
14 Windscreen cowl panel

H.26693

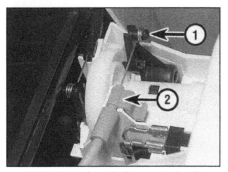

10.3 Heater/ventilation control unit connections

1 Cable end connection
2 Securing clip

10 Heater/ventilation components –
removal and refitting

Heater/ventilation control unit

Removal

1 Remove the facia centre panel assembly, as described in Chapter 11.
2 Carefully pull the heater/ventilation control unit forwards from the facia, taking care not to strain the control cables and wiring.
3 Release the securing clips, and disconnect the control cables from the air distribution and temperature control switches (two cables on the air distribution switch, one cable on the temperature switch), noting their locations **(see illustration)**.
4 Disconnect the wiring plug from the rear of the unit.
5 Disconnect the vacuum pipes from the rear of the air recirculation switch, noting their locations.
6 The heater/ventilation control unit can now be withdrawn from the vehicle.
7 The control unit illumination bulbs can be renewed by disconnecting the wires, and pulling the bulbholder from the rear of the control unit **(see illustration)**. The bulbs are a push-fit in the holders.

Refitting

8 Refitting is a reversal of removal, bearing in mind the following points.

9 Ensure that the control cables are securely reconnected in their correct locations, and that the cable runs are free from kinks and obstructions. Check the operation of the controls before finally refitting the facia centre panel assembly.
10 Refit the facia centre panel assembly as described in Chapter 11.

Heater blower/heated rear screen switch

Removal

11 Carefully prise off the switch knob using a small screwdriver.
12 Release the switch retaining clips and remove the switch.
13 The illumination bulb can now be replaced, if necessary.

Refitting

14 Refitting is a reversal of removal.

Heater/ventilation control cables - renewal

Lower air distribution control cable

15 Pull the heater/ventilation control unit forwards from the facia, as described previously in this Section.
16 Release the securing clips, and disconnect the cable from the rear of the control unit.
17 Follow the run of the cable behind the facia, taking note of its routing, and disconnect the cable from the lever on the air distribution housing. The method of fastening is the same as that used at the control unit.
18 Fit the new cable using a reversal of the removal procedure, noting the following points.
19 Ensure that the cable is correctly routed, and free from kinks and obstructions, and make sure that the cable securing clips are fastened correctly.
20 Refit the control unit as described previously in this Section.

Upper air distribution control cable

21 Remove the instrument panel, as described in Chapter 12.
22 Proceed as described in paragraphs 15 and 16 of this Section.

23 Follow the run of the cable behind the facia, taking note of its routing, and working through the instrument panel aperture, disconnect the end of the cable from the lever on the air distribution housing. Note that the method of fastening is the same as that used at the control unit.
24 Proceed as described in paragraphs 18 to 20 of this Section.
25 Refit the instrument panel as described in Chapter 12.

Air temperature control cable

26 Release the securing clips, and remove the lower cover panel from under the passenger's side facia.
27 Where applicable, remove the securing screws, and withdraw the oddments tray from under the glovebox.
28 Proceed as described in paragraphs 15 and 16 of this Section.
29 Follow the run of the cable behind the facia, taking note of its routing, and working up behind the passenger's footwell, disconnect the end of the cable from the lever on the air distribution housing. Note that the method of fastening is the same as that used at the control unit.
30 Proceed as described in paragraphs 18 to 20 of this Section.
31 Refit the glovebox and the facia lower cover panel using a reversal of the removal procedure.

Heater blower motor

Removal

32 Disconnect the battery negative lead.
33 Remove the pollen filter, as described in Chapter 1.
34 Remove the windscreen wiper arms, with reference to Chapter 12 if necessary.
35 Remove the windscreen cowl panel, as described in Chapter 11.
36 Disconnect the blower motor wiring plug, then prise the wiring grommet from the pollen filter housing, and pull the wiring through the aperture in the housing **(see illustration)**.
37 Similarly, disconnect the vacuum pipes from the connector at the front of the housing, noting their routing **(see illustration)**.
38 Unscrew the four securing bolts (two at the front, and two at the rear), and manipulate

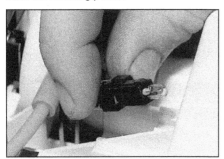

10.7 Pulling the heater control switch illumination bulbholder from the rear of the control unit

10.36 Disconnecting the heater blower motor wiring plug

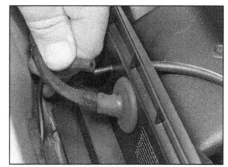

10.37 Disconnecting a vacuum pipe from the connector in the blower motor housing

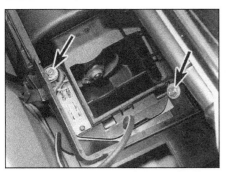

10.38a Pollen filter housing assembly securing bolts (arrowed)

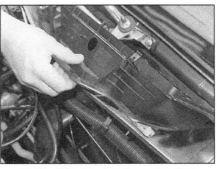

10.38b Withdrawing the pollen filter housing assembly from the scuttle

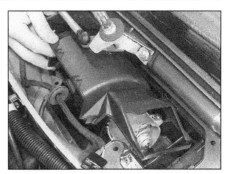

10.39 Removing the blower motor upper cover

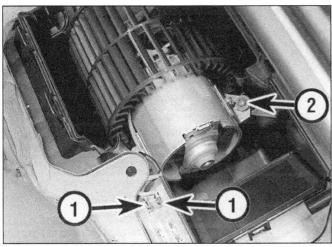

10.40 Heater blower motor fixings

1 Wires   *2 Motor securing screw*

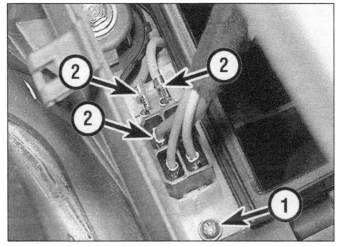

10.46a Heater blower motor wiring

1 Resistor securing screw   *2 Wiring plugs*

the pollen filter housing assembly from the scuttle **(see illustrations)**.
39 Release the two securing clips, and remove the blower motor upper cover **(see illustration)**.
40 Disconnect the two blower motor wires from the blower motor resistor, then remove the two blower motor securing screws, and carefully withdraw the motor assembly from its location **(see illustration)**.

Refitting

41 Refitting is a reversal of removal, bearing in mind the following points.
42 Ensure that the wiring and the vacuum pipes are securely reconnected and correctly routed.
43 Ensure that all panels are securely refitted, and that the weatherstrips are correctly engaged with the panels.
44 Refit the windscreen wiper arms with reference to Chapter 12.

Heater blower motor resistor

Removal

45 Remove the pollen filter, as described in Chapter 1, to expose the resistor.

46 Remove the single securing screw, then disconnect the wiring, and remove the resistor **(see illustrations)**.

Refitting

47 Refitting is a reversal of removal.

Heater matrix

Removal

48 Either drain the cooling system as described in Chapter 1, or clamp the heater hoses (working in the engine compartment) at

10.46b Removing the heater blower motor resistor

the bulkhead to reduce coolant loss when the hoses are disconnected.
49 Place a container beneath the heater hoses, then disconnect the hoses from the heater matrix stubs. Allow the coolant to drain into the container.
50 Remove the centre console, as described in Chapter 11.
51 Carefully detach the two tubes from the bottom of the air ducts in front of the heater matrix housing **(see illustration)**.
52 Remove the five screws securing the

10.51 Detach the two tubes (arrowed) from the bottom of the air ducts

10.52a Remove the front . . .

10.52b . . . and rear heater matrix lower cover securing screws . . .

10.52c . . . and lower the cover

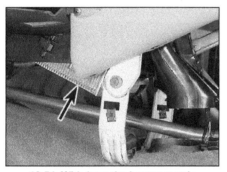

10.54 Withdraw the heater matrix (arrowed) from its housing

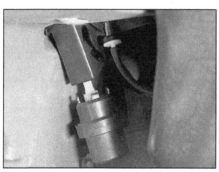

10.60 Air recirculation vacuum unit

10.64 Removing a facia ventilation nozzle

heater matrix lower cover (the front screw also secures the air ducts), then lift up the air ducts to enable the lower cover to be withdrawn **(see illustrations)**.

53 At this stage, it is advisable to lay a piece of plastic sheeting or similar under the heater matrix to prevent any coolant which may be released as the matrix is withdrawn from damaging the carpet.

54 Carefully withdraw the heater matrix from its housing (noting that the metal fins are sharp, and can easily be damaged), and withdraw it from the vehicle **(see illustration)**.

Refitting

55 Refitting is a reversal of removal, noting the following points.

56 Make sure that the tubes are securely refitted to the air ducts.

57 Ensure that the coolant hoses are securely reconnected to the heater matrix stubs.

58 On completion, where applicable, refill the cooling system as described in Chapter 1.

Air recirculation vacuum unit

Removal

59 Remove the glovebox, as described in Chapter 11, Section 32.

60 Reach up behind the facia, and locate the vacuum unit **(see illustration)**; access is limited.

61 Unclip the actuating rod from the end of the unit, and disconnect the vacuum hose.

62 Unclip the vacuum unit from its mounting.

Refitting

63 Refitting is a reversal of removal.

Heater/ventilation vents

Ventilation nozzles

64 Carefully release the relevant nozzle from the facia, using a screwdriver with a piece of card under the blade, to avoid damage to the facia trim, then withdraw the nozzle **(see illustration)**.

65 Simply push the nozzle into its housing in the facia until the securing lugs click into place.

Driver's side ventilation nozzle housing

66 Remove the steering column shrouds, as described in Chapter 11, Section 32.

67 Remove the instrument panel surround, as described in Chapter 11, Section 32.

68 Remove the ventilation nozzle, as described previously in this Section.

69 Remove the lighting rotary switch, as described in Chapter 12, Section 5.

70 Remove the upper nozzle housing securing screw (located at the top of the nozzle aperture), and the lower securing screw (located at the bottom of the lighting switch aperture) **(see illustration)**.

71 Carefully pull out the housing securing clip, accessible from behind the left-hand side (right-hand-drive models), or the right-hand side (left-hand-drive models) of the housing, as applicable **(see illustration)**.

72 Carefully withdraw the housing from the facia, and unclip the wiring plugs from the rear of the housing **(see illustration)**.

10.70 Removing the driver's side ventilation nozzle housing upper securing screw

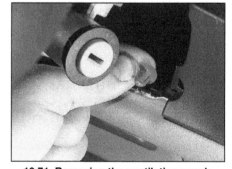

10.71 Removing the ventilation nozzle housing securing clip

73 The remaining switches can be removed from the housing by carefully pushing them out through the front of the housing from behind **(see illustration)**.

74 Refitting is a reversal of removal, but ensure that the housing engages correctly with the air duct in the facia.

Passenger's side ventilation nozzle housing

75 Remove the glovebox, as described in Chapter 11, Section 32.

76 Remove the ventilation nozzle, as described previously in this Section.

77 Remove the upper housing securing screw (located at the top of the nozzle aperture), and the lower securing screw (located at the bottom of the housing, in the glovebox aperture), then carefully withdraw the housing from the facia.

78 Refitting is a reversal of removal, but ensure that the housing engages correctly with the air duct in the facia.

11 Heated front seat components - removal and refitting
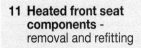

Heater switch

Removal

1 Disconnect the battery negative lead.

2 Using a length of wire, make up a hooked tool similar to that shown **(see illustration)**.

3 Carefully slide the tool round the top edge of the switch to release the securing lugs, then pull the switch forwards from the centre console.

4 Disconnect the wiring plug from the rear of the switch, and remove the switch.

Refitting

5 Refitting is a reversal of removal.

Heater mat

6 For access to the heater mats, the seat must be dismantled, and the upholstery must be removed (by unstitching). The procedure for this involves removing the seat back, which is secured by rivets.

7 Due to the difficulty involved in removing the upholstery, and the possible risk of injury to the vehicle occupants, should the seat be reassembled incorrectly, this task is considered to be beyond the scope of this manual.

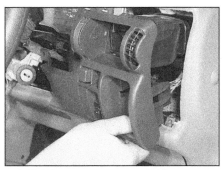

10.72 Withdrawing the ventilation nozzle housing from the facia

12 Air conditioning system - general information and precautions

General information

1 An air conditioning system is available on some models. It enables the temperature of incoming air to be lowered; it also dehumidifies the air, which makes for rapid demisting and increased comfort.

2 The cooling side of the system works in the same way as a domestic refrigerator. Refrigerant gas is drawn into a belt-driven compressor, and passes into a condenser in front of the radiator, where it loses heat and becomes liquid. The liquid passes through an expansion valve to an evaporator, where it changes from liquid under high pressure to gas under low pressure. This change is accompanied by a drop in temperature, which cools the evaporator. The refrigerant returns to the compressor and the cycle begins again.

3 Air blown through the evaporator passes to the air distribution unit, where it is mixed with hot air blown through the heater matrix, to achieve the desired temperature in the passenger compartment.

4 The heating side of the system works in the same way as on models without air conditioning.

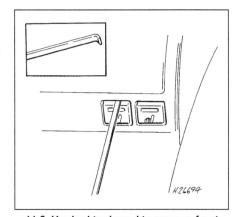

11.2 Hooked tool used to remove front seat heater switches

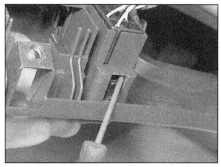

10.73 Levering the headlight aim adjustment switch from the ventilation nozzle housing

Precautions

⚠ **Warning: The refrigerant is potentially dangerous, and should only be handled by qualified persons. If it is splashed onto the skin, it can cause frostbite. It is not itself poisonous, but in the presence of a naked flame (including a cigarette) it forms a poisonous gas.**

5 Uncontrolled discharging of the refrigerant is dangerous, and damaging to the environment. It follows that any work on the air conditioning system which involves opening the refrigerant circuit **must** only be carried out by a Vauxhall/Opel dealer or an air conditioning specialist.

6 Do not operate the air conditioning system if it is known to be short of refrigerant; the compressor may be damaged.

13 Air conditioning system - component removal and refitting

⚠ **Warning: Do not attempt to open the refrigerant circuit. Refer to the precautions at the end of Section 12.**

The only operation which can be carried out easily without discharging the refrigerant is renewal of the compressor drivebelt, which is described in Chapter 1. All other operations must be referred to a Vauxhall/Opel dealer or an air conditioning specialist.

If necessary, the compressor can be unbolted and moved aside, without disconnecting the refrigerant lines, after removing the drivebelt.

Notes

Chapter 4 Part A:
Fuel and exhaust systems - carburettor models

Contents

Degrees of difficulty

| Easy, suitable for novice with little experience | | Fairly easy, suitable for beginner with some experience | | Fairly difficult, suitable for competent DIY mechanic | | Difficult, suitable for experienced DIY mechanic | | Very difficult, suitable for expert DIY or professional | |

Specifications

System type

Carburettor type .... Pierburg 2E3
Application * .... 14 NV engine
Choke type .... Automatic

* For details of engine code location, see 'Buying spare parts and vehicle identification numbers'.

Carburettor data

Idle speed .... 925 ± 25 rpm
Idle mixture CO content .... 1.0 ± 0.5%
Fast idle speed .... 2200 to 2600 rpm
Choke valve gap .... 1.5 to 3.5 mm
Choke pull-down gap:
 'Small' .... 1.7 to 2.1 mm
 'Large' .... 2.5 to 2.9 mm
Idle fuel jet 45
Idle air bleed 130

	Primary	Secondary
Venturi diameter	20.0 mm	24.0 mm
Main jet	X95	X110

Torque wrench settings

	Nm	lbf ft
Exhaust downpipe to manifold bolts	25	18
Exhaust manifold nuts	22	16
Fuel pump bolts	18	13
Fuel tank mounting strap nuts	20	15
Inlet manifold nuts	22	16

1 General information and precautions

General information

The fuel system on carburettor models comprises a fuel tank, a fuel pump, a vapour separator (not fitted to all models), a down-draught carburettor, and a thermostatically-controlled air cleaner.

The fuel tank is mounted under the rear of the vehicle, forward of the rear suspension. The tank is ventilated to the atmosphere, and is filled from the right-hand side of the vehicle through a simple filler pipe. The fuel gauge sender unit is mounted inside the tank.

The fuel pump is a mechanical diaphragm type, operated by a pushrod which is in turn actuated by a lobe on the camshaft.

The fuel vapour separator (where fitted) is used to stabilise the fuel supply to the carburettor. Vapour is purged from the carburettor fuel supply, thus improving hot starting qualities.

The carburettor is a Pierburg 2E3 type, a full description of which is given in Section 12.

The air cleaner has a vacuum-controlled air intake, supplying a blend of hot and cold air to suit the prevailing engine operating conditions.

Precautions

Certain adjustment points in the fuel system are protected by tamperproof caps, plugs or seals. In some countries it is an offence to drive a vehicle with broken or missing tamperproof seals. Before disturbing a tamperproof seal, check that no local or national laws will be broken by doing so, and fit a new tamperproof seal after adjustment is complete where this is required by law. Do not break tamperproof seals on a vehicle which is still under warranty.

When working on fuel system components, scrupulous cleanliness must be observed, and care must be taken not to introduce any foreign matter into fuel lines or components. Carburettors in particular are delicate instruments, and care should be taken not to disturb any components unnecessarily. Before attempting work on a carburettor, ensure that the relevant spares are available. If the problems persist, it is recommended that the advice of a Vauxhall/Opel dealer or carburettor specialist is sought. Most dealers will be able to provide carburettor re-jetting and servicing facilities, and if necessary it should be possible to buy a reconditioned carburettor.

Refer to Chapter 5B for precautions to be observed when working on vehicles fitted with electronic control units.

⚠️ *Warning: Many of the procedures in this Chapter require the removal of fuel lines and connections which may result in some fuel spillage. Before carrying out any operation on the fuel system refer to the precautions given in 'Safety first!' at the beginning of this manual, and follow them implicitly. Petrol is a highly dangerous and volatile liquid and the precautions necessary when handling it cannot be overstressed.*

2 Unleaded petrol - general information and usage

Note: *The information given in this Section is correct at the time of writing, and applies only to petrol currently available in the EC. If in any doubt as to the suitability of petrol or if using the vehicle outside the EC, consult a Vauxhall/Opel dealer or one of the motoring organisations for advice on the petrol available, and their suitability for your vehicle.*

Vauxhall/Opel recommend the use of 95 RON (Premium) unleaded petrol in carburettor models; 98 RON (Super or 'Super Plus') unleaded petrol can be used without modification.

97 or 98 RON leaded petrol can be used without modification in carburettor models not equipped with a catalytic converter. **Do not use leaded petrol in models equipped with a catalytic converter, or the (expensive) catalyst unit will be ruined.**

3 Air cleaner intake air temperature control system - testing

1 The air cleaner is thermostatically-controlled, to provide air at the most suitable temperature for combustion with minimum exhaust emission levels.
2 The optimum air temperature is achieved by drawing in cold air from an air intake at the front of the vehicle, and blending it with hot air from a shroud on the exhaust manifold. The proportion of hot air and cold air is varied by the position of a flap valve in the air cleaner intake spout, which is controlled by a vacuum diaphragm unit. The vacuum applied to the diaphragm type is regulated by a heat sensor located within the air cleaner body.
3 To check the operation of the air temperature control, the engine must be cold. First check the position of the flap valve. Disconnect the hot air tube from the air cleaner spout, and check (by probing with a finger) that the flap is closed to admit only cold air from outside the vehicle **(see illustrations)**. Start the engine, and check that the flap now opens to admit only hot air from the exhaust manifold.
4 Temporarily reconnect the hot air tube to the air cleaner spout.
5 Run the engine until it reaches normal operating temperature.
6 Disconnect the hot air tube again, and check that the flap is now closed to admit only cold air from outside the vehicle, or in hot weather, a mixture of hot and cold air. Reconnect the hot air tube after making the check.
7 If the flap does not function correctly, the air cleaner must be renewed, as parts are not available individually.

4 Air cleaner housing assembly - removal and refitting

Removal

1 Disconnect the air hose from the airbox on the carburettor.
2 Remove the air cleaner filter element, as described in Chapter 1.
3 Slacken the air cleaner housing assembly securing nuts (one front and one rear), and pull the assembly from the body panel.

Refitting

4 Refitting is a reversal of removal.

5 Fuel pump - testing, removal and refitting

Note: *Refer to the warning note in Section 1 before proceeding.*

Testing

1 Disconnect the ignition coil HT lead.
2 Place a wad of clean rag under the pump outlet, then disconnect the pump outlet hose. Be prepared for fuel spillage, and take adequate fire precautions.

3.3a Exhaust manifold-to-air cleaner hot air tube

3.3b Checking the operation of the air cleaner flap valve

5.7 Disconnecting a fuel hose from the fuel pump

3 Have an assistant crank the engine on the starter. Well-defined spurts of fuel should be ejected from the pump outlet - if not, the pump is probably faulty (or the tank is empty). Dispose of the fuel-soaked rag safely.

4 No spare parts are available for the pump, and if faulty, the unit must be renewed.

Removal

5 The fuel pump is located at the right-hand end of the camshaft housing.

6 Disconnect the battery negative lead.

7 Disconnect the fuel hoses from the pump **(see illustration)**. If necessary, label the hoses so that they can be reconnected to their original locations. Be prepared for fuel spillage, and take adequate fire precautions. Plug the open ends of the hoses to prevent dirt ingress and further fuel spillage.

8 Unscrew the two securing bolts, and withdraw the pump from the camshaft housing **(see illustration)**.

9 Recover the plastic insulating block.

Refitting

10 Refitting is a reversal of removal, but ensure that the fuel hoses are reconnected to their correct locations as noted during removal, and tighten the securing bolts to the specified torque.

11 Run the engine and check for leaks on completion. If leakage is evident, stop the engine immediately and rectify the problem without delay. Note that the engine may take a longer time than usual to start when the pump has been removed as the pump refills with fuel.

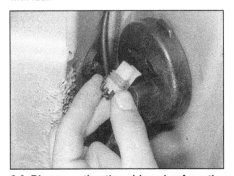

6.6 Disconnecting the wiring plug from the fuel gauge sender unit

5.8 Withdrawing the fuel pump and plastic insulating block

6 Fuel gauge sender unit - removal and refitting

Note: *Refer to the warning in Section 1 before proceeding.*

Removal

1 Disconnect the battery negative lead.

2 Siphon out any remaining fuel in the tank through the filler pipe. Siphon the fuel into a clean metal container that can be sealed.

3 Chock the front wheels, then jack up the rear of the vehicle and support securely on axle stands (see *"Jacking and vehicle support"*).

4 The sender unit is located in the front face of the fuel tank.

5 Make alignment marks on the sender unit and the fuel tank so that the unit can be refitted in its original position.

6 Disconnect the wiring plug from the sender unit **(see illustration)**.

7 Pull back the plastic cover **(see illustration)**, then disconnect the fuel hose(s) from the sender unit. Be prepared for fuel spillage, and take adequate fire precautions. Plug the open end(s) of the hose(s) to prevent dirt ingress and further fuel loss.

8 To remove the sender unit, engage a flat piece of metal as a lever between two of the slots on the sender unit rim, and turn the sender unit anti-clockwise.

9 Withdraw the unit carefully, to avoid bending the float arm.

10 Remove the sealing ring.

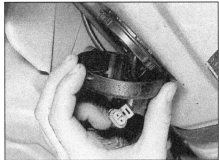

6.7 Pulling the plastic cover from the fuel gauge sender unit

Refitting

11 Refitting is a reversal of removal, remembering the following points.

12 Examine the condition of the sealing ring and renew if necessary.

13 Ensure that the marks made on the sender unit and fuel tank before removal are aligned.

14 Ensure that the hoses are reconnected to their correct locations as noted during removal.

15 On completion, fill the fuel tank, then run the engine and check for leaks. Also check that the fuel gauge reads correctly. If leakage is evident, stop the engine immediately and rectify the problem without delay. Note that the engine may take a longer time than usual to start when the sender unit has been removed, as the fuel pump refills with fuel.

7 Fuel vapour separator - removal and refitting

Note: *Refer to the warning in Section 1 before proceeding.*

Removal

1 Where fitted, the vapour separator is located on a bracket attached to the side of the carburettor.

2 Note the locations of the three fuel hoses, labelling them if necessary to aid refitting, then disconnect the hoses from the vapour separator. Be prepared for fuel spillage, and take adequate fire precautions. Clamp or plug the open ends of the hoses, to prevent dirt ingress and further fuel spillage.

3 Remove the two securing screws, and lift the vapour separator from its bracket.

Refitting

4 Check the body of the separator for cracks or leaks before refitting, and renew if necessary.

5 Refitting is a reversal of removal, but ensure that the three fuel hoses are connected to their correct locations as noted during removal.

8 Fuel filter - removal and refitting

Removal

1 The fuel filter is located in the carburettor fuel inlet pipe.

2 Disconnect the trunking from the air cleaner, then disconnect the vacuum pipe and breather hose from the airbox. Extract the three securing screws and lift off the airbox, complete with air trunking.

3 Place a wad of rag under the fuel inlet pipe at the carburettor to catch any fuel that may be spilled during the procedure.

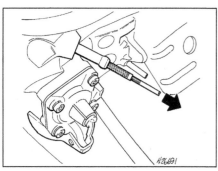

8.5 Removing the fuel filter from the carburettor fuel inlet pipe

4 Disconnect the fuel inlet hose from the carburettor. Be prepared for fuel spillage, and clamp or plug the end of the hose to reduce unnecessary fuel loss. Take adequate fire precautions.

5 To remove the filter, carefully screw an M3 bolt approximately 5.0 mm into the end of the filter, and pull on the bolt to withdraw the filter from the end of the inlet pipe **(see illustration)**.

Refitting

6 Push the new filter into the inlet pipe, ensuring that it engages securely, then reconnect the fuel inlet hose, and refit the airbox.

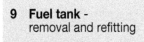

9 Fuel tank -
removal and refitting
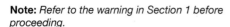

Note: *Refer to the warning in Section 1 before proceeding.*

Saloon and Hatchback models

Removal

1 Disconnect the battery negative lead.
2 Proceed as described in Section 6, paragraphs 1 to 3 inclusive.
3 Disconnect the exhaust system front flexible joint (see Section 23). Suspend the front section of the exhaust system with wire or string from the underbody.
4 Disconnect the rear section of the exhaust system from its rubber mountings, and allow it

to rest on the rear suspension torsion beam. It is advisable to support the centre section of the exhaust system with wire or string from the underbody to avoid straining the system.
5 Release the handbrake cables from the clips on the tank (right-hand cable) and tank securing strap (left-hand cable), and move them clear of the tank **(see illustration)**. On certain models, it may be necessary to slacken the cable adjuster to enable the cables to be moved clear of the tank (see Chapter 9).
6 Where applicable, remove the fuel filter from the side of the fuel tank. Refer to Section 8.
7 Clamp the fuel hose(s) running to the fuel gauge sender unit. This is located in the right-hand side of the tank. Then position a container under the sender unit to catch the fuel which will be released as the hose(s) are disconnected.
8 Pull back the plastic cover, then disconnect the hose(s) from the sender unit. Be prepared for fuel spillage, and take adequate fire precautions.
9 Disconnect the wiring plug from the fuel gauge sender unit. Disconnect the hose and wiring from the fuel pump, if applicable.
10 Disconnect the filler and vent hoses from the rear of the fuel tank **(see illustration)**.
11 Support the weight of the fuel tank on a jack with interposed block of wood.
12 Unscrew the securing nuts from the tank mounting straps **(see illustration)**, then remove the straps and lower the tank sufficiently to enable the disconnection of the remaining vent hose(s).
13 With the aid of an assistant, carefully lower the tank, and withdraw it from under the vehicle. Note that as the tank is withdrawn, some residual fuel may be released.

Refitting

14 If the tank contains sediment or water, it may be cleaned out using two or three rinses with clean fuel. Shake vigorously using several changes of fuel, but before doing so, remove the fuel gauge sender unit, as described in Section 6. *This procedure should be carried out in a well-ventilated area, and it is vital to take adequate fire precautions.*
15 Any repairs to the fuel tank should be carried out by a professional. **Do not** under any circumstances attempt to weld or solder a

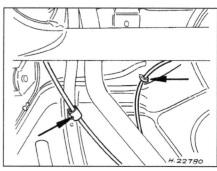

9.5 Handbrake cables (arrowed) clipped to fuel tank and tank securing strap - Saloon and Hatchback models

fuel tank. Removal of all residual fuel vapours requires several hours of specialist cleaning.
16 Refitting is a reversal of removal, remembering the following points.
17 Ensure that all hoses and pipes are securely reconnected to their correct locations, as noted before removal.
18 Where applicable, refit the fuel filter. Refer to Section 8.
19 If the handbrake cable adjuster has been slackened, adjust the handbrake cables as described in Chapter 9.
20 On completion, fill the fuel tank, then run the engine and check for leaks. If leakage is evident, stop the engine immediately and rectify the problem without delay. Note that the engine may take a longer time than usual to start, as the pump refills with fuel.

Estate and Van models

Removal

21 Proceed as described in Section 6, paragraphs 1 to 3 inclusive.
22 Disconnect the filler and vent hoses from the side of the tank.
23 Disconnect the hoses shown **(see illustration)** from the fuel filler assembly.
24 Support the weight of the fuel tank on a jack with interposed block of wood.
25 Unscrew the securing bolts from the tank mounting straps, then remove the straps, and with the aid of an assistant, carefully lower the tank and withdraw it from under the vehicle. Note that as the tank is withdrawn, some residual fuel may be released.

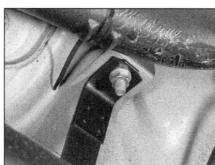

9.10 Filler and vent hose connections at rear of fuel tank - Hatchback model

9.12 Fuel tank mounting strap nut

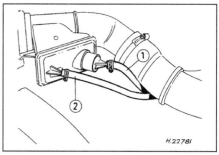

9.23 Disconnect the hoses (1 and 2) from the fuel filler assembly - Estate and Van models

10.2 Removing an airbox securing screw

10.3a Extract the throttle cable end clip . . .

10.3b . . . and slide the grommet from the bracket

Refitting

26 Refer to paragraphs 14 and 15.

27 Refitting is a reversal of removal, but ensure that all hoses and pipes are securely reconnected to their correct locations, as noted before removal.

28 On completion, fill the fuel tank, then run the engine and check for leaks. If leakage is evident, stop the engine immediately and rectify the problem without delay. Note that the engine may take a longer time than usual to start, as the pump refills with fuel.

10 Throttle cable -
removal, refitting and adjustment

Removal

1 Disconnect the air trunking from the air cleaner, then disconnect the vacuum pipe and breather hose from the airbox.

2 Extract the three securing screws **(see illustration)** and lift off the airbox, complete with the air trunking.

3 Extract the clip from the cable end fitting at the bracket on the carburettor, then slide the cable end grommet from the bracket **(see illustrations)**.

4 Slide the cable end from the throttle valve lever on the carburettor.

5 Working inside the vehicle, release the securing clips, and remove the lower trim panel from the driver's footwell **(see illustration)**.

6 Pull the cable retainer from the top of the pedal, and disconnect the cable end from the pedal.

7 Make a careful note of the cable routing, then withdraw the cable through the bulkhead into the engine compartment.

Refitting

8 Refitting is a reversal of removal, remembering the following points.

9 Ensure that the cable is correctly routed, as noted before removal.

10 Ensure that the bulkhead grommet is correctly seated in its aperture.

11 On completion, check the throttle mechanism for satisfactory operation, and if necessary adjust the cable, as described in the following paragraphs.

Adjustment

12 Two points of cable adjustment are provided. A stop screw is located on the pedal arm to control the fully released position of the pedal stop. A clip is located on a threaded section of the cable sheath at the bracket on the carburettor, to adjust the cable free play **(see illustration)**.

13 The cable should be adjusted so that when the throttle pedal is released, there is very slight free play in the cable at the carburettor end.

14 Check that when the throttle pedal is fully depressed, the throttle valve is fully open. Adjust the position of the clip on the cable sheath and the pedal stop screw, as necessary.

11 Throttle pedal -
removal and refitting

Removal

1 Working inside the vehicle, release the securing clips, and remove the lower trim panel from the driver's footwell.

2 Pull the cable retainer from the top of the pedal, and disconnect the cable end from the pedal.

3 Extract the circlip from the right-hand end of the pedal pivot shaft, then slide out the pivot shaft from the left-hand side of the pedal pivot bracket **(see illustration)**. Recover the pivot bushes and the pedal return spring.

Refitting

4 Before refitting the pedal components, examine the pivot bushes for wear, and renew if necessary.

5 Refitting is a reversal of removal, but on completion check the throttle mechanism for satisfactory operation, and check the throttle cable adjustment, as described in Section 10.

12 Carburettor -
general information

1 The Pierburg 2E3 carburettor is of twin-venturi, fixed-jet sequential throttle type **(see illustrations overleaf)**. The primary throttle

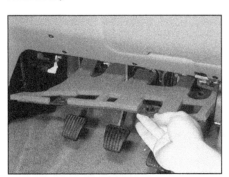

10.5 Removing the lower trim panel from the driver's footwell

10.12 Throttle pedal stop screw

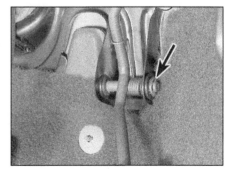

11.3 Throttle pedal pivot assembly - circlip arrowed

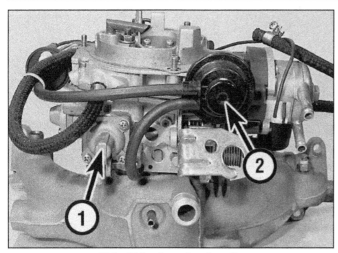

12.1a Side view of carburettor

1 Accelerator pump   *2 Main choke pull-down*
                                diaphragm unit

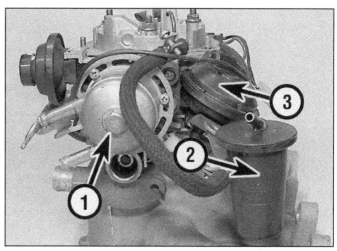

12.1b Side view of carburettor

1 Automatic choke housing   *3 Secondary throttle valve*
2 Vapour separator

valve operates alone except at high speeds and loads, when the secondary throttle valve is operated, until at full-throttle, both are fully open. This arrangement allows good fuel economy during light acceleration and cruising, but also gives maximum power at full-throttle. The secondary throttle valve is vacuum-operated, according to the vacuum produced in the primary venturi. The primary throttle barrel and venturi diameters are smaller than their secondary counterparts. The carburettor is a complicated instrument, with various refinements and sub-systems added to achieve improved driveability, economy and exhaust emission levels.

2 A separate idle system operates independently from the main jet system, supplying fuel controlled by a mixture control screw.

3 The main jets are calibrated to suit engine requirements at mid-range throttle openings. To provide the necessary fuel enrichment at full-throttle, a vacuum-operated power valve

is used. The valve provides extra fuel under the low vacuum conditions associated with wide throttle openings.

4 To provide an enriched mixture during acceleration, an accelerator pump delivers extra fuel to the primary main venturi. The accelerator pump is operated mechanically by a cam on the throttle linkage.

5 A fully automatic choke is fitted, operated by a coolant and electrically heated bi-metal coil. When the engine is cold, the bi-metal coil is fully wound up, holding the choke plate (fitted to the primary barrel) closed. As the engine warms up, the bi-metal coil is heated and therefore unwinds, progressively opening the choke plate. A vacuum-operated pull-down system is employed, whereby, if the engine is under choke but is only cruising (i.e. not under heavy load), the choke plate is opened against the action of the bi-metal coil. The pull-down system prevents an over-rich mixture, which would otherwise reduce fuel economy and may cause unnecessary engine wear when the engine is cold. A secondary pull-down solenoid is fitted, which operates in conjunction with the main diaphragm unit to modify the pull-down characteristics, improving fuel economy.

6 An unusual feature of the Pierburg carburettor is that the float level is set in production, and cannot be adjusted.

13 Carburettor - removal and refitting

Note: *Refer to the warning in Section 1 before proceeding. New gasket(s) must be used when refitting the carburettor.*

Removal

1 Disconnect the battery negative lead.

2 Disconnect the trunking from the air cleaner, then disconnect the vacuum pipe and breather hose from the airbox. Extract the three securing screws and lift off the airbox, complete with air trunking.

3 Disconnect the fuel supply hose from the carburettor, or disconnect the fuel supply and return hoses from the vapour separator, as applicable. Be prepared for fuel spillage, and take adequate fire precautions. Clamp or plug the end of the hose(s), to prevent dirt ingress and further fuel spillage.

4 Extract the clip from the throttle cable end fitting at the bracket on the carburettor, then slide the cable end grommet from the bracket, and slide the cable end from the throttle valve lever.

5 Disconnect the coolant hoses from the automatic choke housing, noting their locations as an aid to refitting **(see illustration)**. Be prepared for coolant spillage, and clamp or plug the hoses, or secure them with their ends facing upwards, to prevent further coolant loss.

6 Disconnect the two vacuum pipes from the front of the carburettor, noting their locations and routing for use when refitting **(see illustration)**.

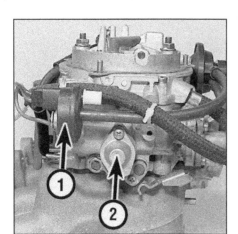

12.1c Side view of carburettor

1 Secondary choke pull-down solenoid
2 Power valve

13.5 Disconnecting the coolant hoses from the automatic choke housing

7 Disconnect the choke heater wiring plug **(see illustration)**.
8 Unscrew the three securing nuts, and withdraw the carburettor from the inlet manifold studs **(see illustration)**.
9 Recover the gasket(s) and insulator block which fit between the carburettor and the inlet manifold.

Refitting

10 Refitting is a reversal of removal, but renew the gasket(s).
11 On completion, carry out the following checks and adjustments.
12 Check the throttle cable free play and adjust if necessary, as described in Section 10.
13 Check and if necessary top-up the coolant level, as described in 'Weekly checks'.
14 Check and if necessary adjust the idle speed and mixture, as described in Chapter 1.

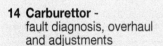
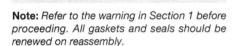

14 Carburettor -
fault diagnosis, overhaul and adjustments

Note: *Refer to the warning in Section 1 before proceeding. All gaskets and seals should be renewed on reassembly.*

Fault diagnosis

1 Faults with the carburettor are usually associated with dirt entering the float chamber and blocking the jets, causing a weak mixture or power failure within a certain engine speed range. If this is the case, then a thorough clean will normally cure the problem. If the carburettor is well worn, uneven running may be caused by air entering through the throttle valve spindle bearings.
2 If a carburettor fault is suspected, always check first (where possible) that the ignition

13.6 Disconnecting a vacuum pipe from the front of the carburettor

timing is correct, and that the spark plugs are in good condition and correctly gapped. Also check that the throttle cable is correctly adjusted, and that the air cleaner filter element is clean. Remember that it is possible that one of the hydraulic valve lifters may be faulty, resulting in an incorrect valve clearance.
3 If careful checking of all the preceding points produces no improvement, the carburettor should be removed for cleaning and overhaul.

Overhaul and adjustments

4 The following paragraphs describe cleaning and adjustment procedures which can be carried out by the home mechanic after the carburettor has been removed from the inlet manifold (see Section 13). If the carburettor is worn or damaged, it should either be renewed or overhauled by a specialist, who will be able to restore the carburettor to its original calibration.
5 With the carburettor removed, clean all external dirt from the carburettor, then remove the four carburettor top cover securing screws, noting their locations, as two lengths of screw are used.

13.7 Disconnecting the choke heater wiring plug

6 Lift off the top cover, and recover the gasket.
7 Access to the carburettor jets in the top cover can now be obtained **(see illustration)**.
8 Blow through the jets and drillings with compressed air (wear eye protection), or air from a foot pump - do not probe them with wire. If the jets are to be removed, unscrew them carefully using tools of the correct size.
9 Remove the fuel filter from the inlet pipe by carefully screwing an M3 bolt approximately 5.0 mm into the end of the filter, and pulling on the bolt to withdraw the filter from the end of the inlet pipe. Push a new filter into the inlet pipe, ensuring that it engages securely.
10 Carefully clean any foreign matter from the float chamber.
11 Removal and refitting of the float and automatic choke unit, and renewal of the various diaphragm units, is described in the following Sections.
12 Further dismantling is not recommended.
13 Reassemble in the reverse order to dismantling. Use new gaskets and seals throughout.
14 Refit the carburettor as described in Section 13.

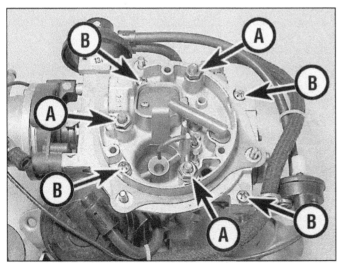

13.8 Carburettor securing nuts (A) and top cover securing screws (B)

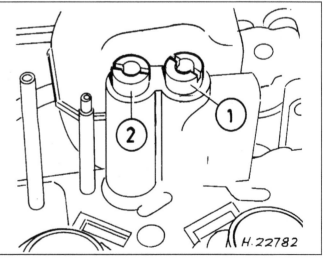

14.7 Main jets in top cover

1 Primary main jet   2 Secondary main jet

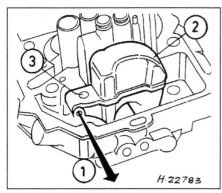

15.11 Float assembly in top cover

| 1 Float retaining | 2 Float |
| pin | 3 Needle valve |

15 Carburettor needle valve and float - removal, inspection and refitting

Note: Refer to the warning in Section 1 before proceeding. A new carburettor top cover gasket should be used on refitting. A tachometer and an exhaust gas analyser will be required to check the idle speed and mixture on completion.

Removal

1 Disconnect the battery negative lead.
2 Disconnect the air trunking from the air cleaner, then disconnect the vacuum pipe and breather hose from the airbox.
3 Extract the three securing screws and lift off the airbox, complete with the air trunking.
4 Thoroughly clean all external dirt from the carburettor.
5 Disconnect the fuel supply hose at the carburettor. Be prepared for fuel spillage, and take adequate fire precautions. Plug the end of hose, to prevent dirt ingress and further fuel spillage.
6 Identify the automatic choke coolant hose locations as an aid to refitting, then disconnect the hoses. Be prepared for

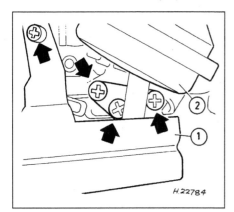

16.6 Secondary throttle valve vacuum diaphragm unit

| 1 Bracket | 2 Diaphragm unit |

coolant spillage, and clamp or plug the hoses, or secure them with their ends facing upwards to prevent further coolant loss.
7 Disconnect the choke heater wiring plug.
8 Disconnect the two vacuum hoses from the choke pull-down unit.
9 Remove the four carburettor top cover securing screws, noting their locations, as two lengths of screw are used.
10 Lift off the top cover, and recover the gasket.
11 Using a pin punch, tap the float retaining pin from the base of the top cover, and lift out the float and needle valve **(see illustration)**.

Inspection

12 Inspect the components for damage, and renew as necessary. Check the needle valve for wear, and check the float for leaks by shaking it to see if it contains petrol.

Refitting

13 Clean the mating faces of the carburettor body and top cover.
14 Refitting is a reversal of removal, remembering the following points.
15 After refitting, check the float and needle valve for full and free movement. Note that no adjustment of the float is possible.
16 Use a new gasket between the top cover and the carburettor body.
17 Ensure that all hoses, pipes and wires are correctly reconnected.
18 On completion, check and if necessary top-up the coolant level, as described in 'Weekly checks' and check and if necessary adjust the idle speed and mixture, as described in Chapter 1.

16 Carburettor secondary throttle valve vacuum diaphragm - renewal

Note: The diaphragm unit must be renewed in its entirety, as no spares are available.
1 Proceed as described in Section 15, paragraphs 2 and 3.
2 Disconnect the diaphragm unit vacuum pipe from the carburettor.
3 Prise the diaphragm operating rod balljoint from the secondary throttle valve linkage.
4 Where applicable, remove the two securing screws and lift the vapour separator from the bracket. Move the vapour separator to one side, taking care not to strain the fuel hoses.
5 If necessary, for improved access, remove the choke housing as described in Section 19, paragraphs 2 and 3.
6 Remove the four securing screws, and withdraw the diaphragm unit, complete with its bracket from the carburettor body **(see illustration)**.
7 Fit the new diaphragm using a reversal of the removal procedure.
8 Where applicable, when refitting the choke bi-metal housing, ensure that the bi-metal spring is correctly engaged with the choke

lever, and align the marks on the bi-metal housing and choke housing as noted before removal.

17 Carburettor power valve diaphragm - renewal

Note: Refer to the warning in Section 1 before proceeding.
1 Disconnect the battery negative lead.
2 Proceed as described in Section 15, paragraphs 2 and 3.
3 Thoroughly clean all external dirt from the area around the power valve housing.
4 Remove the two securing screws, and lift off the power valve cover, spring, and diaphragm assembly **(see illustration)**.
5 Clean the mating faces of the cover and housing.
6 Fit the new diaphragm as follows.
7 Locate the spring on the cover and diaphragm assembly, ensuring that it is correctly seated, then press the diaphragm assembly and cover together. Note that the vacuum hole in the diaphragm must align with the corresponding holes in the housing flange and cover.
8 Further fitting is a reversal of removal, but ensure that the diaphragm is correctly seated.

18 Carburettor accelerator pump diaphragm - renewal

Note: Refer to the warning in Section 1 before proceeding.
1 Proceed as described in Section 15, paragraphs 1 to 3.
2 Thoroughly clean all external dirt from the area around the accelerator pump housing.
3 Remove the four securing screws, and lift off the accelerator pump cover. Recover the diaphragm, spring, valve retainer and valve

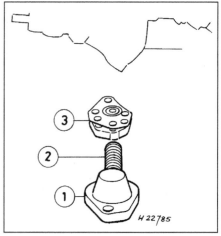

17.4 Power valve components

| 1 Cover | 3 Diaphragm |
| 2 Spring | assembly |

(see illustration). Note the orientation of the valve retainer.

4 Clean the mating faces of the cover and housing.

5 Check the condition of the valve, and renew if necessary.

6 Begin fitting of the new diaphragm by locating the valve, valve retainer and spring in the housing. Note that the valve retainer can only be fitted in one position. The larger diameter of the spring should rest against the valve retainer.

7 Locate the diaphragm on the housing, ensuring that the spring is correctly seated, and refit the cover. Tighten the cover securing screws progressively to avoid distorting the diaphragm.

8 Further fitting is a reversal of removal.

19 Carburettor automatic choke unit - removal, refitting and adjustment

Note: *Refer to the warning in Section 1 before proceeding. A tachometer and an exhaust gas analyser will be required to check the idle speed and mixture on completion. If the coolant housing is removed, new O-rings must be used on refitting.*

Removal

1 Proceed as described in Section 15, paragraphs 1 to 3.

2 Note the position of the bi-metal housing alignment marks as an aid to refitting, if necessary making additional marks for clarity **(see illustration)**. Then remove the three securing screws and lift off the bi-metal housing. Place the housing to one side, taking care not to strain the coolant hoses or electric choke heater wiring.

3 Remove the three screws securing the choke housing to the carburettor body, and withdraw the choke assembly, taking care not to bend the choke operating rod.

4 If it is necessary to remove the bi-metal housing for renewal, continue as follows; otherwise go on to paragraph 8.

5 Identify the automatic choke coolant hose locations as an aid to refitting, then disconnect

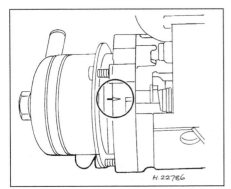

19.2 Automatic choke bi-metal housing alignment marks (circled)

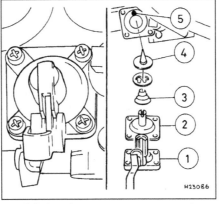

18.3 Accelerator pump components

1	Cover with operating lever	3	Spring
2	Diaphragm	4	Valve
		5	Air passage

the hoses. Be prepared for coolant spillage, and clamp or plug the hoses, or secure them with their ends facing upwards, to prevent further loss of coolant.

6 Disconnect the wiring from the electric choke heater, and withdraw the bi-metal housing.

7 The coolant housing can be separated from the bi-metal housing by unscrewing the central securing bolt. Recover the O-rings from under the bolt head, and from the rim of the coolant housing.

Refitting

8 Begin refitting by locating the choke assembly on the carburettor body, ensuring that the lever on the choke assembly engages with the choke operating rod. Tighten the three securing screws.

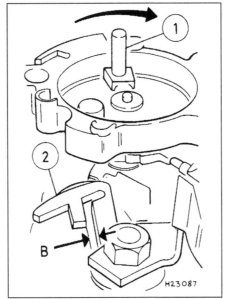

19.18 Choke valve gap adjustment

| 1 | Choke operating lever | 2 | Adjuster segment |
| | | B | Choke valve gap |

9 Check and if necessary adjust the choke valve gap and the fast idle cam position, as described later in this Section.

10 Connect the bi-metal spring to the choke lever, position the bi-metal housing and the choke housing as noted during removal, then tighten the securing screws.

11 Where applicable, refit the coolant housing to the bi-metal housing, using new O-rings if necessary, and reconnect the coolant hoses and the electric choke heater wiring.

12 Further refitting is a reversal of removal, remembering the following points.

13 If the coolant hoses have been disconnected, check the coolant level, as described in 'Weekly checks'.

14 Check and if necessary adjust the fast idle speed, as described later in this Section.

Adjustment

Choke valve gap

15 With the bi-metal housing removed as described previously in this Section, continue as follows.

16 Press the choke operating lever fully clock-wise, and retain it in position with a rubber band.

17 Move the throttle lever to the fully open position, and measure the choke valve gap between the lower side of the choke plate and the wall of the primary barrel. Check that the gap is as given in the Specifications.

18 If necessary, adjust the choke valve gap by bending the segment (2), **(see illustration)**. If the gap is too small, enlarge the gap (B), by levering with a screwdriver. If the gap is too large, decrease gap (B) using a pair of pliers.

19 If no further adjustments are to be carried out, refit the bi-metal housing as described previously in this Section.

Fast idle cam position

20 With the bi-metal housing removed, and the choke valve gap 'A', **(see illustration)** correctly set as described previously in this Section, continue as follows.

19.20 Fast idle cam adjustment

1	Fast idle cam	4	Fast idle speed
2	Adjustment lever		adjustment screw
3	Choke drive lever	A	Choke valve gap

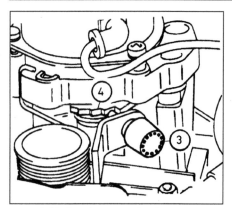

19.27 Fast idle speed adjustment

3 Fast idle speed adjustment screw
4 Fast idle cam - screw positioned on second-highest step

21 Open the throttle valve, then close the choke valve using light finger pressure on the choke drive lever. Close the throttle valve.
22 Check that the fast idle speed adjustment screw is resting against the stop on the second-highest step of the fast idle cam.
23 If adjustment is required, first check that the choke return spring is correctly positioned, then adjust by bending the lever (2).
24 Refit the bi-metal housing as described previously in this Section.

Fast idle speed adjustment

Note: To carry out the adjustment, an accurate tachometer and an exhaust gas analyser will be required.

25 Check the idle speed and mixture, as described in Chapter 1. The idle speed **must** be correct before attempting to check or adjust the fast idle speed.
26 With the engine at normal operating temperature, and a tachometer connected according to the equipment manufacturer's instructions, continue as follows.
27 Position the fast idle speed adjustment screw on the second-highest step of the cam **(see illustration)**.
28 Start the engine without touching the throttle pedal, and check that the fast idle speed is as specified. If adjustment is required, stop the engine, and continue as follows.
29 Remove the tamperproof cap from the

20.11 Secondary choke pull-down solenoid securing screw and earth lead

fast idle speed adjustment screw - ensure that no local or national laws are being broken by doing so **(see illustration)**.
30 Ensure that the adjustment screw is still resting on the second-highest step of the fast idle cam, then start the engine, again without touching the throttle pedal.
31 Turn the adjustment screw using a screwdriver, until the specified fast idle speed is obtained.
32 If the cooling fan cuts in during the adjustment procedure, stop the adjustments, and continue when the cooling fan stops.
33 On completion of adjustment, stop the engine and disconnect the tachometer.
34 Fit a new tamperproof cap to the fast idle speed adjustment screw, where this is required by law.

20 Carburettor automatic choke vacuum pull-down units - removal, refitting and adjustment

Note: Refer to the warning in Section 1 before proceeding. If the main diaphragm unit is removed, a new star clip (securing the main diaphragm unit to the carburettor top cover) will be required on refitting.

Main diaphragm unit

Removal

1 Proceed as described in Section 15, paragraphs 1 to 3.
2 Disconnect the diaphragm unit vacuum pipes.
3 Using a pin punch, tap out the roll pin securing the diaphragm unit to the carburettor top cover.
4 Note the position of the bi-metal housing alignment marks as an aid to refitting (if necessary making additional marks for clarity) then remove the three securing screws, and lift off the bi-metal housing. Place the housing to one side, taking care not to strain the coolant hoses or electric choke heater wiring.
5 Remove the three securing screws securing the choke assembly to the carburettor body. Allow the choke assembly to drop down, but do not disconnect the choke linkage.
6 Remove the star clip which secures the diaphragm unit to the carburettor top cover, and withdraw the diaphragm unit.

Refitting

7 Refitting is a reversal of removal, but use a new star clip to secure the diaphragm unit to the carburettor top cover. Before refitting the airbox to the top of the carburettor, check and if necessary adjust the choke pull-down as described later in this Section.

Secondary pull-down solenoid

Removal

8 This unit operates in conjunction with the main diaphragm unit.
9 To remove the solenoid unit, first continue as described in Section 15, paragraphs 1 to 3.

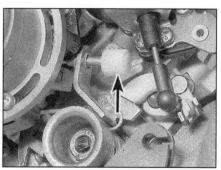

19.29 Tamperproof cap (arrowed) covering fast idle speed adjustment screw

10 Disconnect the diaphragm unit vacuum pipe.
11 Disconnect the wiring plug, then unscrew the securing screw, and withdraw the solenoid unit and its mounting bracket from the carburettor. Note that the securing screw also secures the wiring plug earth lead **(see illustration)**.

Refitting

12 Refitting is a reversal of removal, but ensure that the wiring plug earth lead is in place under the solenoid bracket securing screw.

Vacuum pull-down adjustment

13 With the airbox removed from the top of the carburettor as described in Section 15, paragraphs 2 and 3, continue as follows.
14 Note the position of the bi-metal housing alignment marks as an aid to refitting (if necessary making additional marks for clarity) then remove the three securing screws, and lift off the bi-metal housing. Place the housing to one side, taking care not to strain the coolant hoses or electric choke heater wiring.
15 Position the fast idle speed adjustment screw on the highest step of the fast idle cam, and check that the choke valve is closed.
16 Move the pull-down arm towards the diaphragm unit by pushing on the adjustment screw until resistance is felt. Hold the arm in this position.
17 Using a drill shank of appropriate diameter, or a similar item, measure the clearance between the lower side of the choke plate and the wall of the primary barrel **(see illustration)**.

20.17 Checking the vacuum pull-down gap using a twist drill

21.4 Disconnecting the coolant hose . . .

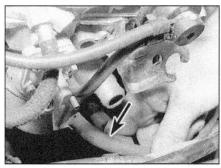

21.5 . . . and the camshaft cover breather hose (arrowed) from the inlet manifold

21.11 Withdrawing the inlet manifold

Check that the clearance is as given for the 'small' choke pull-down gap in the Specifications.
18 If adjustment is necessary, turn the adjustment screw in the appropriate direction, using an Allen key, until the clearance is correct.
19 Now push the pull-down arm towards the diaphragm unit as far as its stop, and hold the arm in this position.
20 As before, measure the clearance between the lower side of the choke plate and the wall of the primary barrel. Check that the clearance is as given for the 'large' choke pull-down gap in the Specifications.
21 If adjustment is necessary, turn the adjustment screw in the appropriate direction until the clearance is correct.
22 Connect the bi-metal spring to the choke lever, position the bi-metal housing on the choke housing, and loosely fit the securing screws. Align the marks on the bi-metal housing and the choke housing as noted during removal, then tighten the securing screws.
23 Refit the airbox to the top of the carburettor on completion.

21 Inlet manifold – removal and refitting

Note: *Refer to the warning in Section 1 before starting work. A new manifold gasket must be used on refitting.*

Removal

1 Disconnect the battery negative lead.
2 Drain the cooling system as described in Chapter 1.
3 Proceed as described in Section 13, paragraphs 2 to 7 inclusive, ignoring the reference to coolant spillage in paragraph 5.
4 Disconnect the coolant hose from the rear of the manifold **(see illustration)**.
5 Where applicable, disconnect the camshaft cover breather hose from the rear of the manifold **(see illustration)**.
6 Unscrew the union and disconnect the

brake servo vacuum hose from the manifold.
7 Disconnect the wiring from the temperature gauge sender.
8 Unscrew and remove the top alternator mounting nut and bolt.
9 Disconnect and remove the stub hose that connects the crankcase breather tube to the rear of the camshaft housing.
10 Make a final check to ensure that all relevant hoses, pipes and wires have been disconnected.
11 Unscrew the securing nuts, and withdraw the manifold from the cylinder head **(see illustration)**. Note the position of the rear engine lifting bracket, which is secured by one of the manifold nuts, and recover the manifold gasket.
12 It is possible that some of the manifold studs may be unscrewed from the cylinder head when the manifold securing nuts are unscrewed. In this event, the studs should be screwed back into the cylinder head once the manifold has been removed, using two manifold nuts locked together.
13 If desired, the carburettor can be removed from the manifold with reference to Section 13.

Refitting

14 Refitting is a reversal of removal, remembering the following points.
15 If the carburettor has been removed from the manifold, refit it using a new gasket.
16 If the alternator mounting bracket has been unbolted from the manifold, refit it before refitting the manifold, as access to the securing bolt is limited once the manifold is in place.
17 Refit the manifold using a new gasket, and ensure that the engine lifting bracket is in place under the relevant manifold nut.
18 Ensure that all relevant hoses, pipes and wires are correctly reconnected.
19 Refill the cooling system as described in Chapter 1.
20 Check the throttle cable free play and adjust if necessary, as described in Section 10.
21 If the carburettor has been disturbed, check and if necessary, adjust the idle speed and mixture, as described in Chapter 1.

22 Exhaust manifold – removal and refitting

Note: *New manifold-to-cylinder head and manifold-to-downpipe gaskets must be used on refitting.*

Removal

1 Disconnect the battery negative lead.
2 Disconnect the HT leads from the spark plugs, if necessary labelling them to ensure refitting to their correct cylinders.
3 Loosen the clamp screw and disconnect the air cleaner hot air tube from the shroud on the manifold, if applicable.
4 Remove the securing screws and withdraw the hot air shroud from the manifold.
5 Working under the manifold, unscrew and remove the four bolts securing the exhaust downpipe to the manifold.
6 Separate the downpipe from the manifold, and support with wire or string. Do not allow the front section of the exhaust system to hang under its own weight. Recover the gasket.
7 Unscrew the securing nuts, and withdraw the manifold from the cylinder head. Note the position of the front engine lifting bracket, which is secured by one of the manifold studs, and recover the manifold gasket.
8 It is possible that some of the manifold studs may be unscrewed from the cylinder head when the manifold securing nuts are unscrewed. If this happens, screw the studs back into the cylinder head once the manifold has been removed, using two manifold nuts locked together.

Refitting

9 Refit the manifold using a new gasket, and ensure that the engine lifting bracket is in place under the relevant manifold nut.
10 Reconnect the exhaust downpipe to the manifold, using a new gasket.
11 Further refitting is a reversal of removal.

23.8 Exhaust front section-to-cylinder block bracket

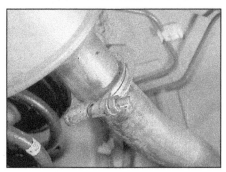

23.16 Exhaust centre section-to-rear section clamp

23 Exhaust system –
general information
and component renewal

General information

1 Periodically, the exhaust system should be checked for signs of leaks or damage. Also inspect the system rubber mountings, and renew if necessary.

2 Small holes or cracks can be repaired using exhaust repair products, such as paste or bandage.

3 The original factory-fitted exhaust system consists of four separate sections, all of which can be renewed individually.

4 Before renewing an individual section of the exhaust system, it is wise to inspect the remaining sections. If corrosion or damage is evident on more than one section of the system, it may prove more economical to renew the entire system.

5 Individual sections of the system can be renewed as follows.

Component renewal

Note: *All relevant gaskets and/or sealing rings should be renewed on refitting.*

Front section

6 Raise the vehicle, and support securely on axle stands (see "*Jacking and vehicle support*").

7 Unscrew the two securing bolts and disconnect the exhaust front section from the front expansion box at the flexible joint. Recover the sealing ring and the springs.

8 Unbolt the exhaust front section from the bracket on the cylinder block **(see illustration)**.

9 Unscrew and remove the bolts securing the downpipe to the exhaust manifold, and withdraw the exhaust front section. Recover the downpipe-to-manifold gasket, and where applicable, recover the springs from the bolts.

10 Refitting is a reversal of removal, but use a new gasket when reconnecting the downpipe to the manifold, and a new sealing ring when connecting the joint.

Front expansion box

11 Proceed as described in paragraphs 6 and 7.

12 Unscrew the securing bolts (and nuts, where applicable), and disconnect the front expansion box from the exhaust centre section. Recover the sealing ring/gasket and, where applicable, the springs.

13 Withdraw the expansion box from under the vehicle.

14 Refitting is a reversal of removal, but use new sealing rings or gaskets, as applicable.

Centre section

15 Raise the vehicle, and support securely on axle stands (see "*Jacking and vehicle support*").

16 Unscrew the clamp bolt, and disconnect the exhaust centre section from the rear section **(see illustration)**. If necessary, tap round the joint with a hammer to break the seal, and gently prise the two sections apart. Note that the end of the centre section fits inside the rear section, to form a sleeve joint.

17 Unscrew the securing bolts (and nuts, where applicable), and disconnect the exhaust centre section from the front expansion box. Recover the sealing ring/gasket and, where applicable, the springs.

18 Release the exhaust centre section from its rubber mountings on the underbody, and withdraw it from the vehicle.

19 Refitting is a reversal of removal, but use a new sealing ring when connecting the flexible joint, and lubricate the pipes with exhaust assembly paste when connecting the centre section to the rear section.

Rear section

20 Disconnect the exhaust rear section from the centre section, as described in paragraphs 15 and 16.

21 Release the exhaust rear section from its rubber mountings on the underbody, and withdraw it from the vehicle.

22 Refitting is a reversal of removal, but lubricate the pipes with exhaust assembly paste when connecting the rear section to the centre section.

Chapter 4 Part B:
Fuel and exhaust systems - fuel injection models

Contents

Degrees of difficulty

Easy, suitable for novice with little experience	**Fairly easy,** suitable for beginner with some experience	**Fairly difficult,** suitable for competent DIY mechanic	**Difficult,** suitable for experienced DIY mechanic 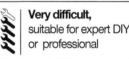	**Very difficult,** suitable for expert DIY or professional

Specifications

General

Injection system type*

C 14 NZ, X 14 NZ, C 16 NZ, X 16 SZ, X 16 SZR and C 18 NZ . . . .   Multec Central Fuel Injection (CFi)
14 SE, C 14 SE and C 16 SE . . . .   Multec M, Multi-Point Injection (MPi)
X 14 XE and X 16 XEL . . . .   Multec S (MPi)
C 18 XE . . . .   Simtec 56.0 (MPi)
C 18 XEL and X 20 XEV . . . .   Simtec 56.1 (MPi)
X 18 XE . . . .   Simtec 56.5 (MPi)
C 20 NE . . . .   Motronic M 1.5 (MPi)
C 20 XE (up to 1993) . . . .   Motronic M 2.5 (MPi)
C 20 XE (from 1993) . . . .   Motronic M 2.8 (MPi)
* For details of engine code location, see 'Buying spare parts and vehicle identification numbers'.

Fuel octane rating*

Unleaded* . . . .   95 RON (Premium)
Leaded . . . .   98 RON (Super)
*Models fitted with a catalytic converter (engine code prefixed by 'C' or 'X'), must **only** be operated on unleaded fuel.

Fuel pump

Delivery quantity . . . .   85.0 litres/hour at 12 volts

Fuel pressure

Note: *Pressure regulator vacuum hose connected.*
Models with central fuel injection (CFi) . . . .   0.76 bar
Models with multi-point injection (MPi) . . . .   3.0 bar

Torque wrench settings

	Nm	lbf ft
Camshaft sensor:		
Multec-S	5	4
Motronic 2.8 and Simtec	6	5
Camshaft sensor housing (Motronic 2.8)	15	11
Crankshaft speed/position sensor:		
Multec CFi, Multec M and Motronic 1.5	6	5
Multec S, Motronic 2.5, 2.8 and Simtec	8	6
Exhaust downpipe to manifold	25	18
Exhaust manifold	22	16
Fuel injection unit (Multec CFi)	22	16
Fuel injection unit upper section to lower section (Multec CFi)	6	5
Fuel rail securing bolts:		
Multec M	9	7
Motronic 1.5, 2.8, Multec S and Simtec	8	6
Fuel pressure regulator to housing (Multec CFi)	2.5	2
Fuel pressure regulator to fuel rail:		
Multec M and Multec S	8	6
Motronic 2.5	4	3
Idle speed control motor to housing (Multec CFi)	2.5	2
Inlet manifold:		
X 14 XE engines:		
Inlet manifold	8	6
Inlet manifold flange	20	15
X 16 XEL engines:		
Upper section of manifold	8	6
Lower section of manifold	20	15
All engines except X 14 XE and X 16 XEL	22	16
Inlet manifold air intake shroud:		
C 18 NZ and C 20 NE engines	8	6
Intake air temperature sensor to intake pipe (Multec M)	27	20
Knock sensor:		
Multec CFi and Multec S	13	10
Motronic 2.5 and 2.8, and Simtec	20	15
Oxygen sensor (refer to text)	30	22
Throttle body:		
Multec S	8	6
Multec M, Motronic and Simtec	9	7

1 General information and precautions

General information

There are four basic types of fuel injection system used in the Astra range. They are the Multec CFi, Multec MPi, Bosch Motronic MPi and the Simtec MPi. The systems are described in further detail in Section 10.

Fuel is supplied from a tank mounted under the rear of the vehicle, by an electric fuel pump mounted in the tank. The fuel passes through a filter, to the fuel injection system, which incorporates various sensors and actuators, and an Electronic Control Unit (ECU).

The inducted air passes through an air cleaner, which incorporates a paper filter element. On CFi models, the air cleaner has a vacuum-controlled air intake, supplying a blend of hot and cold air to suit the engine operating conditions.

The ECU controls both the fuel injection system and the ignition system. Combining the two into a complete engine management system. Refer to Chapter 5B for details of the ignition side of the system.

The exhaust system is similar to that described for carburettor models in Part A of this Chapter, but a catalytic converter is incorporated to reduce exhaust gas emissions.

Precautions

Refer to the precautions and warning given in Part A, Section 1 of this Chapter, but note that the fuel injection system is pressurised - extra care must be taken when disconnecting the fuel lines. When disconnecting a fuel line union or hose, loosen the union or clamp screw slowly, to avoid a sudden release of pressure which may cause the fuel to spray out.

On all fuel injection models, before disconnecting any fuel lines, the system must be depressurised by removing the fuel pump relay (see Chapter 12), and cranking the engine on the starter motor for at least 5 seconds.

After carrying out any work involving disconnection of fuel lines, it is advisable to check the connections for leaks, pressurising the system by switching the ignition on and off several times.

Electronic control units are very sensitive components, and certain precautions must be taken to avoid damage to the unit when working on a vehicle equipped with an engine management system, as follows.

When carrying out welding operations on the vehicle using electric welding equipment, the battery and alternator should be disconnected.

Although the underbonnet-mounted modules will tolerate normal underbonnet conditions, they can be adversely affected by excess heat or moisture. If using welding equipment or pressure-washing equipment near an electronic module, take care not to direct heat, or jets of water or steam, at the module. If this cannot be avoided, remove the module from the vehicle and protect its wiring plug with a plastic bag.

Before disconnecting any wiring, or removing components, always ensure that the ignition is switched off.

Do not attempt to improvise fault diagnosis procedures using a test light or multimeter, as irreparable damage could be caused to the module.

After working on fuel injection or engine management system components, ensure that all wiring is correctly reconnected before reconnecting the battery or switching on the ignition.

2 Unleaded petrol –
general information and usage

Note: *The information given in this Section is correct at the time of writing, and applies only to petrols currently available in the EC. If in any doubt as to the suitability of petrol, or if using the vehicle outside the EC, consult a Vauxhall/Opel dealer or one of the motoring organisations for advice on the petrols available, and their suitability for your vehicle.*

1 Vauxhall/Opel recommend the use of 95 RON ('Premium') unleaded petrol for all fuel injection models.

2 Certain models (see Specifications) can also be operated on 98 RON ('Super' or 'Super Plus') unleaded petrol, by reversing the position of the octane coding plug in its connector on the battery tray **(see illustration)**. Where applicable, the plug is marked '95' on one side, which corresponds to the position for use with 95 RON (Premium) unleaded petrol, and '98' on the other side, which corresponds to the position for use with 98 RON ('Super' or 'Super Plus') unleaded petrol.

3 If necessary (for example, when travelling in territories where 95 RON unleaded petrol is not available), certain models (see Specifications) can be operated on 91 RON unleaded petrol by using a special octane coding plug available from Vauxhall/Opel dealers.

4 Leaded petrol **must not** be used in fuel injection models, as irreparable (and expensive) damage will be caused to the catalytic converter.

3 Air cleaner assembly components –
removal and refitting

Airbox – models with Multec CFi fuel system

Removal

1 Disconnect the breather hose from the airbox.

2 Disconnect the two vacuum pipes from the airbox, noting their locations.

3 Loosen the clamp screw, and disconnect the air trunking from the end of the airbox.

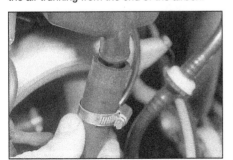

3.10 Disconnecting the hose from the airbox - Motronic M 2.5 models

2.2 Octane coding plug - shown set for 95 RON petrol

4 Remove the two securing screws, and lift the airbox from the fuel injection unit. Recover the sealing ring.

Refitting

5 Refitting is a reversal of removal, bearing in mind the following points.

6 Inspect the sealing ring for damage or deterioration, and renew if necessary. Ensure that the sealing ring locates correctly in the groove in the base of the airbox.

7 Reconnect the vacuum pipes as noted before removal.

Airbox – models with Motronic fuel system

Note: *Sealing cement (GM P/N 90293725, or equivalent) will be required to coat the sealing ring seating area in the airbox on refitting.*

Removal

8 Loosen the clamp screw securing the air trunking to the left-hand side of the air flow meter.

9 Using an Allen key or hexagon bit, unscrew the four bolts securing the airbox to the throttle body **(see illustration)**.

10 Lift the airbox from the top of the throttle body, and disconnect the hose from the base of the airbox **(see illustration)**.

11 Withdraw the airbox, and recover the sealing ring from the base of the airbox if it is loose.

Refitting

12 Before beginning refitting, remove the sealing ring from the base of the airbox, if not already done **(see illustration)**.

13 Examine the sealing ring, and if it is worn or damaged, renew it.

14 Thoroughly clean the sealing ring seating

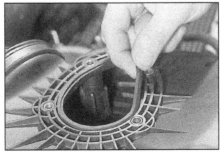

3.12 Removing the sealing ring from the base of the airbox - Motronic M 2.5 models

3.9 Unscrewing an airbox securing bolt - Motronic M 2.5 models

area in the airbox, then liberally coat the seating face with a cement (GM P/N 90293725, or equivalent).

15 Fit the sealing ring to the airbox, ensuring that it is correctly seated, then refit the assembly using a reversal of the removal procedure.

Air cleaner assembly

Removal

16 Disconnect the air hose from the airbox or the throttle body, as applicable.

17 Note that on some models, the air mass meter is attached to the air cleaner cover, and the air temperature sensor is located in the air trunking. Disconnect the battery negative lead, and disconnect the relevant sensor wiring plug when removing the air cleaner or the air trunking.

18 Remove the air cleaner filter element, as described in Chapter 1.

19 Slacken the air cleaner assembly securing nuts (one front and one rear), and pull the assembly from the body panel.

Refitting

20 Refitting is a reversal of removal.

Air cleaner resonator box

Removal

21 On certain models, the base of the air cleaner housing clips into a resonator box mounted under the front wing.

22 Remove the air cleaner assembly as described previously in this Section.

23 For easier access, remove the front wheel arch liner, (see Chapter 11, Section 25).

24 Remove the single securing screw, and lower the resonator box from the wheel arch **(see illustration)**.

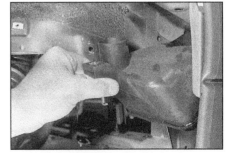

3.24 Withdrawing the air cleaner resonator box from under the wheel arch

4.9 Plastic cover removed to expose fuel pump - Hatchback model

Refitting

25 Refitting is a reversal of removal. However, ensure that there is a firm connection between the resonator and the lower part of the air cleaner housing.

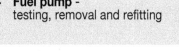

4 Fuel pump - testing, removal and refitting

Note: *Refer to the precautions given in Section 1 before starting work. A new gasket must be used on refitting the pump, and sealing compound will be required to coat the securing bolt threads.*

Saloon and Hatchback models

Testing

1 If the pump is functioning, it should be possible to hear it 'buzzing' by listening under the rear of the vehicle when the ignition is switched on. Unless the engine is started, the fuel pump should switch off after approximately one second. If the noise produced is excessive, this may be due to a faulty pump.
2 If the pump appears to have failed completely, check the wiring to the pump, and check the appropriate fuse and relay.

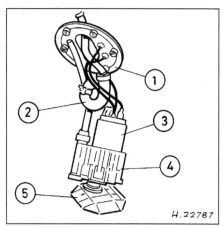

4.20 Fuel pump assembly

1 Mounting plate   *4 Rubber sleeve*
2 Fuel hose   *5 Fuel filter*
3 Pump

3 To test the performance of the pump, special equipment is required, and it is recommended that any suspected faults are referred to a Vauxhall/Opel dealer.

Removal

4 Depressurize the fuel system by removing the fuel pump relay (see Chapter 12), and cranking the engine on the starter motor for at least 5 seconds.
5 Disconnect the battery negative lead.
6 Siphon out any remaining fuel in the tank through the filler pipe. Siphon the fuel into a clean metal container which can be sealed.
7 Fold the rear sear cushions forwards.
8 Lift the carpet panel on the right-hand side of the floor to expose the plastic fuel pump cover.
9 Carefully prise the plastic cover from the floor to expose the fuel pump **(see illustration)**.
10 Disconnect the pump wiring plug.
11 Release the hose clip, and carefully disconnect the fuel hose from the top of the pump. Be prepared for fuel spillage. Clamp or plug the open end of the hose to prevent dirt ingress and further fuel spillage.
12 Unscrew the six securing bolts and washers, and carefully withdraw the pump assembly from the fuel tank. Again, be prepared for the release of fuel, and take precautions.
13 If required, the fuel pump can be detached from the assembly for renewal as follows.
14 Pull the fuel filter from the bottom of the pump.
15 Release the hose clip, and disconnect the fuel hose from the top of the pump.
16 Take note of the positions of the two pump wires to aid correct refitting, then using a soldering iron, de-solder the two wires from the top of the pump.
17 Carefully slide the pump from its rubber mounting sleeve.

Refitting

18 Refitting is a reversal of removal, remembering the following points.
19 If the pump has been detached from the assembly, make sure that the wires are securely soldered to the pump in their correct locations when reassembling.
20 Inspect the filter at the bottom of the pump for excessive contamination or blockage, and renew if necessary **(see illustration)**.
21 Use a new pump gasket.
22 Clean the threads of the pump securing bolts thoroughly, and coat them with a sealing compound before refitting.

Estate and Van models

Testing

23 Proceed as described in paragraphs 1 to 3.

Removal

24 Chock the front wheels, then jack up the

rear of the vehicle and support securely on axle stands (see "*Jacking and vehicle support*").
25 The fuel pump is located in the front end of the fuel tank, under the vehicle **(see illustration)**.
26 Proceed as described in paragraphs 10 to 17 inclusive.

Refitting

27 Proceed as described in paragraphs 18 to 22 inclusive.

5 Fuel gauge sender unit - removal and refitting

Refer to Section 6 in Part A of this Chapter.

6 Fuel filter – removal and refitting

Refer to '*Fuel filter renewal*' in Chapter 1.

7 Fuel tank – removal and refitting

Proceed as described in Section 9 in Part A of this Chapter, but disconnect the fuel hose and the wiring plug from the fuel pump with reference to Section 4.

8 Throttle cable – removal, refitting and adjustment

Removal and refitting

1 Refer to Section 10 in Part A of this Chapter, but note the following.
2 Where applicable, ignore the reference to removing the airbox.
3 For 'carburettor' substitute 'throttle body' or 'fuel injection unit' as applicable, and note that the cable bracket is bolted to the inlet manifold.

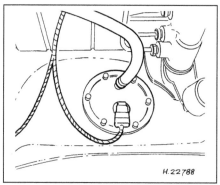

4.25 Fuel pump location in fuel tank - Estate and Van models

4 On some models, the throttle cable end connects to a balljoint on the throttle valve lever, and is retained by a clip. The cable is also retained by a grommet that locates in a bracket attached to the inlet manifold **(see illustrations)**.

Adjustment

5 Refer to Section 10 in Part A of this Chapter, but for 'carburettor' substitute 'throttle body' or 'fuel injection unit', as applicable.

9 Throttle pedal –
removal and refitting

Refer to Section 11 in Part A of this Chapter.

10 Fuel systems –
general information

Multec CFi

1 The injection system is under the overall control of the Multec engine management system which also controls the ignition system (see Chapter 5B).

2 Fuel is supplied from the rear-mounted fuel tank by an electric pump mounted in the tank, via a fuel filter to the Multec injection unit. A fuel pressure regulator mounted on the injection unit maintains a constant fuel pressure to the fuel injector. Excess fuel is returned from the regulator to the tank.

3 The fuel injection unit (resembling a carburettor) houses the throttle valve, idle speed control motor, throttle position sensor, fuel injector and a pressure regulator.

4 The duration of the electrical pulse, supplied to the fuel injector, determines the quantity of fuel injected. The pulse duration is computed by the ECU, based on the information received from the following sensors **(see illustration)**.

a) *Throttle position sensor (all engines).*
b) *Idle speed control motor (all engines).*
c) *Coolant temperature sensor (all engines).*
d) *Oxygen sensor (all engines).*
e) *Manifold absolute pressure (MAP) sensor (C14 NZ, X 14 NZ, C 16 NZ and C 18 NZ engines).*
f) *Distributor (C 14 NZ, X 14 NZ and C 16 NZ engines).*
g) *Crankshaft speed/position sensor (X 16 SZ, X 16 SZR and C 18 NZ engines).*
h) *Knock sensor (X 16 SZ and X 16 SZR).*

5 A catalytic converter is fitted to reduce harmful exhaust gas emissions.

Multec M MPi

6 The injection system is under the overall control of the Multec engine management system which also controls the ignition system (see Chapter 5B).

8.4a Releasing the throttle cable balljoint clip . . .

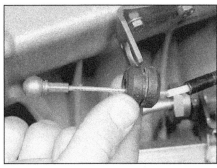

8.4b . . . and releasing the cable grommet from its bracket – 1.6 litre SOHC engine

7 Fuel is supplied from the rear-mounted fuel tank, through a fuel filter and a pressure regulator, to the fuel rail. Excess fuel is returned from the regulator to the tank. The fuel rail acts as a reservoir for the four fuel injectors. Fuel is then injected into the cylinder inlet tracts, upstream of the inlet valves. The fuel injectors operate in pairs. The injectors for cylinder Nos 1 and 2 operate simultaneously and similarly the injectors for cylinder Nos 3 and 4 operate simultaneously.

8 The duration of the electrical pulses to the

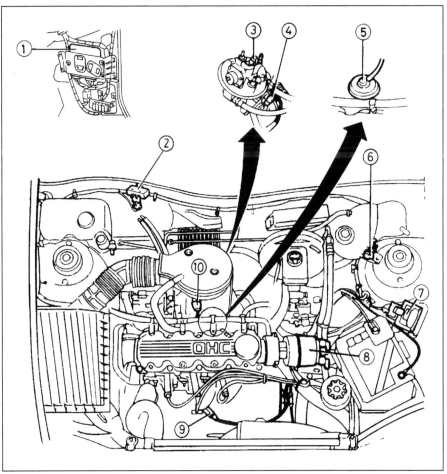

10.4 Multec CFi single-point fuel injection system

1 *Electronic control unit (in right-hand footwell)*
2 *Manifold absolute pressure (MAP) sensor*
3 *Fuel injector*
4 *Throttle position sensor*
5 *Exhaust gas recirculation valve (1.6 litre model only)*
6 *Octane rating plug (see Chapter 5)*
7 *Ignition coil*
8 *Distributor*
9 *Exhaust gas oxygen sensor*
10 *Idle speed control motor*

fuel injectors determines the quantity of fuel injected. The pulse duration is computed by the ECU, based on the information received from the following sensors **(see illustration)**.

a) Manifold absolute pressure (MAP) sensor (all engines).
b) Throttle position sensor (all engines).
c) Idle speed control motor (all engines).
d) Intake air temperature sensor (all engines).
e) Coolant temperature sensor (all engines).
f) Oxygen sensor (all engines except 14 SE).
g) Distributor (14 SE engines, and pre-1993 C 14 SE engines).
h) Crankshaft speed/position sensor (1993-on C 14 SE engines, and C 16 SE engines).

9 Information from the throttle position sensor is also used to cut off the fuel supply on the overrun, thus improving fuel economy and reducing exhaust gas emissions.
10 There is no provision for the direct adjustment of idle speed.
11 A catalytic converter is fitted to all except 14 SE engine models to reduce harmful exhaust gas emissions.

Multec-S MPi

12 Apart from the location of the components, this system is basically the same as the previously-described Multec M system. The main difference is that each fuel injector is triggered individually, in sequence, just before the relevant inlet valves open.
13 In addition to the components listed for the Multec M system, the system also incorporates a knock sensor which detects pre-ignition (pinking), and a camshaft sensor.

Motronic MPi

14 The Bosch Motronic system is available in three versions depending on model. Motronic M 1.5 is used on C 20 NE models, Motronic M 2.5 is used on pre-1993 C 20 XE models and Motronic M 2.8 is used on C 20 XE models from 1993. The system is under the overall control of the Motronic engine management system, which also controls the ignition system (see Chapter 5B).
15 Fuel is supplied from the rear-mounted fuel tank by an electric pump, mounted in the tank, through a fuel filter and a fuel pressure regulator, to a fuel rail. Excess fuel is returned from the regulator to the tank. The fuel rail acts as a reservoir for the four fuel injectors, which inject fuel into the cylinder inlet tracts, upstream of the inlet valves. On C 20 NE models, the fuel injectors receive an electrical pulse once per crankshaft revolution, which operates all four injectors simultaneously. On C 20 XE models, sequential fuel injection is used. Each injector receives an individual electrical pulse, allowing the four injectors to operate independently, which enables finer control of the fuel supply to each cylinder. The duration of the electrical pulse determines the quantity of fuel injected and pulse duration is computed by the Motronic ECU, based on the information received from the various sensors **(see illustrations)**.

a) Air mass meter (all engines).
b) Intake air temperature sensor (all engines).
c) Throttle position sensor (all engines).
d) Coolant temperature sensor (all engines).
e) Knock sensor (C 20 XE engines).
f) Distributor (C 20 NE engines).
g) Crankshaft speed/position sensor (pre-1993 C 20 XE engines).
h) Camshaft position sensor (C 20 XE engines from 1993).
i) Oxygen sensor (all engines).

16 The throttle body contains two throttle valves which open progressively, allowing high torque at part throttle, and high-speed 'breathing' capacity at full-throttle.
17 Some models are fitted with electronic traction control (ETC, or TC). This system operates by modulating a throttle valve to control engine power during wheelspin conditions. The traction control throttle valve operates independently from the Motronic system, and further details can be found in Section 22.
18 A catalytic converter is fitted to reduce harmful exhaust gas emissions.

Simtec MPi

19 This system operates in a similar manner to the Motronic systems described previously, but is slightly more advanced.
20 The Simtec engine management system controls the fuel and ignition systems using information from the following sensors.

a) Air mass meter (all engines).
b) Intake air temperature sensor (all engines).
c) Throttle position sensor (all engines).
d) Coolant temperature sensor (all engines).

10.8 Multec M MPi multi-point fuel injection system

1 Electronic control unit (in right-hand footwell)
2 Manifold absolute pressure (MAP) sensor
3 Fuel tank vent valve
4 Throttle position sensor
5 Idle speed control motor
6 Octane rating plug
7 Fuel pressure regulator
8 Fuel injectors
9 Distributor
10 Intake air temperature sensor
11 Exhaust gas oxygen sensor
12 Crankshaft speed/position sensor

10.15a Motronic M 1.5 fuel injection system components

1 Air flow meter (hot film mass)
2 Intake air temperature sensor
3 Throttle position sensor
4 Idle speed control valve
5 Distributor
6 Fuel tank vent valve
7 Coolant temperature sensor

10.15b Motronic M 2.5 fuel injection system components

1 Electronic control unit (in right-hand footwell)
2 Air flow meter (hot wire mass)
3 Fuel pressure regulator
4 Throttle body
5 Fuel tank vent valve
6 Fuel injection wiring harness housing
7 Coolant temperature sensor
8 Knock sensor
9 Idle speed control valve
10 Crankshaft speed/position sensor

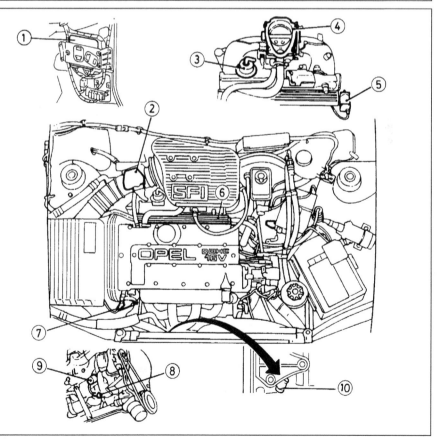

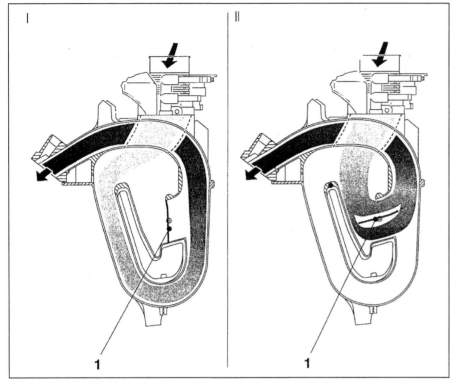

10.22 Variable tract inlet manifold – Simtec 56.5 system

I Long intake path   *II Short intake path*   *1 Switchover valve*

e) *Crankshaft speed/position sensor (all engines).*
f) *Camshaft position sensor (all engines).*
g) *Oxygen sensor (all engines).*

21 A catalytic converter is fitted to reduce harmful exhaust gas emissions.

22 On 1.8 litre DOHC engines fitted with the Simtec 56.5 system, a variable tract inlet manifold is fitted to help increase torque output at low engine speeds. Each manifold tract is fitted with a valve. The valve is controlled by the ECU via a solenoid valve and vacuum diaphragm unit **(see illustration)**.

23 At low engine speeds (below approximately 3600 rpm) the valves remain closed. The air entering the engine is then forced to take the long inlet path through the manifold which leads to an increase in engine torque output.

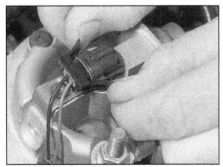

12.4 Releasing the fuel injector wiring plug retaining lugs – Multec CFi models

24 At higher engine speeds, the ECU switches the solenoid valve which then allows vacuum to act on the diaphragm unit. The diaphragm unit is linked to the valve assemblies and opens up each of the four valves, allowing the air passing through the manifold to take the shorter inlet path which is more suited to higher engine speeds.

11 Fuel injection system components - testing

1 Apart from the basic electrical tests outlined in Chapter 12, and the ignition system checks given in Chapter 5B, the individual fuel system components cannot easily be tested by the home mechanic.

2 In most cases, if a fault does occur, the ECU will allow the engine to run. It will use a back-up programme of stored values to keep the engine running, albeit at reduced efficiency and possible driveability. While the fault might be evident to the driver, it could easily be masked by the back-up programme in such a way that fault diagnosis becomes very difficult.

3 The ECUs have a self-analysis function, which stores fault codes in the module memory, and these fault codes can be decoded using specialist test equipment.

4 If a fault occurs (which may be indicated by the illumination of the engine warning light on the instrument panel), and the cause is not

immediately obvious, it is worth carrying out the checks described in the following paragraphs. If these checks do not resolve the problem, the best course of action is to have the complete system checked using a suitable fault code reader or specialist diagnostic equipment.

5 If a fault arises, first check that it is not due to poor maintenance. Check that the air cleaner element is clean and that the spark plugs are in good condition and correctly gapped. Ensure also that the crankcase ventilation system hoses are clear of obstructions and undamaged (see Part C of this Chapter) and that the throttle cable is correctly adjusted (see Section 8).

6 If the engine is running very roughly, carry out a compression test (see Chapter 2A) and remember that one of the hydraulic valve lifters may be faulty, producing an incorrect valve clearance.

7 If the problem is thought to be due to a dirty or blocked fuel injector, try using a fuel injector cleaning product (which is normally added to the contents of the fuel tank) according to the product manufacturer's instructions.

8 If the fault persists, check the ignition system components (as far as possible), as described in Chapter 5B.

9 If the fault is still not eliminated, work methodically through the system, checking all fuses, wiring connectors, wiring, vacuum hoses, looking for any signs of poor connections, damage, dirt, leaks or other faults.

10 Once the system components have been checked for signs of obvious faults, take the vehicle to a suitably equipped Vauxhall/Opel dealer for the full system to be checked using the specialist diagnostic equipment.

11 Do not attempt to check any of the components, particularly the ECU, using anything other than the correct test equipment, as serious (and possibly expensive!) damage to the components could result.

12 Fuel injection system components (Multec CFi single-point) – removal and refitting

Fuel injection unit

Note: *Refer to the precautions given in Section 1 before starting work. All gaskets and seals must be renewed on refitting, and locking compound will be required to coat the fuel injection unit securing nut threads.*

Removal

1 Depressurise the fuel system by removing the fuel pump relay (see Chapter 12), and cranking the engine on the starter motor for a minimum of 5 seconds.

2 Disconnect the battery negative lead.

3 Remove the airbox from the top of the fuel injection unit, as described in Section 3.

4 Release the securing lugs, and disconnect the wiring plug from the fuel injector **(see illustration)**.

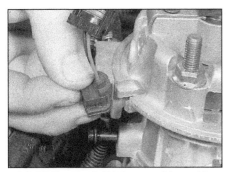

12.5 Sliding the fuel injector wiring rubber grommet from the fuel injection unit – Multec CFi models

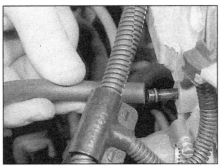

12.9 Disconnecting the MAP sensor hose from the fuel injection unit – Multec CFi models

12.10 Disconnecting the operating rod (arrowed) from the throttle valve lever- Multec CFi models

5 Remove the rubber seal from the top of the fuel injection unit (if not already done), then slide the fuel injector wiring rubber grommet from the slot in the side of the fuel injection unit **(see illustration)**. Move the wiring to one side.

6 Disconnect the wiring plugs from the idle speed control motor and the throttle position sensor.

7 Disconnect the fuel feed and return hoses from the fuel injection unit, noting their locations to aid refitting. Be prepared for fuel spillage, and take adequate fire precautions. Clamp or plug the open ends of the hoses to minimise further fuel loss.

8 Disconnect the vacuum hoses from the fuel injection unit, noting their locations and routing to ensure correct refitting.

9 Disconnect the MAP sensor hose from the rear of the fuel injection unit **(see illustration)**.

10 Disconnect the operating rod from the throttle valve lever **(see illustration)**.

11 Make a final check to ensure that all relevant hoses and wires have been disconnected to facilitate removal of the fuel injection unit.

12 Unscrew the two securing nuts and recover the washers, and recover the sleeves that fit over the manifold studs, then carefully lift the fuel injection unit from the inlet manifold **(see illustrations)**. Recover the gasket.

13 The fuel injection unit may now be split into its upper and lower sections by removing the two securing screws **(see illustration)**. The vacuum hose flange and the fuel hose unions can also be removed if desired.

Refitting

14 Refitting is a reversal of removal, bearing in mind the following points.

15 Where applicable, when reassembling the two sections of the fuel injection unit, use a new gasket. Similarly, where applicable use a new gasket when refitting the vacuum hose flange. If the fuel hose unions have been removed, make sure that the washers are in place when refitting.

16 Refit the fuel injection unit to the manifold using a new gasket, ensuring that the sleeves are in place over the manifold studs. Coat the

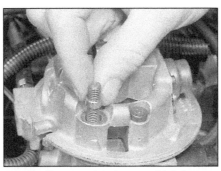

12.12a Recover the sleeves which fit over the manifold studs – Multec CFi models

threads of the securing nuts with a thread-locking compound before fitting. Ensure that the washers are in place under the nuts.

17 Ensure that all hoses are reconnected and routed correctly, as noted before removal. Note that the vacuum hoses should be connected as shown **(see illustration)**.

18 On completion, check and if necessary adjust the throttle cable freeplay as described in Section 8.

Fuel injector

Note: *Refer to the precautions given in Section 1 before starting work. If the original injector is being refitted, new O-rings must be used. Suitable thread-locking compound will be required to coat the clamp bracket screw threads.*

12.13 Removing a fuel injection unit upper-to-lower section securing screw – Multec CFi models

12.12b Lifting the fuel injection unit from the inlet manifold – Multec CFi models

Removal

19 Depressurise the fuel system by removing the fuel pump relay (see Chapter 12), and cranking the engine on the starter motor for a minimum of 5 seconds.

20 Disconnect the battery negative lead.

21 Remove the airbox from the top of the fuel injection unit, as described in Section 3.

22 Squeeze the securing lugs, and disconnect the wiring plug from the fuel injector.

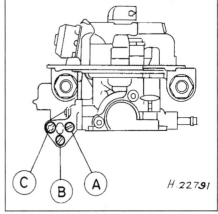

12.17 Vacuum hose connections at fuel injection unit – Multec CFi models

A Intake air temperature control
B Exhaust gas recirculation (where applicable)
C Fuel tank vent valve (where applicable)

12.23a Remove the securing screw . . .

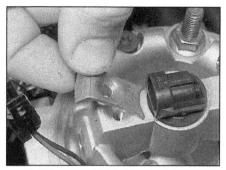

12.23b . . . and withdraw the injector clamp bracket – Multec CFi models

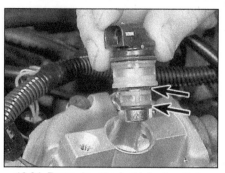

12.24 Removing the fuel injector. Note O-rings (arrowed) – Multec CFi models

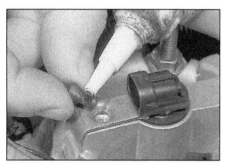

12.28 Coat the fuel injector clamp bracket screw with locking compound – Multec CFi models

12.32 Removing the fuel pressure regulator cover – Multec CFi models

23 Remove the Torx type securing screw, and withdraw the injector clamp bracket **(see illustrations)**.
24 Carefully withdraw the injector from the fuel injection unit **(see illustration)**.

Refitting

25 If the original injector is to be refitted, renew the two O-rings at the base of the injector.
26 Carefully install the injector in the fuel injection unit, with the wiring socket pointing towards the clamp bracket screw hole.
27 Refit the injector clamp bracket, ensuring that it engages correctly with the injector (the bracket should engage with the slot below the wiring socket in the injector).
28 Coat the threads of the clamp bracket screw with a thread-locking compound, then refit and tighten the screw **(see illustration)**.
29 Reconnect the injector wiring plug, and reconnect the battery negative lead.

Fuel pressure regulator

Note: *Refer to the precautions given in Section 1 before starting work. The pressure regulator diaphragm must be renewed whenever the regulator cover is removed. Thread-locking compound will be required to coat the regulator cover securing bolts.*

Removal

30 Depressurise the fuel system by removing the fuel pump relay (see Chapter 12), and cranking the engine on the starter motor for a minimum of 5 seconds.
31 Remove the airbox from the top of the fuel injection unit, as described in Section 3.
32 Unscrew the four Torx type pressure regulator cover securing bolts, and carefully withdraw the cover **(see illustration)**.
33 Recover the spring seat and spring assembly, and lift out the diaphragm **(see illustration)**.

Refitting

34 Refitting is a reversal of removal, but ensure that the diaphragm is correctly located in the groove in the fuel injection unit, and coat the threads of the cover securing bolts with a thread locking compound before fitting.

Throttle position sensor

Note: *Thread-locking compound will be required to coat the sensor securing bolt threads on refitting.*

Removal

35 Disconnect the battery negative lead.
36 Remove the airbox from the top of the fuel injection unit, as described in Section 3.
37 Disconnect the wiring plug from the throttle position sensor **(see illustration)**.

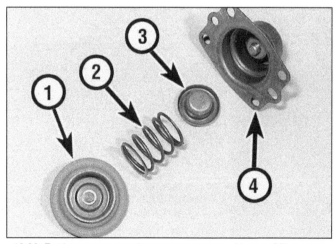

12.33 Fuel pressure regulator components – Multec CFi models

1 Diaphragm   2 Spring   3 Spring seat   4 Cover

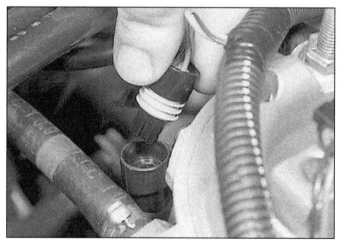

12.37 Disconnecting the throttle position sensor wiring plug – Multec CFi models

12.38 Removing the throttle position sensor – Multec CFi models

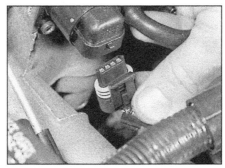

12.44 Disconnecting the wiring plug from the idle speed control motor – Multec CFi models

12.45a Remove the securing screws . . .

12.45b . . . and withdraw the idle speed control motor. Note O-ring (arrowed) – Multec CFi models

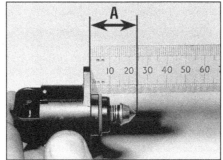

12.47 Measure the distance (A) between the end of the idle speed control motor piston and the end face of the motor body flange – Multec CFi models

12.50 Inlet manifold pressure sensor location (water deflector lifted for access) - Multec CFi models

38 Remove the two securing screws, and withdraw the sensor from its housing in the fuel injection unit **(see illustration)**.

Refitting

39 Ensure that the throttle valve is closed, then refit the sensor to the housing, making sure that the sensor arm is correctly engaged with the throttle valve shaft.
40 Coat the sensor securing bolts with thread-locking compound, then insert and tighten them.
41 Further refitting is a reversal of removal.

Idle speed control motor

Note: *A new O-ring must be used on refitting, and thread-locking compound will be required to coat the motor securing bolt threads.*

Removal

42 Disconnect the battery negative lead.
43 Remove the airbox from the top of the fuel injection unit, as described in Section 3.
44 Release the securing lugs, and disconnect the wiring plug from the idle speed control motor **(see illustration)**.
45 Remove the two securing screws, and withdraw the motor from the side of the fuel injection unit. Where applicable, recover the O-ring seal **(see illustrations)**.

Refitting

46 Refitting is a reversal of removal, bearing in mind the following points.
47 To avoid damaging the housing during

refitting, the distance between the end of the motor piston and the end face of the motor body flange should not be greater than 28.0 mm **(see illustration)**. Measure the distance shown, and if greater than specified, carefully push the piston into the motor body as far as its stop.
48 Refit the motor using a new O-ring seal, with the wiring socket facing downwards.
49 Coat the threads of the motor securing bolts with a thread-locking compound before fitting.

Manifold absolute pressure (MAP) sensor

Removal

50 The sensor is located on the engine compartment bulkhead, under the edge of the water deflector **(see illustration)**.
51 Disconnect the battery negative lead.
52 Lift up the edge of the water deflector for access to the sensor.
53 Disconnect the sensor wiring plug and the vacuum pipe.
54 Pull the sensor upwards to release it from its bracket, and withdraw it from the vehicle.

Refitting

55 Refitting is a reversal of removal.

Coolant temperature sensor

Note: *A new sealing ring must be used on refitting. On Multec-S models, easier access to this sensor can be gained with the air cleaner assembly was removed.*

Removal

56 The sensor is located in the rear right-hand side of the inlet manifold.
57 Disconnect the battery negative lead.
58 Partially drain the cooling system, as described in Chapter 1.
59 Disconnect the sensor wiring plug **(see illustration)**.
60 Unscrew the sensor, and withdraw it. Recover the sealing ring where applicable.

Refitting

61 Refitting is a reversal of removal, but use a new sealing ring.
62 On completion, top-up the cooling system as described in 'Weekly checks'.

12.59 Disconnecting the coolant temperature sensor wiring plug – 1.4 litre SOHC engine

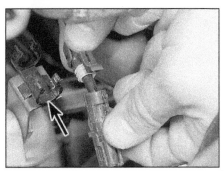

12.64 Disconnecting the oxygen sensor wiring connector. Note connector bracket location on transmission (arrowed) – 1.4 litre SOHC engine

Oxygen sensor

Note: *If the original sensor is to be re-used, the threads must be lubricated with special grease (Vauxhall/Opel Part No 90295397) on refitting. Do not expose the sensor to fuel or silicone. This sensor is also known as a 'Lambda' sensor.*

Removal

63 Start the engine, and run it until it reaches normal operating temperature. Stop the engine.
64 Disconnect the battery negative lead, then trace the wiring back from the oxygen sensor, and disconnect the sensor wiring plug, noting its location **(see illustration)**.
65 Using a spanner, unscrew the sensor from the exhaust manifold.

 Warning: It is advisable to wear gloves, as the exhaust system will be extremely hot.

66 Withdraw the sensor and its wiring, taking care not to burn the wiring on the exhaust system. Take note of the routing of the wiring.

Refitting

67 The sensor must be refitted with the engine and exhaust system still at normal operating temperature.
68 If a new sensor is being fitted, it will be supplied with the threads coated in a special grease, to prevent the sensor seizing in the exhaust manifold.
69 If the original sensor is being refitted, clean the threads carefully. The threads must

12.75 Unscrewing the crankshaft speed/position sensor securing screw (engine mounting bracket and power steering pump removed) – 1.8 litre SOHC engine

be coated with special grease (Vauxhall/Opel Part No 90295397). Use only the specified grease, which consists of liquid graphite and glass beads. As the exhaust system heats up, the graphite will burn off, leaving the glass beads between the threads to prevent the sensor from seizing.
70 Refitting is a reversal of removal.

Crankshaft speed/position sensor – 1.8 litre engines

Note: *A new sealing ring may be required on refitting.*

Removal

71 The sensor is located on the exhaust manifold side of the engine, in the lower cylinder block, behind the oil pump.
72 Disconnect the battery negative lead.
73 Where applicable, release the relevant outer timing belt cover securing clips, and unclip the sensor wiring from the timing belt cover.
74 Disconnect the sensor wiring connector, noting its location.
75 Unscrew the securing screw, and withdraw the sensor from the cylinder block **(see illustration)**.

Refitting

76 Examine the sensor sealing ring, and renew if necessary **(see illustration)**.
77 Refitting is a reversal of removal, ensuring that the sensor wiring is correctly located on

the timing belt cover (where applicable), and that the wiring connector is correctly located.

Electronic control unit (ECU)

Note: *On early 1.6 and 1.8 litre models, the control unit consists of two components - the basic control unit, and the programme memory, which clips into a circuit board in the control unit. The two components can be renewed independently, if a fault is suspected, but the source of the fault can only be established using specialist test equipment available to a Vauxhall/Opel dealer. On 1.4 litre models, the two components cannot be separated, and the complete unit must be renewed if a fault is suspected.*

Removal

78 The control unit is located behind the right-hand footwell side/sill trim panel.
79 Disconnect the battery negative lead.
80 Remove the footwell side/sill trim panel, as described in Chapter 11, Section 30.
81 Where applicable, unscrew the two securing nuts, and pull the wiring plug bracket from the footwell to allow sufficient access to enable the control unit to be withdrawn **(see illustration)**.
82 On certain left-hand-drive models, it may be necessary to remove the glovebox (see Chapter 11, Section 32) to allow access to the control unit.
83 Reach up into the footwell and locate the control unit.
84 Unscrew or unclip (as applicable) the control unit bracket, then lower the bracket, and disconnect the wiring plug(s) from the control unit. Take care not to touch the plug contacts.
85 Unclip the control unit from the bracket, noting its orientation.
86 On early 1.6 and 1.8 litre models, the programme memory can be unclipped from its circuit board in the control unit, after removing the cover from the rear of the control unit. The cover is secured by two screws **(see illustrations)**.

Refitting

87 Refitting is a reversal of removal. Ensure that the wiring plug(s) is/are securely reconnected.

12.76 Examine the crankshaft speed/position sensor O-ring

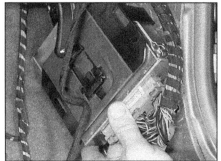

12.81 Lowering the fuel injection control unit and bracket assembly from the footwell

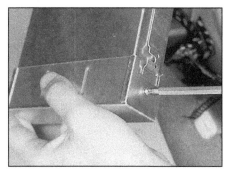

12.86a Remove the control unit rear cover . . .

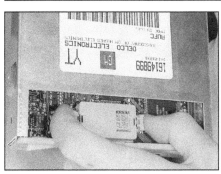

12.86b . . . for access to the programme memory

Fuel pump relay

Removal

88 The fuel pump relay is located in the engine compartment fuse/relay box.
89 Unclip the cover from the fuse/relay box. The fuel pump relay is coloured purple. Ensure that the ignition is switched off, then pull out the relay.

Refitting

90 Refitting is a reversal of removal.

Exhaust gas recirculation system components (1.6 and 1.8 litre models)

91 Refer to Part C of this Chapter.

Fuel evaporation control system components

92 Refer to Part C of this Chapter.

---

13 Fuel injection system components (Multec M multipoint) – removal and refitting

Throttle body

Note: A new gasket must be used on refitting.

Removal

1 Disconnect the battery negative lead.
2 Loosen the clamp screws securing the air trunking to the throttle body and the air cleaner cover, then withdraw the air trunking (see illustration).

13.4 Disconnecting the fuel tank vent valve vacuum hose from the throttle body - Multec M MPi models

13.2 Loosening an air trunking clamp screw

3 Disconnect the camshaft cover breather hoses from the throttle body (see illustration).
4 Disconnect the fuel tank vent valve vacuum hose from the throttle body (see illustration).
5 Disconnect the manifold absolute pressure (MAP) sensor vacuum hose from the throttle body.
6 Disconnect the coolant hoses from the throttle body. Be prepared for coolant spillage, and clamp or plug the open ends of the hoses, to prevent further coolant loss.
7 Disconnect the wiring plugs from the throttle position sensor and the idle speed control motor.
8 Release the securing clip, then disconnect the throttle cable end balljoint from the throttle valve lever.
9 Slide the throttle cable grommet from the bracket on the inlet manifold, then unhook the throttle return spring from the bracket. If necessary, unhook the spring from the grommet in the throttle valve linkage, and lay the spring to one side out of the way (in this case, note the orientation of the spring to enable correct refitting), (see illustration).
10 Make a final check to ensure that all relevant hoses and wires have been disconnected to facilitate removal of the throttle body.
11 Unscrew the four securing nuts, and withdraw the throttle body from the inlet manifold.
12 Recover the gasket.
13 The throttle position sensor and the idle speed control motor can be removed from the throttle body as described later in this Section.

Refitting

14 Refitting is a reversal of removal, bearing in mind the following points.
15 Where applicable, refit the throttle position sensor and/or the idle speed control motor, as described later in this Section.
16 Thoroughly clean the mating faces of the throttle body and inlet manifold, and refit the throttle body using a new gasket.
17 Ensure that all wires and hoses are correctly reconnected and routed.
18 Check and if necessary top-up the coolant level, as described in 'Weekly checks'.
19 On completion, check and if necessary adjust the throttle cable freeplay as described in Section 8.

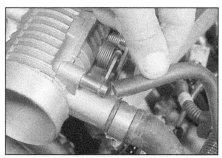

13.3 Disconnecting a camshaft cover breather hose from the throttle body - Multec M MPi models

Fuel injectors

Note: Refer to the precautions given in Section 1 before starting work. The seals at both ends of the fuel injector(s) must be renewed on refitting.

Removal

20 Depressurise the fuel system by removing the fuel pump relay (see Chapter 12), and cranking the engine on the starter motor for a minimum of 5 seconds.
21 Disconnect the battery negative lead.
22 Place a wad of rag beneath the fuel pipe union at the fuel pressure regulator and then relieve and remaining pressure in the fuel system by slowly loosening the fuel pipe union. Two open-ended spanners will be required so one can be used to counterhold the regulator as the union is loosened. Be prepared for fuel spillage, and take adequate fire precautions. Tighten the union when the pressure has been released.
23 Disconnect the wiring plugs from the fuel injectors, then move the wiring clear of the fuel rail (see illustration overleaf).
24 Disconnect the vacuum pipe from the end of the fuel pressure regulator.
25 Remove the two fuel rail securing bolts, then lift the fuel rail complete with fuel injectors sufficiently to enable the injector(s) to be removed (see illustrations overleaf). Take care not to strain the fuel hoses which run under the fuel rail. Be prepared for fuel spillage, and take adequate fire precautions.

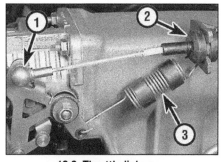

13.9 Throttle linkage - Multec M MPi models

1 Cable end balljoint
2 Cable grommet
3 Throttle return spring (note orientation)

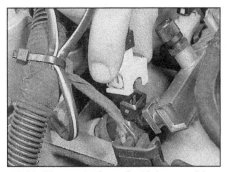

13.23 Disconnecting a fuel injector wiring plug - Multec M MPi models

13.25a Fuel rail securing bolts (arrowed) - Multec M MPi models

13.25b Lifting the fuel rail from the inlet manifold - Multec M MPi models

26 To remove an injector from the fuel rail, prise out the metal securing clip using a screwdriver or a pair of pliers, then pull the injector from the fuel rail **(see illustrations)**.

27 Overhaul of the fuel injectors is not possible, as no spares are available. If faulty, an injector must be renewed.

28 The fuel rail assembly can be removed from the vehicle, after disconnecting the two fuel hoses, which are connected to fuel supply and return pipes under the fuel rail. Access to the two hoses is most easily obtained from under the vehicle. Mark the hoses for position before disconnecting them, to ensure that they are reconnected correctly.

Refitting

29 Begin refitting by fitting new seals to both ends of the fuel injector(s).

30 Refitting is a reversal of removal, ensuring that all pipes and wires are correctly reconnected.

Fuel pressure regulator

Note: *Refer to the precautions given in Section 1 before starting work. New sealing rings must be used on refitting.*

Removal

31 Depressurise the fuel system by removing the fuel pump relay (see Chapter 12), and cranking the engine on the starter motor for a minimum of 5 seconds.

32 Disconnect the battery negative lead.

33 Disconnect the vacuum hose from the end of the pressure regulator, then slacken the fuel pressure regulator fuel pipe union nut (counterhold the union with a second spanner), and disconnect the fuel pipe from the regulator **(see illustration)**. Be prepared for fuel spillage, and take adequate fire precautions. Plug the open end of the pipe to prevent dirt entry and fuel loss.

34 Unscrew the securing bolt, and pull the

pressure regulator from the fuel pipe and the fuel rail **(see illustration)**.

Refitting

35 Refitting is a reversal of removal, but use new sealing rings on the regulator connections to the fuel pipe and the fuel rail.

Throttle position sensor

Removal

36 Disconnect the battery negative lead.

37 Release the securing clips, and disconnect the wiring plug from the throttle position sensor.

38 Remove the three securing screws, and withdraw the sensor from the throttle body.

Refitting

39 Refitting is a reversal of removal, but ensure that the sensor wiper engages correctly with the throttle valve shaft, and ensure that the sensor is correctly seated in its location on the throttle body.

Idle speed control motor

Note: *A new sealing ring may be required on refitting.*

Removal

40 Disconnect the battery negative lead.

41 Release the securing clip, and disconnect the wiring plug from the idle speed control motor **(see illustration)**.

42 Remove the two securing screws, and withdraw the motor. Where applicable, recover the O-ring seal.

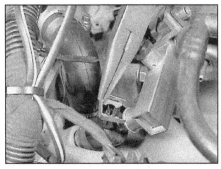

13.26a Removing a fuel injector securing clip - Multec M MPi models

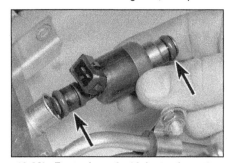

13.26b Removing a fuel injector from the fuel rail. O-rings arrowed - Multec M MPi models

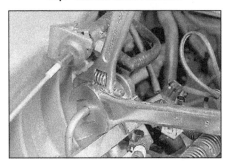

13.33 Loosening the fuel pressure regulator fuel pipe union - Multec M MPi models

13.34 Removing the fuel pressure regulator - Multec M MPi models

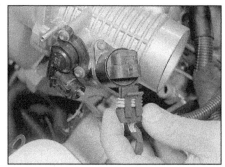

13.41 Disconnecting the idle speed control motor wiring plug - Multec M MPi models

Refitting

43 Before refitting the motor, examine the condition of the sealing ring, and renew if necessary.

44 Refitting is a reversal of removal, ensuring that the sealing ring is correctly located, and that the motor wiring socket faces downwards.

Manifold absolute pressure (MAP) sensor

45 Proceed as described in Section 12 for Multec CFi models.

Coolant temperature sensor

46 Proceed as described in Section 12 for Multec CFi models, but note that the sensor is located in the left-hand end face of the cylinder head, beneath the distributor or coil (as applicable).

Oxygen sensor

47 Proceed as described in Section 12 for Multec CFi models.

Crankshaft speed/position sensor

Note: *A new sealing ring may be required on refitting.*

Removal

48 The sensor is located in a bracket bolted to the lower cylinder block, on the inlet manifold side of the engine, next to the crankshaft pulley **(see illustration)**.

49 Disconnect the battery negative lead.

50 Disconnect the sensor wiring connector, which is attached to a bracket on the camshaft cover. Release the connector from the bracket.

51 Access to the sensor is most easily obtained from under the vehicle. If desired, raise the front of the vehicle and support securely on axle stands (see *"Jacking and vehicle support"*).

52 Remove the securing screw, and withdraw the sensor from its bracket. Note the routing of the wiring to aid refitting.

Refitting

53 Examine the sensor sealing ring, and renew if necessary.

54 Refitting is a reversal of removal, ensuring that the wiring and the wiring connector are correctly located.

55 On completion, check the gap between the end face of the sensor and the toothed sensor wheel attached to the crankshaft pulley, using a feeler gauge. The gap should be as given in the Specifications. If the gap is not as specified, the sensor mounting bracket must be renewed, as no adjustment is possible.

Intake air temperature sensor

Removal

56 The sensor is located in the left-hand end of the inlet manifold plenum.

13.48 Inductive pulse pick-up sensor location viewed from underneath vehicle (securing bolt arrowed) - Multec M MPi models

57 Disconnect the battery negative lead.

58 Disconnect the sensor wiring plug **(see illustration)**.

59 Unscrew the sensor from the manifold.

Refitting

60 Refitting is a reversal of removal.

Electronic control unit

61 Proceed as described in Section 12 for Multec CFi models, noting that the basic control unit and the programme memory can be renewed independently.

Fuel pump relay

62 Proceed as described in Section 12 for Multec CFi models.

Fuel evaporation control system components

63 Refer to Part C of this Chapter.

---

14 Fuel injection system components (Multec S multi-point) – removal and refitting

---

Throttle body – 1.4 litre engines

Note: *Refer to the precautions given in Section 1 before starting work. A new throttle body gasket will be required on refitting.*

Removal

1 Depressurise the fuel system by removing

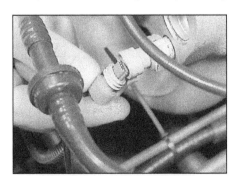

13.58 Disconnecting the intake air temperature sensor wiring plug - Multec M MPi models

the fuel pump relay (see Chapter 12), and cranking the engine on the starter motor for a minimum of 5 seconds.

2 Disconnect the battery negative lead.

3 Remove the engine oil filler cap and the engine cover, then disconnect the two breather hoses from the rear of the camshaft cover.

4 Disconnect the wiring plug from the intake air temperature sensor, then slacken the hose clips, and remove the air cleaner-to-throttle body air intake trunking.

5 Disconnect the throttle cable from the throttle lever and bracket on the throttle body, with reference to Section 8.

6 Release the camshaft sensor wiring connector and the secondary air injection switchover valve wiring plugs from the bracket on the throttle body.

7 Disconnect the wiring plugs from the throttle position sensor and the idle speed control motor.

8 Partially drain the cooling system as described in Chapter 1, then disconnect the coolant hoses from the throttle body. Be prepared for coolant spillage.

9 Disconnect the charcoal canister purge valve hose from the throttle body.

10 Unscrew the securing bolts, and remove the throttle body from the inlet manifold. Recover the gasket, where applicable.

Refitting

11 Commence refitting by thoroughly cleaning the mating faces of the throttle body and the manifold.

12 Refitting is a reversal of removal, bearing in mind the following points.

13 Fit the throttle body using a new gasket, and tighten the securing bolts to the specified torque.

14 Ensure that all hoses and wiring plugs are securely reconnected.

15 Reconnect and if necessary adjust the throttle cable as described in Section 8.

16 On completion, check the coolant level and top up if necessary, as described in *'Weekly checks'*.

Throttle body – 1.6 litre engines

Note: *Refer to the precautions given in Section 1 before starting work. A new throttle body gasket will be required on refitting.*

Removal

17 Proceed as described in paragraphs 1 and 2.

18 Remove the engine oil filler cap then undo the retaining screws and lift off the engine cover. Refit the oil filler cap.

19 Slacken and remove the bolts securing the wiring harness plastic tray to the rear of the inlet manifold. Starting at the front and working back, disconnect the wiring connectors from the oxygen sensor, DIS module, carbon canister purge valve and the various connectors on the left-hand side of the manifold. Unscrew the nuts securing the

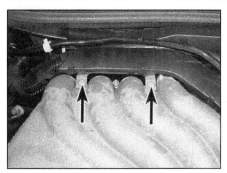

14.19a Undo the retaining bolts . . .

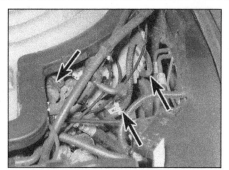

14.19b . . . then disconnect the various wiring connectors (arrowed) . . .

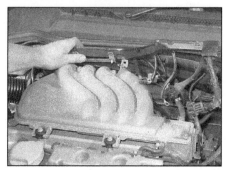

14.19c . . . and free the wiring harness tray from the manifold – 1.6 litre engine

earth leads to the cylinder head and manifold, then unclip the wiring harness plastic tray and position it clear of the manifold **(see illustrations)**.
20 Remove the DIS module as described in Chapter 5B.
21 Unclip the carbon canister purge valve from the left-hand end of the manifold and disconnect the valve hose from the manifold **(see illustration)**.
22 Slacken the union nut and disconnect the brake servo hose from the manifold. Also disconnect the breather/vacuum hoses located next to the servo union **(see illustration)**.
23 Slacken the retaining clip and disconnect the air intake duct from the throttle body.
24 Slacken and remove the bolts securing the throttle cable mounting bracket to the manifold. Disconnect the throttle cable from the throttle lever and bracket, with reference to Section 8.
25 Slacken and remove the throttle body retaining bolts and free the throttle body from the manifold. Recover the gasket and discard it, a new one should be used on refitting.
26 Slacken the union nuts and disconnect the fuel hoses from the fuel rail. Counterhold the fuel rail adapters with an open-ended spanner whilst the union nuts are slackened.
27 Rotate the throttle body until access can be gained to the coolant hose connections. Identify the hoses to aid refitting, then release the securing clips and disconnect the hoses from the throttle body. Plug the ends of the hoses to minimise coolant loss.

28 Disconnect the wiring connectors from the throttle position sensor and the idle speed control motor, then manoeuvre the throttle body from the engine compartment.

Refitting

29 Refitting is the reverse of removal, bearing in mind the following points.
 a) *Ensure that the wiring connectors and coolant hoses are correctly and securely reconnected before bolting the throttle body to the manifold.*
 b) *Fit a new gasket and tighten the throttle body bolts to the specified torque.*
 c) *Tighten the fuel hose union nuts securely.*
 d) *Ensure all hoses are correctly and securely reconnected.*
 e) *Reconnect and if necessary adjust the throttle cable as described in Section 8.*

Fuel injectors – 1.4 litre engines

Note: *If a faulty injector is suspected, before condemning the injector, it is worth trying the effect of one of the proprietary injector-cleaning treatments. New injector sealing rings will be required on refitting.*

Removal

30 Depressurise the fuel system by removing the fuel pump relay (see Chapter 12), and cranking the engine on the starter motor for a minimum of 5 seconds.
31 Disconnect the battery negative lead.
32 Remove the engine oil filler cap then undo the retaining screws and lift off the engine cover. Refit the oil filler cap.
33 Disconnect the breather hoses from the

rear of the camshaft cover.
34 Disconnect the wiring plug from the intake air temperature sensor, then release the hose clips and disconnect the air inlet trunking from the air cleaner and the throttle body. Remove the trunking.
35 Disconnect and release all relevant wiring plugs and wires from the wiring harness plastic tray above the injectors.
36 Release the securing clips and disconnect the fuel injector wiring plugs, then lay the wiring harness plastic tray clear of the working area, towards the rear of the engine, complete with the wiring harness.
37 Unscrew the two fuel rail securing bolts, then carefully lift the fuel rail/injector assembly from the manifold. Remove the lower sealing rings from the injectors and discard them; they must be renewed whenever they are disturbed.
38 Slide off the relevant retaining clip and withdraw the injector from the fuel rail. Remove the upper sealing ring from the injector and discard it; all disturbed sealing rings must be renewed.

Refitting

39 Refitting is a reversal of the removal procedure, noting the following points.
 a) *Renew all disturbed sealing rings and apply a smear of engine oil to them to aid installation.*
 b) *Ease the injector(s) into the fuel rail, ensuring that the sealing ring(s) remain correctly seated, and secure in position with the retaining clips.*
 c) *On refitting the fuel rail, take care not to damage the injectors and ensure that all sealing rings remain in position. Once the fuel rail is correctly seated, tighten its retaining bolts to the specified torque.*
 d) *On completion start the engine and check for fuel leaks.*

Fuel injectors – 1.6 litre engines

Note: *If a faulty injector is suspected, before condemning the injector, it is worth trying the effect of one of the proprietary injector-cleaning treatments. New injector sealing rings will be required on refitting.*

Removal

40 Proceed as described in paragraphs 17 and 18.

14.21 Unclip the purge valve from the left-hand side of the manifold – 1.6 litre engine

14.22 Disconnect the brake servo hose (1) and breather/vacuum hose (2) from the manifold – 1.6 litre engine

14.53 The fuel pressure regulator (arrowed) is located on the left-hand end of the fuel rail – 1.6 litre engine

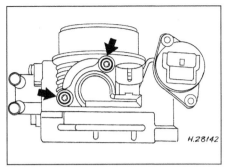

14.59 Throttle position sensor retaining screws (arrowed) – 1.6 litre engine (shown with throttle body removed)

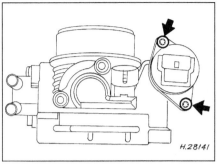

14.64 Idle speed control motor retaining screws (arrowed) – 1.6 litre engine (shown with throttle body removed)

41 Remove the upper section of the inlet manifold as described in Section 19.

42 Disconnect the wiring connectors from the four injectors, then free the wiring harness from the fuel rail.

43 Unscrew the union nuts and disconnect the fuel hoses from the fuel rail. Whilst the unions are being slackened, counterhold the fuel rail adapters with an open-ended spanner. Be prepared for fuel spillage and take adequate fire precautions.

44 Slacken and remove the three fuel rail retaining bolts, then carefully ease the fuel rail/injector assembly out of position and remove it from the manifold. Remove the lower sealing rings from the injectors and discard them; they must be renewed whenever they are disturbed.

45 Slide off the relevant retaining clip and withdraw the injector from the fuel rail. Remove the upper sealing ring from the injector and discard it; all disturbed sealing rings must be renewed.

Refitting

46 Refitting is a reversal of the removal procedure, noting the following points.

a) Renew all disturbed sealing rings and apply a smear of engine oil to them to aid installation.

b) Ease the injector(s) into the fuel rail, ensuring that the sealing ring(s) remain correctly seated, and secure in position with the retaining clips.

c) On refitting the fuel rail, take care not to damage the injectors and ensure that all sealing rings remain in position. Once the fuel rail is correctly seated, tighten its retaining bolts to the specified torque.

d) On completion start the engine and check for fuel leaks.

Fuel pressure regulator – 1.4 litre engines

Note: New O-ring seals must be used on refitting.

Removal

47 Proceed as described in paragraphs 1 and 2.

48 Disconnect the vacuum hose from the regulator.

49 Unscrew the clamp screw, and remove the clamp securing the regulator to the fuel rail.

50 Note the fitted position of the regulator, then carefully pull the regulator from the fuel rail. Discard the O-ring seals – new ones must be used on refitting.

Refitting

51 Refitting is a reversal of removal, but fit new O-ring seals to the regulator, and ensure that the regulator is correctly positioned as noted before removal. On completion, start the engine and check for leaks.

Fuel pressure regulator – 1.6 litre engines

Note: A new sealing ring will be required on refitting.

Removal

52 Proceed as described in paragraphs 1 and 2.

53 Access to the fuel regulator is poor and can be improved slightly by freeing the wiring harness plastic tray from the inlet manifold (see Section 19) **(see illustration)**.

54 Counterhold the regulator with an open-ended spanner, and unscrew the fuel hose union nut. Disconnect the fuel hose and the vacuum hose from the regulator. Be prepared for fuel spillage.

55 Slacken and remove the retaining bolt and free the wiring bracket from the fuel rail.

56 Ease the regulator out from the end of the fuel rail and remove it along with its sealing ring.

Refitting

57 Refitting is the reverse of removal, using a new sealing ring. On completion start the engine and check for fuel leaks.

Throttle position sensor

Note: Thread-locking compound will be required to coat the threads of the sensor securing screws on refitting.

Removal

58 On 1.6 litre engines, remove the throttle body as described previously in this Section.

59 Disconnect the sensor wiring plug (if not already done), then unscrew the securing screws, and withdraw the sensor from the throttle body **(see illustration)**.

Refitting

60 Refit the sensor, ensuring that the sensor wiper engages correctly with the throttle valve spindle.

61 Apply thread-locking compound to the securing screws, then refit and tighten them securely. Where applicable, reconnect the sensor wiring plug.

62 On 1.6 litre engines, refit the throttle body as described previously in this Section.

Idle speed control motor

Note: Thread-locking compound will be required to coat the threads of the motor securing screws on refitting.

Removal

63 On 1.6 litre engines, remove the throttle body as described previously in this Section.

64 Disconnect the idle speed control motor wiring plug (if not already done), then unscrew the securing screws, and withdraw the idle speed control motor from the throttle body **(see illustration)**. Recover the sealing ring.

Refitting

65 Refitting is a reversal of removal, bearing in mind the following points.

a) Check the condition of the sealing ring and renew if necessary.

b) Before refitting, check that the motor plunger tip does not extend more than 33 mm from the motor mounting flange **(see illustration)**. If necessary, gently push the

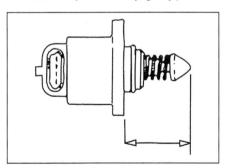

14.65 Idle speed control motor plunger maximum extension is 33.0 mm – Multec S models

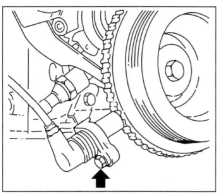

14.75 Crankshaft speed/position sensor securing bolt (arrowed) – Multec S models

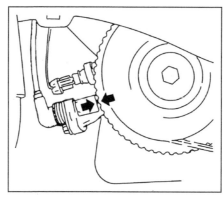

14.76 Crankshaft speed position sensor air gap (arrowed) – Multec S models

plunger into the body until it is correctly positioned. Failure to do this could lead to the motor being damaged
c) Ensure that the motor is fitted with the wiring connector facing downwards.
d) Coat the threads of the securing screws with thread-locking compound.
e) On 1.6 litre engines, refit the throttle body as described previously in this Section.

Manifold absolute pressure (MAP) sensor

66 Proceed as described in Section 12 for Multec CFi models.

Coolant temperature sensor

67 Proceed as described in Section 12 for Multec CFi models, but note that the sensor is located in the thermostat housing. Access can be improved by removing the air cleaner assembly as described in Section 3.

Oxygen sensor

68 Proceed as described in Section 12 for Multec CFi models.

Crankshaft speed/position sensor

Removal

69 Disconnect the battery negative lead.
70 To improve access to the sensor wiring connector, release the wiring harness plastic tray from its mountings.
71 Trace the wiring back from the sensor,

then unclip the sensor wiring connector from the bracket in the engine compartment, and separate the two halves of the connector.
72 Make a careful note of the routing of the sensor wiring.
73 If desired, to assist routing the wiring on refitting, tie a length of string, approximately 2.0 metres in length, to the sensor wiring plug.
74 Working at the sensor end of the wiring, carefully pull the wiring down from the engine compartment, and where applicable, untie the string and leave it in place to assist refitting.
75 Unscrew the sensor securing bolt, and withdraw the sensor from the bracket on the oil pump **(see illustration)**.

Refitting

76 Refitting is a reversal of removal, bearing in mind the following points.
a) Where applicable, use the string to pull the wiring into position in the engine compartment.
b) On completion, measure the air gap between the end of the sensor and the sensor wheel teeth, using feeler gauges. The gap should be 1.0 ± 0.7 mm. If the gap is not as specified, renew the pick-up bracket **(see illustration)**.

Intake air temperature sensor

Removal

77 Disconnect the battery negative lead.
78 Disconnect the wiring plug from the sensor, which is located in the air intake pipe.

79 Carefully pull the sensor out of the rubber sealing ring, then pull out the sealing ring, taking care not to damage it.

Refitting

80 Fit the sealing ring to the sensor, ensuring that the ring is fitted with the flange nearest the wiring connector end of the sensor **(see illustration)**.
81 Carefully push the sensor and ring, into the air intake pipe.
82 Reconnect the sensor wiring plug and reconnect the battery negative lead.

Camshaft sensor

Removal

83 Disconnect the battery negative lead.
84 Release the camshaft sensor wiring connector from the bracket on the fuel rail, and separate the two halves of the connector.
85 Remove the timing belt upper cover as described in Chapter 2B.
86 Unclip the sensor wiring from the timing belt cover, noting its routing.
87 Unscrew the two securing bolts, and withdraw the sensor from the cylinder head **(see illustration)**.

Refitting

88 Refitting is a reversal of removal, but ensure that the sensor wiring is routed as noted before removal.

Knock sensor

Removal

89 Apply the handbrake, then jack up the front of the vehicle and support it on axle stands (see "*Jacking and vehicle support*"). The knock sensor is located at the rear of the cylinder block, just to the right of the starter motor, and is accessible from underneath the vehicle.
90 Trace the wiring back from the sensor, noting its routing, and separate the two halves of the wiring connector.
91 Slacken and remove the retaining bolt and remove the sensor from the engine.

Refitting

92 On refitting ensure that the mating surfaces of the sensor and cylinder block are clean and dry, then fit the sensor and tighten its retaining bolt to the specified torque. Ensure that the wiring is correctly routed and securely reconnected, then lower the vehicle to the ground.

Electronic control unit (ECU)

93 Proceed as described in Section 12 for Multec CFi models, noting the following points.
a) Remove the fuel pump relay from its socket below the ECU before removing the ECU.
b) On models up to mid-1996, if a new ECU is obtained, it will be supplied without programme memory and knock control modules, which plug into the main ECU (the modules are fitted behind a panel in

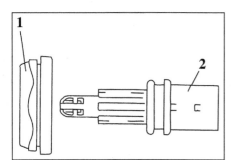

14.80 The sealing ring should be fitted with the flange (1) nearest the wiring connector end (2) of the sensor

14.87 Removing the camshaft sensor – 1.6 litre engine

the ECU). In this case, these modules must be transferred from the old ECU. After transferring the modules, transfer the part and code number information from the old ECU to the new unit for future reference.

c) On models from mid-1996, the ECU is a sealed unit, and if the programme memory or knock modules are faulty, the complete ECU must be renewed. The new ECU must be programmed to suit the vehicle to which it is being fitted, using special Vauxhall/Opel equipment.

Fuel pump relay

Removal

94 The relay is located with the ECU behind the right-hand footwell side panel. Remove the footwell/side trim panel as described in Chapter 11, Section 30.
95 Pull the relay from its connector, and remove it.

Refitting

96 Refitting is a reversal of removal.

Fuel evaporation control system components

97 Refer to Part C of this Chapter.

Exhaust gas recirculation system components

98 Refer to Part C of this Chapter.

Secondary air injection system components

99 Refer to Part C of this Chapter.

---

15 Fuel injection system components (Motronic M 1.5 multipoint) – removal and refitting

Throttle body

Note: A new gasket must be used on refitting.

Removal

1 Disconnect the battery negative lead.
2 Release the securing clip, and disconnect the wiring plug from the intake air temperature sensor (mounted in the air trunking). Pull on the plug, not on the wiring.
3 Loosen the clamp screws securing the air trunking to the throttle body and the air mass meter, then withdraw the air trunking.
4 Disconnect the idle speed control valve hose from the throttle body.
5 Disconnect the camshaft cover breather hose from the throttle body.
6 Disconnect the fuel tank vent valve vacuum hose from the throttle body.
7 Disconnect the coolant hoses from the throttle body. Be prepared for coolant spillage, and clamp or plug the open ends of the hoses, to prevent further coolant loss.
8 Release the securing clip, and disconnect the wiring plug from the throttle position sensor.

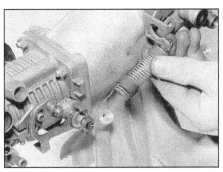

15.10 Unhooking the throttle return spring from the bracket on the inlet manifold - Motronic M 1.5 models

9 Release the securing clip, then disconnect the throttle cable end balljoint from the throttle valve lever.
10 Slide the throttle cable grommet from the bracket on the inlet manifold, then unhook the throttle return spring from the bracket. If desired, unhook the spring from the grommet in the throttle valve linkage, and lay the spring to one side out of the way (in this case, note the orientation of the spring to enable correct refitting), **(see illustration)**.
11 Make a final check to ensure that all relevant hoses and wires have been disconnected to facilitate removal of the throttle body.
12 Unscrew the four securing nuts **(see illustration)**, and withdraw the throttle body from the inlet manifold. Access to the lower nuts may be restricted by the two fuel hoses, and it may be necessary to move the hoses to one side to improve access. Take care not to strain the hoses.
13 Recover the gasket.
14 The throttle position sensor can be removed from the throttle body, as described later in this Section.

Refitting

15 Refitting is a reversal of removal, bearing in mind the following points.
16 Where applicable, refit the throttle position sensor as described later in this Section.
17 Thoroughly clean the mating faces of the throttle body and inlet manifold, and refit the throttle body using a new gasket.
18 Ensure that all wires and hoses are correctly reconnected and routed.
19 Check and if necessary top-up the coolant level, as described in 'Weekly checks'.
20 On completion, check and if necessary adjust the throttle cable freeplay, as described in Section 8.

Fuel injectors

Note: Refer to the precautions, given in Section 1, before starting work. The seals at both ends of the fuel injector/s) must be renewed on refitting.

Removal

21 Depressurise the fuel system by removing the fuel pump relay (see Chapter 12), and

15.12 Unscrewing a throttle body securing nut (arrowed) - Motronic M 1.5 models

cranking the engine on the starter motor for a minimum of 5 seconds.
22 Disconnect the battery negative lead.
23 Unscrew the union nut, and disconnect the brake servo vacuum hose from the inlet manifold.
24 Remove the idle speed control valve, complete with hoses, as described later in this Section.
25 Disconnect the vacuum hose from the top of the fuel pressure regulator.
26 Disconnect the wiring harness housing from the fuel injectors, and move it to one side, taking care not to strain the wiring. Pull up on the wiring harness housing, and compress the wiring plug securing clips to release the harness housing from the injectors.
27 Remove the four bolts from the brackets securing the fuel rail to the inlet manifold, then lift the fuel rail complete with fuel injectors sufficiently to enable the injector(s) to be removed. Take care not to strain the fuel hoses. Be prepared for fuel spillage, and take adequate fire precautions.
28 To remove an injector from the fuel rail, prise out the metal securing clip using a screwdriver, then pull the injector from the fuel rail.
29 Overhaul of the fuel injectors is not possible, as no spares are available. If faulty, an injector must be renewed.

Refitting

30 Begin refitting by fitting new seals to both ends of the fuel injector(s) **(see illustration)**.

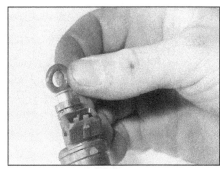

15.30 Fitting a new O-ring to a fuel injector - Motronic M 1.5 models

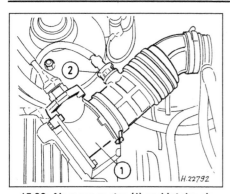

15.39 Air mass meter (1) and intake air temperature sensor (2) – Motronic M 1.5 models

31 Refitting is a reversal of removal, ensuring that all hoses, pipes and wires are correctly reconnected.

Fuel pressure regulator

Note: *Refer to the precautions given in Section 1 before starting work.*

Removal

32 Disconnect the battery negative lead.
33 For improved access, remove the idle speed control valve as described later in this Section, then disconnect the wiring harness from the fuel injectors and move it to one side, taking care not to strain the wiring. Pull on the wiring harness housing, and compress the wiring plug retaining clips to release the harness housing from the injectors.
34 Position a wad of rag beneath the pressure regulator, to absorb any fuel which may be released as the regulator is removed.
35 Slowly loosen the clamp screws and disconnect the fuel hoses from the regulator. Be prepared for fuel spillage, and take adequate fire precautions.
36 Disconnect the vacuum hose from the top of the regulator, and withdraw the regulator.

Refitting

37 Refitting is a reversal of removal.

Air mass meter

Note: *A new sealing ring must be used on refitting, and thread-locking compound will be required to coat the securing bolts.*

15.47 Disconnecting the wiring plug from the idle speed control valve - Motronic M 1.5 models

Removal

38 Disconnect the battery negative lead.
39 Release the securing clip, and disconnect the wiring plug from the intake air temperature sensor (mounted in the air trunking). Pull on the plug, not on the wiring **(see illustration)**.
40 Similarly, disconnect the wiring plug from the air flow meter.
41 Loosen the clamp screws securing the air trunking to the throttle body and the air flow meter, then withdraw the air trunking.
42 Remove the air cleaner cover, complete with the air flow meter, with reference to Section 3.
43 Unscrew the two securing bolts, and remove the air mass meter from the air cleaner cover **(see illustration)**. Recover the sealing ring.

Refitting

44 Refitting is a reversal of removal, but use a new sealing ring when fitting the air mass meter to the air cleaner cover, and coat the securing bolt threads with thread-locking compound.

Throttle position sensor

45 Proceed as described in Section 13 for Multec M models.

Idle speed control valve

Removal

46 Disconnect the battery negative lead.
47 Release the retaining clip, and disconnect the wiring plug from the idle speed control valve **(see illustration)**.
48 The valve can be removed complete with its connecting hoses, or separately, leaving the hoses in place.
49 Loosen the relevant clamp screws, then disconnect the hoses and withdraw the valve **(see illustration)**.

Refitting

50 Refitting is a reversal of removal.

Coolant temperature sensor

51 Proceed as described in Section 12 for Multec CFi models, but note that the sensor is located in the end of the thermostat housing on the inlet manifold side of the engine, below

15.49 Withdrawing the idle speed control valve complete with hoses - Motronic M 1.5 models

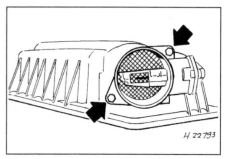

15.43 Air mass meter securing screws (arrowed) – Motronic M 1.5 models

the alternator upper mounting bracket **(see illustration)**.

Oxygen sensor

52 Proceed as described in Section 12 for Multec CFi models, but note that the sensor is mounted in the exhaust front section, and access is obtained from underneath the vehicle. If desired, raise the front of the vehicle and support securely on axle stands (see *"Jacking and vehicle support"*).

Crankshaft speed/position sensor

53 Proceed as described in Section 12 for 1.8 litre Multec CFi models.

Intake air temperature sensor

54 Proceed as described in Section 13 for Multec M models, but note that the sensor is located in the air trunking between the inlet manifold and the air mass meter. Take care not to damage the air trunking.

Electronic control unit (ECU)

55 Proceed as described in Section 12 for Multec CFi models, ignoring the references to the basic control unit and the programme memory.

Fuel pump relay

56 Proceed as described in Section 12 for Multec CFi models.

Fuel evaporation control system components

57 Refer to Part C of this Chapter.

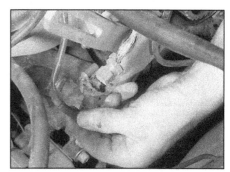

15.51 Disconnecting the coolant temperature sensor wiring plug – Motronic M 1.5 models

16.5 Disconnecting the throttle cable from the throttle valve lever - Motronic M 2.5 models

16.6 Disconnect the breather hose from the throttle body - Motronic M 2.5 models

16.8 Two of the main throttle body securing nuts (arrowed) - Motronic M 2.5 models

16 Fuel injection system components (Motronic M 2.5/M 2.8 multi-point) – removal and refitting

Main throttle body

Note: *A new gasket must be used on refitting.*

Removal

1 Disconnect the battery negative lead.
2 Remove the airbox assembly from the top of the throttle body, as described in Section 3.
3 Release the securing clip, and disconnect the wiring plug from the throttle position sensor. Pull on the plug, not on the wiring.
4 Unscrew the retaining nut, and detach the fuel hose bracket from the left-hand side of the throttle body.
5 Slide the throttle cable end from the throttle valve lever **(see illustration)**.
6 Disconnect the breather hose from the front of the throttle body **(see illustration)**.
7 Make a final check to ensure that all relevant hoses, pipes and wires have been disconnected and moved clear of the throttle body.
8 Unscrew the four securing nuts, and remove the throttle body from the inlet manifold **(see illustration)**. Recover the gasket.
9 If desired, the throttle position sensor can be removed from the throttle body, as described later in this Section.
10 **Do not** under any circumstances attempt to adjust the throttle valve linkage. It the throttle valve linkage is faulty, refer the problem to a Vauxhall/Opel dealer.

Refitting

11 Refitting is a reversal of removal, bearing in mind the following points.
12 On models with Motronic M 2.5 fuel injection, before refitting the throttle body, check the adjustment of the throttle position sensor, as described in paragraphs 61 to 63 of this Section.
13 Thoroughly clean the mating faces of the throttle body and electronic traction control (ETC) throttle housing (if applicable), and refit the throttle body using a new gasket.
14 Ensure that all hoses, pipes and wires are correctly reconnected and routed.
15 Refit the airbox as described in Section 3.
16 On completion, check and if necessary adjust the throttle cable freeplay, as described in Section 8.

Electronic traction control (ETC) throttle housing

17 Refer to Section 22.

Fuel injectors

Note: *Refer to the precautions given in Section 1 before starting work. The seals at both ends of the fuel injector(s) must be renewed on refitting.*

Removal

18 Disconnect the battery negative lead.
19 Remove the airbox, as described in Section 3.
20 Position a wad of rag beneath one of the fuel hose unions on the fuel rail, to absorb the fuel which will be released as the union is disconnected.

21 Slowly loosen the fuel hose union to relieve the pressure in the fuel line, then disconnect the hose from the fuel rail **(see illustration)**. Be prepared for fuel spillage, and take adequate fire precautions. Clamp or plug the end of the fuel hose, to prevent dirt ingress and further fuel spillage.
22 Repeat paragraphs 3 and 4 for the remaining fuel hose-to-fuel rail union.
23 Disconnect the two breather hoses from the rear of the camshaft cover. Disconnect the larger hose from the throttle body, and remove the hose completely.
24 Disconnect the vacuum pipe from the top of the fuel pressure regulator.
25 Disconnect the wiring plug from the air flow meter. Recover the sealing ring.
26 Disconnect the wiring plug from the throttle position sensor.
27 Slide the end of the throttle cable from the throttle valve lever on the throttle body, then unbolt the cable bracket from the inlet manifold, and move it to one side.
28 Disconnect the wiring harness from the fuel injectors, and move it to one side, taking care not to strain the wiring. Pull up on the wiring harness housing, and compress the wiring plug retaining clips to release the housing from the injectors **(see illustration)**.
29 Unscrew and remove the two fuel rail securing nuts, and withdraw the fuel rail complete with fuel injectors from the inlet manifold. Note the position of the earth leads on the fuel rail securing studs **(see illustration)**.

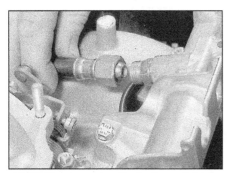

16.21 Disconnecting the fuel supply hose from the fuel rail - Motronic M 2.5 models

16.28 Lifting the wiring harness housing from the fuel injectors - Motronic M 2.5 models

16.29 Fuel rail securing nut (arrowed). Note position of earth lead - Motronic M 2.5 models

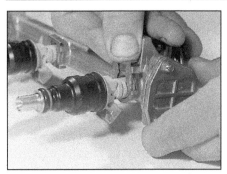

16.30a Prise out the metal securing clip . . .

16.30b . . . and pull the injector from the fuel rail - Motronic M 2.5 models

16.43 Disconnecting the vacuum pipe from the fuel pressure regulator - Motronic M 2.5 models

30 To remove an injector from the fuel rail, prise out the metal securing clip, then pull the injector from the fuel rail **(see illustrations)**.

31 Overhaul of the fuel injectors is not possible, as no spares are available. If faulty, an injector must be renewed.

Refitting

32 Begin refitting by fitting new seals to both ends of the fuel injector(s).

33 Further refitting is a reversal of removal, bearing in mind the following points.

34 Where applicable, the wiring plug strip for the injectors must firmly 'snap' into place.

35 Ensure that all hoses, pipes and wires are correctly reconnected.

36 Refit the airbox as described in Section 3.

37 On completion, check and if necessary adjust the throttle cable freeplay, as described in Section 8.

Fuel pressure regulator

Note: *Refer to the precautions given in Section 1 before starting work.*

Removal

38 Depressurise the fuel system by removing the fuel pump relay (see Chapter 12), and cranking the engine on the starter motor for a minimum of 5 seconds.

39 Disconnect the battery negative lead.

40 Remove the airbox from the top of the throttle housing, as described in Section 3.

41 Release the retaining clip, and disconnect the wiring plug from the air mass meter. Pull on the plug, not on the wiring. Where applicable, recover the sealing ring.

42 Release the retaining clip, and disconnect

the wiring plug from the throttle position sensor.

43 Disconnect the vacuum pipe from the top of the fuel pressure regulator **(see illustration)**.

44 Position a wad of rag beneath the regulator, to absorb the fuel which will be released as the regulator is removed.

45 Using a spanner or socket, and working underneath the regulator, unscrew the Torx type securing bolts, then withdraw the regulator. Be prepared for fuel spillage, and take adequate fire precautions.

Refitting

46 Refitting is a reversal of removal, remembering the following points.

47 Ensure that all wires, pipes and hoses are correctly reconnected.

48 Refit the airbox as described in Section 3.

Air mass meter

Removal

49 Disconnect the battery negative lead.

50 Note the orientation of the meter assembly in the air trunking.

51 Release the retaining clip, and disconnect the wiring plug from the air flow meter **(see illustration)**. Pull on the plug, not on the wiring. Recover the sealing ring, where applicable.

52 Loosen the clamp screws, disconnect the air trunking from either end of the meter, then withdraw the meter.

53 No dismantling of the air mass meter is possible. If faulty replace the complete assembly.

Refitting

54 Inspect the condition of the wiring plug sealing ring and renew if necessary.

55 Refitting is a reversal of removal, but ensure that the meter is orientated as noted before removal, and ensure that the hose connections are correctly seated in the recesses on the meter.

Throttle position sensor – Motronic M 2.5

Removal

56 Disconnect the battery negative lead.

57 Remove the airbox as described in Section 3, and the air mass meter as described previously in this Section. Note that if the connecting air trunking is left in place, the two components can be removed as an assembly.

58 Release the retaining clip, and disconnect the wiring plug from the throttle position sensor **(see illustration)**.

59 Remove the two securing screws and withdraw the sensor from the throttle body.

Refitting

60 Refit the sensor, but before tightening the securing screws, adjust the position of the sensor as follows.

61 Turn the sensor body anti-clockwise until resistance is felt then tighten the securing screws.

62 When the throttle valve is opened, an audible click should be noticeable from the sensor, and similarly, this should be repeated as the throttle valve is closed.

63 If necessary, adjust the position of the sensor until a click is heard just as the throttle valve begins to open.

64 Refit the air mass meter as described previously in this Section, and the airbox as described in Section 3.

Throttle position sensor – Motronic M 2.8

Removal

65 Disconnect the battery negative lead.

66 Disconnect the intake air temperature sensor and the air mass meter wiring plugs.

67 Remove the airbox, as described in Section 3.

16.51 Disconnecting the wiring plug from the air mass meter – Motronic M 2.5 models

16.58 Throttle position sensor (arrowed) - Motronic M 2.5 models

68 Disconnect the throttle position sensor wiring plug.
69 Unscrew the two securing screws and remove the sensor from the throttle body.

Refitting

70 Refitting is a reversal of removal, but ensure that all wiring plugs are securely reconnected.

Idle speed control valve

Removal

71 Disconnect the battery negative lead.
72 Loosen the clamp screw, and disconnect the hose from underneath the airbox on the throttle body. Remove the clamp from the hose.
73 Apply the handbrake, then jack up the front of the vehicle, and support securely on axle stands (see "*Jacking and vehicle support*").
74 Remove the engine undershield, if fitted, as described in Chapter 11, Section 25.
75 Working underneath the vehicle, disconnect the wiring plug from the idle speed control valve, which is located underneath the inlet manifold, above the starter motor **(see illustration)**.
76 Loosen the clamp screw and disconnect the remaining idle speed control valve hose from the inlet manifold, then withdraw the valve downwards, complete with the hoses.
77 If the hoses are to be removed from the valve, mark their locations before removal so that they can be correctly reconnected. Once the valve has been refitted, it is extremely difficult to swap the hose positions.

Refitting

78 Refitting is a reversal of removal, but ensure that the valve rests horizontally, with the wiring routed over the top of the coolant hose. If the wiring is routed under the coolant hose, this may cause the valve to be bent downwards, resulting in a restriction or fracture in the air hose to the inlet manifold.

Crankshaft speed/position sensor – Motronic M 2.5

79 Proceed as described in Section 12 for 1.8 litre Multec CFi models.

Crankshaft speed/position sensor – Motronic M 2.8

Removal

80 Disconnect the battery negative lead.
81 Trace the wiring back from the sensor, and locate the sensor wiring connector, which is located between the air cleaner housing and the front suspension turret. Separate the two halves of the connector.
82 Release the sensor wiring from its retaining straps and brackets, noting the routing.
83 Two different types of power steering pump bracket may be fitted, one with a small aperture in the rear of the bracket, and one with a large aperture **(see illustration)**. On

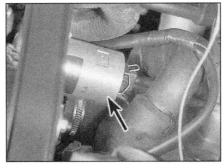

16.75 Idle speed control valve (arrowed) - Motronic M 2.5 models

models fitted with a bracket with a small aperture, the power steering pump (there is no need to disconnect the fluid lines) and bracket must be unbolted and moved to one side to allow the sensor wiring to pass through. Refer to Chapter 10 as necessary.
84 Unscrew the securing screw, and withdraw the sensor from the cylinder block.

Refitting

85 Refitting is a reversal of removal, but when refitting and reconnecting the wiring, ensure that the wiring cannot foul against any moving or hot parts, i.e. drivebelts or exhaust. Where applicable, refit the power steering pump with reference to Chapter 10.

Coolant temperature sensor

86 Proceed as described in Section 12 for Multec CFi models, but note that the sensor is located in the end of the thermostat housing on the inlet manifold side of the engine **(see illustration)**.

Oxygen sensor

87 Proceed as described in Section 12 for Multec CFi models, but note that the sensor is mounted in the exhaust front section, and access is obtained from underneath the vehicle. If desired, raise the front of the vehicle and support securely on axle stands (see "*Jacking and vehicle support*") **(see illustration)**.

Intake air temperature sensor

88 Proceed as described in Section 13 for Multec M models, but note that the sensor is

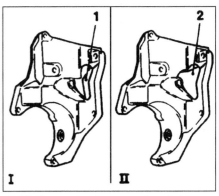

16.83 Power steering pump bracket types – Motronic M 2.8 models

I   Version with small aperture (1)
II Version with large aperture (2)

located in the air trunking between the inlet manifold and the air mass meter. Take care not to damage the air trunking.

Knock sensor

Removal

89 The sensor is located on the lower inlet manifold side of the cylinder block, below the idle speed control valve, and (unless the inlet manifold has been removed) is only accessible from below the vehicle.
90 Disconnect the battery negative lead.
91 Apply the handbrake, then jack up the front of the vehicle and support securely on axle stands (see "*Jacking and vehicle support*").
92 Remove the engine undershield, as described in Chapter 11, Section 25.
93 Disconnect the sensor wiring plug.
94 Unscrew the securing bolt, and withdraw the sensor from the cylinder block.

Refitting

95 Refitting is a reversal of the removal procedure, but make sure that the sensor and its seat are perfectly clean, and that the sensor is secured firmly. Failure to observe these points could result in damage to the engine, as a poorly mounted sensor will not detect 'knocking', and the appropriate ignition correction will not be applied.

16.86 Coolant temperature sensor – Motronic M 2.5 models

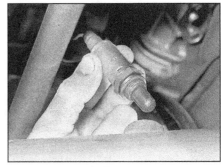

16.87 Removing the oxygen sensor – Motronic M 2.5 models

Camshaft sensor – Motronic M 2.8

Note: *A new sealing ring will be required when refitting the disc.*

Removal

96 Disconnect the battery negative lead, then disconnect the sensor wiring plug.

97 Unscrew the securing bolt, and withdraw the sensor from the housing on the cylinder head **(see illustration)**. Recover the sealing ring

Refitting

98 Refitting is a reversal of the removal procedure, but use a new sensor sealing ring.

Electronic control unit (ECU)

99 Proceed as described in Section 12 for Multec CFi models, ignoring the references to the basic control unit and the programme memory.

Fuel pump relay

Removal

100 The relay is located with the ECU behind the right-hand footwell side panel. Remove the footwell/side trim panel as described in Chapter 11, Section 30.

101 Pull the relay from its connector, and remove it.

Refitting

102 Refitting is a reversal of removal.

Fuel evaporation control system components

103 Refer to Part C of this Chapter.

Exhaust gas recirculation system components

104 Refer to Part C of this Chapter.

Secondary air injection system components

105 Refer to Part C of this Chapter.

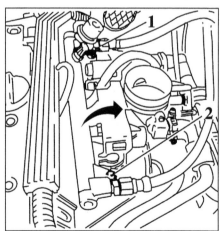

17.20 Releasing the fuel rail - Simtec models

1 Securing pin   2 Securing bolt

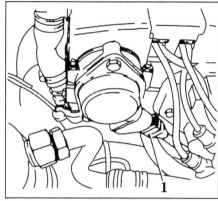

16.97 Camshaft sensor location - Motronic 2.8 models

1 Camshaft sensor

17 Fuel injection system components (Simtec multi-point) – removal and refitting

Throttle body

Note: *A new gasket will be required on refitting.*

Removal

1 Disconnect the battery negative lead.

2 Disconnect the two breather hoses from the camshaft cover.

3 On models from mid-1996, locate the knock sensor wiring connector which is attached to a bracket next to the throttle body, then separate the two halves of the connector and release the connector from the bracket.

4 Disconnect the wiring plugs from the idle speed control motor and the throttle position sensor.

5 Disconnect the throttle cable from the throttle lever and locating bracket, with reference to Section 8.

6 Disconnect the fuel pressure regulator vacuum hose and the fuel tank vent valve vacuum hose from the throttle body.

7 Partially drain the cooling system as described in Chapter 1, and disconnect the coolant hoses from the throttle body.

8 Unscrew the four securing nuts, and remove the throttle body. Recover the gasket.

Refitting

9 Refitting is a reversal of removal, bearing in mind the following points.

a) *Thoroughly clean the mating faces of the throttle body and manifold, then refit the throttle body using a new gasket.*

b) *Reconnect the throttle cable and check the adjustment with reference to Section 8.*

c) *Check the coolant level and top up if necessary as described in 'Weekly checks'.*

Fuel injectors

Note: *Refer to the precautions given in Section 1 before starting work. New injector seals will be required on refitting.*

Removal

10 Depressurise the fuel system by removing the fuel pump relay (see Chapter 12), and cranking the engine on the starter motor for a minimum of 5 seconds.

11 Disconnect the battery negative lead, then disconnect the wiring plugs from the intake air temperature sensor, the air mass meter, and the idle speed control motor.

12 Disconnect the two breather hoses from the camshaft cover.

13 Release the securing clips, then remove the air cleaner-to-throttle body air intake trunking.

14 Disconnect the vacuum hose from the fuel pressure regulator.

15 Remove the securing screw and disconnect the earth wire from the fuel rail.

16 Disconnect the throttle cable from the throttle lever and locating bracket, with reference to Section 8.

17 Position a wad of clean rag around the fuel pressure check connector on the fuel rail, to absorb any fuel that may be released. Remove the cap from the pressure check connector, then carefully depress the valve to release any remaining pressure in the fuel system. Be prepared for fuel spillage, and take adequate fire precautions.

18 The injector wiring housing must now be removed from the top of the injectors. Simultaneously press the Nos 1 and 4 cylinder injector wiring plug retaining clips towards the fuel rail (using a screwdriver if necessary), and pull the wiring housing from the injectors.

19 On models up to mid-1996, disconnect the crankshaft speed/position sensor and the knock sensor wiring plugs from the wiring housing. Move the wiring housing clear of the working area.

20 Unscrew the fuel rail securing bolt and remove the pin, then lift the fuel rail/injector assembly from the manifold **(see illustration)**.

21 To remove an injector from the fuel rail, prise out the metal securing clip, then pull the injector from the fuel rail **(see illustration)**.

22 Overhaul of the fuel injectors is not possible, as no spares are available. If faulty, an injector must be renewed.

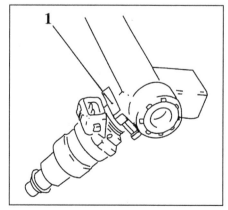

17.21 Fuel injector securing clip (1) - Simtec models

Refitting

23 Begin refitting by fitting new seals to both ends of the fuel injector(s).

24 Further refitting is a reversal of removal, bearing in mind the following points.

a) When refitting the injector wiring housing to the injectors, make sure that the wiring plug retaining clips are correctly aligned to allow the housing to 'snap' into place on the injectors.

b) Reconnect the throttle cable and check the adjustment with reference to Section 8.

Fuel pressure regulator

Note: Refer to the precautions given in Section 1 before starting work. New pressure regulator O-rings will be required on refitting.

Removal

25 Depressurise the fuel system by removing the fuel pump relay (see Chapter 12), and cranking the engine on the starter motor for a minimum of 5 seconds, then disconnect the battery negative lead.

26 Disconnect the breather hose from the camshaft cover to improve access to the pressure regulator.

27 Disconnect the vacuum hose from the pressure regulator.

28 Slacken the clamp screw, and carefully remove the pressure regulator mounting clamp.

29 Make alignment marks between the pressure regulator and the fuel rail to ensure correct refitting, then carefully pull the pressure regulator from the fuel rail. Remove the O-rings and discard them – new ones must be used on refitting.

Refitting

30 Commence refitting by fitting new O-rings to the pressure regulator.

31 Refitting is a reversal of removal, but ensure that the marks made on the pressure regulator and fuel rail before removal are aligned.

Throttle position sensor

Removal

32 Disconnect the sensor wiring plug, then disconnect the sensor wiring plug.

33 Unscrew the securing screws, and withdraw the sensor from the throttle body.

Refitting

34 Refit the sensor, ensuring that the sensor wiper engages correctly with the throttle valve spindle.

35 Apply thread-locking compound to the securing screws, then refit and tighten them securely. Reconnect the sensor wiring plug, then reconnect the battery negative lead.

Idle speed control motor

Note: A new idle speed control motor gasket will be required on refitting.

Removal

36 Disconnect the battery negative lead, then disconnect the wiring plugs from the intake air

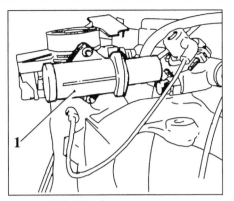

17.39 Idle air stepper motor - Simtec models

1 Motor

temperature sensor and the air mass meter.

37 Disconnect the breather hose from the camshaft cover, then release the securing clips, and remove the air cleaner-to-throttle body air intake trunking.

38 Disconnect the wiring plug from the idle speed control motor.

39 Unscrew the two securing bolts, and remove the idle speed control motor from the throttle body **(see illustration)**. Recover the gasket.

Refitting

40 Commence refitting by thoroughly cleaning the mating faces of the motor and the throttle body.

41 Refitting is a reversal of removal, but use a new gasket.

Coolant temperature sensor

42 Proceed as described in Section 12 for Multec CFi models, but note that the sensor is located in the coolant flange, next to the DIS module.

Oxygen sensor

43 Proceed as described in Section 12 for Multec CFi models, but note that the sensor is mounted in the exhaust front section, and

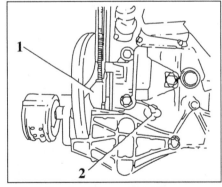

17.49 Crankshaft speed/position sensor (models without air conditioning) - Simtec models

1 Power steering pump bracket
2 Crankshaft speed/position sensor

access is obtained from underneath the vehicle. If desired, raise the front of the vehicle and support securely on axle stands (see "*Jacking and vehicle support*").

Crankshaft speed/position sensor – models without air conditioning

Removal

44 Disconnect the battery negative lead.

45 On models up to mid-1996, proceed as follows.

a) Simultaneously press the Nos 1 and 4 cylinder injector wiring plug retaining clips towards the fuel rail (using a screwdriver if necessary), and pull the wiring housing from the injectors.

b) Disconnect the crankshaft speed/position sensor wiring plug from the wiring housing.

46 On models from mid-1996, trace the wiring back from the crankshaft speed/position sensor and separate the two halves of the wiring connector.

47 Release the crankshaft speed/position sensor wiring from any brackets and clips.

48 Remove the air cleaner assembly as described in Section 3.

49 Remove the power steering pump (there is no need to disconnect the fluid lines) as described in Chapter 10, then unbolt the power steering pump bracket from the engine. The sensor wiring runs between the cylinder block and the power steering pump bracket **(see illustration)**.

50 Unscrew the securing screw, and withdraw the sensor from the cylinder block, noting the routing of the wiring.

Refitting

51 Refitting is a reversal of removal, but when refitting and reconnecting the wiring, ensure that the wiring cannot foul against any moving or hot parts, ie. drivebelts or exhaust. Refit the power steering pump with reference to Chapter 10.

Crankshaft speed/position sensor – models with air conditioning

Removal

52 Proceed as described in paragraphs 44 to 46.

53 Tie a length of sting or cable (approx. 2 m long) to the free end of the sensor wiring.

54 Release the sensor wiring from the clips on the timing belt cover, noting its routing.

55 If the oil level dipstick is located at the front right-hand side of the cylinder block, pull out the dipstick and its tube. Recover the O-rings.

56 Remove the exhaust front section as described later in this Section.

57 Working under the vehicle, unscrew the securing screw and withdraw the sensor from the cylinder block. Pull the wiring down from the top of the engine compartment, then untie the string and leave it in place to aid refitting.

Refitting

58 Refitting is a reversal of removal, bearing in mind the following points.
a) *Where applicable, use the string to pull the wiring into position in the engine compartment.*
b) *Refit the exhaust front section as described later in this Section.*
c) *Where applicable, refit the dipstick tube using new O-rings.*

Intake air temperature sensor

59 Proceed as described in Section 14 for Multec S models.

Camshaft sensor

Removal

60 Remove the securing screws, and withdraw the HT lead cover from the top of the camshaft cover.
61 Disconnect the battery negative lead, then disconnect the camshaft sensor wiring connector.
62 Remove the outer timing belt cover as described in Chapter 2B.
63 Unscrew the securing bolt, then withdraw the camshaft sensor upwards from the cylinder head.

Refitting

64 Refitting is a reversal of removal.

Knock sensor

65 The sensor is located on the lower inlet manifold side of the cylinder block, and (unless the inlet manifold has been removed) is only accessible from below the vehicle.
66 Disconnect the battery negative lead.
67 On models up to mid-1996, proceed as follows.
a) *Simultaneously press the Nos 1 and 4 cylinder injector wiring plug retaining clips towards the fuel rail (using a screwdriver if necessary), and pull the wiring housing from the injectors.*
b) *Disconnect the knock sensor wiring plug from the wiring housing.*
68 On models from mid-1996, trace the wiring back from the knock sensor and separate the two halves of the wiring connector.
69 Apply the handbrake, then jack up the front of the vehicle and support securely on axle stands (see *"Jacking and vehicle support"*).
70 Remove the engine undershield, as described in Chapter 11, Section 25.
71 Disconnect the sensor wiring plug.
72 Unscrew the securing bolt, and withdraw the sensor from the cylinder block.

Refitting

73 Refitting is a reversal of the removal procedure, but make sure that the sensor and its seat are perfectly clean, and that the sensor is secured firmly. Failure to observe these points could result in damage to the engine, as a poorly mounted sensor will not

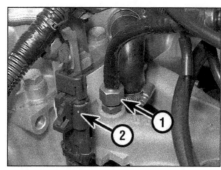

18.11 Brake servo hose union nut (1) and wiring connector (2) attached to left-hand end of inlet manifold – Multec CFi model

detect 'knocking', and the appropriate ignition correction will not be applied.

Electronic control unit (ECU)

74 Proceed as described in Section 12 for Multec CFi models, ignoring the references to the basic control unit and the programme memory.

Fuel pump relay

Removal

75 The relay is located with the ECU behind the right-hand footwell side panel. Remove the footwell/side trim panel as described in Chapter 11, Section 30.
76 Pull the relay from its connector, and remove it.

Refitting

77 Refitting is a reversal of removal.

Fuel evaporation control system components

78 Refer to Part C of this Chapter.

Exhaust gas recirculation system components

79 Refer to Part C of this Chapter.

Secondary air injection system components

80 Refer to Part C of this Chapter.

18.17 Earth wire (arrowed) attached to upper alternator mounting – Multec CFi model

18 Inlet manifold (SOHC engines) – removal and refitting

Multec CFi single-point fuel injection

Note: *Refer to the precautions given in Section 1 before starting work. A new gasket must be used on refitting.*

Removal

1 Depressurise the fuel system by removing the fuel pump relay (see Chapter 12), and cranking the engine on the starter motor for a minimum of 5 seconds.
2 Disconnect the battery negative lead.
3 Remove the airbox from the top of the fuel injection unit, as described in Section 3.
4 Release the securing lugs, and disconnect the wiring plug from the fuel injector.
5 Remove the rubber seal from the top of the fuel injection unit (if not already done), then slide the fuel injector wiring rubber grommet from the slot in the side of the fuel injection unit. Move the wiring to one side.
6 Disconnect the wiring plugs from the idle speed control motor and the throttle position sensor.
7 Disconnect the fuel feed and return hoses from the fuel injection unit, noting their locations to aid refitting. Be prepared for fuel spillage, and take adequate fire precautions. Clamp or plug the open ends of the hoses to minimise further fuel loss.
8 Disconnect the vacuum hoses from the fuel injection unit, noting their locations and routing to ensure correct refitting.
9 Disconnect the MAP sensor hose from the rear of the fuel injection unit.
10 Release the securing clip, then disconnect the throttle cable end balljoint from the throttle valve lever. Slide the throttle cable grommet from the bracket on the inlet manifold, and move the throttle cable to one side out of the way.
11 Unscrew the union nut, and disconnect the brake servo vacuum hose from the inlet manifold **(see illustration)**.
12 Where applicable, disconnect the hose from the exhaust gas recirculation valve.
13 Disconnect the wiring from the temperature gauge sender.
14 Where applicable, disconnect the wiring from the coolant temperature sensor.
15 Separate the two halves of the wiring connector located in the bracket attached to the left-hand end of the inlet manifold. Unclip the connector from the bracket.
16 Partially drain the cooling system as described in Chapter 1, then disconnect the coolant hose from the rear of the inlet manifold. Be prepared for coolant spillage, and plug the open end of the hose to reduce coolant loss.
17 Unscrew and remove the top alternator mounting nut and bolt, noting the location of the earth wire on the bolt **(see illustration)**.

18 Make a final check to ensure that all relevant hoses, pipes and wires have been disconnected.

19 Unscrew the securing nuts, and withdraw the manifold from the cylinder head. Recover the gasket.

20 It is possible that some of the manifold studs may be unscrewed from the cylinder head when the manifold securing nuts are unscrewed. In this event, the studs should be screwed back into the cylinder head once the manifold has been removed, using two manifold nuts locked together.

21 If desired, the ancillary components can be removed from the manifold with reference to the relevant Sections of this Chapter.

Refitting

22 Refitting is a reversal of removal, remembering the following points.

23 Where applicable, refit any ancillary components to the manifold, with reference to the relevant Sections of this Chapter.

24 If the alternator mounting bracket has been unbolted from the manifold, refit it before refitting the manifold, as access is limited once the manifold is in place.

25 Refit the manifold using a new gasket, and tighten the securing nuts to the specified torque.

26 Ensure that all relevant hoses, pipes and wires are correctly reconnected and routed.

27 On completion, check and if necessary top-up the coolant level, as described in 'Weekly checks'.

28 Check and if necessary, adjust the throttle cable freeplay, as described in Section 8.

Multec M multi-point fuel injection

Note: *Refer to the precautions given in Section 1 before starting work. A new gasket must be used on refitting.*

Removal

29 Depressurise the fuel system by removing the fuel pump relay (see Chapter 12), and cranking the engine on the starter motor for a minimum of 5 seconds, then disconnect the battery negative lead.

30 Release the securing clip, then disconnect the throttle cable end balljoint from the throttle valve lever. Slide the throttle cable grommet

18.32 Brake servo hose union nut (arrowed) – Multec M MPi model

from the bracket on the inlet manifold, and move the throttle cable to one side out of the way.

31 Loosen the clamp screw, and disconnect the air trunking from the throttle body.

32 Unscrew the union nut, and disconnect the brake servo vacuum hose from the inlet manifold **(see illustration)**.

33 Disconnect the camshaft cover breather hoses from the throttle body.

34 Disconnect the vacuum hoses from the throttle body, noting their locations to aid refitting.

35 Disconnect the coolant hoses from the throttle body (two hoses) and the inlet manifold (one hose), noting their locations to aid refitting. Be prepared for coolant spillage, and clamp or plug the open ends of the hoses, to prevent further coolant loss. Where applicable, unclip the coolant hose from the rear of the manifold.

36 Disconnect the wiring plugs from the throttle position sensor and the idle speed control motor in the throttle housing, and from the intake air temperature sensor in the inlet manifold plenum chamber.

37 Unscrew the two securing bolts, and disconnect the two earth leads from the right-hand end of the cylinder head **(see illustration)**.

38 Disconnect the earth lead from the engine lifting eye bolt at the left-hand end of the inlet manifold.

39 Disconnect the wiring from the coolant temperature gauge sender in the inlet manifold.

18.37 Earth lead securing bolts (arrowed) at right-hand end of cylinder head – Multec M MPi model

40 Disconnect the wiring plugs from the fuel injectors.

41 Separate the two halves of the wiring connector located in the bracket attached to the upper left-hand inlet manifold stud.

42 Disconnect the fuel hoses from the fuel pipes under the fuel rail, noting their locations to ensure correct refitting. Access is most easily obtained from under the vehicle. Loosen the clamp screws slowly, to release any remaining pressure in the system. Be prepared for fuel spillage, and take adequate fire precautions. Clamp or plug the open ends of the hoses to prevent dirt ingress and further fuel leakage **(see illustrations)**.

43 Unscrew and remove the top alternator mounting nut and bolt.

44 Make a final check to ensure that all relevant hoses, pipes and wires have been disconnected.

45 Proceed as described in paragraphs 19 to 21 inclusive **(see illustration)**.

Refitting

46 Refitting is as described previously in this Section for Multec CFi single-point fuel injection models.

Motronic M 1.5 multi-point fuel injection system

Note: *Refer to the precautions given in Section 1 before starting work. New gaskets must be used on refitting.*

Removal

47 Depressurise the fuel system by removing the fuel pump relay (see Chapter 12), and

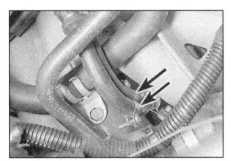

18.42a Fuel pipe connections (arrowed) under inlet manifold (viewed from underneath vehicle) – Multec M MPi model

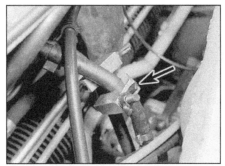

18.42b Clamp the fuel hoses (arrowed) to prevent fuel spillage

18.45 Lifting the inlet manifold from the engine – Multec M MPi model

18.60a Unscrewing an inlet manifold securing nut – Motronic M 1.5 model

18.60b Removing the inlet manifold – Motronic M 1.5 model

cranking the engine on the starter motor for a minimum of 5 seconds, then disconnect the battery negative lead.

48 Remove the idle speed control valve and its hoses, referring to Section 15, if necessary.

49 Release the securing clip, then disconnect the throttle cable and balljoint from the throttle valve lever. Slide the throttle cable grommet from the bracket on the inlet manifold, and move the cable to one side out of the way.

50 Loosen the clamp screw, and disconnect the air trunking from the throttle body.

51 Unscrew the union nut, and disconnect the brake servo vacuum hose from the inlet manifold.

52 Disconnect the camshaft cover breather hose from the throttle body.

53 Disconnect the coolant hoses from the throttle body. Be prepared for coolant spillage, and clamp or plug the open ends of the hoses to prevent further coolant loss.

54 Disconnect the wiring plug from the throttle position sensor.

55 Disconnect the vacuum pipe from the top of the fuel pressure regulator.

56 Disconnect the wiring harness housing from the fuel injectors, and move it to one side, taking care not to strain the wiring. Pull up on the wiring harness housing, and compress the wiring plug retaining clips to release the harness housing from the injectors.

57 Disconnect the fuel hoses from the fuel rail. Loosen the clamps slowly, to release any remaining pressure in the fuel system. Be

19.15 Alternator upper mounting bracket securing bolts (arrowed) – 1.4 litre Multec S MPi model

prepared for fuel spillage, and take adequate fire precautions. Clamp or plug the open ends of the hoses, to prevent dirt ingress and further fuel leakage.

58 Unscrew and remove the top alternator mounting nut and bolt.

59 Make a final check to ensure that all relevant hoses, pipes and wires have been disconnected.

60 Proceed as described in paragraphs 19 to 21 inclusive **(see illustrations)**.

Refitting

61 Refitting is as described for Multec CFi models, in paragraphs 22 to 28.

19 Inlet manifold (DOHC engines) – removal and refitting

Multec S multi-point fuel injection (1.4 litre engines) – inlet manifold

Note: *Refer to the precautions given in Section 1 before starting work. A new gasket must be used on refitting.*

Removal

1 Depressurise the fuel system by removing the fuel pump relay (see Chapter 12), and cranking the engine on the starter motor for a minimum of 5 seconds, then disconnect the battery negative lead.

2 Remove the air cleaner as described in Section 3.

3 Remove the alternator drivebelt as described in Chapter 1.

4 Remove the engine oil filler cap, then remove the engine cover and refit the oil filler cap.

5 Disconnect the wiring plug from the intake air temperature sensor.

6 Disconnect the two breather hoses from the camshaft cover.

7 Loosen the clamp, and disconnect the air intake trunking from the throttle body.

8 Work along the plastic wiring housing at the rear of the engine and disconnect all the wiring connectors from the wiring housing and its wiring harness, noting the locations of the connectors to aid refitting.

9 Depress the securing clips, and release the wiring housing from the fuel injectors, then move the housing clear of the working area, towards the rear of the engine.

10 Disconnect the vacuum hose from the fuel tank vent valve.

11 Disconnect the throttle cable from the throttle lever and bracket with reference to Section 8.

12 Disconnect the brake servo vacuum hose and the manifold absolute pressure (MAP) sensor vacuum hoses from the manifold.

13 Partially drain the cooling system as described in Chapter 1, then disconnect the coolant hoses from the throttle body.

14 Unscrew the union nuts and disconnect the fuel hoses from the fuel rail and fuel pressure regulator. Be prepared for fuel spillage and take adequate fire precautions.

15 Unscrew the securing bolts, and remove the alternator upper mounting bracket, then unscrew the lower alternator mounting bolt, and pivot the alternator towards the rear of the engine **(see illustration)**.

16 If not already done, apply the handbrake, then jack up the front of the vehicle and support securely on axle stands (see *"Jacking and vehicle support"*).

17 Working underneath the vehicle, unbolt the inlet manifold support bracket from the manifold and the cylinder block.

18 Unscrew the securing bolts, and remove the manifold from the manifold mounting flange. Recover the gasket.

Refitting

19 Commence refitting by thoroughly cleaning the mating faces of the manifold and the manifold mounting flange.

20 Refitting is a reversal of removal, bearing in mind the following points.

a) Fit the manifold using a new gasket.

b) Ensure that all wiring plugs and vacuum hoses are correctly reconnected and routed as noted before removal.

c) Check and if necessary top up the coolant level as described in 'Weekly checks'.

d) Refit and tension the alternator drivebelt as described in Chapter 1.

Multec S multi-point fuel injection (1.4 litre engines) – inlet manifold mounting flange

Note: *A new gasket will be required on refitting.*

Removal

21 Remove the inlet manifold as described previously in this Section.

22 Disconnect the coolant hose from the manifold flange. Be prepared for coolant spillage.

23 Unscrew the securing nuts, and remove the manifold flange from the cylinder head. It is possible that some of the manifold studs may be unscrewed from the cylinder head when the manifold securing nuts are unscrewed. In this event, the studs should be screwed back into the cylinder head once the manifold has been removed, using two manifold nuts locked together.

24 Unbolt the coolant flange from the cylinder head, then remove the manifold/coolant flange gasket **(see illustration)**.

Refitting

25 Commence refitting by thoroughly cleaning the mating faces of the manifold flange, coolant flange and cylinder head.
26 Refitting is a reversal of removal, but use a new gasket, and refit the inlet manifold as described previously in this Section.

Multec S multi-point fuel injection (1.6 litre engines) – upper section of inlet manifold

Note: *A new gasket will be required on refitting.*

Removal

27 Disconnect the battery negative lead.
28 Remove the engine oil filler cap, then remove the engine cover, and refit the oil filler cap.
29 Work along the plastic wiring housing at the rear of the engine and disconnect all the wiring connectors from the wiring housing and its wiring harness, noting the locations of the connectors to aid refitting.
30 Release the wiring housing from the three securing clips, then move the housing clear of the working area, towards the rear of the engine.
31 Disconnect the following vacuum hoses from the inlet manifold, noting their locations to aid refitting.
a) Engine breather hose.
b) Secondary air injection switchover valve hose.
c) Brake servo hose.
d) Manifold absolute pressure (MAP) sensor hose.
e) Charcoal canister hose.
32 Slide the fuel tank vent valve upwards from its mounting bracket, and move the valve to one side.
33 Disconnect the fuel pressure regulator vacuum hose from the inlet manifold **(see illustration)**.
34 Slacken the clip securing the intake air trunking to the top section of the manifold.
35 Unscrew the 5 bolts securing the upper section of the manifold to the lower section, and the two bolts securing the upper section of the manifold to the camshaft cover, then lift off the upper section of the manifold. Recover the gasket.

Refitting

36 Commence refitting by thoroughly cleaning the mating faces of the upper and lower sections of the manifold.
37 Refitting is a reversal of removal, bearing in mind the following points.
a) Use a new gasket between the upper and lower sections of the manifold.
b) Ensure that all vacuum hoses and wiring plugs are correctly reconnected as noted before removal.

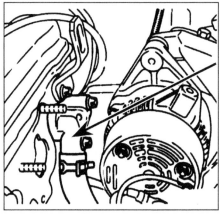

19.24 Unbolt the coolant flange (arrowed) from the cylinder head – 1.4 litre Multec S MPi model

Multec S multi-point fuel injection (1.6 litre engines) – lower section of inlet manifold

Note: *Refer to the precautions given in Section 1 before starting work. A new gasket must be used on refitting.*

Removal

38 Depressurise the fuel system by removing the fuel pump relay (see Chapter 12), and cranking the engine on the starter motor for a minimum of 5 seconds.
39 Remove the air cleaner as described in Section 3.
40 Remove the upper section of the inlet manifold as described previously in this Section.
41 Unscrew the union nuts and disconnect the fuel hoses from the fuel rail and fuel pressure regulator. Be prepared for fuel spillage and take adequate fire precautions.
42 Slacken the clamp, and disconnect the air intake trunking from the throttle body.
43 Separate the two halves of the crankshaft speed/position sensor wiring connector, located at the bracket above the fuel pressure regulator, then release the connector from the bracket, and feed the wiring down between the inlet manifold ducts, noting its routing.
44 Remove the securing screw(s) and release the plastic wiring housing from the throttle body. Lay the wiring housing clear of the

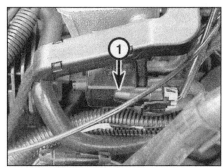

19.33 Charcoal canister vacuum hose (1) – 1.6 litre Multec S MPi model

working area, towards the rear of the engine compartment.
45 Disconnect the throttle cable from the throttle lever and bracket, and move the cable clear of the working area, with reference to Section 8.
46 Unscrew the securing bolts, and remove the throttle body. Lower the throttle body and leave it in the engine compartment.
47 Disconnect the wiring plugs from the idle speed control motor and the throttle position sensor.
48 Unscrew the securing bolts, and remove the throttle body flange from the lower section of the inlet manifold, noting the locations of the bolts (different lengths of bolts are used).
49 Drain the cooling system as described in Chapter 1.
50 Remove the alternator drivebelt as described in Chapter 1.
51 Unbolt the alternator upper mounting bracket, then slacken the lower alternator mounting bolt, and pivot the alternator towards the rear of the engine.
52 Unbolt the plastic wiring housing bracket from the lower part of the manifold, and lay it towards the rear of the engine compartment.
53 Disconnect the coolant hose from the lower part of the inlet manifold.
54 Unscrew the securing nuts, and remove the lower part of the manifold from the cylinder head.
55 Unbolt the coolant flange from the cylinder head, then remove the manifold/coolant flange gasket.

Refitting

56 Commence refitting by thoroughly cleaning the mating faces of the manifold flange, coolant flange and cylinder head.
57 Refitting is a reversal of removal, bearing in mind the following points.
a) Use a new gasket.
b) Refit and tension the alternator drivebelt with reference to Chapter 1.
c) Refill the cooling system as described in Chapter 1.
d) Ensure that the throttle body flange bolts are refitted to their correct locations as noted before removal.
e) Ensure that all wiring plugs and hoses are correctly reconnected and routed as noted before removal.
f) Refit the upper section of the inlet manifold as described previously in this Section.

Motronic M 2.5 and M 2.8 multi-point fuel injection systems

Note: *Refer to the precautions given in Section 1 before starting work. New gaskets must be used on refitting.*

Removal

58 Depressurise the fuel system by removing the fuel pump relay (see Chapter 12), and cranking the engine on the starter motor for a minimum of 5 seconds, then disconnect the battery negative lead.

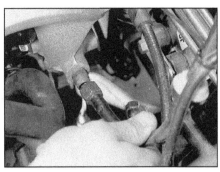

19.71 Disconnecting the brake servo hose from the inlet manifold – Motronic M 2.5 model

59 Disconnect the wiring from the air mass meter. Recover the sealing ring, where applicable.

60 Loosen the clamp screw securing the air trunking to the right-hand end of the air mass meter.

61 Using an Allen key or hexagon bit, unscrew the four bolts securing the airbox to the throttle body. Lift the airbox from the throttle body, and disconnect the hose from the base of the airbox, then withdraw the airbox/air mass meter assembly.

62 Disconnect the wiring plug from the throttle position sensor and intake air temperature sensor (if applicable).

63 Slide the throttle cable end from the throttle valve lever, then pull the cable end grommet from the bracket on the inlet manifold, and move the throttle cable to one side out of the way.

64 Disconnect the two breather hoses from the rear of the camshaft cover. Disconnect the larger hose from the main throttle body, and remove the hose completely.

65 Position a piece of cloth beneath one of the fuel hose unions on the fuel rail, to absorb the fuel that will be released as the union is disconnected.

66 Slowly loosen the fuel hose unions, to gradually relieve any remaining pressure in the fuel feed line, then disconnect the hose from the fuel rail. Be prepared for fuel spillage, and

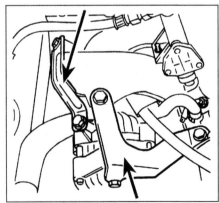

19.76 Remove the alternator upper support brackets (arrowed) – Motronic M 2.8 models

take adequate fire precautions. Plug the end of the fuel hose, to prevent dirt ingress and further fuel leakage.

67 Repeat paragraphs 65 and 66 for the remaining fuel hose-to-fuel rail union.

68 Where applicable, disconnect the vacuum pipes from the front of the electronic traction control (ETC) throttle housing.

69 Where applicable, disconnect the coolant hoses from the ETC throttle valve housing, noting their locations and routing to aid correct refitting. Be prepared for coolant spillage, and clamp or plug the open ends of the hoses to minimise coolant loss.

70 Disconnect the wiring harness housing from the fuel injectors, and move it to one side, taking care not to strain the wiring. Pull up on the wiring harness housing, and compress the wiring plug retaining clips to release the housing from the injectors.

71 Unscrew the union nut, and disconnect the brake servo vacuum hose from the left-hand side of the inlet manifold **(see illustration)**.

72 Unscrew the retaining nut, and remove the fuel hose bracket from the left-hand side of the throttle body.

73 Unscrew the securing nuts, and disconnect the earth leads from the fuel rail securing studs at either end of the fuel rail.

74 Unscrew the securing bolt, and remove the cable/hose bracket from the left-hand end of the inlet manifold.

75 Remove the idle speed control valve, as described in Section 16.

76 Remove the alternator drivebelt as described in Chapter 1, then unscrew and remove the top alternator mounting nut and bolt. On models with Motronic M 2.8 fuel injection, unbolt the remove the alternator upper support brackets **(see illustration)**.

77 Make a final check to ensure that all relevant hoses, pipes and wires have been disconnected.

78 Unscrew the securing nuts, and withdraw the manifold from the cylinder head. Recover the gasket.

79 It is possible that some of the manifold studs may be unscrewed from the cylinder head when the manifold securing nuts are unscrewed. In this event, the studs should be screwed back into the cylinder head once the manifold has been removed, using two manifold nuts locked together.

80 If desired, the ancillary components can be removed from the manifold with reference to the relevant Sections of this Chapter.

Refitting

81 Refitting is a reversal of removal, remembering the following points.
 a) *Where applicable, refit any ancillary components to the manifold, with reference to the relevant Sections of this Chapter.*
 b) *If the alternator mounting bracket has been unbolted from the manifold, refit it before refitting the manifold, as access is limited once the manifold is in place.*

 c) *Refit the manifold using a new gasket, and tighten the securing nuts to the specified torque.*
 d) *Ensure that all relevant hoses, pipes and wires are correctly reconnected and routed.*
 e) *Make sure that the ETC throttle housing coolant hoses are correctly routed and reconnected, as noted before removal.*
 f) *On completion, check and if necessary top-up the coolant level, as described in 'Weekly checks'.*

Simtec multi-point fuel injection systems

Note: *Refer to the precautions given in Section 1 before starting work. New gaskets must be used on refitting.*

Removal

82 Depressurise the fuel system by removing the fuel pump relay (see Chapter 12), and cranking the engine on the starter motor for a minimum of 5 seconds.

83 Disconnect the battery negative lead.

84 Remove the air cleaner assembly as described in Section 3.

85 Disconnect the wiring plugs from the intake air temperature sensor and the air mass meter.

86 Disconnect the two breather hoses from the camshaft cover, and disconnect the air intake trunking from the throttle body.

87 Disconnect the throttle cable from the throttle lever and the support bracket(s), with reference to Section 8.

88 Unscrew the union nuts and disconnect the fuel supply and return hoses from the fuel rail. Be prepared for fuel spillage and take adequate fire precautions.

89 Disconnect the wiring plug from the idle speed control motor, and unbolt the earth wiring from the inlet manifold.

90 Work along the plastic wiring housing at the rear of the engine and disconnect all the wiring connectors from the wiring housing and its wiring harness, noting the locations of the connectors to aid refitting. Note that it may not be possible to disconnect the knock sensor and crankshaft speed/position sensor wiring plugs until the wiring housing has been removed.

91 Simultaneously press the Nos 1 and 4 cylinder injector wiring plug retaining clips towards the fuel rail (using a screwdriver if necessary), and pull the wiring housing from the injectors.

92 Partially drain the cooling system as described in Chapter 1, then disconnect the coolant hoses from the throttle body.

93 Disconnect the following vacuum hoses from the inlet manifold.
 a) *Brake servo hose.*
 b) *Exhaust gas recirculation (EGR) vacuum hose.*
 c) *Fuel tank vent valve hose.*
 d) *Secondary air injection combination valve (where applicable).*

94 Unbolt and remove the upper alternator support brackets, then remove the alternator drivebelt as described in Chapter 1.

95 Slacken the lower alternator mounting bolt, then pivot the alternator back towards the engine.

96 If not already done, apply the handbrake, then jack up the front of the vehicle and support securely on axle stands (see *"Jacking and vehicle support"*).

97 Working under the vehicle, unbolt the inlet manifold support bracket from the manifold and the cylinder block, and remove the bracket.

98 Make a final check to ensure that all relevant hoses, pipes and wires have been disconnected.

99 Proceed as described in paragraphs 77 to 79 inclusive.

Refitting

100 Commence refitting by thoroughly cleaning the mating faces of the manifold and cylinder head.

101 Refitting is a reversal of removal, bearing in mind the following points.

a) *Refit and tension the alternator drivebelt with reference to Chapter 1.*
b) *Ensure that all hoses and wiring plugs are correctly reconnected and routed as noted before removal.*
c) *Check the coolant level and top up if necessary as described in "Weekly checks".*
d) *Reconnect the throttle cable and check the adjustment with reference to Section 8.*

---

20 Exhaust manifold – removal and refitting

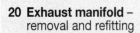

Removal

Note: *A new gasket will be required on refitting.*

1 On all except C 20 XE engines, proceed as follows. On C 20 XE engines, a tubular exhaust manifold is fitted, which incorporates the front section of the exhaust system – refer to Section 21 for details of removal and refitting.

2 Where applicable, disconnect the oxygen sensor wiring plug.

3 Where applicable, unbolt the heat shield from the manifold **(see illustration)**.

4 Where applicable, disconnect the hot air hose from the shroud on the exhaust manifold.

5 Where applicable, remove the secondary air injection pipe as described in Part C of this Chapter.

6 Disconnect the exhaust front section from the manifold as described in Section 21.

7 Unscrew the securing nuts, and withdraw the manifold from the cylinder head. Recover the gasket(s) **(see illustrations)**.

20.3 Exhaust manifold heat shield securing bolts (arrowed) – 1.6 litre SOHC engine

8 It is possible that some of the manifold studs may be unscrewed from the cylinder head when the manifold securing nuts are unscrewed. In this event, the studs should be screwed back into the cylinder head once the manifold has been removed, using two manifold nuts locked together.

Refitting

9 Commence refitting by thoroughly cleaning the mating faces of the manifold and cylinder head.

10 Refitting is a reversal of removal, bearing in mind the following points **(see illustration)**.

a) *Use a new gasket.*
b) *Tighten the securing nuts to the specified torque.*
c) *Reconnect the exhaust front section to the manifold with reference to Section 21.*
d) *Where applicable, refit the secondary air injection pipe as described in Part C of this Chapter.*

---

21 Exhaust system – general information and component renewal

General information

All except C 20 XE engine models

1 Refer to Part A, Section 23 of this Chapter, noting the following points.

2 The original factory-fitted exhaust system consists of four separate sections (including

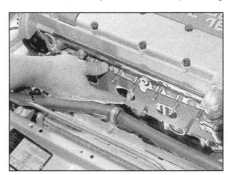

20.7b . . . and recover the gasket – 1.6 litre SOHC engine

the catalytic converter), all of which can be renewed individually **(see illustration overleaf)**. The manufacturers do not specify any renewal intervals for the catalytic converter. An exhaust gas oxygen sensor is fitted in the exhaust front section on some models.

3 When inspecting the exhaust system, also inspect the catalytic converter for signs of damage or corrosion. At the same time, inspect the oxygen sensor and its wiring for signs of damage.

C 20 XE engine models

4 Refer to the preceding information for other models, but note that a tubular exhaust manifold is fitted, which incorporates the front section of the exhaust system.

Component renewal

Note: *All relevant gaskets and/or sealing rings should be renewed on refitting.*

Front section – all except C 20 XE engine models

5 Raise the vehicle, and support securely on axle stands (see *"Jacking and vehicle support"*).

6 Where applicable, disconnect the oxygen sensor wiring plug, which is usually attached to a bracket secured to one of the top engine-to-gearbox bolts.

7 Unscrew the two securing bolts, and disconnect the exhaust front section from the catalytic converter. Recover the sealing ring and, where applicable, the springs.

20.7a Withdraw the exhaust manifold . . .

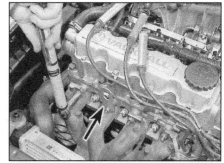

20.10 Tightening an exhaust manifold securing nut. Note position of engine lifting bracket (arrowed) – 1.6 litre SOHC engine

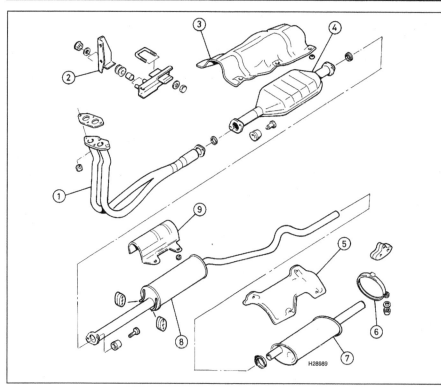

21.2 Typical exhaust system with catalytic converter

1 Front downpipe
2 Front downpipe mounting bracket
3 Heatshield – catalytic converter
4 Catalytic converter
5 Heatshield – rear silencer
6 Clamp
7 Rear silencer and tailpipe
8 Front silencer and intermediate pipe
9 Heatshield – front silencer

21.10a Exhaust front section-to-manifold joint – 1.4 litre SOHC engine model

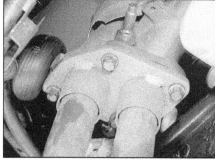

21.10b Exhaust front section-to-manifold joint – 1.6 litre SOHC engine model

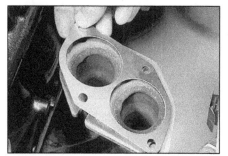

21.10c Fitting a new exhaust front section-to-manifold gasket – 1.6 litre SOHC engine model

21.10d Use a new sealing ring when connecting the exhaust front section to the catalytic converter

21.8 Exhaust front section mounting and joint – 1.6 litre SOHC engine model

1 Bracket   2 Sprung joint

8 Unbolt the exhaust front section from the bracket on the cylinder block (see illustration).
9 Unscrew and remove the bolts securing the downpipe to the exhaust manifold, and withdraw the exhaust front section. Recover the downpipe-to-manifold gasket, and where applicable, recover the springs from the bolts.
10 Refitting is a reversal of removal, but use a new gasket when reconnecting the downpipe to the manifold, and a new sealing ring when connecting the joint to the catalytic converter (see illustrations).

Front section – C 20 XE engine models

11 Proceed as described in paragraphs 5 an 6.
12 Remove the engine undershield, as described in Chapter 11, Section 25.
13 Unscrew the two securing bolts, and disconnect the exhaust front section from the catalytic converter at the flexible joint. Recover the sealing ring and springs.
14 Unbolt the exhaust front section from the bracket on the cylinder block.
15 Working in the engine compartment, remove the bolts securing the exhaust manifold heat shield to the cylinder head (see illustration).
16 Unscrew the two lower exhaust manifold securing nuts that also secure the heat shield brackets, and withdraw the heat shield.
17 Unscrew the remaining manifold securing nuts, then withdraw the manifold/exhaust front section from the vehicle. Recover the manifold gasket.

21.15 Unscrewing an exhaust manifold heat shield bolt – C 20 XE engine model

18 It is possible that some of the manifold studs may be unscrewed from the cylinder head when the manifold securing nuts are unscrewed. In this event, the studs should be screwed back into the cylinder head once the manifold has been removed, using two manifold nuts locked together.

19 Refitting is a reversal of removal, but use a new manifold gasket, and use a new sealing ring when reconnecting the flexible joint.

Catalytic converter

20 Proceed as described for the front expansion box in Part A, Section 23 of this Chapter. The internal components of the catalytic converter are fragile – take care not to strike it during removal, and do not drip it once removed.

Centre section

21 Refer to Part A, Section 23 of this Chapter, noting that the front end of the centre section must be disconnected from the catalytic converter instead of the front expansion box.

Rear section

22 Refer to Part A, Section 23 of this Chapter.

22 Electronic traction control (ETC) system – general information

1 An electronic traction control (ETC) system is fitted to certain DOHC engine models. The system monitors the traction provided by the driven (front) wheels, preventing the wheels from spinning, regardless of the road conditions and the grip of the tyres. This is particularly beneficial in helping to increase traction when driving on slippery roads due to rain, snow, or ice.

2 The ETC system is controlled by an electronic control unit, which receives information from the engine management and ABS system electronic control units (ECUs). The four ABS wheel sensors (see Chapter 9) continuously monitor the traction of the front wheels by comparing the speeds of the front wheels with those of the rear wheels. Immediately a difference in speed is registered between the front and rear wheels, a signal is fed to the ETC electronic control unit. The ETC control unit activates an auxiliary throttle valve, which reduces the engine speed (and thus torque) to optimum levels in relation to the rotation of the wheels, even though the driver may be applying full-throttle (main throttle valve fully open). In exceptional circumstances, such as when driving away from rest using full-throttle on an icy surface, the ETC control unit supplies a signal to the engine management ECU to interrupt the fuel injection and ignition systems intermittently, reducing engine torque more rapidly **(see illustration)**.

3 The ETC system throttle valve is mounted in

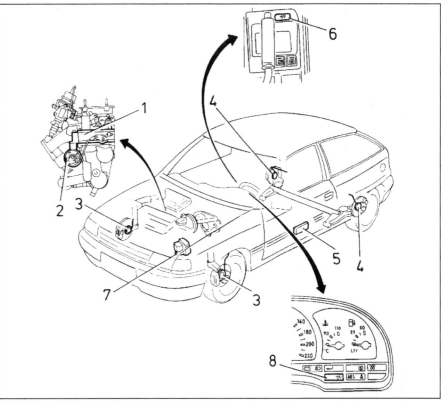

22.2 Electronic Traction Control (ETC) system

1	Throttle housing	5	Electronic control unit
2	Throttle valve control motor	6	Control button
3	Front wheel ABS sensor	7	ABS hydraulic modulator
4	Rear wheel ABS sensor (see Chapter 10)	8	Warning light

a housing fitted between the main throttle body and the inlet manifold. The throttle valve is actuated by a control motor, through a coupling rod. A position sensor is incorporated in the control motor to provide the traction control unit with information on the ETC throttle valve position.

4 If desired, the system can be switched off by using a button mounted in the centre console. This may be beneficial in certain circumstances such as when driving in deep snow, or when 'digging' the vehicle out of soft ground.

23 Electronic traction control (ETC) system components – removal and refitting

Throttle housing

Note: New gaskets must be used on refitting.

Removal

1 Disconnect the battery negative lead.
2 Remove the main throttle body, as described in Section 16 or 17, as applicable.
3 Disconnect the camshaft cover breather hose from the right-hand side of the ETC throttle valve housing.

4 Disconnect the coolant hoses from the ETC throttle valve housing, noting their locations and routing to aid correct refitting. Be prepared for coolant spillage, and clamp or plug the open ends of the hoses to minimise coolant loss.

5 Unscrew and remove the two bolts securing the throttle valve control motor to the throttle valve housing.

6 Disconnect the two vacuum hoses from the front of the throttle valve housing, noting their locations to aid refitting.

7 Disconnect the throttle valve actuating rod from the lever on the side of the throttle valve housing **(see illustration)**.

23.7 Throttle valve operating rod connection (arrowed) to ETC throttle valve

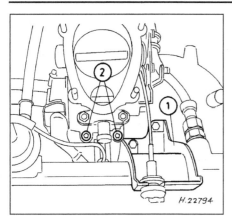

23.24 ETC throttle valve control motor securing screws (2) and throttle cable bracket (1)

8 Lift the ETC throttle valve housing from the inlet manifold. Recover the gasket.

Refitting

9 Before commencing refitting, thoroughly clean the mating surfaces of the ETC throttle valve housing and the inlet manifold.

10 Fit the ETC throttle valve housing to the inlet manifold, using a new gasket.

11 Further refitting is a reversal of removal, remembering the following points.

12 Ensure that the coolant hoses are correctly reconnected and routed, as noted before removal.

13 When reconnecting the throttle valve actuating rod to the lever on the throttle valve housing, ensure that the retaining clip engages.

14 When reconnecting the vacuum hoses to the throttle valve housing, ensure that they are correctly positioned as noted previously.

15 Refit the main throttle body, using a new gasket, as described in Section 16 or 17, as applicable.

16 On completion, check the coolant level and top-up if necessary, as described in 'Weekly checks'.

Throttle valve control motor

Removal

17 Disconnect the battery negative lead.

18 Remove the airbox from the top of the throttle body, as described in Section 3.

19 Disconnect the crankcase ventilation hose from the main throttle body.

20 Loosen the alternator mounting bolts, then remove the top mounting bolt, slip the drivebelt from the alternator pulley, and swing the alternator to one side, away from the engine.

21 Unscrew the two securing screws, and detach the throttle cable bracket from the inlet manifold.

22 Disconnect the throttle valve control motor wiring plug, which is accessible from the alternator side of the throttle housing.

23 Disconnect the ETC throttle valve operating rod from the throttle valve.

24 Unscrew and remove the two bolts securing the throttle valve control motor to the ETC throttle valve housing, then carefully withdraw the motor assembly **(see illustration)**.

25 If the throttle valve operating rod is disconnected from the motor, take careful note of the orientation of the rod, to enable correct refitting **(see illustration)**.

Refitting

26 Refitting is a reversal of removal, remembering the following points.

27 Where applicable, ensure that the throttle valve operating rod is correctly orientated, as noted before removal.

28 Before tightening the alternator mounting

bolts, tension the drivebelt as described in Chapter 1.

29 Refit the airbox as described in Section 3.

Electronic control unit (ECU)

Removal

30 The ETC control unit is located inside the vehicle, next to the left-hand front seat, beneath a cover in the sill.

31 Ensure that the ignition is switched off, then disconnect the battery negative lead.

32 Prise up the two flaps which conceal the control unit cover securing nuts, then remove the securing nuts **(see illustration)**.

33 Carefully withdraw the control unit cover, noting that it clips into the seat runner cover panel.

34 Pull the control unit from its location, then remove the wiring plug securing screw, release the clips to disconnect the wiring plug, and withdraw the unit **(see illustration)**.

Refitting

35 Refitting is a reversal of removal, ensuring that the cover engages correctly with the seat runner cover panel.

Manual override switch

Removal

36 The switch is located in the centre console.

37 Disconnect the battery negative lead.

38 Carefully prise the central storage tray from the centre console.

39 Disconnect the wiring from the switch.

40 Carefully push the switch out through the top of the centre console.

Refitting

41 Refitting is a reversal of removal.

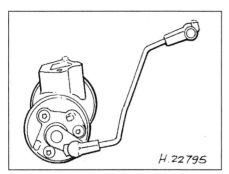

23.25 ETC throttle valve control motor assembly

23.32 ETC electronic control unit cover securing nuts

23.34 Withdrawing the ETC electronic control unit

Chapter 4 Part C:
Emission control systems

Contents

Degrees of difficulty

Easy, suitable for novice with little experience		Fairly easy, suitable for beginner with some experience		Fairly difficult, suitable for competent DIY mechanic		Difficult, suitable for experienced DIY mechanic		Very difficult, suitable for expert DIY or professional	

Specifications

Torque wrench settings	Nm	lbf ft
Exhaust gas recirculation valve securing bolts	20	15
Secondary air injection metal pipe to exhaust manifold:		
X 14 XE and X 16 XEL engines	20	15
X 18 XE and X 20 XEV engines	8	6
Secondary air injection pump to bracket	10	7
Secondary air injection pump bracket	20	15

1 General information and precautions

General information

All models can be operated on unleaded petrol (models with a catalytic converter can **only** be operated on unleaded petrol), but additionally, various systems may be fitted (depending on model) to reduce the emission of pollution into the atmosphere. The systems are described in more detail in the following paragraphs. All models are fitted with a crankcase emission control system.

Crankcase emission control system

A crankcase ventilation system is fitted to all models, but the systems differ in detail according to model.

Oil fumes and blow-by gases (combustion gases that have passed by the piston rings) are drawn from the crankcase into the area of the cylinder head above the camshaft(s) through a hose. From here, the gases are drawn into the inlet manifold/throttle body (as applicable) and/or the air box on the carburettor/throttle body, where they are mixed with fresh air/ fuel mixture and burnt, hence reducing harmful exhaust emissions.

Certain models may have a mesh filter inside the camshaft cover, which should be cleaned in paraffin if clogging is evident.

Exhaust emission control system

To minimise the level of exhaust gas pollutants released into the atmosphere, all fuel-injected models are fitted with a catalytic converter (see Part B of this Chapter), located in the exhaust system. A 'closed loop' system is used, in which an exhaust gas oxygen sensor, mounted in the exhaust manifold or downpipe (depending on model), provides a signal to the fuel system electronic control unit. This enables it to adjust the air/fuel mixture ratio within very fine limits. This enables the catalytic converter to operate at its optimum efficiency at all times.

The oxygen sensor senses the level of oxygen in the exhaust gas, which is proportional to the air/fuel mixture ratio. A rich mixture produces exhaust gases with a low oxygen content, and the oxygen content rises as the mixture weakens. The catalyst operates at maximum efficiency when the air/fuel mixture ratio is at the chemically correct ratio for the complete combustion of petrol, and the output produced by the oxygen sensor allows the electronic control unit to maintain air/fuel ratio very close to the optimum value under all engine operating conditions.

Fuel evaporation control system

To minimise the escape into the atmosphere of unburnt hydrocarbons, a fuel evaporation control system is fitted to certain models. The fuel tank filler cap is sealed, to prevent the release of fuel vapour into the atmosphere, and a charcoal canister is mounted under the right-hand wheel arch, to collect the fuel vapours that would otherwise be released from the tank when the vehicle is parked. The vapours are stored in the canister until a vent valve is operated by manifold vacuum, or by the fuel system ECU (depending on model). The vent valve releases the vapours into the engine inlet tract where they are burnt during the normal combustion process.

Exhaust gas recirculation system

The exhaust gas recirculation system is designed to recirculate small quantities of exhaust gas into the inlet tract and therefore into the combustion process. This process reduces the level of oxides of nitrogen present in the final exhaust gas that is released into the atmosphere. The volume of exhaust gas recirculated is controlled by manifold vacuum through a valve mounted in the inlet manifold.

A tract in the cylinder head allows exhaust gas to pass from the exhaust side of the cylinder head to the exhaust gas recirculation valve in the inlet manifold.

Secondary air injection system

The secondary air injection system uses an electric air pump to inject air into the exhaust manifold under certain driving conditions. This raises the exhaust gas temperature, which oxidises a higher proportion of the pollutants in the exhaust gases, therefore reducing harmful emissions from the exhaust system. The system also helps the catalytic converter to reach an efficient operating temperature more quickly.

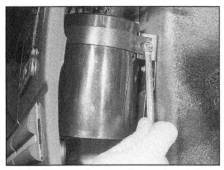

4.4a Unscrewing the charcoal canister clamp nut

4.4b Withdrawing the charcoal canister

Precautions

During operation, the catalytic converter reaches very high temperatures, and this should be remembered when parking the car. Try to avoid parking the vehicle on dry grass, etc, which may present a fire hazard if the catalyst is at working temperature.

When carrying out any work under the vehicle, remember that the catalyst will take a considerable time to cool down from its working temperature when the engine has been running. Take precautions to avoid the possibility of burns and the risk of fire.

If a fault in the ignition system is suspected, rectify the problem or seek advice as soon as possible, particularly in the case of misfiring, as damage to the catalyst may result.

If unburnt fuel enters the catalytic converter, the fuel may burn in the catalyst, resulting in overheating and serious damage to the converter. To avoid this possibility, the following should be avoided.

a) *Frequent cold starts in succession.*
b) *Operation of the starter motor for an excessively long time (fuel is injected during the starting process).*
c) *Allowing the fuel level in the fuel tank to become excessively low (an irregular fuel supply may cause overheating).*
d) *Starting the engine by push or tow-starting (unburnt fuel may enter the converter). Always use jump leads as an alternative.*

To avoid damage to the catalyst, the engine must be regularly serviced, and unleaded petrol must **always** be used. Leaded petrol will 'poison' the catalyst, and **must not** be used.

2 Crankcase emission control system components – testing, removal and refitting

Testing

1 If the system is thought to be faulty, firstly, check that the hoses are unobstructed. On high-mileage vehicles, particularly when regularly used for short journeys, a jelly-like deposit may be evident inside the crankcase emission control system hoses. If excessive deposits are present, the relevant hose(s) should be removed and cleaned.

2 Periodically inspect the system hoses for security and damage, and renew them as necessary. Note that damaged or loose hoses can cause various engine running problems (erratic idle speed, stalling, etc.) which can be difficult to trace.

Removal and refitting

3 The crankcase breather tube can be unbolted from the cylinder block after disconnecting the hose. Use a new gasket when refitting. Note that on certain engines, the dipstick tube is integral with the crankcase breather tube.

4 Certain models have a mesh filter inside the camshaft cover, which should be cleaned in paraffin if clogging is evident. For access to the filter, remove the camshaft cover as described in Chapter 2A or 2B, as applicable. The filter can be removed from the camshaft cover for cleaning after unscrewing the securing screws.

3 Exhaust emission control system components – testing, removal and refitting

Testing

1 The system can only be tested accurately using specialist diagnostic equipment. Any suspected faults should be referred to a Vauxhall/Opel dealer.

4.6 Fuel tank vent valve - Multec CFi model

Removal and refitting

2 Refer to the relevant Section in Part B of this Chapter.

4 Fuel evaporation control system components – testing, removal and refitting

Testing

1 If the system is thought to be faulty, disconnect the hoses from the charcoal canister and vent valve, and check that the hoses are clear by blowing through them. If necessary, clean or renew the hoses.

2 If the vent valve or the charcoal canister itself are thought to be faulty, the only course of action available is renewal.

Removal and refitting

Charcoal canister

3 Remove the wheel arch liner from the front right-hand wheel arch, as described in Chapter 11, Section 25.

4 Unscrew the securing nut, and detach the clamp strap securing the canister to the bracket under the wheel arch. Withdraw the canister and disconnect the hoses **(see illustrations)**.

5 Refitting is a reversal of the removal procedure.

Fuel tank vent valve – Multec CFi and Multec M MPi fuel injection systems

6 The valve is located under the water deflector on the engine compartment bulkhead **(see illustration)**.

7 To remove the valve, lift the water deflector to expose the valve, then disconnect the three hoses, noting their locations to ensure correct refitting, and withdraw the valve from the bulkhead (release the securing clip, where applicable).

8 Refitting is a reversal of removal, ensuring that the hoses are reconnected correctly, as noted before removal.

Fuel tank vent valve – Multec S fuel injection system (1.4 litre engines)

9 The valve is mounted on the left-hand side of the inlet manifold.

10 If desired, to improve access remove the inlet air trunking.

11 To remove the valve, ensure that the ignition is switched off, then depress the retaining clip and disconnect the wiring connector from the valve.

12 Disconnect the hoses from the valve, noting their locations.

13 Using a small screwdriver, bend up the valve retaining tang on the mounting bracket, then remove the valve from the bracket.

14 Refitting is a reversal of removal, but before fitting the valve, bend the retaining tang on the bracket back to its original

position, and ensure that the vacuum hoses are correctly reconnected.

Fuel tank vent valve – Multec S fuel injection system (1.6 litre engines)

15 The valve is located at the rear of the inlet manifold.

16 Slacken and remove the bolts securing the wiring harness plastic tray to the rear of the inlet manifold. Starting at the front and working back, disconnect the wiring connectors from the oxygen sensor, DIS module, carbon canister purge valve and the various connectors on the left-hand side of the manifold. Unscrew the nuts securing the earth leads to the cylinder head and manifold, then unclip the wiring harness plastic tray and position it clear of the manifold.

17 Proceed as described in paragraphs 11 to 14.

18 On completion, refit the wiring harness plastic tray, ensuring that all wiring connectors are correctly reconnected.

Fuel tank vent valve – Motronic M 1.5 fuel injection system

19 The valve is located in a bracket attached to the rear of the cylinder head.

20 Disconnect the battery negative lead.

21 Disconnect the wiring plug from the fuel tank vent valve.

22 Disconnect the two hoses from the valve, noting their locations to ensure correct refitting.

23 Unclip the valve from its bracket, and withdraw it.

24 Refitting is a reversal of removal, ensuring that the hoses are reconnected as noted before removal.

Fuel tank vent valve – Motronic M 2.5 and M 2.8 fuel injection systems

25 The fuel tank vent valve is located at the rear left-hand side of the engine **(see illustration)**.

26 Disconnect the battery negative lead.

27 Disconnect the wiring plug from the valve.

28 Disconnect the two hoses from the valve, noting their locations to aid refitting.

29 Remove the securing screw, and withdraw the valve from its bracket.

30 Refitting is a reversal of removal, ensuring that the hoses are reconnected as noted before removal.

Fuel tank vent valve – Simtec fuel injection system

31 The fuel tank vent valve is located to the rear of the DIS module, at the left-hand end of the cylinder head.

32 Disconnect the wiring plug from the DIS module.

33 Disconnect the two vacuum hoses from the valve, noting their locations.

34 Disconnect the wiring plug from the vent valve, then unclip the valve from the mounting bracket.

35 Refitting is a reversal of removal, ensuring that the vacuum hoses are correctly reconnected.

5 Exhaust gas recirculation system components – testing, removal and refitting

Testing

1 Start the engine, and run it until it reaches normal operating temperature.

2 Stop the engine, and remove the airbox from the top of the fuel injection unit, as described in Chapter 4B, Section 3.

3 Connect an accurate tachometer to the engine according to the equipment manufacturer's instructions.

4 Disconnect the vacuum hose from the valve, then start the engine and record the idle speed.

5 Disconnect the vacuum hose from the valve, then apply vacuum to the valve using a vacuum hand pump. When the vacuum is applied, the idle speed should drop by at least 100 rpm.

6 If the idle speed does not drop as described previously, firstly, check the valve vacuum hose for obstructions and leaks. Clean the hose or renew it if necessary.

7 If the hose is in good condition, and a fault is still suspected, it is likely that the valve is faulty. In this case, clean and if necessary renew the valve as described in the relevant Section.

8 Disconnect the tachometer, reconnect the vacuum hose and refit the airbox on completion.

Removal and refitting

Exhaust gas recirculation valve – C 16 NZ and C 18 NZ engines

Note: *A new gasket will be required on refitting.*

9 Remove the airbox from the top of the fuel injection unit, as described in Chapter 4B, Section 3.

10 Disconnect the vacuum hose from the valve.

11 Unscrew the two securing bolts, and withdraw the valve from the inlet manifold. Recover the gasket.

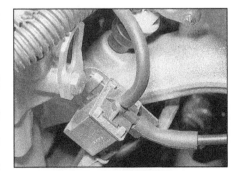

4.25 Fuel tank vent valve - Motronic M 2.5 model

12 Carefully clean the mating faces of the housing and the valve using a stiff brush.

13 If the original valve is to be refitted, clean all deposits from the valve seat using a brush or a pointed tool. Take great care not to damage the valve seat.

14 Refit the valve using a new gasket, then refit the vacuum hose and the airbox.

Exhaust gas recirculation valve – X 16 SZ and X 16 SZR engines

Note: *A new gasket will be required on refitting.*

15 Ensure that the ignition is switched off, then disconnect the wiring plug from the exhaust gas recirculation valve.

16 Proceed as described in paragraphs 11 to 13.

17 Refit the valve using a new gasket, then reconnect the valve wiring plug.

Exhaust gas recirculation valve – X 14 XE engines

Note: *A new gasket will be required on refitting.*

18 The valve is located at the rear left-hand corner of the cylinder head.

19 Remove the engine oil filler cap, then remove the engine cover, and refit the oil filler cap.

20 Ensure that the ignition is switched off, then disconnect the wiring plug from the valve.

21 Unscrew the two securing bolts, then remove the exhaust gas recirculation valve, noting its orientation. Recover the gasket.

22 Proceed as described in paragraphs 12 and 13.

23 Refit the valve using a new gasket. Ensure that the valve is correctly orientated as noted before removal. Reconnect the wiring plug and refit the engine cover.

Exhaust gas recirculation valve – X 16 XEL engines

Note: *A new gasket will be required on refitting.*

24 Depressurise the fuel system by removing the fuel pump relay (see Chapter 12), and cranking the engine on the starter motor for a minimum of 5 seconds.

25 Disconnect the battery negative lead.

26 Slacken the clamp, and disconnect the air intake trunking from the air cleaner housing.

27 Disconnect the intake air temperature sensor wiring connector.

28 Unscrew the bolt securing the air intake trunking to the lower section of the inlet manifold.

29 Disconnect the engine breather hose from the air intake trunking, then slacken the clamp and disconnect the trunking from the throttle body. Remove the trunking.

30 Ensure that the ignition is switched off, then disconnect the wiring plug from the valve.

31 Unscrew the two securing bolts, then remove the exhaust gas recirculation valve, noting its orientation. Recover the gasket.

32 Proceed as described in paragraphs 12 and 13.

33 Refit the valve using a new gasket. Ensure that the valve is correctly orientated as noted before removal. Reconnect the wiring plug.

34 The remainder of the refitting procedure is a reversal of removal.

Exhaust gas recirculation valve – X 18 XE and X 20 XEV engines

Note: *A new gasket will be required on refitting.*

35 The valve is located at the left-hand end of the cylinder head, in front of the DIS module.

36 Ensure that the ignition is switched off, then disconnect the vacuum hose and the wiring plug from the valve.

37 Unscrew the two securing bolts, and withdraw the valve. Recover the gasket.

38 Proceed as described in paragraphs 12 and 13.

39 Refitting is a reversal of removal, but refit the valve using a new gasket, and ensure that the valve is correctly orientated as noted before removal.

Exhaust gas recirculation control module – X 16 SZ engines

40 The module is located at the left-hand side of the engine compartment, in front of the suspension turret.

41 Unclip the knock sensor module from its mounting bracket, and move the module to one side.

42 Ensure that the ignition is switched off, then disconnect the wiring plug from the exhaust gas recirculation module, and unclip the module from its mounting bracket.

43 Refitting is a reversal of removal.

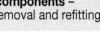

6 Secondary air injection system components – testing, removal and refitting

Testing

1 The system can only be tested accurately using specialist diagnostic equipment. Any suspected faults should be referred to a Vauxhall/Opel dealer.

Removal and refitting

Note: *Always ensure that all hoses in the secondary air injection system are fitted dry. Do not use any lubricants (eg, soapy water, grease, etc) to ease assembly.*

Secondary air injection pump

2 Apply the handbrake, then jack up the front of the vehicle and support it securely on axle stands.

3 Remove the left-hand front wheel and the wheel arch liner.

4 Loosen the securing clamp, and disconnect air hose from the pump.

5 Disconnect the battery negative lead, then disconnect the wiring plugs from the pump and the horn.

6.18 Secondary air injection switchover valve – X 16 XEL engines up to mid-1996

1 Servo hose connection
2 AIR combination valve connection

6 Unscrew the two upper securing nuts, and slacken the lower securing nut, and lower the pump and its mounting bracket from under the wheel arch.

7 To separate the pump from its bracket, proceed as follows.

 a) *Unclip the wiring plug from the pump assembly.*
 b) *Slacken the clamps, and disconnect the air hose from the pump and the pump air cleaner.*
 c) *Make alignment marks between the pump and bracket to ensure correct refitting, then unscrew the securing bolts, and remove the pump from the mounting bracket.*
 d) *Refit the pump to the bracket using a reversal of the removal procedure. Make sure that the marks made on the pump and bracket before removal are aligned.*

8 Refitting of the pump is a reversal of removal.

Secondary air injection pump air filter

9 Remove the pump as described previously in this Section.

10 Slacken the clamp, and disconnect the pump air hose from the air filter.

11 Slacken the securing nut, and remove the air filter from the pump mounting bracket.

12 Refitting is a reversal of removal.

Secondary air injection switchover valve – X 14 XE engines

13 The valve is attached to the inlet manifold.

6.28 Secondary air injection combination valve – X 16 XEL engine

14 Disconnect the vacuum hoses from the valve, noting their locations to ensure correct refitting.

15 Disconnect the battery negative lead, then disconnect the wiring plug from the valve.

16 Unclip the valve from the inlet manifold.

17 Refitting is a reversal of removal, but ensure that the vacuum hoses are correctly reconnected as noted before removal.

Secondary air injection switchover valve – X 16 XEL engines up to mid-1996

18 The valve is located at the front of the engine compartment, to the right of the power steering fluid reservoir **(see illustration)**.

19 Proceed as described in paragraphs 14 and 15.

20 Unscrew the two bolts securing the valve to its mounting bracket, then remove the valve.

21 Refitting is a reversal of removal, but ensure that the vacuum hoses are correctly reconnected as noted before removal.

Secondary air injection switchover valve – X 16 XEL engines from mid-1996

22 The valve is located at the rear of the inlet manifold.

23 Slacken and remove the bolts securing the wiring harness plastic tray to the rear of the inlet manifold. Starting at the front and working back, disconnect the wiring connectors from the oxygen sensor, DIS module, carbon canister purge valve and the various connectors on the left-hand side of the manifold. Unscrew the nuts securing the earth leads to the cylinder head and manifold, then unclip the wiring harness plastic tray and position it clear of the manifold.

24 Proceed as described in paragraphs 14 and 15.

25 Unscrew the two securing bolts, and remove the valve from the lower section of the inlet manifold.

26 Refitting is a reversal of removal, but ensure that the vacuum hoses are correctly reconnected as noted before removal.

Secondary air injection switchover valve – X 18 XE and X 20 XEV engines

27 Proceed as described in paragraphs 13 to 17 for X 14 XE engines.

Secondary air injection combination valve – X 14 XE and X 16 XEL engines

Note: *A new gasket will be required on refitting.*

28 The valve is located at the front of the engine above the exhaust manifold **(see illustration)**.

29 Disconnect the vacuum hose and the air hose from the valve.

30 Note the fitted position of the valve, then unscrew the two securing bolts, and remove the valve from the air injection pipe. Recover the gasket.

31 Thoroughly clean the mating faces of the valve and the air injection pipe.

32 Refitting is a reversal of removal, but use a new gasket, and ensure that the valve is positioned as noted before removal.

Secondary air injection combination valve – X 18 XE and X 20 XEV engines

Note: *A new gasket will be required on refitting.*

33 The valve is located at the front left-hand corner of the engine.

34 Proceed as described in paragraphs 29 to 32 for X 18 XE and X 20 XEV engines.

Secondary air injection pipe – X 14 XE and X 16 XEL engines

Note: *A new gasket, and suitable high-temp-erature grease will be required on refitting.*

35 Remove the secondary air injection combination valve as described previously in this Section.

36 Unscrew the two securing bolts, and remove the air injection pipe support bracket.

37 Unscrew the two securing bolts, and remove the exhaust manifold heat shield.

38 Unscrew the securing bolts, and disconnect the air injection pipe from the exhaust manifold. Recover the gasket.

39 Refitting is a reversal of removal, bearing in mind the following points.

  a) Ensure that the mating faces are clean and dry, and use a new gasket.

  b) Apply a smear of high-temperature grease to the threads of the pipe retaining bolts prior to refitting.

Secondary air injection pipe – X 18 XE and X 20 XEV engines

Note: *A new gasket, and suitable high-temp-erature grease will be required on refitting.*

40 Unscrew the two securing bolts, and remove the exhaust manifold heat shield.

41 Unscrew the secondary air injection combination valve securing bolts, then unscrew the securing bolts, and remove the air injection pipe. Recover the gasket.

42 Proceed as described in paragraph 39.

Notes

Chapter 5 Part A:
Starting and charging systems

Contents

Degrees of difficulty

Easy, suitable for novice with little experience	Fairly easy, suitable for beginner with some experience	Fairly difficult, suitable for competent DIY mechanic	Difficult, suitable for experienced DIY mechanic	Very difficult, suitable for expert DIY or professional

Specifications

Battery

Type	Maintenance free (sealed for life) lead acid
Capacity	36, 44, 66 or 70 amps

Alternator

Type	Bosch or Delco-Remy
Output	55 or 70 amps, depending on model
Minimum brush length:	
Bosch alternator (all except code number 0 120 488 193)	5.0 mm
Bosch alternator (code number 0 120 488 193)	11.0 to 12.0 mm
Delco-Remy alternator	12.0 mm overall length

Starter motor

Type	Pre-engaged Bosch, Delco-Remy or Valeo
Brush minimum length:	
Bosch DM starter motor	3.0 mm
Bosch DW starter motor	8.0 mm
Delco-Remy starter motor (all except code number 09 000 756)	4.0 mm
Delco-Remy starter motor (code number 09 000 756)	8.5 mm
Valeo type starter motor	No data available at time of writing

Torque wrench settings

	Nm	lbf ft
Alternator mounting bolts:		
M8 bolts	30	22
M10 bolts	40	29
Starter motor to cylinder block:		
SOHC engines:		
Engine side	45	32
Transmission side	60	43
1.6 litre DOHC engine	25	19
1.8 and 2.0 litre DOHC engines	45	33

1 General information and precautions

General information

The engine electrical system consists mainly of the charging and starting systems. Because of their engine-related functions, these components are covered separately from the body electrical devices such as the lights, instruments, etc (which are covered in Chapter 12). Refer to Part B of this Chapter for information on the ignition system.

The electrical system is of the 12-volt negative earth type.

The battery is of the low maintenance or 'maintenance-free' (sealed for life) type and is charged by the alternator, which is belt-driven from the crankshaft pulley.

The starter motor is of the pre-engaged type incorporating an integral solenoid. On starting, the solenoid moves the drive pinion into engagement with the flywheel ring gear before the starter motor is energised. Once the engine has started, a one-way clutch prevents the motor armature being driven by the engine until the pinion disengages from the flywheel.

Precautions

Further details of the various systems are given in the relevant Sections of this Chapter. While some repair procedures are given, the usual course of action is to renew the component concerned. The owner whose interest extends beyond mere component renewal should obtain a copy of the *"Automobile Electrical & Electronic Systems Manual"*, available from the publishers of this manual.

It is necessary to take extra care when working on the electrical system to avoid damage to semi-conductor devices (diodes and transistors), and to avoid the risk of personal injury. In addition to the precautions given in *"Safety first!"* at the beginning of this manual, observe the following when working on the system:

Always remove rings, watches, etc before working on the electrical system. Even with the battery disconnected, capacitive discharge could occur if a component's live terminal is earthed through a metal object. This could cause a shock or nasty burn.

Do not reverse the battery connections. Components such as the alternator, electronic control units, or any other components having semi-conductor circuitry could be irreparably damaged.

If the engine is being started using jump leads and a slave battery, connect the batteries *positive-to-positive* and *negative-to-negative* (see *"Jump starting"*). This also applies when connecting a battery charger.

Never disconnect the battery terminals, the alternator, any electrical wiring or any test instruments when the engine is running.

Do not allow the engine to turn the alternator when the alternator is not connected.

Never 'test' for alternator output by 'flashing' the output lead to earth.

Never use an ohmmeter of the type incorporating a hand-cranked generator for circuit or continuity testing.

Always ensure that the battery negative lead is disconnected when working on the electrical system.

Before using electric-arc welding equipment on the car, disconnect the battery, alternator and components such as the fuel injection/ignition electronic control unit to protect them from the risk of damage.

The radio/cassette unit fitted as standard equipment by Vauxhall/Opel is equipped with a built-in security code to deter thieves. If the power source to the unit is cut, the anti-theft system will activate. Even if the power source is immediately reconnected, the radio/cassette unit will not function until the correct security code has been entered. Therefore, if you do not know the correct security code for the radio/cassette unit do not disconnect the battery negative terminal of the battery or remove the radio/cassette unit from the vehicle. Refer to the *"Disconnecting the battery"* Section for further information.

2 Electrical fault finding – general information

Refer to Chapter 12.

3 Battery – testing and charging

Traditional-style and low maintenance battery - testing

1 If the vehicle covers a small annual mileage, it is worthwhile checking the specific gravity of the electrolyte every three months to determine the state of charge of the battery.

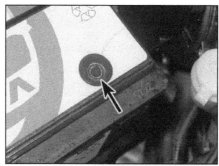

3.5 Battery charge condition indicator (arrowed) – 'Delco' type battery

Use a hydrometer to make the check and compare the results with the following table. Note that the specific gravity readings assume an electrolyte temperature of 15°C (60°F); for every 10°C (18°F) below 15°C (60°F) subtract 0.007. For every 10°C (18°F) above 15°C (60°F) add 0.007.

Ambient temperature - 25°C (77°F)

	above	below
Charged	1.210 to 1.230	1.270 to 1.290
70% charged	1.170 to 1.190	1.230 to 1.250
Discharged	1.050 to 1.070	1.110 to 1.130

2 If the battery condition is suspect, first check the specific gravity of electrolyte in each cell. A variation of 0.040 or more between any cells indicates loss of electrolyte or deterioration of the internal plates.

3 If the specific gravity variation is 0.040 or more, the battery should be renewed. If the cell variation is satisfactory but the battery is discharged, it should be charged as described later in this Section.

Maintenance-free battery - testing

4 In cases where a 'sealed for life' maintenance-free battery is fitted, topping-up and testing of the electrolyte in each cell is not possible. The condition of the battery can therefore only be tested using a battery condition indicator or a voltmeter.

5 Certain models may be fitted with a 'Delco' type maintenance-free battery, with a built-in charge condition indicator. The indicator is located in the top of the battery casing, and indicates the condition of the battery from its colour **(see illustration)**. If the indicator shows green, then the battery is in a good state of charge. If the indicator turns darker, eventually to black, then the battery requires charging, as described later in this Section. If the indicator shows clear/yellow, then the electrolyte level in the battery is too low to allow further use, and the battery should be renewed. **Do not** attempt to charge, load or jump start a battery when the indicator shows clear/yellow.

6 If testing the battery using a voltmeter, connect the voltmeter across the battery and compare the result with those given in the Specifications under 'charge condition'. The test is only accurate if the battery has not been subjected to any kind of charge for the previous six hours. If this is not the case, switch on the headlights for 30 seconds, then wait four to five minutes before testing the battery after switching off the headlights. All other electrical circuits must be switched off, so check that the doors and tailgate are fully shut when making the test.

7 If the voltage reading is less than 12.2 volts, then the battery is discharged, whilst a reading of 12.2 to 12.4 volts indicates a partially discharged condition.

8 If the battery is to be charged, remove it from the vehicle (Section 4) and charge it as described later in this Section.

Traditional-style and low maintenance battery - charging

Note: *The following is intended as a guide only. Always refer to the manufacturer's recommendations (often printed on a label attached to the battery) before charging a battery.*

9 Charge the battery at a rate of 3.5 to 4 amps and continue to charge the battery at this rate until no further rise in specific gravity is noted over a four hour period.

10 Alternatively, a trickle charger charging at the rate of 1.5 amps can safely be used overnight.

11 Specially rapid 'boost' charges which are claimed to restore the power of the battery in 1 to 2 hours are not recommended, as they can cause serious damage to the battery plates through overheating.

12 While charging the battery, note that the temperature of the electrolyte should never exceed 37.8°C (100°F).

Maintenance-free battery - charging

Note: *The following is intended as a guide only. Always refer to the manufacturer's recommendations (often printed on a label attached to the battery) before charging a battery.*

13 This battery type takes considerably longer to fully recharge than the standard type, the time taken being dependent on the extent of discharge, but it can take anything up to three days.

14 A constant voltage type charger is required, to be set, when connected, to 13.9 to 14.9 volts with a charger current below 25 amps. Using this method, the battery should be usable within three hours, giving a voltage reading of 12.5 volts, but this is for a partially discharged battery and, as mentioned, full charging can take considerably longer.

15 If the battery is to be charged from a fully discharged state (condition reading less than 12.2 volts), have it recharged by your Vauxhall dealer or local automotive electrician, as the charge rate is higher and constant supervision during charging is necessary.

4 Battery - removal and refitting

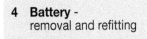

Removal

1 The battery is located at the front left-hand corner of the engine compartment.

2 Disconnect the negative (earth or "-") lead first, by unscrewing the retaining nut and removing the terminal clamp.

3 Disconnect the positive terminal lead(s) in the same way.

4 Unscrew the clamp bolt sufficiently to enable the battery to be lifted from its location. Keep the battery upright, to avoid spilling electrolyte on the bodywork.

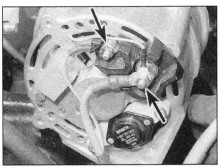

6.3 Wiring connections (arrowed) at rear of alternator (Bosch type) – SOHC engines with 'V' drivebelt

Refitting

5 Refitting is a reversal of removal, but smear petroleum jelly on the terminals when reconnecting the leads. Always reconnect the positive lead first, and the negative lead last.

5 Charging system - testing

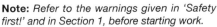

Note: *Refer to the warnings given in 'Safety first!' and in Section 1, before starting work.*

1 If the ignition warning light fails to illuminate when the ignition is switched on, first check the alternator wiring connections for security. If satisfactory, check that the warning light bulb has not blown, and that the bulbholder is secure in its location in the instrument panel. If the light still fails to illuminate, check the continuity of the warning light feed wire from the alternator to the bulbholder. If all is satisfactory, the alternator is at fault, and should be renewed or taken to an auto-electrician for testing and repair.

2 If the ignition warning light illuminates when the engine is running, stop the engine and check that the alternator drivebelt is correctly tensioned (Chapter 1) and that the alternator connections are secure. If all is so far satisfactory, check the alternator brushes (see Section 7 or 8, as applicable). If the fault persists, the alternator should be renewed, or taken to an auto-electrician for testing and repair.

3 If the alternator output is suspect even though the warning light functions correctly, the regulated voltage may be checked as follows.

4 Connect a voltmeter across the battery terminals and start the engine.

5 Increase the engine speed until the voltmeter reading remains steady; the reading should be approximately 12 to 13 volts, and no more than 14 volts.

6 Switch on as many electrical accessories (e.g., the headlights, heated rear window and heater blower) as possible, and check that the alternator maintains the regulated voltage at around 13 to 14 volts.

7 If the regulated voltage is not as stated, the

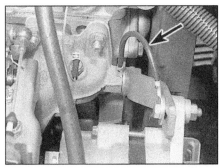

6.5 Earth strap (arrowed) attached to top alternator mounting bolt – SOHC engines with 'V' drivebelt

fault may be due to worn brushes, weak brush springs, a faulty voltage regulator, a faulty diode, a severed phase winding, or worn or damaged slip rings. The brushes may be checked (see Section 7 or 8), but if the fault persists, the alternator should be renewed or taken to an auto-electrician for testing and repair.

6 Alternator - removal and refitting

SOHC engine models with 'V' drivebelt

Removal

1 Disconnect the battery leads.

2 For improved access, remove the air intake pipe and the air cleaner assembly, as described in Chapter 4A or 4B.

3 Disconnect the wires from their terminals on the rear of the alternator, noting their locations, or disconnect the wiring plug, as applicable **(see illustration)**.

4 Mark the running direction on the drivebelt, before removing it as described in Chapter 1.

5 Unscrew the two mounting bolts and nuts, and recover any washers and insulating bushes, noting their locations. Note the earth strap attached to the top mounting bolts on certain models **(see illustration)**.

6 Withdraw the alternator **(see illustration)**, taking care not to knock or drop it, as this can cause irreparable damage.

6.6 Withdrawing the alternator – SOHC engines with 'V' drivebelt

Refitting

7 Refitting is a reversal of removal, remembering the following points.

8 Where applicable, ensure that the earth lead is in place on the top mounting bolt.

9 Before tightening the mounting bolts and nuts, refit and tension the drivebelt, as described in Chapter 1.

SOHC engine models with 'ribbed' drivebelt

Removal

10 Proceed as described in paragraphs 1 to 4.

11 Unscrew the securing bolts and remove the brackets securing the alternator to the inlet manifold and cylinder head. Note that the bolts securing the brackets to the alternator are of different lengths.

12 Unscrew the lower alternator mounting bolt, and lift the alternator from the engine compartment.

Refitting

13 Proceed as described in paragraphs 7 to 9.

1.4 and 1.6 litre DOHC engines

Removal

14 Proceed as described in paragraphs 1 and 2.

15 Mark the running direction on the drivebelt, before removing it as described in Chapter 1.

16 Unscrew the upper alternator mounting bolt, then unscrew the lower bolts securing the alternator mounting bracket to the engine.

17 Support the alternator, then unscrew the securing nuts (where applicable) and disconnect the wires from their terminals on the rear of the alternator, noting their locations.

18 Withdraw the alternator, complete with its mounting bracket.

Refitting

19 Proceed as described in paragraphs 7 to 9.

1.8 and 2.0 litre DOHC engine models with 'V' drivebelt

Removal

20 Disconnect the battery leads.

21 For improved access, slacken the hose clips, and remove the intake air trunking connecting the air cleaner to the throttle body.

22 Unscrew the alternator upper mounting bolt, then pivot the alternator and remove the drivebelt.

23 Disconnect the wires from their terminals on the rear of the alternator, noting their locations, or disconnect the wiring plug, as applicable.

24 Unscrew the alternator lower mounting bolt, and remove the alternator.

Refitting

25 Proceed as described in paragraphs 7 to 9.

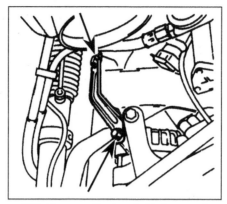

6.33 Unscrew the two bolts (arrowed) securing the alternator rear support bracket – 1.8 and 2.0 DOHC engines with 'ribbed' drivebelt

1.8 and 2.0 litre DOHC engine models with 'ribbed' drivebelt

Removal

26 Disconnect the battery leads.

27 On all except C 20 XE engines, proceed as follows.

a) Disconnect the wiring plug from the intake air temperature sensor and the air mass meter, and disconnect the engine breather hose from the intake air trunking.

b) Slacken the hose clips, and remove the intake air trunking connecting the air cleaner to the throttle body.

28 On C 20 XE engines, proceed as follows.

a) Disconnect the air intake trunking from the air cleaner housing.

b) Disconnect the air mass meter wiring plug.

c) Where applicable, disconnect the wiring plug from the intake air temperature sensor.

d) Remove the air box, complete with the air trunking, from the top of the throttle body, as described in Chapter 4B.

29 Remove the air cleaner assembly as described in Chapter 4B.

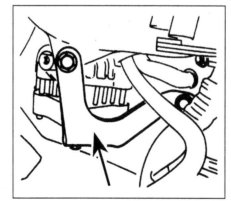

6.34 Top alternator support bracket (arrowed) - 1.8 and 2.0 DOHC engines with 'ribbed' drivebelt

30 Mark the running direction on the drivebelt, before removing it as described in Chapter 1.

31 Disconnect the wires from their terminals on the rear of the alternator, noting their locations, or disconnect the wiring plug, as applicable.

32 Unscrew the lower alternator mounting bolt.

33 Unscrew the two bolts securing the alternator rear support bracket, and remove the support bracket **(see illustration)**.

34 Unscrew the bolts securing the top alternator support bracket to the inlet manifold and the alternator (note that the bolts are of different lengths), then remove the support bracket, and withdraw the alternator **(see illustration)**.

Refitting

35 Refitting is a reversal of removal, but refit the drivebelt as described in Chapter 1.

---

7 Alternator brushes and regulator (Delco-Remy) - removal and refitting

Removal

1 The brush holder and voltage regulator are combined in a single assembly. For access to the assembly, the alternator must be partially dismantled as follows. If the voltage regulator is faulty, the complete assembly must be renewed.

2 Remove the alternator as described in Section 6.

3 Scribe a line across the drive end housing and the slip ring end housing, to ensure correct alignment when reassembling.

4 Unscrew the three through-bolts, and prise the drive end housing and rotor away from the slip ring end housing and stator **(see illustration)**.

5 Check the condition of the slip rings, and if necessary clean with a rag or very fine glass paper **(see illustration)**.

6 Remove the three nuts and washers securing the stator leads to the rectifier, and lift away the stator assembly **(see illustration)**.

7.4 Separating the drive end housing from the slip ring end housing – Delco-Remy type alternator

7.5 Alternator slip rings (arrowed) - Delco-Remy type alternator

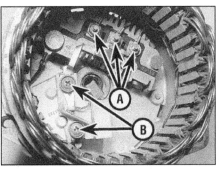

7.6 Stator lead securing nuts (A) and brush holder/voltage regulator securing screws (B) - Delco-Remy type alternator

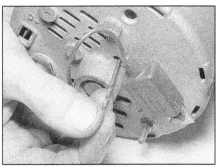

7.16 Removing drill bit used to hold brushes in retracted position - Delco-Remy type alternator

7 Remove the terminal screw, and lift out the diode assembly.

8 Extract the two screws securing the brush holder and voltage regulator to the slip ring end housing, and remove the brush holder assembly. Note the insulation washers under the screw heads.

9 Check that the brushes move freely in their guides, and that the brush lengths are within the limits given in the Specifications. If any doubt exists regarding the condition of the brushes, the best policy is to renew them.

10 To fit new brushes, unsolder the old brush leads from the brush holder, and solder on the new leads in exactly the same place.

11 Check that the new brushes move freely in the guides.

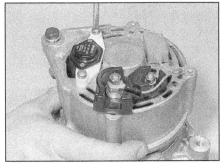

8.5a Remove the securing screws . . .

Refitting

12 Before refitting the brush holder assembly, retain the brushes in the retracted position using a stiff piece of wire or a twist drill.

13 Refit the brush holder assembly so that the wire or drill protrudes through the slot in the slip ring end housing, and tighten the securing screws.

14 Refit the diode assembly and the stator assembly to the housing, ensuring that the stator leads are in their correct positions, and refit the terminal screw and nuts.

15 Assemble the drive end housing and rotor to the slip ring end housing, ensuring that the previously made marks are still aligned. Insert and tighten the three through-bolts.

16 Pull the wire or drill, as applicable, from the slot in the slip ring end housing, so that the brushes rest on the rotor slip rings **(see illustration)**.

17 Refit the alternator, (see Section 6).

---

8   Alternator brushes and regulator (Bosch) - removal and refitting

Removal

1 The brush holder and voltage regulator are combined in a single assembly, which is bolted to the rear of the alternator. If the voltage regulator is faulty, the complete assembly must be renewed.

2 Disconnect the air trunking from the air cleaner, and from the airbox or throttle body, as applicable, and remove it for improved access.

3 Disconnect the battery negative lead.

4 To improve access further, the alternator can be removed, as described in Section 6.

5 Remove the two securing screws, and withdraw the brush holder/voltage regulator assembly **(see illustrations)**.

6 Check that the brushes move freely in their guides, and that the brush lengths are within the limits given in the Specifications **(see illustration)**. If any doubt exists regarding the condition of the brushes, the best policy is to renew them as follows.

7 Hold the brush wire with a pair of pliers, and unsolder it from the brush holder. Lift away the brush. Repeat for the remaining brush.

Refitting

8 Note that whenever new brushes are fitted, new brush springs should also be fitted.

9 With the new springs fitted to the brush holder, insert the new brushes, and check that they move freely in their guides. If they bind, lightly polish with a very fine file or glass paper.

10 Solder the brush wire ends to the brush holder, taking care not to allow solder to pass to the stranded wire.

11 Check the condition of the slip rings, and if necessary clean them with a rag or very fine glass paper **(see illustration)**.

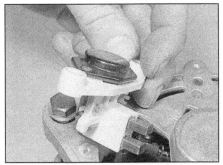

8.5b . . . and withdraw the brush holder/voltage regulator - Bosch type alternator

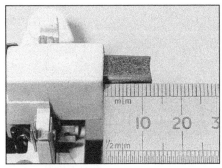

8.6 Measuring the length of an alternator brush - Bosch type alternator

8.11 Alternator slip rings (arrowed) - Bosch type alternator

12 Refit the brush holder/voltage regulator assembly, and tighten the securing screws.
13 Where applicable, refit the alternator, as described in Section 6.
14 Reconnect the battery leads.
15 Refit the air trunking.

9 Starting system - testing

Note: *Refer to the precautions given in 'Safety first!' and in Section 1 before starting work.*
1 If the starter motor fails to operate when the ignition key is turned to the appropriate position, the following possible causes may be to blame.
  a) *The battery is faulty.*
  b) *The electrical connections between the switch, solenoid battery and starter motor are somewhere failing to pass the necessary current from the battery through the starter to earth.*
  c) *The solenoid is faulty.*
  d) *The starter motor is mechanically or electrically defective.*
2 To check the battery, switch on the headlights. If they dim after a few seconds, this indicates that the battery is discharged - recharge (see Section 3) or renew the battery. If the headlights glow brightly, operate the ignition switch and observe the lights. If they dim, then this indicates that current is reaching the starter motor, therefore the fault must lie in the starter motor. If the lights continue to glow brightly (and no clicking sound can be heard from the starter motor solenoid), this indicates that there is a fault in the circuit or solenoid - see following paragraphs. If the starter motor turns slowly when operated, but the battery is in good condition, then this indicates that either the starter motor is faulty, or there is considerable resistance somewhere in the circuit.
3 If a fault in the circuit is suspected, disconnect the battery leads (including the earth connection to the body), the starter/ solenoid wiring and the engine/ transmission earth strap. Thoroughly clean the connections, reconnect the leads and wiring, then use a voltmeter or test light to check that full battery voltage is available at the battery positive lead connection to the solenoid, and that the earth is sound. Smear petroleum jelly around the battery terminals to prevent corrosion - corroded connections are amongst the most frequent causes of electrical system faults.
4 If the battery and all connections are in good condition, check the circuit by disconnecting the wire from the solenoid blade terminal. Connect a voltmeter or test light between the wire end and a good earth (such as the battery negative terminal), and check that the wire is live when the ignition switch is turned to the 'start' position. If it is, then the circuit is sound - if not, continue on to paragraph 5.

10.5 Starter motor solenoid wiring connections

5 The solenoid contacts can be checked by connecting a voltmeter or test light between the battery positive feed connection on the starter side of the solenoid, and earth. When the ignition switch is turned to the 'start' position, there should be a reading or lighted bulb, as applicable. If there is no reading or lighted bulb, the solenoid is faulty and should be renewed.
6 If the circuit and solenoid are proved sound, the fault must lie in the starter motor.

10 Starter motor - removal and refitting

Removal

1 Disconnect the battery negative lead.
2 Apply the handbrake, then jack up the front of the vehicle, and support securely on axle stands (see *"Jacking and vehicle support"*).
3 Where fitted, remove the engine under-shield, as described in Chapter 11, Section 25.
4 On 1.8 and 2.0 litre DOHC engines, if necessary to improve access, disconnect the brake servo vacuum hose, and unbolt the inlet manifold-to-cylinder block support bracket.
5 Note the wiring connections on the solenoid, then disconnect them **(see illustration)**.
6 Where applicable, unscrew the bolt securing the starter motor mounting bracket to the cylinder block.
7 Unscrew the two starter motor mounting bolts, noting that the top bolt on some models is fitted from the transmission side, and also

10.7 Starter motor top bolt (arrowed) - viewed from above

secures the wiring harness bracket **(see illustration)**. Where applicable, also note the location of the engine earth strap, which may be secured by one of the starter motor mounting bolts on certain models.
8 Withdraw the starter motor.

Refitting

9 Refitting is a reversal of removal, but where applicable, ensure that the wiring harness bracket is in place on the top mounting bolt, and tighten all bolts to the specified torque.

11 Starter motor - testing and overhaul

If the starter motor is thought to be suspect, it should be removed from the vehicle and taken to an auto-electrician for testing. Most auto-electricians will be able to supply and fit brushes at a reasonable cost. However, check on the cost of repairs before continuing as it may prove more economical to obtain a new or exchange motor.

12 Ignition switch - removal and refitting

Refer to Chapter 12, Section 5.

13 Oil pressure warning light switch - removal and refitting

Removal

1 The switch is screwed into the end of the oil pump, on the inlet manifold side of the engine.
2 Disconnect the battery negative lead.
3 On most models, access to the switch can be obtained from above, but on some models improved access can be obtained by jacking up the front of the vehicle, and supporting securely on axle stands, then removing the right-hand roadwheel (see *"Jacking and vehicle support"*). Where fitted, remove the access hatch from the engine undershield **(see illustration)**.

13.3 Low oil pressure warning light switch viewed from underneath vehicle - C 20 XE engine

**14.1 Engine oil level sensor –
C 20 XE engine**

4 Disconnect the wiring from the switch.
5 Place a container under the switch to catch the oil that will be released as the switch is removed.

6 Using a spanner, unscrew the switch. Be prepared for oil spillage, and plug the hole in the oil pump to minimise oil loss and prevent dirt ingress.

Refitting

7 Refitting is a reversal of removal, but on completion check and if necessary top-up the engine oil level as described in "*Weekly checks*".

14 Oil level sensor -
removal and refitting

Removal

1 If fitted, the engine oil level sensor is located in the front face of the sump **(see illustration)**.
2 Where fitted, remove the access hatch from the engine undershield.
3 Disconnect the battery negative lead, then disconnect the wiring plug from the sensor.
4 Place a container under the sump, to catch any oil that may be released as the sensor is unscrewed.
5 Unscrew the securing screws, and withdraw the sensor from the sump.
6 Recover the sealing ring.

Refitting

7 Refitting is a reversal of removal, but before refitting the sensor, examine the condition of the sealing ring, and renew if necessary.

Notes

Chapter 5 Part B:
Ignition systems

Contents

Degrees of difficulty

Easy, suitable for novice with little experience	**Fairly easy,** suitable for beginner with some experience	**Fairly difficult,** suitable for competent DIY mechanic	**Difficult,** suitable for experienced DIY mechanic	**Very difficult,** suitable for expert DIY or professional 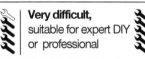

Specifications

Ignition system

Type:*

14 NV	Bosch High Energy Ignition (HEI) inductive discharge distributor system
14 SE, C 14 SE (up to 1993), C 14 NZ, X 14 NZ, C 16 NZ and C 20 XE (up to 1993) engines	Multec Microprocessor-controlled Spark Timing System (MSTS) with 'Hall-effect' distributor
X 14 XE, C 16 SE, X 16 SZ, X 16 SZR, X 16 XEL, C 18 XE, C 18 XEL, X 18 XE, C 20 XE (from 1993) and X 20 XEV engines . .	Direct Ignition System (DIS)
C 14 SE (from 1993), C 18 NZ, and C 20 NE engines	Crankshaft speed/position sensor and high voltage distributor components

* For details of engine code location, refer to the Reference part of this manual.

Firing order

All models	1 - 3 - 4 - 2

Location of No 1 cylinder

All models	Timing belt end of engine

Ignition timing (stroboscopic, at idle speed, vacuum hose disconnected)*

14 NV engines	5° BTDC
C 14 NZ, C 14 SE (pre-1993) and C 16 NZ engines	10° BTDC**
All other engines	Controlled by the ECU (Electronic Control Unit)

* For details of engine code location, refer to the Reference part of this manual.
** Checking and basic adjustment only possible using special equipment.

Distributor

Direction of rotor arm rotation	Anti-clockwise (viewed from cap)

Torque wrench setting	**Nm**	**lbf ft**
Spark plugs	25	18

1 General information and precautions

General information

The ignition system is responsible for igniting the air/fuel mixture in each cylinder at the correct moment, in relation to engine speed and load. A number of different types of ignition systems are fitted to models within the Astra range, ranging from a basic breakerless electronic system, to a fully integrated engine management system controlling both ignition and fuel injection systems. Each system is described in further detail later in this Section.

The ignition system is based on feeding low-tension voltage from the battery to the coil, where it is converted into high-tension voltage. The high-tension voltage is powerful enough to jump the spark plug gap in the cylinders many times a second under high compression pressures, providing that the system is in good condition. The low-tension (or primary) circuit consists of the battery, the lead to the ignition switch, the lead from the ignition switch to the low-tension coil windings, and also to the supply terminal on the electronic module, and the lead from the low-tension coil windings to the control terminal on the electronic module. The high-tension (or secondary) circuit consists of the high-tension coil windings, the HT (high-tension) lead from the coil to the distributor cap (where applicable), the rotor arm (where applicable), the HT leads to the spark plugs, and the spark plugs.

The system functions in the following manner. Current flowing through the low-tension coil windings produces a magnetic field around the high-tension windings. As the engine rotates, a sensor produces an electrical impulse that is amplified in the electronic module and used to switch off the low-tension circuit.

The subsequent collapse of the magnetic field over the high-tension windings produces a high-tension voltage, which is then fed to the relevant spark plug(s), either directly from the coil, or through the distributor cap and rotor arm, as applicable. The low-tension circuit is automatically switched on again by the electronic module, to allow the magnetic field to build up again before the firing of the next spark plug(s). The ignition is advanced and retarded automatically, to ensure that the spark occurs at the correct instant in relation to the engine speed and load.

HEI (High-Energy Ignition) system – carburettor engines

This system comprises of a breakerless distributor and an electronic switching and amplifier module along with the coil and spark plugs.

The electrical impulse which is required to switch off the low-tension circuit is generated by a magnetic trigger coil in the distributor.

The ignition advance is a function of the distributor, and is controlled both mechanically and by a vacuum-operated system.

Multec MSTS (Microprocessor-controlled Spark Timing System) – Multec CFi engines

The Multec engine management system controls both the ignition and fuel injection systems, and comprises various sensors and actuators (described in Chapter 4B), and the Multec ECU, along with the coil, electronic module, and spark plugs.

On 1.4 and 1.6 litre engines, the electrical impulse which is required to switch off the low-tension circuit is generated by a sensor in the distributor.

On 1.8 litre engines, the electrical impulse which is required to switch off the low-tension circuit is generated by a crankshaft speed/position sensor, which is activated by a toothed wheel on the crankshaft. The distributor consists simply of a rotor arm and distributor cap, and is used solely to distribute the HT current to the spark plugs.

The control unit selects the optimum ignition advance setting based on the information received from the various sensors. The degree of advance can thus be constantly varied to suit the prevailing engine conditions. The control unit also provides outputs to control the fuel injection system, which is described in Chapter 4B.

Multec MSTS (Microprocessor-controlled Spark Timing System) – Multec M and Multec S MPi models

The system is similar to that described previously for CFi models, but note the following differences.

The electrical impulse which is required to switch off the low-tension circuit is generated by a crankshaft speed/position sensor, similar to that described previously for 1.8 litre CFi engines.

On 1.4 litre SOHC engines, the distributor consists simply of a rotor arm and distributor cap, and is used solely to distribute the HT current to the spark plugs.

On 1.6 litre SOHC engines, and DOHC engines, a DIS (Direct Ignition System) module is used in place of the distributor and the coil. The DIS module is attached to the camshaft housing in the position normally occupied by the distributor, and consists of two ignition coils and an electronic control module, housed in a cast casing. Each ignition coil supplies two spark plugs with HT voltage one spark is provided in a cylinder with its piston on the compression stroke, and one spark is provided to a cylinder with its piston on the exhaust stroke. This means that a 'wasted spark' is supplied to one cylinder during each ignition cycle, but this has no detrimental effect. This system has the advantage that there are no moving parts therefore there is no wear, and the system is largely maintenance-free.

Motronic M 1.5 system

This Motronic engine management system controls both the ignition and fuel injection systems, and comprises various sensors and actuators (described in Chapter 4B), and the Multec ECU, along with the coil, distributor components, and spark plugs.

The electrical impulse which is required to switch off the low-tension circuit is generated by a crankshaft speed/position sensor, similar to that described previously for 1.8 litre CFi engines.

The distributor consists simply of a rotor arm and distributor cap, and is used solely to distribute the HT current to the spark plugs.

The ECU selects the optimum ignition advance setting, based on the information received from the various sensors. The degree of advance can thus be constantly varied to suit the prevailing engine conditions. The ECU also provides outputs to control the fuel injection system, which is described in Chapter 4B.

Motronic M 2.5 system

The system is similar to the Motronic M 1.5 system described previously, with the following differences.

Besides the crankshaft speed/position sensor, a 'Hall-effect' distributor is fitted. The electrical impulse which is required to switch off the ignition low-tension circuit is generated by the crankshaft speed/position sensor, and the sensor in the distributor provides a cylinder recognition signal.

Additionally, the Motronic ECU receives information from a cylinder block-mounted knock sensor (see Chapter 4B), which senses 'knocking' (or pre-ignition) just as it begins to occur, enabling the ECU to retard the ignition timing, thus preventing engine damage.

Motronic M 2.8 system

From mid-1993, the Motronic M 2.5 system fitted to C 20 XE models was superseded by the Motronic M 2.8 system.

A DIS (Direct Ignition System) module is used in place of the distributor and coil. The DIS system is as described previously for Multec M and Multec S MPi models.

Simtec system

This system, like the previously described Motronic types, controls both the ignition and fuel injection systems, and comprises various sensors and actuators (described in Chapter 4B), and the Simtec ECU, along with a DIS module and spark plugs. The DIS system is as described previously for Multec M and Multec S MPi models.

Precautions

⚠ **Warning: Before carrying out any work on the electrical system, read through the precautions given in 'Safety first!' at the beginning of this manual.**

⚠ **Warning: The HT voltage generated by an electronic ignition system is extremely high and, in certain circumstances, could prove fatal. Take care to avoid receiving electric shocks from the HT side of the ignition system. Do not handle HT leads, or touch the distributor or coil when the engine is running. If tracing faults in the HT circuit use well-insulated tools to manipulate live leads. Persons with surgically implanted cardiac pacemaker devices should keep well away from the Ignition circuits, components and test equipment.**

It is necessary to take extra care when working on the electrical system to avoid damage to semi-conductor devices (diodes and transistors), and to avoid the risk of personal injury. Along with the precautions given in 'Safety first!' at the beginning of this manual, observe the following when working on the system.

Always remove rings, watches, etc., before working on the electrical system. Even with the battery disconnected, capacitive discharge could occur if a component's live terminal is earthed through a metal object. This could cause a shock or nasty burn.

Do not reverse the battery connections. Components such as the alternator, fuel injection/ignition system ECU (where applicable), or any other components having semi-conductor circuitry could be irreparably damaged.

If the engine is being started using jump leads and a slave battery, connect the batteries positive-to-positive and negative-to-negative. This also applies when connecting a battery charger.

Never disconnect the battery terminals, the alternator, any electrical wiring or any test instruments when the engine is running.

Do not allow the engine to turn the alternator when the alternator is not connected.

Never 'test' for alternator output by 'shorting' the output lead to earth.

Never use an ohmmeter of the type incorporating a hand-cranked generator for circuit or continuity testing.

Always ensure that the battery negative lead is disconnected when working on the electrical system.

Before using electric-arc welding equip-ment on the car, disconnect the battery, alternator and components such as the fuel injection/ ignition system ECU (where applicable), to protect them from the risk of damage.

Refer to the precautions to be observed when working on models fitted with an ECU, given in Chapter 4B.

2 Ignition system - testing

Carburettor engines

Note: *Refer to the warning given in Section 1 before starting work.*

1 The components of the electronic ignition system are normally very reliable; most faults are far more likely to be due to loose or dirty connections or to 'tracking' of HT voltage due to dirt, dampness or damaged insulation than to the failure of any of the system components. **Always** check all wiring thoroughly before condemning an electrical component, and work methodically to eliminate all other possibilities before deciding that a particular component is faulty.

2 The practice of checking for a spark by holding the live end of a HT lead a short distance away from the engine is not recommended - not only is there a high risk of a powerful electric shock, but the coil or electronic module may be damaged.

Engine fails to start

3 If the engine either will not turn over at all, or only turns over very slowly, check the battery and starter motor. Connect a voltmeter across the battery terminals (meter positive probe to battery positive terminal), disconnect the ignition coil HT lead from the distributor cap and earth it, then note the voltage reading obtained while turning over the engine on the starter for around ten seconds (no more). If the reading obtained is less than approximately 8 volts, check the battery, starter motor and charging system.

4 If the engine turns over at normal speed, but will not start, check the HT circuit by connecting a timing light (following the equipment manufacturer's instructions) and turning the engine over on the starter motor; if the light flashes, voltage is reaching the spark plugs, so these should be checked first. If the light does not flash, check the HT leads themselves, followed by the distributor cap, carbon brush and rotor arm (see Chapter 1 and Section 3). Additionally, use an ohmmeter or continuity tester to check that there is no continuity between any of the distributor cap contacts. Similarly, check that there is no continuity between the rotor arm body and its metal contact - note that the arm has a built-in resistance.

5 If there is a spark, check the fuel system for faults (see Chapter 4A).

6 If there is still no spark, check the voltage at the ignition coil '+ ' terminal (black wires), which should be the same as the battery voltage (i.e., at least 11.5 volts). If the voltage at the coil is significantly (more than 1.0 volt) less than that at the battery, check the feed back through the fusebox and ignition switch to the battery and its earth until the fault is found.

7 If the feed to the coil is sound, check the coil windings, as described in Section 4. Renew the coil if faulty, but be careful to check carefully the condition of the LT connections themselves before doing so, to ensure that the fault is not due to dirty or loose connections.

8 If the coil is in good condition, the fault is probably within the electronic module or the distributor. To check the module and distributor, connect a test meter across the coil LT terminals, according to the equipment manufacturer's instructions. If the ignition is switched on, and the engine is turned over on the starter motor, the meter voltage readings should fluctuate each time the module triggers a HT pulse in the coil. If the meter reading fluctuates as the engine is turned over, the electronic module and the distributor are sound.

9 If the electronic module and distributor are sound, and the entire LT circuit is in good condition, the fault, if it lies in the ignition system, must be in the HT circuit components. These should be checked carefully, as outlined previously.

Engine misfires

10 An irregular misfire suggests either a loose connection or intermittent fault in the primary circuit, or a HT fault on the coil side of the rotor arm.

11 With the ignition switched off, check carefully through the system, ensuring that all connections are clean and securely fastened. If the equipment is available, check the LT circuit, as described previously in paragraphs 6 to 8 inclusive.

12 Check that the coil, the distributor cap and the HT leads are clean and dry. Check the leads themselves and the spark plugs (by substitution if necessary), then check the distributor cap, carbon brush and rotor arm.

13 Regular misfiring is almost certainly due to a fault in the distributor cap, HT leads or spark plugs. Use a timing light (see paragraph 4) to check whether HT voltage is present at all leads.

14 If HT voltage is not present on any particular lead, the fault will be in that lead or in the distributor cap. If HT voltage is present on all leads, the fault will be in the spark plugs; check and renew them if there is any doubt about their condition.

15 If no HT voltage is present, check the coil, as the secondary windings may be breaking down under load.

Fuel injection engines

Note: *On models fitted with DIS modules, testing should only be carried out on using the appropriate specialist test equipment.*

16 The general comments made previously for carburettor engines apply equally to the fuel injection engines, but note that extreme care should be taken when testing the system, as the ECU is very sensitive, and if damaged, it may prove very costly to renew.

17 If in any doubt as to test procedures, or if the correct equipment is not available, entrust testing and fault diagnosis to a Vauxhall/Opel dealer. It is far better to pay the labour charges involved in having the car checked by someone suitably qualified, than to risk damage to the system or to yourself.

18 At the time of writing, test equipment, including ECU fault code readers, were being released by certain companies to the general public. If using such equipment, follow the manufacturers instructions carefully. A list of the fault codes should also be supplied with the equipment.

Engine fails to start

19 Check whether the fault lies in the ignition system, by following the procedure described in paragraphs 3 and 4, and check the HT circuit as described.

20 If the HT circuit appears to be sound, the feed to the coil can be checked as described in paragraph 6. Note that the ECU controls the coil feed. **Do not** attempt to 'test' the ECU with anything other than the appropriate test equipment, which will be available only at a suitably equipped Vauxhall/Opel dealer. If any of the wires are to be checked which run to the ECU (although this is not recommended without the correct test equipment), always first unplug the relevant connector from the control unit (with the ignition switched off) so that there is no risk of the unit being damaged by the application of incorrect voltages from the test equipment.

21 If all components have been checked for signs of obvious faults, such as dirty or loose connections, damp, or 'tracking', and have been tested as far as possible, but the system is still thought to be faulty, the vehicle must be taken to a Vauxhall/Opel dealer for testing using the appropriate equipment.

Engine misfires

22 Refer to paragraphs 10 to 15, but note that the possible causes of partial failures that may result in a misfire are far too numerous to be eliminated without using test equipment. Once the ignition system components have been checked for signs of obvious faults, such as dirty or loose connections, damp, or 'tracking', and have been tested as far as possible, but the system is still thought to be faulty, take the vehicle to a Vauxhall/Opel dealer for the full engine management system to be tested using the appropriate equipment.

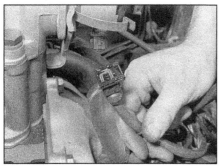

3.4 Disconnecting the distributor wiring plug – carburettor engine

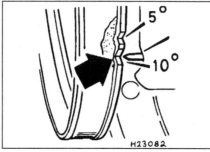

3.7 Timing pointer on rear timing belt cover aligned with 10° BTDC notch in crankshaft pulley – carburettor engine

3.8a Unscrew the clamp nut . . .

3 Distributor - removal, overhaul and refitting

Carburettor engines

Removal

1 Disconnect the battery negative lead.
2 If necessary, identify each HT lead for position to aid correct refitting, then disconnect the leads from the spark plugs by pulling on the connectors, not on the leads. Similarly, disconnect the HT lead from the coil. Pull the leads from the clips on the camshaft cover.
3 Release the two securing clips using a screwdriver, and lift the distributor cap, complete with HT leads, from the distributor.
4 Disconnect the distributor wiring plug **(see illustration)**.
5 Disconnect the vacuum pipe from the diaphragm unit on the side of the distributor.
6 If the original distributor is to be refitted, make alignment marks between the distributor body and the camshaft housing, so that the distributor can be refitted in its original position.
7 Using a socket or spanner on the crankshaft pulley bolt, or by engaging top gear (manual transmission) and pushing the vehicle backwards or forwards as necessary (with the handbrake released!), turn the crankshaft to bring No 1 piston to the firing point. No 1 piston is at the firing point when:
a) The timing pointer on the rear timing belt

cover is aligned with the 10° BTDC notch in the crankshaft pulley (see illustration).
b) The tip of the rotor arm is pointing to the position occupied by the No 1 cylinder HT lead terminal in the distributor cap.
c) The rotor arm is aligned with the notch in the distributor body (remove the rotor arm and plastic shield, then refit the rotor arm to check the alignment with the notch).

8 Unscrew the clamp nut and remove the clamp plate, then withdraw the distributor from the camshaft housing **(see illustrations)**.

Overhaul

9 With the distributor removed, pull off the rotor arm, and remove the plastic shield.
10 Although the top bearing plate can be removed after unscrewing the two securing screws - this is of academic interest, as other than the vacuum diaphragm unit, no spares are available for the distributor, and no adjustments are required.
11 The vacuum diaphragm unit can be removed by extracting the two securing screws and unhooking the operating arm from the distributor baseplate. Note that the screws are of differing lengths; the longer screw also secures one of the distributor cap clips.
12 The vacuum unit can be tested by applying suction to the vacuum port, and checking that the operating rod moves into the unit as suction is applied. Remove the suction, and check that the operating rod returns to its original position. If the operating rod does not move as described, renew the vacuum unit.

13 Check the distributor cap for corrosion of the segments, and for signs of tracking, indicated by a thin black line between the segments. Make sure that the carbon brush in the centre of the cap moves freely, and stands proud of the surface of the cap. Renew the cap if necessary.
14 If the metal portion of the rotor arm is badly burnt or loose, renew it. If slightly burnt or corroded, it may be cleaned with a fine file.
15 Examine the seal ring at the rear of the distributor body, and renew if necessary.
16 Reassembly is a reversal of dismantling, ensuring that the vacuum unit operating arm is correctly engaged with the peg on the baseplate several attempts may be required to reconnect it **(see illustration)**.

Refitting

17 Begin refitting by checking that No 1 cylinder is still at the firing point (see paragraph 7). The relevant timing marks should be aligned. If the engine has been turned whilst the distributor has been removed, check that No 1 cylinder is on its firing stroke by removing No 1 cylinder spark

3.8b . . . remove the clamp plate . . .

3.8c . . . and withdraw the distributor - 14 NV models

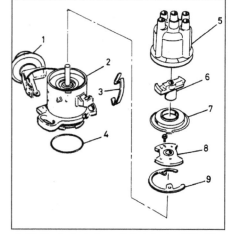

3.16 Exploded view of distributor fitted to 14 NV models

1 Vacuum diaphragm unit	*5 Distributor cap*
2 Body	*6 Rotor arm*
3 Cap retaining clip	*7 Plastic shield*
4 Seal ring	*8 Top bearing plate*
	9 Abutment ring

3.28 Removing the distributor cap –
1.4 litre fuel injection model

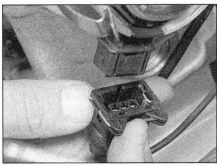

3.29 Disconnecting the distributor wiring
plug – 1.4 litre Multec CFi model

3.30a Alignment marks (circled) between
distributor body and camshaft housing –
1.4 litre Multec CFi model

3.30b Rotor arm aligned with arrow
(circled) stamped on distributor body –
1.4 litre Multec CFi model

3.30c Remove the plastic shield . . .

3.30d . . . and check that the rotor arm is
aligned with the notch (circled) in the
distributor body rim –
1.4 litre Multec M MPi model

plug and placing a finger over the plug hole. Turn the crankshaft until compression can be felt which indicates that No 1 piston is rising on its compression stroke. Continue turning the crankshaft until the relevant timing marks are in alignment.

18 Turn the rotor arm to the position noted in paragraph 7(c), and hold the rotor arm in this position as the distributor is fitted, noting that the distributor driveshaft will only engage with the camshaft in one position. If the original distributor is being refitted, align the marks made on the distributor body and camshaft housing before removal.

19 Refit the clamp plate and nut, but do not fully tighten the nut at this stage.

20 Remove the rotor arm, then refit the plastic shield and the rotor arm.

21 Reconnect the vacuum pipe to the diaphragm unit.

22 Reconnect the distributor wiring plug.

23 Refit the distributor cap, ensuring that the HT leads are correctly reconnected.

24 Reconnect the battery negative lead.

25 Check and if necessary adjust the ignition timing, as described in Chapter 1.

1.4 and 1.6 litre fuel injection models

Removal

26 Proceed as described in paragraphs 1 and 2.

27 Note that various types of distributor may be fitted, depending on model.

28 Loosen the two securing screws, or release the two securing clips using a screwdriver, as applicable, and remove the distributor cap, complete with HT leads, from the distributor **(see illustration)**.

29 Where applicable, disconnect the distributor wiring plug **(see illustration)**.

30 Continue as described in paragraphs 6 to 8 inclusive, noting the following points **(see illustrations)**:

a) Some distributors may already have alignment marks on the distributor body and camshaft housing.

b) On certain distributors, No 1 piston is at the firing point when the rotor arm is aligned with the TDC arrow stamped on the distributor body (in place of a notch in the distributor body).

Overhaul

31 On some Bosch distributors, the plastic drive collar can be renewed if necessary after driving out the securing roll pin **(see illustration)**, but otherwise no spare parts are available for the distributors, and if faulty, the complete unit must be renewed. The distributor cap and rotor arm can be examined as described in paragraphs 13 and 14.

3.30e Removing the clamp plate . . .

3.30f . . . and withdrawing the distributor –
1.4 litre Multec M MPi model

3.31 Driving out the distributor drive collar
roll pin – 1.4 litre Multec M MPi model

3.36 Unscrewing a distributor cap securing screw – 2.0 litre SOHC engine

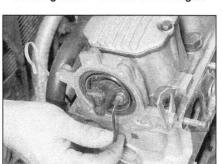

3.38a Extract the securing screws . . .

3.37 Removing the plastic shield from the rotor arm housing – 2.0 litre SOHC engine

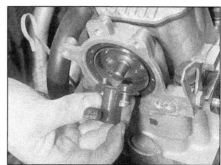

3.38b . . . and withdraw the rotor arm – 2.0 litre SOHC engine

Refitting

32 Where applicable, examine the condition of the O-ring seal at the base of the distributor, and renew if necessary.
33 Proceed as described in paragraphs 17 to 24 inclusive, noting the points made in paragraph 30.

1.8 and 2.0 litre SOHC engines

Removal

34 The distributor consists simply of a cap, rotor arm and plastic shield, mounted on the end of the camshaft housing, which can be removed as follows.

35 Proceed as described in paragraphs 1 and 2.
36 Using a Torx socket, unscrew the three captive securing screws (see illustration), and withdraw the distributor cap (complete with HT leads) from the distributor.
37 Withdraw the plastic shield from the rotor arm housing. The shield is an interference fit in the housing, via an O-ring seal located in a groove in its periphery. Ease out the shield, taking care not to damage the rotor arm (see illustration).
38 Using an Allen key or hexagon bit, extract the two securing screws and withdraw the rotor arm, leaving the metal rotor hub in the housing (see illustrations).

Overhaul

39 Examine the distributor cap and rotor arm as described in paragraphs 13 and 14.

Refitting

40 Examine the O-ring on the plastic shield, and renew if necessary.
41 Refitting is a reversal of removal, noting that the rotor arm can only be fitted in one position. If necessary, turn the metal rotor hub so that the screw holes align with those in the rotor arm and the end of the camshaft. Ensure that the HT leads are correctly reconnected.

DOHC engines

Removal

42 Disconnect the battery negative lead.
43 Remove the securing screws and lift the spark plug cover from the camshaft cover, then disconnect the HT leads from the spark plugs, and unclip the leads from the bracket on the end of the camshaft cover. Also disconnect the HT lead from the coil. Identify the leads for position if necessary, to aid refitting.
44 Using a Torx socket, unscrew the three captive securing screws, and withdraw the distributor cap (complete with HT leads) from the distributor.
45 Disconnect the distributor wiring plug.
46 Unscrew the two bolts securing the distributor to the cylinder head, and withdraw the distributor. Note that the offset peg on the distributor drive engages with the corresponding hole in the end of the camshaft (see illustrations).

Overhaul

47 No spare parts are available for the distributor, and if faulty, the complete unit must be renewed. The distributor cap and rotor arm can be examined as described in paragraphs 13 and 14.

Refitting

48 Examine the condition of the O-ring seal at the base of the distributor, and renew if necessary.

3.46a Unscrewing a distributor securing bolt – DOHC engine

3.46b Offset peg (A) engages with hole (B) in camshaft – DOHC engine

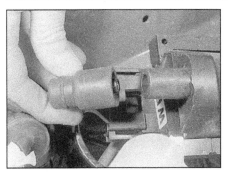

4.3 Disconnecting the HT lead from the coil – 1.4 litre Multec M MPi model

4.4 Disconnecting the coil wiring plug . . .

4.5 . . . and the amplifier module wiring plug – 1.4 litre Multec M MPi model

49 Refitting is a reversal of removal, noting that the distributor can only be fitted in one position.

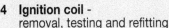
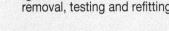

4 Ignition coil - removal, testing and refitting

Note: *For details of the DIS module, refer to Section 6.*

Removal

1 The coil is mounted on the left-hand side of the engine compartment, in front of the suspension turret.
2 Disconnect the battery negative lead.
3 Disconnect the HT lead from the coil **(see illustration)**.
4 Disconnect the LT wires from the coil, and/or disconnect the coil wiring plug, as applicable **(see illustration)**. Note that the LT wires may be secured with spade connectors or by nuts depending on model. Where applicable, make a note of the LT wire connections to aid refitting.
5 Where applicable, disconnect the wiring plug from the ignition amplifier module mounted under the coil **(see illustration)**.
6 Unscrew the two coil securing bolts, and withdraw the coil, complete with the amplifier module and mounting plate, where applicable **(see illustrations)**. Note that on certain models fitted with power steering, one of the coil securing bolts also secures the power steering fluid reservoir bracket. Also note the location of the coil suppressor that may be secured by one of the coil securing screws on certain models.
7 Where applicable, disengage the coil from the amplifier module mounting plate.
8 On models with a cylindrical type coil, the mounting clamp can be removed from the coil by loosening the clamp nut.

Testing

9 Connect an ohmmeter between both LT terminals, and check the primary windings for continuity. Connect the ohmmeter between the HT terminal and either LT terminal, and check the secondary windings for continuity. If there is no continuity, the coil should be renewed.

10 Using an ohmmeter or a continuity tester, check that there is no continuity between the HT terminal and the coil body. If there is continuity, the coil should be renewed.

Refitting

11 Refitting is a reversal of removal, ensuring that (where applicable) the coil suppressor is in position before fitting the coil securing bolts. Ensure that all wiring is correctly reconnected as noted before removal, and that all connections are secure.

5 Ignition amplifier module - removal and refitting

Removal

1 Where applicable, the amplifier module is located on a bracket under the ignition coil.
2 Remove the ignition coil and amplifier module mounting bracket, as described in Section 4.
3 The module can be removed from the mounting plate by unscrewing the two securing screws **(see illustration)**.

Refitting

4 Before refitting the module, special heat-sink compound should be applied to the mounting plate to improve heat dissipation. If a new module is being fitted, it should be supplied with heat sink compound. Similar compounds can be bought from DIY electrical shops.
5 Refit the coil mounting plate and coil assembly, as described in Section 4.

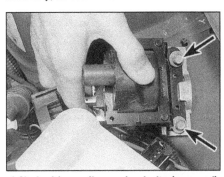

4.6b Ignition coil securing bolts (arrowed) – 1.4 litre Multec M MPi model

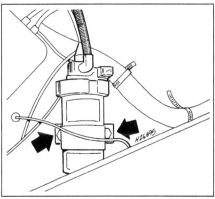

4.6a Cylindrical type ignition coil mounting bolts (arrowed) – carburettor engine

6 DIS (Direct Ignition System) module - removal, testing and refitting

Removal

1 The DIS module is mounted on the left-hand end of the camshaft housing or cylinder head, in the position normally occupied by the distributor, or on the coolant flange at the left-hand end of the cylinder head on models with a Simtec engine management system.
2 Disconnect the battery negative lead.
3 Disconnect the HT leads from the DIS module, noting their locations to ensure correct refitting. Note that the HT lead cylinder numbers are stamped into the coil casing **(see illustration overleaf)**.

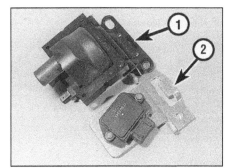

5.3 Ignition coil (1) and amplifier module and mounting bracket (2)

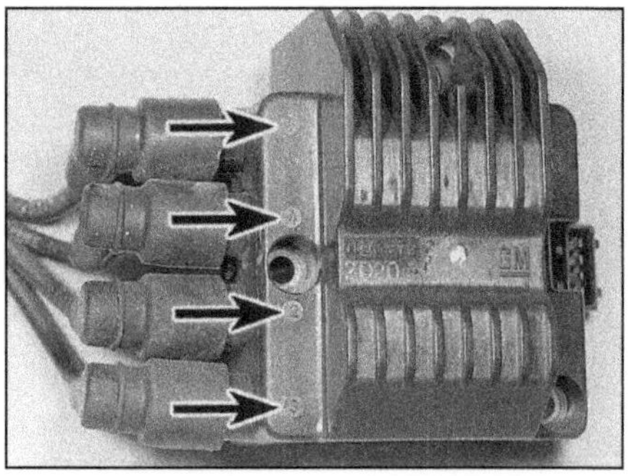

6.3 HT lead cylinder numbers (arrowed) marked on DIS module (shown removed) – 1.6 litre Multec M MPi model

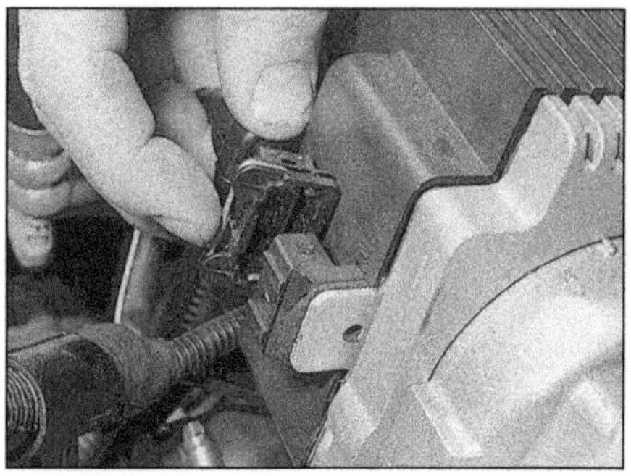

6.4 Disconnecting the DIS module wiring plug – 1.6 litre Multec M MPi model

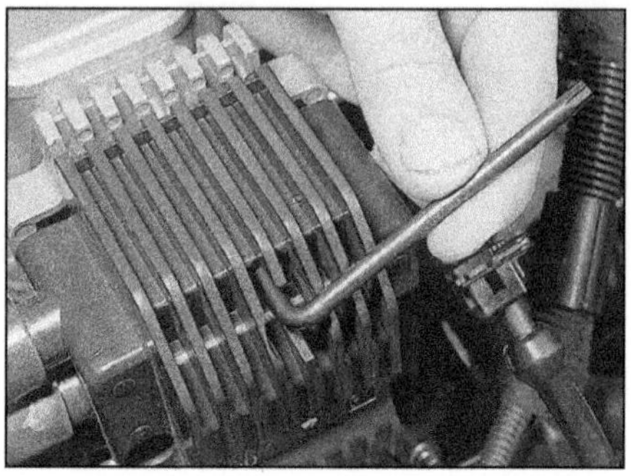

6.5 Unscrewing a DIS module securing screw – 1.6 litre Multec M MPi model

4 Disconnect the coil wiring plug(s) **(see illustration)**.

5 Unscrew the securing screws, and remove the DIS module from its mounting plate **(see illustration)**.

Testing

6 Due to the construction of the DIS module, testing should be carried out using the appropriate specialist test equipment available to a Vauxhall/Opel dealer.

Refitting

7 Refitting is a reversal of removal.

Chapter 6
Clutch

Contents

Degrees of difficulty

Easy, suitable for novice with little experience	**Fairly easy,** suitable for beginner with some experience	**Fairly difficult,** suitable for competent DIY mechanic 🔧	**Difficult,** suitable for experienced DIY mechanic 🔧	**Very difficult,** suitable for expert DIY or professional 🔧

Specifications

Clutch disc

Diameter:

1.4 litre SOHC engines	190 mm
1.4 litre DOHC and all 1.6 litre engines	200 mm
1.8 and 2.0 litre engines (except C 20 XE)	216 mm
C 20 XE engines	228 mm
Lining thickness (new all models)	3.5 mm

Torque wrench settings

	Nm	lbf ft
Bellhousing cover plate:		
Alloy type	6	4
Steel type	12	9
Clutch cover to flywheel	15	11
Clutch fork to release lever	35	26
Differential housing cover plate bolts:		
All except F18 and F18+ transmissions:		
Steel plate	30	22
Alloy plate	18	13
F18 and F18+ transmissions	40	30
Input shaft socket-headed screw	15	11
Transmission endplate bolts:		
M7 bolts	15	11
M8 bolts	20	15
Transmission to cylinder block bolts	75	55

1 General information

All manual transmission models are fitted with a single dry plate clutch, which consists of five main components; friction disc, pressure plate, diaphragm spring, cover and release bearing.

The friction disc is free to slide along the splines of the transmission input shaft, and is held in position between the flywheel and the pressure plate by the pressure exerted on the pressure plate by the diaphragm spring. Friction lining material is riveted to both sides of the friction disc, and spring cushioning between the friction linings and the hub absorbs transmission shocks, and helps to ensure a smooth take-up of power as the clutch is engaged.

The diaphragm spring is mounted on pins, and is held in place in the cover by annular fulcrum rings.

The release bearing is located on a guide sleeve at the front of the transmission, and the bearing is free to slide on the sleeve, under the action of the release arm that pivots inside the clutch bellhousing.

The release arm is operated by the clutch pedal, by way of a cable. As wear takes place on the friction disc over a period of time, the clutch pedal will rise progressively, relative to its original position. No periodic adjustment of the clutch cable is specified by the manufacturers.

When the clutch pedal is depressed, the release arm is actuated by means of the cable. The release arm pushes the release bearing forwards, to bear against the centre of the diaphragm spring, thus pushing the centre of the diaphragm spring inwards. The diaphragm spring acts against the fulcrum rings in the cover. So, as the centre of the spring is pushed in, the outside of the spring is pushed out, thus allowing the pressure plate to move backwards away from the friction disc.

When the clutch pedal is released, the diaphragm spring forces the pressure plate into contact with the friction linings on the friction disc, and simultaneously pushes the friction disc forwards on its splines, forcing it against the flywheel. The friction disc is now firmly sandwiched between the pressure plate and the flywheel, and drive is taken up.

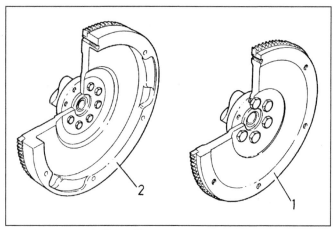

1.9 Two different types of flywheel

1   Standard flywheel

2   'Pot-type' flywheel introduced
on some models during 1992

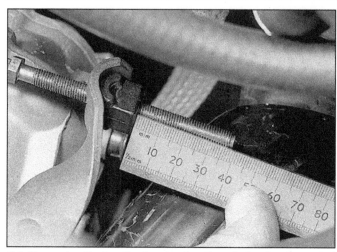

2.1 Measuring the length of protruding threaded rod at the end of the clutch cable

On certain models, the clutch assembly, release bearing and guide sleeve oil seal can be renewed without removing the engine or transmission from the vehicle.

During 1992, certain models were progressively fitted with a 'pot type' flywheel **(see illustration)**. This design assists in smoother running and reduces transmission vibration. On these vehicles, the transmission must be removed to replace the clutch.

2 Clutch cable - removal and refitting

Removal

1 Working in the engine compartment, measure the length of the threaded rod protruding through the plastic block at the release arm end of the cable **(see illustration)**. This will enable approximate pre-setting of the cable when refitting.
2 Remove the clip from the threaded rod at the release arm, then slide the rod from the release arm **(see illustration)**. Push the release arm

towards the engine, and if necessary slacken the cable adjuster, to aid removal.
3 Pull the cable assembly from the lug on the clutch bellhousing **(see illustration)**.
4 Working inside the vehicle, release the securing clips, and remove the lower trim panel from the driver's footwell.
5 Unhook the return spring from the clutch pedal, and disconnect the cable end from the pedal. Note that the end of the return spring retains the cable end in the pedal. Access is limited, and it may prove easier to remove the clutch pedal, as described in Section 3, before disconnecting the cable.
6 The cable assembly can now be withdrawn into the engine compartment, by pulling it through the bulkhead. Take care not to damage the bulkhead grommet as the cable is withdrawn.

Refitting

7 Refitting is a reversal of removal, remembering the following points.
8 Position the threaded rod so that the length of thread protruding through the plastic block is as noted before removal, then adjust the cable as described in Chapter 1.

9 Ensure that the bulkhead grommet is correctly seated.

3 Clutch pedal - removal and refitting

Removal

1 Proceed as described in Section 2, paragraphs 1 and 2.
2 Working inside the vehicle, release the securing clips, and remove the lower trim panel from the driver's footwell.
3 Remove the locking clip from the right-hand end of the pedal pivot shaft **(see illustration)**, then unscrew the pedal retaining nut and recover the washer(s).
4 Push the pivot shaft out of the pedal bracket (to the left), then lower the pedal and return spring. Note the position of any washers and/or spacers on the pivot shaft, so that they can be refitted in their original positions.
5 Disconnect the cable end from the pedal by releasing the return spring, and withdraw the pedal and return spring from the vehicle **(see illustrations)**.

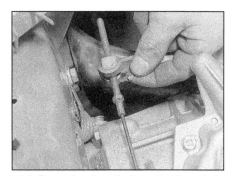

2.2 Removing the clip from the threaded rod at the release arm

2.3 Clutch cable attachment to lug on bellhousing

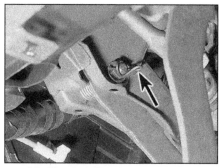

3.3 Clutch pedal pivot locking clip (arrowed)

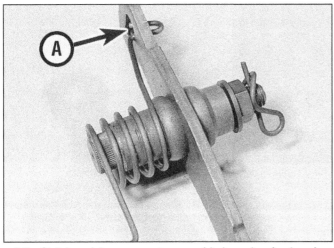

3.5a Clutch pedal components assembled as when in place in vehicle. Clutch cable is retained by return spring at 'A'

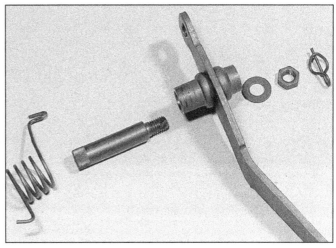

3.5b Clutch pedal pivot components

Refitting

6 Refitting is a reversal of removal, but before inserting the pedal pivot shaft, smear the surface with a little molybdenum disulphide grease.

7 On completion, adjust the clutch cable if necessary, as described in Chapter 1.

4 Clutch assembly (standard flywheel) - removal, inspection and refitting

⚠ **Warning: Dust created by clutch wear and deposited on the clutch components may contain asbestos, which is a health hazard. DO NOT blow it out with compressed air, or inhale any of it. DO NOT use petrol (or petroleum-based solvents) to clean off the dust. Brake system cleaner or methylated spirit should be used to flush the dust into a container. After the clutch components are wiped clean with rags, dispose of the contaminated rags and cleaner in a sealed, marked container.**

Note: *During 1992, certain models were progressively fitted with a 'pot-type' flywheel during production. The 'pot-type' flywheel is significantly thicker than the standard item, and consequently there is insufficient clearance between the flywheel and the clutch bellhousing to enable the clutch to be removed with the engine and transmission in the vehicle. Before attempting to remove the clutch, remove the clutch bellhousing cover plate and examine the flywheel to ascertain which type is fitted, then continue as follows for models with a standard flywheel, or as described in Section 5 for models with a 'pot-type' flywheel. Vauxhall/Opel recommend the use of special tools for this procedure. However, an alternative method is described in the text. It is suggested that this Section is read thoroughly before work starts, so that tools can be made available as required.*

Removal

1 Where applicable, remove the left-hand front wheel trim, then loosen the roadwheel bolts. Apply the handbrake, jack up the front of the vehicle, and support securely on axle stands (see "*Jacking and vehicle support*"). Remove the roadwheel for improved access. Where fitted, remove the engine undershield with reference to Chapter 11, Section 25.

2 Unscrew the securing bolts, and remove the cover plate from the base of the clutch bellhousing **(see illustration)**.

3 For improved access, remove the wheel arch liner, as described in Chapter 11, Section 25.

4 Unscrew the retaining nut and disconnect the earth strap from the transmission endplate, where fitted **(see illustration)**.

5 Place a container beneath the transmission endplate, to catch any escaping oil. Then unscrew the securing bolts and remove the endplate **(see illustration)**. Note the location of the bolts (including the stud for the earth strap, where applicable), as two different lengths are used.

6 Remove the gasket.

7 Extract the circlip from inside the end of the transmission input shaft, using a pair of circlip pliers **(see illustration)**.

4.2 Removing the cover plate from the clutch bellhousing

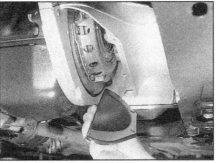

4.4 Earth strap on transmission endplate

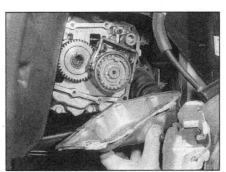

4.5 Removing the transmission endplate

4.7 Extract the circlip (arrowed) from the end of the transmission input shaft

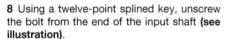

4.8 Unscrew the bolt from the end of the input shaft

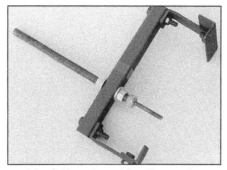

4.9a Self-made tool for disengaging transmission input shaft from clutch

4.9b Disengaging the input shaft from the clutch using the self-made tool

8 Using a twelve-point splined key, unscrew the bolt from the end of the input shaft **(see illustration)**.

9 The input shaft can now be pulled from the splined hub of the clutch friction disc. The manufacturers specify the use of special tools for this operation (GM tool Nos KM-556-1-A and KM-556-4), but an alternative can be made, as shown **(see illustrations)**. The tool bolts into place on the end of the transmission, using the endplate securing bolts. Tool dimensions will vary according to transmission type.

10 Alternatively, screw an M7 bolt into the end of the input shaft, and use the bolt to pull the shaft out to its stop. It is likely that the input shaft will be a very tight fit, in which case it may prove difficult to withdraw, without using the special tool previously described. In extreme cases, a slide hammer can be attached to the end of the shaft to enable it to

be withdrawn. Using this method may damage transmission components, use only when absolutely necessary.

11 Before the clutch assembly can be removed, the pressure plate must be compressed against the tension of the diaphragm spring. Otherwise the assembly will be too thick to be withdrawn through the space between the flywheel and the edge of the bellhousing.

12 Three special clamps are available from the manufacturers for this purpose (GM tool No KM-526-A), but alternatives can be made up from strips of metal. The clamps should be U-shaped, and conform to the dimensions given below and as shown **(see illustration)**. Bevel the edges of the clamps to ease fitting, and cut a slot in one of the U-legs to clear the pressure plate rivets.

  a) Thickness of metal strip - 3.0 mm
  b) Distance between U-legs - 15.0 mm

13 Have an assistant depress the clutch pedal fully, then fit each clamp securely over the edge of the cover pressure plate, fitting the clamps in the slots around the rim of the cover **(see illustrations)**. Turn the crankshaft using a socket or spanner on the pulley/gear bolt, to bring each clamp location into view.

14 Once the clamps have been fitted, have the assistant release the clutch pedal.

15 Progressively loosen and remove the six bolts and spring washers that secure the clutch cover to the flywheel. As previously, turn the crankshaft to bring each bolt into view. Where applicable (and if the original clutch is to be refitted), note the position of the mark on the flywheel that aligns with the notch in the rim of the clutch cover **(see illustrations)**.

16 The clutch assembly can now be withdrawn downwards from the bellhousing **(see illustration)**. Be prepared to catch the

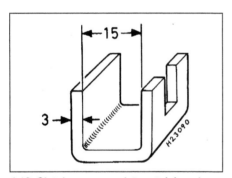

4.12 Clutch pressure plate retaining clamp dimensions - in mm

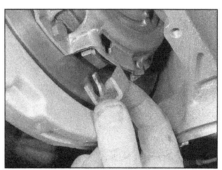

4.13a Fitting a clamp . . .

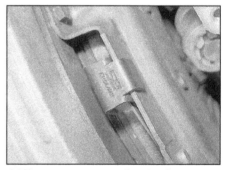

4.13b . . . to compress the clutch pressure plate prior to removal

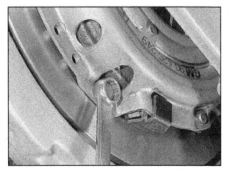

4.15a Loosening a clutch cover to flywheel bolt

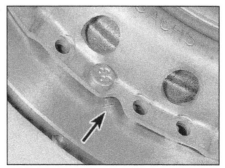

4.15b Stamped mark on flywheel (arrowed) aligned with notch in clutch cover

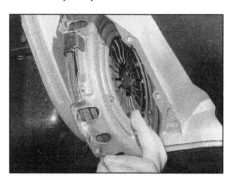

4.16 Withdrawing the clutch assembly from the bellhousing

clutch friction disc, which may drop out of the cover as it is withdrawn, and note which way round the friction disc is fitted. The greater projecting side of the hub faces away from the flywheel.

17 The pressure plate can be compressed against the tension of the diaphragm spring, in a vice fitted with soft jaw protectors, in order to remove the clamps.

Inspection

18 With the clutch assembly removed, clean off all traces of dust using a dry cloth. Although most friction discs now have asbestos-free linings, some do not, and it is wise to take precautions. Asbestos dust is harmful and must not be inhaled.

19 Examine the linings of the clutch disc for wear and loose rivets, and the disc for distortion, cracks, broken torsion springs and worn splines. The surface of the friction linings may be glazed, but as long as the friction material pattern can be clearly seen, this is satisfactory. If there is any sign of oil contamination, indicated by a continuous, or patchy, shiny black discoloration, the disc must be renewed. The source of the contamination must be traced and rectified before fitting new clutch components. Typically, a leaking crankshaft oil seal or transmission input shaft oil seal or both, may need replacing (refer to Chapters 2C and 7A, as appropriate). The disc must also be renewed if the lining thickness has worn down to, or just above, the level of the rivet heads.

20 Check the machined faces of the flywheel and pressure plate. If either is grooved, or heavily scored, renewal is necessary. The pressure plate must also be renewed if any cracks are apparent, or if the diaphragm spring is damaged or its pressure suspect.

21 With the clutch removed, check the condition of the release bearing, as described in Section 6.

Refitting

Note: *The circlip in the end of the input shaft and the transmission endplate gasket should be renewed on reassembly.*

22 Some replacement clutch assemblies are supplied with the pressure plate already compressed using the three clamps described in paragraph 12. If not, the pressure plate should be compressed against the tension of the diaphragm spring. Use a vice fitted with soft jaw protectors and the clamps used during removal.

23 It is important to ensure that no oil or grease gets onto the friction disc linings, or the pressure plate and flywheel faces. Refit the clutch assembly with clean hands. Wipe down the pressure plate and flywheel faces with a clean rag before refitting.

24 Apply a smear of long-life grease (molybdenum disulphide), to the splines of the friction disc hub, then offer the disc to the flywheel, with the greater projecting side of the hub facing away from the flywheel. Hold the friction disc against the flywheel while the pressure plate assembly is fitted into position.

25 The input shaft must now be pushed through the hub of the friction disc, until its end engages in the spigot bearing in the end of the crankshaft. **Under no circumstances** must the shaft be hammered home, as transmission damage may result. If the input shaft cannot be pushed home by hand, steady pressure should be exerted on the end of the shaft. The manufacturers specify the use of a special tool for this operation (tool No KM-564), but the improvised tool used to withdraw the shaft during the removal procedure can be used by repositioning the nut.

26 With the input shaft pushed fully home, position the pressure plate assembly so that the mark on the flywheel is in alignment with the notch on the rim. Then refit and progressively tighten the six clutch cover to flywheel bolts (ensuring that the spring washers are fitted) in a diagonal sequence. Turn the crankshaft, using a socket or spanner on the pulley/gear bolt, to gain access to each bolt in turn, and finally tighten all the bolts to the specified torque.

27 Have an assistant depress the clutch pedal. Then remove the three clamps from the edge of the pressure plate, again turning the crankshaft for access to each clamp.

28 Once the clamps have been removed, have the assistant release the clutch pedal.

29 Refit the screw to the end of the transmission input shaft, then fit a new circlip.

30 Using a new gasket, refit the transmission endplate, and tighten the securing bolts to the specified torque. Where applicable, ensure that the studded bolt that retains the earth strap is fitted to its correct location, as noted during removal.

31 Where applicable, reconnect the transmission earth strap, and fit the retaining nut.

32 Refit the cover plate to the base of the clutch bellhousing, and tighten the securing bolts. Where applicable, refit the wheel arch liner.

33 Refit the roadwheel, then lower the vehicle to the ground and finally tighten the roadwheel bolts. Refit the wheel trim and undershield, as applicable.

34 Check the clutch cable adjustment, as described in Chapter 1.

35 Check and if necessary top-up the transmission oil level, as described in Chapter 1.

5 Clutch assembly ('pot-type' flywheel) - removal, inspection and refitting

Removal

1 Due to the design of the 'pot-type' flywheel, there is insufficient space for the clutch to be withdrawn through the aperture in the clutch bellhousing, as described for models with a flat flywheel.

2 Unless the complete engine and transmission assembly is to be removed from the vehicle, access to the clutch can be obtained by removing the engine or (with most models) the transmission (refer to Chapters 2C and 7A).

3 With the engine or transmission removed, continue as follows.

4 Where applicable (and if the original clutch is to be refitted), note the position of the mark on the flywheel that aligns with the notch in the rim of the clutch cover. Then progressively unscrew the six bolts and spring washers that secure the clutch cover to the flywheel.

5 With all the bolts removed, lift off the clutch assembly. Be prepared to catch the friction disc as the cover assembly is lifted from the flywheel, and note which way round the friction disc is fitted. The greater projecting side of the hub should face away from the flywheel.

Inspection

6 Inspect the clutch as described in Section 4.

Refitting

7 Proceed as described in Section 4, paragraphs 23 and 24.

8 Fit the clutch cover assembly, where applicable aligning the mark on the flywheel with the notch in the rim of the clutch cover. Insert the six bolts and spring washers, and tighten them finger-tight, so that the friction disc is gripped, but can still be moved.

9 The friction disc must now be centralised, so that when the engine and transmission are mated, the transmission input shaft splines will pass through the splines in the friction disc hub.

10 Centralisation can be carried out by inserting a round bar or a long screwdriver through the hole in the centre of the friction disc, so that the end of the bar rests in the spigot bearing in the centre of the crankshaft. Where possible, use a blunt instrument, but if a screwdriver is used, wrap tape around the blade to prevent damage to the bearing surface. Moving the bar sideways or up and down as necessary, move the friction disc in whichever direction is necessary to achieve centralisation. With the bar removed, view the friction disc hub in relation to the hole in the centre of the crankshaft and the circle created by the ends of the diaphragm spring fingers. When the hub appears exactly in the centre, all is correct. Alternatively, if a clutch alignment tool can be obtained, this will eliminate all the guesswork, and obviate the need for visual alignment.

11 Tighten the cover retaining bolts gradually in a diagonal sequence, to the specified torque. Remove the alignment tool.

12 Refit the engine or the transmission, as described in Chapter 2C or 7A.

13 On completion, check the clutch cable adjustment, as described in Chapter 1.

6.3 Unscrewing the clamp bolt securing the release fork to the release arm pivot shaft (model with a standard flywheel)

6.5 Withdrawing the clutch release bearing (model with a standard flywheel)

6 Clutch release bearing - removal, inspection and refitting

Note: *Refer to the note at the beginning of Section 4 before proceeding.*

Removal

1 On models with a standard flywheel, access to the release bearing can be obtained with the engine and transmission in the vehicle, after removing the clutch assembly, as described in Section 4, although access is improved if the transmission is removed.

2 On models with a 'pot-type' flywheel, the transmission (on some models, the engine and transmission) must be removed for access to the release bearing. Refer to Chapters 7A, and 2C, as applicable.

3 Unscrew the clamp bolt securing the release fork to the release arm pivot shaft **(see illustration)**.

4 If not already done, disconnect the clutch cable, from the release arm, by removing the clip from the threaded rod, and then sliding the threaded rod from the release arm.

5 Pull the release arm pivot shaft up and out of the bellhousing, then withdraw the release fork and the bearing **(see illustration)**. Where necessary, slide the bearing from the release fork, and where applicable, pull the bearing from the plastic collar.

6 If desired, the transmission input shaft oil seal can be renewed after removing the release bearing guide sleeve, as described in Chapter 7A.

Inspection

7 Spin the release bearing, and check it for excessive roughness. Hold the outer race, and attempt to move it laterally against the inner race. If any excessive movement or roughness is evident, renew the bearing. If a new clutch has been fitted, it is wise to renew the release bearing as a matter of course.

8 The nylon bushes supporting the release arm pivot shaft can be renewed if necessary, by tapping them from their lugs in the bellhousing using a drift. This is likely to be difficult if the transmission is still in the vehicle. Drive the new bushes into position, ensuring that their locating tabs engage with the slots in the bellhousing lugs.

Refitting

9 Refitting of the release bearing and arm is a reversal of the removal procedure, remembering the following points.

10 Lightly smear the inner surfaces of the release arm pivot bushes, and the outer surfaces of the release bearing guide sleeve, with long-life grease (molybdenum disulphide).

11 Where applicable, fit the release bearing to the plastic collar. Then fit the release bearing and fork together, and tighten the release fork clamp bolt to the specified torque.

12 Refit the clutch as described in Section 4, or refit the transmission as described in Chapter 7A, as applicable.

13 On completion, check the clutch cable adjustment as described in Chapter 1.

Chapter 7 Part A:
Manual transmission

Contents

Degrees of difficulty

Easy, suitable for novice with little experience		Fairly easy, suitable for beginner with some experience		Fairly difficult, suitable for competent DIY mechanic		Difficult, suitable for experienced DIY mechanic		Very difficult, suitable for expert DIY or professional	

Specifications

Manufacturer's designation

Note: *The transmission code is either cast into the casing, or can be found on a plate fixed to the end shield.*

	Transmission codes	Final drive ratio
14 NV, C 14 NZ and X 14 NZ:		
Up to 1994	F 10	4.18 : 1
From 1994	F 13	4.18 : 1
14 SE and C 14 SE:		
Up to 1994	F 10	3.94/4.18 : 1
From 1994:		
Sports models	F 13 or F 15 Close Ratio (CR)	3.94 : 1
X 14 XE and C 16 NZ	F 13	4.18/3.94/3.74 : 1
C 16 SE	F 13, F 13 CR or F 15 CR	3.94/3.74 : 1
X 16 SZ and X 16 SZR	F 13 or F 13 CR	3.74 : 1
X 16 XEL	F 15 or F 15 CR	3.55 : 1
C 18 NZ, C 18 XE, C 18 XEL and C 20 NE	F 16, F 16 CR, F 18 or F 18 CR	3.55/3.57/3.72/3.74 :1
X 18 XE	F 18 CR	3.57 : 1
C 20 XE	F 20 CR and F 18 CR	3.42/3.45 : 1
X 20 XEV	F 18	3.45 : 1

Torque wrench settings

	Nm	lbf ft
Clutch release bearing guide sleeve bolts	5	4
Differential housing cover plate bolts:		
All except F 18 and F 18+ transmissions:		
Steel plate	30	22
Alloy plate	18	13
F 18 and F 18+ transmissions	40	30
Engine-to-transmission bolts	75	55
Engine/transmission mounting bracket-to-transmission bolts	60	44
Gear selector rod clamp bolt	15	11
Gearchange lever housing to floorpan	6	4
Input shaft socket headed screw	15	11
Left-hand engine/transmission mounting-to-transmission bracket bolts	60	44
Left-hand engine/transmission mounting-to-body bolts*	65	48
Rear engine/transmission mounting-to-crossmember bolts	40	30
Rear engine/transmission mounting-to-transmission bracket bolts	45	33
Reversing light switch	20	15
Speedometer drive retaining plate bolt	4	3
Sump to transmission bolts (1.6 litre DOHC engines)	40	30
Transmission endplate bolts:		
M7 bolts	15	11
M8 bolts	20	15

*Use new bolts

3.1 Gear selector rod-to-clamp sleeve clamp bolt (arrowed)

3.2 Extract the plug from the adjuster hole . . .

3.3 . . . and insert a twist drill to engage with the selector lever

1 General description

A five-speed transmission is fitted to all models. Six different types of transmission are used, depending on the model and the power output of the engine fitted (see Specifications), but there are only minor internal differences between the transmission types.

Drive from the clutch is picked up by the input shaft, which runs in parallel with the mainshaft. The input shaft and mainshaft gears are in constant mesh, and selection of gears is by sliding synchromesh hubs, which lock the appropriate mainshaft gear to the mainshaft.

The 5th speed components are located in an extension housing at the end of the transmission.

Reverse gear is obtained by sliding an idler gear into mesh with two straight-cut gears on the input shaft and mainshaft.

All the forward gear teeth are helically-cut, to reduce noise and to improve wear characteristics.

The differential is mounted in the main transmission casing, and drive is transmitted to the differential by a pinion gear on the end of the mainshaft. The inboard ends of the driveshafts locate directly into the differential. The transmission and differential unit share the same lubricating oil.

Gear selection is by a floor-mounted gearchange lever, through a remote control linkage.

3.5 Arrow on gearchange lever aligned with notch in reverse stop

2 Transmission oil - draining and refilling

Draining

1 Where fitted, remove the engine undershield as described in Chapter 11, Section 25.
2 Place a container under the differential cover plate, then unscrew the securing bolts, and withdraw the cover plate, allowing the transmission oil to drain into the container.
3 Refit the differential cover plate, and tighten the securing bolts when the oil has drained.
4 Where applicable, do not refit the engine undershield until the transmission has been refilled with oil.

Refilling

5 Proceed as described for the transmission oil level check in Chapter 1.

3 Gearchange linkage/mechanism - adjustment

Note: *A new plug should be fitted to the gear linkage adjuster hole in the gear selector cover on completion of adjustment.*

1 Working in the engine compartment, loosen the clamp bolt securing the gear selector rod to the clamp sleeve **(see illustration)**.
2 Extract the plug from the adjuster hole in the gear selector cover **(see illustration)**.
3 Looking towards the engine compartment bulkhead, grip the gear selector rod. Twist it clockwise until a 4.5 mm diameter twist drill can be inserted through the adjuster hole in the gear selector cover, to engage with the hole in the selector lever **(see illustration)**.
4 Working inside the vehicle, pull back on the front edge of the gearchange lever gaiter, and free its lower end from the centre console, to allow access to the base of the gearchange lever.
5 The help of an assistant will now be required, to hold the gearchange lever in neutral in the 1st/2nd gear plane. The lever should be resting against the reverse stop, and the arrow and notch should be aligned as shown **(see illustration)**.

6 Without moving the gearchange lever, tighten the clamp bolt securing the gear selector rod to the clamp sleeve in the engine compartment.
7 Check that the free play between the hook (A) and the stop (B) at the base of the gearchange lever is as specified **(see illustration)**.
8 Refit the gearchange lever gaiter to the centre console.
9 Remove the twist drill from the adjuster hole in the gear selector cover, and seal the hole with a **new** plug.
10 Finally check that all gears can be engaged easily with the vehicle at rest, engine running, and clutch pedal depressed.

4 Gearchange lever - removal, overhaul and refitting

Removal

1 Ensure that the lever is in the neutral position.
2 Pull back on the front edge of the gearchange lever gaiter, and free its lower end from the centre console to allow access to base of the lever.
3 Release the clip from the base of the lever shaft, then withdraw the pivot pin, and lift out the lever **(see illustrations)**.

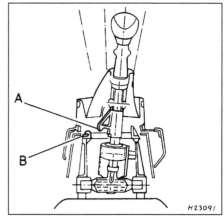

3.7 Gearchange lever free play between hook (A) and stop (B) should be a maximum of 3.0 mm

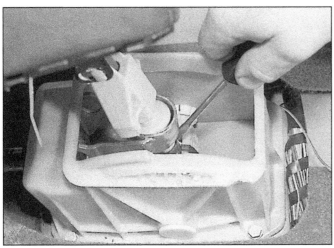

4.3a Release the clip from the base of the gearchange lever shaft . . .

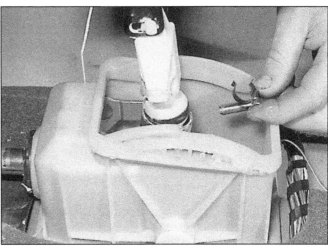

4.3b . . . then withdraw the pivot pin

Overhaul

4 To renew the gearchange lever gaiter and/or the knob, continue as follows.

5 On models with a plastic lever knob, immerse the knob in hot water (approximately 80°C) for a few minutes, then twist the knob and tap it from the lever. On models with a leather-covered lever knob, clamp the lever in a vice fitted with soft jaw protectors, and place an open-ended spanner under the metal insert at the bottom of the knob, then tap the knob from the lever, using the spanner as an insulator to protect the knob. There is a strong possibility that the knob will be destroyed during the removal process.

6 If renewing the gaiter, slide the old gaiter from the lever, and fit the new one. Use a little liquid detergent to aid fitting if necessary.

7 Refit the knob (or fit the new knob, as applicable). When fitting a plastic knob, preheat it in hot water, as during removal. When fitting a leather-covered knob, preheat the metal insert at the base of the knob using a hair drier or hot-air gun. Ensure that the knob is fitted the correct way round.

Refitting

8 Refitting is a reversal of removal.

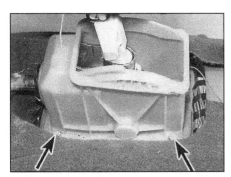

5.4 Gear lever housing securing bolts (arrowed)

5 Gearchange lever housing assembly - removal, overhaul and refitting

Removal

1 Working in the engine compartment, loosen the clamp bolt securing the gear selector rod to the clamp sleeve.

2 Remove the gearchange lever, as described previously in Section 4.

3 Remove the centre console, as described in Chapter 11.

4 Unscrew the four bolts securing the gearchange lever housing to the floorpan (see illustration).

5 The housing and clamp sleeve can now be withdrawn. Pull the assembly towards the rear of the vehicle, to feed the clamp sleeve through the bulkhead. As the clamp sleeve is fed through the bulkhead, have an assistant remove the clamp from the end of the clamp sleeve in the engine compartment, to avoid damage to the rubber boot on the bulkhead.

Overhaul

6 The rubber boot can be renewed by pulling the old boot from the bulkhead, and pushing the new boot into position, ensuring that it is correctly seated.

7 The clamp sleeve bush in the gearchange lever housing can be renewed after sliding the clamp sleeve from the housing. Prise the bush insert from the front of the housing, then prise the bush from the insert. Fit the new bush using a reversal of the removal procedure, but lubricate the inside of the bush with a little silicone grease.

Refitting

8 Refitting of the assembly is a reversal of removal, but before tightening the clamp bolt, adjust the gear selector linkage as described in Section 3.

6 Gear selector linkage - removal, overhaul and refitting

Removal

1 Loosen the clamp bolt securing the clamp sleeve to the linkage.

2 Prise off the securing clip, then withdraw the pivot pin from the linkage universal joint.

3 Release the spring clip, the pull the bellcrank pivot pin from the bracket on the rear engine/transmission mounting (see illustration).

4 Withdraw the linkage from the vehicle.

Overhaul

5 Check the linkage components for wear, and renew as necessary. The pivot bushes can be renewed by prising out the old bushes and pressing in the new, and the link can be renewed by pulling it from the balljoints. Further dismantling is not recommended.

Refitting

6 Refitting is a reversal of removal, but before tightening the clamp bolt, adjust the gear selector linkage as described in Section 3.

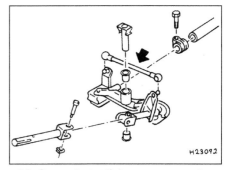

6.3 Gear selector linkage components - link rod arrowed

7.2 Disconnecting the speedometer cable from the transmission

7.3a Unbolt the retaining plate . . .

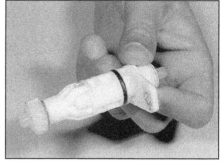

7.3b . . . and withdraw the speedometer drive assembly

7 Speedometer drive - removal and refitting

Removal

1 Where applicable, disconnect the battery negative lead, and disconnect the wiring plug from the vehicle speed sensor.
2 Unscrew the securing sleeve, and disconnect the speedometer cable from the top of the transmission **(see illustration)**.
3 Unbolt the retaining plate, and withdraw the speedometer drive assembly **(see illustrations)**.
4 The speedometer driven gear can be withdrawn from its sleeve, in which case note the thrustwasher under the gear **(see illustration)**.

Refitting

5 If the driven gear has been removed from the sleeve, lubricate the gear shaft with a little silicon grease, then slide the gear into the sleeve, ensuring that the thrustwasher is in place on the gear shaft.
6 Inspect the O-ring seal on the sleeve, and renew if worn or damaged.
7 Further refitting is a reversal of removal.

8 Differential side (driveshaft) oil seals - removal and refitting

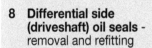

Note: *A balljoint separator tool will be required for this operation. The driveshaft snap-ring(s) and lower arm-to-suspension strut balljoint locking pin(s) must be renewed on reassembly.*

Removal

1 Jack up the front of the vehicle, and support securely on axle stands, then remove the roadwheel.
2 Drain the transmission oil, as described in Section 2.
3 Extract the locking pin, then unscrew the castellated nut from the lower arm-to-suspension strut balljoint.
4 Using a balljoint separator tool, disconnect the lower arm-to-suspension strut balljoint.

5 A tool will now be required to release the inner end of the driveshaft from the differential. To release the right-hand driveshaft, a flat steel bar with a good chamfer on one end can be used. On certain models, the left-hand driveshaft may be more difficult to release, and a square- or rectangular-section bar will be required.
6 Lever between the driveshaft and the differential housing to release the driveshaft snap-ring from the differential. Oil will probably be released as the driveshaft is withdrawn from the differential, even though the transmission has been drained. Support the driveshaft by suspending it with wire or string, and do not allow it to hang under its own weight.
7 Prise the now-exposed oil seal from the differential, using a screwdriver or similar instrument **(see illustration)**.

Refitting

8 Smear the sealing lip of the new oil seal with a little transmission oil. Then using a metal tube or socket of similar diameter, drive the new seal into the differential until the outer surface of the seal is flush with the outer surface of the differential casing **(see illustration)**.
9 Fit a new snap-ring to the inboard end of the driveshaft, then push the driveshaft into the differential as far as possible.
10 Place a screwdriver or similar tool on the weld bead of the inner driveshaft joint, **not** the

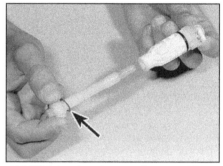

7.4 Withdrawing the speedometer driven gear from its sleeve. Note thrustwasher (arrowed)

metal cover, and drive the shaft into the differential until the retaining snap-ring engages positively. Pull on the **outer** circumference of the joint to check the engagement.
11 Reconnect the lower arm-to-suspension strut balljoint, then fit the castellated nut and tighten to the specified torque. Secure the nut with a new locking pin.
12 Refit the roadwheel, then lower the vehicle to the ground, and finally tighten the roadwheel bolts. Refit the wheel trim, where applicable.
13 Refill the transmission with oil, as described in Section 2.

8.7 Prising out a differential side oil seal

8.8 Driving a new differential side oil seal into position

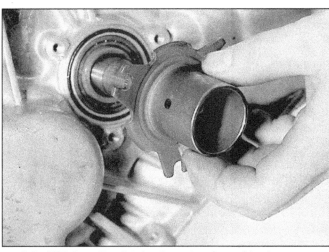

9.2a Withdraw the clutch release bearing guide sleeve . . .

9.2b . . . and recover the O-ring

9 Input shaft (clutch) oil seal - removal and refitting

Note: *A new clutch release bearing guide sleeve O-ring must be used on refitting.*

Removal

1 Remove the clutch release bearing and fork, as described in Chapter 6.
2 Unscrew the securing bolts, and withdraw the clutch release bearing guide sleeve from the bellhousing. Recover the O-ring that fits between the guide sleeve and the bellhousing **(see illustrations)**.
3 Drive the old oil seal from the guide sleeve **(see illustration)**, and fit a new seal using a tube or socket.

Refitting

4 Press the new seal into position - do not drive it in, as the seal is easily damaged.
5 Fill the space between the lips of the new seal with lithium-based grease, then refit the guide sleeve, using a new O-ring. The O-ring should be fitted dry.
6 Refit the guide sleeve to the bellhousing, and tighten the securing bolts.
7 Refit the clutch release bearing and fork, as described in Chapter 6.

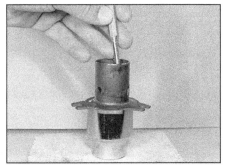

9.3 Driving the oil seal from the clutch release bearing guide sleeve

10 Reversing light switch - testing, removal and refitting

Testing

1 The reversing light circuit is operated by a plunger-type switch, mounted in the front of the transmission casing.
2 To test the switch, disconnect the wiring, and use a meter or a battery-and-bulb test circuit to check for continuity between the switch terminals. Continuity should only exist when reverse gear is selected. If this is not the case, and there are no obvious breaks or other damage to the wires, the switch is faulty and must be renewed.

Removal

3 The reversing light switch is located in the front of the transmission casing, and is accessible from the engine compartment.
4 Disconnect the battery negative lead, then disconnect the wiring from the switch **(see illustration)**.
5 Unscrew the switch from the transmission.

Refitting

6 Refitting is a reversal of removal.

11 Transmission assembly - removal and refitting

Note: *This is an involved procedure, and it is easier in many cases to remove the transmission with the engine as an assembly, as described in Chapter 2C. If removing the transmission on its own, it is suggested that this Section is read through thoroughly before starting work. Various components must be renewed on reassembly, a hoist or similar equipment will be required to support the engine, and a special tool will be required to engage the transmission input shaft with the clutch on refitting.*

Removal

Note: *New left-hand engine/transmission mounting to body bolts, new driveshaft snaprings, and a new transmission endplate gasket must be used on refitting.*
1 Disconnect the battery negative lead. Where fitted, remove the cover from the top of the engine.
2 Working in the engine compartment, loosen the clamp bolt securing the gear selector rod to the linkage, then pull the selector tube towards the engine compartment bulkhead to separate it from the linkage.
3 Remove the retaining clip, then slide the clutch cable from the release lever, pushing the release lever back towards the bulkhead if necessary, to allow the cable to be disconnected. Pull the cable support from the bracket on the transmission casing, then move the cable to one side out of the way, taking note of its routing.
4 Disconnect the wiring from the reversing light switch, which is located at the front of the transmission casing, above the left-hand mounting bracket.
5 Where applicable, disconnect the wiring from the vehicle speed sensor and, on 2.0 litre engines, where applicable, separate the two halves of the oxygen sensor wiring connector, located behind the coolant expansion tank.

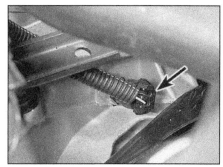

10.4 Reversing light switch wiring connector (arrowed)

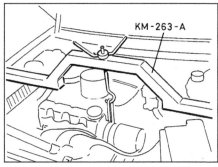

11.8 Vauxhall special tool No KM-263 used to support engine

6 Unscrew the securing sleeve, and disconnect the speedometer cable from the top of the transmission.

7 On all except 1.6 litre DOHC engine models, unscrew and remove the three upper engine-to-transmission bolts, noting the locations of any brackets or clips attached to the bolts. On 1.6 litre DOHC engine models, the three upper bolts can only be removed after the front suspension subframe has been removed.

8 The engine must now be supported from its left-hand lifting bracket. Ideally, the engine should be supported using a strong wooden or metal beam, resting on blocks positioned securely in the channels at the sides of the engine compartment. The Vauxhall/Opel special tool designed specifically for this purpose is shown **(see illustration)**. Alternatively, the engine can be supported using a hoist and lifting tackle. However, in this case, the hoist must be of such a design to enable the engine to be supported with the vehicle raised off the ground, leaving sufficient clearance to withdraw the transmission from under the front of the vehicle.

9 Jack up the front of the vehicle, and support securely on axle stands. Note that the vehicle must be raised sufficiently high to enable the transmission to be withdrawn from under the front of the vehicle.

10 Where fitted, remove the engine undershield, with reference to Chapter 11, Section 25.

11 Ensure that the engine is adequately supported, as described in paragraph 8, then remove the front suspension subframe, as described in Chapter 10.

12 Drain the transmission oil, as described in Section 2.

13 The inner ends of the driveshafts from the differential, now need to be released. To release the right-hand driveshaft, a flat steel bar with a good chamfer on one end can be used. On certain models, the left-hand driveshaft may be more difficult to release, and a square or rectangular section bar may be required.

14 Lever between the driveshaft and the differential housing to release the driveshaft snap-ring from the differential. Oil will probably be released as the driveshaft is withdrawn from the differential, even though the transmission has been drained. Support the driveshafts by
suspending them with wire or string, and do not allow them to hang under their own weight.

15 Where applicable, unscrew the retaining nut, and disconnect the earth strap from the transmission endplate.

16 Place a container beneath the transmission endplate, to catch the oil that will be released, then unscrew the securing bolts and remove the endplate. Note the location of the bolts (including the stud for the earth strap, where applicable), as two different lengths are used.

17 Recover the gasket.

18 Extract the circlip from the end of the transmission input shaft, using a pair of circlip pliers.

19 Using a twelve-point splined key, unscrew the bolt from the end of the input shaft.

20 The input shaft can now be pulled out of engagement with the splined hub of the clutch friction disc. The manufacturers specify the use of special tools for this operation (Vauxhall/Opel tool Nos KM-556-1-A and KM-556-4, but an alternative can be improvised (refer to Chapter 6 for details). The tool bolts into place on the end of the transmission, using the endplate securing bolts. Tool dimensions will vary according to transmission type.

21 Alternatively, screw an M7 bolt into the end of the input shaft, and use the bolt to pull the shaft out to its stop. It is likely that the input shaft will be a very tight fit, in which case it may prove difficult to withdraw, without using the special tool previously described. In extreme cases, a slide hammer can be attached to the end of the shaft to enable it to be withdrawn, although this is not to be recommended, as damage to the transmission components may result.

22 Support the transmission with a trolley jack, with an interposed block of wood to spread the load.

23 Remove the left-hand engine/transmission mounting completely, by unscrewing the two bolts securing the rubber mounting to the vehicle body, and the three bolts securing the mounting bracket to the transmission. On 1.6 litre DOHC engine models, remove the three upper transmission to engine bolts and loosen the wheel arch liner fixings **(see illustrations)**.

24 On all except 1.6 litre DOHC engine models, unscrew the securing bolts, and remove the cover plate from the base of the

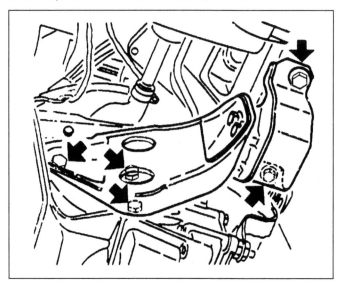

11.23a Remove the left-hand engine/transmission mounting by unscrewing the five bolts (arrowed)

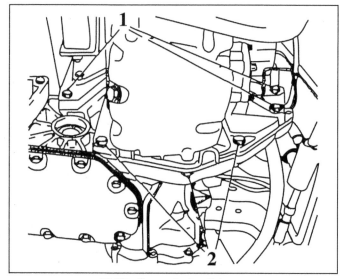

**11.23b Transmission fixings –
1.6 litre DOHC engine models**

1 Cylinder block to   2 Sump to transmission
   transmission bolts (3)   bolts (3)

clutch bellhousing. On 1.6 litre DOHC engine models, unscrew the three bolts securing the transmission to the cylinder block, and the three bolts securing the transmission to the sump.

25 Ensure that the transmission is adequately supported, then unscrew and remove the remaining engine-to-transmission bolts.

26 The transmission can now be lowered and withdrawn from under the front of the vehicle. The help of an assistant will greatly ease this operation.

Refitting

27 Before starting the refitting operations, check that the two original bolts that secured the left-hand engine/transmission mounting to the vehicle body rotate freely in their threaded bores in the body. If necessary, re-cut the threaded bores, using an M10 x 1.25 mm tap.

28 Begin refitting by positioning the transmission under the front of the vehicle, and support with a trolley jack and interposed block of wood, as during removal.

29 Raise the transmission sufficiently to enable the lower engine-to-transmission bolts to be fitted, then refit the bolts. On all except 1.6 litre DOHC engine models, do not fully retighten the bolts at this stage (on 1.6 litre DOHC engine models, the bolts must be tightened at this stage).

30 Refit the left-hand engine/transmission mounting, using two new bolts to secure the rubber mounting to the vehicle body. Tighten all bolts to the specified torque.

31 On all except 1.6 litre DOHC engine models, tighten the previously fitted lower engine-to-transmission bolts to the specified torque, then withdraw the trolley jack from under the transmission.

32 The transmission input shaft must now be pushed through the hub of the clutch friction disc, until its end engages in the spigot bearing in the end of the crankshaft. **Under no circumstances** must the shaft be hammered home, as transmission damage may result. If the input shaft cannot be pushed home by hand, steady pressure should be exerted on the end of the shaft. The manufacturers specify the use of a special tool for this operation (tool No KM-564), but the improvised tool used to withdraw the shaft during the removal procedure can be used by repositioning the nut (see Chapter 6).

33 Refit the bolt to the end of the input shaft, then fit a new circlip.

34 Using a new gasket, refit the transmission endplate, and tighten the securing bolts to the specified torque. Where applicable, ensure that the studded bolt that retains the earth

strap is fitted to its correct location, as noted during removal.

35 Where applicable, reconnect the transmission earth strap, and fit the retaining nut.

36 Refit the cover plate to the base of the clutch bellhousing, and tighten the securing bolts.

37 Fit new snap-rings to the inboards end of the driveshafts, then push the driveshafts into the differential as far as possible.

38 Place a screwdriver or similar tool on the weld bead of each inner driveshaft joint, **not** the metal cover, and drive the shaft into the differential until the retaining snap-ring engages positively. Pull on the **outer** circumference of the joint to check the engagement.

39 Refit the front suspension subframe, as described in Chapter 10.

40 Refit the front wheels.

41 If a hoist and lifting tackle has been used to support the engine, either disconnect the lifting tackle, or lower the hoist sufficiently to enable the vehicle to be lowered to the ground.

42 Lower the vehicle to the ground, and remove or disconnect the equipment used to support the engine, if not already done.

43 Refit the three upper engine-to-transmission bolts, and tighten them to the specified torque.

44 Reconnect the speedometer cable, and tighten the securing sleeve.

45 Where applicable, reconnect the wiring to the vehicle speed sensor.

46 Reconnect the reversing light switch wiring.

47 Refit the clutch cable support to the bracket on the transmission casing, then reconnect the cable to the release lever, and adjust the cable as described in Chapter 1. Ensure that the cable is routed as noted during removal.

48 Reconnect the gear selector rod to the linkage, then adjust the linkage as described in Section 3, before tightening the clamp bolt.

49 Refill the transmission with oil, as described in Chapter 1.

50 Reconnect the battery negative lead.

12 Transmission overhaul - general

The complete overhaul of a manual transmission is a complicated task, requiring a number of special tools. Previous experience is a great help. It is therefore recommended

that owners remove the transmission themselves, if wished, but then either fit a new or reconditioned unit, or have the existing unit overhauled by a Vauxhall/Opel dealer or transmission specialist.

The dismantling of the transmission into its major assemblies is a reasonably straightforward operation, and can be carried out to enable an assessment of wear or damage to be made. From this assessment, a decision can be taken as to whether or not to proceed with a full overhaul. Note however that any overhaul work will require the dismantling and reassembly of many small and intricate assemblies, as well as the taking of certain measurements to assess wear.

This will require a number of special tools, and previous experience will prove invaluable. As a minimum, the following tools will be required:

a) Internal and external circlip pliers
b) A selection of pin punches
c) A selection of Torx and splined bits
d) A bearing puller
e) A hydraulic press
f) A slide hammer
g) A selection of heat-sensitive marker pencils

While the 'Fault finding' part of this manual should help to isolate most transmission faults to enable a decision to be taken on what course of action to follow, remember that economic considerations may rule out an apparently-simple repair. For example, a common reason for transmission dismantling is to renew the synchromesh units, wear or faults in these assemblies being indicated by noise when changing gear. Jumping out of gear or similar gear selection faults may be due to worn selector forks, or synchro-sleeves. General noise during operation may be due to worn bearings, shafts or gears. The cumulative cost of renewing all worn components may make it more economical to renew the transmission complete.

To establish whether transmission overhaul is economically viable, first establish the cost of a complete replacement transmission, comparing the cost of a new unit with that of an exchange reconditioned unit (if available), or even a good second-hand unit (with a guarantee) from a vehicle breaker. Compare these costs with the likely cost of the replacement parts which will be required if the existing transmission is overhauled; do not forget to include all items that must be renewed when they are disturbed, such as oil seals, O-rings, roll pins, circlips, snap-rings, etc.

Notes

Chapter 7 Part B:
Automatic transmission

Contents

Degrees of difficulty

Easy, suitable for novice with little experience		Fairly easy, suitable for beginner with some experience		Fairly difficult, suitable for competent DIY mechanic		Difficult, suitable for experienced DIY mechanic		Very difficult, suitable for expert DIY or professional	

Specifications

Transmission code

Except C 18 NZ and X 20 XEV	AF 13
C 18 NZ and X 20 XEV	AF 20

Torque wrench settings

	Nm	lbf ft
Actuating lever to selector lever shaft	16	12
Converter bellhousing cover plate bolts	7	5
Cooler pipe unions	22	16
Dipstick and filler tube nut	20	15
Drain plug	35	26
Engine bracket, front left to transmission	60	44
Mounting to front chassis *	65	48
Temperature sensor	25	18
Temperature sensor cover plate to transmission	25	18
Torque converter to driveplate (refer to text) *	50	37
Transmission to engine	75	55
Selector cable clamp bolt	6	4
Speed sensor	6	4
Starter inhibitor/reversing light switch securing nut	25	18
Starter inhibitor switch/reversing light switch to selector lever shaft nut	8	6

* Use new bolts

1 General description

A 4-speed fully automatic transmission is available as an option on certain models. The transmission consists of a torque converter, an epicyclic geartrain and hydraulically operated clutches and brakes. The differential is integral with the transmission, and is similar to that used in manual transmission models.

The torque converter provides a fluid coupling between the engine and transmission that acts as an automatic 'clutch', and provides a degree of torque multiplication when accelerating.

The epicyclic geartrain provides either one of the four forward gear ratios, or reverse gear, according to which of its component parts are held stationary or allowed to turn. The components of the geartrain are held or released by brakes and clutches, which are activated by a hydraulic control unit. A fluid pump within the transmission provides the necessary hydraulic pressure to operate the brakes and clutches.

The transmission is electronically controlled, and three driving modes; 'Economy', 'Sport' and 'Winter' are provided. The transmission electronic control unit operates in conjunction with the engine electronic control unit to control the gearchanges. The electronic control unit receives information on transmission fluid temperature, throttle position, engine coolant temperature, and input versus output speed. The control unit controls the hydraulically operated clutches and brakes through four solenoids. The control system can also retard the engine ignition timing, by way of the engine electronic control unit, to allow smoother gearchanges (see illustrations overleaf).

During 1993, the AF 13 transmission was introduced. Although based on the previous AF 20 unit, it is more compact and includes an electronic reverse pawl. This prevents reverse gear being selected, if the forward motion is greater than 5 mph.

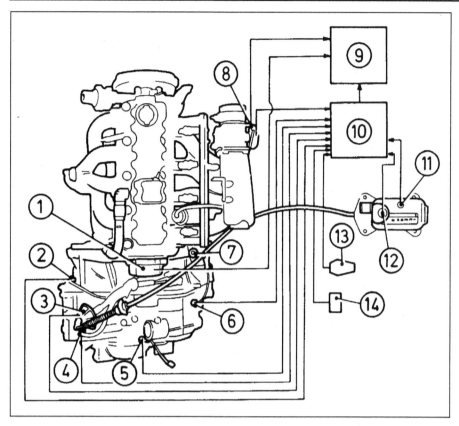

 1.4a Electronic control system -
AF 20 models

1 Distributor
2 Transmission fluid temperature sensor
3 Starter inhibitor/reversing light switch
4 Connection for pressure-regulating
  solenoids
5 Transmission input speed sensor
6 Transmission output sensor
7 Speedometer cable connection
8 Throttle position sensor
9 Engine electronic control unit
10 Automatic transmission electronic
   control unit
11 'Winter' mode switch
12 'Economy/Sport' mode switch
13 Kickdown switch
14 Brake light switch

Due to the complexity of the automatic transmission, any repair or overhaul work must be entrusted to a Vauxhall/Opel dealer, with the necessary specialist equipment and knowledge for fault diagnosis and repair.

2 Selector cable - removal, refitting and adjustment

Removal

1 Apply the handbrake, and ensure that the transmission selector lever is in position 'P'.
2 Disconnect the battery negative lead.
3 Remove the retaining clamp and the washer, and disconnect the selector cable from the actuating lever on the transmission.
4 Unscrew the securing nuts, and withdraw the cable mounting bracket from the transmission.
5 Remove the centre console, as described in Chapter 11.
6 Slacken the cable clamp bolt and unscrew the cable locknut, items 1 and 2 (see illustration), then withdraw the cable, and pull it through the bulkhead into the engine compartment, prising out the bulkhead grommet where necessary.

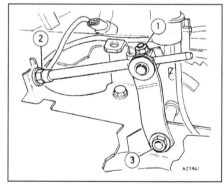

2.6 Automatic transmission selector cable connection at selector lever

| 1 Cable clamp | 2 Cable locknut |
| bolt | 3 Lever pivot nut |

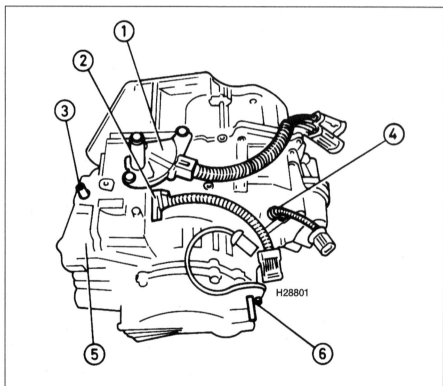

1.4b External electrical components - AF 13 models

1 Selector lever position switch	4 Input speed sensor
2 Solenoid valves wiring harness	5 Valve body cover
3 Transmission vent	6 Output speed sensor

Refitting

7 Refitting is a reversal of the removal procedure, but make sure that the bulkhead grommet is correctly located, and before tightening the cable clamp bolt and refitting the selector cover, adjust the cable as described in the following paragraphs.

Adjustment

8 Working in the engine compartment, check that the actuating lever on the transmission moves to the appropriate position, while an assistant moves the selector lever inside the vehicle through the full range of positions. Note that positions 'P' and 'N' are marked on the transmission, but the remaining positions are unmarked.

9 If adjustment is required, move the selector lever to position 'P'. Check that the lever is locked in position 'P' by attempting to move the lever backwards and forwards without lifting the lever knob.

10 Working inside the vehicle, release the transmission selector cover from the centre console (the cover is secured by clips on either side), then rotate the cover until the cable clamp bolt aperture is visible.

11 Using a long reach socket, slacken the cable clamp bolt **(see illustration)**.

12 Again working in the engine compartment, turn the actuating lever on the transmission to the right (i.e., towards the battery holder), until it reaches its stop.

13 Attempt to turn the front roadwheels, and check that the parking pawl engages, locking the wheels in position.

14 Have the assistant hold the actuating lever against the stop, while the cable clamp bolt inside the vehicle is tightened to the specified torque.

15 Recheck the selector operation, as described in paragraph 1.

16 Refit the selector cover on completion.

3 Selector lever assembly - removal and refitting

Removal

1 Apply the handbrake, and ensure that the transmission selector lever is in position 'P'.

2 Disconnect the battery negative lead.

3 Release the transmission selector cover from the centre console (the cover is secured by clips at either side). Pull the illumination light bulb holder from the selector cover, and disconnect the transmission 'Winter' mode switch wiring connector.

4 Slacken the selector cable clamp bolt and unscrew the cable locknut (items 1 and 2 in illustration 2.6), then disconnect the cable from the selector lever assembly.

5 Disconnect the transmission 'Economy/ Sport' mode switch wiring connector.

6 Unscrew the securing nut, and slide the

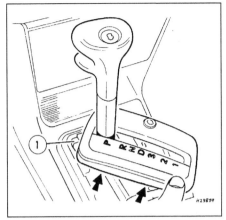

2.11 Automatic transmission selector cable adjustment

1 Long-reach socket can be inserted through aperture to slacken cable clamp bolt
Selector cover clips arrowed

selector lever from the end of the pivot shaft, then withdraw the assembly.

7 No attempt should be made to dismantle the assembly.

Refitting

8 Refitting is a reversal of removal, but on completion, adjust the cable as described in Section 2.

4 Differential side (driveshaft) oil seals - renewal

1 The procedure is as described for the manual transmission in Chapter 7A, remembering the following points.

a) Drain the transmission fluid into a container by removing the drain plug located at the lower right-hand side of the transmission housing **(see illustration)**.

b) Smear the sealing ring of the new oil seal with transmission fluid.

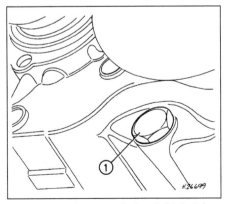

4.1 Automatic transmission fluid draining

1 Drain plug

c) On completion, refill the transmission through the dipstick tube with the correct quantity and type of fluid, and check the level as described in Chapter 1.

5 Fluid cooler information - general

The transmission fluid cooler is an integral part of the radiator assembly, and removal and refitting is described in Chapter 3.

The hoses running from the transmission to the cooler should be checked at regular intervals, and renewed if there is any doubt about their condition.

Always take note of the pipe and hose connections before disturbing them, and take note of the hose routing.

To minimise the loss of fluid, and to prevent the entry of dirt into the system, clamp the hoses before disconnecting them, and plug the unions once the hoses have been disconnected.

When reconnecting the hoses, ensure that they are connected to their original locations, and route them so that they are not kinked or twisted. Also allow for the movement of the engine on its mountings, ensuring that the hoses will not be stretched or fouled by surrounding components.

Always renew the sealing washers if the banjo union bolts are disturbed, and tighten the bolts to their specified torque wrench setting. Be particularly careful when tightening the cooler unions.

6 Kickdown switch - removal, refitting and adjustment

Removal

1 Disconnect the battery negative lead.

2 Release the carpet from the retainer under the throttle pedal, and lift the carpet to expose the switch mounting.

3 Disconnect the switch wiring, then unclip the switch from its retainer.

Refitting

4 Refitting is a reversal of removal, but push the switch into the retainer as far as the stop, and check the switch adjustment as described in the following paragraphs.

Adjustment

5 Working in the engine compartment, where applicable, remove the airbox from the top of the fuel injection unit, to enable the throttle valve to be observed.

6 Have an assistant depress the throttle pedal until it contacts the switch on the vehicle floor, then check that the throttle valve is fully open, and that the pedal acts squarely on the centre of the switch button.

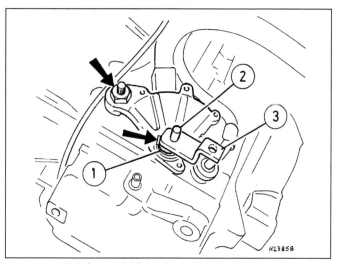

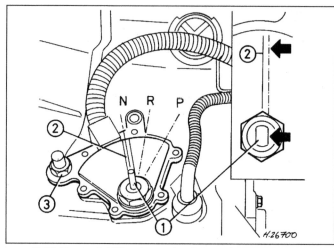

7.6 Starter inhibitor/reversing light switch

1 *Large nut*   2 *Selector lever shaft*   3 *Actuating lever*

Arrows indicate switch mountings

7.15 Starter inhibitor/reversing light switch adjustment

1 *Selector lever shaft*   2 *Groove switch housing*   3 *Switch securing nut*

Arrows show shaft in alignment with groove in switch housing

7 If the pedal/switch button contact point requires adjustment, this must be carried out by adjusting the throttle cable free play - see Chapter 4A or 4B.

7 Starter inhibitor/reversing light switch - removal, refitting and adjustment

Note: *The dipstick tube O-ring must be renewed on refitting.*

Removal

1 Apply the handbrake and select position 'N' with the gear selector lever.
2 Disconnect the battery negative lead.
3 Working in the engine compartment, unscrew the securing nut from the starter inhibitor/reversing light switch mounting stud, and withdraw the dipstick tube upwards from the transmission.
4 Remove the retaining clamp and the washer, and disconnect the selector cable from the actuating lever on the transmission.
5 Disconnect the wiring from the switch.
6 Using pliers to counterhold the shaft, unscrew the nut securing the actuating lever to the selector lever shaft, then remove the locking plate and unscrew the large nut and washer securing the switch to the shaft **(see illustration)**.
7 Unscrew the nut securing the switch to the transmission, and withdraw the switch.

Refitting

8 Ensure that the selector lever shaft is in position 'N' (the third detent from the front). Lower the switch onto the shaft and rotate it until the shaft's flattened surface is aligned with the groove in the switch housing. Then refit the nut that secures the switch to the transmission, and tighten it to the specified torque.

9 Refit the washer, then refit and tighten the large nut securing the switch to the selector lever shaft. Tighten the nut to the specified torque wrench setting, then refit the locking plate.
10 Refit the nut securing the actuating lever to the selector lever shaft. Use pliers to counterhold the shaft as the nut is tightened, as during removal.
11 Refit the dipstick tube, using a new O-ring, then refit and tighten the securing nut.
12 Reconnect the switch wiring, and the battery negative lead.
13 Reconnect the selector cable to the actuating lever on the transmission, and adjust the cable as described in Section 2.

Adjustment

14 Remove the retaining clamp and the washer, and disconnect the selector cable from the actuating lever on the transmission.
15 Move the actuating lever fully to the right

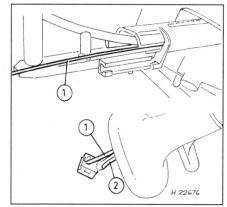

8.2 Removing the transmission mode switches

1 *Welding rod*   2 *Soldered switch connectors*

against the stop, then turn the lever back two notches to position 'N' **(see illustration)**.
16 Observe the end of the selector lever shaft. The shaft's flattened surface should be aligned with the groove in the switch housing. If necessary, loosen the nut securing the switch to the transmission, and turn the switch until the alignment is correct.
17 On completion of adjustment, tighten the switch securing nut to the specified torque.
18 Reconnect the selector cable to the actuating lever on the transmission, and adjust the cable as described in Section 2.

8 Transmission 'mode' switches - removal and refitting

'Economy'/'Sport' mode switch

Removal

1 Remove the selector lever assembly as described in Section 3.
2 Using a length of welding rod or a similar tool inserted through the lower end of the selector lever, push out the switch **(see illustration)**.
3 Note the wiring connections, then carefully unsolder the wires from the switch.

Refitting

4 Refitting is a reversal of removal, but ensure that the wiring connections are correct, as noted before removal, and refit the selector lever assembly as described in Section 3.

'Winter' mode switch

Removal

5 Disconnect the battery negative lead.
6 Release the transmission selector cover from the centre console (the cover is secured

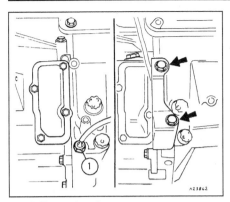

9.2 Removing the temperature sensor

1 *Temperature sensor* *Shield securing bolts arrowed*

by clips on either side), then carefully push the switch from the selector cover, and disconnect the wiring plug.

Refitting

7 Refitting is a reversal of removal.

9 Fluid temperature sensor - removal and refitting

Note: *A new sensor sealing ring must be used on refitting.*

Removal

1 Disconnect the battery negative lead.
2 Unscrew the two securing nuts, and remove the sensor shield from the front of the transmission **(see illustration)**.
3 Disconnect the sensor wiring connector.
4 Unscrew the sensor, and withdraw it from the transmission. Be prepared for fluid spillage, and plug the aperture in the transmission to prevent dirt ingress and minimise fluid loss. Recover the sealing ring.

Refitting

5 Refitting is a reversal of removal, using a new sealing ring. On completion, check the fluid level and top-up if necessary as described in Chapter 1.

10 Input/output speed sensors - removal and refitting

Note: *A new sensor sealing ring must be used on refitting.*

Removal

1 The speed sensors are located in the upper face of the transmission casing. The input speed sensor is nearest to the left-hand end of the transmission **(see illustration)**.
2 Disconnect the battery negative lead.
3 Disconnect the relevant wiring connector.
4 Unscrew the sensor securing screw, and withdraw the sensor from the transmission.

Be prepared for fluid spillage, and plug the aperture in the transmission to prevent dirt ingress and minimise fluid loss. Recover the sealing ring.

Refitting

5 Refitting is a reversal of removal, using a new sealing ring. On completion, check the fluid level and top-up if necessary, as described in Chapter 1.

11 Electronic control unit - removal and refitting

Removal

1 The electronic control unit is located behind the glovebox on the passenger's side of the facia **(see illustration)**.
2 Disconnect the battery negative lead.
3 Remove the glovebox as described in Chapter 11.
4 Disconnect the wiring plug from the control unit.
5 Release the control unit from its securing bracket, and withdraw it from the facia.

Refitting

6 Refitting is a reversal of removal.

12 Transmission assembly - removal and refitting

Note: *This is an involved procedure, and it is easier in many cases to remove the transmission with the engine as an assembly, as described in Chapter 2C. If removing the transmission on its own, it is suggested that this Section is read through thoroughly before starting work. Various components must be renewed on reassembly and an engine hoist, or equivalent will be required to support the engine.*

Removal

1 Disconnect the battery negative lead.
2 Working in the engine compartment, remove the retaining clamp and the washer, and disconnect the selector cable from the actuating lever on the transmission.
3 Disconnect the vent hose from the transmission (the vent hose is located below the battery tray).
4 Disconnect the transmission wiring harness plug, and unbolt the wiring harness bracket(s) from the transmission, if fitted.
5 Unscrew the securing sleeve, and disconnect the speedometer cable from the top of the transmission.
6 Unscrew and remove the three upper engine to transmission bolts, noting the locations of any brackets or clips attached to the bolts. Remove the oxygen sensor (located behind the coolant expansion tank), if fitted.

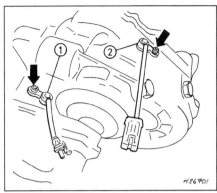

10.1 Speed sensor locations

1 *Input speed sensor* 2 *Output speed*

Securing screws arrowed

7 Proceed as described in Chapter 7A, Section 11, paragraphs 8 to 14, but drain the transmission fluid by removing the drain plug located at the lower right-hand side of the transmission housing.
8 Clamp the transmission fluid cooler hoses, then disconnect them from the transmission, noting their locations. Some AF 13 models are fitted with 'quick release sockets' **(see illustration overleaf)**. These can be released using a small screwdriver. In either case, be prepared for fluid spillage, and plug the open ends of the hoses and transmission to minimise fluid loss and prevent dirt ingress.
9 Unbolt and remove the transmission bellhousing cover plate.
10 If the original torque converter and driveplate are to be refitted, make alignment marks between the torque converter and the driveplate, to ensure that the components are reassembled in their original positions.
11 Working through the bottom of the bellhousing, unscrew the three torque converter to driveplate bolts. It will be necessary to turn the crankshaft using a spanner or socket on the crankshaft pulley or gear bolt (as applicable), to gain access to each bolt in turn through the aperture. Use a

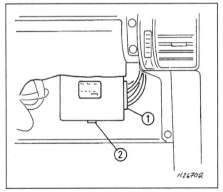

11.1 Automatic transmission electronic control unit location

1 *Wiring plug*
2 *Control unit-to-bracket clip*

screwdriver or a similar tool to jam the driveplate ring gear, preventing the driveplate from rotating as the bolts are loosened. Discard the bolts.

12 Support the transmission with a trolley jack, with an interposed block of wood to spread the load.

13 Remove the left-hand engine/transmission mounting completely, by unscrewing the two bolts securing the rubber mounting to the vehicle body, and the three bolts securing the mounting bracket to the transmission.

14 Ensure that the transmission is adequately supported, then unscrew and remove the remaining engine to transmission bolts. Ensure that the torque converter is held firmly in place in the transmission casing as the engine and transmission are separated, otherwise it could fall out, resulting in fluid spillage and possible damage. Retain the torque converter while the transmission is removed by bolting a strip of metal across the transmission bellhousing end face.

15 The transmission can now be lowered and withdrawn from under the front of the vehicle. The help of an assistant will greatly ease this operation.

Refitting

Note: *New torque converter to driveplate bolts must be used on refitting, and if the original torque converter is being used, an M10 x 1.25 mm tap will be required. New left-hand engine/transmission mounting to body bolts, and new driveshaft snap-rings, must be used on refitting.*

16 If the original torque converter is being refitted, begin refitting by recutting the torque converter to driveplate bolt threads in the torque converter using an M10 x 1.25 mm tap **(see illustration).**

17 If a new transmission is being fitted, the manufacturers recommend that the radiator fluid cooler passages are flushed clean before the new transmission is installed. Ideally, compressed air should be used (in which case, ensure that adequate safety precautions are taken), but alternatively, the cooler can be flushed with clean automatic transmission fluid until all the old fluid has been expelled, and fresh fluid runs clear from the cooler outlet.

18 Begin refitting by positioning the transmission under the front of the vehicle, and support with a trolley jack and interposed block of wood, as during removal.

19 Where applicable, remove the strip of metal retaining the torque converter in the transmission, and hold the torque converter in position as the transmission is mated to the engine.

20 Raise the transmission sufficiently to enable the upper and lower engine to transmission bolts to be fitted, but do not tighten them fully at this stage. Ensure that any brackets or clips noted during removal are in place on the bolts.

21 Refit the left-hand engine/transmission mounting, using two new bolts to secure the rubber mounting to the vehicle body. Tighten all bolts to the specified torque.

22 Tighten the previously fitted engine to transmission bolts to the specified torque, then withdraw the trolley jack from under the transmission.

23 If the original torque converter and driveplate have been refitted, carefully turn the crankshaft to align the marks made before removal, before fitting the torque converter to driveplate bolts.

24 Fit **new** torque converter to driveplate bolts, and tighten them to the specified torque. Turn the crankshaft for access to each

bolt in turn, and prevent the driveplate from turning as during removal.

25 Refit the transmission bellhousing cover plate.

26 Proceed as described in Chapter 7A, Section 11, paragraphs 37 to 42 inclusive.

27 Reconnect the transmission fluid cooler hoses to the transmission, using new sealing washers.

28 Reconnect the speedometer drive cable to the transmission.

29 Refit the transmission harness brackets, and reconnect the wiring harness plug.

30 Reconnect the transmission vent hose.

31 Reconnect the selector cable to the actuating lever on the transmission, and adjust the cable as described in Section 2.

32 Refill the transmission with the specified type and quantity of fluid through the dipstick tube.

33 Reconnect the battery negative lead.

34 On completion, check the transmission fluid level and top-up if necessary, as described in Chapter 1.

13 Transmission overhaul - general

If a fault develops in the transmission, it is first necessary to determine whether it is of an electrical, mechanical or hydraulic nature, and to achieve this, special test equipment is required. It is therefore essential to have the work carried out by a Opel dealer if a transmission fault is suspected.

Do not remove the transmission from the car for possible repair before professional fault diagnosis has been carried out, since most tests require the transmission to be in the vehicle.

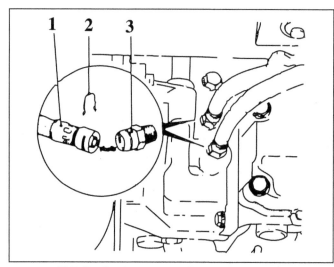

12.8 Cooling hose connections - AF 13 models

1 Cooling hose   2 Retaining clip   3 Union

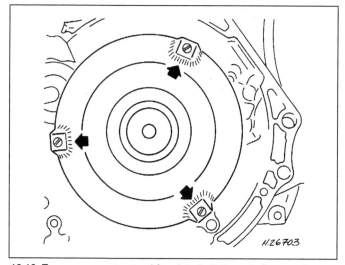

12.16 Torque converter-to-driveplate bolt threads (arrowed) must be recut on refitting

Chapter 8
Driveshafts

Contents

Degrees of difficulty

Easy, suitable for novice with little experience	Fairly easy, suitable for beginner with some experience	Fairly difficult, suitable for competent DIY mechanic	Difficult, suitable for experienced DIY mechanic	Very difficult, suitable for expert DIY or professional

Specifications

Driveshaft joint grease specification .... GM P/N 90094176

Torque wrench settings	Nm	lbf ft
Front hub (refer to text):		
Stage 1	100	74
Stage 2	Loosen nut fully	
Stage 3	20	15
Stage 4	Angle-tighten by a further 80° (plus up to 9° if necessary)	
Lower arm-to-suspension strut balljoint	70	52

1 General description

Drive from the differential is taken to the roadwheels by two open driveshafts with a constant velocity joint at each ends. The driveshafts are splined at both ends.

The inner ends fit into the differential, and are retained by snap-rings, while the outer ends fit into the front hubs, and are retained by the front hub nuts.

The right-hand driveshaft is longer than the left-hand one, due to the position of the differential. Certain models have a two-piece vibration damper fitted to the right-hand driveshaft.

2 Driveshafts - removal and refitting

Note: *A balljoint separator tool will be required for this operation. The following components must be renewed when refitting the driveshaft: hub nut, washer and split pin, driveshaft retaining snap-ring, and lower arm-to-suspension strut balljoint nut locking pin.*

Removal

1 Jack up the front of the vehicle and support securely on axle stands (see "*Jacking and vehicle support*"). Remove the relevant roadwheel.
2 Extract the split pin from the castellated hub nut on the end of the driveshaft.
3 The hub nut must now be loosened. The nut is extremely tight, and an extension bar will be required to loosen it. To prevent the driveshaft from turning, insert two roadwheel bolts, and insert a metal bar between them to counterhold the hub.

2.4 Removing the hub nut and washer from the driveshaft

2.5a Extract the locking pin (arrowed) . . .

2.5b . . . then remove the balljoint castellated nut

2.6 Using a balljoint separator tool to disconnect the balljoint

2.9 Using a steel bar to release the end of the driveshaft from the differential

2.11 Withdrawing the outer end of the driveshaft from the hub

4 Remove the hub nut and washer from the driveshaft **(see illustration)**.

5 Extract the locking pin, then unscrew the castellated nut from the lower arm-to-suspension strut balljoint **(see illustrations)**.

6 Using a balljoint separator tool, disconnect the lower arm-to-suspension strut balljoint **(see illustration)**.

7 Where fitted, remove the engine undershield, as described in Chapter 11, Section 25.

8 A suitable tool will now be required to release the right-hand driveshaft, a flat steel bar with a good chamfer on one end can be used. The left-hand driveshaft may prove more difficult to release, and a square or rectangular section bar may be required.

9 Lever between the driveshaft and the differential housing to release the driveshaft

snap-ring from the differential **(see illustration)**. Have a container available, to catch the oil that will be released as the driveshaft is withdrawn from the differential. Support the driveshaft by suspending it with wire or string, and do not allow it to hang under its own weight.

10 Plug the opening in the differential, to prevent further oil loss and dirt ingress.

11 Withdraw the outer end of the driveshaft from the hub, and remove the driveshaft from the vehicle **(see illustration)**. It should be possible to pull the driveshaft from the hub by hand, but if necessary tap the end of the shaft with a soft-faced mallet to release it.

Caution: Do not use heavy blows, as

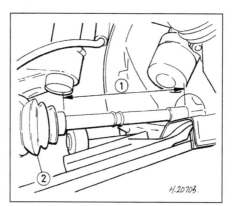

2.13b Driveshaft damper weight distance from outer joint gaiter (2)

1 = 268.0 to 270.0 mm

damage to the driveshaft joints may result. Caution: Do not allow the vehicle to rest on its wheels with one or both driveshaft(s) removed, as damage to the wheel bearing(s) may result.

12 If moving the vehicle is unavoidable, temporarily insert the outer end of the driveshaft(s) in the hub(s) and tighten the hub nut(s). In this case, the inner end(s) of the driveshaft(s) must be supported, for example by suspending with string from the vehicle underbody.

Caution: Do not allow the driveshaft to hang down under its own weight.

13 Certain models have a two-piece vibration damper fitted to the right-hand driveshaft. If the damper is removed for any reason, it is important to refit it so that the distance between the inner end of the outer joint gaiter and the outer face of the damper is as shown **(see illustrations)**.

Refitting

14 Before refitting a driveshaft, make sure that the contact faces of the shaft and the wheel bearing are absolutely clean **(see illustration)**.

15 Begin refitting by applying a little molybdenum disulphide grease to the driveshaft splines, then insert the outer end of the shaft into the hub. Fit a new washer, and screw on a new hub nut finger-tight.

16 Fit a new snap-ring to the inboard end of the driveshaft **(see illustration)**, then remove the plug from the opening in the differential, and push the driveshaft into the differential as far as possible.

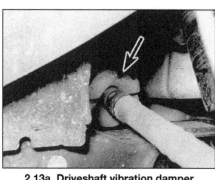

2.13a Driveshaft vibration damper (arrowed) - DOHC model viewed through right-hand wheel arch

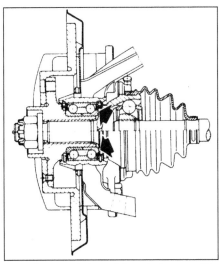

2.14 Sectional view of front hub assembly

Clean the contact faces (arrowed) of the driveshaft and wheel bearing

17 Place a screwdriver or similar tool on the weld bead of the inner driveshaft joint, **not** the metal cover, and drive the shaft into the differential until the retaining snap-ring engages positively. Pull on the **outer** circumference of the joint to check the engagement.

18 Reconnect the lower arm-to-suspension strut balljoint, then fit the castellated nut, and tighten to the specified torque. Secure the nut with a new locking pin.

19 Tighten the new hub nut to the specified torque, in the stages given in the

2.19a Tighten the hub nut to the specified torque . . .

2.19b . . . then through the specified angle (see Specifications)

Specifications. Prevent the driveshaft from turning as during removal **(see illustrations)**. If the holes in the driveshaft for the split pin do not line up with any of the slots in the nut, loosen (**do not** tighten) the nut, until the holes line up with the nearest slots to enable the split pin to be fitted. Use a new split pin, bending over the ends of the pin to secure it.

20 Refit the roadwheel, then lower the vehicle to the ground.

21 Check and if necessary top-up the transmission oil/fluid level, as described in Chapter 1.

22 Where applicable, refit the engine undershield.

3 Driveshaft joint - removal and refitting

Note: *Check to ensure that a new securing circlip is supplied when ordering a new driveshaft joint.*

Removal

1 A worn driveshaft joint must be renewed, as it cannot be overhauled. If driveshaft joint wear is apparent on a vehicle in which the driveshaft has covered more than 80 000 km, the manufacturers recommend that the complete driveshaft is renewed.

2 With the driveshaft removed as described in Section 2, release the metal securing band, and slide the rubber gaiter from the worn joint.

3 Using circlip pliers, expand the circlip that secures the joint to the driveshaft **(see illustration)**.

4 Using a soft-faced mallet, tap the joint from the driveshaft **(see illustration)**.

Refitting

5 Ensure that a new circlip is fitted to the new joint, then tap the new joint onto the driveshaft until the circlip engages in its groove.

6 Pack the joint with the specified grease.

7 Refit the rubber gaiter to the new joint, with reference to Section 4.

8 Refit the driveshaft to the vehicle, as described in Section 2.

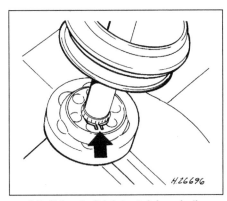

3.3 Driveshaft joint retaining circlip (arrowed)

2.16 Always renew driveshaft retaining snap-ring on refitting

4 Driveshaft joint gaiter - removal and refitting

Removal

1 With the driveshaft removed as described in Section 2, remove the relevant joint as described in Section 3. Note that if both gaiters on a driveshaft are to be renewed, it is only necessary to remove one joint.

2 Release the remaining securing band, and slide the gaiter from the driveshaft.

Refitting

3 Clean the old grease from the joint, then repack the joint with the specified grease. If excessively worn or damaged, the driveshaft joint should be renewed, with reference to Section 3 if necessary.

4 Slide the new gaiter onto the driveshaft so that the smaller diameter opening is located in the groove in the driveshaft.

5 Refit the joint, using a new securing circlip. Tap the joint onto the driveshaft until the circlip engages in its groove.

6 Slide the gaiter over the joint, then squeeze the gaiter to expel as much air as possible.

7 Secure the gaiter using new securing bands. To fit a securing band, wrap it around the gaiter, and while pulling on the band as tight as possible, engage the lug on the end of the band with one of the slots. Use a screwdriver if necessary to push the band as tight as

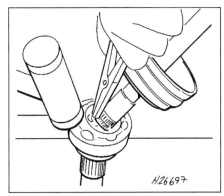

3.4 Tapping joint from driveshaft

possible before engaging the lug and slot. Finally tighten the band by compressing the raised square portion of the band with pliers.

5 Driveshaft overhaul - general

1 If any of the checks in Chapter 1 reveal wear in any driveshaft joint, first remove the roadwheel trim or wheel centre cap, as applicable. If the driveshaft nut staking is still effective, the nut should be correctly tightened. If in doubt, use a torque wrench to check that the nut is securely fastened and re-stake it (see Section 2), then refit the wheel trim or centre cap, as applicable. Repeat this check on the remaining driveshaft nut.

2 Road test the vehicle, and listen for a metallic clicking from the front as the vehicle is driven slowly in a circle on full steering lock. If a clicking noise is heard, this indicates wear in the outer constant velocity joint. This means that the joint must be renewed, as overhaul is not possible (see Section 3).

3 If vibration, consistent with road speed, is felt through the vehicle when accelerating, there is a possibility of wear in the inner constant velocity joints.

Chapter 9
Braking system

Contents

Degrees of difficulty

| Easy, suitable for novice with little experience | | Fairly easy, suitable for beginner with some experience | | Fairly difficult, suitable for competent DIY mechanic | | Difficult, suitable for experienced DIY mechanic | | Very difficult, suitable for expert DIY or professional |  |

Specifications

Front brakes

Disc thickness - new :
Solid discs . . . . 12.7 mm
Vented discs:
  1.4, 1.6 and 1.8 litre SOHC engine models . . . . 20.0 mm
  2.0 litre SOHC engine models and DOHC engine models . . . . . 24.0 mm
Minimum permissible thickness after machining:*
Solid discs . . . . 10.7 mm
Vented discs:
  1.4, 1.6 and 1.8 litre SOHC engine models . . . . 18.0 mm
  2.0 litre SOHC engine models and DOHC engine models . . . . . 22.0 mm
Minimum permissible thickness (at which point discs must be renewed):
Solid discs . . . . 9.7 mm
Vented discs:
  1.4, 1.6 and 1.8 litre SOHC engine models . . . . 17.0 mm
  2.0 litre SOHC engine models and DOHC engine models . . . . . 21.0 mm
Maximum disc run-out . . . . 0.1 mm
*When this dimension is reached, only one further new set of pads is permissible, then renew the discs.

Rear drum brakes

Drum internal diameter:
New . . . . 200.0 mm
Maximum permissible diameter after machining . . . . 201.0 mm

Rear disc brakes

Disc thickness:
New . . . . 10.0 mm
Minimum permissible thickness after machining * . . . . 8.0 mm
Minimum permissible thickness (at which point discs must be renewed)7.0 mm
Maximum disc run-out . . . . 0.1 mm
*When this dimension is reached, only one further new set of pads is permissible, then renew the discs.

Torque wrench settings

	Nm	lbf ft
ABS hydraulic modulator securing nuts	8	6
ABS wheel sensor securing bolt	8	6
Bleed nipples	6	4
Brake drum securing screw	4	3
Brake fluid pipe union nuts	16	12
Brake hose to caliper	40	30
Caliper guide bolt	30	22
Caliper, front to steering knuckle	95	70
Brake master cylinder to servo	22	16
Front brake disc securing screw	4	3
Front brake disc shield screws	4	3
Handbrake lever securing bolts	20	15
Master cylinder (ATE-type) stop-screw	6	4
Pressure regulating valve securing screws (Estate and Van models)	20	15
Rear brake backplate/hub unit securing nuts: *		
Stage 1	50	37
Stage 2	Angle-tighten by a further 30 to 45°	
Rear brake disc securing screw	8	6
Rear caliper mounting	80	59
Rear wheel cylinder bolts	9	7
Servo with bracket to bulkhead	22	16
Servo to bracket	20	15

Use new nuts

1 General information and precautions

General information

The footbrake operates on all four wheels. Solid or ventilated disc brakes are fitted at the front, and self-adjusting drum or solid disc brakes are fitted at the rear, depending on model. Actuation is hydraulic, with vacuum servo assistance. The handbrake is cable-operated, and acts on the rear wheels only.

The hydraulic system is split into two circuits. On non-ABS (Anti-lock Braking System) models, the system is split diagonally, and on ABS models, the system is split front and rear. If there is a brake fluid leak in one circuit, the remaining circuit will still function, so that some braking capability remains.

The brake fluid supply to the rear brakes is regulated so that the front brakes always lock first under heavy braking (this reduces the danger of the car spinning). On Saloon and Hatchback models, the fluid pressure to the rear brakes is controlled by two valves, one for each brake, which are mounted on the rear underbody of the vehicle. On Estate and Van models, the fluid pressure to the rear brakes is controlled by a single load-dependent valve, which acts depending on the loading of the rear suspension.

The brake servo is of the direct-acting type, fitted between the pedal and the master cylinder. The servo is powered by vacuum developed in the inlet manifold. Should the servo fail, the brakes will still operate, but increased pedal pressure will be required.

Refer to Section 25 for further details of the ABS system.

Precautions

When working on any part of the system, work carefully and methodically; also observe scrupulous cleanliness when overhauling any part of the hydraulic system. Always renew components (in axle sets, not just on one wheel, where applicable) if in doubt about their condition, and use only GM replacement parts, or at least those of known good quality. Note the warnings given in 'Safety first' and at the relevant points in this Chapter concerning the dangers of asbestos dust and brake fluid.

2 Hydraulic system - bleeding

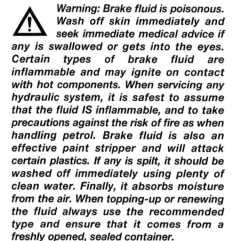

⚠️ *Warning: Brake fluid is poisonous. Wash off skin immediately and seek immediate medical advice if any is swallowed or gets into the eyes. Certain types of brake fluid are inflammable and may ignite on contact with hot components. When servicing any hydraulic system, it is safest to assume that the fluid IS inflammable, and to take precautions against the risk of fire as when handling petrol. Brake fluid is also an effective paint stripper and will attack certain plastics. If any is spilt, it should be washed off immediately using plenty of clean water. Finally, it absorbs moisture from the air. When topping-up or renewing the fluid always use the recommended type and ensure that it comes from a freshly opened, sealed container.*

Caution: Vauxhall/Opel recommend the use of a pressure bleeding kit when bleeding the braking system - see paragraphs 24 to 27.

General

1 The efficient operation of any hydraulic system is only possible after removing all air from the components and circuit. If any of the hydraulic components in the braking system have been removed or disconnected, or if the fluid level has been allowed to fall appreciably, it is inevitable that air will have been introduced into the system. The removal of all this air from the hydraulic system is essential if the brakes are to function correctly, and the process of removing it is known as 'bleeding'.

2 During the bleeding procedure, add only clean, unused brake fluid of the recommended type; never re-use fluid that has already been bled from the system. Ensure that sufficient fluid is available before starting work.

3 If there is any possibility of incorrect fluid already being present in the system, the complete hydraulic circuit must be flushed with fresh fluid of the correct type, and new fluid seals should be fitted to all the components.

4 If brake fluid has been lost from the system, or air has entered due to a leak, ensure that the fault is rectified before continuing further.

5 Park the vehicle on level ground, stop the engine, and select first or reverse gear on manual transmission models (or 'P' on models with automatic transmission), then chock the wheels and release the handbrake.

6 Check that all pipes and hoses are secure, unions tight and bleed nipples closed. Clean any dirt from around the bleed nipples.

7 Top-up the brake fluid reservoir to the 'MAX' level line. Refit the cap loosely and maintain the fluid level above the 'MIN' level line throughout the procedure, or there is a risk of further air entering the system through the reservoir.

8 There are a number of one-man, do-it-yourself brake bleeding kits currently available from motor accessory shops. It is recommended that one of these kits is used whenever possible, as they greatly simplify the bleeding operation, and also reduce the risk of expelled air and fluid being drawn back into the system (see 'Caution' at the start of this Section). If such a kit is not available, the basic (two-man) method must be used, which is described in detail later in this Section.

9 If a kit is to be used, prepare the car as described previously, and follow the kit manufacturer's instructions, as the procedure may vary slightly according to the type being used. Generally, instructions for using a kit will be as outlined below in the relevant sub-Section.

10 Whichever method is used, if the complete system is to be bled, the same sequence must be followed (paragraphs 11 and 12) to ensure the removal of all air from the system.

11 Where an operation has only affected one circuit of the hydraulic system (the system is split diagonally on non-ABS models, and front and rear on models with ABS), then it will only be necessary to bleed the relevant circuit. If the master cylinder has been disconnected and reconnected, or the fluid level has been allowed to fall appreciably, then the complete system must be bled.

12 If the complete system is to be bled, models with ABS should have the front brake circuits bled first.

Bleeding - basic (two-man) method

13 Gather together a clean glass jar, a length of plastic or rubber tubing that will fit the bleed nipples tightly, and a ring spanner to fit the nipples. The help of an assistant will also be required.

14 Remove the dust cap from the first nipple in the sequence **(see illustrations)**. Fit the spanner and tube to the nipple, place the other end of the tube in the jar, and pour in sufficient fluid to cover the end of the tube.

15 Ensure that the brake fluid reservoir level is maintained at least above the 'MIN' level mark throughout this procedure.

16 Have the assistant fully depress the brake pedal several times to build up pressure, then maintain it on the final stroke.

17 While pedal pressure is maintained, unscrew the bleed nipple (approximately one turn) and allow the fluid to flow into the jar. The assistant should maintain pedal pressure, pushing the pedal down to the floor if necessary, and should not release the pedal until instructed to do so. When the flow stops, tighten the bleed nipple again, instruct the assistant to release the pedal slowly, and recheck the reservoir fluid level.

18 Repeat the steps given in paragraphs 16 and 17 until the fluid emerging from the bleed nipple is free from air bubbles.

19 When no more air bubbles appear, tighten

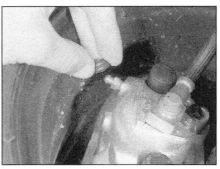

2.14a Removing the dust cap from a front brake caliper bleed nipple

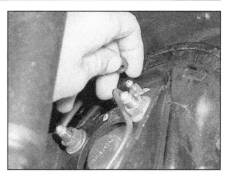

2.14b Removing the dust cap from a rear wheel cylinder bleed nipple - model with rear drum brakes

the bleed nipple securely, remove the tube and spanner, and refit the dust cap. Do not overtighten the bleed nipple.

20 Repeat the procedure on the remaining nipples, until all air is removed from the system and the brake pedal feels firm again.

Bleeding - using a one-way valve kit

21 As the name implies, these kits consist of a length of tubing with a one-way valve fitted to prevent expelled air and fluid being drawn back into the system. Some kits include a clear container that can be positioned so that the air bubbles can be more easily seen flowing from the end of the tube **(see illustration)**.

22 The kit is connected to the bleed nipple, which is then opened. The user returns to the driver's seat and depresses the brake pedal with a smooth, steady stroke and slowly releases it. This is repeated until the expelled fluid is free from air bubbles.

23 Note that although these kits simplify the work, it is easy to forget the brake fluid reservoir fluid level. Ensure that the level is maintained above the 'MIN' level mark at all times, or more air will be drawn into the system.

Bleeding - using a pressure-bleeding kit

24 These kits are usually operated by the pressurised air contained in the spare tyre. Although note that it will probably be necessary to reduce the pressure to a lower limit than normal. Refer to the instructions supplied with the kit.

25 By connecting a pressurised, fluid-filled container to the brake fluid reservoir, bleeding can be carried out simply by opening each nipple in turn (in the specified sequence) and allowing the fluid to flow out until no more air bubbles can be seen in the expelled fluid.

26 This method has the advantage that the large reservoir of fluid provides an additional safeguard against air being drawn into the system during bleeding.

27 Pressure-bleeding is particularly effective when bleeding 'difficult' systems, or when bleeding the complete system at the time of routine fluid renewal.

All methods

28 When bleeding is complete, and firm pedal feel is restored, wash off any spilt fluid, tighten the bleed nipples securely and refit their dust caps. Do not overtighten the bleed nipples.

29 Check the brake fluid level, and top-up if necessary.

30 Discard any brake fluid that has been bled from the system; it will not be fit for re-use.

31 Depress the brake pedal in the normal way to check its 'feel'. If it feels at all spongy, air must still be present in the system, and further bleeding is required. Failure to bleed satisfactorily after a reasonable repetition of the bleeding procedure may be due to worn master cylinder seals.

---

3 Hydraulic pipes and hoses - inspection, removal and refitting

Note: *Refer to the note at the beginning of Section 2 before proceeding.*

Inspection

1 The brake fluid pipes, hoses, hose connections and pipe unions should be regularly examined.

2 First check for signs of leakage at the pipe unions, then examine the flexible hoses for signs of cracking, chafing and fraying.

3 The rigid brake pipes should be examined carefully for signs of dents, corrosion or other

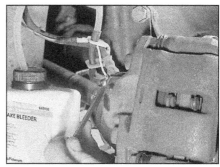

2.21 Bleeding the brake hydraulic system using a typical one-way valve kit

3.4 Using a brake hose clamp will minimise fluid loss when brake flexible hoses are disconnected

damage. Corrosion should be scraped off, and if the depth of pitting is significant, the pipes should be renewed. This is particularly likely in those areas underneath the vehicle body where the pipes are exposed and unprotected.

Removal

4 If any section of pipe or hose is to be removed, the loss of fluid may be reduced by removing the brake fluid reservoir filler cap, placing a piece of polythene over the filler neck and securing it tightly with an elastic band. If a section of pipe is to be disconnected from the master cylinder, the reservoir should be emptied by syphoning out the fluid or drawing out the fluid with a pipette. Alternatively, flexible hoses can be sealed, if required, using a brake hose clamp **(see illustration)**, while metal pipe unions can be plugged (if care is taken not to allow dirt into the system), or

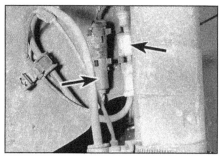

4.2 Pad wear sensor (and ABS wheel sensor) wiring connectors (arrowed) under front wheel arch

4.4a Prise out the dust caps . . .

3.6 Typical brake pipe-to-flexible hose union

capped immediately they are disconnected.
5 To remove a section of pipe, unscrew the union nuts at each end of the pipe, and release the pipe from the clips attaching it to the body. Some union nuts can be very tight, particularly if they are exposed to road dirt, etc., under the vehicle. If an open-ended spanner is used, burring of the flats on the nuts is not uncommon, and for this reason it is preferable to use a split ring spanner that will engage all the flats. If such a spanner is not available, self-locking grips may be used, although this is NOT recommended.
6 To remove a flexible hose, first clean the ends of the hose and the surrounding area, then unscrew the union nut(s)/bolt(s), as applicable, from the hose end(s). Where applicable, unclip the hose from its mounting bracket, and withdraw the hose **(see illustration)**.
7 Brake pipes with flared ends and union nuts in place can be obtained individually or in

4.3 Removing the pad retaining clip from the edge of the caliper

4.4b . . . then remove the caliper guide bolts . . .

sets, from Vauxhall/Opel dealers or accessory shops. The pipe is then bent to shape, using the old pipe as a guide, and is ready for fitting to the car.

Refitting

8 Refitting the pipes and hoses is a reversal of removal. Make sure that brake pipes are securely supported in their clips, and ensure that the hoses are not kinked. Check also that the hoses are clear of all suspension components and underbody fittings, and will remain clear during movement of the suspension and steering. After refitting, remove the polythene from the reservoir, and bleed the brake hydraulic system as described in Section 2.

4 Front brake pads - removal and refitting

⚠️ *Warning: Renew both sets of front brake pads at the same time. Never renew the pads on only one wheel, as the vehicle may pull to one side when braking. Note that the dust created by wear of the pads may contain asbestos, which is a health hazard. Never blow it out with compressed air, and do not inhale it. A filter mask should be worn when working on the brakes. DO NOT use petroleum-based solvents to clean brake parts - use brake cleaner or methylated spirit only.*

Removal

1 Apply the handbrake, then jack up the front of the car, and support securely on axle stands.
2 Where applicable, pull the pad wear sensor from the inboard pad, and disconnect the wiring at the connector under the wheel arch, next to the suspension strut **(see illustration)**. Note the wire routing.
3 Using a screwdriver, prise the pad retaining clip from the outboard edge of the caliper, noting how it is located **(see illustration)**.
4 Prise out the two guide bolt dust caps from the inboard edge of the caliper. Using an Allen key or hexagon bit, unscrew the guide bolts, and lift the caliper and inboard pad from the bracket **(see illustrations)**. Recover the

4.4c . . . and withdraw the caliper and inboard pad

4.5 Pulling the inboard pad from the caliper piston

4.12 Tightening a caliper guide bolt

4.14 Pad retaining clip correctly positioned on caliper

outboard brake pad. Suspend the caliper with wire or string, to avoid straining the brake fluid hose.

5 Pull the inboard pad from the caliper piston, noting that it is retained by a clip attached to the pad backing plate **(see illustration)**.

Refitting

6 Brush the dirt and dust from the caliper, but take care not to inhale it. Carefully remove any rust from the edge of the brake disc.

7 To accommodate the new thicker pads, the caliper piston must be depressed fully into its cylinder bore, using a flat metal bar such as a tyre lever. Do not lever between the piston and disc to depress the piston. The action of depressing the piston will cause the fluid level in the reservoir to rise, so to avoid spillage, syphon out some fluid using a (clean) old battery hydrometer or a pipette.
Caution: It is imperative that the caliper piston is depressed as slowly as possible, using minimal force.

8 Check that the cutaway recesses in the piston are positioned vertically. If necessary, carefully turn the piston to its correct position.

9 Apply a little copper brake grease to the areas on the pad backing plates which contact the caliper and piston.

10 Fit the new inboard pad to the caliper piston, ensuring that the clip is correctly located.

11 Locate the outboard pad on the caliper bracket, with the friction material facing the disc.

12 Refit the caliper to the bracket, and tighten the guide bolts to the specified torque **(see illustration)**.

13 Refit the guide bolt dust caps.

14 Refit the pad retaining clip, locating it as noted before removal **(see illustration)**.

15 Where applicable, fit a new pad wear sensor to the inboard pad, and connect the wiring at the connector under the wheel arch. Route the wiring as noted during removal.

16 Repeat the operations on the remaining side of the vehicle.

17 Refit the roadwheels and lower the vehicle to the ground.

18 Apply the footbrake several times to position the pads against the discs.

19 Check and if necessary top-up the brake fluid level (see "*Weekly checks*").

20 New pads should be carefully bedded-in and, where possible, heavy braking should be avoided during the first 160 km or so after fitting new pads.

5 Front brake caliper - removal, overhaul and refitting

Note: *Refer to the note at the beginning of Section 2, and the warning concerning brake dust at the beginning of Section 4 before proceeding. Before dismantling a caliper, check that replacement parts can be obtained, and retain the old components to compare them with the new ones. New sealing rings must be used on the fluid hose union bolt on refitting.*

Removal

1 Apply the handbrake, then jack up the front of the vehicle, and support securely on axle stands.

2 Remove the brake pads, as described in Section 4.

3 Working under the bonnet, remove the brake fluid reservoir cap, and secure a piece of polythene over the filler neck with a rubber band, or by refitting the cap. This will reduce the loss of fluid during the following procedure.

4 Unscrew the brake fluid hose union bolt from the rear of the caliper, and disconnect the hose. Recover the two sealing rings from the union bolt (one either side of the hose end fitting). Be prepared for fluid spillage, and plug

5.6 Caliper bracket securing bolts (arrowed)

the open ends to prevent dirt ingress and further fluid loss.

5 Withdraw the caliper body from the vehicle.

6 The caliper bracket can be removed from the hub carrier by unscrewing the two securing bolts **(see illustration)**.

Overhaul

7 Brush the dirt from the caliper, but take care not to inhale it.

8 Using a screwdriver, carefully prise the dust seal from the end of the piston and the caliper body, and remove it.

9 Place a thin piece of wood in front of the piston to prevent it from falling out of its bore and sustaining damage, then apply low air pressure – eg, from a foot pump - to the brake fluid union hole in the rear of the caliper body, to eject the piston from its bore.

10 Remove the wood, and carefully withdraw the piston.

11 Carefully prise the seal from the groove in the caliper piston bore, using a plastic or wooden instrument **(see illustration)**.

12 Inspect the surfaces of the piston and its bore in the caliper for scoring, or evidence of metal-to-metal contact. If evident, renew the complete caliper assembly.

13 If the piston and bore are in good condition, discard the seals and obtain a repair kit, which will contain all the necessary renewable items.

14 Clean the piston and cylinder bore with brake fluid or methylated spirit nothing else.

15 Begin reassembly by fitting the dust seal into the caliper bore.

16 Locate the dust seal in its groove in the

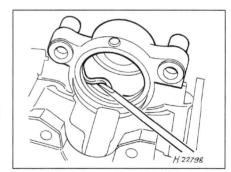

5.11 Prising the seal from the groove in the front caliper piston bore

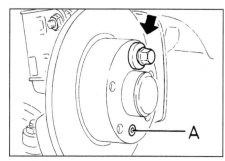

6.2 Refit a wheel bolt and spacer (arrowed) opposite the disc securing screw (A) before checking brake disc run-out

6.11 Unscrewing a front brake disc securing screw

6.15 Removing a rear brake disc

piston. Dip the piston in clean brake fluid, and insert it squarely into the cylinder. Check that the cutaway recesses in the piston are positioned vertically. If necessary, carefully turn the piston to its correct position.

17 When the piston has been partially depressed, engage the dust seal with the rim of the caliper bore.

18 Push the piston further into its bore, but not as far as the stop, ensuring that it does not jam.

19 If desired, the guide bolt sleeves can be renewed. Extract the nylon compression sleeve from within each rubber, then carefully compress the rubber shoulder, and push the rubber through the hole in the caliper body to remove it from the inboard end.

20 Fit the new sleeves using a reversal of the removal procedure.

Refitting

21 Where applicable, refit the caliper bracket to the hub carrier, and tighten the securing bolts to the specified torque.

22 Reconnect the brake fluid hose union, using new sealing rings on the union bolt.

23 Refit the brake pads, as described in Section 4.

24 Remove the polythene from the brake fluid reservoir filler neck, and bleed the relevant brake hydraulic circuit, as described in Section 2.

25 Refit the roadwheel and lower the vehicle to the ground.

6 Brake disc -
inspection, removal and refitting

Note: *Refer to the warning concerning brake dust at the beginning of Section 4 before proceeding.*

Inspection

1 If checking a front disc, apply the handbrake, and if checking a rear disc, chock the front wheels, then jack up the relevant end of the vehicle, and support securely on axle stands.

2 Check that the brake disc securing screw is tight, then fit a spacer approximately 10.0 mm thick to one of the roadwheel bolts, and refit

and tighten the bolt in the hole opposite the disc securing screw **(see illustration)**.

3 Rotate the brake disc, and examine it for deep scoring or grooving. Light scoring is normal, but if excessive, the disc should be removed and either renewed or machined (within the specified limits) by an engineering works.

4 Using a dial gauge, or a flat metal block and feeler gauges, check that the disc run-out does not exceed the figure given in the Specifications.

5 If the disc run-out is excessive, remove the disc as described later in this Section, and check that the disc-to-hub surfaces are perfectly clean.

6 With the disc removed, check the hub run-out. If the run-out exceeds the maximum specified for disc run-out, it is likely that the hub bearings are severely worn or damaged. Refer to Chapter 10 for details of renewal.

7 Refit the disc, and check the disc run-out again. If the hub bearings are in good condition, the fault must lie with the disc, which should be renewed.

Removal

Front disc

8 Where applicable, remove the roadwheel bolt and spacer used when checking the disc.

9 Remove the brake pads, as described in Section 4.

10 Unscrew the two securing bolts, and remove the caliper bracket.

11 Remove the securing screw **(see illustration)**, and withdraw the disc from the hub.

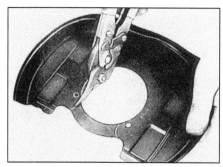

7.5 Cutting a section of metal from a new front brake disc shield prior to fitting

Rear disc

12 Where applicable, remove the roadwheel bolt and spacer used when checking the disc.

13 Remove the brake pads, as described in Section 11.

14 Remove the brake caliper with reference to Section 12, but leave the hydraulic pipe connected. Move the caliper to one side, and suspend it using wire or string to avoid straining the pipe.

15 Remove the securing screw, and withdraw the disc from the hub **(see illustration)**. If the disc is tight, collapse the handbrake shoes by inserting a screwdriver through the adjuster hole in the disc and turning the adjuster wheel.

Refitting

16 Refitting is a reversal of removal, but make sure that the mating faces of the disc and hub are perfectly clean. Refit the brake pads as described in Section 4 or 11, as applicable.

7 Front brake disc shield -
removal and refitting

Note: *Refer to the warning concerning brake dust at the beginning of Section 4 before proceeding.*

Removal

1 Apply the handbrake, then jack up the front of the vehicle, and support securely on axle stands. Remove the relevant roadwheel.

2 Remove the brake disc, (see Section 6).

3 Using a screwdriver inserted through the holes in the hub flange, extract the three screws securing the disc shield to the hub carrier.

4 Using plate shears or an alternative tool, cut a section of metal from the rear edge of the shield to enable the shield to be withdrawn over the hub, then remove the shield.

Refitting

5 If a new shield is to be fitted, cut out a section of metal, as during removal of the old shield, to enable the shield to be fitted **(see illustration)**. De-burr the cut edges, and coat them with anti-corrosion paint.

6 Further refitting is a reversal of removal; refit the brake disc as described in Section 6.

8.5a Release the shoe hold-down cup . . .

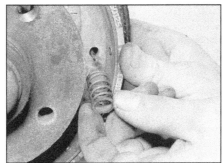

8.5b . . . and withdraw the cup and spring

8.6 Disconnecting the handbrake cable from the operating lever (hub removed for clarity)

8 Rear brake shoes - removal and refitting

Note: *Renew both sets of rear brake shoes at the same time - never renew the shoes on one wheel, as uneven braking may result. Refer to the warning concerning brake dust at the beginning of Section 4 before proceeding.*

Removal

1 Chock the front wheels, then jack up the rear of the vehicle and support securely on axle stands. Remove the rear roadwheels.
2 Working on one side of the vehicle, remove the brake drum, as described in Section 9.
3 Note the location and orientation of all components before dismantling, as an aid to reassembly.
4 Clean the dust and dirt from the drum and shoes, but take care not to inhale it.
5 Remove the shoe hold-down pins, springs and cups by depressing the cups and turning them through 90° using a pair of pliers **(see illustrations)**. Note that the hold-down pins are removed through the rear of the backplate.
6 Disconnect the handbrake cable from the operating lever **(see illustration)**.
7 The upper and lower return springs may now be unhooked and the shoes removed separately, or the assembly of shoes, adjuster strut and springs may be removed together. The second course of action is particularly easy if the hub is removed - see Chapter 10. Take care not to damage the wheel cylinder rubber boots. Before removing the return

springs, note the position and orientation of the springs and adjuster strut.
8 If the shoes are to be removed for some time, fit a stout rubber band or a spring clip to the wheel cylinder, to prevent the pistons from being pushed out of their bores **(see illustration)**. In any event, **do not** press the brake pedal while the drum is removed.

Refitting

9 Clean the dust and dirt from the brake backplate, but take care not to inhale it.
10 Apply a small amount of brake grease to the shoe rubbing areas on the backplate.
11 If the linings removed were contaminated with brake fluid or grease, investigate and rectify any source of contamination before fitting new linings (wheel cylinder or hub bearing oil seal leaking).
12 Although linings are available separately (without shoes), renewal of the shoes complete with linings is to be preferred, unless the necessary skills and equipment are available to fit new linings to the old shoes.
13 If not already done, dismantle the shoes, strut and springs. Note the position and orientation of the components.
14 If both brake assemblies are dismantled at the same time, take care not to mix up the components. Note that the left-hand and right-hand adjuster components are marked; the threaded rod is marked 'L' or 'R', and the other 'handed' components are colour-coded black for the left-hand side, and silver for the right-hand side.
15 Dismantle and clean the adjuster strut. Apply a smear of silicone-based grease to the adjuster threads. If new brake linings or shoes

are to be fitted, the thermo-clip on the adjuster strut must also be renewed **(see illustration)**.
16 Examine the return springs. If they are distorted, or if they have seen extensive service, renewal is advisable. Weak springs may cause the brakes to bind.
17 If a new handbrake operating lever was not supplied with the new shoes (where applicable), transfer the lever from the old shoes. The lever may be secured with a pin and circlip, or by a rivet, which will have to be drilled out.
18 If the components are to be refitted as an assembly, assemble the new shoes, springs and adjuster components. Expand the adjuster strut to ease fitting.
19 Offer the shoes to the brake backplate. Be careful not to damage the wheel cylinder boots, or to displace the pistons. Remember to remove the rubber band or spring clip from the wheel cylinder, where applicable.
20 When the shoes are in position, insert the hold-down pins and secure them with the springs and cups.
21 Reconnect the handbrake cable, then refit the hub, where applicable.
22 If fitting the shoes and springs together as an assembly is found too difficult, it is possible to fit the shoes and secure them with the hold-down pins. Then to fit the adjuster strut and fit the return springs and adjuster.
23 Back off the adjuster wheel to reduce the length of the strut, until the brake drum will pass over the shoes.
24 Make sure that the handbrake operating lever is correctly positioned, with the pin on the edge of the shoe web, not riding on top of it, then refit and secure the brake drum **(see illustration)**.

8.8 Rubber band fitted to wheel cylinder to retain pistons

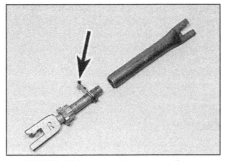

8.15 Right-hand brake shoe adjuster components - thermo-clip arrowed

8.24 Rear drum brake components correctly assembled. Hub removed for clarity

9.3 Removing a brake drum securing screw

25 Repeat the operations on the remaining side of the vehicle.

26 Adjust the brakes by operating the footbrake at least fifteen times. A clicking noise will be heard at the drums, as the automatic adjusters operate. When the clicking stops, adjustment is complete.

27 Check the handbrake cable adjustment, as described in Section 19.

28 Refit the roadwheels, and lower the vehicle to the ground.

29 New brake linings should be carefully bedded-in and, where possible, heavy braking should be avoided during the first 160 km or so after fitting new linings.

9 Rear brake drum - removal, inspection and refitting

Note: *Refer to the warning concerning brake dust at the beginning of Section 4 before proceeding.*

Removal

1 Chock the front wheels, then jack up the rear of the vehicle and support securely on axle stands.

2 Fully release the handbrake.

3 Extract the drum securing screw **(see illustration)**, and remove the drum. If the drum is tight, remove the plug from the inspection hole in the brake backplate, and push the handbrake operating lever towards the brake shoe to move the shoes away from the drums. If necessary, slacken the handbrake cable adjuster (see Section 19).

10.5 Unscrewing the fluid pipe union nut from the rear wheel cylinder

Inspection

4 Brush the dirt and dust from the drum, taking care not to inhale it.

5 Examine the internal friction surfaces of the drum. If they are deeply scored, or so worn that the drum has become ridged to the width of the shoes, then both drums must be renewed.

6 Regrinding of the friction surface is not recommended, since the internal diameter of the drum will no longer be compatible with the shoe friction material contact diameter.

Refitting

7 Refit the brake drum and tighten the securing screw. If necessary, back off the adjuster wheel until the drum will pass over the shoes.

8 Adjust the brakes by operating the footbrake a number of times. A clicking noise will be heard at the drum as the automatic adjuster operates. When the clicking stops, adjustment is complete.

9 Refit the roadwheel and lower the vehicle to the ground.

10 Rear wheel cylinder - removal, overhaul and refitting

Note: *Refer to the note at the beginning of Section 2, and the warning concerning brake dust at the beginning of Section 4 before proceeding. Before dismantling a wheel cylinder, check that replacement parts can be obtained, and retain the old components to compare them with the new ones.*

Removal

1 Chock the front wheels, then jack up the front of the vehicle and support securely on axle stands. Remove the relevant roadwheel.

2 Remove the brake drum, as described in Section 9.

3 Using a pair of pliers, unhook the upper return spring from the brake shoes, noting its orientation, then push the upper ends of the shoes apart until they are clear of the wheel cylinder.

4 Working under the bonnet, remove the brake fluid reservoir cap, and secure a piece of polythene over the filler neck with a rubber band, or by refitting the cap. This will reduce the loss of fluid during the following procedure.

5 Unscrew the brake fluid pipe union nut from the rear of the wheel cylinder, and disconnect the pipe **(see illustration)**. Take care not to strain the pipe. Be prepared for fluid spillage, and plug the open ends to prevent dirt ingress and further fluid loss.

6 Unscrew the two securing bolts from the rear of the brake backplate, and withdraw the wheel cylinder.

Overhaul

7 Brush the dirt and dust from the wheel cylinder, but take care not to inhale it.

8 Pull the rubber dust seals from the ends of the cylinder body.

9 The pistons will normally be ejected by the pressure of the coil spring, but if they are not, tap the end of the cylinder body on a piece of wood, or apply low air pressure - e.g., from a foot pump - to the brake fluid union hole in the rear of the cylinder body, to eject the pistons from their bores.

10 Inspect the surfaces of the pistons and their bores in the cylinder body for scoring, or evidence of metal-to-metal contact. If evident, renew the complete wheel cylinder assembly.

11 If the pistons and bores are in good condition, discard the seals and obtain a repair kit, which will contain all the necessary renewable items **(see illustration)**.

12 Lubricate the piston seals with clean brake fluid, and insert them into the cylinder bores, with the spring between them, using finger pressure only.

13 Dip the pistons in clean brake fluid, and insert them into the cylinder bores.

14 Fit the dust seals, and check that the pistons can move freely in their bores.

Refitting

15 Refit the wheel cylinder to the backplate, and tighten the securing bolts.

16 Reconnect the brake fluid pipe to the cylinder, and tighten the union nut.

17 Push the brake shoes against the pistons, then refit the upper return spring as noted before removal.

18 Refit the brake drum, and tighten the securing screw. If necessary, back off the adjuster wheel until the drum will pass over the shoes.

19 Remove the polythene from the brake fluid reservoir filler neck, and bleed the relevant brake hydraulic circuit, as described in Section 2.

20 Adjust the brakes by operating the footbrake a number of times. A clicking noise will be heard at the drum as the automatic adjuster operates. When the clicking stops, adjustment is complete.

21 Refit the roadwheel and lower the vehicle to the ground.

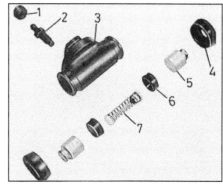

10.11 Exploded view of a rear brake wheel cylinder

1 Dust cap
2 Bleed nipple
3 Cylinder body
4 Dust seal
5 Piston
6 Piston seal
7 Spring

11 Rear brake pads (rear disc brakes) - removal and refitting

Note: *Refer to the warning concerning brake dust at the beginning of Section 6 before proceeding.*

Removal

1 Chock the front wheels, then jack up the rear of the vehicle and support securely on axle stands. Remove the rear roadwheels.
2 Note how the anti-rattle spring is located, then drive out the upper and lower pad retaining pins from the outside of the caliper using a pin punch **(see illustrations)**.
3 Remove the anti-rattle spring.
4 Push the pads away from the disc slightly then, using a pair of pliers, withdraw the outboard pad and, where applicable, the anti-squeal shim that fits between the pad and the caliper body.
5 Withdraw the inboard pad **(see illustration)** and, where applicable, the anti-squeal shim.
6 Brush the dust and dirt from the caliper, but take care not to inhale it. Carefully remove any rust from the edge of the brake disc.

Refitting

7 To accommodate the new thicker pads, the caliper piston must be depressed fully into its cylinder bore, using a flat metal bar such as a tyre lever. Do not lever between the piston and the disc to depress the piston. The action of depressing the piston will cause the fluid level in the reservoir to rise, so to avoid spillage, syphon out some fluid using a (clean) old battery hydrometer or a teat pipette.
Caution: It is imperative that the caliper piston is depressed as slowly as possible, using minimal force.
8 Check that the cutaway recesses in the pistons are positioned downwards, at approximately 23° to the horizontal. A template made of card may be used to check the setting **(see illustration)**. If necessary, carefully turn the pistons to their correct positions.
9 Apply a little brake grease to the top and bottom edges of the backplates on the new brake pads.

11.2a Rear brake pad anti-rattle spring correctly located. Note lower pad retaining pin has been partially removed

10 Locate the new pads and the anti-squeal shims in the caliper. Ensure that the friction material faces the disc, and check that the pads are free to move slightly.
11 Locate the anti-rattle spring on the pads, then insert the pad retaining pins from the inside edge of the caliper, while depressing the spring. Tap the pins firmly into the caliper.
12 Repeat the operations on the remaining side of the vehicle.
13 Refit the roadwheels, and lower the vehicle to the ground.
14 Apply the footbrake hard several times to position the pads against the discs.
15 Check and if necessary top-up the brake fluid level.
16 New brake pads should be carefully bedded-in and, where possible, heavy braking should be avoided during the first 100 miles (160 km) or so after fitting new pads.

12 Rear brake caliper (rear disc brakes) - removal, overhaul and refitting

Note: *Refer to the note at the beginning of Section 2, and the warning concerning brake dust at the beginning of Section 4 before proceeding. Before dismantling a caliper, check that replacement parts can be obtained, and retain the old components to compare them with the new ones.*

Removal

1 Chock the front wheels, then jack up the rear of the vehicle and support securely on

11.2b Driving out the upper pad retaining pin

axle stands. Remove the relevant roadwheel.
2 Remove the brake pads, as described in Section 11.
3 Working under the bonnet, remove the brake fluid reservoir cap, and secure a piece of polythene over the filler neck with a rubber band, or by refitting the cap. This will reduce the loss of fluid during the following procedure.
4 Unscrew the brake fluid pipe union nut from the rear of the caliper, and disconnect the pipe. Take care not to strain the pipe. Be prepared for fluid spillage, and plug the open ends to prevent dirt ingress and further fluid loss.
5 Unscrew the two mounting bolts and withdraw the caliper from the vehicle **(see illustration)**.

Overhaul

6 Brush the dirt and dust from the caliper, but take care not to inhale it.
7 Note that no attempt must be made to separate the two halves of the caliper.
8 Using a screwdriver, prise the dust seal retaining clips from the piston dust seals, then carefully prise off the dust seals.
9 Using a clamp, clamp one of the pistons in its fully retracted position. Then apply low air pressure - e.g. from a foot pump - to the brake fluid union hole in the rear of the caliper body, to eject the remaining piston from its bore. Take care not to drop the piston, as it may result in damage.
10 Temporarily close off the bore of the removed piston, using a flat piece of wood or similar improvised tool. Then remove the

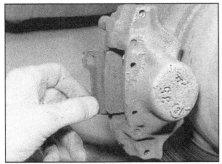

11.5 Removing the rear inboard brake pad

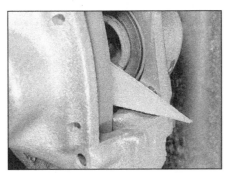

11.8 Checking a rear caliper piston cutaway recess angle with a card template

12.5 Rear brake caliper mounting bolts (arrowed)

clamp from the remaining piston, and again apply air pressure to the caliper union to eject the piston.

11 Carefully prise the seals from the grooves in the caliper piston bores, using a plastic or wooden instrument.

12 Inspect the surfaces of the pistons and their bores in the caliper for scoring, or evidence of metal-to-metal contact. If evident, renew the complete caliper assembly.

13 If the pistons and bores are in good condition, discard the seals, and obtain a repair kit, which will contain all the necessary renewable items. Also obtain a tube of brake cylinder paste.

14 Clean the piston and cylinder bore with brake fluid or methylated spirit - nothing else.

15 Apply a little brake cylinder paste to the pistons, cylinder bores, and piston seals.

16 Begin reassembly by fitting the seals to the grooves in the caliper bores.

17 Locate the dust seals in their grooves in the pistons, then insert the pistons carefully into their bores until they enter the seals. It may be necessary to rotate the pistons to prevent them from jamming in the seals.

18 When the pistons have been partially depressed, engage the dust seals with the rims of the caliper bores, and refit the retaining clips.

Refitting

19 Refit the caliper, and tighten the securing bolts to the specified torque.

20 Reconnect the brake fluid pipe to the caliper, and tighten the union nut.

21 Refit the brake pads, as described in Section 11.

22 Refit the roadwheel, and lower the vehicle to the ground.

23 Remove the polythene from the brake

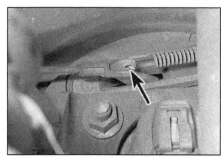

13.4 Handbrake cable and return spring connection to handbrake operating lever - model with rear disc brakes

fluid reservoir filler neck, and bleed the relevant brake hydraulic circuit, as described in Section 2.

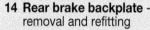

13 Handbrake shoes (rear disc brakes) - removal and refitting

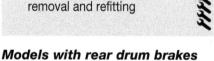

Note: *Refer to the warning concerning brake dust at the beginning of Section 4 before proceeding.*

Removal

1 Jack up the vehicle, and support on axle stands positioned under the body side members (see "*Jacking and vehicle support*").

2 Remove the brake disc, as described in Section 6.

3 Clean the dust and dirt from the various components, but take care not to inhale it.

4 Disconnect the handbrake cable and the return spring from the handbrake operating lever at the brake backplate (see illustration). If necessary, slacken the handbrake cable adjustment, with reference to Section 19.

5 Remove the shoe hold-down pins, springs and cups by depressing the cups and turning them through 90° using a pair of pliers. Note that the hold-down pins are removed through the rear of the brake backplate.

6 The shoes, adjuster, handbrake operating lever and return springs can now be removed together as an assembly.

7 Note the position and orientation of all components, then unhook the upper and lower return springs from the shoes, and recover the handbrake operating lever and the adjuster (see illustration).

Refitting

8 Apply a little brake grease to the threads of the adjuster, then screw it together to its minimum length. Also apply a little brake grease to the shoe rubbing areas on the backplate.

9 Fit one of the new brake shoes, and secure it to the backplate with the hold-down pin, spring and cup.

10 Locate the handbrake operating lever in position.

11 Fit the remaining brake shoe, and secure with the hold-down pin, spring and cup.

12 Hook the upper return spring onto the shoes.

13 Fit the adjuster between the lower ends of the shoes, as noted before dismantling, then fit the lower return spring.

14 Reconnect the handbrake cable and the return spring to the handbrake operating lever.

15 Refit the brake disc, as described in Section 6, but do not refit the roadwheel at this stage.

16 Repeat the operations on the remaining side of the vehicle.

17 Check the handbrake cable adjustment, as described in Section 19.

18 Refit the roadwheels, and lower the vehicle to the ground.

14 Rear brake backplate - removal and refitting

Models with rear drum brakes

Removal

1 Chock the front wheels, then jack up the rear of the vehicle, and support securely on axle stands (see "*Jacking and vehicle support*"). Remove the relevant roadwheel.

2 Remove the brake shoes, as described in Section 8.

3 Remove the rear wheel cylinder, as described in Section 10.

4 Using a pair of pliers, prise out the clip securing the handbrake cable to the backplate.

5 Remove the rear hub unit, as described in Chapter 10, and withdraw the backplate.

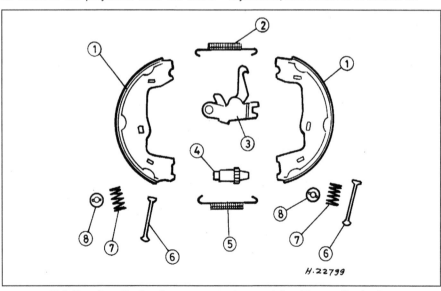

H.22799

13.7 Rear handbrake shoe components - models with rear disc brakes

1 Brake shoes	*4 Adjuster*	*7 Hold-down spring*
2 Upper return spring	*5 Lower return spring*	*8 Hold-down clip*
3 Handbrake operating lever	*6 Hold-down pin*	

Refitting

6 Fit the backplate and the rear hub unit, with reference to Chapter 10, using new nuts tightened in the two stages given in the Specifications.
7 Locate the handbrake cable in the backplate, and refit the securing clip.
8 Refit the rear wheel cylinder, as described in Section 10.
9 Refit the brake shoes, as described in Section 8.
10 Before refitting the roadwheel and lowering the vehicle to the ground, check and if necessary adjust the handbrake, as described in Section 19.
11 Bleed the relevant brake hydraulic circuit, as described in Section 2.

Models with rear disc brakes

Removal

12 Chock the front wheels, then jack up the rear of the vehicle, and support securely on axle stands (see "*Jacking and vehicle support*"). Remove the relevant roadwheel.
13 Remove the brake disc, as described in Section 6.
14 Remove the handbrake shoes, as described in Section 13.
15 Remove the rear hub unit, as described in Chapter 10, and withdraw the brake backplate.

Refitting

16 Fit the backplate and the rear hub unit, with reference to Chapter 10, using new nuts tightened in the two stages given in the Specifications.
17 Refit the handbrake shoes, as described in Section 13.
18 Refit the brake disc, as described in Section 6.
19 Before refitting the roadwheel and lowering the vehicle to the ground, check and if necessary adjust the handbrake, as described in Section 19.

15 Brake pedal - removal and refitting
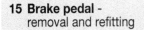

Removal

1 Disconnect the battery negative lead.
2 Remove the lower trim panel from the driver's footwell.
3 Disconnect the wiring plug from the brake light switch, then twist the switch anti-clockwise and remove it from its bracket.
4 Pull the spring clip from the right-hand end of the servo fork-to-pedal pivot pin (see illustration).
5 Using a pair of pliers, pull back the end of the pedal return spring from the pedal, to enable the servo fork-to-pedal pivot pin to be removed. Withdraw the pivot pin (see illustration).

15.4 Brake servo fork-to-pedal pivot pin spring clip (arrowed)

6 Pull the locking clip from the left-hand end of the pedal pivot pin.
7 Unscrew the nut from the left-hand end of the pivot pin, then slide the pivot pin from the right-hand end of the pedal mounting bracket. If necessary, tap the end of the pivot pin with a soft-faced hammer to free the splines from the mounting bracket. Recover any washers that may be positioned on the pivot pin, noting their locations.
8 Withdraw the pedal and return spring.

Refitting

9 Refitting is a reversal of removal, remembering the following points.
10 Ensure that the pedal return spring is correctly located on the pedal before refitting.
11 Coat the pedal pivot pin with a little molybdenum disulphide grease.
12 Ensure that any washers on the pedal pivot pin are positioned as noted before removal.

16 Servo unit - testing, removal and refitting

Right-hand-drive models

Testing

1 To test the operation of the servo unit, depress the footbrake four or five times to exhaust the vacuum, then start the engine while keeping the footbrake depressed. As the engine starts, there should be a noticeable 'give' in the brake pedal as vacuum builds up. Allow the engine to run for at least two minutes, and then switch it off. If the brake pedal is now depressed again, it should be possible to detect a hiss from the servo when the pedal is depressed. After about four or five applications, no further hissing will be heard, and the pedal will feel considerably firmer.

Removal

Note: *When refitting, sealing compound (Vauxhall/Opel P/N 90485251 or equivalent) will be required to coat the mating faces of the servo mounting bracket, and thread-locking compound will be required to coat the servo securing bolts.*

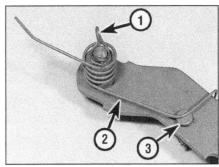

15.5 Brake pedal assembly removed from vehicle

1 Locking clip
2 Pedal return spring
3 Pedal pivot pin

2 Disconnect the battery negative lead.
3 Working inside the vehicle, release the securing clips, and remove the lower trim panel from the driver's footwell.
4 Disconnect the wiring plug from the brake light switch, then twist the switch anti-clockwise and remove it from its bracket.
5 Pull the spring clip from right-hand end of the servo fork-to-pedal pivot pin.
6 Using a pair of pliers, pull back the end of the pedal return spring from the pedal, to enable the servo fork-to-pedal pin to be removed. Withdraw the pivot pin.
7 Remove the windscreen cowl trim panel, as described in Chapter 11, then remove the windscreen wiper motor and linkage, as described in Chapter 12.
8 Remove the washer fluid reservoir, as described in Chapter 12.
9 Disconnect the vacuum pipe from the brake servo.
10 Unscrew the two securing nuts, and carefully withdraw the brake master cylinder from the studs on the servo. Move the master cylinder forwards slightly, taking care not to strain the brake pipes.
11 Remove the two plugs covering the servo securing bolts from the cowl panel (see illustration).
12 Using an Allen key or hexagon bit, unscrew the servo securing bolts and remove them completely (see illustration overleaf), then lift the servo complete with mounting bracket from

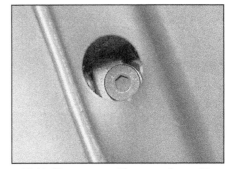

16.11 Plug removed from cowl panel to expose brake servo securing bolt

16.12 Unscrewing a brake servo securing bolt

16.16 Measuring the servo operating fork dimension using a bolt inserted through the pivot pin hole

the bulkhead. Note that the bracket may stick to the bulkhead, as it is fitted with sealing compound.

13 The mounting bracket can be removed from the servo by unscrewing the four securing nuts. Note that the bracket will stick to the servo, as it is fitted with sealing compound.

14 The servo cannot be overhauled, and if faulty, the complete unit must be renewed.

Refitting

15 Before refitting the servo, check that the operating fork dimension is correct, as follows.

16 Measure the distance from the end face of the servo casing to the centre of the pivot pin hole in the end of the operating fork. The distance should be 147.70 mm. To make accurate measurement easier, insert a bolt or bar of diameter through the pivot pin hole, and measure to the centre of the bolt or bar **(see illustration)**.

17 If adjustment is necessary, slacken the locknut, turn the fork to give the specified dimension, then tighten the locknut.

18 Coat the mating surfaces of the mounting bracket with sealing compound (Vauxhall/Opel P/N 90485251 or equivalent), then refit the bracket to the servo.

19 Coat the threads of the servo securing bolts with thread-locking fluid, then fit the servo to the bulkhead and tighten the securing bolts.

20 Refit the securing bolt cover plugs to the cowl panel.

21 Refit the master cylinder to the servo, and tighten the securing nuts to the specified torque.

22 Reconnect the vacuum pipe to the servo.

23 Refit the washer fluid reservoir.

24 Refit the windscreen wiper motor and linkage, as described in Chapter 12, then refit the windscreen cowl trim panel.

25 Further refitting is a reversal of removal. On completion, check the operation of the servo, as described in paragraph 16.

Left-hand-drive models

Note: *New self-locking nuts will be required when refitting the servo mounting bracket to the bulkhead.*

Testing

26 Refer to paragraph 1.

Removal

27 Proceed as described in paragraphs 2 to 6 inclusive.

28 Disconnect the vacuum pipe from the brake servo.

29 Unscrew the two securing nuts, and carefully withdraw the brake master cylinder from the studs on the servo. Move the master cylinder forwards slightly, taking care not to strain the brake pipes.

30 Unscrew the four servo bracket securing nuts from the bulkhead (a flexible socket coupling will be required to reach the lower bolt), then tilt the servo/bracket assembly, and withdraw it upwards from the engine compartment **(see illustration)**.

31 The mounting bracket can be removed from the servo by unscrewing the four securing nuts. The rubber sleeve can now be removed from the brake servo.

32 To remove the operating fork from the servo operating rod sleeve, prise out the securing clip **(see illustration)**.

Refitting

33 Before refitting the servo, check that the operating fork dimension is correct, as follows.

34 Measure the distance from the end face of the servo casing to the centre of the pivot pin hole in the end of the operating fork. The distance should be 255.5 mm **(see illustration)**. To make accurate measurement easier, insert a bolt or bar of diameter through the pivot pin hole, and measure to the centre of the bolt or bar.

35 If adjustment is necessary, slacken the locknut on the operating rod sleeve, turn the fork to give the specified dimension, then tighten the locknut.

36 Where applicable, refit the rubber sleeve, and refit the servo to the mounting bracket. Tighten the servo-to-mounting bracket nuts to the specified torque.

37 Lower the servo and mounting bracket and servo assembly into position, then refit the assembly to the bulkhead, using new self-locking nuts, and tighten the nuts to the specified torque.

38 Refit the master cylinder to the servo, and tighten the securing nuts to the specified torque.

39 Reconnect the vacuum pipe to the servo.

40 Further refitting is a reversal of removal. On completion, check the operation of the servo, as described in paragraph 1.

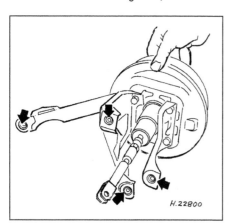

16.30 Brake servo and mounting bracket removed showing securing nut locations (arrowed) - left-hand-drive models

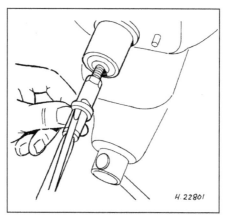

16.32 Prising out the securing clip to remove the operating fork from the servo operating rod sleeve - left-hand-drive models

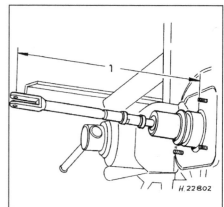

16.34 Brake servo operating fork dimension (1) on left-hand-drive models

17 Servo non-return valve - testing, removal and refitting

Testing

1 The function of the valve is to allow air to flow in one direction only, out of the servo unit. If the valve allows air to flow in both directions, it is faulty, and must be renewed.

2 To test the valve, first remove the hose/valve assembly, as described later in this Section.

3 Blow through the hose on the servo side of the valve; air should pass freely through the valve.

4 Now blow through the hose on the inlet manifold side of the valve; no air should pass through.

5 If the valve is faulty, it must be renewed.

Removal

6 The plastic valve is located in the vacuum hose running from the inlet manifold to the brake servo.

7 Although the valve is available separately from the hoses, to remove the valve, the hoses must be cut, and therefore renewed on reassembly. If the valve is to be renewed, it is therefore easier to remove the complete hose/valve assembly, and renew it complete.

8 To remove the assembly, carefully unplug the hose adaptor from the vacuum servo unit, then unscrew the hose union from the inlet manifold, and withdraw the assembly.

Refitting

9 Refitting is a reversal of removal, but when reconnecting the hose adaptor to the servo, take care not to damage or distort the sealing grommet, and on completion, start the engine and check for air leaks.

18 Master cylinder - removal, overhaul and refitting

Note: *Refer to the note at the beginning of Section 2 before proceeding.*

Removal

1 Disconnect the battery negative lead.

2 Depress the footbrake pedal several times to dissipate the vacuum in the servo unit.

3 Disconnect the wiring plug from the brake fluid level sensor in the reservoir filler cap.

4 If possible, use a pipette or a (clean) old battery hydrometer to remove the brake fluid from the reservoir. This will reduce the loss of fluid later in the procedure.

5 Position a container beneath the master cylinder, to catch the brake fluid that will be released.

6 Identify the brake fluid pipes for position, then unscrew the union nuts and disconnect the pipes from the master cylinder.

7 Unscrew the two securing nuts, and withdraw the master cylinder from the studs on the vacuum servo unit.

8 Clean the external surfaces of the cylinder, then using a screwdriver, carefully prise the fluid reservoir and its seals from the top of the cylinder.

Overhaul

Note: *Check availability of parts before overhauling the master cylinder. Compare the new parts with the old ones before fitting.*

9 On models with a conventional (non-ABS) braking system, the master cylinder can be overhauled, as described in the following paragraphs. No overhaul of the master cylinder is possible on models with ABS.

10 With the master cylinder removed, continue as follows, according to type.

GMF type master cylinder

11 Clamp the master cylinder in a soft-jawed vice.

12 Carefully prise out the sealing ring from the end of the cylinder bore.

13 Depress the primary piston slightly using a piece of wood or plastic. Then hold the piston in the depressed position by inserting a smooth pin or rod of 3.0 mm diameter through the primary fluid reservoir port in the cylinder **(see illustration)**.

14 Extract the circlip from the end of the cylinder bore using a screwdriver. Take care not to damage the piston or cylinder bore.

15 Withdraw the pin or rod retaining the piston.

16 Withdraw the primary piston assembly from the cylinder, if necessary tapping the cylinder on a wooden block to free the piston from the bore.

17 Apply low air pressure - e.g. from a foot pump - to the front fluid reservoir port in the cylinder, to eject the secondary piston assembly.

18 Clean all the components, in clean brake fluid or methylated spirit only, and examine them for wear and damage. In particular, check the surfaces of the pistons and cylinder bore for scoring and corrosion **(see illustration)**. If the bore shows signs of wear, renew the complete master cylinder assembly.

19 If the cylinder bore is in good condition, obtain a repair kit, which will contain all the necessary renewable items. A Vauxhall/Opel dealer will be able to supply a pre-assembled kit of parts, which should be fitted as follows.

20 Lubricate the cylinder bore with clean brake fluid or brake grease, then clamp the cylinder in a soft-jawed vice, with the bore horizontal.

21 Remove the plug from the end of the assembly tube, and insert the short part of the tube into the cylinder bore as far as the shoulder on the tube.

22 Use a piece of wood or plastic to push the components out of the tube and into the cylinder bore. Then hold the primary piston in

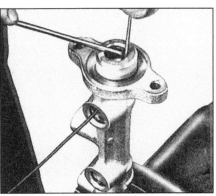

18.13 Holding the primary piston depressed while extracting the circlip from the cylinder body - GMF type master cylinder

the depressed position by inserting the pin or rod used during dismantling through the cylinder primary fluid reservoir port.

23 Fit a new circlip to the end of the cylinder bore, ensuring that it seats correctly, and that the piston is free to move.

24 Depress the primary piston, and withdraw the pin or rod from the fluid reservoir port.

25 Fit a new sealing ring to the end of the cylinder bore.

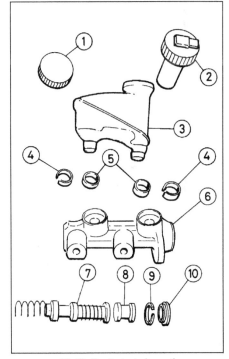

18.18 Exploded view of GMF type master cylinder

1 Filler cap (standard)	5 Fluid reservoir seals
2 Filler cap (with fluid level sensor)	6 Cylinder body
3 Fluid reservoir	7 Secondary piston and springs
4 Fluid reservoir retaining clips	8 Primary piston
	9 Circlip
	10 Sealing ring

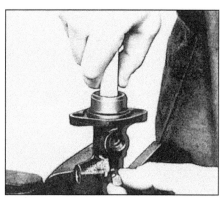

18.30 Depressing the secondary piston while extracting the stop-screw - ATE type master cylinder

ATE type master cylinder

26 Clamp the master cylinder in a soft-jawed vice.

27 Carefully prise out the sealing ring from the end of the cylinder bore.

28 Depress the primary piston slightly using a piece of wood or plastic, then extract the circlip from the end of the cylinder bore.

29 Withdraw the primary piston assembly, noting the location of the stopwashers.

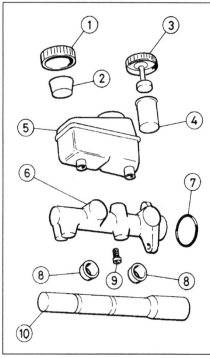

18.32 Exploded view of ATE type master cylinder

1 *Filler cap (standard)*
2 *Strainer*
3 *Filler cap (with fluid level sensor)*
4 *Guide sleeve for float*
5 *Fluid reservoir*
6 *Cylinder body*
7 *Sealing ring*
8 *Fluid reservoir seals*
9 *Stop-screw*
10 *Repair kit assembly*

30 Depress the secondary piston, again using a piece of wood or plastic, and withdraw the stop-screw from the end of the cylinder body **(see illustration)**.

31 Withdraw the secondary piston assembly from the cylinder, if necessary tapping the cylinder on a wooden block to free the piston from the bore.

32 Clean all the components, using clean brake fluid or methylated spirit only, and examine them for wear and damage. In particular, check the surfaces of the pistons and cylinder bores for scoring and corrosion **(see illustration)**. If the bore shows signs of wear, renew the complete master cylinder assembly.

33 If the cylinder bore is in good condition, obtain a repair kit, which will contain all the necessary renewable items. A Vauxhall/Opel dealer will supply a pre-assembled kit of parts, which should be fitted as follows.

34 Lubricate the cylinder bore with clean brake fluid or brake grease, then clamp the cylinder in a soft-jawed vice, with the bore horizontal.

35 Fit a new sealing ring to the stop-screw, then screw it into the cylinder body a little way, but not so far that it protrudes into the bore.

36 Remove the plugs from the ends of the assembly tube, then remove all the components from the short part of the tube, and push the short part into the long part until they are flush.

37 Insert the assembly tube into the cylinder bore as far as the collar on the short sleeve. Then use a piece of wood or plastic to push the secondary piston assembly into the bore until it contacts the end of the cylinder.

38 Lightly tighten the stop-screw, then withdraw the piece of wood or plastic and the assembly tube, and fully tighten the stop-screw.

39 Reposition the master cylinder in the vice, with the bore facing upwards.

40 Smear the primary piston skirt and the seal grooves with the special grease provided in the repair kit. Fit the stop-washer to the piston.

41 Adjust the assembly tube so that the end of the long part is flush with the inner shoulder of the short part.

42 Fit the front seal to the primary piston, with the open end of the seal facing the front of the master cylinder.

43 Place the assembly tube over the cylinder to compress the seal, insert the piston and tube part way into the bore, and withdraw the tube.

44 Place the intermediate ring on the primary piston, then fit the remaining seal using the assembly tube as described previously.

45 Place the stop-washer on the primary piston, then depress the piston slightly using a piece of wood or plastic, and fit a new circlip to the end of the cylinder bore. Ensure that the circlip is correctly seated, and that the piston is free to move.

46 Fit a new sealing ring to the end of the cylinder bore.

Refitting

47 Refitting is a reversal of removal, but on completion, bleed the complete brake hydraulic system, as described in Section 2.

19 Handbrake - adjustment

Models with rear drum brakes

1 The handbrake will normally be kept in correct adjustment by the self-adjusting action of the rear brake shoes. However, due to cable stretch over a period of time, the travel of the handbrake lever may become excessive, in which case the following operations should be carried out.

2 Chock the front wheels, then jack up the rear of the vehicle, and support securely on axle. Remove the rear roadwheels.

3 Fully release the handbrake.

4 On models with a catalytic converter, unscrew the securing nuts, and withdraw the exhaust centre box heat shield by carefully sliding it round the centre box.

5 Turn the adjuster nut on the now-exposed cable adjuster **(see illustration)**, until the brake shoes can just be heard to rub when the rear wheels are turned by hand in the normal direction of rotation.

6 Loosen the adjuster nut until the wheels are just free to turn.

7 The handbrake must start to operate with the lever on the second notch of the ratchet.

8 On completion of adjustment, check the handbrake cables for free movement, and apply a little grease to the adjuster threads to prevent corrosion.

9 Where applicable, refit the exhaust heat shield.

10 Refit the roadwheels, and lower the vehicle to the ground.

Models with rear disc brakes

11 Chock the front wheels, then jack up the rear of the vehicle, and support securely on axle stands (see *"Jacking and vehicle support"*). Remove the rear roadwheels.

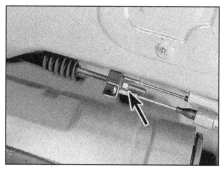

19.5 Handbrake cable adjuster nut (arrowed)

12 Pull the handbrake lever as far as the second notch on the ratchet.

13 On models with a catalytic converter, unscrew the securing nuts, and withdraw the exhaust centre box heat shield by carefully sliding it round the centre box.

14 Loosen the nut on the now-exposed cable adjuster.

15 Using a screwdriver inserted through the adjuster hole in one of the discs, turn the adjuster wheel until the brake shoes can just be heard to rub when the disc is turned by hand in the normal direction of rotation **(see illustration)**.

16 Turn the adjuster wheel back until the disc is just free to turn.

17 Repeat paragraphs 15 and 16 on the remaining side of the vehicle.

18 Tighten the nut on the cable adjuster until the brake shoes just begin to operate. Check that the shoes operate equally on both wheels.

19 Fully release the handbrake, then apply it again.

20 The discs must lock when the handbrake lever reaches the sixth notch on the ratchet. If necessary, turn the nut on the adjuster to achieve this.

21 Where applicable, refit the exhaust heat shield.

22 Refit the roadwheels, and lower the vehicle to the ground.

20 Handbrake lever -
removal, overhaul and refitting

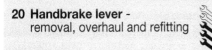

Note: *A new self-locking nut must be used to secure the handbrake cable to the operating rod on refitting.*

Removal

1 Disconnect the battery negative lead.

2 Jack up the vehicle, and support on axle stands positioned under the body side members (see "*Jacking and vehicle support*").

3 On models with a catalytic converter, unscrew the securing nuts, and withdraw the exhaust centre box heat shield by carefully sliding it round the centre box.

4 Note the length of exposed thread on the

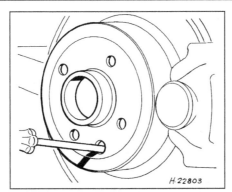

19.15 Using a screwdriver to turn the handbrake adjuster wheel - models with rear disc brakes

now-exposed handbrake cable adjuster, then remove the adjuster nut to enable the cable bracket to be disconnected from the handbrake lever operating rod.

5 Disconnect the cable bracket from the operating rod, and slide the rubber sealing grommet from the underbody and the operating rod.

6 Remove the passenger's seat on right-hand-drive models, or the driver's seat on left-hand-drive models (as applicable), as described in Chapter 11. Pay particular attention to the warning given regarding the seat belt tensioner mechanism.

7 Remove the centre console, as described in Chapter 11.

8 Carefully lift up the carpet around the handbrake lever housing, to expose the two handbrake lever securing bolts **(see illustration)**. Alternatively, slits can be cut in the carpet for access to the bolts.

9 Unscrew the securing bolts, and withdraw the handbrake lever sufficiently to disconnect the handbrake 'on' warning light switch wiring.

10 Disconnect the wiring, and withdraw the handbrake lever and operating rod from the vehicle.

Overhaul

11 A worn ratchet segment can be renewed by driving the securing sleeve from the handbrake lever, using a metal rod or a bolt of suitable diameter.

12 Drive the new sleeve supplied with the new segment into the lever to permit a little play between the segment and lever **(see illustration)**.

13 A new pawl can be fitted if the original pivot rivet is drilled out **(see illustration)**.

14 Rivet the new pawl so that it is still free to move.

15 The handbrake 'on' warning light switch can be removed from the lever assembly after unscrewing the securing bolt.

Refitting

16 Refitting is a reversal of removal, remembering the following points.

17 Refit the seat as described in Chapter 11.

18 Use a new self-locking nut to secure the handbrake cable bracket to the operating rod, and screw the nut onto the rod to the position noted before removal.

19 Before lowering the vehicle to the ground, adjust the handbrake, as described in Section 19.

21 Handbrake cables -
removal and refitting

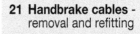

Models with rear drum brakes

Note: *A new self-locking nut must be used to secure the handbrake cable to the operating rod on refitting.*

Removal

1 The handbrake cable assembly consists of two cables (one running to each rear brake assembly), attached to a bracket on the handbrake lever operating rod. The two cables cannot be removed separately, and the complete cable assembly must therefore be removed as a unit.

2 Jack up the vehicle, and support on axle stands positioned under the body side members (see "*Jacking and vehicle support*").

3 On models with a catalytic converter, unscrew the securing nuts, and withdraw the exhaust centre box heat shield by carefully sliding it round the centre box.

4 Note the length of exposed thread on the now-exposed handbrake cable adjuster, then

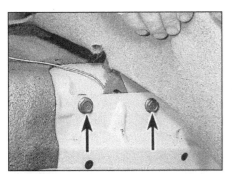

20.8 Carpet pulled back to expose handbrake lever securing bolts (arrowed)

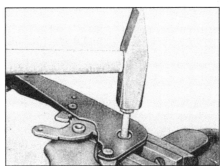

20.12 Driving in the handbrake lever ratchet segment securing sleeve

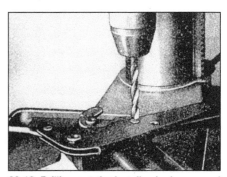

20.13 Drilling out the handbrake lever pawl pivot pin

21.7 Removing a handbrake cable securing clip (arrowed) from the brake backplate - model with rear drum brakes

remove the adjuster nut to enable the cable bracket to be disconnected from the handbrake lever operating rod.

5 Disconnect the cable bracket from the operating rod.

6 Remove the brake shoes, and disconnect the handbrake cables from the shoes, as described in Section 8.

7 Using a pair of pliers, prise out the clips (one for each cable) which secure the handbrake cables to the brake backplates **(see illustration)**.

8 Detach the cables from the guides on the underbody and rear suspension. Note that the cables can be fed through certain guides, but in some cases, the guide brackets must be bent away from the underbody to allow the cable to be withdrawn.

9 Withdraw the cable assembly from the vehicle.

Refitting

10 Refitting is a reversal of removal, remembering the following points.

11 Ensure that the cables are routed as noted before removal.

12 Refit the brake shoes, as described in Section 8.

13 Use a new self-locking nut to secure the handbrake cable bracket to the operating rod, and screw the nut onto the rod to the position noted before removal.

14 Before refitting the roadwheels and lowering the vehicle to the ground, adjust the handbrake, as described in Section 19.

22.1 Rear brake pressure-regulating valve (arrowed) - Hatchback model

Models with rear disc brakes

Note: *A new self-locking nut must be used to secure the handbrake cable to the operating rod on refitting.*

Removal

15 The procedure is as described for models with rear drum brakes, remembering the following points.

16 Ignore the references to removal and refitting of the brake drum.

17 Note that there is no lockplate securing the handbrake cable to the brake backplate, but the return spring must be unhooked from the cable end.

Refitting

18 Refitting is a reversal of removal, remembering the following points.

19 Ensure that the cables are routed as noted before removal.

20 Use a new self-locking nut to secure the handbrake cable bracket to the operating rod, and screw the nut onto the rod to the position noted before removal.

21 Before refitting the roadwheels and lowering the vehicle to the ground, adjust the handbrake, as described in Section 19.

22 Rear brake pressure-regulating valve - removal, refitting and adjustment

Saloon and Hatchback models

Note: *Refer to the note at the beginning of Section 2 before proceeding. Note also that the valves must only be renewed in pairs, and both valves must be of the same calibration.*

Removal

1 Two valves are fitted, one for each hydraulic circuit, located under the rear of the vehicle **(see illustration)**.

2 Chock the front wheels, then jack up the rear of the car and support securely on axle stands.

3 Working under the bonnet, remove the brake fluid reservoir cap, and secure a piece of polythene over the filler neck with a rubber band, or by refitting the cap. This will reduce the loss of fluid during the following procedure.

4 Working under the rear of the vehicle, unscrew the union nut, and disconnect the brake pipe from one of the valves. Be prepared for fluid spillage, and plug the open end of the pipe to prevent dirt ingress and further fluid spillage.

5 Similarly, disconnect the flexible hose from the valve.

6 Pull the valve retaining clip from the bracket on the underbody, noting that on certain models, the retaining clip also secures the ABS sensor wiring, and withdraw the valve.

7 Repeat the procedure for the remaining valve.

Refitting

8 Refitting is a reversal of removal, but on completion, remove the polythene from the brake fluid reservoir filler neck, and bleed the complete hydraulic system, as described in Section 2.

Adjustment

9 The valves are calibrated at the factory, and no adjustment is possible.

Estate and Van models

Removal

10 A single tandem valve is used, which is located under the rear of the vehicle, above the rear suspension torsion beam.

11 Proceed as described in paragraphs 2 and 3.

12 Unhook the spring from the valve operating lever.

13 Unscrew the union nuts, and disconnect the brake pipes from the valve. Be prepared for fluid spillage, and plug the open ends of the pipes to prevent dirt ingress and further fluid spillage. Note that the union nuts differ in size, to ensure correct reconnection.

14 Remove the two securing screws, and withdraw the valve from its bracket on the underbody.

15 If the valve is to be renewed, the protective shield should be removed from the old valve and transferred to the new valve. The shield is secured by a single nut.

Refitting

16 Fit the valve to the bracket on the underbody, and tighten the two securing bolts.

17 Reconnect the two brake pipes to the valve, and tighten the union nuts. Note that the two union nuts differ in size; also take care not to overtighten the nuts.

18 Reconnect the spring to the valve operating lever.

19 Refit the roadwheels, and lower the vehicle to the ground.

20 Bleed the complete hydraulic system, as described in Section 2, then refer to Chapter 1 and adjust the valve.

Adjustment

21 Refer to Chapter 1.

23 Brake light switch - removal and refitting

Removal

1 Disconnect the battery negative lead.

2 Release the securing clips, and remove the lower trim panel from under the driver's side facia.

3 Disconnect the wiring plug from the brake light switch, then twist the switch anti-clockwise and remove it from its bracket **(see illustration)**.

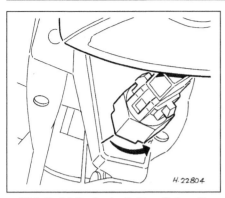

23.3 Twist the brake light switch anti-clockwise to remove it from its bracket

4 No adjustment of the switch is possible, except by bending the bracket, which is not recommended.

Refitting

5 Refitting is a reversal of removal.

24 Braking system warning lights - general

Brake lights

1 The brake light circuit is controlled by a plunger-type switch mounted on the brake pedal bracket.
2 If the switch is thought to be faulty, it can be tested by disconnecting the wires and connecting either a multi-meter (set to the resistance function) or a battery-and-bulb test circuit, across the switch terminals. The switch should allow current to flow only when its plunger is extended. If the switch is faulty, it must be renewed.
3 Details for removal and refitting of the switch are given in Section 23.

Low fluid level warning light

4 The warning light circuit is activated by a float-type sensor attached to the brake fluid reservoir filler cap.
5 If the sensor is thought to be faulty, unscrew the filler cap, and connect the test equipment described in paragraph 2 across the sensor terminals on the cap. The sensor should allow current to flow only when the float is hanging at the bottom of its travel. If the sensor is faulty, the complete filler cap/sensor assembly must be renewed.

Handbrake 'on' warning light

6 The warning light is activated by a plunger-type switch mounted at the base of the handbrake lever.
7 The switch should illuminate whenever the handbrake is applied, and should extinguish when the handbrake is released.
8 If the switch is thought to be faulty, remove it as described in Section 20, and connect the test equipment described previously in

paragraph 2. The switch should only allow current to flow only when the plunger is fully extended. If the switch is faulty, it must be renewed.

ABS warning light

9 The ABS warning light will illuminate when the ignition is first switched on, and should extinguish after a few seconds. If the warning light stays on, or comes on whilst driving, this indicates a fault in the system. The vehicle is still safe to drive (the conventional braking system will still be effective); however, at the earliest opportunity, take the vehicle to a Vauxhall/Opel dealer, and have the complete system tested using the dedicated test equipment.

Check control unit warnings

10 On models fitted with a check control system, warnings are provided to indicate front disc pad wear, and brake light bulb failure. Further details of this system can be found in Chapter 12, Section 14.

25 Anti-lock braking system (ABS) – general information and precautions

General information

ABS (Anti-lock Braking System) is fitted as standard on certain models, and is available as an option for all others.

The system comprises an electronic control unit, roadwheel sensors, hydraulic modulator, and the necessary valves and relays. The purpose of the system is to prevent wheel(s) locking during heavy brake applications. This is achieved by automatic release of the brake on the locked wheel, followed by reapplication of the brake. This procedure is carried out several times a second by the hydraulic modulator. The modulator is controlled by the electronic control unit, which itself receives signals from the wheel sensors, which monitor the locked or unlocked state of the wheels. The two front brakes are modulated separately, but the two rear brakes are modulated together. The ABS unit is fitted between the brake master cylinder and the brakes, the vacuum servo and master cylinder being of similar type for both non-ABS and ABS models.

The front wheel sensors are mounted on the hub carriers, and monitor the rotation of the wheels through toothed discs on the driveshafts. The rear wheel sensors are integral with the rear hub units.

Precautions

If the ABS develops a fault, the complete system should be tested by a Vauxhall/Opel dealer, who will have the necessary specialist equipment to make a quick and accurate diagnosis of the problem. Due to the special equipment required, it is not practical for the

DIY mechanic to carry out the test procedure.

To prevent possible damage to the electronic control unit, always disconnect the control unit wiring plug before carrying out electrical welding work.

It is recommended that the control unit is removed if the vehicle is to be subjected to high temperatures, as may be encountered (for instance) during certain paint-drying processes.

If using steam-cleaning equipment, do not aim the water/steam jet directly at the control unit.

Do not disconnect the control unit wiring plug with the ignition switched on.

Do not use a battery booster to start the engine.

After working on the ABS system components, ensure that all wiring plugs are correctly reconnected, and ideally, have the complete system tested by a Vauxhall/Opel dealer using dedicated ABS test equipment at the earliest opportunity.

On models with Electronic Traction Control (ETC), the ABS wheel sensors also send signals to the ETC system.

26 Anti-lock braking system (ABS) components – removal and refitting

Hydraulic modulator

Note: *Refer to the note at the beginning of Section 2 before proceeding.*

Removal

1 Disconnect the battery negative lead.
2 Remove the brake fluid reservoir cap, and secure a piece of polythene over the filler neck with a rubber band, or by refitting the cap. This will reduce the loss of fluid during the following procedure.
3 Remove the securing screw, and withdraw the plastic cover from the hydraulic modulator **(see illustration)**.
4 Disconnect the control unit wiring plug, and the solenoid valve wiring plug. Note that the control unit wiring plug is secured by a screw **(see illustrations overleaf)**.
5 Unscrew the brake fluid pipe union nuts, and disconnect the pipes from the modulator.

26.3 Withdrawing the plastic cover from the ABS hydraulic modulator

26.4a Removing the ABS control unit wiring plug securing screw

26.4b Disconnecting the ABS solenoid valve wiring plug

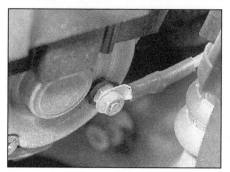

26.6a ABS hydraulic modulator earth lead and securing nut

Be prepared for fluid spillage, and plug the open ends to prevent dirt ingress and further fluid loss. Move the pipes just clear of the modulator, taking care not to strain them.

6 Unscrew the three securing nuts, then tilt the modulator slightly, and withdraw it upwards from its bracket, sufficiently to gain access to the earth lead securing nut at the lower front edge of the modulator **(see illustrations)**.

7 Unscrew the securing nut and disconnect the earth lead, then withdraw the modulator from the vehicle, taking care not to spill brake fluid on the vehicle paintwork.

8 If a new modulator is to be fitted, pull the two relays from the top of the old modulator, and transfer them to the new unit. No attempt must be made to dismantle the modulator.

Refitting

9 Before refitting the modulator, check that the bolts securing the mounting bracket to the body panel are tight, and that the modulator rubber mountings are in good condition. Renew the rubber mountings if necessary.

10 Refitting is a reversal of removal, remembering the following points.

11 Make sure that the earth lead is reconnected before fitting the modulator to its mounting bracket.

12 On completion, remove the polythene sheet from the brake fluid reservoir filler neck, and bleed the complete hydraulic system, as described in Section 2.

13 Check that the ABS warning light

extinguishes when first starting the engine after the modulator has been removed. At the earliest opportunity, take the vehicle to a Vauxhall/Opel dealer, and have the complete system tested using the dedicated test equipment.

Front wheel sensor

Removal

14 Disconnect the battery negative lead.

15 Apply the handbrake, then jack up the front of the vehicle, and support securely on axle stands (see "Jacking and vehicle support").

16 Unclip the sensor wiring connector from the retaining clip under the wheel arch, then separate the two halves of the wiring connector, prising them apart with a screwdriver if necessary.

17 Using an Allen key or hexagon bit, unscrew the bolt securing the wheel sensor to the mounting bracket **(see illustration)**, then carefully lever the sensor from the bracket using a screwdriver. Recover the sealing ring.

Refitting

18 Examine the condition of the sealing ring, and renew if necessary.

19 Refitting is a reversal of removal, remembering the following points.

20 Smear a little grease on the sensor casing before fitting it to the bracket.

21 Check that the ABS warning light extinguishes when first starting the engine. At the earliest opportunity, take the vehicle to a Vauxhall/Opel dealer, and have the complete

system tested using the dedicated test equipment.

Rear wheel sensor

22 The rear wheel sensors are integral with the rear hub assemblies, and cannot be separated from the hub assemblies. For details of rear hub removal and refitting, refer to Chapter 10.

Electronic control unit

Note: Refer to the precautions concerning the ABS system given in Section 25 before proceeding.

Removal

23 Ensure that the ignition is switched off, then disconnect the battery negative lead.

24 The module is attached to the hydraulic modulator assembly in the engine compartment.

25 Remove the securing screw, and withdraw the plastic cover from the hydraulic modulator.

26 Disconnect the control unit wiring plug, and the solenoid valve wiring plug **(see illustration)**.

27 Remove the two relays from the top of the assembly.

28 Disconnect the remaining wiring plug from the control unit.

29 Unscrew the seven securing screws, and withdraw the control unit from the modulator assembly.

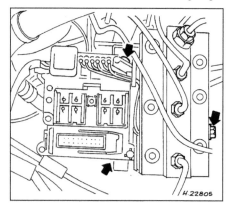

26.6b ABS hydraulic modulator securing nuts (arrowed)

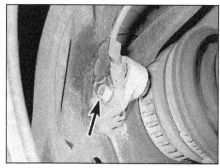

26.17 ABS front wheel sensor securing bolt (arrowed)

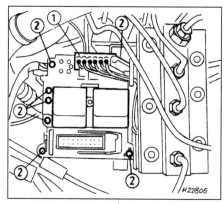

26.26 ABS electronic control unit

1 Wiring plug   2 Securing screws

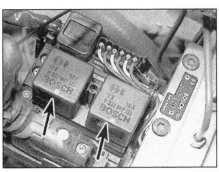

26.31 ABS relays (arrowed)

Refitting

30 Refitting is a reversal of removal, but take care not to overtighten the control unit securing screws.

Relays

Removal

31 Two relays are used, one for the solenoid valve, and one for the pump motor; both relays are mounted on the control unit **(see illustration)**.

32 Disconnect the battery negative lead.

33 Remove the securing screw, and withdraw the plastic cover from the hydraulic modulator.

34 Pull out the appropriate relay.

Refitting

35 Refitting is a reversal of removal.

36 Check that the ABS warning light extinguishes when first starting the engine. At the earliest opportunity, take the vehicle to a Vauxhall/Opel dealer, and have the complete system tested using the dedicated test equipment.

Notes

Chapter 10
Suspension and steering

Contents

Degrees of difficulty

Easy, suitable for novice with little experience		Fairly easy, suitable for beginner with some experience		Fairly difficult, suitable for competent DIY mechanic		Difficult, suitable for experienced DIY mechanic		Very difficult, suitable for expert DIY or professional	

Specifications

Front suspension
Type . . . . Independent, with McPherson struts and anti-roll bar

Rear suspension
Type . . . . Semi-independent torsion beam, with trailing arms, coil springs and
telescopic shock absorbers. Anti-roll bar(s) on certain models. Manual
level control system available on certain models

Steering
Type . . . . Rack-and-pinion. Power assistance available on certain models

Tyres
Size:
  51/2J x 13 wheels . . . . 155 R13 78S/T or 175/70 R13 82T/H
  51/2J x 14 wheels . . . . 175/65 R14 82T/H, 175/70 R14 84T, 185/60 R14 82 H, 185/60 R14
                                                                         82T/H or 195/60 R14 85H/V *
  6J x 15 wheels . . . . 195/55 R15 84 H/V or 205/50 R15 85V
  * Only permissible for use with Vauxhall/Opel snow chains

Roadwheels

Type . . . . Steel or alloy
Size . . . . 51/2J x 13, 51/2J x 14 or 6J x 15

Wheel alignment and steering angles

Front camber angle (laden* - not adjustable):
    All models . . . . 1°50' negative to 0°20' negative
    Maximum camber variation between sides . . . . 1° 00'
Front castor angle (laden* - not adjustable):
    Saloon and Hatchback models . . . . 1°15' positive to 3°15' positive
    Estate and Van models . . . . 0°30' positive to 2°30' positive
    Maximum castor variation between sides . . . . 1°
Front toe setting (all models) . . . . 0° 25' toe-out to 0° 5' toe-out
Rear wheel camber angle (not adjustable) . . . . 2 °10' negative to 1°10' negative
Rear wheel toe setting (not adjustable) . . . . 10' toe-out to 40' toe-in
* For the purposes of these figures, a vehicle is considered to be 'laden' when it has a load equivalent to 70.0 kg in each front seat.

Torque wrench settings

	Nm	lbf ft
Front suspension		
Anti-roll bar-to-lower arm locknuts*	20	15
Anti-roll bar-to-subframe bolts	20	15
Balljoint-to-lower arm nuts	60	44
Front hub nut (refer to text):*		
Stage 1	100	74
Stage 2	Loosen nut fully	
Stage 3	20	15
Stage 4	Angle-tighten by a further 80° (plus another 9° if necessary)	
Lower arm damper weight bolts (where applicable)	20	15
Lower arm-to-front subframe (horizontal) pivot bolt: *		
Stage 1	100	74
Stage 2	Angle-tighten by a further 60°	
Stage 3	Angle-tighten by a further 15°	
Lower arm-to-front subframe rear bolt (subframe-to-underbody rear bolt): *		
Stage 1	100	74
Stage 2	Angle-tighten by a further 75°	
Stage 3	Angle-tighten by a further 15°	
Lower arm-to-suspension strut balljoint nut *	70	52
Suspension strut piston rod nut	55	
Suspension strut ring nut	200	148
Suspension strut upper mounting nuts	30	22
Subframe-to-underbody bolts: *		
Front bolts (not applicable to certain early models - refer to text) . . .	115	85
Centre bolts (front bolts on early models - refer to text)	170	125
Rear bolts (lower arm-to-front subframe rear bolts):		
Stage 1	100	74
Stage 2	Angle-tighten by a further 75°	
Stage 3	Angle-tighten by a further 15°	
Rear suspension		
Additional anti-roll bar securing bolts (if fitted): *		
Stage 1	60	44
Stage 2	Angle-tighten a further 60°	
Stage 3	Angle-tighten a further 15°	
Main anti-roll bar securing bolts: *		
Stage 1	30	22
Stage 2	Angle-tighten a further 30°	
Stage 3	Angle-tighten a further 15°	
Rear hub unit securing nuts (refer to text): *		
Stage 1	50	37
Stage 2	Angle-tighten by a further 30°	
Stage 3	Angle-tighten by a further 15°	
Shock absorber lower mounting bolt (Saloon and Hatchback models)70	52	
Shock absorber lower mounting nut (Estate and Van models)	12	9
Shock absorber top mounting nut (Saloon and Hatchback models) . . .	20	15
Shock absorber upper mounting bolt	70	52
Trailing arm-to-underbody fixings	105	77

Torque wrench settings (continued)

	Nm	lbf ft
Steering		
Power steering fluid pipe unions	28	21
Power steering pump mounting bolts:		
SOHC models:		
with V-belts	30	22
with ribbed V-belts	20	15
DOHC models:		
with V-belts	30	22
Bolts 'A' and 'C' (refer to text)	25	18
Bolt 'B' (refer to text)	40	30
with ribbed V-belts	20	15
Bolts 'A' and 'C' (refer to text)	25	18
Bolt 'B' (refer to text)	18	13
Power steering pump pulley bolts (1.4 and 1.6 litre, V-belt models) ...	25	18
Steering column fixings	22	16
Steering gear damper adjuster locknut	60	44
Steering gear pinion nut	40	30
Steering gear pinion-to-rubber coupling pinch-bolt	22	16
Steering gear-to-bulkhead fixings	22	16
Steering shaft-to-rubber coupling pinch-bolt	22	16
Steering wheel retaining nut	25	18
Tie-rod end clamp bolts	20	15
Tie-rod-to-steering gear bolts	95	70
Tie-rod end-to-suspension strut balljoint nut	60	44
Roadwheels		
Roadwheel bolts	See Chapter 1	

* Use new bolts/nuts, as applicable.

1 General information

1 The front suspension consists of MacPherson struts, lower arms, and an anti-roll bar. The lower arms and the anti-roll bar are mounted on a detachable U-shaped front subframe, which also carries the rear engine/transmission mounting **(see illustration)**.

2 Each lower arm is attached to the subframe by a horizontal front bush and a vertical rear bush.

3 The hub carriers are mounted between the lower ends of the MacPherson struts and the lower arms, and carry the double-row ball type wheel bearings and the brake assemblies.

4 The rear suspension is of semi-independent type, consisting of a torsion beam and trailing arms, with double-conical coil springs and telescopic shock absorbers, and (on certain models) an anti-roll bar. The front ends of the trailing arms are attached to the vehicle underbody by horizontal bushes, and the rear ends are located by the shock absorbers, which are bolted to the underbody at their upper ends. The coil springs are mounted independently of the shock absorbers, and act directly between the trailing arms and the underbody. Certain models are fitted with an anti-roll bar, which is mounted between the torsion beam and the trailing arms. DOHC models are fitted with twin rear anti-roll bars.

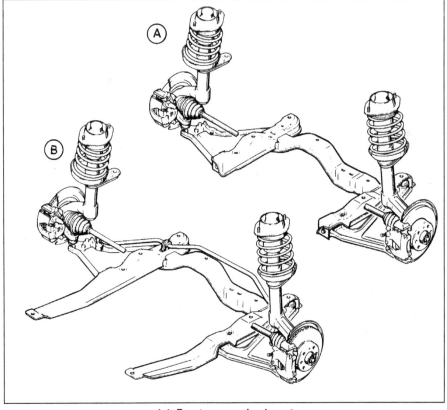

1.1 Front suspension layout

A   Early models (see Section 10)   B   Later models

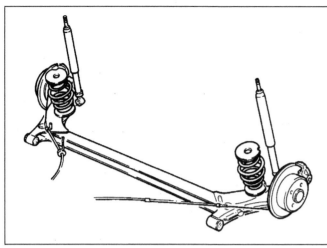

**1.4a Rear suspension layout -
Saloon and Hatchback models with rear disc brakes**

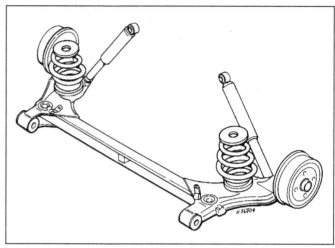

**1.4b Rear suspension layout -
Estate and Van models with rear drum brakes**

On all models, each rear wheel bearing, hub and stub axle assembly is manufactured as a sealed unit, which cannot be dismantled **(see illustrations)**.

5 A manual rear suspension level control system is available on Estate and Van models. The system operates using compressed air-filled shock absorbers. The rear suspension level is adjusted by altering the air pressure in the shock absorbers, through a valve located in the luggage compartment.

6 The steering gear is of rack-and-pinion type. Movement is transmitted to the front wheels via tie-rods, which are connected to the rack through a sliding sleeve at their inner ends, and to the suspension struts via balljoints at their outer ends.

7 The steering column consists of an outer column that incorporates a collapsible section, and a shaft connected to a flexible coupling at its lower end.

8 Power steering is fitted as standard to certain models, and is available as an option on others. The power steering is hydraulically operated, and pressure is supplied by a fluid pump driven by way of a drivebelt from the engine crankshaft. On certain larger-engined models, fluid cooler pipes are mounted beneath the radiator to keep the temperature of the hydraulic fluid within operating limits.

2 Front suspension strut - removal and refitting

Note: A balljoint separator tool will be required during this procedure. The tie-rod end balljoint nut, lower arm-to-suspension strut balljoint nut locking pin, and the hub nut, washer and split pin, must be renewed on refitting.

Removal

1 Apply the handbrake, then jack up the front of the vehicle and support securely on axle stands (see "Jacking and vehicle support"). Remove the relevant roadwheel.

2 Where applicable, remove the ABS wheel sensor from the hub carrier, referring to Chapter 9 if necessary, and disconnect the wiring from the strut.

3 Remove the brake caliper from the hub carrier, as described in Chapter 9. The caliper can be suspended out of the way, using wire or string, to avoid the need to disconnect the hydraulic fluid hose.

4 Unscrew and remove the self-locking nut from the tie-rod end-to-suspension strut balljoint.

5 Using a balljoint separator tool, disconnect the tie-rod end-to-suspension strut balljoint.

6 Extract the split pin from the castellated hub nut on the end of the driveshaft.

7 The hub nut must now be loosened. The nut is extremely tight, and an extension bar will be required to loosen it. To prevent the driveshaft from turning, insert two roadwheel bolts, and insert a metal bar between them to counterhold the hub.

8 Remove the hub nut and washer from the driveshaft.

9 Extract the locking pin, then unscrew the castellated nut from the lower arm-to-suspension strut balljoint.

10 Using a balljoint separator tool, disconnect the lower arm-to-suspension strut balljoint.

11 Withdraw the outer end of the driveshaft from the hub. It should be possible to pull the driveshaft from the hub by hand, but if necessary tap the end of the shaft with a soft-faced mallet to release it. **Do not** use heavy blows, as damage to the driveshaft joints may result. Support the driveshaft by suspending it with wire or string - **do not** allow the driveshaft to hang down under its own weight.

12 Working in the engine compartment, unscrew the two nuts securing the suspension strut to the suspension turret **(see illustration)**. Support the suspension strut as the nuts are unscrewed, as once the nuts have been removed, the strut is free to drop from the vehicle.

13 Withdraw the suspension strut/hub carrier assembly from the vehicle **(see illustration)**.

Refitting

14 Locate the top end of the strut in the suspension turret, then refit the securing nuts and tighten them to the specified torque.

15 Apply a little molybdenum disulphide grease to the driveshaft splines, then insert the outer end of the shaft into the hub. Fit a new washer, and screw on a new hub nut finger-tight.

16 Reconnect the lower arm-to-suspension strut balljoint, then fit the castellated nut, and tighten to the specified torque. Secure the nut with a new locking pin.

2.12 Suspension strut securing nuts (arrowed)

2.13 Withdrawing the suspension strut/hub carrier assembly

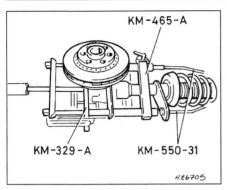

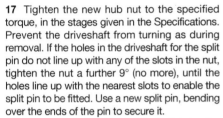

3.3 Vauxhall/Opel spring compressor tool components in position on front suspension strut

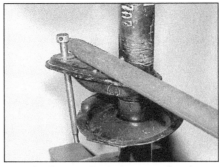

3.9a One method of unscrewing the suspension strut ring nut

3.9b Removing the ring nut . . .

17 Tighten the new hub nut to the specified torque, in the stages given in the Specifications. Prevent the driveshaft from turning as during removal. If the holes in the driveshaft for the split pin do not line up with any of the slots in the nut, tighten the nut a further 9° (no more), until the holes line up with the nearest slots to enable the split pin to be fitted. Use a new split pin, bending over the ends of the pin to secure it.

18 Reconnect the tie-rod balljoint to the suspension strut, and tighten a new self-locking nut to the specified torque.

19 Refit the brake caliper to the hub carrier, as described in Chapter 9.

20 Where applicable, refit the ABS wheel sensor to the hub carrier, referring to Chapter 9 if necessary, and reconnect the wiring to the strut.

21 Refit the roadwheel, and lower the vehicle to the ground.

22 On completion, check and if necessary adjust the front wheel alignment, as described in Section 35.

3 Front suspension strut - overhaul

Note: *A spring compressor tool will be required for this operation.*

1 With the strut removed as described in Section 2, proceed as follows.

2 The hub, wheel bearing and brake disc shield can be removed, as described in Section 4.

3 With the suspension strut resting on a bench or clamped in a vice, fit a spring compressor tool, and compress the coil spring to relieve the pressure on the upper spring seat. Ensure that the compressor tool is securely located on the spring according to the tool manufacturer's instructions **(see illustration).**

4 Prise out the plastic cover from the top of the strut.

5 Hold the strut piston rod with a socket, and unscrew the piston rod nut.

6 Lift off the strut upper mounting rubber and the bearing.

7 Lift off the upper spring seat and damper ring, then carefully release the spring compressor and remove the spring. Note which way round the spring is fitted.

8 Slide the bellows, and the rubber buffer that fits inside the bellows, from the strut.

9 To remove the shock absorber cartridge, the ring nut must be unscrewed from the top of the strut tube. This nut is extremely tight. One method that can be used to unscrew the nut is to invert the strut and clamp the nut in a vice. Then lever the strut round using a long bar and a bolt passed through the tie-rod bracket **(see illustrations).**

10 With the ring nut removed, the shock absorber cartridge can be withdrawn **(see illustration).**

11 The shock absorber can be tested by clamping the lower end in a vice, then fully extending and contracting the shock absorber several times. Any evidence of jerky movement or lack of resistance indicates the need for renewal.

12 Examine all components for wear or damage, and renew as necessary. Pay particular attention to the mounting rubber and the bearing **(see illustration).**

13 Begin reassembly by sliding the shock absorber cartridge into the strut and refitting the ring nut. Do not remove the wax coating from the nut.

14 Clamp the strut in a vice, and tighten the ring nut to the specified torque, using a large long-reach socket.

15 Refit and compress the coil spring, ensuring that the lower end of the spring rests against the lug on the lower spring seat.

16 Refit the rubber buffer and the bellows.

17 Refit the upper spring seat and the damper ring.

18 Lubricate the bearing with a little grease, then refit it with the visible part of the bearing race uppermost.

19 Refit the strut upper mounting rubber.

20 Counterhold the strut piston rod, and tighten the piston rod nut to the specified torque. This can be achieved by holding the piston rod using a splined key fitted to a torque wrench, and tightening the nut using a spanner until the specified torque is reached.

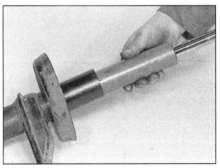

3.10 . . . and withdrawing the shock absorber cartridge

21 Carefully release and remove the spring compressor tool, ensuring that the spring seats correctly at top and bottom. Ensure that the lower end of the spring still rests against the lug on the lower spring seat.

22 Refit the strut, as described in Section 2.

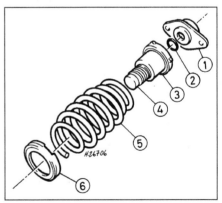

3.12 Front suspension strut components

1 Upper mounting rubber assembly
2 Bearing
3 Upper spring seat and damper ring
4 Bellows and rubber buffer
5 Spring
6 Lower spring seat

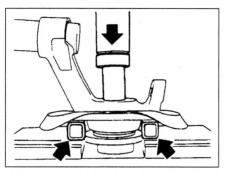

4.3 Pressing the front hub from the wheel bearing

4.4 Removing the half inner bearing race from the hub

4.5 Removing a brake disc shield securing screw

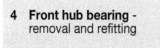

4 Front hub bearing - removal and refitting

Note: *The bearing will probably be destroyed during the removal operation. The use of a puller will greatly ease the procedure.*

Removal

1 Remove the relevant suspension strut/hub carrier assembly, as described in Section 2.
2 Unscrew the securing screw, and remove the brake disc from the hub.
3 Support the hub carrier on two metal bars

4.6a Extracting the outer bearing retaining circlip

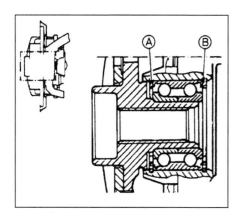

4.6b Cross-sectional view of front wheel bearing/hub assembly

A   *Outer bearing retaining circlip*
B   *Inner bearing retaining circlip*

positioned as shown **(see illustration)**, then, using a metal bar, press or drive the hub from the wheel bearing. Alternatively, screw two roadwheel bolts into the hub and, using progressively thicker packing pieces, tighten the bolts to force the hub from the bearing. Note that one half of the inner bearing race will remain on the hub .
4 Using a puller, pull the half inner bearing race from the hub **(see illustration)**. Alternatively, support the bearing race on thin metal bars, and press or drive the hub from the bearing race.
5 Remove the three securing screws **(see illustration)**, and lift the brake disc shield from the hub carrier.
6 Extract the inner and outer bearing retaining circlips **(see illustrations)**.
7 Using a puller, pull the bearing from the hub carrier, applying pressure to the outer race. Alternatively, support the hub carrier, and press or drive out the bearing.

Refitting

8 Before installing the new bearing, thoroughly clean the bearing location in the hub carrier, and fit the outer bearing retaining circlip 'A' (see illustration 4.6b). Note that the circlip tabs should be positioned towards the bottom of the hub carrier.
9 Press or drive the new bearing into position until it contacts the outer circlip, applying pressure to the outer race **(see illustration)**.
10 Fit the inner bearing retaining circlip, with the tabs positioned towards the bottom of the hub carrier.
11 Fit the brake disc shield.

4.9 Fitting a new front wheel bearing using a socket, nut, bolt, washers and a length of bar

12 Press or draw the hub into the bearing. The bearing inner track **must** be supported during this operation. This can be achieved using a socket, long bolt, washer, and a length of bar as shown **(see illustration)**.
13 Refit the brake disc.
14 Refit the suspension strut/hub carrier assembly, as described in Section 2.

5 Front suspension lower arm - removal and refitting

Note: *A balljoint separator tool will be required for this operation. The lower arm rear pivot bolt, lower arm-to-suspension strut balljoint nut locking pin, and anti-roll bar-to-lower arm securing nuts and locknuts must be renewed on refitting.*
Note: *Regular inspection of the front suspension lower arms is recommended in order to detect damage or distortion which could eventually lead to failure. Any sign of cracking, creasing or other damage should be investigated and the arm renewed if necessary. If in doubt, consult your Vauxhall/Opel dealer for advice.*

Removal

1 Apply the handbrake, then jack up the front of the vehicle, and support securely on axle stands (see "*Jacking and vehicle support*"). Remove the relevant roadwheel.
2 Unscrew and discard the nuts securing the end of the anti-roll bar to the lower arm. Note that the nut that rests against the dished

4.12 Drawing the hub into the bearing using improvised tools

5.5 Lower arm front pivot bolt (arrowed)

washer is a conventional nut, and the second nut is a locknut. Recover the dished washers and the mounting rubbers.
3 Extract the locking pin, then unscrew the castellated nut from the lower arm-to-suspension strut balljoint.
4 Using a balljoint separator tool, disconnect the lower arm-to-suspension strut balljoint.
5 Unscrew and remove the two pivot bolts securing the lower arm to the subframe **(see illustration)**. Note that the rear pivot bolt also secures the subframe to the underbody. Both bolts are very tight, and an extension bar will probably be required to loosen them.
6 Pull the lower arm from the subframe, and withdraw it from the vehicle.

Refitting

7 Note that on certain models, a damper weight may be bolted to the right-hand lower arm. If the right-hand lower arm is to be renewed on such a vehicle, it is important to ensure that the damper weight is transferred to the new arm.
8 Note that the metal sleeves in the rear mounting bush can be discarded when refitting the lower arm.
9 Begin refitting by pushing the lower arm into position in the subframe.
10 Fit the two pivot bolts, then hold the lower arm in a horizontal position, and tighten the bolts to the specified torque. Note that a new rear pivot bolt must be used, and the new bolt must be tightened to the specified torque in the three stages given in the Specifications.
11 Reconnect the lower arm-to-suspension strut balljoint, and tighten the castellated nut to the specified torque. Secure the nut with a new locking pin.
12 Reconnect the end of the anti-roll bar to the lower arm, noting that the dished washers that retain the mounting rubbers should be fitted with their concave sides facing towards the lower arm.
13 Fit a new anti-roll bar-to-lower arm securing nut, and tighten it to give the specified rubber bush compression shown **(see illustration)**. If necessary, renew the rubber bushes.
14 Fit a new anti-roll bar-to-lower arm locknut, and tighten it to the specified torque.
15 Refit the roadwheel and lower the vehicle to the ground.

16 On completion, check and if necessary adjust the front wheel alignment, as described in Section 35.

6 Front suspension lower arm bushes - renewal

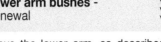

1 Remove the lower arm, as described in Section 5.
2 The bushes are a tight fit in the lower arm, and must be pressed out.
3 If a press is not available, the bushes can be drawn out using a long bolt, nut, washers and a socket or length of metal tubing.
4 The vertical bush should be pressed out through the top of the lower arm, from below, and the horizontal bush should pressed out towards the front of the lower arm, from the rear.
5 Lubricate the new bushes using soapy water, then fit them to the lower arm, using the method described in paragraph 3.
6 The new vertical bush should be pressed into the lower arm from below, and the new horizontal bush should be pressed into the lower arm from front to rear. The horizontal bush should project from the lower arm equally at both ends.
7 Refit the lower arm, as described in Section 5.

7 Front suspension lower arm balljoint - renewal

Note: *Three special bolts, spring washers and nuts (available from Vauxhall/Opel dealers) will be required when fitting the new balljoint.*
1 Remove the lower arm, as described in Section 5.
2 Mount the lower arm in a vice, then drill the heads from the three rivets that secure the balljoint to the lower arm, using a 12 mm diameter drill.
3 If necessary, tap the rivets from the lower arm, then remove the balljoint.
4 The new balljoint should be fitted using three special bolts, spring washers and nuts, available from a Vauxhall/Opel parts centre.
5 Ensure that the balljoint is fitted the correct

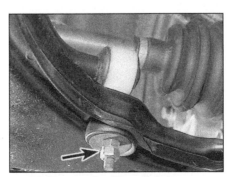

8.5 Front anti-roll bar-to-lower arm securing nuts (arrowed)

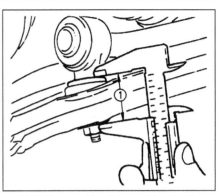

5.13 Front anti-roll bar rubber bush compression (1) should be 38.0 to 39.0 mm

way up, noting that the securing nuts should be positioned on the underside of the lower arm.
6 Tighten the balljoint-to-lower arm nuts to the specified torque.
7 Refit the lower arm, as described in Section 5.

8 Front anti-roll bar - removal and refitting

Note: *A hoist or similar lifting equipment will be required to support the engine during this procedure. The rear subframe securing bolts, and the anti-roll bar-to-lower arm securing nuts and locknuts, must be renewed on refitting.*

Removal

1 Before removing the anti-roll bar, the engine must be supported from its left-hand lifting bracket. Ideally, the engine should be supported using a strong wooden or metal beam resting on blocks positioned securely in the channels at the sides of the engine compartment. The Vauxhall/Opel special tool designed specifically for this purpose is shown in Chapter 7A. Alternatively, the engine can be supported using a hoist and lifting tackle. However, in this case, the hoist must be of such a design as to enable the engine to be supported with the vehicle raised off the ground, leaving sufficient clearance to lower the front subframe.
2 Apply the handbrake, then jack up the front of the vehicle, and support securely on axle stands (see *"Jacking and vehicle support"*). Remove the front roadwheels.
3 Where applicable, remove the engine undershield, as described in Chapter 11, Section 25.
4 For improved access, remove the front section of the exhaust system, as described in Chapter 4A, Section 23 or Chapter 4B, Section 21.
5 Working under the vehicle, unscrew and remove the nuts securing the ends of the anti-roll bar to the lower arms. Recover the dished washers and mounting rubbers **(see illustration)**.

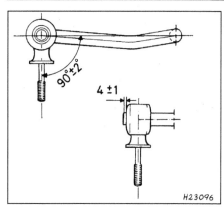

9.6 Correct position of end link on front anti-roll bar

Dimensions in mm

6 Ensure that the engine is adequately supported, then unscrew and remove the two nuts and washers securing the engine/transmission rear mounting to the subframe.

7 Support the subframe on a trolley jack, with an interposed wooden beam to spread the load.

8 Unscrew and remove the two rear and two centre bolts securing the subframe to the vehicle underbody. Note that the rear bolts also secure the lower arms to the subframe. The bolts are very tight, and an extension bar will probably be required to loosen them. **Note:** *On certain early left-hand-drive models, a short front subframe was used, which was secured by four bolts instead of six. On these models, remove all four subframe securing bolts, and lower the complete subframe from the vehicle.*

9 Loosen, but do not remove, the two front subframe-to-underbody securing bolts (not applicable to certain early left-hand-drive models - see paragraph 8).

10 Carefully lower the subframe until the anti-roll bar-to-subframe bolts are accessible, then unscrew and remove the bolts.

11 Lift the anti-roll bar from the subframe and the lower arms, and withdraw it from the vehicle.

Refitting

12 The anti-roll bar mounting bushes can be renewed, as described in Section 9.

13 Refitting is a reversal of removal, remembering the following points.

14 When refitting the subframe to the underbody, use new rear securing bolts, and tighten them to the specified torque in the three stages given in the Specifications.

15 Reconnect the ends of the anti-roll bar to the lower arms, noting that the dished washers that retain the mounting rubbers should be fitted with their concave sides facing towards the lower arm.

16 Fit new anti-roll bar-to-lower arm securing nuts, and tighten them to give the specified rubber bush compression as described in paragraph 13 of Section 5. If necessary, renew the rubber bushes.

17 Fit new anti-roll bar-to-lower arm locknuts, and tighten them to the specified torque.

18 Tighten all nuts and bolts to the specified torques.

19 Where applicable, refit the front section of the exhaust system, with reference to Chapter 4A, Section 23 or Chapter 4B, Section 21.

9 Front anti-roll bar bushes - renewal

Note: *The use of a balljoint separator tool will greatly ease this procedure.*

1 Remove the anti-roll bar, as described in Section 8.

2 If an anti-roll bar end link bush (between the end link and the anti-roll bar) requires renewal, the complete end link must be renewed.

3 To remove an end link, mount the anti-roll bar in a vice, then, using a balljoint separator tool and progressively thicker packing pieces, remove the end link from the end of the anti-roll bar. Alternatively, the end link can be removed by driving it from the anti-roll bar using light hammer blows on a drift, although this is likely to cause damage to the end link unless carried out with extreme care.

4 If necessary, repeat the procedure on the remaining end link.

5 With either end link removed, the anti-roll bar-to-subframe mounting bushes can be renewed, by sliding the bushes along the bar and manipulating them until they can be withdrawn from the end of the bar. Fit the new bushes in a similar way.

6 Press or drive the end link(s) onto the anti-roll bar, to the position shown **(see illustration)**. Use a metal tube or socket to avoid damage to the end link(s).

7 Before refitting the anti-roll bar, examine the anti-roll bar-to-lower arm bushes, and renew if necessary.

8 Refit the anti-roll bar, as described in Section 8.

10 Front suspension subframe - removal and refitting

Note: *A hoist or similar lifting equipment will be required to support the engine during this procedure; a balljoint separator tool will also be required. The subframe securing bolts, and the lower arm-to-suspension strut balljoint nut locking pins, must be renewed on refitting.*

Removal

1 The subframe is removed complete with the lower arms and the anti-roll bar, as an assembly.

2 Before removing the subframe, the engine must be supported from its left-hand lifting bracket. Ideally, the engine should be supported using a strong wooden or metal beam resting on blocks positioned securely in the channels at the sides of the engine

compartment. The Vauxhall/Opel special tool designed specifically for this purpose is shown in Chapter 7A. Alternatively, the engine can be supported using a hoist and lifting tackle. However, in this case, the hoist must be of such a design as to enable the engine to be supported with the vehicle raised off the ground, leaving sufficient clearance to withdraw the subframe from under the front of the vehicle.

3 Apply the handbrake, then jack up the front of the vehicle and support securely on axle stands (see "*Jacking and vehicle support*"). Remove the front roadwheels.

4 Where applicable, remove the engine undershield, as described in Chapter 11.

5 Remove the front section of the exhaust system, referring to Chapter 4A, Section 23 or Chapter 4B, Section 21. Where applicable, unbolt the oil cooler hose bracket from the right-hand side of the subframe.

6 Working on one side of the vehicle, extract the locking pin, then unscrew the castellated nut from the lower arm-to-suspension strut balljoint.

7 Using a balljoint separator tool, disconnect the lower arm-to-suspension strut balljoint.

8 Repeat paragraphs 6 and 7 for the remaining lower arm.

9 Ensure that the engine is adequately supported, then unscrew and remove the two nuts and washers securing the rear engine/transmission mounting to the subframe.

10 Support the subframe on a trolley jack, with an interposed wooden beam to prevent the subframe from tipping as it is withdrawn.

11 Unscrew and remove the six bolts securing the subframe to the vehicle underbody. *Note that on certain early models, a short front subframe was used, which was secured by four bolts instead of six. On these models, remove all four subframe securing bolts. Note that the rear bolts also secure the lower arms to the subframe* **(see illustrations)**. The bolts are very tight, and an extension bar will probably be required to loosen them.

12 Lower the jack supporting the subframe, and withdraw the assembly from under the front of the vehicle.

13 The anti-roll bar and/or the lower arms can be removed from the subframe, referring to Section 8 and/or Section 5, as applicable.

10.11a Front subframe front securing bolt (arrowed)

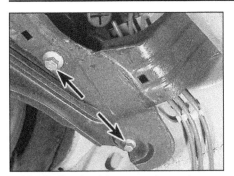

10.11b Front subframe centre and rear securing bolts (arrowed)

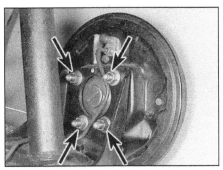

11.6a Rear hub securing nuts (arrowed) - model with rear drum brakes

11.6b Removing a rear hub - model with rear drum brakes

Refitting

14 Refitting is a reversal of removal, bearing in mind the following points.

15 If the anti-roll bar and/or the lower arms have been removed from the subframe, refit them with reference to Section 8 and/or Section 5, as applicable.

16 Fit new subframe securing bolts, and tighten them to the specified torque given in the Specifications. Note that the rear subframe/lower arm securing bolts must be tightened in three stages.

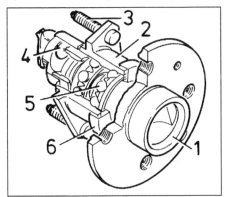

11.6c Sectional view of rear hub assembly

1 Hub
2 Stub axle
3 Threaded bolt
4 Dust cap with integral ABS wheel sensor
5 Bearings
6 Oil seal

11.8 Tightening a rear hub nut using an angle gauge

17 Secure the lower arm-to-suspension strut balljoint nuts with new locking pins.

18 Refit the front section of the exhaust system, referring to Chapter 4A, Section 23 or Chapter 4B, Section 21 and, where applicable, refit the oil cooler bracket to the subframe, followed by the engine undershield.

11 Rear hub - removal and refitting

Note: *The hub unit securing nuts must be renewed on refitting.*

Removal

1 Chock the front wheels, then jack up the rear of the vehicle and support securely on axle stands (see *"Jacking and vehicle support"*). Remove the relevant roadwheel.

2 On models with rear drum brakes, remove the brake drum, as described in Chapter 9.

3 On models with rear disc brakes, remove the brake caliper and the brake disc, as described in Chapter 9. The caliper can be suspended out of the way, using wire or string, to avoid the need to disconnect the hydraulic fluid pipe.

4 On models with rear disc brakes, disconnect the return spring from the handbrake shoe lever and the brake backplate.

5 On models with ABS, disconnect the ABS sensor wiring plug at the rear of the hub assembly.

6 Unscrew the four securing nuts, and withdraw the hub assembly **(see illustrations)**. On models with rear disc brakes, the hub assembly can be withdrawn complete with the brake backplate, in which case, detach the handbrake cable from the handbrake shoe lever as the hub assembly is withdrawn. On models with rear drum brakes, the brake backplate can be left attached to the rear suspension torsion beam.

Refitting

7 Refitting is a reversal of removal, remembering the following points.

8 New hub unit securing nuts must be used, and they must be tightened in the three stages given in the Specifications. Note that a

socket extension and a universal joint may be required, to enable the use of an angle gauge **(see illustration)**.

9 On models with rear disc brakes, where applicable, make sure that the handbrake cable and the return spring are correctly reconnected.

10 On models with rear disc brakes, refit the brake disc and the brake caliper as described in Chapter 9.

11 On models with rear drum brakes, refit the brake drum as described in Chapter 9.

12 Before refitting the roadwheel and lowering the vehicle to the ground, check the handbrake cable adjustment, as described in Chapter 9.

12 Rear shock absorber - removal, inspection and refitting

Note: *Only one shock absorber should be removed at a time. Shock absorbers should be renewed in pairs.*

Saloon and Hatchback models

Removal

1 Working in the luggage compartment, pull the plastic cover from the shock absorber top mounting.

2 Counterhold the shock absorber piston rod, and unscrew the shock absorber top mounting nut **(see illustration)**. Remove the washer and the upper mounting rubber.

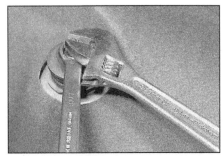

12.2 Unscrewing a rear shock absorber top mounting nut while counter-holding the piston rod - Hatchback model

12.4 Rear shock absorber lower securing bolt - Hatchback model

3 For improved access, drive the rear of the vehicle up onto ramps, and chock the front wheels. Alternatively, chock the front wheels, then jack up the rear of the vehicle, and support securely on axle stands (see "*Jacking and vehicle support*"). If the vehicle is jacked up, the relevant trailing arm **must be** supported with a jack as the vehicle is raised, to prevent the trailing arm being forced down by the coil spring.
4 Unscrew and remove the bolt securing the lower end of the shock absorber to the trailing arm **(see illustration)**.
5 Compress the shock absorber by hand, if necessary prising the lower end to free it from the trailing arm.
6 Withdraw the shock absorber from under the vehicle, and recover the remaining mounting rubber and the spacer sleeve from the top of the shock absorber.

Inspection

7 Examine the shock absorber mounting rubbers for wear or damage, and renew if necessary.
8 The shock absorber can be tested by clamping the lower mounting eye in a vice, then fully extending and compressing the shock absorber several times. Any evidence of jerky movement or lack of resistance indicates the need for renewal.

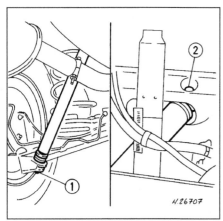

12.14 Rear shock absorber mountings - Estate and Van models

1 Lower mounting   *2 Upper mounting*

Refitting

9 Refitting is a reversal of removal, but tighten the shock absorber lower mounting bolt to the specified torque.

Estate and Van models

Removal

10 On models with manual rear suspension level control, depressurise the system by releasing the air through the valve in the luggage compartment.
11 Proceed as described in paragraph 3.
12 Where applicable, disconnect the manual suspension level control air line from the shock absorber.
13 Counterhold the shock absorber piston rod, and unscrew the shock absorber lower mounting nut from the trailing arm. Remove the washer and the upper mounting rubber.
14 Unscrew and remove the bolt securing the upper end of the shock absorber to the vehicle underbody **(see illustration)**.
15 Compress the shock absorber by hand, if necessary prising the upper end to free it from the body.
16 Withdraw the shock absorber from under the vehicle, and recover the remaining mounting rubber and the spacer sleeve from the lower end of the shock absorber.

Inspection

17 Proceed as described in paragraphs 7 and 8, but clamp the upper mounting eye in the vice when testing the shock absorber.

Refitting

18 Refitting is a reversal of removal, remembering the following points.
19 Where applicable, ensure that the shock absorber is fitted with the air line union facing the correct way round.
20 Tighten the shock absorber upper mounting bolt to the specified torque.
21 On models with manual rear suspension level control, pressurise the system to 0.8 bars, and check for air leaks.

13 Rear shock absorber mounting rubbers - renewal

Note: *Only one shock absorber should be disconnected at a time.*

Saloon and Hatchback models

1 The mounting bush in the shock absorber lower eye is not available separately, and if worn or damaged, the complete shock absorber must be renewed.
2 The shock absorber upper mounting rubbers can be renewed without removing the shock absorber as follows.
3 Proceed as described in Section 12, paragraphs 1 and 2.
4 With the roadwheels resting on the ground, jack up the rear of the vehicle slightly, to enable the shock absorber to be compressed

sufficiently by hand to release the top mounting from the body.
5 Remove the remaining mounting rubber from the top of the shock absorber.
6 Fit the new mounting rubbers using a reversal of the removal procedure.

Estate and Van models

7 The mounting bush in the shock absorber upper eye is not available separately, and if worn or damaged, the complete shock absorber must be renewed.
8 The shock absorber lower mounting rubbers can be renewed without removing the shock absorber as follows.
9 On models with manual rear suspension level control, depressurise the system by releasing the air through the valve in the luggage compartment.
10 Counterhold the shock absorber piston rod, and unscrew the shock absorber lower mounting nut from the trailing arm. Remove the washer and mounting rubber.
11 Compress the shock absorber by hand sufficiently to release the lower end from the trailing arm.
12 Remove the remaining mounting rubber and the spacer sleeve from the lower end of the shock absorber.
13 Fit the new mounting rubbers using a reversal of the removal procedure.
14 On models with manual rear suspension level control, pressurise the system to 0.8 bars on completion.

14 Rear suspension coil spring - removal and refitting

Note: *Due to the design of the rear suspension, it is important to note that only one coil spring should be removed at a time. Note that the rear springs should be renewed in pairs, and if the springs are to be renewed, it is advisable to renew the spring damping rubbers at the same time.*

Removal

1 On models with manual rear suspension level control, depressurise the system by releasing the air through the valve in the luggage compartment.
2 Chock the front wheels, then jack up the rear of the vehicle, and support securely on axle stands (see "*Jacking and vehicle support*").
3 Raise the relevant trailing arm slightly using a jack.
4 Unscrew and remove the bolt and washer securing the lower end of the shock absorber to the trailing arm, and free the lower end of the shock absorber.
5 Carefully lower the jack supporting the trailing arm, and remove the coil spring and its damping rubbers. Lever the trailing arm downwards slightly if necessary to remove the spring.

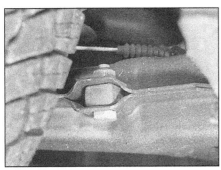

15.3 Rear anti-roll bar securing nut and bolt

15.5 Rear anti-roll bar insulation rubber (arrowed)

15.12 Additional rear anti-roll bar securing bolts (arrowed)

Refitting

6 Refitting is a reversal of removal, remembering the following points.
7 Ensure that the spring locates correctly on the trailing arm and the underbody.
8 Tighten the shock absorber lower mounting bolt to the specified torque.
9 If the springs are to be renewed, repeat the procedure on the remaining side of the vehicle.
10 On models with manual rear suspension level control, pressurise the system to 0.8 bars on completion.

15 Rear anti-roll bar(s) - removal and refitting

Main anti-roll bar

Note: *New anti-roll bar securing nuts and bolts must be used on refitting.*

Removal

1 On all models fitted with a rear anti-roll bar, the anti-roll bar is located inside the rear suspension torsion beam. On some models, an additional rear anti-roll bar is fitted, which is bolted to the exterior of the torsion beam - removal and refitting is described in the following sub-Section.
2 Chock the front wheels, then jack up the rear of the vehicle, and support securely on axle stands (see *"Jacking and vehicle support"*). Remove one of the rear roadwheels.
3 Working at one end of the anti-roll bar, counterhold the securing bolt, while unscrewing the securing nut (see illustration).
4 Repeat the procedure for the remaining securing nut at the other end of the anti-roll bar.
5 Prise the anti-roll bar insulation rubber from the centre of the torsion beam (see illustration).
6 Working at the side of the vehicle from which the wheel has been removed, draw the anti-roll bar out through the end of the torsion beam.

Refitting

7 Refitting is a reversal of removal, remembering the following points.
8 To ease refitting, lightly coat the anti-roll bar with a lubricant, such as light oil.

9 Ensure that the insulation rubber is correctly refitted to the centre of the torsion beam.
10 Use new anti-roll bar securing nuts and bolts. Counterhold the securing nuts, while tightening the bolts in the three stages given in the Specifications.

Additional anti-roll bar

Note: *New anti-roll bar securing nuts and bolts must be used on refitting.*

Removal

11 To improve access, chock the front wheels, then jack up the rear of the vehicle, and support securely on axle stands (see *"Jacking and vehicle support"*).
12 Unscrew the four securing bolts - two at each end of the anti-roll bar (see illustration) while counter-holding the nuts, and lower the anti-roll bar from the torsion beam.

Refitting

13 Refitting is a reversal of removal, but use new securing nuts and bolts. Counterhold the securing nuts, while tightening the bolts in the three stages given in the Specifications.

16 Rear suspension torsion beam/trailing arms assembly - removal and refitting

Removal

1 Chock the front wheels, then jack up the rear of the vehicle, and support securely on axle stands (see *"Jacking and vehicle support"*). Remove the rear roadwheels.
2 On models with manual rear suspension level control, depressurise the system by releasing the air through the valve in the luggage compartment.
3 On models with a catalytic converter, unbolt and remove the exhaust centre box heat shield.
4 Note the length of exposed thread on the now-exposed handbrake cable adjuster, then remove the adjuster nut to enable the cable bracket to be disconnected from the handbrake lever operating rod.
5 Release the handbrake cables from the brackets on the underbody.

6 Working in the engine compartment, remove the filler cap from the brake hydraulic fluid reservoir, then place a piece of polythene across the top of the reservoir filler hole, and refit the filler cap. This will minimise fluid loss when the brake lines are disconnected.
7 Disconnect the flexible hoses from the rigid brake pipes at the front edge of each trailing arm. Be prepared for fluid loss, and plug the open ends of the pipes and hoses, to prevent dirt ingress and further fluid loss.
8 Where applicable, disconnect the wiring plugs from the ABS wheel sensors, and release the wiring from the brackets on the trailing arms.
9 On Estate and Van models, disconnect the brake pressure-regulating valve spring from the bracket on the torsion beam.
10 Loosen, but do not remove, the nuts and bolts securing the front ends of the trailing arms to the vehicle underbody (see illustration).
11 Support the torsion beam with a trolley jack and interposed block of wood. Position the jack securely under the centre of the torsion beam.
12 On Saloon and Hatchback models, unscrew and remove the bolts securing the lower ends of the shock absorbers to the trailing arms.
13 On Estate and Van models, counterhold the shock absorber piston rods, and unscrew the nuts securing the lower ends of the shock absorbers to the trailing arms.
14 Gently lower the jack supporting the torsion beam, until the coil springs can be

16.10 Trailing arm-to-underbody securing nut (arrowed) viewed through rear wheel arch

removed. Remove the coil springs, referring to Section 14 if necessary.

15 Ensure that the torsion beam is adequately supported, then remove the nuts and bolts securing the front ends of the trailing arms to the vehicle underbody. The help of an assistant will greatly ease this task - ensure that the torsion beam does not slip off the jack.

16 Withdraw the torsion beam/trailing arms assembly from under the rear of the vehicle.

17 If desired, the brake components can be removed from the trailing arms, referring to the relevant Sections of Chapter 9. The hub units can be removed referring to Section 11, and where applicable, the anti-roll bar(s) can be removed with reference to Section 15.

18 If necessary, the trailing arm bushes can be renewed, referring to Section 17.

Refitting

19 Start reassembly by refitting any components that were removed from the torsion beam/trailing arms assembly, referring to the relevant Sections of this Chapter and/or Chapter 9, as applicable.

20 Support the torsion beam/trailing arms assembly on the trolley jack, and position the assembly under the rear of the vehicle.

21 Raise the jack, and fit the bolts and nuts that secure the front ends of the trailing arms to the underbody. Do not fully tighten the fixings at this stage.

22 Refit the coil springs, referring to Section 14 if necessary.

23 Raise the rear ends of the trailing arms, and refit the bolts or nuts, as applicable, securing the lower ends of the shock absorbers to the trailing arms. Tighten the fixings to the specified torque, counter-holding the shock absorber piston rod on Estate and Van models. Withdraw the jack from under the rear of the vehicle.

24 Where applicable, reconnect the ABS wheel sensor wiring, and refit the wiring to the brackets on the trailing arms.

25 Remove the plugs from the brake pipes and hoses, and reconnect the unions.

26 Refit the handbrake cables to the brackets on the underbody, then reconnect the handbrake cable bracket to the handbrake lever operating rod.

27 Fit a new handbrake cable adjuster nut, and screw the nut onto the rod to the position noted before removal. Check the handbrake adjustment, as described in Chapter 9.

28 On models with a catalytic converter, refit the exhaust centre box heat shield.

29 On Estate and Van models, reconnect the brake pressure-regulating valve spring to the bracket on the torsion beam.

30 Refit the roadwheels, and lower the vehicle to the ground.

31 On models with manual rear suspension level control, pressurise the system to 0.8 bar.

32 Remove the chocks from the front wheels.

33 Ensure that the vehicle is parked on level ground, then with the equivalent of a load of 70.0 kg in each front seat, 'bounce' the vehicle to settle the suspension.

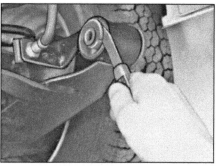

17.10 Cutting the inner flange from a trailing arm bush

34 Without disturbing the position of the vehicle, place chocks at the front and rear edges of the front wheels, to prevent the vehicle from moving.

35 Working under the rear of the vehicle, tighten the fixings securing the front ends of the trailing arms to the underbody to the specified torque.

36 Finally, recheck the handbrake cable adjustment, then remove the polythene from beneath the brake hydraulic fluid reservoir cap, and bleed the complete brake hydraulic system, as described in Chapter 9.

37 On Estate and Van models, check the adjustment of the brake pressure-regulating valve, as described in Chapter 1.

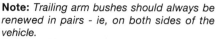

17 Rear suspension trailing arm bushes - renewal

Note: *Trailing arm bushes should always be renewed in pairs - ie, on both sides of the vehicle.*

1 The trailing arm bushes can be renewed without removing the torsion beam/trailing arms assembly from the vehicle, as follows.

2 Chock the front wheels, then jack up the rear of the vehicle, and support securely on axle stands (see *"Jacking and vehicle support"*). Remove the rear roadwheels.

3 On models with manual rear suspension level control, depressurise the system by releasing the air through the valve in the luggage compartment.

4 On Estate and Van models, disconnect the brake pressure-regulating valve spring from the bracket on the torsion beam.

5 Unclip the flexible hoses and the rear ends of the rigid brake pipes from the vehicle underbody. Also unclip the handbrake cables and ABS sensor wiring, where applicable.

6 Support the torsion beam with a trolley jack and interposed block of wood. Position the jack under the centre of the torsion beam.

7 Unscrew and remove the nuts and bolts securing the trailing arms to the underbody.

8 Gently lower the jack until the trailing arm bushes are accessible, then support the torsion beam on axle stands (see *"Jacking and vehicle support"*). Take care not to strain the brake pipes.

9 A special Vauxhall/Opel tool is available for removal and refitting of the bushes, but an alternative can be improvised using a long bolt, nut, washers, and a length of metal tubing or a socket.

10 Where applicable, before removing a bush, cut the flange from the inner end of the bush using a sharp knife **(see illustration)**.

11 Removal of the bush will be made easier if the bush housing in the trailing arm is heated to approximately 70°C using a heat gun or a hairdryer. **Do not** use a naked flame, due to the close proximity of the fuel tank.

12 Draw the bush from the trailing arm using the tool described in paragraph 9.

13 Lubricate the new bush with a little soapy water, then draw it into position, ensuring that the narrow part of the bush points upwards.

14 Repeat the procedure on the remaining trailing arm.

15 Raise the torsion beam using the jack, and fit the bolts and nuts that secure the front ends of the trailing arms to the underbody. Do not fully tighten the fixings at this stage. Withdraw the axle stands (see *"Jacking and vehicle support"*).

16 Clip the rigid brake pipes and the flexible hoses to the vehicle underbody.

17 On Estate and Van models, reconnect the brake pressure-regulating valve spring to the bracket on the torsion beam.

18 Proceed as described in Section 16, paragraphs 30 to 35 inclusive.

19 On Estate and Van models, check the adjustment of the brake pressure-regulating valve, as described in Chapter 1.

18 Rear suspension level control system – general information

The suspension level control system is manually operated, and the level is adjusted by altering the air pressure in the rear shock absorbers, through a valve located in the luggage compartment.

For safety reasons, if the vehicle is to be driven fully loaded, the level control system must not be fully pressurised with the vehicle in the unladen condition.

To adjust the system, continue as follows.

With the vehicle unladen, use a tyre pressure gauge on the air valve to check that the system pressure is 0.8 bar. Adjust if necessary.

With the vehicle standing on a level surface, measure the distance from the centre of the rear bumper to the ground. Subtract 50.0 mm from the distance measured, and note the new value.

Load the vehicle, and if necessary increase the pressure in the system until the noted value for the bumper height is reached. Do not exceed a pressure of 5.0 bars.

After unloading the vehicle, depressurise the system to the minimum pressure of 0.8 bar.

Do not drive an unladen vehicle with the system fully pressurised.

19 Rear suspension level control system components - removal and refitting

Air valve

Removal

1 Working in the luggage compartment, pull back the floor covering for access to the air valve.
2 Fully depressurise the system.
3 Remove the cap and retaining sleeve from the valve, then compress the retaining lugs and push the valve downwards, taking care not to damage the air lines **(see illustration)**.
4 Unscrew the air line unions from the valve, and then withdraw the valve from the vehicle.

Refitting

5 Refitting is a reversal of removal, but on completion, pressurise the system and check for air leaks.

Air lines

Removal

6 To remove an air line, first fully depressurise the system.
7 Unscrew the unions at the shock absorber and air valve, then release the air line from the clips on the vehicle underbody.

Refitting

8 Refitting is a reversal of removal, but on completion, pressurise the system and check for air leaks.

Shock absorbers

9 Removal and refitting of the shock absorbers is covered in Section 12.

20 Steering wheel - removal and refitting

Models without driver's airbag

Note: *A two-legged puller will be required for this operation.*

Removal

1 Disconnect the battery negative lead.
2 Set the front wheels in the straight-ahead position, and unless it is unavoidable, do not move them until the steering wheel has been refitted.
3 Prise the horn push pad from the centre of the steering wheel, and disconnect the wiring.
4 Using a screwdriver, prise back the tabs on the lockwasher securing the steering wheel retaining nut.
5 Unscrew and remove the steering wheel retaining nut and the lockwasher.
6 Make alignment marks between the steering wheel and the end of the column shaft.
7 A small two-legged puller must now be fitted to the steering wheel to pull it from the

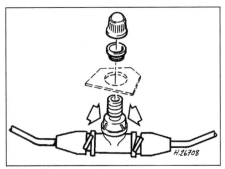

19.3 Rear suspension level control system air valve. Compress retaining lugs (arrowed) to remove valve

column shaft. Note that the steering wheel is a very tight fit on the shaft.

Refitting

8 Begin refitting by gently tapping the steering wheel into position on the column shaft, using a metal tube or socket, and ensuring that the marks made before removal are aligned. Before tapping the wheel fully home, check the centralisation, as described in Section 21.
9 Refit the lockwasher and the steering wheel retaining nut, and tighten the nut to the specified torque. Bend up the lockwasher tabs to secure the nut.
10 Refit the horn push pad, ensuring that the wiring is securely connected, and reconnect the battery negative lead.

Models with driver's airbag

Note: *Read the precautions given in Chapter 12, Section 30, before starting work. A two-legged puller will be required for this operation.*

Removal

11 Remove the driver's airbag unit as described in Chapter 12.
12 Remove the steering column shrouds, as described in Chapter 11, Section 32.
13 Remove the cable-tie and disconnect the plug connection for the airbag contact unit and horn.
14 Ensure that the front wheels are in the straight ahead position.

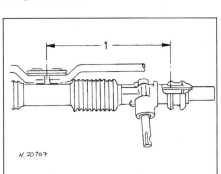

21.1a Steering gear centralised for setting of steering wheel straight-ahead position - right-hand-drive shown

1 = 325.0 mm

15 Proceed as described in paragraphs 4 to 7. Note that the steering wheel is removed complete with the airbag contact unit.

Refitting

16 Proceed as described in paragraphs 8 and 9.
17 Reconnect the plug connection for the airbag contact unit and the horn, and secure with a new cable-tie. Ensure that the wiring loom is routed below the ignition switch.
18 Refit the steering column shrouds.
19 Refit the airbag unit as described in Chapter 12.

21 Steering wheel - centralising

1 The steering straight-ahead position is achieved when the reference dimension between the centre of the tie-rod-to-steering gear bolt locking plate(s), and the centre of the rib on the right-hand steering gear mounting clamp (right-hand-drive models), or the left-hand steering gear mounting clamp (left-hand-drive models), as applicable, is as shown. In this position, the flexible rubber coupling upper pinch-bolt should lie horizontally on top of the steering shaft **(see illustrations)**.
2 Check that the steering wheel is centralised.
3 If the steering wheel is off-centre by more than 5°, it should be removed, then moved the required number of splines on the column shaft to achieve centralisation, and refitted as described in Section 20.

22 Steering column lock - removal and refitting

Removal

1 Disconnect the battery negative lead.
2 Remove the steering column shrouds, as described in Chapter 11, Section 32.
3 Insert the ignition key into the ignition switch, and turn it to position 'II'.

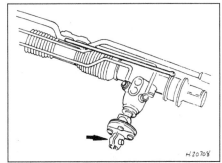

21.1b Flexible coupling upper pinch-bolt alignment (arrowed) with steering gear centralised - right-hand-drive shown

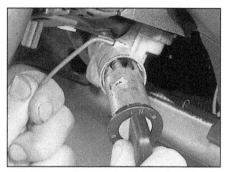

22.4 Removing the steering column lock cylinder

4 Insert a thin rod into the hole in the lock housing, then press the rod to release the detent spring, and pull out the lock cylinder using the key **(see illustration)**.

5 Removal and refitting of the lock housing is described in Section 24 as part of the steering column dismantling and reassembly procedure.

Refitting

6 Where applicable refit the lock housing as described in Section 24.

7 Refit the lock cylinder, with the key in position 'II' by simply pushing it into position in the housing. Turn the key back to position '0', and remove it.

8 Further refitting is a reversal of removal.

23 Steering column - removal and refitting

Removal

Note: *A bolt/stud extractor will be required for this operation. A new shear-head bolt must be used on refitting.*

1 Disconnect the battery negative lead.

2 Set the front wheels in the straight-ahead position.

3 Working in the drivers footwell, release the securing clips and remove the lower trim panel.

4 Remove the steering wheel as described in Section 20, for improved access.

5 Remove the steering column lock as described in Section 22.

6 Depress the retaining clips release the two stalk switches from the steering column, then disconnect the wiring plugs and withdraw the switches.

7 Unclip the fusebox cover and unclip the blanking cover from the aperture in the facia panel below the steering column.

8 Working at the lower end of the steering shaft, unscrew and remove the upper pinch-bolt securing the steering shaft to the flexible rubber coupling **(see illustration)**.

9 Locate the plastic disc that should be fitted loosely to the lower end of the steering shaft and push it up the shaft until it engages with the steering column tube.

10 Using a socket and extension bar, unscrew the bolt securing the steering column to the facia bracket **(see illustration)**.

11 Two fixings must now be extracted from the column upper mounting bracket. A conventional nut is used on one side of the column (the left-hand side on right-hand-drive models, or the right-hand side on left-hand-drive models) and a shear-head type bolt is used on the remaining side.

12 The shear-head type bolt must be removed by centre-punching, drilling off the head and then using a bolt/stud extractor. When drilling the bolt take care not to damage the facia panel **(see illustration)**.

13 Withdraw the column assembly into the vehicle interior and then remove it from the vehicle. Handle the column carefully avoiding knocks or impact of any kind, which may damage the collapsible section of the column.

14 If desired, the column can be dismantled as described in Section 24.

Refitting

15 Begin refitting by ensuring that the roadwheels are still in the straight-ahead position and that the plastic disc on the steering shaft is engaged with the column tube.

16 The flexible coupling should be positioned so that the upper pinch-bolt will be horizontal on top of the steering shaft.

17 Offer the column into position and reconnect the flexible coupling. Refit the pinch-bolt, but do not fully tighten it at this stage.

18 Loosely fit the upper mounting fixings using a new shear-head bolt.

19 Refit the bolt securing the steering column to the facia bracket and tighten to the specified torque.

20 Tighten the upper mounting fixings. The shear-head bolt should be tightened until the head breaks off and the conventional nut should be tightened to the specified torque.

21 Pull upwards on the steering shaft until the shaft contacts the bearing stop then tighten the flexible coupling upper pinch-bolt.

22 Prise the plastic centring disc from the base of the column tube and leave it loose on the steering shaft.

23 Further refitting is a reversal of the removal procedure. Refit the steering wheel as described in Section 20.

24 On completion, first manoeuvre the vehicle at low speed, then carry out a test drive along a route with several corners and check that the steering mechanism operates smoothly.

24 Steering column - dismantling and reassembly

Dismantling

1 If the steering column is in position in the vehicle, continue as described in Section 22 paragraphs 1 to 4 inclusive.

2 Prise out the ignition switch housing safety plugs, then turn the housing anti-clockwise, and pull it from the steering column.

3 The bearing can be removed from the ignition switch housing by prising apart the two bearing fixing catches, and pressing or driving out the bearing with a piece of tubing on the bearing outer race. When pressing in the new bearing, make sure that the thrustwasher and contact springs are correctly located **(see illustration)**.

4 The ignition switch is secured to the lock housing by two grub screws. Remove the screws to extract the switch. It is recommended that the switch and the lock cylinder are not both removed at the same time, otherwise their mutual alignment will be lost **(see illustration)**.

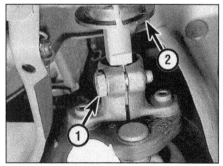

23.8 Steering shaft flexible rubber coupling pinch-bolt (1) and plastic disc (2)

23.10 Steering column-to-facia bracket securing bolt (arrowed) viewed through instrument panel aperture

23.12 Drilling out the steering column shear-head bolt - right-hand-drive model

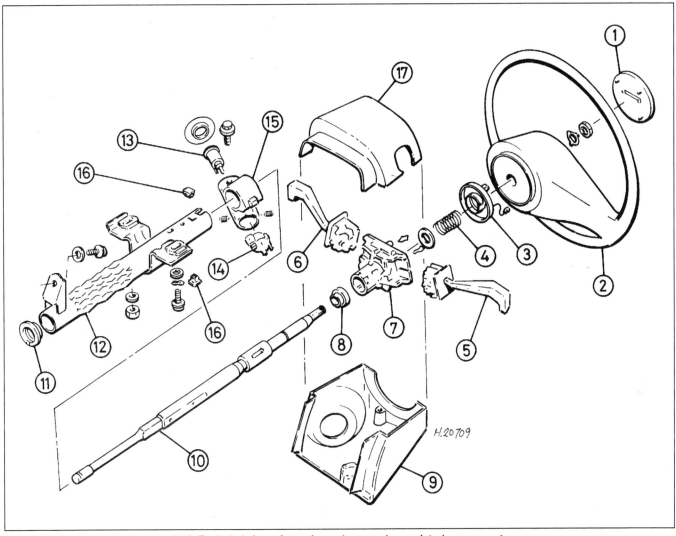

24.3 Exploded view of steering column and associated components

1 Horn push pad	6 Wash/wipe switch	11 Centralising plastic	15 Lock housing
2 Steering wheel	7 Switch housing	disc	16 Switch housing safety
3 Cam assembly	8 Bearing	12 Column tube	plugs
4 Spring	9 Lower column shroud	13 Lock barrel	17 Upper column shroud
5 Lighting switch	10 Steering shaft	14 Lock barrel	

5 If the steering column is in position in the vehicle, unscrew and remove the upper pinch-bolt from the steering shaft flexible coupling in the driver's footwell.

6 Withdraw the steering shaft from the steering column tube.

Reassembly

7 Begin reassembly by fitting the plastic centring disc, which will be supplied with a new column or steering shaft, into the base of the column tube.

8 Insert the shaft into the column tube, and if the column is in position in the vehicle, engage the bottom end of the shaft with the flexible coupling and refit the upper pinch-bolt, but do not tighten it at this stage.

9 Where applicable, refit the ignition switch, and tighten the grub screws.

10 Refit the ignition switch housing, using new safety plugs.

11 If the column is in position in the vehicle, pull upwards on the steering shaft until the shaft contacts the bearing stop, then tighten the flexible coupling upper pinch-bolt. Ensure that the roadwheels are in the straight-ahead position, and that the flexible coupling is positioned so that the upper pinch-bolt is horizontal on top of the steering shaft.

12 Where applicable, further reassembly is a reversal of dismantling. Refit the steering wheel, as described in Section 20.

13 On completion, first manoeuvre the vehicle at low speed, then carry out a test drive along a route with several corners, and check that the steering mechanism operates smoothly.

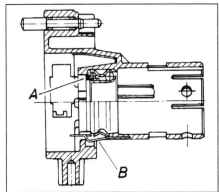

24.4 Sectional view of ignition switch housing

A Thrustwasher   B Contact springs

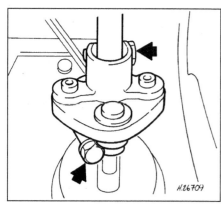

25.3 Steering shaft flexible rubber coupling pinch-bolts (arrowed)

25 Steering shaft flexible rubber coupling - renewal

1 Set the front wheels in the straight-ahead position.
2 Working in the driver's footwell, release the securing clips, and remove the lower trim panel.
3 Unscrew and remove the two pinch-bolts securing the rubber coupling to the steering shaft and the steering gear pinion shaft **(see illustration)**.
4 Unscrew the bolts securing the steering gear to the bulkhead in the engine compartment, then move the steering gear away from the bulkhead sufficiently to disconnect the coupling from the steering gear pinion.
5 Pull the coupling from the steering shaft, noting which way round it is fitted.
6 Check that the steering wheel and the front wheels are still in the straight-ahead position.
7 Fit the coupling to the steering gear pinion, and tighten the clamp bolt.
8 Push the steering gear back into position on the bulkhead, ensure that the steering shaft engages with the coupling, then tighten the steering gear securing bolts to the specified torque.
9 Pull upwards on the steering shaft until the shaft contacts the bearing stop, then tighten the flexible coupling upper pinch-bolt.
10 Check that the steering wheel is centralised, as described in Section 21.

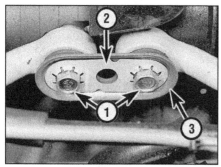

27.6 Tie-rod-to-steering gear bolts (1), locking plate (2) and spacer plate (3)

26 Steering gear rubber bellows - renewal

Note: *New bellows securing clips will be required when refitting.*
1 Remove the steering gear, as described in Section 27.
2 Remove the mounting clamp and rubber from the left-hand end of the steering gear on right-hand-drive models, or from the right-hand end of the steering gear on left-hand-drive models, as applicable.
3 On power steering gear, disconnect the fluid pipe unions from the left-hand end of the steering gear (right-hand-drive models), or the right-hand end of the steering gear (left-hand-drive models).
4 Remove the outer bellows securing clips from each end of the steering gear, then slide off the bellows/tube assembly.
5 Remove the inner bellows securing clips, and separate the bellows from the tube.
6 Fit the new bellows to the tube, using new clips. The clips should be positioned so that when the steering gear is fitted to the vehicle, the ends of the clips point upwards.
7 Fit the bellows/tube assembly to the steering gear, and secure with new clips, again positioned with the ends of the clips pointing upwards. Ensure that the bellows are not twisted.
8 On power steering gear, reconnect the fluid pipe unions, using new O-rings.
9 Refit the mounting clamp and rubber, then refit the steering gear, as described in Section 27.

27 Steering gear - removal and refitting

Note: *New steering gear-to-bulkhead bolts, and a new tie-rod-to-steering gear locking plate must be used on refitting. On models with power steering, the fluid hose-to-pipe O-ring(s) must be renewed on refitting.*

Removal

1 Disconnect the battery negative lead.

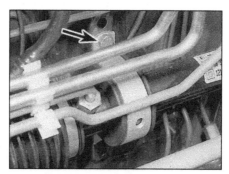

27.10 Steering gear clamp bolt (arrowed) - model with power steering

2 Set the front wheels in the straight-ahead position.
3 Where applicable, remove the airbox from the top of the carburettor or throttle body (see Chapter 4A or 4B, as applicable).
4 Remove the coolant expansion tank, as described in Chapter 3. On certain models, it may be possible to move the expansion tank sufficiently to allow access for removal of the steering gear without disconnecting the hoses.
5 Where applicable, disconnect the wiring harness from the anti-theft alarm switch on the left-hand suspension turret, and move the harness clear of the steering gear. Alternatively, the switch can be removed.
6 Prise the locking plate from the tie-rod-to-steering gear bolts, then unscrew and remove the bolts, and recover the washers and spacer plate **(see illustration)**.
7 On models with power steering, disconnect the fluid hoses from the pipes at the left-hand side of the engine compartment (next to the coolant expansion tank location). Recover the O-ring(s) where applicable. Be prepared for fluid spillage, and plug the open ends of the pipes and hoses to prevent dirt ingress and further fluid loss.
8 Working in the driver's footwell, release the securing clips, and remove the lower trim panel.
9 Unscrew and remove the upper pinch-bolt securing the steering shaft to the flexible rubber coupling.
10 Working in the engine compartment, unbolt the two clamps securing the steering gear to the bulkhead **(see illustration)**. Then push the right-hand end of the steering gear through the large rubber grommet in the right-hand wheel arch, and manipulate the steering gear upwards out of the engine compartment. The help of an assistant may be required to release the flexible rubber coupling from the steering shaft as the steering gear is withdrawn. Note that on some models, various wires and hoses may be secured to the steering gear with cable ties - ensure that, where applicable, all wires and hoses are freed before the steering gear is removed.

Refitting

11 Refitting is a reversal of removal, remembering the following points.
12 Use new mounting bolts to secure the steering gear clamps to the bulkhead.
13 Reconnect the flexible rubber-coupling to the steering shaft (with the rack and steering wheel centralised) so that the upper pinch-bolt lies horizontally on top of the steering shaft (see illustration 21.1b).
14 On models with power steering, renew the O-ring(s) when reconnecting the fluid hoses to the pipes.
15 The tie-rod-to-steering gear locking plate must be renewed on refitting.
16 Where applicable, after refitting the expansion tank, top-up the coolant level as described in "Weekly checks".

30.3 Removing the power steering pump pulley – 1.6 litre engine with 'V' drivebelt

30.6a Unscrewing the power steering pump fluid pipe union (arrowed) – 1.6 litre engine with 'V' drivebelt

30.6b Power steering pump fluid pipe and hose ends covered to prevent dirt ingress and fluid loss

17 On models with power steering, on completion, bleed the hydraulic system, as described in Section 29.

18 On completion, check the steering wheel centralisation, as described in Section 21.

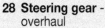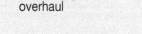

28 Steering gear - overhaul

Manual steering gear

1 Examine the steering gear assembly for signs of wear or damage. Check that the rack moves freely throughout the full length of its travel, with no signs of roughness or excessive free play between the steering gear pinion and rack. It is possible to overhaul the steering gear assembly housing components, but this task should be entrusted to a Vauxhall/Opel dealer.

2 The only components which can be renewed easily by the home mechanic are the steering gear rubber bellows, the tie-rod balljoints and the tie-rods (see Sections 26, 33 and 34 respectively).

Power steering gear

3 Overhaul of the power steering gear is not recommended by the manufacturers, and no adjustment should be attempted.

4 Fluid leaks from the hydraulic fluid pipe unions can normally be corrected by renewing the union seals with the rack installed.

5 Rubber bellows renewal is covered in Section 26.

6 Any faults with the steering gear should be referred to a Vauxhall/Opel dealer, although renewal of the complete assembly will probably be the only course of action available.

29 Power steering hydraulic system - bleeding

1 With the engine stopped, initially fill the reservoir to the level of the 'MAX' mark on the dipstick attached to the reservoir filler cap.

2 Start the engine, and immediately top-up

the fluid level to the 'MIN' mark on the dipstick. **Do not** allow the reservoir to run dry at any time. The help of an assistant will ease this operation.

3 With the engine running at idle speed, turn the steering wheel slowly two or three times approximately 45° to the left and right of the centre, then turn the wheel twice from lock to lock. Do not hold the wheel on either lock, as this imposes strain on the hydraulic system.

4 Stop the engine, and check the fluid level. With the fluid at operating temperature (80°C), the level should be on the 'MAX' mark, and with the fluid cold (20°C), the level should be on the 'MIN' mark. Top-up if necessary.

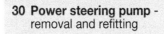

30 Power steering pump - removal and refitting

1.4 and 1.6 litre engine models, with 'V' power steering pump drivebelt

Note: A new fluid pipe union O-ring must be used on refitting.

Removal

1 For improved access, remove the air cleaner casing from the right-hand front wing panel, as described in Chapter 4A or 4B.

2 Remove the power steering pump drivebelt, as described in Chapter 1.

3 Counterhold the power steering pump pulley, using an old drivebelt, then unscrew

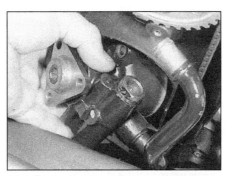

30.7 Removing the power steering pump – 1.6 litre engine with 'V' drivebelt

the three pulley securing bolts, and remove the pulley (see illustration).

4 To improve access, remove the upper outer timing belt cover, as described in Chapter 2A or 2B, as applicable.

5 Unscrew and remove the securing bolts, and carefully manipulate the pump from its location.

6 Have ready a suitable container to catch escaping fluid, then disconnect the fluid pipe union and the flexible fluid hose from the pump. Be prepared for fluid spillage, and plug or cover the open ends of the pump, pipe and hose, to prevent dirt ingress and further fluid loss (see illustrations).

7 Withdraw the pump from the engine compartment. Take care not to damage the bodywork, as there is very little clearance to withdraw the pump (see illustration).

8 No overhaul of the pump is possible, and if faulty, a new unit must be fitted.

Refitting

9 Refitting is a reversal of removal, but renew the O-ring when reconnecting the fluid pipe union (see illustration), and refit and tension the power steering pump drivebelt, as described in Chapter 1.

10 On completion, top-up the power steering fluid level (see "Weekly checks"), and bleed the fluid circuit as described in Section 29.

Models with 'ribbed' power steering pump drivebelt

Note: A new fluid pipe union O-ring must be used on refitting.

30.9 Renew the power steering pump fluid pipe O-ring (arrowed) on refitting

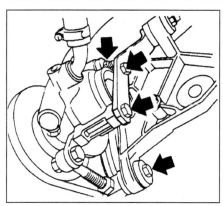

30.14 Power steering pump mounting bolts (arrowed) - SOHC ribbed V-belt model

Removal

11 On SOHC engine models, for improved access to the pump, apply the handbrake, then jack up the front of the vehicle and support securely on axle stands (see "*Jacking and vehicle support*").

12 Proceed as described in paragraphs 1 and 2.

13 Have ready a suitable container to catch escaping fluid, then disconnect the fluid pipe union and the flexible fluid hose from the pump. Be prepared for fluid spillage, and plug or cover the open ends of the pump, pipe and hose, to prevent dirt ingress and further fluid loss.

14 Unscrew and remove the securing bolts, and carefully manipulate the pump from its location **(see illustration)**. Remove the pump downwards for SOHC engine models, or upwards for DOHC engine models.

15 No overhaul of the pump is possible, and if faulty, a new unit must be fitted.

Refitting

16 Proceed as described in paragraphs 9 and 10.

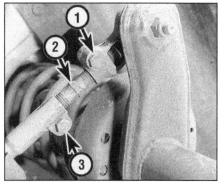

33.2 Tie-rod end viewed from underneath

1 Tie-rod end clamp bolt
2 Threaded adjuster pin
3 Tie-rod clamp bolt

32.3 Power steering fluid cooler pipes (arrowed) viewed from underneath vehicle

31 Power steering fluid reservoir - removal and refitting

Removal

1 The reservoir can be removed from the mounting bracket by unscrewing the clamp screw and removing the clamp.

2 Have a container ready to catch the fluid, then disconnect the fluid hoses from the reservoir, and drain the fluid. Plug the open ends of the hoses, to prevent dirt ingress and further fluid loss.

3 If desired, the mounting bracket can be unbolted from the body panel, but note that on certain models, the bolts securing the bracket also secure the ignition coil and suppressor - refer to Chapter 3 if necessary. Where applicable, unclip the brake fluid pipes and any wiring from the bracket before removal.

Refitting

4 Refitting is a reversal of removal, but on completion, bleed the fluid circuit, as described in Section 29.

32 Power steering fluid cooler pipes - removal and refitting

Note: *New fluid pipe union O-rings must be used on refitting.*

Removal

1 For improved access, apply the handbrake, then jack up the front of the vehicle, and support securely on axle stands (see "*Jacking and vehicle support*").

2 Where applicable, remove the engine undershield, as described in Chapter 11, Section 25.

3 Disconnect the fluid cooler pipe unions **(see illustration)**. Be prepared for fluid spillage, and plug the open ends of the pipes, to prevent dirt ingress and further fluid loss. Recover the O-rings.

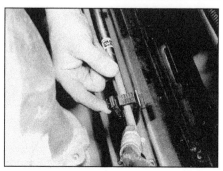

32.4 Releasing a power steering fluid cooler pipe securing clip (viewed from above with radiator removed)

4 Release the three plastic clips securing the pipes to the lower body panel **(see illustration)**, then manipulate the pipes from the engine compartment.

Refitting

5 Refitting is a reversal of removal, but renew the O-rings when reconnecting the fluid pipe unions.

6 On completion, top-up the fluid level, and bleed the fluid circuit as described in Section 29.

33 Tie-rod end/balljoint - removal and refitting

Note: *A balljoint separator tool will be required for this operation. A new tie-rod end balljoint nut must be used on refitting.*

Removal

1 Apply the handbrake, then jack up the front of the vehicle and support securely on axle stands (see "*Jacking and vehicle support*"). Remove the relevant front roadwheel.

2 Loosen the tie-rod end clamp bolt, which secures the tie-rod end to the threaded adjuster pin on the tie-rod **(see illustration)**.

3 Unscrew the self-locking nut from the tie-rod end-to-suspension strut balljoint.

4 Using a balljoint separator tool, disconnect the tie-rod end-to-suspension strut balljoint **(see illustration)**.

33.4 Using a balljoint separator tool to disconnect the tie-rod end-to-suspension strut balljoint

5 Note the position of the tie-rod end on the adjuster pin, either by marking the pin with paint or tape, or by counting the number of threads exposed, then unscrew the tie-rod end from the tie-rod.

6 Note that the tie-rod ends are 'handed'. The right-hand tie-rod end is marked 'R', but the left-hand tie-rod end has no marking.

Refitting

7 Begin refitting by screwing the tie-rod end onto the adjuster pin to approximately the same position as was noted during removal.

8 Reconnect the tie-rod end balljoint to the suspension strut, and tighten a new self-locking nut to the specified torque.

9 Tighten the tie-rod end clamp bolt.

10 Refit the roadwheel and lower the vehicle to the ground.

11 Check the front wheel alignment, as described in Section 35, and adjust if necessary. No harm will result from driving the vehicle a short distance to have the alignment checked.

34 Tie-rod -
removal and refitting

Note: *A new tie-rod end-to-steering gear locking plate, and where applicable, a new tie-rod end balljoint nut, must be used on refitting.*

Removal

1 The tie-rod can either be removed leaving the tie-rod end in place, or as an assembly with the tie-rod end.

2 Apply the handbrake, then jack up the front of the vehicle and support securely on axle stands (see *"Jacking and vehicle support"*). Remove the relevant front roadwheel.

3 If the tie-rod is to be removed complete with the tie-rod end, continue as described in Section 33, paragraphs 3 and 4.

4 If the tie-rod is to be removed independently of the tie-rod end, loosen the tie-rod clamp bolt, which secures the tie-rod to the threaded adjuster pin on the tie-rod end.

5 Prise the locking plate from the tie-rod end-to-steering gear bolts, then unscrew and remove the bolts, and recover the washers and spacer plate.

6 If the tie-rod is being removed complete with the tie-rod end, the assembly can now be withdrawn from the vehicle.

7 If the tie-rod is to be removed independently of the tie-rod end, note the position of the tie-rod end on the adjuster pin. Do this either, by marking the pin with paint or tape, or by counting the number of threads exposed, then unscrew the tie-rod from the tie-rod end, and withdraw it from the vehicle.

Refitting

8 Refitting is a reversal of removal, remembering the following points.

9 The tie-rod-to-steering gear bolt locking plate must be renewed on refitting.

10 If the tie-rod is being refitted complete with the tie-rod end, reconnect the tie-rod end balljoint to the suspension strut, and tighten a new self-locking nut to the specified torque.

11 If the tie-rod is being refitted with the tie-rod end already in place on the vehicle, screw the tie-rod onto the adjuster pin to approximately the same position as noted during removal, and tighten the clamp bolt.

12 On completion, check the front wheel alignment, as described in Section 35, and adjust if necessary. No harm will result from driving the vehicle a short distance to have the alignment checked.

35 Wheel alignment and steering angles -
general

1 Accurate front wheel alignment is essential for precise steering and handling, and for even tyre wear. Before carrying out any checking or adjusting operations, make sure that the tyres are correctly inflated. Also check that all steering and suspension joints and linkages are in sound condition, and that the wheels are not buckled or distorted, particularly around the rims. It will also be necessary to have the vehicle positioned on flat, level ground, with enough space to push the car backwards and forwards through about half its length.

2 Front wheel alignment consists of four factors **(see illustration)**:

Camber is the angle at which the roadwheels are set from the vertical, when viewed from the front or rear of the vehicle. Positive camber is the angle (in degrees) that the wheels are tilted outwards at the top from the vertical.

Castor is the angle between the steering axis and a vertical line when viewed from each side of the vehicle. Positive castor is indicated when the steering axis is inclined towards the rear of the vehicle at its upper end.

Steering axis inclination is the angle, when viewed from the front or rear of the vehicle, between the vertical and an imaginary line drawn between the upper and lower front suspension strut mountings.

Toe setting is the amount by which the distance between the front inside edges of the roadwheels differs from that between the rear inside edges, when measured at hub height. If the distance between the front edges is less than at the rear, the wheels are said to 'toe-in'. If it is greater than at the rear, the wheels are said to 'toe-out'.

3 Camber, castor and steering axis inclination are set during manufacture, and are not adjustable. Unless the vehicle has suffered accident damage, or there is gross wear in the suspension mountings or joints, it can be assumed that these settings are correct. If for any reason it is believed that they are not correct, the task of checking them should be left to a Vauxhall/Opel dealer, who will have the necessary special equipment needed to measure the small angles involved.

4 It is, however, within the scope of the home mechanic to check and adjust the front wheel toe setting. To do this, a tracking gauge must first be obtained. Two types of gauge are available, and can be obtained from motor accessory shops. The first type measures the distance between the front and rear inside edges of the roadwheels, as previously described, with the vehicle stationary. The

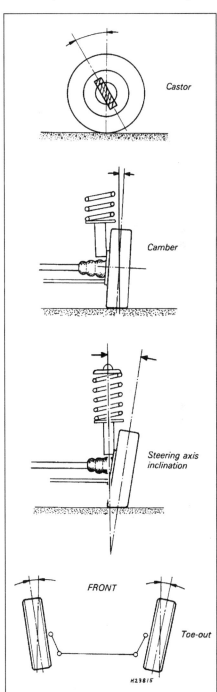

35.2 Wheel alignment and steering angles

second type, known as a 'scuff plate', measures the actual position of the contact surface of the tyre, in relation to the road surface, with the vehicle in motion. This is achieved by pushing or driving the front tyre over a plate, which then moves slightly according to the scuff of the tyre, and shows this movement on a scale. Both types have their advantages and disadvantages, but either can give satisfactory results if used correctly and carefully. Alternatively, a tracking gauge can be fabricated from a length of steel tubing, suitably cranked to clear the sump and clutch bellhousing, with a set screw and locknut at one end.

5 Many tyre specialists will also check toe settings free, or for a nominal charge.

6 Make sure that the steering is in the straight-ahead position when making measurements.

7 If adjustment is found to be necessary, clean the ends of the tie-rods in the area around the adjustment pin and clamp bolts.

8 Slacken the clamp bolts (one on each tie-rod balljoint, and one on each tie-rod), and turn the adjustment pin on each tie-rod by the same amount in the same direction. Only turn each pin by a quarter of a turn at a time before rechecking.

9 When adjustment is correct, tighten the clamp bolts to the specified torque. Check that the tie-rod lengths are equal to within 5.0 mm, and that the steering wheel spokes are in the correct straight-ahead position.

Chapter 11
Bodywork and fittings

Contents

Degrees of difficulty

Easy, suitable for novice with little experience	Fairly easy, suitable for beginner with some experience	Fairly difficult, suitable for competent DIY mechanic	Difficult, suitable for experienced DIY mechanic	Very difficult, suitable for expert DIY or professional

Specifications

Torque wrench settings	Nm	lbf ft
Front seat securing bolts	20	15
Seat belt mounting bolts	35	26
Seat belt height adjuster securing bolts	20	15

1 General description

The bodyshell and floorpan are manufactured from pressed-steel, and together make up the vehicle's structure, without the need for a separate chassis. The Astra is available in 4-door Saloon, 3- and 5-door Hatchback, 5-door Estate and 2-door Van body styles.

Various areas of the structure are strengthened to provide for suspension, steering and engine mounting points, and load distribution. One notable feature of all Astra models is the use of tubular reinforcing bars in the doors, to provide the occupants with additional protection if there is a side impact.

Extensive corrosion protection is applied to all new vehicles. Various anti-corrosion preparations are used, including galvanising, zinc phosphatisation, and PVC underseal. Protective wax is injected into the box sections and other hollow cavities.

Extensive use is made of plastic for peripheral components, such as the radiator grille, bumpers and wheel trims, and for much of the interior trim.

Interior fittings are to a high standard on all models, and a wide range of optional equipment is available throughout the range.

2 Maintenance - bodywork and underframe

Cleaning the vehicle's exterior

The general condition of a vehicle's bodywork is the one thing that significantly affects its value. Maintenance is easy but needs to be regular. Neglect, particularly after minor damage, can lead quickly to further deterioration and costly repair bills. It is important also to keep watch on those parts of the vehicle not immediately visible, for instance the underbody, inside all the wheel arches and the lower part of the engine compartment.

The basic maintenance routine for the bodywork is washing preferably with a lot of water, from a hose. This will remove all the loose solids that may have stuck to the vehicle. It is important to flush these off in such a way as to prevent grit from scratching the finish. The wheel arches and underbody need washing in the same way to remove any accumulated mud, which will retain moisture and tend to encourage rust, particularly in winter, when it is essential that any salt (from that put down on the roads) is washed off. Paradoxically enough, the best time to clean the underbody and wheel arches is in wet weather, when the mud is thoroughly wet and soft. In very wet weather, the underbody is usually cleaned automatically of large accumulations; this is therefore a good time for inspection.

If the vehicle is very dirty, especially underneath or in the engine compartment, it is tempting to use one of the pressure-washers or steam-cleaners available on garage forecourts, while these are quick and effective, especially for the removal of the accumulation of oily grime which sometimes is allowed to become thick in certain areas, their usage does have some disadvantages. If caked-on dirt is simply blasted off the paintwork, its finish soon becomes scratched and dull, and the pressure can allow water to penetrate door and window seals and the lock mechanisms; if the full force of such a jet is directed at the vehicle's underbody, the wax-based protective coating can easily be damaged, and water (with whatever cleaning solvent is used) could be forced into crevices or components that it would not normally reach. Similarly, if such equipment is used to clean the engine compartment, water can be forced into the components of the fuel and electrical systems, and the protective coating can be removed that is applied to many small components during manufacture; this may therefore actually promote corrosion (especially inside electrical connectors) and initiate engine problems or other electrical faults. Also, if the jet is pointed directly at any of the oil seals, water can be forced past the seal lips and into the engine or transmission. Great care is required, therefore, if such equipment is used and, in general, regular cleaning by such methods should be avoided.

A much better solution in the long term is just to flush away as much loose dirt as possible using a hose alone, even if this leaves the engine compartment looking 'dirty'. If an oil leak has developed, or if any other accumulation of oil or grease is to be removed, there are one or two excellent grease solvents available that can be brush-applied. The dirt can then be simply hosed off. Take care to replace the wax-based protective coat, if this was affected by the solvent.

Normal washing of the vehicle's bodywork is best carried out using cold or warm water, with a proprietary vehicle shampoo, tar spots can be removed by using white spirit, followed by soapy water to remove all traces of spirit. Try to keep water out of the bonnet air inlets, and check afterwards that the heater air inlet box drain tube is clear, so that any water has drained out of the box.

After washing the paintwork, wipe off with a chamois leather to give an unspotted clear finish. A coat of clear protective wax polish will give added protection against chemical pollutants in the air. If the paintwork sheen has dulled or oxidised, use a cleaner/polisher combination to restore the brilliance of the shine. This requires a little effort, but such dulling is usually caused because regular washing has been neglected. Care needs to be taken with metallic paintwork, as special non-abrasive cleaner/polisher is required to avoid damage to the finish.

Any polished metals should be treated in the same way as paintwork.

Windscreens and windows can be kept clear of the smeary film that often appears with proprietary glass cleaner. Never use any form of wax or other body or chromium polish on glass.

Exterior paintwork and body panels check

Once the vehicle has been washed, and all tar spots and other surface blemishes have been cleaned off, check carefully all paintwork, looking closely for chips or scratches; check with particular care vulnerable areas such as the front (bonnet and spoiler) and around the wheel arches. Any damage to the paintwork must be rectified as soon as possible, to comply with the terms of the manufacturer's cosmetic and anti-corrosion warranties; check with a Vauxhall/Opel dealer for details.

If a chip or (light) scratch is found that is recent and still free from rust, it can be touched-up using the appropriate touch-up pencil; these can be obtained from Vauxhall/ Opel dealers. Any more serious damage, or rusted stone chips, can be repaired as described in Section 4, but if damage or corrosion is so severe that a panel must be renewed, seek professional advice as soon as possible.

Always check that the door and ventilator opening drain holes and pipes are completely clear, so that water can drain out.

Underbody sealer check

The wax-based underbody protective coating should be inspected annually, preferably just before Winter. Wash the underbody down as thoroughly but gently as possible (see the above concerning steam cleaners, etc.) and any damage to the coating repaired. If any of the body panels are disturbed for repair or renewed, do not forget to replace the coating and to inject wax into door panels, sills, box sections, etc., to maintain the level of protection provided by the vehicle manufacturer.

3 Maintenance - upholstery and carpets

Mats and carpets should be brushed or vacuum-cleaned regularly, to keep them free of grit. If they are badly stained, remove them from the vehicle for scrubbing or sponging, and make quite sure they are dry before refitting. Seats and interior trim panels can be kept clean by wiping with a damp cloth. If they do become stained (which can be more apparent on light-coloured upholstery), use a little liquid detergent and a soft nail brush to scour the grime out of the grain of the material. Do not forget to keep the headlining clean in the same way as the upholstery. When using liquid cleaners inside the vehicle, do not over-wet the surfaces being cleaned. Excessive damp could get into the seams and padded interior, causing stains, offensive odours or even rot. If the inside of the vehicle gets wet accidentally, it is worthwhile taking some trouble to dry it out properly, particularly where carpets are involved. *Do not leave oil or electric heaters inside the vehicle for this purpose.*

4 Minor body damage - repair

Note: *For more detailed information about bodywork repair, Haynes Publishing produce a book titled "The Car Bodywork Repair Manual" (Book No 9864). This incorporates information on such aspects as rust treatment, painting and glass-fibre repairs, as well as details on more ambitious repairs involving welding and panel beating.*

Repairs of minor scratches in bodywork

If the scratch is very superficial, and does not penetrate to the metal of the bodywork, repair is very simple. Lightly rub the area of the scratch with a paintwork renovator, or a very fine cutting paste, to remove loose paint from the scratch, and to clear the surrounding bodywork of wax polish. Rinse the area with clean water.

Apply touch-up paint to the scratch using a fine paint brush; continue to apply fine layers of paint until the surface of the paint in the scratch is level with the surrounding paintwork. Allow the new paint at least two weeks to harden, then blend it into the surrounding paintwork by rubbing the scratch area with a paintwork renovator or a very fine cutting paste. Finally, apply wax polish.

Where the scratch has penetrated right through to the metal of the bodywork, causing the metal to rust, a different repair technique is required. Remove any loose rust from the bottom of the scratch with a penknife, then apply rust-inhibiting paint to prevent the formation of rust in the future. Using a rubber or nylon applicator, fill the scratch with bodystopper paste. If required, this paste can be mixed with cellulose thinners to provide a very thin paste that is ideal for filling narrow scratches. Before the stopper-paste in the scratch hardens, wrap a piece of smooth cotton rag around the top of a finger. Dip the finger in cellulose thinners, and quickly sweep it across the surface of the stopper-paste in the scratch; this will ensure that the surface of the stopper-paste is slightly hollowed. The scratch can now be painted over as described earlier in this Section.

Repairs of dents in bodywork

When deep denting of the vehicle's bodywork has taken place, the first task is to pull the dent out, until the affected bodywork almost attains its original shape. There is little point in trying to restore the original shape completely, as the metal in the damaged area will have stretched on impact, and cannot be reshaped fully to its original contour. It is better to bring the level of the dent up to a point that is about 3 mm below the level of the surrounding bodywork. In cases where the dent is very shallow anyway, it is not worth trying to pull it out at all. If the underside of the dent is accessible, it can be hammered out gently from behind, using a mallet with a wooden or plastic head. Whilst doing this, hold a block of wood firmly against the outside of the panel, to absorb the impact from the hammer blows and thus prevent a large area of the bodywork from being 'belled-out'.

Should the dent be in a section of the bodywork that has a double skin, or some other factor making it inaccessible from behind, a different technique is called for. Drill several small holes through the metal inside the area - particularly in the deeper section. Then screw long self-tapping screws into the holes, just sufficiently for them to gain a good purchase in the metal. Now the dent can be pulled out by pulling on the protruding heads of the screws with a pair of pliers.

The next stage of the repair is the removal of the paint from the damaged area, and from an inch or so of the surrounding 'sound' bodywork. This is accomplished most easily by using a wire brush or abrasive pad on a power drill, although it can be done just as effectively by hand, using sheets of abrasive paper. To complete the preparation for filling, score the surface of the bare metal with a screwdriver or the tang of a file, or alternatively, drill small holes in the affected area. This will provide a good 'key' for the filler paste.

To complete the repair, see the Section on filling and respraying.

Repairs of rust holes or gashes in bodywork

Remove all paint from the affected area, and from an inch or so of the surrounding 'sound' bodywork, using an abrasive pad or a wire brush on a power drill. If these are not available, a few sheets of abrasive paper will do the job most effectively. With the paint removed, you will be able to judge the severity of the corrosion, and therefore decide whether to renew the whole panel (if this is possible) or to repair the affected area. New body panels are not as expensive as most people think, and it is often quicker and more satisfactory to fit a new panel than to attempt to repair large areas of corrosion.

Remove all fittings from the affected area, except those which will act as a guide to the original shape of the damaged bodywork (e.g. headlight shells, etc.). Then, using tin snips or a hacksaw blade, remove all loose metal and any other metal badly affected by corrosion. Hammer the edges of the hole inwards, to create a slight depression for the filler paste.

Wire-brush the affected area to remove the powdery rust from the surface of the remaining metal. Paint the affected area with rust-inhibiting paint, if the back of the rusted area is accessible, treat this also.

Before filling can take place, it will be necessary to block the hole in some way. This can be achieved with aluminium or plastic mesh, or aluminium tape.

Aluminium or plastic mesh, or glass-fibre matting, is probably the best material to use for a large hole. Cut a piece to the approximate size and shape of the hole to be filled, then position it in the hole so that its edges are below the level of the surrounding bodywork. It can be retained in position by several blobs of filler paste around its periphery.

Aluminium tape should be used for small or very narrow holes. Pull a piece off the roll, trim it to the approximate size and shape required, then pull off the backing paper (if used) and stick the tape over the hole. It can be overlapped if the thickness of one piece is insufficient. Burnish down the edges of the tape with the handle of a screwdriver or similar, to ensure that the tape is securely attached to the metal underneath.

Bodywork repairs - filling and respraying

Before using this Section, see the Sections on dent, deep scratch, rust holes and gash repairs.

Many types of bodyfiller are available, but generally speaking, those proprietary kits that contain a tin of filler paste and a tube of resin hardener are best for this type of repair. A wide, flexible plastic or nylon applicator will be found invaluable for imparting a smooth and well-contoured finish to the surface of the filler.

Mix up a little filler on a clean piece of card or board - measure the hardener carefully (follow the maker's instructions on the pack), otherwise the filler will set too rapidly or too slowly. Using the applicator, apply the filler paste to the prepared area; draw the applicator across the surface of the filler to achieve the correct contour and to level the surface. When a contour that follows the original is achieved, stop working the paste. If you carry on too long, the paste will become sticky and begin to 'pick-up' on the applicator. Continue to add thin layers of filler paste at 20-minute intervals, until the level of the filler is just proud of the surrounding bodywork.

Once the filler has hardened, the excess can be removed using a metal plane or file. From then on, progressively-finer grades of abrasive paper should be used, starting with a 40-grade production paper, and finishing with a 400-grade wet-and-dry paper. Always wrap the abrasive paper around a flat rubber, cork, or wooden block - otherwise the surface of the filler will not be completely flat. During the smoothing of the filler surface, the wet-and-dry paper should be periodically rinsed in water. This will ensure that a very smooth finish is imparted to the filler at the final stage.

At this stage, the 'dent' should be surrounded by a ring of bare metal, which in turn should be encircled by the finely 'feathered' edge of the good paintwork. Rinse the repair area with clean water, until all of the dust produced by the rubbing-down operation has gone.

Spray the whole area with a light coat of primer - this will show up any imperfections in the surface of the filler. Repair these imperfections with fresh filler paste or bodystopper, and again smooth the surface with abrasive paper. If bodystopper is used, it can be mixed with cellulose thinners, to form a thin paste that is ideal for filling small holes.

Repeat this spray-and-repair procedure until you are satisfied that the surface of the filler, and the feathered edge of the paintwork, are perfect. Clean the repair area with clean water, and allow to dry fully.

The repair area is now ready for final spraying. Paint spraying must be carried out in a warm, dry, windless and dust-free atmosphere. This condition can be created artificially if you have access to a large indoor working area, but if you are forced to work in the open, you will have to pick your day very carefully. If you are working indoors, dousing the floor in the work area with water will help to settle the dust that would otherwise be in the atmosphere. If the repair area is confined to one body panel, mask off the surrounding panels; this will help to minimise the effects of a slight mis-match in paint colours. Bodywork fittings (e.g. chrome strips, door handles, etc.), will also need to be masked off. Use genuine masking tape, and several thicknesses of newspaper, for the masking operations.

Before starting to spray, agitate the aerosol can thoroughly, then spray a test area (an old tin, or similar) until the technique is mastered. Cover the repair area with a thick coat of primer; the thickness should be built up using several thin layers of paint, rather than one thick one. Using 400-grade wet-and-dry paper, rub down the surface of the primer until it is smooth. While doing this, the work area should be thoroughly doused with water, and the wet-and-dry paper periodically rinsed in water. Allow to dry before spraying on more paint.

Spray on the top coat, again building up the thickness by using several thin layers of paint. Start spraying at one edge of the repair area, and then, using a side-to-side motion, work until the whole repair area and about 2 inches of the surrounding original paintwork is covered. Remove all masking material 10 to 15 minutes after spraying on the final coat of paint.

Allow the new paint at least two weeks to harden, then, using a paintwork renovator, or a very fine cutting paste, blend the edges of the paint into the existing paintwork. Finally, apply wax polish.

Plastic components

With the use of more and more plastic body components by the vehicle manufacturers (e.g. bumpers. spoilers, and in some cases major body panels), rectification of more serious damage to such items has become a matter of either entrusting repair work to a specialist in this field, or renewing complete components. Repair of such damage by the DIY owner is not feasible, owing to the cost of the equipment and materials required for effecting such repairs. The basic technique involves making a groove along the line of the crack in the plastic, using a rotary burr in a power drill. The damaged part is then welded back together, using a hot-air gun to heat up and fuse a plastic

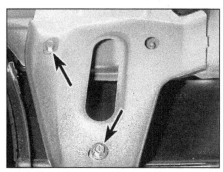

6.5 Front bumper side securing screws (arrowed)

6.6 Front bumper-to-body front panel securing nut

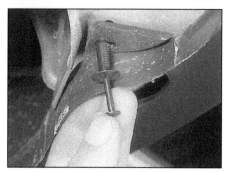

6.7 Removing a front bumper securing clip

filler rod into the groove. Any excess plastic is then removed, and the area rubbed down to a smooth finish. It is important that a filler rod of the correct plastic is used, as body components can be made of a variety of different types (e.g. polycarbonate, ABS, polypropylene).

Damage of a less serious nature (abrasions, minor cracks, etc.), can be repaired by the DIY owner using a two-part epoxy filler repair material. Once mixed in equal proportions, this is used in similar fashion to the bodywork filler used on metal panels. The filler is usually cured in twenty to thirty minutes, ready for sanding and painting.

If the owner is renewing a complete component himself, or if he has repaired it with epoxy filler, he will be left with the problem of finding a paint for finishing which is compatible with the type of plastic used. At one time, the use of a universal paint was not possible, owing to the complex range of plastics encountered in body component applications. Standard paints, generally speaking, will not bond to plastic or rubber satisfactorily. However, it is now possible to obtain a plastic body parts finishing kit that consists of a pre-primer treatment, a primer and coloured top coat. Full instructions are normally supplied with a kit, but basically, the method of use is to first apply the pre-primer to the component concerned, and allow it to dry for up to 30 minutes. Then the primer is applied, and left to dry for about an hour before finally applying the special-coloured top coat. The result is a correctly coloured component, where the paint will flex with the plastic or rubber, a property that standard paint does not normally possess.

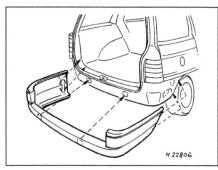

6.12 Rear bumper securing screw and nut locations

5 Major body damage - repair

Where serious damage has occurred, or large areas need renewal due to neglect, it means that complete new panels will need welding-in; this is best left to professionals. If the damage is due to impact, it will also be necessary to check completely the alignment of the bodyshell; this can only be carried out accurately by a Vauxhall/Opel dealer using special jigs. If the body is left misaligned, it is primarily dangerous (as the car will not handle properly) and secondly, uneven stresses will be imposed on the steering, suspension and possibly transmission, causing abnormal wear or complete failure, particularly to items such as the tyres.

6 Bumpers - removal and refitting

Front bumper

Removal

1 The bumper is removed as a complete assembly with the front trim panel; on models with front foglights, disconnect the battery negative lead and disconnect the foglight wiring plugs.
2 For improved access, apply the handbrake, then jack up the front of the vehicle, and support securely on axle stands (see "Jacking and vehicle support").
3 Remove the radiator grille, as described in Section 7.
4 Working under the wheel arches, remove the screws and/or clips, as applicable, securing the rear edges of the bumper to the wheel arch liners.
5 Unscrew the two screws securing each side of the bumper to the brackets on the body **(see illustration)**.
6 Unscrew the two nuts (one at each side of the bumper) securing the bumper to the body front panel **(see illustration)**. Recover the washers.

7 Remove the four plastic clips securing the lower edge of the bumper to the lower body panel. To remove the clips, prise out the central pins, using a screwdriver if necessary, then pull the clips from the bumper **(see illustration)**.
8 Carefully withdraw the bumper from the vehicle.

Refitting
9 Refitting is a reversal of removal.

Rear bumper
Removal
10 The bumper is removed as a complete assembly with the rear trim panel.
11 On Saloon and Hatchback models, remove the rear number plate light(s), as described in Chapter 12, Section 8.
12 Working under the wheel arches, unscrew the two screws securing each side of the bumper to the brackets on the body **(see illustration)**.
13 Where applicable, remove the rear luggage compartment trim panel for access to the bumper-to-rear body panel nuts. On Estate and Van models, note that it will be necessary to lift the spare wheel cover for access to one of the bumper securing nuts.
14 Unscrew the two bumper-to-rear body panel nuts (one at each side of the bumper), **(see illustration)**. Recover the washers.
15 Carefully withdraw the bumper from the vehicle.

Refitting
16 Refitting is a reversal of removal.

6.14 Rear bumper-to-rear body panel securing nut - Hatchback model

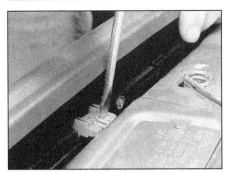

7.2 Releasing a radiator grille upper securing clip

7.3 Radiator grille end securing clip released from below headlight

7.4 Radiator grille lower securing clip released from body front panel

7 Radiator grille - removal and refitting

Removal

1 Open the bonnet.
2 Carefully lever the top of the grille forwards to release the upper securing clips **(see illustration)**.
3 Using a screwdriver, carefully release the clips from each end of the grille, below the headlights **(see illustration)**.
4 Slide the grille towards the right-hand side of the vehicle, to release the lower securing clips, then lift the grille from the vehicle **(see illustration)**.
5 Where applicable, disconnect the fluid hoses from the headlight washer nozzles, which are integral with the grille panel.
6 Carefully manipulate the grille from the front panel, and withdraw it from the vehicle.

Refitting

7 Refitting is a reversal of removal, ensuring that all the clips are positively engaged.

8 Windscreen cowl panel - removal and refitting

Removal

1 Open the bonnet.
2 Remove the windscreen wiper arms, as described in Chapter 12.
3 Unscrew the two large nuts from the windscreen wiper arm spindles.
4 Prise the two screw covers from the cowl panel, and remove the securing screws **(see illustration)**.
5 Note how the cowl panel engages with the weatherstrip at the base of the windscreen. Then carefully release the ends of the cowl panel from the scuttle (the ends of the panel are secured with Velcro strips), and withdraw the panel from the vehicle **(see illustration)**.

Refitting

6 Refitting is a reversal of removal, remembering the following points.

7 Ensure that the panel is correctly engaged with the weatherstrip.
8 Make sure that the ends of the panel are securely held by the Velcro strips.
9 Refit the windscreen wiper arms as described in Chapter 12.

9 Bonnet and hinges - removal and refitting

Bonnet

Removal

1 Open the bonnet and support it in the fully open position.
2 Disconnect the windscreen washer fluid hose from the connector in the bonnet. It is advisable to tie a length of string to the connector, to prevent it from slipping into an inaccessible position in the bonnet.
3 If the original bonnet is to be refitted, mark the position of the hinges on the bonnet, to alignment on refitting.
4 Carefully pull back the insulation blocks from the bonnet hinges.
5 With the help of an assistant, support the weight of the bonnet, then unscrew the securing bolts from the hinges, and lift the bonnet from the vehicle. If the bonnet is to be refitted, rest it carefully on rags or cardboard, to avoid damaging the paint.

Refitting

6 Refitting is a reversal of removal, remembering the following points.

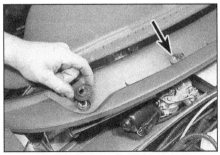

8.4 Removing a windscreen cowl panel securing screw nut from the wiper arm spindle. Cowl panel securing screw arrowed

7 If a new bonnet is to be fitted, transfer all the serviceable fixings (rubber buffers, lock strikers, etc.) to it.
8 Where applicable, align the hinges with the previously made marks on the bonnet.
9 If the lock striker has been disturbed, adjust it to the dimension shown in illustration 10.4, then tighten the locknut.
10 If necessary, adjust the hinge bolts and the front rubber buffers until a good fit is obtained with the bonnet shut.

Hinge

Note: *To secure the hinge on refitting, a new bolt and washer assembly will be required.*

Removal

11 Remove the bonnet, as described previously in this Section.
12 Remove the windscreen cowl panel, as described in Section 8.
13 The bonnet hinges are riveted to the body panels, and to remove a hinge, it will be necessary to drill or grind off the rivet head.
14 With the rivet head removed, tap the rivet from the hinge assembly, and withdraw the hinge.

Refitting

15 When refitting the hinge, a bolt and washer assembly must be used to replace the rivet used originally.
16 Secure the hinge using the bolt and washer assembly (available from a Vauxhall/ Opel dealer), ensuring that the components are located as shown **(see illustration overleaf)**.

8.5 Removing the windscreen cowl panel

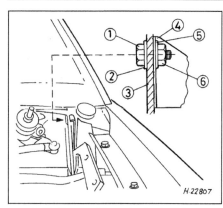

9.16 Bonnet hinge-to-body fixing components

1 Bolt	4 Body bracket
2 Spring washer	5 Washer
3 Hinge	6 Nut

17 Refit the windscreen cowl panel, referring to Section 8.

18 Refit the bonnet as described previously in this Section.

10 Bonnet lock components - removal and refitting

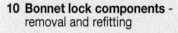

Lock hook

Removal

1 The bonnet lock hook is riveted to the bonnet, and removal involves drilling out the rivet.

Refitting

2 Refitting is a reversal of removal, using a new rivet.

Lock striker

Removal

3 To remove the lock striker from the bonnet, loosen the locknut, then unscrew the striker, and recover the washer and spring.

Refitting

4 Refitting is a reversal of removal, but adjust the striker dimension as shown **(see illustration)**, before tightening the locknut.

12.2 Front door wiring connector

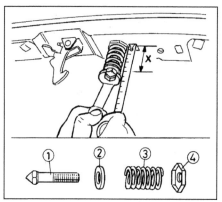

10.4 Bonnet lock striker adjustment

1 Striker	3 Coil spring
2 Washer	4 Locknut

$X = 40$ to 45 mm

Locking spring

Removal

5 Disconnect the end of the bonnet release cable from the spring, then unhook the end of the spring from the slot in the front body panel, taking care not to damage the paint.

Refitting

6 Refitting is a reversal of removal.

11 Bonnet release cable - removal and refitting

Removal

1 Open the bonnet, and support it in the fully open position.

2 Unscrew the release cable clip from the front body panel.

3 Disconnect the end of the release cable from the locking spring under the front body panel.

4 Disconnect the release cable from the release lever in the driver's footwell. If necessary, remove the release lever from its retainer for access to the cable end.

5 Pull the cable assembly through the grommet in the engine compartment bulkhead and into the engine compartment.

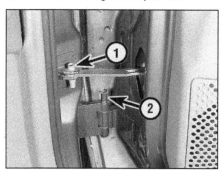

12.3 Front door check-link roll-pin (1) and hinge pin (2)

6 Note the routing of the cable, then release the cable from any remaining clips and cable-ties, and withdraw it from the engine compartment.

Refitting

7 Refitting is a reversal of removal, but ensure that the cable is correctly routed, and on completion, check the release mechanism for satisfactory operation.

12 Doors - removal, refitting and adjustment

Front door

Removal

1 To remove a door, open it fully and support it under its lower edge on blocks or axle stands covered with pads of rag.

2 Disconnect the wiring connector from the front edge of the door. To release the connector, twist the locking collar, then pull the connector from the socket in the door **(see illustration)**.

3 Using a punch, drive the large roll-pin from the door check arm pivot **(see illustration)**.

4 Where applicable, remove the plastic covers from the hinge pins, then drive out the pins using a punch. Have an assistant support the door as the pins are driven out, then withdraw the door from the vehicle.

Refitting

5 Refitting is a reversal of removal, using a new check-link roll-pin.

Adjustment

6 The door hinges are welded onto the door frame and the body pillar, so that there is no provision for adjustment or alignment.

7 If the door can be moved up and down on its hinges due to wear in the hinge pins or their holes, it may be possible to drill out the holes and fit slightly oversize pins. Consult a Vauxhall/Opel dealer for further advice.

8 Door closure may be adjusted by altering the position of the lock striker on the body pillar, using an Allen key or a hexagon bit.

Rear door

Removal

9 On models with central locking, remove the door inner trim panel, as described in Section 30, and disconnect the wiring connector inside the door. Note the routing of the wiring, and the location of the wiring connector, then carefully feed the wiring through the grommet in the front edge of the door.

10 Proceed as described in paragraphs 3 and 4.

Refitting

11 Refitting is a reversal of removal, using a new check-link roll-pin.

12 Where applicable, ensure that the wiring and the connector are routed and located as noted during removal.

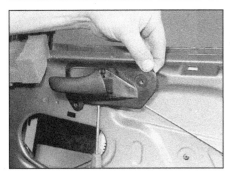

13.2a Releasing a front door interior handle retaining clip

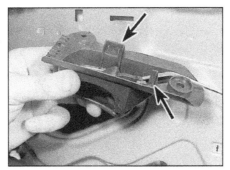

13.2b Front door interior handle - retaining clips (arrowed)

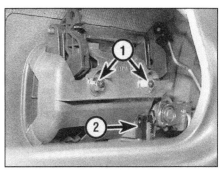

13.5 Front door exterior handle securing nuts (1) and central locking microswitch (2)

13 Door handle and lock components - removal and refitting

Door interior handle

Removal

1 Remove the door inner trim panel, as described in Section 30.
2 Using a screwdriver, carefully release the retaining clips and pull the handle assembly from the door, then unhook the operating rod, and withdraw the assembly (see illustrations).

Refitting

3 Refitting is a reversal of removal, but check the mechanism for satisfactory operation before refitting the door inner trim panel, then refit the trim panel with reference to Section 30.

Front door exterior handle

Removal

4 Remove the door inner trim panel, and peel back the plastic insulating sheet for access to the handle, as described in Section 30.
5 Unscrew the two nuts securing the exterior handle to the door (see illustration).
6 Where applicable, unclip the central locking microswitch from the rear edge of the exterior handle assembly.
7 Release the two lower retaining clips, then manipulate the outer plastic section of the exterior handle assembly through the outside of the door, and disconnect the operating rod (see illustration).

13.7 Withdrawing the outer section of a front door exterior handle

8 Withdraw the inner section of the exterior handle assembly from the inside of the door, and disconnect the lock cylinder operating rod.

Refitting

9 Refitting is a reversal of removal, but check the operation of the mechanism before refitting the door inner trim panel, and refit the trim panel referring to Section 30.

Rear door exterior handle - Saloon and Hatchback models

Removal

10 Remove the door inner trim panel, and peel back the plastic insulating sheet for access to the handle, as described in Section 30.
11 Pull the weatherstrips from the inside and outside lower edges of the window aperture.
12 Unscrew the upper window rear guide rail securing bolt, which is accessible at the rear edge of the window aperture.
13 Unscrew the lower window rear guide rail securing bolt (Torx type), which is accessible through the inner door skin, then withdraw the guide rail from the door. Where applicable, the weatherstrip can be left attached to the guide rail, in which case, position the guide rail to one side out of the way, taking care not to damage the vehicle paintwork.
14 Unscrew the two nuts securing the exterior handle to the door.
15 Release the two lower retaining clips, then manipulate the exterior handle assembly through the outside of the door, and disconnect the operating rods.

Refitting

16 Refitting is a reversal of removal, but check the operation of the mechanism before refitting the door inner trim panel, and refit the trim panel referring to Section 30.

Rear door exterior handle - Estate models

Removal

17 Remove the door inner trim panel, and peel back the plastic insulating sheet for access to the handle, as described in Section 30.
18 Unscrew the two nuts securing the exterior handle to the door.
19 Release the two lower retaining clips, then manipulate the exterior handle assembly

through the outside of the door, and disconnect the operating rods.

Refitting

20 Refitting is a reversal of removal, but check the operation of the mechanism before refitting the door inner trim panel, and refit the trim panel referring to Section 30.

Front door lock

Removal

21 Remove the door inner trim panel, and peel back the plastic insulating sheet from the rear edge of the door, as described in Section 30.
22 Unscrew the window rear guide rail securing bolt from the rear edge of the door, then manipulate the guide rail out through the lower aperture in the door.
23 Where applicable, reach in through the door aperture and unclip the plastic cover from the lock.
24 Working through the apertures in the door, disconnect the three operating rods from the lock assembly.
25 On models with central locking, disconnect the battery negative lead (if not already done), then reach in through the door aperture, and disconnect the wiring plug from the central locking motor (see illustration).
26 Unscrew the three Torx screws securing the lock assembly to the rear edge of the door, then manipulate the lock assembly (complete with the lock button operating rod, and the central locking motor, where applicable) around the window regulator mechanism, and out through the lower door aperture (see illustrations overleaf).

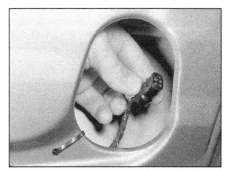

13.25 Disconnecting the central locking motor wiring plug from a front door lock

13.26a Unscrewing a front door lock securing screw

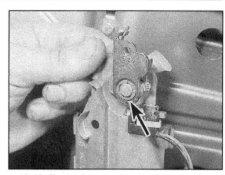

13.26b Withdrawing a front door lock assembly through the lower door aperture

13.43 Front door lock cylinder securing circlip (arrowed)

Refitting

27 Refitting is a reversal of removal, but check the operation of the door lock, handle and window regulator mechanisms before refitting the door trim panel, and refit the trim panel referring to Section 30. If the lock operation is not satisfactory, note that the exterior handle operating rod can be adjusted by turning the knurled plastic adjuster wheel at the end of the rod.

Rear door lock - Saloon and Hatchback models

Removal

28 Fully lower the window, then remove the door inner trim panel and the plastic insulating sheet, as described in Section 30.
29 Pull the weatherstrips from the inside and outside lower edges of the window aperture.
30 Unscrew the upper window rear guide rail securing bolt, which is accessible at the rear edge of the window aperture.
31 Unscrew the lower window rear guide rail securing bolt (Torx type), which is accessible through the inner door skin, then withdraw the guide rail from the door. Where applicable, the weatherstrip can be left attached to the guide rail, in which case, position the guide rail to one side out of the way, taking care not to damage the vehicle paintwork.
32 Where applicable, reach in through the door aperture, and unclip the plastic cover from the lock.
33 Working through the apertures in the door, disconnect the operating rods from the lock assembly.
34 On models with central locking, disconnect the battery negative lead (if not already done), and disconnect the wiring plug from the central locking motor.
35 Unscrew the three Torx screws securing the lock assembly to the rear edge of the door, then manipulate the lock assembly (complete with the lock button operating rod, and the central locking motor, where applicable) around the window regulator mechanism, and out through the lower door aperture.

Refitting

36 Refitting is a reversal of removal, but check the operation of the door lock, handle and window regulator mechanisms before

refitting the door trim panel, and refit the trim panel with reference to Section 30. If the lock operation is not satisfactory, note that the exterior handle operating rod can be adjusted by turning the knurled plastic adjuster wheel at the end of the rod.

Rear door lock - Estate models

Removal

37 Fully lower the window, then remove the door inner trim panel and the plastic insulating sheet, as described in Section 30.
38 Working at the top of the window aperture, remove the two upper rear window rear guide rail securing screws.
39 Working at the bottom of the window aperture, remove the lower rear window guide securing screw, then remove the rear window guide securing bolt and nut, and withdraw the window guide upwards through the window aperture.
40 Proceed as described in paragraphs 32 to 35 inclusive.

Refitting

41 Refitting is a reversal of removal, but check the operation of the door lock, handle and window regulator mechanisms before refitting the door trim panel, and refit the trim panel with reference to Section 30. If the lock operation is not satisfactory, note that the exterior handle operating rod can be adjusted by turning the knurled plastic adjuster wheel at the end of the rod.

Front door lock cylinder

Removal

42 Remove the door exterior handle, as described earlier in this Section.
43 Insert the key into the lock, then extract the circlip from the end of the lock cylinder **(see illustration)**.
44 Withdraw the lock cylinder using the key, and recover the lever assembly.

Refitting

45 Refitting is a reversal of removal, but check the operation of the door lock, handle and window regulator mechanism before refitting the door trim panel, and refit the trim panel with reference to Section 30.

Lock striker

Removal

46 The lock striker is screwed into the door pillar on the body.
47 Before removing the striker, mark its position, so that it can be refitted in exactly the same position.
48 To remove the striker, simply unscrew the securing screw using an Allen key or hexagon bit.

Refitting

49 Refitting is a reversal of removal, but if necessary, adjust the position of the striker to achieve satisfactory closing of the door.

Central locking components

50 Refer to Section 19.

---

14 Door window glass and regulators - removal and refitting

Front door window glass

Removal

1 Remove the door inner trim panel and the plastic insulating sheet, as described in Section 30.
2 Pull the weatherstrips from the inside and outside lower edges of the window aperture. Note that on certain models, it may be necessary to remove the door mirror (see Section 21) to enable removal of the outside weatherstrip **(see illustrations)**.

14.2a Removing the weatherstrip from the inside of the front door window aperture

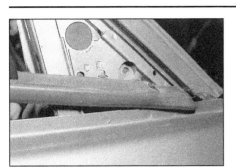

14.2b Removing the weatherstrip from the outside of the front door window aperture (door mirror removed)

14.3a Unscrewing the window rear guide rail securing bolt from the front door . . .

14.3b . . . and withdrawing the rear guide rail

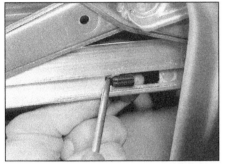

14.5 Prising the end stop from the front door window glass guide channel

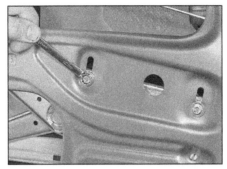

14.6a Unscrewing a front door window lower guide rail securing bolt . . .

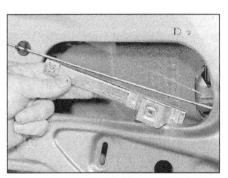

14.6b . . . and withdrawing the lower guide rail

3 Unscrew the window rear guide rail securing bolt from the rear edge of the door, then manipulate the guide rail out through the lower aperture in the door (see illustrations).

4 Where applicable, reconnect the battery negative lead and the electric window switch wiring, and lower the window until the metal guide channel at the bottom edge of the window glass is accessible through the door aperture.

5 Prise the plastic end stop from the window glass guide channel (see illustration).

6 Unscrew the two securing bolts, and remove the window lower guide rail from the door (see illustrations).

7 Manipulate the window regulator mechanism as necessary, and tilt the window glass forwards until it can be withdrawn from outside the door through the window aperture (see illustration).

Refitting

8 Refitting is a reversal of removal, but adjust the angle of the lower guide rail by means of the two securing screws until smooth operation of the window is achieved, and refit the door inner trim panel referring to Section 30.

Rear door window glass - Saloon and Hatchback models

Removal

9 Fully lower the window, then remove the door inner trim panel and the plastic insulating sheet, as described in Section 30.

10 Pull the weatherstrips from the inside and outside lower edges of the window aperture.

11 Unscrew the upper window rear guide rail securing bolt, which is accessible at the rear edge of the window aperture.

12 Unscrew the lower window rear guide rail securing bolt (Torx type), which is accessible through the inner door skin, then withdraw the guide rail from the door (see illustration). Where applicable, the weatherstrip can be left attached to the guide rail, in which case, position the guide rail to one side out of the way, taking care not to damage the vehicle paintwork.

13 Manipulate the window regulator mechanism as necessary, and tilt the window glass forwards until it can be withdrawn from outside the door through the window aperture.

Refitting

14 Refitting is a reversal of removal, but refit the door inner trim panel referring to Section 30.

14.7 Withdrawing the front door window glass

Rear door window sliding glass - Estate models

Removal

15 Proceed as described in paragraphs 9 and 10.

16 Remove the window regulator mechanism, as described later in this Section.

17 Working at the top of the window aperture, remove the two upper rear window rear guide rail securing screws.

18 Working at the bottom of the window aperture, remove the lower rear window guide securing screw, then remove the rear window guide securing bolt and nut, and withdraw the window guide upwards through the window aperture (see illustration overleaf).

19 Withdraw the window glass upwards through the window aperture.

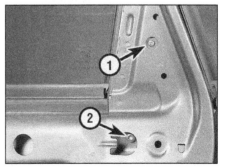

14.12 Upper (1) and lower (2) rear door window rear guide rail securing bolts - Hatchback model

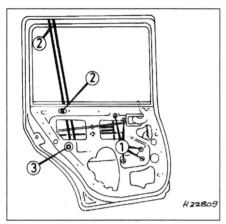

14.18 Rear door rear window guide fixings - Estate models

1 Regulator
  securing rivets
2 Screws
3 Nut and bolt

Refitting

20 Refitting is a reversal of removal, but refit the window regulator mechanism as described in Section 20, and refit the door inner trim panel referring to Section 30.

Rear door window fixed glass - Estate models

Removal

21 Remove the sliding glass, as described previously in this Section.
22 Pull the fixed glass forwards from its surround, and withdraw it from the door.

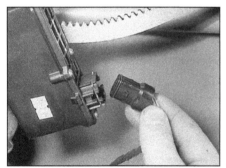

14.29 Disconnecting a front door electric window motor wiring plug

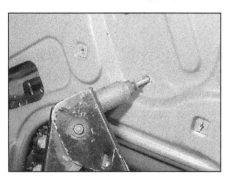

14.33 Fit new rivets to secure the front door window regulator assembly

14.26 Drilling out a front door window regulator securing rivet

Refitting

23 Refitting is a reversal of removal.

Front door window regulator

Removal

24 Lower the window approximately halfway, then remove the door inner trim panel and the plastic insulating sheet, as described in Section 30.
25 Support the window in the half-open position by placing a wooden prop under it, ensuring that the prop is clear of the regulator mechanism.
26 Drill out the four rivets securing the regulator mechanism to the door, using an 8.5 mm diameter drill (see illustration). Take care not to damage the door panel.
27 Prise the plastic end stop from the window glass guide channel.
28 Unscrew the two securing bolts, and

14.30 Withdrawing a front door window regulator assembly

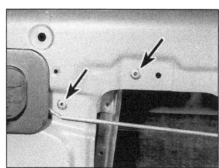

14.36a Rear door window regulator assembly upper . . .

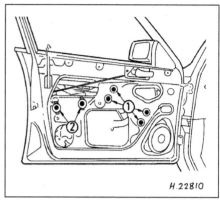

14.28 Front door window regulator securing rivets (1) and window lower guide rail securing bolts (2)

remove the window lower guide rail from the door (see illustration).
29 On models with electric windows, disconnect the battery negative lead (if not already done), then disconnect the wiring plug from the window motor (see illustration).
30 Carefully manipulate the window regulator assembly out through the aperture in the door (see illustration).

Refitting

31 Refitting is a reversal of removal, remembering the following points.
32 Ensure that the regulator arms are correctly positioned in the guide rails before securing the regulator assembly to the door.
33 Secure the regulator assembly to the door, using new rivets (see illustration).
34 Adjust the angle of the lower guide rail by means of the two securing screws, until smooth operation of the window is achieved.
35 Refit the door inner trim panel referring to Section 30.

Rear door window regulator

Removal

36 Proceed as described in paragraphs 24 to 26 inclusive, and paragraphs 29 and 30, noting that the assembly is secured by five rivets (two upper and three lower rivets), (see illustrations).

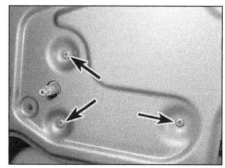

14.36b . . . and lower securing rivets (arrowed)

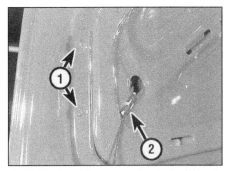

15.4 Boot lid hinge securing bolts (1) and central locking motor wiring (2) - Saloon model

Refitting

37 Refitting is a reversal of removal, remembering the following points.
38 Ensure that the regulator arm is correctly positioned in the guide rail before securing the regulator assembly to the door.
39 Secure the regulator assembly to the door using new rivets.
40 Check the regulator mechanism for satisfactory operation before refitting the door trim panel, then refit the panel referring to Section 30.

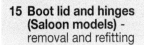

15 Boot lid and hinges (Saloon models) - removal and refitting

Boot lid

Removal

1 Open the boot lid fully.
2 On models with central locking, disconnect the battery negative lead, then disconnect the wiring from the lock motor. If the original boot lid is to be refitted, first tie a length of string to the end of the wiring. Feed the wiring through the boot lid, then untie the string, leaving it in position in the boot lid to assist refitting.
3 Mark the position of the hinges on the boot lid.
4 With the help of an assistant, support the weight of the boot lid, then unscrew the securing bolts from the hinges **(see illustration)**, and lift the boot lid from the vehicle.

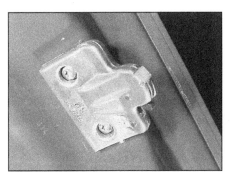

16.5 Boot lid lock - Saloon model

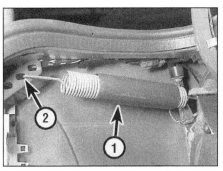

15.13 Boot lid hinge spring (1) - note position of spring in bracket (2) - Saloon model

Refitting

5 If a new boot lid is to be fitted, transfer all the serviceable fittings (rubber buffers, lock mechanism, etc.) to it.
6 Refitting is a reversal of removal, remembering the following points.
7 Align the hinges with the previously made marks on the boot lid.
8 Where applicable, draw the central locking motor wiring through the boot lid, using the string.
9 If necessary, adjust the hinge bolts and the rubber buffers until a good fit is obtained with the boot lid shut.
10 If necessary, adjust the position of the lock striker on the body, to achieve satisfactory lock operation.

Hinge

Removal

11 Remove the boot lid, as described previously in this Section.
12 Remove the rear quarter trim panel, as described in Section 30.
13 Note the position of the hinge counterbalance spring in the bracket on the body, so that it can be refitted in its original position, then unhook the spring from the body **(see illustration)**. Use a lever to release the spring if necessary.
14 Unscrew the securing bolt **(see illustration)**, and remove the hinge from the body.

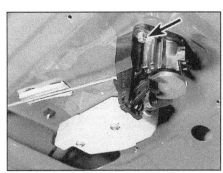

16.9 Lock cylinder securing nut (arrowed) - Saloon model

15.14 Boot lid hinge-to-body securing bolt (arrowed) - Saloon model

Refitting

15 Refitting is a reversal of removal, remembering the following points.
16 Ensure that the counterbalance spring is positioned as noted before removal.
17 Refit the boot lid as described previously in this Section.

16 Boot lid handle and lock components (Saloon models) - removal and refitting

Handle

Removal

1 Open the boot lid, then remove the four securing screws, and withdraw the lock cylinder assembly cover panel.
2 Unscrew the two securing nuts, then withdraw the handle from outside the boot lid. Note that the securing nuts also secure the lock cylinder assembly to the boot lid.

Refitting

3 Refitting is a reversal of removal.

Lock

Removal

4 Proceed as described in paragraph 1.
5 Unscrew the two securing bolts, and withdraw the lock from the boot lid **(see illustration)**.

Refitting

6 Refitting is a reversal of removal, but if necessary, adjust the position of the lock striker on the body, to achieve satisfactory lock operation.

Lock cylinder

Removal

7 Open the boot lid fully.
8 Remove the four securing screws, and withdraw the lock cylinder assembly cover panel.
9 Unscrew the two securing nuts **(see illustration)**, and withdraw the lock cylinder assembly, unhooking the lock operating rod(s) as the assembly is withdrawn. Note that the securing nuts also secure the boot lid handle.

16.13 Boot lid lock striker securing bolt

10 No spare parts are available for the lock cylinder assembly, and if faulty, the complete assembly must be renewed.

Refitting

11 Refitting is a reversal of removal.

Lock striker

Removal

12 The lock striker is screwed into the lower body panel.
13 Remove the securing screws, then unclip the rear boot trim panel to expose the lock striker securing bolt **(see illustration)**.
14 Before removing the striker, mark its position, so that it can be refitted in exactly the same position.
15 To remove the striker, simply unscrew the securing screw.

Refitting

16 Refitting is a reversal of removal, but if necessary, adjust the position of the striker to achieve satisfactory closing of the boot lid.

Central locking motor

17 Refer to Section 19.

17 Tailgate, hinges and support struts - removal and refitting

Tailgate

Removal

1 Open the tailgate fully.
2 Disconnect the battery negative lead.
3 Remove the securing screws, and withdraw the tailgate rear trim panels.
4 Disconnect all the relevant wiring now exposed, and disconnect the washer fluid hose from the washer nozzle.
5 If the original tailgate is to be refitted, tie string to the ends of all the relevant wires, and if necessary the washer fluid hose, then feed the wiring and the hose through the top of the tailgate. Untie the string, leaving it in position in the tailgate to assist refitting.
6 Have an assistant support the weight of the tailgate, then disconnect the tailgate support struts from their mounting balljoints, with reference to paragraph 22.

7 Prise the securing clips from the ends of the tailgate hinge pins **(see illustration)**.
8 With the tailgate adequately supported, tap the hinge pins from the hinges, using a punch, and carefully lift the tailgate from the vehicle.

Refitting

9 If a new tailgate is to be fitted, transfer all serviceable components (rubber buffers, lock mechanism, etc.) to it.
10 Refitting is a reversal of removal, bearing in mind the following points.
11 If the original tailgate is being refitted, draw the wiring and washer fluid hose (where applicable) through the tailgate, using the string.
12 If necessary, adjust the rubber buffers to obtain a good fit when the tailgate is shut.
13 If necessary, adjust the position of the lock striker on the body, to achieve satisfactory lock operation.

Hinge

Removal

14 Remove the tailgate as described previously in this Section.
15 Prise off the rear roof trim panel, taking care not to break the securing clips (see Section 29), and lower the rear headlining slightly for access to the tailgate hinge securing screws.
16 Mark the hinge position on the body.
17 Unscrew the securing screws, and withdraw the hinge.

Refitting

18 Refitting is a reversal of removal, bearing in mind the following points.
19 Align the hinges with the previously made marks on the body.
20 Refit the tailgate as described previously in this Section.

Support strut

Removal

21 Open the tailgate fully, and have an assistant support it.
22 Release the strut from its mounting balljoints by prising the spring clips a little way out **(see illustration)**, and pulling the strut off the balljoints.

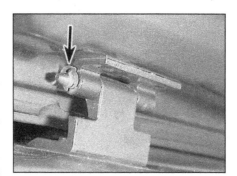

17.7 Tailgate hinge pin securing clip (arrowed) - Hatchback model

Refitting

23 Refitting is a reversal of removal.

18 Tailgate handle and lock components – removal and refitting

Handle - Hatchback models

Removal

1 Open the tailgate, then remove the securing screws and withdraw the tailgate rear trim panel.
2 Working through the aperture in the tailgate, unscrew the two securing nuts, then withdraw the handle from outside the tailgate. Note that the securing nuts also secure the lock cylinder assembly.

Refitting

3 Refitting is a reversal of removal.

Handle - Estate and Van models

Removal

4 Proceed as described in paragraph 1.
5 Remove the tailgate lock cylinder assembly, as described later in this Section.
6 Remove the tailgate wiper motor, as described in Chapter 12.
7 Remove the rear number plate lights, as described in Chapter 12, Section 8.
8 Working through the apertures in the tailgate, unscrew the four securing nuts, and withdraw the handle from outside the tailgate.

Refitting

9 Refitting is a reversal of removal, but refit the tailgate wiper motor as described in Chapter 12.

Lock

Removal

10 Proceed as described in paragraph 1.
11 Working through the aperture in the tailgate, disconnect the operating rod(s) from the lock **(see illustration)**.
12 Unscrew the securing screws (three on Hatchback models, four on Estate models), and withdraw the lock **(see illustration)**.

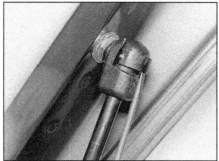

17.22 Prising out a tailgate support strut balljoint clip - Hatchback model

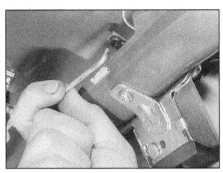

18.11 Disconnecting a tailgate lock operating rod - Hatchback model

18.12 Removing the tailgate lock - Hatchback model

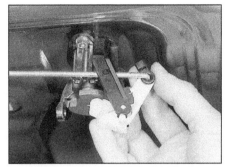

18.15 Disconnecting an operating rod from the lock cylinder assembly - Hatchback model

Refitting

13 Refitting is a reversal of removal, but if necessary, adjust the position of the lock striker on the body, to achieve satisfactory lock operation.

Lock cylinder

Removal

14 Remove the securing screws, and withdraw the tailgate rear trim panel.
15 Disconnect the operating rod(s) from the lock cylinder assembly **(see illustration)**.
16 Unscrew the two securing nuts **(see illustration)**, and withdraw the lock cylinder assembly. Note that on Hatchback models, the securing nuts also secure the tailgate handle.
17 No spare parts are available for the lock cylinder assembly, and if faulty, the complete assembly must be renewed.

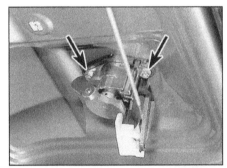

18.16 Lock cylinder assembly securing nuts (arrowed) - Hatchback model

18.22 Tailgate lock striker - Hatchback model

Refitting

18 Refitting is a reversal of removal.

Lock striker

Removal

19 The lock striker is screwed into the lower body panel.
20 Where applicable, extract the securing screws, and remove the luggage compartment rear trim panel for access to the lock striker securing bolts.
21 Before removing the striker, mark its position, so that it can be refitted in exactly the same position.
22 To remove the striker, simply unscrew the securing screws **(see illustration)**.

Refitting

23 Refitting is a reversal of removal, but if necessary, adjust the position of the striker to achieve satisfactory closing of the tailgate.

Central locking motor

24 Refer to Section 19.

19 Central locking system components -
removal and refitting

Electronic control unit

Removal

1 The control unit is located behind the right-hand footwell side/sill trim panel.

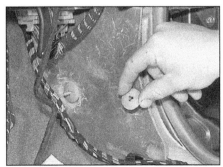

19.5a Pull the securing clips from the studs in the footwell . . .

2 Disconnect the battery negative lead.
3 Remove the footwell side/sill trim panel, as described in Section 30.
4 Where applicable, unscrew the two securing nuts, and pull the wiring plug bracket from the footwell.
5 Pull the two securing clips from the studs in the footwell, and pull the carpet back from the studs to expose the control unit **(see illustrations)**.
6 Unscrew the two securing screws, and lift the unit from its location in the footwell, then disconnect the wiring plug and withdraw the unit.

Refitting

7 Refitting is a reversal of removal.

Microswitches

Removal

8 The microswitches are mounted inside the front doors, at the rear of the exterior handle assemblies.
9 Remove the door inner trim panel, and peel back the plastic insulating sheet sufficiently to gain access to the exterior handle, as described in Section 30.
10 Unclip the microswitch from the rear edge of the exterior handle assembly, disconnect the switch wiring connector from the door wiring harness, then withdraw the switch **(see illustration overleaf)**.

Refitting

11 Refitting is a reversal of removal, but refit

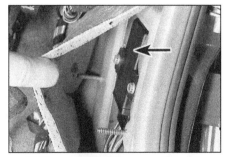

19.5b . . . and pull the carpet back to expose the central locking electronic control unit (arrowed)

19.10 Central locking operating
microswitch (arrowed)

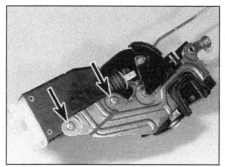

19.14 Central locking motor securing
screws (arrowed)

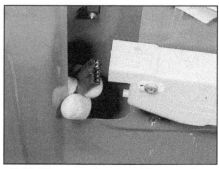

19.19 Disconnecting the wiring plug from
the boot lid lock operating motor -
Saloon model

19.20a Boot lid lock operating motor -
Saloon model

19.20b Removing a tailgate lock operating
motor - Hatchback model

the door inner trim panel as described in
Section 30.

Door lock operating motor

Removal

12 Remove the door lock, as described in
Section 13.

13 Disconnect the lock operating rod from
the motor.

14 Remove the two securing screws, and
withdraw the motor from the lock assembly
(see illustration).

Refitting

15 Refitting is a reversal of removal.

Boot lid/tailgate lock operating motor

Removal

16 Disconnect the battery negative lead.

17 Open the boot or tailgate, as applicable.

18 Remove the securing screws, and
withdraw the lock cylinder assembly cover
(Saloon models), or the tailgate rear trim panel
(Hatchback and Estate models).

19 Disconnect the wiring plug from the motor
(see illustration).

20 Unscrew the two securing screws, and
withdraw the motor from the boot lid or
tailgate, as applicable, unhooking the lock
operating rod as the motor is withdrawn (see
illustrations).

Refitting

21 Refitting is a reversal of removal.

Fuel filler flap operating motor - Saloon and Estate models

Removal

22 Disconnect the battery negative lead.

23 Release the right-hand luggage
compartment side trim panel from the body,
with reference to Section 30.

24 Disconnect the motor wiring plug.

25 Remove the two securing screws, then
carefully manipulate the motor from its
location, disengaging the operating rod as the
unit is withdrawn (see illustration).

Refitting

26 Refitting is a reversal of removal.

Fuel filler flap operating motor - Hatchback models

Removal

27 Disconnect the battery negative lead.

28 Remove the luggage compartment right-
hand side trim panel, referring to Section 30.

29 Remove the right-hand rear light cluster,
as described in Chapter 12, Section 8.

30 Pull back the carpet from the wheel arch
to expose the two lock motor bracket
securing screws (see illustration).

31 Remove the securing screws, then
carefully manipulate the motor and bracket
assembly from its location, disengaging the
operating rod as the unit is withdrawn.
Manipulate the unit out through the rear light
cluster aperture, and disconnect the wiring
plug (see illustration).

32 The motor can be separated from the
bracket by removing the securing screws.

Refitting

33 Refitting is a reversal of removal.

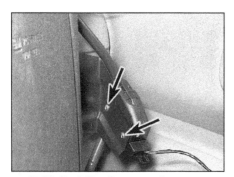

19.25 Fuel filler flap operating motor
securing screws (arrowed) - Saloon model

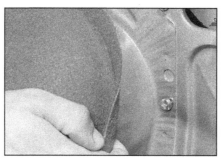

19.30 Pulling back the carpet to expose the
fuel filler flap lock operating motor bracket
securing screws - Hatchback model

19.31 Fuel filler flap operating motor
viewed through rear light cluster aperture

20 Electric window components - removal and refitting

Switches

Removal

1 The switches are located in the driver's and passenger's doors.
2 Remove the door inner trim panel, as described in Section 30.
3 With the wiring connector disconnected, carefully prise the switch assembly from the trim panel **(see illustration)**.

Refitting

4 Refitting is a reversal of removal, but refit the door inner trim panel as described in Section 30.

Window motors

Removal

5 Remove the door window regulator, as described in Section 14.
6 To remove the motor assembly from the regulator, unscrew the three securing screws **(see illustration)**.
7 No spare parts are available for the motor assembly, and if faulty, the complete unit must be renewed.

Refitting

8 Refitting is a reversal of removal, but refit the regulator as described in Section 14.

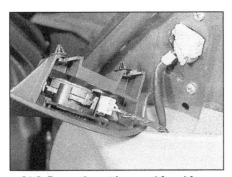

21.3 Door mirror trim panel freed from front edge of door - electric mirror

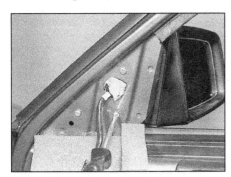

21.4 Unscrewing a door mirror securing screw - electric mirror

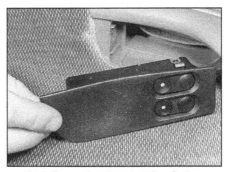

20.3 Removing the electric window operating switch from the driver's door

21 Mirror components - removal and refitting

Door mirror

Removal

1 On models with electric mirrors, disconnect the battery negative lead.
2 Where applicable, on models with manually adjustable mirrors, pull off the adjuster lever.
3 Prise the mirror trim panel from the inside front edge of the door, and disconnect the wiring from the loudspeaker mounted in the trim panel **(see illustration)**.
4 Extract the three now-exposed securing screws, and withdraw the mirror assembly from the door. On models with electric mirrors, disconnect the wiring plug **(see illustration)**.

Refitting

5 Refitting is a reversal of removal, but ensure that the rubber weatherstrip is correctly located on the mirror housing.

Glass renewal

6 The mirror glass can be removed for renewal without removing the mirror. On models with electric mirrors, disconnect the battery negative lead before proceeding.
7 Carefully prise the glass from its balljoints using a screwdriver, and where applicable, disconnect the heater wires from the glass.

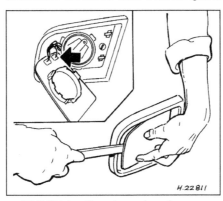

21.7 Prising the mirror glass from an electric mirror - heater wires arrowed

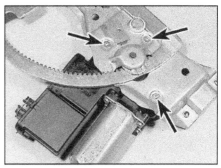

20.6 Electric window operating motor securing screws (arrowed)

Take care, as the glass is easily broken if forced **(see illustration)**.
8 To refit, simply push the glass onto the balljoints (ensuring that the heater wires are connected, where applicable).

Electric mirror operating switch - removal and refitting

9 The switch can be prised from the door inner trim panel, after removing the door inner trim panel (as described in Section 30) and disconnecting the wiring plug **(see illustration)**.
10 After refitting the switch, refit the door inner trim panel as described in Section 30.

Electric mirror motor - removal and refitting

11 Remove the mirror glass, as described previously in this Section.
12 Extract the three motor securing screws, disconnect the wiring plug, then withdraw the motor.
13 Refitting is a reversal of removal, but ensure that the wiring is routed behind the motor, to avoid interfering with the adjustment mechanism.

Interior rear-view mirror

Removal

14 The mirror can be removed from its mounting plate on the windscreen, after unscrewing the mounting screw using a 2 mm Allen key.
15 The mounting plate is fixed to the windscreen using a special adhesive, and should not be disturbed unless necessary.

21.9 Removing the electric mirror operating switch from the door inner trim panel

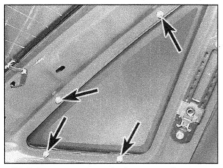

23.2 Rear quarter window securing nuts (arrowed)

Note that there is a risk of cracking the windscreen glass if an attempt is made to remove a securely bonded mounting plate.

Refitting

16 If necessary, the special adhesive required to fix the mounting plate to the windscreen can be obtained from a Vauxhall/Opel dealer.

22 Windscreen and rear window glass - general

Except for the rear quarter windows, all fixed glass is bonded in position, using a special adhesive.

24.4 Prising a plastic trim strip from the guide rail

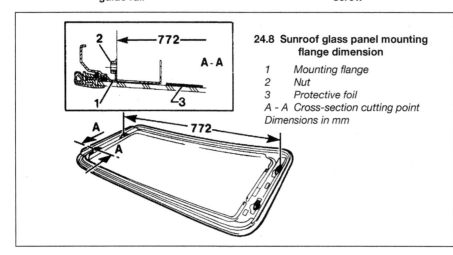

24.8 Sunroof glass panel mounting flange dimension

1   *Mounting flange*
2   *Nut*
3   *Protective foil*
A - A *Cross-section cutting point*
Dimensions in mm

24.2a Extract the four securing screws ...

Special tools, adhesives and expertise are required for successful removal and refitting of glass fixed by this method. Such work must therefore be entrusted to a Vauxhall/Opel dealer, a windscreen specialist, or other competent professional.

23 Rear quarter windows - removal and refitting

Note: *The manufacturers recommend the use of new plastic nuts to secure the glass on refitting.*

Removal

1 Remove the rear quarter trim panel, as described in Section 30.

24.5 Loosening a glass panel securing screw

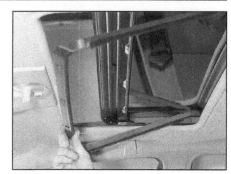

24.2b ... and withdraw the sunroof guide rail plastic surround

2 Have an assistant support the quarter window from outside the vehicle, then unscrew the plastic securing nuts **(see illustration)**, and the bolts, and push the window from the body.

Refitting

3 Refitting is a reversal of removal, but ensure that the seal on the rear of the glass is seated correctly against the body as the window is fitted, and use new plastic nuts to secure the glass.

24 Sunroof components - removal and refitting

Note: *The sunroof is a complex piece of equipment, consisting of a large number of components. It is strongly recommended that the sunroof mechanism is not disturbed unless necessary. If the sunroof mechanism is faulty, or requires overhaul, consult a Vauxhall/ Opel dealer for advice.*

Glass panel

Removal

1 Push the sunshade fully rearwards, and open the glass panel halfway.
2 Extract the four securing screws from the front edge of the guide rail plastic surround, and withdraw the surround down through the sunroof aperture **(see illustrations)**.
3 Move the glass panel forwards, and open it to its tilt position.
4 Prise the plastic trim strips from the guide rails, to expose the glass panel securing screws **(see illustration)**.
5 Extract the three securing screws from each guide rail **(see illustration)** and where applicable, recover the lockwashers.
6 Carefully lift the glass panel from the roof aperture, taking care not to damage the vehicle paintwork.

Refitting

7 Refitting is a reversal of removal, remembering the following points.
8 Before refitting the glass panel, measure the distance between the mounting flanges. Bend the flanges if necessary to achieve the required dimension **(see illustration)**.

9 Where applicable, ensure that the glass panel securing screw lockwashers engage with the locating pins on the guide rails.
10 Before fully tightening the glass panel securing screws, close the panel, and adjust its position to give the dimensions shown **(see illustration)**.
11 If a new glass panel has been fitted, peel off the protective foil on completion of adjustment.

Gutter

Removal

12 Remove the glass panel, as described previously in this Section.
13 Extract the two securing screws, then lift the gutter from the roof aperture.

Refitting

14 Refit the gutter to the roof aperture at an angle, pushing it up to the stop on both sides until the retaining lugs engage with the gutter guides.
15 Refit and tighten the securing screws.
16 Refit and adjust the glass panel, as described previously in this Section.

Sunshade

Removal

17 Remove the glass panel and the gutter, as described previously in this Section.
18 Carefully prise the four sunshade spring clips out of the roof guides (using a plastic or wooden implement to avoid damage), then withdraw the sunshade from the guides **(see illustration)**.

Refitting

19 Refitting is a reversal of removal, but ensure that the spring clips engage correctly with the roof guides.

Crank drive

Removal

20 Prise out the trim, and unscrew the crank handle securing screw. Prise the crank from the drive spindle.
21 Disconnect the battery negative lead, then prise the courtesy light from the roof trim panel, and disconnect the wiring.
22 Remove the two trim panel securing screws, and withdraw the trim panel from the roof.
23 Extract the two securing screws, and remove the crank drive assembly.

Refitting

24 Refitting is a reversal of removal, remembering the following points.
25 Before finally tightening the crank handle, the crank drive must be adjusted as follows.
26 Temporarily refit the crank handle, and position it so that it faces forwards, then depress the locking button.
27 Remove the crank handle and turn the crank drive pinion anti-clockwise by hand as far as the stop.

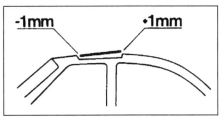

24.10 Sunroof glass panel fitting position

28 Refit the crank handle so that it faces directly forwards, then tighten the securing screw and refit the trim.

25 Body exterior fittings – removal and refitting

Wheel arch liners

1 The plastic wheel arch liners are secured by a combination of self-tapping screws and plastic nuts and clips. Removal and refitting is self-evident, bearing in mind the following points.
2 Some of the securing clips may be held in place using a central pin, which must be tapped out to release the clip.
3 The clips are easily broken during removal, and it is advisable to obtain a few spare clips for possible use when refitting.
4 Certain models may have additional underbody shields and splashguards fitted, which may be attached to the wheel arch liners.

Engine undershield

Removal

5 Apply the handbrake, then jack up the front of the vehicle, and support securely on axle stands (see "Jacking and vehicle support").
6 Where applicable, extract the two securing screws, and remove the oil filter access panel.
7 Working around the edges of the undershield, remove the self-tapping screws that secure the shield to the underbody, noting that some of the screws may also secure the wheel arch liners **(see illustration)**.
8 With the help of an assistant, pull the shield

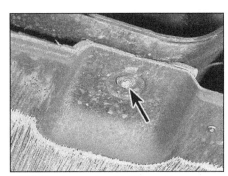

25.7 Engine undershield securing screw (arrowed)

24.18 Sunshade spring clip locations (arrowed)

from the vehicle, and place it to one side to avoid damage.

Refitting

9 Refitting is a reversal of removal.

Fuel filler flap

Removal

10 Open the flap for access to the two securing screws.
11 Remove the securing screws and withdraw the flap.

Refitting

12 Refitting is a reversal of removal.

Boot lid spoiler – Saloon models

Removal

13 Open the boot lid, then remove the securing screws, and withdraw the lock assembly cover panel.
14 Unscrew the three bolts and eight nuts securing the spoiler to the boot lid.
15 On certain models, the spoiler may be retained with adhesive tape, in which case great care mast be taken to avoid damage to the paintwork as the spoiler is removed. One solution is to heat the tape using a hot air gun or a hairdryer, until the heat softens the adhesive sufficiently to enable the spoiler to be easily removed. Take care that the heat does not damage the surrounding paintwork.
16 Withdraw the spoiler from the boot lid.

Refitting

17 Where applicable, clean off all traces of adhesive using white spirit, then wash the area with warm soapy water to remove all traces of spirit. If adhesive tape is used to secure the spoiler, ensure that the relevant surfaces are completely clean, and free from dirt and grease.
18 If adhesive tape is used to refit the spoiler, follow the instructions supplied for refitting (consult a Vauxhall/Opel dealer if necessary). It may be necessary to use a heat source, as during removal, to soften the adhesive before the tape is applied.

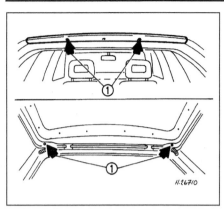

25.22 Tailgate spoiler securing screws (1) - all except 'Sports' models

19 Refit the spoiler, ensuring that it is correctly aligned before pressing firmly into position, and tighten the securing nuts and bolts.
20 Refit the lock assembly cover panel on completion.

Tailgate spoiler (all except 'Sports' models)

Removal

21 Working outside the tailgate, remove the two spoiler securing screws.
22 Open the tailgate, and unscrew the two remaining screws from the corners of the tailgate (see illustration).
23 Refer to paragraph 15.
24 Withdraw the spoiler.
25 The washer nozzle can be prised from the spoiler mounting bracket once the spoiler has been withdrawn.
26 The spoiler mounting bracket can be removed from the tailgate after unscrewing the securing nuts and screws.

Refitting

27 Where applicable, refit the spoiler mounting bracket and the washer nozzle, using a reversal of the removal procedure.
28 Refer to paragraphs 17 and 18.
29 Refit the spoiler, ensuring that it is correctly aligned before pressing firmly into position, and tighten the securing bolts.

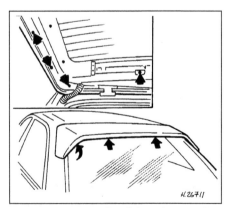

25.31 Tailgate spoiler fixings (arrowed) – 'Sports' models

Tailgate spoiler ('Sports' models)

Removal

30 Open the tailgate, then remove the securing screws, and withdraw the tailgate upper inner trim panel.
31 Working inside the tailgate, and at the outer lower edge of the spoiler, remove the six bolts and four nuts securing the spoiler to the tailgate (see illustration).
32 Proceed as described in paragraphs 23 to 26 inclusive.

Refitting

33 Proceed as described in paragraphs 27 to 29 inclusive.

Side rubbing strips

Removal

34 Apply masking tape along the edge of the strip to be removed, as an aid to correct alignment on refitting.
35 Using a hot air gun or a hairdryer, heat the trim strip until the heat softens the adhesive sufficiently to enable the trim strip to be easily removed. Take care that the heat does not damage the surrounding paintwork.

Refitting

36 Clean off all traces of adhesive using white spirit, then wash the area with warm soapy water to remove all traces of spirit. Ensure that the surface to which the new strip is to be fitted is completely clean, and free from dirt and grease.
37 Use the heat gun or hairdryer to heat the new trim strip to approximately 80°C, then peel off the protective foil, and press the trim strip firmly into position, using the masking tape as a guide. Remove the masking tape when the strip is secured.

Badges

Removal

38 The various badges are secured with adhesives. To remove them, either soften the adhesive using a hot air gun or hairdryer (taking care to avoid damage to the paintwork), or separate the badge from the body by 'sawing' through the adhesive using a length of nylon cord.

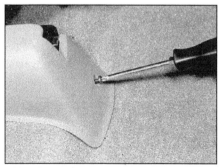

26.1 Removing the securing screw from the outer seat rail trim

Refitting

39 Clean off all traces of adhesive using white spirit, then wash the area with warm soapy water to remove all traces of spirit. Ensure that the surface to which the new badge is to be fastened is completely clean, and free from grease and dirt.
40 Use the hot air gun to soften the adhesive on the new badge, then press it firmly into position.

Side skirts and additional spoilers

41 On certain models, body kits may be fitted, comprising side skirts and an additional tailgate spoiler.
42 These components are secured by a combination of screws, adhesive and rivets. Although the basic principles described in this Section for other similar components apply, it is advisable to entrust removal and refitting to a Vauxhall/Opel dealer or a bodywork specialist. Great care is required to avoid damage to the surrounding paintwork and the components themselves.

---

26 Seats –
removal and refitting

Front seat

⚠️ *Warning: The seat belt tensioners fitted to the front seat assemblies may cause injury if triggered inadvertently. Before carrying out any work on the front seats, the safety fork must be inserted into the seat belt tensioner cylinder, to prevent the possibility of the tensioner being triggered (see paragraphs 3 and 4 below). Seats should always be transported and installed with the safety fork in place. If a seat is to be disposed of, the tensioner must be triggered before the seat is removed from the vehicle, by inserting the safety fork, and striking the tensioner tube sharply with a hammer. If the tensioner has been triggered due to a sudden impact or accident, the unit must be renewed, as it cannot be reset. Due to safety considerations, tensioner renewal should be entrusted to a Vauxhall/Opel dealer.*

Removal

Note: *The manufacturers recommend the use of new bolts when refitting the seats.*
1 Remove the single securing screw from the front edge of the outer seat rail trim (see illustration), then withdraw the trim.
2 Release the securing clips, and unclip the trim from the rear edge of the inner seat rail (see illustration).
3 Locate the plastic safety fork for the seat belt tensioner, which is usually taped to the outside of the tensioner cylinder (see illustration).

26.2 Releasing the clips from the inner seat rail trim piece

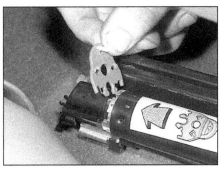

26.3 Inserting the safety fork into its slot in the seat belt tensioner cylinder

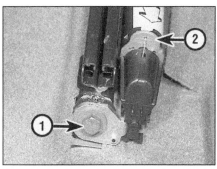

26.5a Front outer seat rail securing bolt (1) - note seat belt tensioner safety fork (2) engaged in slot

4 Insert the safety fork into the slot provided in the tensioner cylinder, ensuring that the fork engages securely.
5 Remove the four bolts that secure the seat rails to the floor, then withdraw the seat, complete with rails **(see illustrations)**. Recover the washers and plates.
6 Withdraw the seat, complete with the rails, from the vehicle.
7 If desired, the seat can be separated from the rails for attention to the adjustment mechanism.

Refitting

8 Refitting is a reversal of removal, bearing in mind the following points.
9 Use new seat securing bolts, and tighten them in the sequence shown **(see illustration)**.
10 Before refitting the trim panels to the seat rails, remove the safety fork from the seat belt tensioner cylinder, and tape it to the outside of the cylinder.

Rear seat cushion

Removal

11 With the seats in their raised position, where applicable, unclip the trim panel from the front of the hinge **(see illustration)**.
12 Prise the securing clips from the ends of the hinge pins **(see illustration)**, then withdraw the pins from the hinges.

26.5b Rear outer seat rail securing bolt - note washer and plate

26.5c Rear inner seat rail securing bolt

13 With the hinge pins removed, the seat cushion can be withdrawn from the vehicle.

Refitting

14 Refitting is a reversal of removal.

Rear seat back

Removal

15 Fold down the seat back.
16 Carefully release the securing clips, using a forked tool or a screwdriver, and pull back the trim covering the hinges on the seat back.
17 Unscrew the two bolts at each side, securing the seat back to the hinges, then withdraw the seat back from the vehicle.

Refitting

18 Refitting is a reversal of removal.

27 Seat belt tensioner system – general information

1 All models are fitted with a front seat belt tensioner system, which is designed to instantaneously take up any slack in the seat belt in the case of a sudden frontal impact, therefore reducing the possibility of injury to the front seat occupants. Each front seat is fitted with its own system, the components of which are mounted in the seat frame **(see illustration overleaf)**.
2 The seat belt tensioner is triggered by a frontal impact causing a deceleration of six times the force of gravity or greater. Lesser impacts, including impacts from behind, will not trigger the system.

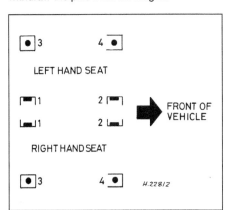

26.9 Tightening sequence for front seat bolts

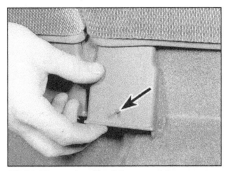

26.11 Removing the trim panel from a rear seat cushion hinge - note securing clip (arrowed)

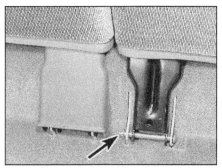

26.12 Rear seat cushion hinge pin securing clip (arrowed)

3 When the system is triggered, a pre-tensioned spring draws back the seat belt through a cable attached to a fulcrum, which acts on the seat belt stalk mounted on the seat frame. The cable and fulcrum can move by up to 80.0 mm, which therefore reduces the slack in the seat belt around the shoulders and waist of the occupant by a similar amount.

4 There is a risk of injury if the system is triggered inadvertently when working on the vehicle, and it is therefore strongly recommended that any work involving the seat belt tensioner system is entrusted to a Vauxhall/Opel dealer. Refer to the warning given at the beginning of Section 26 before contemplating any work on the front seats.

28 Seat belt components - removal and refitting

Front seat belt – all models except 3-door Hatchback

Removal

1 Remove the B-pillar lower trim panel, as described in Section 30.

2 Prise off the trim, and unbolt the seat belt upper mounting from the B-pillar. Recover the spacer.

3 Unbolt the lower seat belt mounting from the body, and recover the spacer and washers, noting their locations.

4 Unscrew the securing bolt **(see illustration)**, withdraw the inertia reel unit

28.4 B-pillar lower trim panel removed to expose inertia reel unit and seat belt lower mounting securing bolts (arrowed)

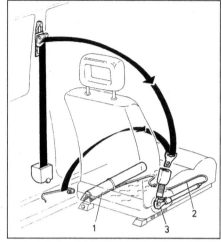

27.1 Front seat belt tensioner system

1 Spring   2 Cable   3 Fulcrum

from the B-pillar, then withdraw the seat belt assembly from the vehicle.

Refitting

5 Refitting is a reversal of removal, but make sure that the belt is fitted untwisted, and ensure that the washers and spacers on the upper and lower mountings are fitted as noted before removal. Tighten all fixings to the specified torque.

Front seat belt - 3-door Hatchback models

Removal

6 Prise off the trim, and unbolt the seat belt upper mounting from the B-pillar. Recover the spacer.

7 Remove the rear side trim panel, as described in Section 30.

8 Unscrew the securing bolt, withdraw the inertia reel unit from the B-pillar, then withdraw the seat belt assembly from the vehicle.

Refitting

9 Refitting is a reversal of removal, but tighten all fixings to the specified torque.

Front seat belt height adjuster

Removal

10 Remove the B-pillar upper trim panel, as described in Section 30.

11 Remove the two Torx type securing bolts, and withdraw the height adjuster assembly from the B-pillar.

Refitting

12 Refitting is a reversal of removal, but ensure that the height adjuster is fitted the correct way up. The top of the adjuster is marked with two arrows, which should point towards the vehicle roof.

Front seat belt tensioner

13 The front seat belt tensioner mechanism is mounted on the front seat frame. Due to safety considerations (refer to the warning at the beginning of Section 26), no attempt should be made to carry out work on the tensioner mechanism. Any problems should be referred to a Vauxhall/Opel dealer.

Rear seat belt

Removal

14 Fold the rear seat cushion forwards for access to the seat belt lower mountings.

15 Prise up the carpet to expose the seat belt lower mounting bolt(s), then unscrew the relevant bolt(s) from the floor. Note the location of any spacers and washers on the mounting bolt(s).

16 If removing one of the side inertia reel seat belts, continue as follows.

17 Prise off the trim, and unbolt the seat belt upper mounting from the body pillar **(see illustration)**. Recover the spacer.

18 On Saloon and 5-door Hatchback models, remove the rear quarter trim panel, as described in Section 30.

19 On 3-door Hatchback models, remove the rear parcel shelf support panel, as described in Section 30.

20 On Estate and Van models, remove the luggage compartment side trim panel, referring to Section 30.

21 On Saloon models, remove the luggage compartment side trim panel, referring to Section 30.

22 Unscrew the inertia reel unit securing bolt - accessible from the luggage compartment on Saloon models **(see illustrations)** - remove the inertia reel unit from the body, then withdraw the seat belt assembly from the vehicle.

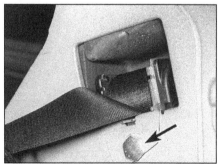

28.17 Prising the trim from a rear seat belt upper mounting

28.22a Rear seat belt inertia reel securing bolt (arrowed) - 5-door Hatchback model

28.22b Rear seat belt inertia reel securing bolt (arrowed) - Saloon model

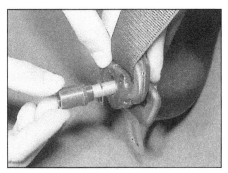

28.23 Fitting a rear seat belt upper mounting spacer and washer

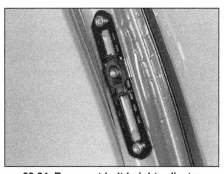

28.24 Rear seat belt height adjuster assembly

29.4 Using a forked tool to remove a trim panel securing clip

Refitting

23 Refitting is a reversal of removal, but make sure that the belt is fitted untwisted, and ensure that the washers and spacers on the upper (where applicable) and lower mountings are fitted as noted before removal **(see illustration)**. Tighten all fixings to the specified torque.

Rear seat belt height adjuster

24 The procedure is as described in paragraphs 10 to 12 for the front seat belt height adjuster, but for access to the height adjuster, remove the rear quarter trim panel (see Section 30) instead of the B-pillar trim panel **(see illustration)**.

29 Interior trim – general information

Interior trim panels

1 The interior trim panels are all secured using either screws or various types of plastic fasteners.

2 To remove a panel, study it carefully, noting how it is secured. Often, other panels or ancillary components must be removed before a particular panel can be withdrawn, such as seat belt mountings, grab handles, etc.

3 Once any such components have been removed, check that there are no other panels overlapping the one to be removed; usually there is a sequence that has to be followed, which will become obvious on close inspection.

4 Remove all obvious fasteners, such as screws, many of which may have plastic covers fitted. If the panel cannot be freed, it is probably secured by hidden clips or fasteners on the rear of the panel. Such fasteners are usually situated around the edge of the panel, and can be prised up to release them. Note that plastic clips can break quite easily so it is advisable to have a few replacement clips of the correct type available for refitting. Generally, the best way of releasing such clips is to use a forked tool **(see illustration)**. If this is not available, an old, broad-bladed screwdriver with the edges rounded-off and

wrapped in insulating tape will serve as a good substitute.

5 The following Section and the accompanying illustrations and photographs describe removal and refitting of all the major trim panels. Note that the type and number of fasteners used often varies during the production run of a particular model, and differences may be noted to the procedures provided for certain vehicles.

6 When removing a panel, **never** use excessive force, or the panel may be damaged. Always check carefully that all fasteners have been removed or released before attempting to withdraw a panel.

7 Refitting is the reverse of the removal procedure; secure the fasteners by pressing them firmly into place, and ensure that all disturbed components are correctly secured to prevent rattles. If adhesives were found at any point during removal, use white spirit to remove all traces of old adhesive, then wash off all traces of spirit using soapy water. Use a trim adhesive (a Vauxhall/Opel dealer should be able to recommend a proprietary product) on reassembly.

Carpets

8 The passenger compartment floor carpet is divided into two pieces, front and rear, and each section is secured by plastic clips.

9 Carpet removal and refitting is reasonably straightforward, but very time-consuming because many of the adjoining trim panels must be removed first, as must components such as the seats and their mountings, the centre console, etc.

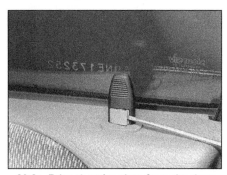

30.2a Prise the trim plate from the door lock button . . .

Headlining

10 The headlining is clipped to the roof, and can be withdrawn only once all fittings such as the grab handles, sunvisors, sunroof trim (where applicable), door pillar trim panels, rear quarter trim panels, weatherstrips, etc., have been removed or prised clear.

11 Note that headlining removal requires considerable skill and patience if it is to be carried out without damage, and is therefore best entrusted to an expert.

30 Interior trim panels - removal and refitting

Front door inner trim panel

Removal

1 Disconnect the battery negative lead.

2 Prise the trim plate from the door lock button in the top rear edge of the door, then pull the lock button from the operating rod **(see illustrations)**.

3 On models with manually operated windows, release the securing clip, and remove the window regulator handle. To release the securing clip, insert a length of wire with a hooked end between the handle and the trim bezel on the door trim panel, and manipulate it to free the securing clip from the handle. Take care not to damage the door trim panel. Recover the trim bezel.

4 Where applicable (manually adjustable mirrors), pull off the door mirror adjuster lever,

30.2b . . . and pull the lock button from the operating rod

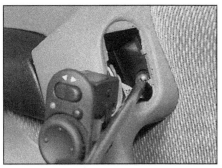

30.5 Unscrewing the front door inner trim panel upper securing screw

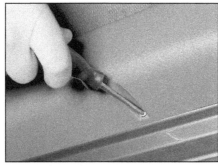

30.6a Removing a front door inner trim panel lower securing screw

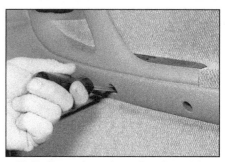

30.6b Removing a front door inner trim panel securing screw from armrest/handgrip

then prise the door mirror trim panel from the door, and disconnect the wiring from the loudspeaker mounted in the trim panel.

5 Prise the door mirror switch (driver's door), electric window switch (passenger door), or the blanking plate, as applicable, from the door handle surround to expose the upper door trim panel securing screw. Remove the screw **(see illustration)**.

6 Remove the five remaining trim panel securing screws, which are located along the bottom edge of the door (three screws), and around the bottom edge of the armrest (two screws), **(see illustrations)**.

7 The plastic clips securing the trim panel to the door must now be released. This can be done using a screwdriver, but it is preferable to use a forked tool, to minimise the possibility of damage to the trim panel and the clips. The clips are located around the outer edge of the trim panel.

8 Once the clips have been released, pull the trim panel away from the door.

9 When working on models with electric door mirrors and/or electric windows, it will be necessary to disconnect the wiring plugs as the trim panel is withdrawn. Note the position of the wiring connector(s) in the bracket(s) on the door **(see illustrations)**.

10 Withdraw the trim panel from the door.

11 The plastic insulating sheet can be peeled from the door **(see illustration)**. Peel the sheet back slowly to prevent damage to the sealant, and take care not to damage the sheet.

Refitting

12 Refitting is a reversal of removal, bearing in mind the following points.

13 If the plastic insulating sheet has been removed from the door, make sure that it is refitted intact, and securely fixed to the door. If the sheet was removed carefully, there

should be no need to use new sealant when refitting the sheet. If the sheet is damaged or detached, rainwater may leak into the vehicle or damage the door trim.

14 Where applicable, ensure that the wiring connector(s) is/are positioned correctly in the bracket(s) on the door before refitting the trim panel.

15 Ensure that all the trim panel securing clips engage as the panel is refitted, and if any of the clips were broken during removal, renew them on refitting.

Rear door inner trim panel

Removal

16 Proceed as described in paragraphs 2 and 3 **(see illustration)**.

17 Prise the plastic surround from the door interior handle **(see illustration)**.

18 Prise the trim panel from the lower rear edge of the window aperture **(see illustration)**.

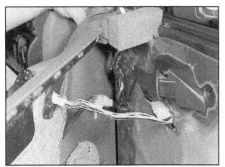

30.9a Front door inner trim panel removed to expose wiring connectors

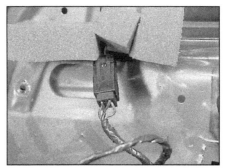

30.9b Electric door mirror wiring connector locates under foam padding

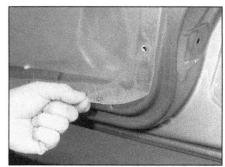

30.11 Peeling the plastic insulating sheet from the door

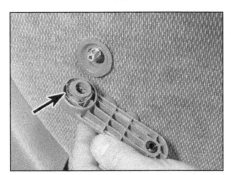

30.16 Removing the rear window regulator handle - securing clip arrowed

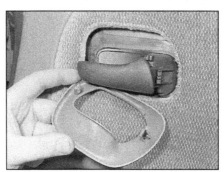

30.17 Removing the plastic surround from the rear door interior handle

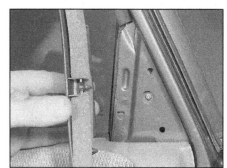

30.18 Removing the trim panel from the edge of the rear door window aperture

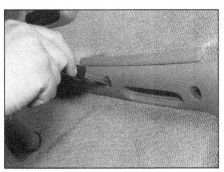

30.19 Removing a rear door inner trim panel securing screw

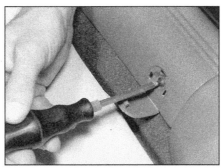

30.23 Unscrewing a front footwell side/sill trim panel securing screw

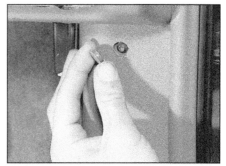

30.24a Removing the cover from the front footwell side/sill trim panel securing screw

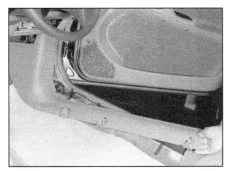

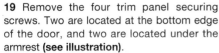

30.24b Removing a front footwell side/sill trim panel (front seat removed)

30.30 Removing the seat belt mounting rail securing bolt and spacer plate - 3-door Hatchback model

30.31 Removing the seat belt mounting rail - 3-door Hatchback model

19 Remove the four trim panel securing screws. Two are located at the bottom edge of the door, and two are located under the armrest **(see illustration)**.
20 Proceed as described in paragraphs 7 and 8.
21 Withdraw the trim panel from the door.

Refitting

22 Proceed as described in paragraphs 12 to 15 inclusive.

Front footwell side/sill trim panel

Removal

23 Working along the sill, prise down the three cover panels, and remove the three securing screws **(see illustration)**.
24 Working at the upper front edge of the panel, prise out the cover and extract the

remaining securing screw, then withdraw the panel **(see illustrations)**.

Refitting

25 Refitting is a reversal of removal.

Rear sill trim panel – all models except 3-door Hatchback

Removal

26 Fold the rear seat cushion forwards.
27 Working along the sill, prise down the two cover panels and remove the two securing screws, then withdraw the panel.

Refitting

28 Refitting is a reversal of removal.

Rear sill trim panel - 3-door Hatchback models

Removal

29 Prise down the covers, and remove the

two rear securing screws from the front footwell side/sill trim panel.
30 Prise down the cover, and unscrew the bolt securing the seat belt lower mounting rail to the sill. Recover the spacer plate **(see illustration)**.
31 Pull the rear of the seat belt mounting rail from the hole in the sill trim panel and slip the lower end of the seat belt webbing from the rail **(see illustration)**.
32 Fold the rear seat cushion forwards.
33 Prise out the covers, and extract the two trim panel securing screws then carefully withdraw the panel, sliding the front edge of the panel from under the front footwell side/sill trim panel **(see illustrations)**.

Refitting

34 Refitting is a reversal of removal, tightening the seat belt mounting rail bolt to the specified torque.

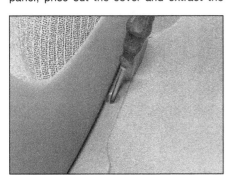

30.33a Remove the rear sill trim panel rear. . .

30.33b . . . and front securing screws . . .

30.33c . . . and withdraw the panel - 3-door Hatchback model

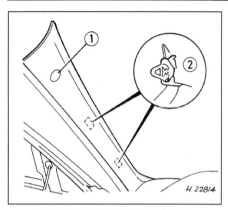

30.36 A-pillar trim panel fixings

1 Screw and cover   *2 Clips*

A-pillar trim panel

Removal

35 Prise out the cover, and remove the securing screw from the top of the trim panel.
36 Carefully prise the panel from the pillar to release the two securing clips **(see illustration)**.

Refitting

37 Refitting is a reversal of removal.

B-pillar lower trim panel – all models except 3-door Hatchback

Removal

38 Prise down the cover, and remove the front securing screw from the rear sill trim panel.
39 Open the front and rear doors, and prise the weatherstrips from the edges of the B-pillar.
40 Carefully prise the panel from the pillar, recovering the securing clips, where applicable.

Refitting

41 Refitting is a reversal of removal.

B-pillar upper trim panel – all models except 3-door Hatchback

Removal

42 Remove the B-pillar lower trim panel, as described previously in this Section.

30.56 Unscrewing a rear side trim panel securing screw - 3-door Hatchback model

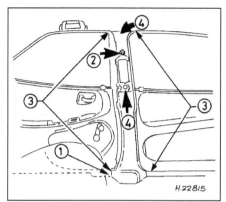

30.44 B-pillar upper trim panel fixings - all models except 3-door Hatchback

1 Rear sill panel securing screw
2 Seat belt upper mounting bolt
3 Weather seals
4 Trim panel securing screws

43 Prise off the trim, and unbolt the seat belt upper mounting from the B-pillar. Recover the spacer.
44 Prise out the covers, and remove the two securing screws from the upper trim panel (one at the top and one at the bottom) **(see illustration)**.
45 Carefully prise the panel from the pillar.

Refitting

46 Refitting is a reversal of removal, tightening the seat belt mounting to the specified torque.

B-pillar upper trim panel - 3-door Hatchback models

Removal

47 Remove the rear side trim panel, as described later in this Section.
48 Prise off the trim, and unbolt the seat belt upper mounting from the B-pillar. Recover the spacer.
49 Extract the two securing screws, and remove the grab handle from the top of the B-pillar upper trim panel.
50 Extract the securing screw, and remove the coat hook from the B-pillar **(see illustration)**.
51 Prise out the cover, and remove the lower securing screw from the trim panel.
52 Carefully prise the panel from the body, releasing the clip from the rear end of the panel as it is withdrawn.

Refitting

53 Refitting is a reversal of removal, tightening the seat belt mounting to the specified torque.

Rear side trim panel - 3-door Hatchback models

Removal

54 Remove the rear sill trim panel, as described previously in this Section.
55 Open the door, and carefully pull the

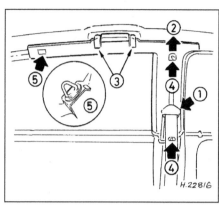

30.50 B-pillar upper trim panel fixings - 3-door Hatchback models

1 Seat belt upper mounting bolt
2 Coat hook
3 Grab handle
4 Trim panel securing screws
5 Trim panel securing clip

weatherstrip from the front of the rear trim panel.
56 Prise out the cover, and remove the securing screw from the rear of the side trim panel **(see illustration)**.
57 Carefully pull the panel from the body to release the securing clips **(see illustration)**.

Refitting

58 Refitting is a reversal of removal.

Rear parcel shelf support panel - 3-door Hatchback models

Removal

59 Open the tailgate, then remove the parcel shelf, and fold the rear seat back forwards.
60 Working in the luggage compartment, disconnect the wiring from the loudspeaker.
61 Working inside the rear of the vehicle, where applicable prise out the cover, and remove the trim panel securing screw.
62 Working in the luggage compartment, remove the five remaining panel securing screws.
63 Carefully pull the panel from the body, releasing the retaining clip at the front of the panel as it is pulled free.

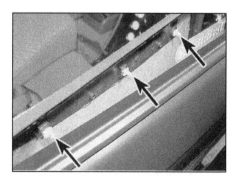

30.57 Rear side trim panel removed to expose securing clips (arrowed - viewed through rear window) - 3-door Hatchback model

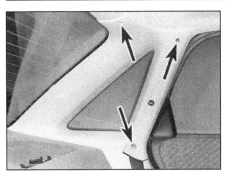

30.69 Rear quarter trim panel securing
screw locations (arrowed) - Saloon model

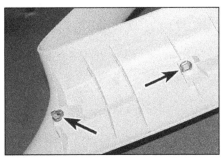

30.70 Rear quarter trim panel removed to
show two of the securing clips (arrowed) -
Saloon model

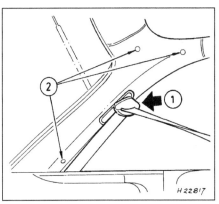

30.74 Rear quarter (C-pillar) trim panel
fixings - 3-door Hatchback models

1 Seat belt upper mounting
2 Trim panel securing screws and covers

64 Pass the seat belt webbing and the wiring through the holes in the panel, and withdraw the panel from the vehicle.

Refitting

65 Refitting is a reversal of removal.

Rear quarter trim panel - Saloon models

Removal

66 Fold the rear seat back forwards.
67 Prise off the trim, and unbolt the seat belt upper mounting from the C-pillar. Recover the spacer.
68 Open the rear door, and carefully prise the weatherstrip from the front edge of the trim panel.
69 Where applicable, prise out the covers, and remove the three trim panel securing screws (two upper screws, and one lower screw), (see illustration).
70 Carefully pull the panel from the body to release the securing clips, passing the seat belt webbing through the slot in the panel as it is withdrawn (see illustration).

Refitting

71 Refitting is a reversal of removal, tightening the seat belt mounting to the specified torque.

Rear quarter (C-pillar) trim panel - 3-door Hatchback models

Removal

72 Prise off the trim, and unbolt the seat belt

upper mounting from the C-pillar. Recover the spacer.
73 Open the tailgate, and carefully prise the weatherstrip from the rear edge of the trim panel.
74 Prise out the covers, remove the three securing screws, then withdraw the panel (see illustration).

Refitting

75 Refitting is a reversal of removal, tightening the seat belt mounting to the specified torque.

Rear quarter trim panel - 5-door Hatchback models

Removal

76 Remove the rear parcel shelf, and fold the rear seat back forwards.
77 Prise off the trim, and unbolt the seat belt upper mounting from the C-pillar. Recover the spacer.
78 Open the rear door and the tailgate, and carefully prise the weatherstrips from the edges of the trim panel.
79 Working in the luggage compartment, disconnect the wiring from the loudspeaker.
80 Working inside the rear of the vehicle, where applicable prise out the covers, and remove the four trim panel securing screws.
81 Working in the luggage compartment, remove the five remaining panel securing screws (see illustration).
82 Carefully pull the panel from the body, releasing the retaining clip at the front of the panel as it is pulled free (see illustration).
83 Pass the seat belt webbing and the wiring

through the holes in the panel, and withdraw the panel from the vehicle.

Refitting

84 Refitting is a reversal of removal, tightening the seat belt mounting to the specified torque.

Rear quarter trim panel - Estate models

Removal

85 Fold the rear seat back forwards.
86 Prise off the trim, and unbolt the seat belt upper mounting from the C-pillar. Recover the spacer.
87 Open the rear door and the tailgate, and carefully prise the weatherstrips from the edges of the trim panel.
88 Where applicable, remove the luggage retaining net and the luggage compartment cover.
89 Prise off the covers, and remove the three trim panel securing screws.
90 Carefully pull the panel from the body to release the securing clips, and withdraw the panel from the vehicle (see illustration).

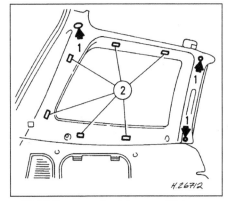

30.90 Rear quarter trim panel fixings -
Estate models

1 Securing screws and covers
2 Clips

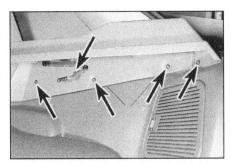

30.81 Rear quarter trim panel securing
screws (arrowed) -
5-door Hatchback model

30.82 Removing the rear quarter trim
panel - 5-door Hatchback model

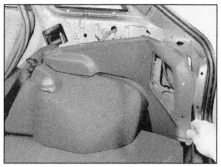

30.93 Removing the luggage compartment side trim panel - 5-door Hatchback model

Refitting

91 Refitting is reversal of removal, tightening the seat belt mounting to the specified torque.

Luggage compartment, tailgate and boot lid trim panels

92 The luggage compartment trim panels on all models are secured by a combination of plastic clips and/or screws. Removal and refitting of the panels is self-explanatory, remembering the points made in Section 29, and the following additional points.

93 To remove the luggage compartment side trim panel on Hatchback and Estate models, it will first be necessary to remove the rear quarter trim panel, as described previously in this Section **(see illustration)**.

94 Various fittings, such as the luggage compartment light, and the first aid kit retaining strap bolt, may have to be removed before certain panels can be freed.

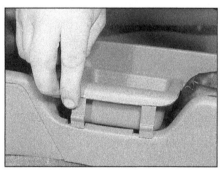

31.3 Removing the central storage tray from the centre console

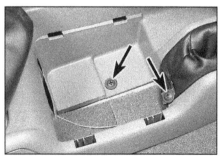

31.7 Central storage tray removed to expose centre console securing screws (arrowed)

31 Centre console - removal and refitting

Removal

1 Disconnect the battery negative lead.
2 Carefully prise the rear ashtray from the centre console.
3 Similarly, remove the central storage tray from the centre console **(see illustration)**. Note that on models fitted with heated front seats and/or electronic traction control, it will be necessary to disconnect the battery negative lead and then disconnect the wiring from the relevant switches located in the storage tray, before the tray can be removed.
4 Release the handbrake lever gaiter from the centre console, and on manual gearbox models, release the gear lever gaiter from the centre console.
5 On models with automatic transmission, release the transmission selector cover from the centre console (the cover is secured by clips at either side). Pull the illumination light bulbholder from the selector cover, and disconnect the transmission 'Winter' mode switch wiring connector.
6 Remove the two securing screws from the rear ashtray housing **(see illustration)**.
7 Remove the two securing screws from the central storage tray housing **(see illustration)**.
8 Remove the two screws from the front of the centre console assembly one screw on each side **(see illustration)**. Then slide the assembly rearwards, and pull the cigarette

31.6 Rear ashtray removed to expose rear centre console securing screws

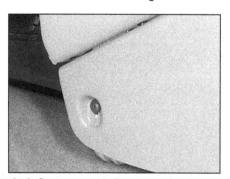

31.8 Centre console front securing screw

lighter plug and the illumination bulb from the rear of the assembly.
9 Withdraw the assembly, manipulating the gear lever gaiter/selector lever and cover (as applicable) through the aperture in the centre console, and sliding the handbrake lever gaiter from the assembly as it is withdrawn.

Refitting

10 Refitting is a reversal of removal.

32 Facia panels - removal and refitting

Note: *When removing facia panels, note the locations of the securing screws, as several different types of screw are used.*

Facia centre panel assembly

Removal

1 Disconnect the battery negative lead.
2 Remove the steering column shrouds and the instrument panel surround, as described later in this Section.
3 Remove the lighting control stalk (right-hand-drive models), or the wash/wipe control stalk (left-hand-drive models), as applicable, as described in Chapter 12, Section 5.
4 Remove the hazard warning light switch, as described in Chapter 12, Section 5.
5 Remove the radio/cassette player, and the multi-function display, as described in Chapter 12.
6 Remove the centre facia ventilation nozzles, as described in Chapter 3.
7 Working through the centre facia ventilation nozzle apertures, carefully release the securing clip, using a screwdriver or a similar tool, and disconnect the vent flap actuating rod **(see illustration)**.
8 Remove the two lower facia panel securing screws, visible at the bottom of the panel **(see illustration)**.
9 Carefully pull off the heater air distribution and temperature control switch knobs, to expose two of the facia panel securing screws, then extract the screws **(see illustrations)**.
10 Turn the heater blower switch knob to position '3', then insert a small screwdriver or

32.7 Releasing the centre facia ventilation vent flap actuating rod

32.8 Unscrewing a facia centre panel lower securing screw

32.9a Pull off the heater switch knobs . . .

32.9b . . . and extract the facia centre panel securing screws

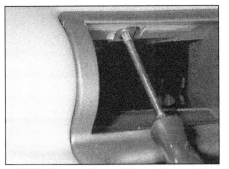

32.11 Unscrewing a facia centre panel upper securing screw

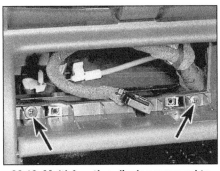

32.12 Multi-function display removed to expose facia centre panel securing screws (arrowed)

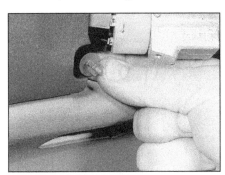

32.13 Removing the facia centre panel securing clip

a rod through the hole in the bottom of the switch knob to depress the knob retaining clip. Pull the knob from the switch.

11 Remove the two upper facia panel

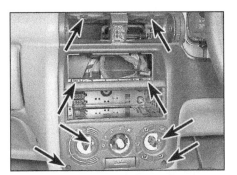

32.14a Facia centre panel securing screws (arrowed)

securing screws, accessible through the centre facia ventilation nozzle apertures **(see illustration)**.

12 Remove the two centre facia panel securing screws, accessible through the multi-function display aperture **(see illustration)**.

13 Carefully pull out the facia panel securing clip, accessible from behind the right-hand side (right-hand-drive models), or the left-hand side (left-hand-drive models) of the panel, as applicable **(see illustration)**.

14 The facia centre panel assembly can now be carefully withdrawn from the facia. As the assembly is withdrawn, disconnect the radio aerial lead, the radio/cassette unit wiring plug, and the hazard warning light switch wiring plug from the rear of the assembly **(see illustrations)**.

Refitting

15 Refitting is a reversal of removal, remembering the following points.

16 Make sure that all electrical plugs are securely reconnected to the rear of the assembly, and as the assembly is refitted, feed the multi-function display wiring through the multi-function display aperture, to aid subsequent reconnection.

17 Ensure that the centre vent flap actuating rod is securely reconnected, before refitting the ventilation nozzles.

Steering column shrouds

Removal

18 Disconnect the battery negative lead.

19 Turn the steering wheel to expose the two front steering column shroud securing screw covers.

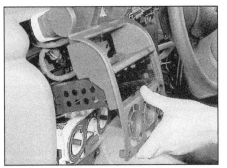

32.14b Withdrawing the facia centre panel assembly

32.14c Disconnecting the radio/cassette unit wiring plug . . .

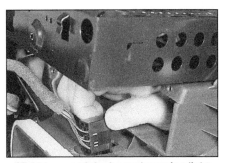

32.14d . . . and the hazard warning light switch wiring plug from the rear of the facia centre panel assembly

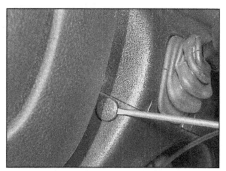

32.20a Prise out the covers . . .

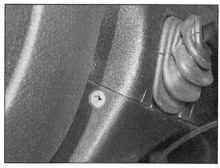

32.20b . . . to expose the front steering column shroud securing screws

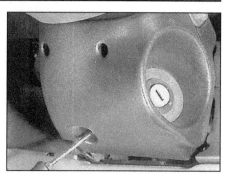

32.21 Unscrewing a steering column shroud lower securing screw

20 Prise out the covers, then remove the securing screws **(see illustrations)**.
21 Working under the lower steering column shroud, remove the three lower securing screws, noting their locations, as the screws are of different lengths **(see illustration)**.
22 Pull the rubber grommet from the ignition switch.
23 Unclip the lower shroud from the upper shroud (two clips at the back, and one each side), and withdraw the lower shroud **(see illustration)**.
24 Unhook the stalk switch gaiters from the upper shroud, and withdraw the upper shroud **(see illustration)**.

Refitting

25 Refitting is a reversal of removal, but ensure that the stalk switch gaiters and ignition switch grommet are correctly located, and make sure that the lower shroud securing screws are refitted to their original locations.

Instrument panel surround

Removal

26 Remove the steering column shrouds, as described earlier in this Section.
27 Where applicable, prise out the screw covers, then remove the four (two upper and two lower) securing screws, and withdraw the instrument panel surround **(see illustrations)**.

Refitting

28 Refitting is a reversal of removal.

Ventilation nozzles

29 Refer to Chapter 3.

Driver's side ventilation nozzle housing

30 This housing also houses the lighting switch, headlight aim adjustment switch, and foglight switch(es). Removal and refitting of the panel is described in Chapter 3.

Passenger's side ventilation nozzle housing

31 Refer to Chapter 3.

Glovebox

Note: *If a passenger's side airbag is fitted, read the warning in Chapter 12, Section 30, before starting work.*

Removal

32 With the glovebox lid closed, unscrew the two lower securing screws, which are accessible below the glovebox.
33 Open the glovebox lid, and prise the glovebox light from its location in the side of the glovebox. Disconnect the wiring, and remove the light assembly.
34 Unscrew the two upper securing screws, which are now accessible at the top of the glovebox.
35 Withdraw the glovebox from the facia, feeding the light through the aperture in the side of the glovebox as it is withdrawn **(see illustration)**.

Refitting

36 Refitting is a reversal of removal.

Glovebox lock cylinder

Removal

37 Squeeze the two securing lugs together, and remove the cover from the glovebox catch.
38 Insert the key into the lock cylinder, then turn the key and cylinder to the locked position, and pull the lock cylinder from its housing using the key.

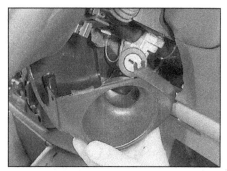

32.23 Withdrawing the lower steering column shroud

32.24 Withdrawing the upper steering column shroud

32.27a Unscrewing an instrument panel surround lower securing screw

32.27b Withdrawing the instrument panel surround

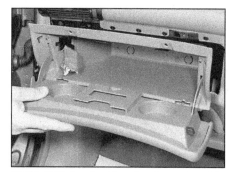

32.35 Withdrawing the glovebox assembly

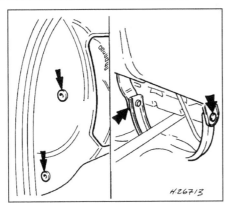

32.50 Facia internal fixing screws (arrowed)

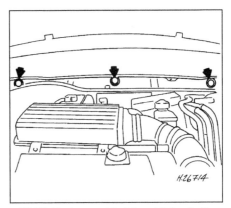

32.52 Facia panel bulkhead fixing bolts (arrowed)

Refitting

39 Refitting is a reversal of removal.

Footwell lower trim panels

Removal

40 The footwell lower trim panels are attached to the bottom of the facia by plastic securing clips.
41 To remove a panel, release the clips by turning them with a screwdriver, then withdraw the panel from underneath the facia.

Refitting

42 Refitting is a reversal of removal.

Complete facia assembly

Removal

43 Disconnect the battery negative lead.
44 Remove the centre console, as described in Section 31.
45 Remove the facia centre panel assembly, the steering column shrouds, the footwell lower trim panels, the glovebox, and the instrument panel surround, as described in earlier in this Section.
46 Remove the heater/ventilation control unit, and the driver's side ventilation nozzle housing, as described in Chapter 3.
47 Remove the steering wheel, as described in Chapter 10.
48 Remove the steering column stalk switches, the instrument panel, and the fusebox, as described in Chapter 12.
49 Open the front doors, then prise out the covers, and unscrew the two securing screws from each side of the facia.
50 Working under the centre of the facia, unscrew the two lower facia securing screws from the mounting bracket **(see illustration)**.
51 Remove the windscreen wiper motor and linkage, as described in Chapter 12.
52 Unscrew the three facia panel securing bolts from the engine compartment bulkhead **(see illustration)**.
53 With the aid of an assistant, withdraw the facia assembly into the interior of the vehicle, and carefully disconnect all wiring and hoses from the rear of the facia.
54 Check that all relevant wiring and hoses have been disconnected, then manipulate the facia out through one of the front door apertures.

Refitting

55 Refitting is a reversal of removal, remembering the following points.
56 Make sure that all relevant wiring and hoses are securely reconnected, and routed so that they are not under strain.
57 Refit the windscreen wiper motor and linkage as described in Chapter 12.
58 Refit the instrument panel as described in Chapter 12.
59 Refit the steering wheel as described in Chapter 10.
60 Refit the heater/ventilation control unit, and the driver's side ventilation nozzle housing, as described in Chapter 3.
61 Refit the facia centre panel assembly, as described earlier in this Section.

Notes

Chapter 12
Body electrical systems

Contents

Degrees of difficulty

| Easy, suitable for novice with little experience | | Fairly easy, suitable for beginner with some experience | | Fairly difficult, suitable for competent DIY mechanic | | Difficult, suitable for experienced DIY mechanic | 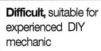 | Very difficult, suitable for expert DIY or professional | 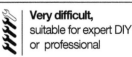 |

Specifications

Fuses - fusebox with 30 fuse locations

Fuse No	Rating (amps)	Circuit(s) protected
1	20	Central door locking
2	20	Fuel pump
3	30	Horn, windscreen and tailgate wash/wipe systems
4	10	Left-hand headlight dipped beam, left-hand headlight aim adjustment motor, bulb failure sensor
5	10	Right-hand headlight dipped beam, right-hand headlight aim adjustment motor, bulb failure sensor
6	10	Automatic transmission ECU, anti-lock braking system ECU
7	10	Warning lights, 'headlights on' warning buzzer, electric mirrors, glovebox light, radio/cassette player, facia switch illumination bulbs, heated rear window
8	20	Tow bar coupling
9	-	Unused
10	-	Unused
11	-	Unused
12	10	Left-hand headlight main beam
13	10	Right-hand headlight main beam, headlight main beam warning light
14	15	TC control unit
15	30	Electric window motors
16	-	Unused
17	20	Front foglights
18	10	Left-hand sidelight, left-hand tail light, bulb failure sensor
19	10	Right-hand sidelight, right-hand tail light, number plate light(s), bulb failure sensor, facia switch illumination bulbs, centre console switch illumination bulbs, radio/cassette player, headlight washer pump, 'headlights on' warning buzzer
20	20	Central door locking, carburettor automatic choke, automatic transmission switch, reversing lights, cigarette lighter, seat heating
21	-	Unused
22	10	Anti-theft alarm horn
23	-	Unused
24	20	Electric aerial, direction indicators, radio/cassette player, interior lights
25	10	Automatic transmission ECU
26	-	Unused
27	10	Daytime running lights (Norway and Sweden only)
28	15	Brake lamps, ABS/TC/AT control units, hazard warning switch
29	10	Rear foglamps and switch
30	20	Heated rear window

Fuses - fusebox with 28 fuse locations

All fuse ratings and circuits protected as for fusebox with 30 fuse locations, except for the following.

Fuse No	Rating (amps)	Circuit(s) protected
9	15	Electronic traction control ECU
10	30	Electric window motors
11	10	Rear foglights
14	30	Heater blower motor
15	30	Cooling fan
16	30	Heated rear window
22	-	Unused
23	30	Headlight washer system

Torque wrench settings

	Nm	lbf ft
Airbag unit to steering wheel	10	7
Airbag control unit	10	7
Passenger's side airbag to bracket	8	6

1 General information and precautions

⚠ *Warning: Before carrying out any work on the electrical system, read through the precautions given in 'Safety first!' at the beginning of this manual, and in Chapter 5A and 5B.*

The electrical system is of 12-volt negative earth type. Power for the lights and all electrical accessories is supplied by a lead/acid type battery, which is charged by the alternator.

This Chapter covers repair and service procedures for the various electrical components not associated with engine. Information on the battery, alternator and starter motor can be found in Chapter 5A.

It should be noted that, prior to working on any component in the electrical system, the battery negative terminal should first be disconnected, to prevent the possibility of electrical short-circuits and/or fires.

Caution: Before disconnecting the battery, refer to the information given in 'Disconnecting the battery' in the Reference Section of this manual.

2 Electrical fault finding – general information

General

A typical electrical circuit consists of an electrical component, any switches, relays, motors, fuses, fusible links or circuit breakers related to that component, and the wiring and connectors that link the component to both the battery and the chassis. To help to pinpoint a problem in an electrical circuit, wiring diagrams are included at the end of this manual.

Before attempting to diagnose an electrical fault, first study the appropriate wiring diagram to obtain a complete understanding of the components included in the particular circuit concerned. The possible sources of a fault can be narrowed down by noting if other components related to the circuit are operating properly. If several components or circuits fail at one time, the problem is likely to be related to a shared fuse or earth connection.

Electrical problems usually stem from simple causes, such as loose or corroded connections, a faulty earth connection, a blown fuse, a melted fusible link, or a faulty relay (refer to Section 3 for details of testing relays). Visually inspect the condition of all fuses, wires and connections in a problem circuit before testing the components. Use the wiring diagrams to determine which terminal connections will need to be checked, to pinpoint the trouble-spot.

The basic tools required for electrical fault-finding include a circuit tester or voltmeter (a 12-volt bulb with a set of test leads can also be used for certain tests); a self-powered test light (sometimes known as a continuity tester); an ohmmeter (to measure resistance); a battery and set of test leads; and a jumper wire, preferably with a circuit breaker or fuse incorporated, which can be used to bypass suspect wires or electrical components. Before attempting to locate a problem with test instruments, use the wiring diagram to determine where to make the connections.

To find the source of an intermittent wiring fault (usually due to a poor or dirty connection, or damaged wiring insulation), a 'wiggle' test can be performed on the wiring. This involves wiggling the wiring by hand to see if the fault occurs as the wiring is moved. It should be possible to narrow down the source of the fault to a particular section of wiring. This method of testing can be used in conjunction with any of the tests described in the following sub-Sections.

Apart from problems due to poor connections, two basic types of fault can occur in an electrical circuit - open-circuit, or short-circuit.

Open-circuit faults are caused by a break somewhere in the circuit, which prevents current from flowing. An open-circuit fault will prevent a component from working, but will not cause the relevant circuit fuse to blow.

Short-circuit faults are caused by a 'short' somewhere in the circuit, which allows the current flowing in the circuit to 'escape' along an alternative route, usually to earth. Short-circuit faults are normally caused by a breakdown in wiring insulation, which allows a feed wire to touch either another wire, or an earthed component such as the bodyshell. A short-circuit fault will normally cause the relevant circuit fuse to blow.

Finding an open-circuit

To check for an open-circuit, connect one lead of a circuit tester or voltmeter to either the negative battery terminal or a known good earth.

Connect the other lead to a connector in the circuit being tested, preferably nearest to the battery or fuse.

Switch on the circuit, remembering that some circuits are live only when the ignition switch is moved to a particular position.

If voltage is present (indicated either by the tester bulb lighting or a voltmeter reading, as applicable), this means that the section of the circuit between the relevant connector and the battery is problem-free.

Continue to check the remainder of the circuit in the same fashion.

When a point is reached at which no voltage is present, the problem must lie between that point and the previous test point with voltage. Most problems can be traced to a broken, corroded or loose connection.

Finding a short-circuit

To check for a short-circuit, first disconnect the load (s), from the circuit (loads are the components that draw current from a circuit, such as bulbs, motors, heating elements, etc.).

Remove the relevant fuse from the circuit, and connect a circuit tester or voltmeter to the fuse connections.

Switch on the circuit, remembering that some circuits are live only when the ignition switch is moved to a particular position.

If voltage is present (indicated either by the tester bulb lighting or a voltmeter reading, as applicable), this means that there is a short-circuit.

If no voltage is present, but the fuse still blows with the load(s) connected, this indicates an internal fault in the load(s).

Finding an earth fault

The battery negative terminal is connected to 'earth' - the metal of the engine/transmission and the car body - and most systems are wired so that they only receive a positive feed, the current returning through the metal of the car body. This means that the component mounting and the body form part of that circuit. Loose or corroded mountings can therefore cause a range of electrical faults, ranging from total failure of a circuit, to a puzzling partial fault. In particular, lights may shine dimly (especially when another circuit sharing the same earth point is in operation), motors (e.g. wiper motors or the radiator cooling fan motor) may run slowly, and the operation of one circuit may have an apparently unrelated effect on another. Note that on many vehicles, earth straps are used between certain components, such as the engine/transmission and the body, usually where there is no metal-to-metal contact between components due to flexible rubber mountings, etc.

To check whether a component is properly earthed, disconnect the battery, and connect one lead of an ohmmeter to a known good earth point. Connect the other lead to the wire or earth connection being tested. The resistance reading should be zero; if not, check the connection as follows.

If an earth connection is thought to be faulty, dismantle the connection, and clean back to bare metal both the bodyshell and the wire terminal or the component earth connection mating surface. Be careful to remove all traces of dirt and corrosion, then use a knife to trim away any paint, so that a clean metal-to-metal joint is made. On reassembly, tighten the joint fasteners securely; if a wire terminal is being refitted, use serrated washers between the terminal and the bodyshell, to ensure a clean and secure connection. When the connection is re-made, prevent the onset of corrosion in the future by applying a coat of petroleum jelly or silicone-based grease. Alternatively, (at regular intervals) spray on a proprietary ignition sealer or a water-dispersant lubricant.

3.3 Removing the cover from the secondary fusebox on the engine compartment bulkhead – 2.0 litre DOHC engine model

3 Fuses and relays – general information

Fuses

1 Fuses are designed to break a circuit when a predetermined current is reached, to protect components that may be damaged by excessive current flow. Any excessive current flow will be due to a fault in the circuit - usually a short-circuit (see Section 2).

2 The main fuses are located in the fusebox, at the lower driver's side of the facia, under a removable cover.

3 On certain models, additional fuses are located in a secondary fusebox mounted on the engine compartment bulkhead (see illustration).

4 The circuits protected by the various fuses are marked on the inside of the fusebox cover.

5 A blown fuse can be recognised from its melted or broken wiring.

6 To remove a fuse, first ensure that the relevant circuit is switched off.

7 Pull off the fusebox cover, and pull the relevant fuse from its location in the fusebox.

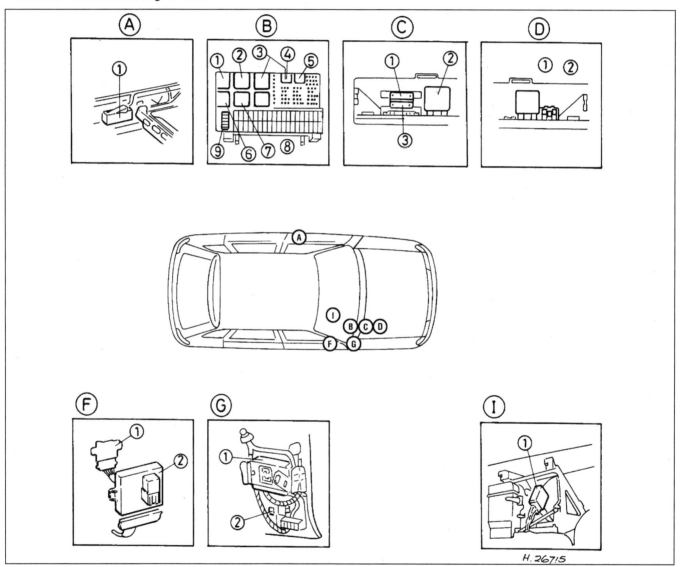

3.11a Schematic view of fuse and relay locations

A Left-hand sill panel	5 Rear foglight relay	2 Starter motor relay
1 Traction control ECU	6 Windscreen wash/wipe relay	3 Heater blower motor fuse
B Fusebox - front view	7 Heated rear window relay	**D Fusebox - rear view**
1 Door mirror heater relay	8 Warning buzzer	1 Starter motor relay
2 Direction indicator relay	9 Diagnostic plug	2 Anti-theft alarm fuse
3 Tailgate wash/wipe relay	**C Fusebox - rear view**	**F Right-hand footwell**
4 Front foglight relay	1 Cooling fan fuse	1 Central door locking ECU

2 Anti-theft alarm ECU	
G Right-hand footwell	
1 Engine management ECU	
2 Fuel pump relay	
I Steering column bracket	
1 Driving light relay (Sweden and Norway only)	

H.26715

8 Before renewing a blown fuse, try to trace and rectify the cause, and always use a fuse of the correct rating. Fuses rarely blow without good reason - do not renew the same fuse more than once without finding the source of the problem. If the same fuse is blowing regularly, it could be that the associated wiring is getting too hot, with attendant fire risks (see ''Safety first!''). Never substitute a fuse of a higher rating, or make temporary repairs using wire or metal foil, as more serious damage or even fire could result.

9 Note that the fuses are colour-coded as follows. Refer to the Specifications for details of the fuse ratings and the circuits protected.

Red   10A
Blue   15A
Yellow 20A
Green 30A

Relays

10 A relay is an electrically operated switch, which is used for the following reasons.

  a) A relay can switch a heavy current remotely from the circuit in which the current is flowing, therefore allowing the use of lighter gauge wiring and switch contacts.

  b) A relay can receive more than one control input, unlike a mechanical switch.

  c) A relay can have a 'timer' function e.g., intermittent wiper relay.

11 The main relays are located in the fusebox, above the fuses **(see illustrations)**. Additional relays are located in various positions, as shown in the accompanying illustrations.

12 If a circuit controlled by a relay develops a fault, and the relay is suspect, operate the circuit. If the relay is functioning, it should be possible to hear the relay click as it is energised. If this is the case, the fault lies with the components or wiring in the system. If the relay is not being energised, then either the relay is not receiving a main supply or switching voltage, or the relay itself is faulty. (Do not overlook the relay socket terminals when tracing faults.) Testing is by the substitution of a known good unit, but be careful; while some relays are identical in appearance and in operation, others look similar, but perform different functions.

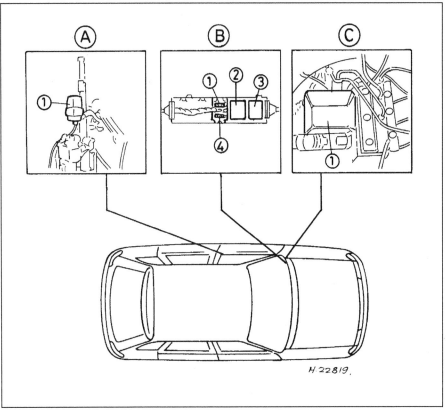

3.11b Schematic view of fuse and relay locations

A Left-hand rear wing
1 Electric aerial relay
B Engine compartment bulkhead
1 Headlight wash system fuse
2 Headlight wash system relay
3 Horn relay
4 Horn fuse
C Engine compartment
1 Anti-lock braking system ECU

3.11c Relays located above fuses in fusebox

4 Fusebox - removal and refitting

Removal

1 Disconnect the battery negative lead.
2 Pull off the fusebox cover.
3 Unscrew the two securing screws **(see illustration)**, then release the assembly from the retaining brackets, and lower the assembly sufficiently to enable the wiring plugs to be disconnected.
4 Disconnect the wiring plugs, carefully noting their locations if there is likely to be any confusion on refitting, then withdraw the assembly from the facia.

Refitting

5 Refitting is a reversal of removal.

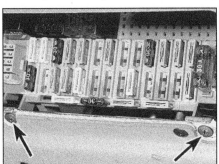

4.3 Fusebox cover removed to expose securing screws (arrowed)

5 Switches - removal and refitting

Ignition switch

Removal

1 Disconnect the battery negative lead.
2 Remove the steering column shrouds, as described in Chapter 11, Section 32.
3 The ignition switch is secured to the steering lock housing by two grub screws.
4 Disconnect the wiring, and remove the screws to extract the switch **(see illustrations overleaf)**. It is recommended that the switch and the lock cylinder are not both removed at the same time, or their mutual alignment will be lost.

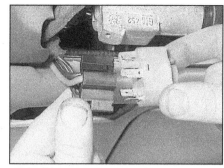

5.4a Ignition switch grub screw location (arrowed)

5.4b Disconnecting the wiring plug from the ignition switch

5.7 Withdrawing a stalk switch from the steering column

5.8 Disconnecting a stalk switch wiring plug

5.11 Releasing the lighting switch knob retaining clip

5.12 Removing the lighting switch

Refitting

5 Refitting is a reversal of removal.

Steering column stalk switches

Removal

6 Proceed as described in paragraphs 1 and 2.
7 Depress the retaining clips, and release the relevant switch from the steering column (see illustration).
8 Disconnect the wiring plug(s) and withdraw the switch (see illustration).

Refitting

9 Refitting is a reversal of removal.

Lighting switch

Removal

10 Disconnect the battery negative lead.
11 Insert a small screwdriver or rod through the hole in the bottom of the switch knob to

depress the knob retaining clip (see illustration). Pull the knob from the switch.
12 Press the two now-exposed switch securing clips towards the switch spindle (see illustration), then pull the switch from the facia and disconnect the wiring plug.
13 Note that the switch assembly cannot be dismantled, and if any part of the switch is faulty, the complete assembly must be renewed.

Refitting

14 Refitting is a reversal of removal.

Facia push-button switches

Removal

15 Disconnect the battery negative lead.
16 Using a screwdriver, carefully prise the switch from the facia, taking care not to damage the facia trim, and where applicable disconnect the wiring plug (see illustrations).

Refitting

17 Refitting is a reversal of removal.

Headlight aim adjustment switch

18 The procedure is as described previously in this Section for the facia push-button switches.

Hazard warning flasher switch

Removal

19 Disconnect the battery negative lead.
20 Move the switch to the 'on' position.
21 Using a screwdriver, carefully prise off the switch button to expose the switch.
22 Again using a screwdriver, carefully prise the switch from its housing.

Refitting

23 Refitting is a reversal of removal.

Horn switch

24 Carefully prise the centre pad from the steering wheel, and disconnect the wire.
25 If desired, the horn switch contact assembly can be removed from the centre of the steering wheel, after removing the steering wheel as described in Chapter 10.

Brake light switch

Removal

26 Disconnect the battery negative lead.
27 Working in the driver's footwell, release the securing clips, and remove the lower trim panel.
28 The switch is mounted in a bracket next to the steering column, at the top of the brake pedal.

5.16a Carefully prise the switch free . . .

5.16b . . . and withdraw it from the facia

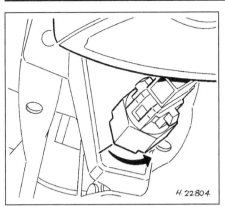

5.30 Brake light switch location (arrowed) - twist switch anti-clockwise to remove

29 Disconnect the wiring plug from the switch.
30 Twist the switch anti-clockwise, and withdraw it from the bracket **(see illustration)**.

Refitting

31 Refitting is a reversal of removal, but note that the brake lights should come on when the brake pedal is pressed down by about 15 to 20 mm. The switch can only be adjusted by carefully bending the mounting bracket, but this is not recommended.

Handbrake 'on' warning light switch

32 The procedure is described in Chapter 9, as part of the handbrake lever removal, overhaul and refitting procedure.

Reversing light switch

33 Refer to Chapter 7A.

Low oil pressure warning light switch

34 Refer to Chapter 5A.

Heater blower motor switch

35 Refer to Chapter 3.

Central locking operating switches

36 Refer to Chapter 11.

Electric window operating switches

37 Refer to Chapter 11.

6.2 Disconnecting the wiring plug from a headlight bulb

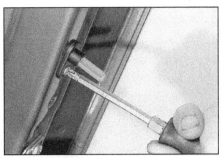

5.45a Removing the luggage compartment light switch securing screw - Hatchback model

Electric door mirror switch

38 Refer to Chapter 11.

Seat heating switches

39 The procedure is as described previously in this Section for the facia push-button switches.

Courtesy light switches

Removal

40 The courtesy light switches are located in the door pillars, at the front of the doors.
41 Disconnect the battery negative lead.
42 Open the relevant door.
43 Remove the securing screw, then pull the switch from the door pillar, and disconnect the wiring. If there is a danger of the wiring falling back inside the door pillar, tie a piece of string to it.

Refitting

44 Refitting is a reversal of removal.

Luggage compartment light switch

45 The switch is located at the bottom of the tailgate on Hatchback, Estate and Van models, and at the front left-hand corner of the luggage compartment on Saloon models **(see illustrations)**.
46 Removal and refitting is as described previously in this Section, for the courtesy light switches.

Glovebox light switch

47 The switch is integral with the light assembly, and is operated by the left-hand glovebox hinge.

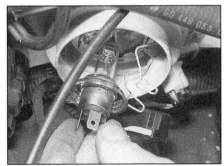

6.4 Removing a headlight bulb

5.45b Luggage compartment light switch location - Saloon model

48 Removal and refitting of the assembly is described in Section 7.

Electronic traction control manual override switch

49 The procedure is described in Chapter 4B.

Automatic transmission switches

50 Refer to Chapter 7B.

---

6 Bulbs (exterior lights) - renewal

General

1 Whenever a bulb is renewed, note the following points.
  a) *Disconnect the battery negative lead before starting work.*
  b) *Remember that if the light has recently been in use, the bulb may be extremely hot.*
  c) *Always check the bulb contacts and/or holder (as applicable). Ensure that there is clean metal-to-metal contact between the bulb contacts and the contacts in the holder, and/or the holder and the wiring plug. Clean off any corrosion or dirt before fitting a new bulb.*
  d) *Always ensure that the new bulb is of the correct rating, and that it is completely clean before fitting; this applies particularly to headlight bulbs.*

Headlight

Note: *It may be necessary to remove the air filter assembly, to replace the driver's side headlight bulb (refer to Chapter 4A or 4B).*
2 Working in the engine compartment, pull the wiring plug from the rear of the headlight bulb **(see illustration)**.
3 Pull the rubber cover from the rear of the headlight.
4 Release the bulb retaining spring clip, then grasp the bulb by its contacts and carefully withdraw it from the headlight unit **(see illustration)**.
5 When handling the new bulb, use a tissue or clean cloth to avoid touching the glass with the fingers; moisture and grease from the skin can cause blackening and rapid failure of this type of bulb. If the glass is accidentally touched, wipe it clean using methylated spirit.

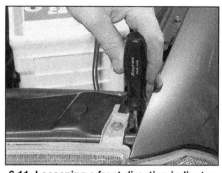

6.8 Removing a sidelight bulbholder

6.11 Loosening a front direction indicator unit securing screw

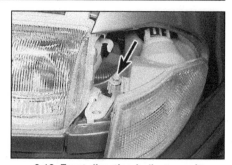

6.12 Front direction indicator unit withdrawn, exposing securing screw (arrowed)

6 Refitting is a reversal of removal, but make sure that the locating lugs on the bulb engage with the cut-outs in the headlight reflector, and ensure that the rubber cover is securely located over the rear of the headlight unit.

Front sidelight

7 Working in the engine compartment, locate the sidelight bulbholder, which is positioned in the lower rear of the headlight unit, on the side nearest the radiator grille.
8 Push the bulbholder into the headlight unit, and twist it anti-clockwise to remove it (see illustration).
9 The bulb is a push-fit in the holder.
10 Refitting is a reversal of removal.

Front direction indicator light

11 Working in the engine compartment, loosen, but do not remove the screw securing the top of the direction indicator unit to the

headlight (see illustration).
12 Withdraw the direction indicator unit forwards from the front wing, taking care not to strain the wiring (see illustration).
13 Push the bulbholder into the light unit, and twist it anti-clockwise to remove it.
14 The bulb is a bayonet fit in the bulbholder.
15 Refitting is a reversal of removal.

Front direction indicator side repeater light

16 Twist the light lens anti-clockwise, and pull it from the light (see illustration).
17 The bulb is a push-fit in the light.
18 Refitting is a reversal of removal, but ensure that the rubber sealing ring is correctly seated between the lens and the body panel.

Front foglight

19 To improve access, apply the handbrake, then jack up the front of the vehicle, and

support securely on axle stands (see "Jacking and vehicle support").
20 Remove the plastic cover from the rear of the light unit by twisting it anti-clockwise, and pulling it free (see illustration).
21 Release the retaining clip, then withdraw the bulb and disconnect the wiring.
22 Refitting is a reversal of removal.

Rear light cluster

23 Working in the luggage compartment, unclip the cover from the rear of the light unit.
24 On Saloon and Hatchback models, release the securing lug, and on Estate and Van models, squeeze the two securing clips towards the centre of the bulbholder, then withdraw the bulbholder from the light unit, taking care not to strain the wiring (see illustrations).
25 The bulbs are a bayonet fit in the bulbholder (see illustration). Note that the brake/tail light bulb has offset bayonet pins, so that it can only be fitted in one position; ensure that the correct type of replacement is obtained.
26 Refitting is a reversal of removal.

Rear number plate light - Saloon and Hatchback models (except 'Sports' models)

27 Using a thin-bladed screwdriver, carefully prise the light surround from the bumper (see illustration).
28 Pull the light assembly from the bumper, taking care not to strain the wiring.
29 Unclip the cover from the light unit, to expose the bulb (see illustration).

6.16 Removing the front direction indicator side repeater light lens

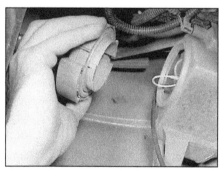

6.20 Removing the rear cover from a front foglight

6.24a Rear light bulbholder securing lug (arrowed) - Hatchback model

6.24b Removing a rear light bulbholder - Saloon model

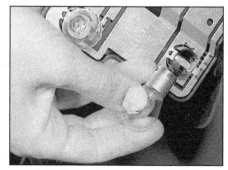

6.25 Removing a rear light bulb - Hatchback model

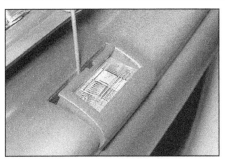

6.27 Prising the rear number plate light surround from the bumper - Hatchback model

30 The bulb is a bayonet fit in the light unit.
31 Refitting is a reversal of removal.

Rear number plate light – 'Sports' models

32 Proceed as described in paragraph 27.
33 Remove the bulb by carefully prising it from its location with a screwdriver.
34 Refitting is a reversal of removal.

Rear number plate light - Estate and Van models

35 Remove the two screws securing the relevant light to the tailgate handle assembly, and lower the light from the tailgate.
36 Carefully prise the bulb from the light.
37 Refitting is a reversal of removal.

7 Bulbs (interior lights) - renewal

General

1 Refer to Section 6, paragraph 1.

Courtesy lights and rear reading lights

2 Using a thin-bladed screwdriver, carefully prise the light from its location **(see illustrations)**.
3 Where applicable, unclip the shield from the bulb, then remove the bulb by carefully prising it from the contacts in the light unit **(see illustration)**.

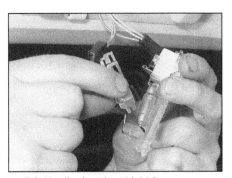

7.3 Unclipping the shield from a rear reading light bulb

6.29 Removing the cover from the rear number plate light unit

4 Refitting is a reversal of removal.

Glovebox light

5 Proceed as described previously in this Section for the courtesy light **(see illustration)**.

Luggage compartment light

6 Proceed as described previously in this Section for the courtesy light **(see illustration)**.

Instrument illumination and warning light bulbs

7 The procedure is described in Section 12.

Heater/ventilation control illumination light bulb

8 The procedure is described as part of the heater/ventilation control unit removal and refitting procedure in Chapter 3.

Cigarette lighter illumination light bulb

9 The procedure is described as part of the cigarette lighter removal and refitting procedure in Section 17.

Facia panel/centre console switch illumination bulbs

10 If a bulb fails in one of these switches, the complete switch assembly must be renewed as described in Section 5, as no individual spare parts are available.

7.5 Glovebox light assembly withdrawn from its location

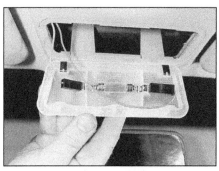

7.2a Withdrawing the front courtesy light to expose the bulb

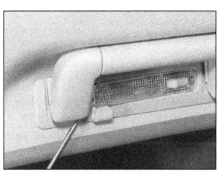

7.2b Prising a rear reading light from its location

8 Exterior light units - removal and refitting

Headlight unit

Removal

1 Disconnect the battery negative lead.
2 Remove the radiator grille panel, as described in Chapter 11.
3 Working in the engine compartment, loosen, but do not remove the screw securing the top of the direction indicator unit to the headlight.
4 Withdraw the direction indicator unit forwards from the front wing, and disconnect the wiring plug.

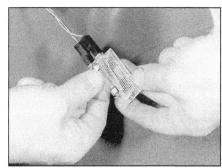

7.6 Withdrawing a luggage compartment light bulb

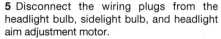

8.6a Headlight securing screws (arrowed)

8.6b Withdrawing a headlight

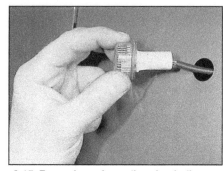

8.15 Removing a front direction indicator side repeater light

5 Disconnect the wiring plugs from the headlight bulb, sidelight bulb, and headlight aim adjustment motor.
6 Remove the three securing screws (two upper screws, and a single lower screw), and withdraw the headlight unit **(see illustrations)**.
7 With the exception of the bulbs and the aim adjustment motor, no headlight components are available separately, and if faulty or damaged, the complete unit must be renewed.

Refitting

8 Refitting is a reversal of removal, but on completion have the headlight beam alignment checked, referring to Section 9.

Front direction indicator unit

Removal

9 Disconnect the battery negative lead.
10 Proceed as described in paragraphs 3 and 4.

Refitting

11 Refitting is a reversal of removal.

Front direction indicator side repeater light

Removal

12 Disconnect the battery negative lead.
13 Remove the wheel arch liner, as described in Chapter 11, Section 25.
14 Working in the engine compartment, locate the repeater light wiring connector, and separate the two halves of the connector.
15 Working under the wheel arch, depress the retaining tabs and manipulate the light unit through the outside of the wing, pulling the

wiring and the grommet from the inner wing panel **(see illustration)**.
16 The lens can be removed from the light by twisting it to release the retaining clips.
17 Check the condition of the rubber sealing ring, and renew if necessary.

Refitting

18 Refitting is a reversal of removal.

Front foglight

Removal

19 Disconnect the battery negative lead.
20 For improved access, apply the handbrake, then jack up the front of the vehicle, and support securely on axle stands (see "*Jacking and vehicle support*").
21 Working behind the front spoiler, disconnect the foglight wiring plug.
22 Unscrew the three securing screws (two at the bottom of the light, and one well hidden above the light), and withdraw the light from the front bumper/spoiler assembly **(see illustration)**.

Refitting

23 Refitting is a reversal of removal.

Rear light cluster

Removal

24 Disconnect the battery negative lead.
25 Working in the luggage compartment, unclip the cover from the rear of the light unit.
26 On Saloon and Hatchback models, release the securing lug, and on Estate and Van models, squeeze the two securing clips

towards the centre of the bulbholder. Then withdraw the bulbholder from the light unit, taking care not to strain the wiring.
27 On Saloon and Hatchback models, remove the four light cluster securing screws, and on Estate and Van models, remove the three securing screws (one upper screw, and two lower screws). Withdraw the light cluster from outside the rear wing panel **(see illustrations)**.
28 Note that the lens cannot be renewed separately, and if damaged, the complete light cluster must be renewed.

Refitting

29 Refitting is a reversal of removal.

Rear number plate light - Saloon and Hatchback models

Removal

30 Using a thin-bladed screwdriver, carefully prise the light surround from the bumper.
31 Pull the light assembly from the bumper, and disconnect the wiring.

Refitting

32 Refitting is a reversal of removal.

Rear number plate light - Estate and Van models

Removal

33 Remove the two screws securing the relevant light assembly to the tailgate handle.
34 Pull the light assembly from the handle, and disconnect the wiring.

Refitting

35 Refitting is a reversal of removal.

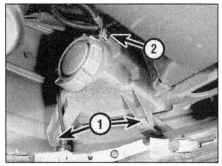

8.22 Front foglight lower securing screws (1) and wiring plug (2)

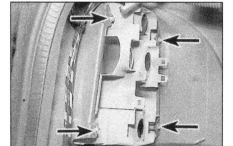

8.27a Rear light cluster securing screws (arrowed) - Saloon model

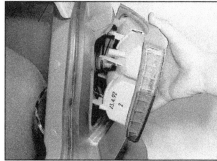

8.27b Removing a rear light cluster - Hatchback model

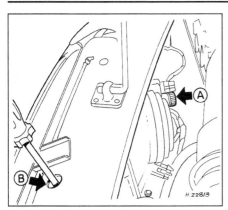

9.3 Headlight beam adjustment screws

A   Vertical adjustment
B   Horizontal adjustment

9 Headlight beam alignment - general

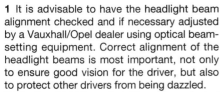

1 It is advisable to have the headlight beam alignment checked and if necessary adjusted by a Vauxhall/Opel dealer using optical beam-setting equipment. Correct alignment of the headlight beams is most important, not only to ensure good vision for the driver, but also to protect other drivers from being dazzled.

2 The headlight beam height may be adjusted to compensate for the load being carried by using the headlight aim adjustment control on the facia. The settings provided by this control are as follows:

0 Driver's seat occupied.
1 All seats occupied.
2 All seats occupied and load in luggage compartment
3 Driver's seat occupied and load in luggage compartment.

3 In an emergency, adjustment of the headlights may be made by turning the adjuster screws on the top and rear of each headlight unit. The top screw controls horizontal adjustment, and the rear screw controls vertical adjustment **(see illustration)**.

4 If an adjustment is made, the alignment should be checked using beam-setting equipment at the earliest opportunity. Note that when using beam-setting equipment, the headlight aim adjustment control should be set to position '0'.

10 Headlight aim adjustment motor - removal and refitting

Removal

1 Remove the headlight unit, as described in Section 8.

2 Remove the sidelight bulbholder assembly, referring to Section 6 if necessary.

3 Turn the motor through approximately 60° towards the top of the headlight. Then carefully push the headlight reflector assembly away from the motor, and hold it in position, so that the motor and the balljoint are pushed partially out of the headlight assembly **(see illustration)**.

4 On models with 'Carello' headlights, carefully pull the motor and balljoint assembly from the headlight **(see illustration)**.

5 On models with 'Bosch' headlights, release the balljoint using a small screwdriver, then carefully pull the motor and balljoint assembly from the headlight **(see illustration)**.

Refitting

6 Carefully push the headlight reflector assembly away from the motor location, ensuring that on models with 'Carello' type headlights, the ball socket is open, as shown **(see illustration)**, (otherwise irreparable damage could be caused to the headlight). Also hold the reflector in position while pushing the motor balljoint into place.

7 With the balljoint reconnected, lock the motor in position by twisting it towards the bottom of the headlight.

8 Refit the sidelight bulbholder, then refit the headlight as described in Section 8.

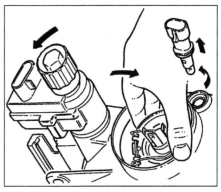

10.3 Remove the sidelight bulbholder, turn the headlight aim adjustment motor, and push the reflector assembly to one side

11 Instrument panel - removal and refitting

Removal

1 Disconnect the battery negative lead.

2 Working in the engine compartment, unscrew the securing sleeve, and disconnect the speedometer cable from the gearbox /transmission.

3 Remove the steering column shrouds, as described in Chapter 11, Section 32.

4 Where applicable, prise out the screw covers, then remove the four (two upper and two lower) securing screws, and withdraw the instrument panel surround.

5 Remove the three (one upper and two lower) instrument panel securing screws **(see illustration overleaf)**, and carefully pull the instrument panel forwards from the facia.

6 Push down (towards the back of the speed-ometer) on the catch securing the speedometer cable to the rear of the speedometer, and release the speedometer cable **(see illustration overleaf)**.

7 Release the retaining clips, and disconnect the wiring plugs from the rear of the instrument panel **(see illustration overleaf)**.

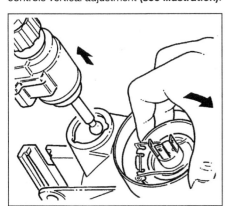

10.4 Pull the headlight aim adjustment motor from the headlight - 'Carello' type headlight

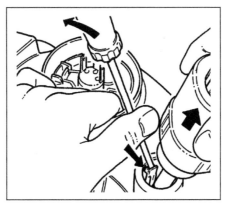

10.5 Release the headlight aim adjustment motor balljoint using a screwdriver - 'Bosch' type headlight

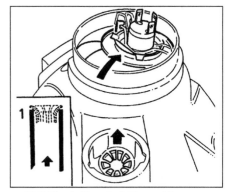

10.6 The ball socket (1) must be open before pushing the headlight aim adjustment motor balljoint into place - 'Carello' type headlight

11.5 Unscrewing a lower instrument panel securing screw

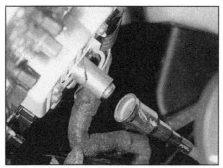

11.6 Speedometer cable disconnected from speedometer

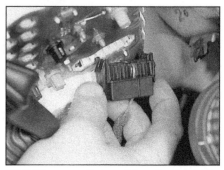

11.7 Disconnecting a wiring plug from the rear of the instrument panel

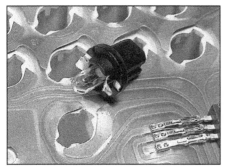

12.2 Warning light bulb withdrawn from its location in the instrument panel

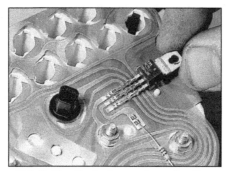

12.5 Pulling the instrument panel voltage stabiliser from the printed circuit board

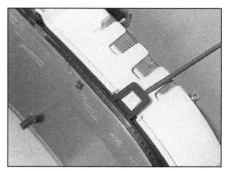

12.8 Releasing an instrument panel shroud retaining clip

8 Withdraw the instrument panel.

Refitting

9 Refitting is a reversal of removal, but ensure that the speedometer cable is not twisted or kinked between the instrument panel and the bulkhead as the panel is refitted.

12 Instrument panel components - removal and refitting

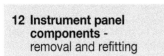

General

1 With the instrument panel removed as described in Section 11, continue as follows.

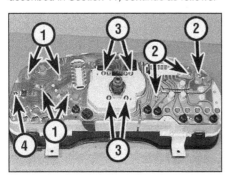

12.11 Rear view of instrument panel - model with tachometer

1 *Fuel and temperature gauge securing nuts*
2 *Tachometer securing nuts*
3 *Speedometer securing screws*
4 *Voltage stabiliser securing screw*

Panel illumination and warning light bulbs

Removal

2 Twist the relevant bulbholder anti-clockwise, and withdraw it from the printed circuit board on the rear of the instrument panel (see illustration).
3 The bulbs are integral with the bulbholders, and must be renewed as a unit.

Refitting

4 Refitting is a reversal of removal.

Voltage stabiliser

Removal

5 Remove the single securing screw from the rear of the instrument panel, then pull the voltage stabiliser from the contacts on the printed circuit board (see illustration).

Refitting

6 Refitting is a reversal of removal, but take care not to damage the contacts on the voltage stabiliser and printed circuit board.

Fuel and temperature gauges - models without tachometer

Removal

7 Pull the tripmeter reset pin from the front of the panel.
8 Release the two retaining clips at the top of the panel, and remove the panel shroud (see illustration).
9 Unscrew the two securing nuts, and withdraw the relevant gauge through the front of the instrument panel.

Refitting

10 Refitting is a reversal of removal.

Fuel and temperature gauge assembly - models with tachometer

11 The procedure is as described in paragraphs 7 to 10 inclusive, except that the gauge assembly is secured by four nuts (see illustration).

Tachometer

12 The procedure is as described in paragraphs 7 to 10 inclusive, except that the tachometer is secured by three nuts.

Speedometer

Removal

13 Proceed as described in paragraphs 7 and 8.
14 Extract the four securing screws from the rear of the panel, and withdraw the speedometer from the front of the panel.

Refitting

15 Refitting is a reversal of removal.

Printed circuit board

Removal

16 Remove all bulbs and instruments, and the voltage stabiliser, as described previously in this Section.
17 Carefully peel the printed circuit board from the instrument panel.

Refitting

18 Refitting is a reversal of removal, but ensure that the printed circuit board is seated correctly on the rear of the instrument panel.

13 Clock/multi-function display - removal and refitting

Removal

1 Disconnect the battery negative lead.
2 Remove the radio/cassette player, as described in Section 25.
3 Remove the rubber mat from the tray in front of the clock/multifunction display **(see illustration)**.
4 Remove the two central now-exposed screws **(see illustration)**.
5 Reach up through the radio/cassette player aperture, and push the clock/multi-function display from the facia **(see illustration)**.
6 Disconnect the wiring plug, and withdraw the unit.

Refitting

7 Refitting is a reversal of removal, but refit the radio/cassette player as described in Section 25.

14 Auxiliary warning system – general information

The auxiliary warning system displays information on the multifunction display, to warn the driver of low engine oil level, low engine coolant level, low washer fluid level, brake pad wear, brake light bulb failure, and dipped headlight beam/tail light bulb failure.

Warnings are displayed automatically on the multi-function display, and the warnings will override any other information displayed.

Removal and refitting procedures for the auxiliary warning system components are given in Section 15.

15 Auxiliary warning system components - removal and refitting

Control module

1 The control module is integral with the multi-function display. Refer to Section 13 for details of removal and refitting.

Multi-function display

2 Refer to Section 13.

Coolant level sensor

Note: *Refer to the precautions given in Chapter 3, Section 1 before removing the sensor.*

Removal

3 The coolant level sensor is integral with the expansion tank filler cap.

13.3 Removing the rubber mat from the tray in front of the clock/multi-function display

4 Before removing the filler cap/coolant level sensor assembly, disconnect the battery negative lead, and disconnect the wiring plug from the top of the sensor.

Refitting

5 Refitting is a reversal of removal.

Washer fluid level sensor

Removal

6 If possible, drain the fluid reservoir by operating the washers, to minimise fluid loss when the level sensor is removed.
7 Disconnect the battery negative lead.
8 Disconnect the wiring plug from the sensor, which is mounted in the side of the washer fluid reservoir.
9 Unscrew the sensor from the reservoir.

Refitting

10 Refitting is a reversal of removal.

Brake fluid level sensor

⚠ *Warning: Brake fluid is poisonous. Wash off skin immediately and seek immediate medical advice if any is swallowed or gets into the eyes. Certain types of brake fluid are inflammable and may ignite on contact with hot components. When servicing any hydraulic system, it is safest to assume that the fluid IS inflammable, and to take precautions against the risk of fire as when handling petrol. Brake fluid is also an effective paint stripper and will attack certain plastics. If any is spilt, it should be washed off immediately using plenty of clean water. Finally, it absorbs moisture from the air. When topping-up or*

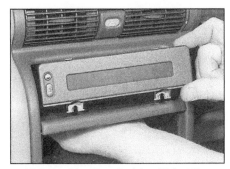

13.5 Pushing the clock/multi-function display from the facia

13.4 Unscrewing a clock/multifunction display securing screw

renewing the fluid always use the recommended type and ensure that it comes from a freshly opened, sealed container.

Removal

11 The brake fluid level warning sensor is integral with the brake hydraulic fluid reservoir filler cap.
12 Before removing the filler cap/level sensor assembly, disconnect the battery negative lead, and disconnect the wiring plug from the top of the sensor.

Refitting

13 Refitting is a reversal of removal.

Engine oil level sensor

14 Refer to Chapter 5A.

Brake pad wear sensors

15 The sensors take the form of wires located in the front brake pads.
16 Removal and refitting are described in Chapter 9 as part of the front brake pad renewal procedure.

Outside air temperature sensor

Removal

17 The sensor is clipped into the lower edge of the front spoiler.
18 Disconnect the battery negative lead.
19 For improved access, apply the handbrake, then jack up the front of the vehicle, and support securely on axle stands (see "*Jacking and vehicle support*").
20 Unclip the sensor from the spoiler, then disconnect the wiring connector, noting its location **(see illustration)**.

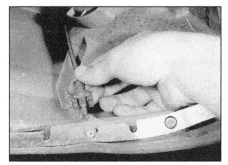

15.20 Unclipping the outside air temperature sensor from the spoiler

18.4 Horn location viewed with radiator grille panel removed (securing nut arrowed) - model with single-tone horn

Refitting

21 Refitting is a reversal of removal, ensuring that the wiring connector is located as noted before removal.

16 Trip computer - general

The trip computer displays information on the multi-function display, to indicate fuel consumption, average speed, range, outside air temperature, and elapsed time (stopwatch). The information to be displayed is selected using two push-buttons on the end of the right-hand steering column stalk switch.

The trip computer operates in conjunction with the auxiliary warning system, and any warning display will take priority over the trip computer display.

Details for removal and refitting of the auxiliary warning system components are given in Section 15.

17 Cigarette lighter - removal and refitting

Removal

1 Disconnect the battery negative lead.
2 Remove the centre console, as described in Chapter 11.

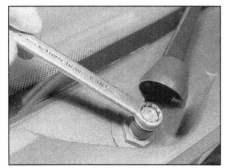

20.2a Unscrewing a windscreen wiper arm securing nut

18.9 Horn location (arrowed) - model with multi-tone horns

3 To remove the cigarette lighter assembly, simply pull it from the illumination ring assembly. The illumination ring assembly can be removed, by pulling it from the housing after depressing the retaining clips.

Refitting

4 Refitting is a reversal of removal.

18 Horn - removal and refitting

Models with single-tone horn

Removal

1 Disconnect the battery negative lead.
2 Remove the radiator grille, as described in Chapter 11.
3 Disconnect the wiring from the rear of the horn.
4 Unscrew the securing nut, and withdraw the horn from its bracket (see illustration).

Refitting

5 Refitting is a reversal of removal.

Models with multi-tone horns

Removal

6 Disconnect the battery negative lead.
7 Apply the handbrake, then jack up the front of the vehicle, and support securely on axle stands (see "Jacking and vehicle support").

20.2b Removing the tailgate wiper arm securing nut and washer - Hatchback model

8 Working at the front of the left-hand wheel arch, disconnect the wiring from the relevant horn.
9 Unscrew the relevant securing nut, and withdraw the horn from its bracket (see illustration).
10 On certain models, access to the horn mounting nuts may be easier if the complete horn assembly is first removed by unscrewing the bracket securing nut.

Refitting

11 Refitting is a reversal of removal.

19 Speedometer drive cable - removal and refitting

Removal

1 Remove the instrument panel, as described in Section 11.
2 Carefully pull the speedometer cable through the bulkhead into the engine compartment, noting its routing. It will probably be necessary to prise the cable grommet from the bulkhead.
3 The cable can now be withdrawn from the vehicle, noting its routing so that it can be refitted in the same position.

Refitting

4 Refitting is a reversal of removal, ensuring that the cable is correctly routed. Make sure that the cable is not kinked or twisted between the instrument panel and the bulkhead as the instrument panel is refitted, and ensure that the cable grommet is securely located in the bulkhead.

20 Wiper arms - removal and refitting

Removal

1 The wiper motor should be in the parked position before removing the wiper arm.

 HAYNES HiNT *Mark the position of the blade on the glass with adhesive tape, as a guide to refitting.*

2 Lift the hinged cover, and remove the nut and washer securing the arm to the spindle (see illustrations).
3 Prise the arm from the spindle, using a screwdriver if necessary - take care not to damage the trim or paintwork.

Refitting

4 Refitting is a reversal of removal, positioning the arms so that the blades align with the tape applied to the glass before removal. Note that the driver's side windscreen wiper blade is fitted with a wind deflector.

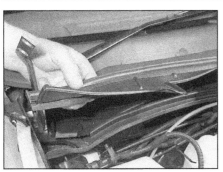

21.3a Removing the front . . .

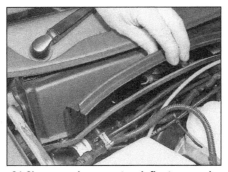

21.3b . . . and rear water deflector panels from the scuttle

21.5 Disconnecting the wiring plug from the windscreen wiper motor

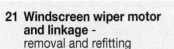

21 Windscreen wiper motor and linkage -
removal and refitting

Removal

1 Disconnect the battery negative lead.
2 Remove the windscreen wiper arms with reference to Section 20.
3 Remove the scuttle water deflector panels, noting how they are located over the flanges on the scuttle **(see illustrations)**.
4 Remove the windscreen cowl panel, as described in Chapter 11.
5 Disconnect the wiring plug from the motor **(see illustration)**.
6 Unscrew the three securing bolts, and withdraw the complete motor and linkage assembly from the scuttle **(see illustration)**.

Refitting

7 Refitting is a reversal of removal, remembering the following points.
8 Refit the windscreen cowl panel, as described in Chapter 11.
9 Refit the windscreen wiper arms with reference to Section 20.

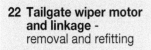

22 Tailgate wiper motor and linkage -
removal and refitting

Removal

1 Disconnect the battery negative lead.

22.3 Removing the plastic cover from the tailgate wiper spindle - Hatchback model

2 Remove the tailgate wiper arm, as described in Section 20.
3 Remove the plastic cover from the end of the wiper spindle, then unscrew the spindle nut and recover the washer **(see illustration)**.
4 Remove the tailgate trim panel, as described in Chapter 11, Section 17.
5 Locate the motor wiring connector, and separate the two halves of the connector **(see illustration)**.
6 Unscrew the two securing bolts, noting the locations of any earth wires secured by the bolts **(see illustration)**, and withdraw the motor assembly from the tailgate. Note that the spindle mounting rubbers may be released from the tailgate as the assembly is withdrawn.

Refitting

7 Refitting is a reversal of removal, ensuring that the spindle mounting rubbers are correctly located in the tailgate aperture, and that any earth wires are located as noted before removal.

23 Windscreen/tailgate washer system components -
removal and refitting

Fluid reservoir

Removal

1 Disconnect the battery negative lead.
2 Working in the engine compartment, disconnect the wiring plug(s) from the fluid

22.5 Tailgate wiper motor wiring connector - Hatchback model

21.6 Withdrawing the windscreen wiper motor and linkage assembly

pump(s) in the reservoir.
3 Disconnect the fluid hose(s) from the pump(s). Be prepared for fluid spillage.
4 Remove the securing screw from the front right-hand edge of the reservoir, and withdraw the reservoir from the engine compartment.
Refitting
5 Refitting is a reversal of removal.

Fluid pump

Removal

6 Disconnect the battery negative lead.
7 Working in the engine compartment, disconnect the wiring plug from the pump.
8 Disconnect the fluid hose(s) from the pump. Be prepared for fluid spillage.
9 Pull the pump from the reservoir, being prepared for fluid spillage if the reservoir still contains fluid.

22.6 Tailgate wiper motor securing bolts (arrowed)

25.3 Unscrewing a grub screw from the radio/cassette player

25.5 Withdrawing the radio/cassette player from the facia

Refitting

10 Examine the condition of gauze filter at the end of the pump pick-up tube, and clean or renew if necessary.
11 Refitting is a reversal of removal, ensuring that the pump is securely seated in the reservoir.

Windscreen washer nozzle

Removal

12 Carefully prise the nozzle from the bonnet, taking care not to damage the paintwork.
13 Disconnect the fluid hose, and withdraw the nozzle.

Refitting

14 To refit, reconnect the washer hose to the nozzle, and push the nozzle into its locating hole.
15 The nozzle can be adjusted by inserting a pin into the jet, and swivelling it to the required position.

Tailgate washer nozzle - Hatchback models

Removal

16 The washer nozzle can be removed after removing the tailgate spoiler as described in Chapter 11, Section 25. Take care to prevent the end of the fluid hose from dropping into the tailgate.

Refitting

17 Refitting is a reversal of removal, but refit the spoiler as described in Chapter 11, Section 25 and note that the nozzle can be adjusted by inserting a pin into the jet and swivelling it to the desired position.

Tailgate washer nozzle - Estate models

Removal

18 Open the tailgate, and remove the upper tailgate interior trim panel, referring to Chapter 11, Section 17.
19 Disconnect the fluid hose from the rear of the nozzle, then push the nozzle out through the tailgate.

Refitting

20 Refitting is a reversal of removal.

24 Headlight washer system components - removal and refitting

Washer nozzles

Removal

1 Remove the radiator grille, as described in Chapter 11.
2 Remove the two securing screws, and withdraw the nozzles from the radiator grille.

Refitting

3 Refitting is a reversal of removal.
4 The nozzles can be adjusted by inserting a pin into the jet, and swivelling it to the desired position.

Fluid reservoir

Removal

5 The headlight washer fluid reservoir is located at the rear left-hand corner of the engine compartment.
6 Disconnect the battery negative lead.
7 Working in the engine compartment, unscrew the filler neck from the top of the reservoir.
8 Remove the wheel arch liner, as described in Chapter 11, Section 25.
9 Remove the three reservoir securing screws, and manipulate the reservoir as necessary to disconnect the pump wiring plug and the fluid hose. Be prepared for fluid spillage as the hose is disconnected.

26.4 Removing a front treble loudspeaker from the mirror trim panel

10 Withdraw the reservoir from under the wheel arch.

Refitting

11 Refitting is a reversal of removal.

Fluid pump

Removal

12 Remove the fluid reservoir, as described previously in this Section.
13 Pull the pump from the reservoir, being prepared for fluid spillage if the reservoir still contains fluid.

Refitting

14 Examine the condition of the pump-to-reservoir sealing grommet, and renew if necessary.
15 Refitting is a reversal of removal.

25 Radio/cassette player - removal and refitting

Removal

1 All the radio/cassette players have DIN standard fixings. Two special tools, obtainable from in-car entertainment specialists, are required for removal.
2 Disconnect the battery negative lead.
3 Unscrew the four grub screws from the corners of the radio/cassette player, using an Allen key or hexagon bit (see illustration).
4 Insert the tools into the holes exposed by removal of the grub screws, and push them until they snap into place. Pull the tools rearwards (away from the facia) to release the unit.
5 Pull the unit forwards, and withdraw it from the facia (see illustration).

Refitting

6 To refit the radio/cassette player, simply push the unit into the facia until the retaining lugs snap into place, then refit the grub screws.

26 Loudspeakers - removal and refitting

Front treble loudspeaker ('tweeter')

Removal

1 Disconnect the battery negative lead.
2 Carefully prise the door mirror trim panel from the door.
3 Disconnect the wiring plug from the speaker.
4 Carefully push the speaker from its location in the trim panel (see illustration).

Refitting

5 Refitting is a reversal of removal.

26.7 Removing the front bass loudspeaker trim panel from the door

Front bass loudspeaker ('woofer')

Removal

6 Disconnect the battery negative lead.
7 Carefully unclip the speaker trim panel from the door to expose the speaker **(see illustration)**.
8 Remove the three securing screws, then withdraw the speaker from the door and disconnect the wiring.

Refitting

9 Refitting is a reversal of removal.

Rear loudspeaker - Saloon models

Removal

10 Disconnect the battery negative lead.
11 Working in the luggage compartment, disconnect the wiring plug from the speaker.
12 Working inside the vehicle, carefully prise the speaker cover from the rear parcel shelf (slide the cover towards the centre of the vehicle to remove it), **(see illustration)**.
13 Unscrew the four now-exposed speaker securing screws, and carefully withdraw the speaker into the luggage compartment **(see illustration)**.

Refitting

14 Refitting is a reversal of removal.

Rear loudspeaker - Hatchback models

Removal

15 Disconnect the battery negative lead.
16 Working in the luggage compartment, disconnect the wiring plug from the speaker.

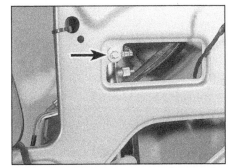

27.9a Electric aerial earth lead (arrowed) - Hatchback model

26.12 Removing the rear loudspeaker cover from the parcel shelf (viewed through rear window) - Saloon model

17 Remove the four securing screws, and withdraw the speaker from under the rear parcel shelf **(see illustration)**.

Refitting

18 Refitting is a reversal of removal.

Rear loudspeaker - Estate and Van models

Removal

19 Disconnect the battery negative lead.
20 Remove the tailgate lower trim panel, as described in Chapter 11, Section 17.
21 Remove the three securing screws, then withdraw the speaker from the tailgate, and disconnect the wiring.

Refitting

22 Refitting is a reversal of removal.

27 Radio aerial - removal and refitting

Saloon models

Removal

1 On models fitted with an electrically operated aerial, make sure that the aerial is fully retracted, then disconnect the battery negative lead.
2 Remove the luggage compartment rear trim panel, and the left-hand side trim panel, as described in Chapter 11.
3 Where applicable, remove the screw securing the aerial earth lead to the body panel.

27.9b Lower the aerial to disconnect the aerial lead (arrowed) . . .

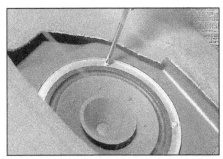

26.13 Removing a rear loudspeaker securing screw (viewed through rear window) - Saloon model

26.17 Removing a rear loudspeaker - Hatchback model

4 Remove the screw securing the lower end of the aerial to the body panel, then pull the aerial through the grommet in the rear wing panel, and lower it sufficiently to disconnect the aerial lead and, where applicable, the motor wiring plug.
5 Withdraw the aerial into the luggage compartment.

Refitting

6 Refitting is a reversal of removal, but ensure that the aerial grommet is correctly seated in the rear wing panel.

Hatchback models (except 'Sports' models)

Removal

7 Proceed as described in paragraphs 1 and 2.
8 Remove the left-hand rear light cluster, as described in Section 8.
9 Proceed as described in paragraphs 3 and 4 **(see illustrations)**.

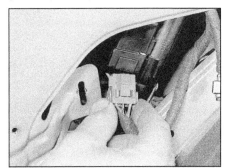

27.9c . . . and the motor wiring plug - Hatchback model

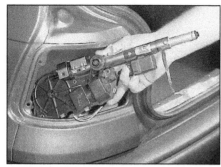

27.10 Withdrawing the aerial assembly through the rear light cluster aperture - Hatchback model

10 Carefully manipulate the aerial assembly to enable it to be withdrawn from the vehicle through the rear light cluster aperture **(see illustration)**.

Refitting

11 Refer to paragraph 6.

Estate and 'Sports' Hatchback models

Removal

12 Remove the headlining with reference to Chapter 11, Section 29.
13 Working through the access hole in the roof, disconnect the aerial lead from the base of the aerial.
14 Unscrew the aerial securing nut, and withdraw the aerial from the roof.

Refitting

15 Refitting is a reversal of removal.

Electric aerial mast

Removal

16 The mast on 'factory fitted', fully automatic electric aerials, can be replaced separately.
17 Extend the aerial as far as possible, by switching on the radio.
18 Unscrew the mounting nut.
19 Pull the sprung sleeve upwards and clear of its base.
20 The assembly can now be removed from the clutch mechanism, by pulling the assembly upwards.

Refitting

21 Insert the ball end of the mast assembly into the base.
22 Carefully push the mast assembly down as far as possible, until it engages into the clutch mechanism.
23 Switch the radio off to retract the aerial.
24 If the aerial does not fully retract into its base, guide the remaining mast into the base by hand.
25 Insert the sprung sleeve into the base and tighten the mounting nut.
26 Check that the aerial works properly by turning the radio on and off a few times.

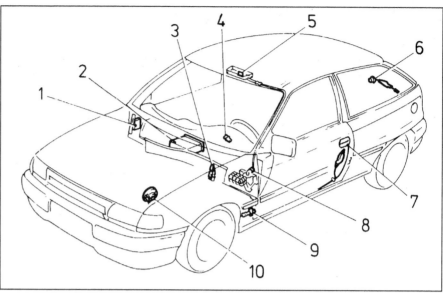

28.2 Anti-theft alarm system components

1 Electronic control unit	5 LED integral with courtesy light	8 Relay (isolates starter motor)
2 Radio/cassette sensor	6 Tailgate/boot lid switch	9 Courtesy light switch
3 Bonnet switch	7 Door lock switch	10 Horn
4 Ignition switch		

28 Anti-theft alarm system - general

1 Certain models are fitted with an anti-theft alarm system as standard equipment.
2 The alarm system operates in conjunction with the central locking system switches, and is triggered by opening of the doors, bonnet, and boot lid/tailgate, or by interference with the radio/cassette player **(see illustration)**.

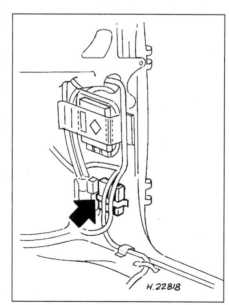

29.1 Anti-theft alarm electronic control unit location (arrowed) in right-hand footwell

3 The alarm features a self-diagnostic function, and any faults should be referred to a Vauxhall/Opel dealer, who will have access to the necessary specialist diagnostic equipment.

29 Anti-theft alarm system components - removal and refitting

Electronic control unit

Removal

1 The control unit is located behind the right-hand footwell side/sill trim panel **(see illustration)**.
2 Disconnect the battery negative lead.
3 Remove the footwell side/sill trim panel, as described in Chapter 11, Section 30.
4 Unscrew the two plastic securing nuts, then lift the control unit from the footwell, disconnect the wiring plug, and withdraw the unit.

Refitting

5 Refitting is a reversal of removal.

Bonnet switch

Removal

6 Disconnect the battery negative lead.
7 Using a screwdriver, carefully release the securing clip, and withdraw the switch from its bracket on the suspension turret **(see illustration)**.
8 Disconnect the wiring plug, and withdraw the switch.

Refitting

9 Refitting is a reversal of removal.

Horn

Removal

10 The horn is located on the left-hand inner front wing panel, next to the battery **(see illustration)**.

11 Disconnect the battery negative lead, then disconnect the wiring from the horn.

12 Unscrew the securing nut, and withdraw the horn from its mounting bracket. Alternatively, unscrew the securing bolt, and withdraw the mounting bracket complete with the horn.

Refitting

13 Refitting is a reversal of removal.

30 Airbag system - general

General information

A driver's side airbag is fitted as standard equipment on all models. The airbag is fitted to the steering wheel centre pad. Similarly, a passenger's side airbag is also fitted as standard equipment, or as an option, depending on model.

The system is armed only when the ignition is switched on, however, a reserve power source maintains a power supply to the system in the event of a break in the main electrical supply. The system is activated by a 'g' sensor (deceleration sensor), incorporated in the electronic control unit.

The airbags are inflated by gas generators, which force the bags out from their locations in the steering wheel, and the passenger's side facia, where applicable.

In the event of a fault occurring in the airbag system (warning light illuminated on the instrument panel), seek the advice of a Vauxhall/Opel dealer.

Precautions

⚠ **Warning: The following precautions must be observed when working on vehicles equipped with an airbag system, to prevent the possibility of personal injury.**

General precautions

The following precautions **must** be observed when carrying out work on a vehicle equipped with an airbag.

a) Do not disconnect the battery with the engine running.

b) Before carrying out any work in the vicinity of the airbag, removal of any of the airbag components, or any welding work on the vehicle, de-activate the system as described in the following sub-Section.

29.7 Anti-theft alarm bonnet switch (arrowed)

c) Do not attempt to test any of the airbag system circuits using test meters or any other test equipment.

d) If the airbag warning light comes on, or any fault in the system is suspected, consult a Vauxhall/Opel dealer without delay. **Do not** attempt to carry out fault diagnosis, or any dismantling of the components.

Precautions to be taken when handling an airbag

a) Transport the airbag by itself, bag upward.

b) Do not put your arms around the airbag.

c) Carry the airbag close to the body, bag outward.

d) Do not drop the airbag or expose it to impacts.

e) Do not attempt to dismantle the airbag unit.

f) Do not connect any form of electrical equipment to any part of the airbag circuit.

g) Do not allow any solvents or cleaning agents to contact the airbag assembly. The unit must be cleaned using only a damp cloth.

Precautions to be taken when storing an airbag unit

a) Store the unit in a cupboard with the airbag upward.

b) Do not expose the airbag to temperatures above 90°C.

29.10 Anti-theft alarm horn (arrowed)

c) Do not expose the airbag to flames.

d) Do not attempt to dispose of the airbag - consult a Vauxhall/Opel dealer.

e) Never refit an airbag which is known to be faulty or damaged.

De-activation of airbag system

The system must be de-activated as follows, before carrying out any work on the airbag components or surrounding area.

a) Switch off the ignition.

b) Remove the ignition key.

c) Switch off all electrical equipment.

d) Disconnect the battery negative lead (see Chapter 5A).

e) Insulate the battery negative terminal and the end of the battery negative lead to prevent any possibility of contact.

f) Wait for at least one minute before carrying out any further work. This will allow the system capacitor to discharge.

31 Airbag unit (driver's side) - removal and refitting

⚠ **Warning: Read the precautions given in Section 30, before starting work. Stand the unit with the cover uppermost and do not expose it to heat sources more than 100°C. Do not attempt to open or repair the airbag unit, or apply any voltage to it. Do not use any airbag unit that is visibly damaged or has been tampered with.**

Note: On power steering models in particular, it will be advantageous to jack up the front of the car and support it on axle stands placed under the body side members, so that the steering wheel can be turned more easily.

Removal

1 De-activate the airbag system as described in Section 30.

2 Check that the front wheel are pointing in the straight-ahead position, then turn the steering wheel 90° clockwise so that the left-hand spoke is accessible from the rear.

3 Using a Torx type socket, unscrew the airbag retaining bolt from the underside of the steering wheel.

4 Turn the steering wheel 180° anti-clockwise so that the right-hand spoke is accessible from the rear.

5 Unscrew the second airbag retaining bolt from the rear of the steering wheel.

6 Return the steering wheel to the straight-ahead position then carefully lift the airbag unit from the steering wheel.

7 Disconnect the wiring plug from the rear of the airbag, and remove the airbag from the car.

Refitting

8 Refitting is a reversal of removal.

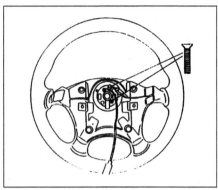

32.3 Airbag contact unit securing screws (arrowed)

32 Airbag contact unit - removal and refitting

> ⚠ **Warning: Read the precautions given in Section 30 before starting work.**

Removal

1 Remove the airbag as described in Section 31, and the steering wheel as described in Chapter 10.

2 Disconnect the horn wiring harness connector, it not already done.

3 Unscrew the two securing screws, and withdraw the contact unit from the steering wheel, noting its orientation to aid refitting **(see illustration)**.

Refitting

4 Refit the contact unit, and tighten the securing screws, ensuring that the unit is orientated as noted before removal.

5 If a new contact unit has been fitted, remove the safety screw.

6 Reconnect the horn wiring connector.

7 Refit the steering wheel as described in Chapter 10, then refit the airbag as described in Section 31.

33 Airbag unit (passenger's side) - removal and refitting

> ⚠ **Warning: Read the precautions given in Section 30 before starting work.**

Note: *If the airbag has been deployed, the unit brackets must be renewed – this work should be carried out by a Vauxhall/Opel dealer. The airbag unit securing nuts must be renewed when refitting.*

Removal

1 De-activate the airbag system as described in Section 30.

2 Remove the windscreen cowl panel, and the glovebox assembly, as described in Chapter 11.

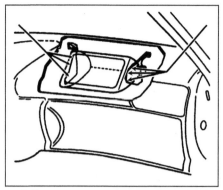

33.8 Passenger's side airbag unit securing nuts (arrowed) – left-hand-drive model shown

3 Remove the passenger's side ventilation nozzle housing, as described in Chapter 3.

4 Remove the passenger's side footwell lower trim panel, as described in Chapter 11, Section 30.

5 Remove the storage tray from the passenger's side facia.

6 Remove the air ducts for the footwell air duct and the passenger's side ventilation nozzle, noting their locations to aid refitting.

7 Disconnect the airbag unit wiring connector.

8 Unscrew the six securing nuts, and withdraw the airbag unit from the facia **(see illustration)**.

Refitting

9 Refitting is a reversal of removal, but use new securing nuts, and tighten the nuts to the specified torque.

34 Airbag control unit - removal and refitting

> ⚠ **Warning: Read the precautions given in Section 30 before starting work.**

Removal

1 De-activate the airbag system (Section 30).

2 Remove the centre console as described in Chapter 11.

3 Disconnect the control unit wiring plug, then unscrew the three securing nuts and remove the control unit from the vehicle floor **(see illustration)**.

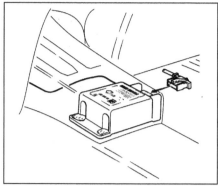

34.3 Airbag control unit location

Refitting

4 Refitting is a reversal of removal.

35 Wiring diagrams - explanatory notes

Two wiring diagrams are provided for models up to 1994, one diagram for early models with 30 fuses in the fusebox, and one for later models with 28 fuses in the fusebox **(see illustration)**.

All wiring diagrams are of the current flow type, each circuit being shown in the simplest possible form. Note that since the diagrams were originally produced in Germany (to the DIN standard), all wire colours and abbreviations used on the diagrams are in German; refer to the information given on the next page for clarification.

The bottom line of the diagram represents the earth (or negative) connection; the numbers below this line are track numbers, enabling circuits and components to be located using the key.

The lines at the top of the diagram represent live feed (or positive) connection points. The line marked '30' is live at all times, that marked '15' is live only when the ignition is switched on.

Numbers on the diagram that are framed in square boxes at the end of a wire indicate the track reference number at which that particular wire is continued. At the point indicated, another framed number will appear, referring back to the previous circuit.

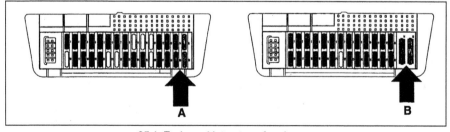

35.1 Early and later type fuseboxes

A Early models with 30 fuses   *B Later models with 28 fuses*

Explanation of abbreviations used

Note: *The following list is included for guidance only - a comprehensive list was not available at time of writing.*

ABS	Anti-lock braking system	HS	Heated rear window	PBSL	Parking/brake lockout
AC	Air conditioning	HW	Rear screen wiper	P/N	Park/Neutral (starter inhibitor - automatic transmission)
AT	Automatic transmission	HZG	Heating		
ATC	Automatic temperature control	INS	Instrument	POT	Potentiometer
AZV	Trailer hitch	IRL	Interior light	RC	Ride control
BR	On-board computer	KAT	Catalytic converter	RFS	Reversing lights
CC	Check control	KBS	Wiring harness	RHD	Right-hand drive
CRC	Cruise control	KV	Contact, distributor	S	Sweden
D	Diesel	L3.1	Fuel injection (Bosch L3.1-Jetronic)	SD	Sliding sunroof
DID	Dual information display	LCD	LCD instrument	SH	Seat heating
DIS	Direct ignition system	LHD	Left-hand drive	SRA	Headlight washer
DS	Theft protection	LWR	Headlamp range control	TANK	Fuel gauge
DWA	Anti-theft warning system	M1.5	Fuel injection (Bosch Motronic M1.5)	TD	Turbodiesel
DZM	Tachometer	M2.5	Fuel injection (Bosch Motronic M2.5)	TEMP	Temperature gauge
EFC	Electric folding roof (Convertible)	MID	Multi-information display	TFL	Day running lights
EKS	Pinch guard (electric windows)	MOT	Motronic system (general)	TKS	Door courtesy light switch
EMP	Radio/cassette	MT	Manual transmission	TSZI	High-energy ignition (HEI)
ETC	Electronic traction control	MUL	Fuel injection (Multec)	VGS	Carburettor
EUR	Euronorm engine	N	Norway	WEG	Mileometer frequency sensor
EZ +	El Plus with self-diagnosis	NSL	Rear foglight	WHR	Vehicle level control
EZV	Ecotronic	NSW	Foglight	WS	Warning buzzer
FH	Electric windows	OEL	Oil level check (oil pressure)	ZV	Central locking
GB	Great Britain	OPT	Optional equipment	ZYL	Cylinder
HRL	Luggage compartment lamp			4WD	Four-wheel-drive

Wiring identification

Example: GE WS 1.5
GE - Basic colour
WS - Identification colour
1.5 - Wirecross-section (mm²)

Colour code

BL	Blue	GN	Green	HBL	Light blue	RT	Red	VI	Violet
BR	Brown	GR	Grey	LI	Lilac	SW	Black	WS	White
GE	Yellow								

Circuit interconnections

A framed number - eg 180 - refers to a grid reference (track) at which the circuit is continued

Key to wiring diagrams for models up to 1994

Not all items fitted to all models   *Models*   with earlier 30-fuse type fusebox   **Models with later 28-fuse type fusebox*

No	Description	Track
E01	Sidelight, left	604
E02	Tail light, left	501, 602
E03	Number plate light	613 to 616
E04	Sidelight, right	609
E05	Tail light, right	503, 611
E07	Headlight main beam, left	629
E08	Headlight main beam, right	631
E09	Headlight dipped beam, left	505, 630
E10	Headlight dipped beam, right	507, 632
E11	Instrument lighting	546
E12	Automatic transmission selector illumination	296, 297
E13	Luggage compartment light	687
E14	Interior light	689, 750, 752
E15	Glovebox light	857
E16	Cigarette lighter illumination	855
E17	Reversing light, left	698
E18	Reversing light, right	699
E19	Heated rear window	756
E20	Foglight, front left	650
E21	Foglight, front right	651
E24	Foglight, rear left	645
E25	Seat heating, left	860
E27	Rear reading light, left	692
E28	Rear reading light, right	694
E30	Seat heating, right	864
E34	Heater control illumination	756
E39	Foglight, rear right	646
F01 to F30	Fuses in fusebox	Various
F14**	Heater blower fuse ('maxi' type)	762
F35	Voltage stabiliser	548
F36	Fuel filter heating fuse (diesel, engine compartment)	450, 495
F38**	Anti-theft alarm horn fuse	743
F41	Glow plug fuse ('maxi' type, engine compartment)	440, 487
F42	Fuse, radiator cooling fan	120
F45	Horn fuse	830
F46*	Heater blower fuse ('maxi' type)	762
F48*	Anti-theft alarm horn fuse	743
G01	Battery	100
G02	Alternator	115
G06	Alternator (diesel)	469 to 472
H01	Radio/cassette	571 to 587
H02	Horn (single-tone)	826
H03	Direction indicator warning light	554
H04	Oil pressure warning light	561
H05	Brake fluid warning light	563
H06	Hazard flashers warning light	674
H07	Alternator/no-charge warning light	565
H08	Headlight main beam warning light	558
H09	Stop-light, left	509, 659
H10	Stop-light, right	511, 660
H11	Direction indicator light, front left	675
H12	Direction indicator light, rear left	676
H13	Direction indicator light, front right	683
H14	Direction indicator light, rear right	684
H15	Low fuel/fuel reserve warning light	551
H16	Glow plug warning light	539
H17	Trailer direction indicator warning light	542
H18	Horn (twin-tone)	830
H19	Headlights 'on' warning buzzer	695, 696
H21	Handbrake 'on' warning light	566
H25	Heated mirror warning light	842
H26	ABS warning light	537
H30	Engine warning light	559

No	Description	Track
H33	Direction indicator side repeater light left	679
H34	Direction indicator side repeater light right	681
H37	Loudspeaker, front left	576, 577
H38	Loudspeaker, front right	581 582
H39	Loudspeaker, rear left	576 577
H40	Loudspeaker, rear right	581, 582
H42	Automatic transmission warning light	540
H47	Anti-theft alarm horn	743
H48	Horn (twin-tone)	832
H51	Electronic traction control (ETC) warning light	538
H52	Tweeter, front left	576
H53	Tweeter, front right	581
K01	Heated rear window relay	756, 757
K03	Relay, starter (anti-theft warning unit, 70A)	111, 112
K05	Front foglight relay	651, 652
K08	Intermittent wiper relay (windscreen)	803 to 806
K10	Direction indicator flasher unit	670 to 672
K20	Ignition module/ignition coil	137 to 141, 170 to 172, 239, 240, 302, 303, 362 to 365
K25	Glow time relay (70A)	437 to 440
K30	Intermittent wiper relay (tailgate)	813 to 815
K35	Heated mirror relay	847 to 849
K37	Central door locking control unit	705 to 711
K57	Multec single-point control unit	175 to 194, 211 to 230, 242 to 261
K58	Fuel pump relay (Multec single-point)	196, 197, 231, 232, 261, 262, 332, 333
K59	Day running light relay	619 to 625
K61	Motronic control unit	367 to 397, 402 to 426
K63	Twin-tone horn relay	829,830
K68	Fuel injection unit relay	395 to 399, 428 to 432
K76	Glow time control unit	479 to 484
K77	Glow plug relay	486, 487
K78	Pre-resistor relay	489,490
K79	Charging indicator relay	472 to 474
K80	Fuel filter heating relay (diesel)	449, 450, 494, 495
K82	Engine speed relay	444, 445
K85	Automatic transmission control unit	271 to 294
K89	Rear foglight relay	639 to 641
K91	Multec multi-point control unit	305 to 332, 345
K94	Anti-theft alarm control unit	737 to 750
K95	ETC system control unit	926 to 941
K97	Headlight washer delay relay	820 to 822
L01	Ignition coil	138, 172, 205, 239, 303, 362, 406
L02	Ignition coil (DIS)	338 to 343
M01	Starter motor	105, 106
M02	Windscreen wiper motor	801 to 804
M03	Heater blower motor	761 to 763
M04*	Radiator cooling fan motor	120, 123
M04**	Radiator cooling fan motor	120, 123, 127
M08	Tailgate wiper motor	811 to 813
M15	Electric window motor, front passenger door	783, 785
M18	Central locking motor, driver's door	706 to 709
M19	Central locking motor, left rear door	717 to 719
M20	Central locking motor, right rear door	721 to 723
M21	Fuel pump	197, 232, 262, 333, 399, 429
M24	Headlight washer pump	822
M26	Electric aerial motor	587, 588
M26.1	Electric aerial motor relay	590
M30	Electric mirror (driver's side)	838 to 841
M31	Electric mirror (passenger side)	844 to 847
M32	Central locking motor, front passenger door	717 to 720
M33	Idle speed actuator/power unit	377, 378, 414, 415
M39	Headlight levelling motor, left	592 to 594
M40	Headlight levelling motor, right	596 to 598
M41	Central locking motor, fuel filler flap	725,726

Key to wiring diagrams for models up to 1994

Not all items fitted to all models   *Models   with earlier 30-fuse type fusebox   **Models with later 28-fuse type fusebox*

No	Description	Track
M47	Electric window motor, driver's door	773 to 776
M55	Windscreen/tailgate washer pump	817
M60	Central locking motor, boot lid/tailgate	726, 728
M65	Throttle valve actuator (ETC system)	930 to 934
M66	Idle air stepper motor	
	178 to 181, 215 to 218, 249 to 252, 314 to 317	
P01	Fuel gauge	550
P02	Coolant temperature gauge	553
P04	Fuel level sensor	550
P05	Coolant temperature sensor	553
P07	Tachometer	543
P12	Coolant temperature sensor	371 to 373, 413
P13	Ambient air temperature sensor	524
P14	Distance sensor	478, 479
P17	Wheel sensor, front left	910, 953
P18	Wheel sensor, front right	913, 956
P19	Wheel sensor, rear left	916, 959
P20	Wheel sensor, rear right	919, 962
P21	Distance sensor	556
P23	MAP sensor 188 to 190, 217 to 219, 249 to 251, 319 to 321	
P25	Bulb test sensor	500 to 513
P27	Brake pad wear sensor, front left	516
P28	Brake pad wear sensor, front right	516
P29	Inlet manifold temperature sensor	315, 410
P30	Coolant temperature sensor	186, 215, 247, 317
P32	Exhaust gas oxygen sensor (heated)	392, 393, 426, 427
P33	Exhaust gas oxygen sensor	190, 229, 256, 330
P34	Throttle potentiometer	
	191 to 193, 221 to 223, 252 to 254, 323 to 325, 411, 412	
P35	Crankshaft impulse sensor	
	244 to 246, 311 to 313, 381, 383, 421 to 423	
P38	Automatic transmission fluid temperature sensor	290
P44	Air mass meter	394 to 398, 417 to 419
P45	Automatic transmission engine speed sensor	287, 288
P46	Knock sensor	385, 386
P47	Hall sensor (cylinder identification)	388, 389
P48	Automatic transmission distance sensor	285, 286
P55	Coolant temperature sensor	482
P57	Aerial	587
P58	Anti-theft alarm glass breakage sensor, rear left	754
P59	Anti-theft alarm glass breakage sensor, rear right	754
R02	Carburettor pre-heating	135
R03	Cigarette lighter	854
R05	Glow plugs	438 to 440, 485 to 487
R19*	Pre-resistor, radiator cooling fan motor	123
R19**	Pre-resistor, radiator cooling fan motor	123, 127
R22	Glow plug pre-resistor	490
S01	Ignition/starter switch	105, 106
S02	Light switch assembly	
S02.1	Light switch	604 to 607
S02.2	Interior light switch	689
S02.3	Instrument lighting dimmer	533
S03	Heater blower/heated rear window switch	760 to 764
S05	Direction indicator switch assembly	
S05.2	Headlight dipped beam switch	630 to 631
S05.3	Direction indicator switch	682 to 684
S07	Reversing light switch	698
S08	Stop-light switch	660
S09	Wiper switch assembly	
S09.2	Intermittent wiper switch (windscreen)	801 to 804
S09.5	Tailgate wash/wipe switch	814 to 816
S010	Automatic transmission selector switch	271 to 277
S011	Brake fluid level switch	563
S013	Handbrake 'on' switch	566
S014	Oil pressure sender/switch	561

No	Description	Track
S015	Luggage compartment light switch	687
S017	Courtesy light switch, front passenger door	694
S021	Front foglight switch	652 to 654
S022	Rear foglight switch	645 to 647
S029**	Coolant temperature switch	120
S030	Seat heating switch, front left	860 to 862
S031	Courtesy light switch, left rear door	691
S032	Courtesy light switch, right rear door	692
S033	ETC system switch	929, 930
S034	Multi-information display switch	526, 527
S037	Electric window switch assembly (in driver's door)	774, 775
S037.1	Electric window switch, driver's window	774, 775
S037.2	Electric window switch, passenger window	772 to 777
S041	Anti-theft locking switch, driver's door	702 to 704
S042	Front passenger door locking switch	714
S047	Courtesy light switch, driver's door	695, 696
S052	Hazard warning light (hazard flashers) switch	672 to 676
S055	Seat heating switch, front right	864 to 866
S064	Horn switch	826
S068	Electric mirror switch assembly	
S068.1	Electric mirror adjustment switch	836 to 840
S068.2	Electric mirror heating switch	842
S068.3	Electric mirror left/right selector switch	836 to 841
S078	Electric window switch assembly (in passenger door)	782 to 785
S082	Washer fluid level switch	518
S088*	Coolant temperature switch	119 to 124
S088**	Coolant temperature switch	123 to 128
S093	Coolant level switch	520
S095	Engine oil level switch	522
S098	Headlight levelling switch	591 to 593
S104	Automatic transmission kickdown switch	289
S105	Automatic transmission 'Winter' switch	293 to 295
S106	Automatic transmission 'Economy/'Sport' switch	288
S107	Throttle position switch	374 to 379
S120	Anti-theft alarm bonnet switch	739
S127	Boot lid/tailgate central locking switch	735
U04	ABS hydraulic unit	
U04.1	Pump motor relay	902, 903, 945, 946
U04.2	Solenoid valve relay	904, 905, 947, 948
U04.3	Pump motor	902, 945
U04.4	Diode	905, 948
U04.5	Solenoid valve, front left	909, 952
U04.6	Solenoid valve, front right	911, 954
U04.7	Solenoid valve, rear axle	913, 956
U04.8	ABS control unit	906 to 912, 949 to 963
U12	Heated fuel filter assembly	449, 450, 494, 495
U13	Automatic transmission solenoid valve block	280 to 283
U14	Clock display unit	515 to 533
U15	Clock/radio display unit	515 to 533
U16	Clock/radio/computer display unit	515 to 533
U17	Aerial amplifier	584, 585
V01	Brake fluid level test bulb diode	564
V03	Anti-theft alarm light/diode	749
X01	Trailer socket	606, 607, 657, 658
X02 to X90	Wiring connectors	Various
Y05	Fuel solenoid valve	442, 476
Y07	Fuel injectors	323 to 330, 380 to 387, 416 to 423
Y10	Distributor (HEI system)	174 to 179
Y23	Distributor (HEI system)	140 to 144, 201 to 208
Y30	Cold start acceleration valve	445
Y32	Single-point fuel injector	181, 212, 244
Y33	Distributor (MHDI system)	
	237, 303 to 305, 361 to 363, 401	
Y34	Fuel tank ventilation valve	391, 422

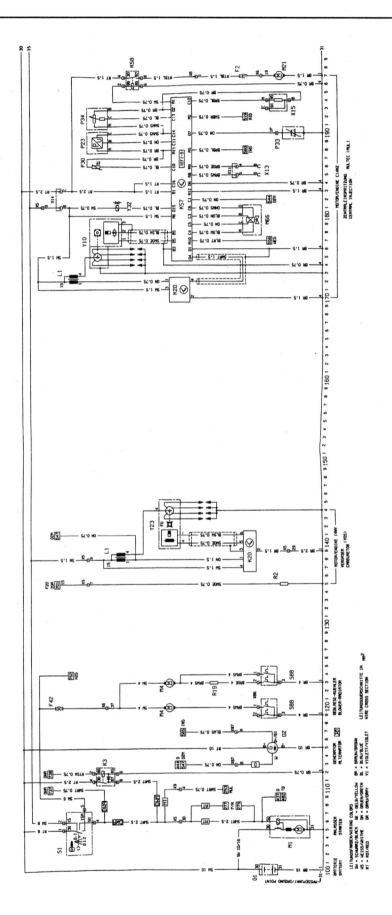

Wiring diagram for models with 30 fuses in fusebox (up to approximately February 1992)

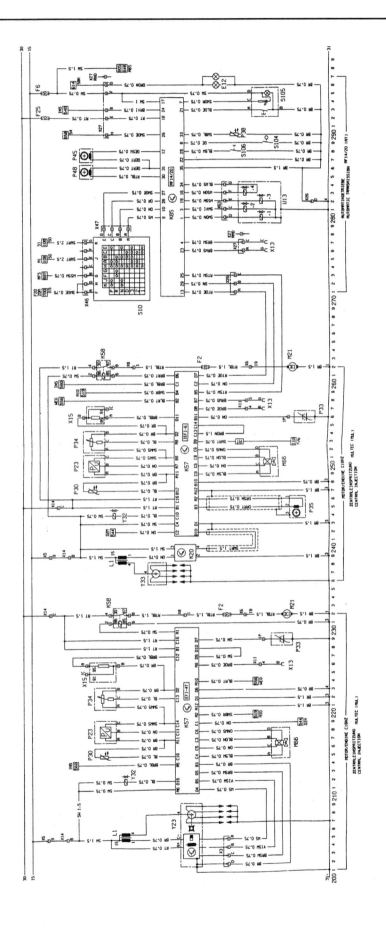

Wiring diagram for models with 30 fuses in fusebox (up to approximately February 1992) – continued

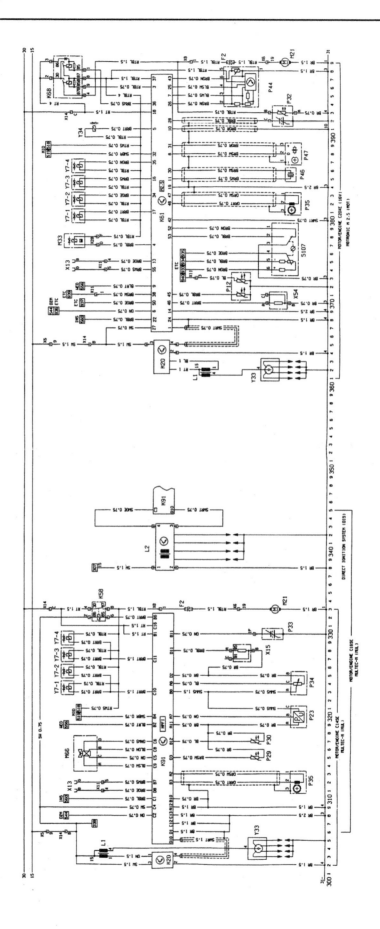

Wiring diagram for models with 30 fuses in fusebox (up to approximately February 1992) – continued

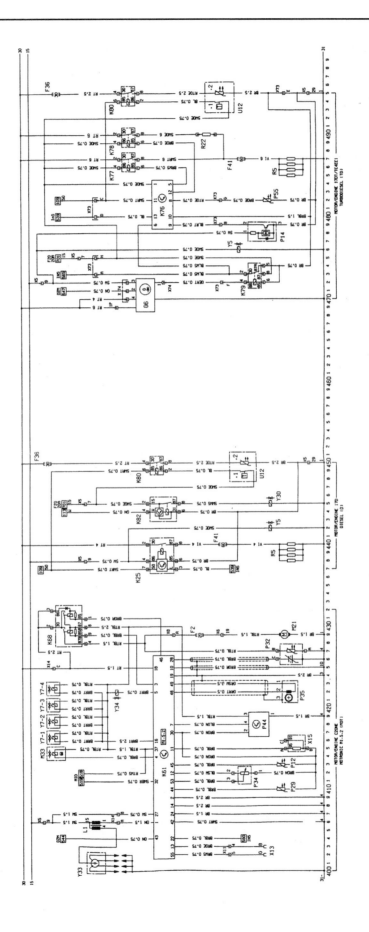

Wiring diagram for models with 30 fuses in fusebox (up to approximately February 1992) – continued

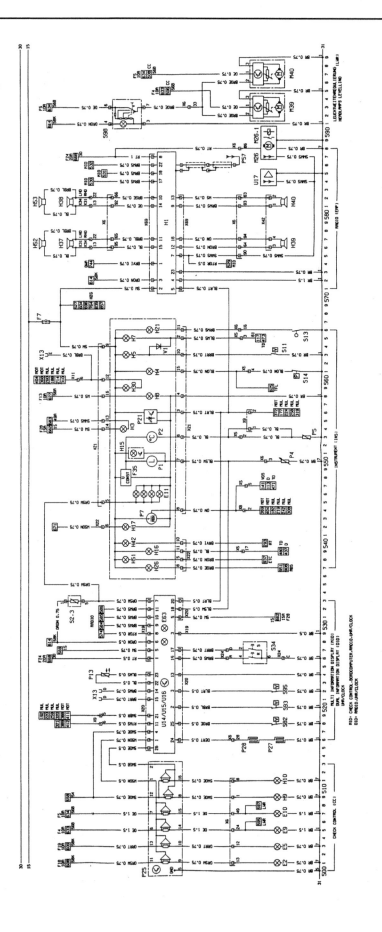

Wiring diagram for models with 30 fuses in fusebox (up to approximately February 1992) – continued

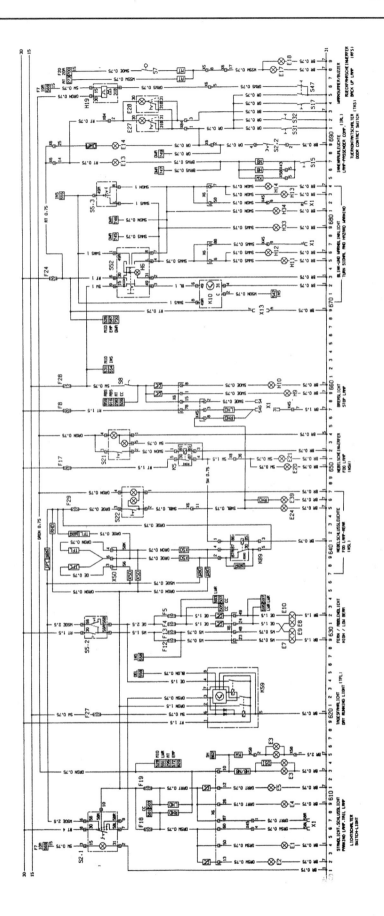

Wiring diagram for models with 30 fuses in fusebox (up to approximately February 1992) – continued

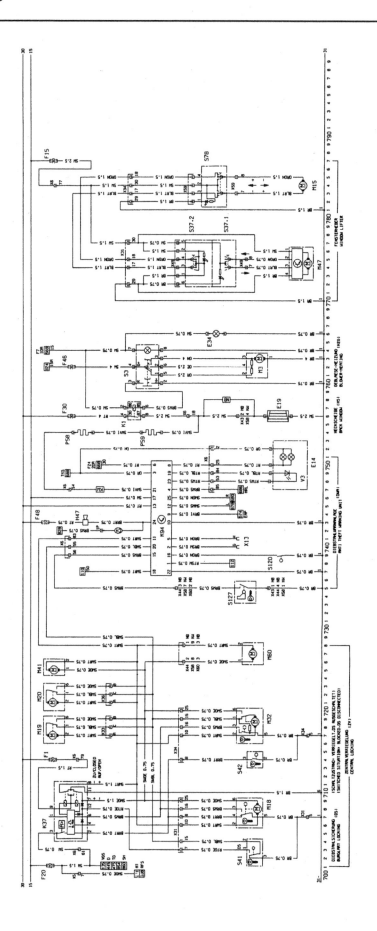

Wiring diagram for models with 30 fuses in fusebox (up to approximately February 1992) – continued

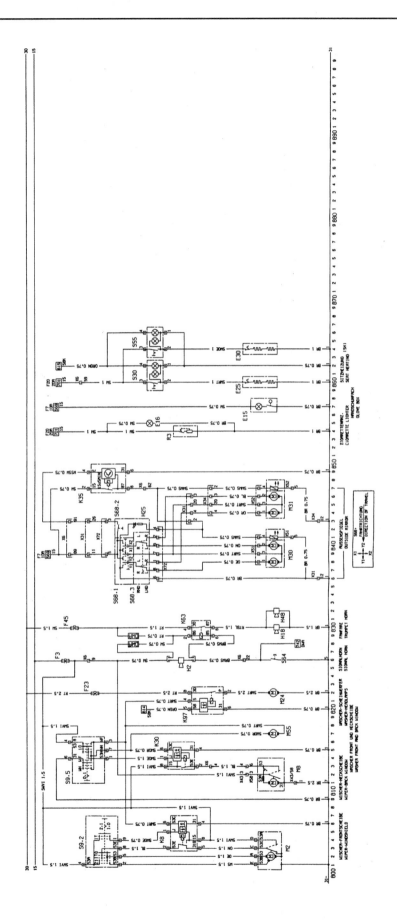

Wiring diagram for models with 30 fuses in fusebox (up to approximately February 1992) – continued

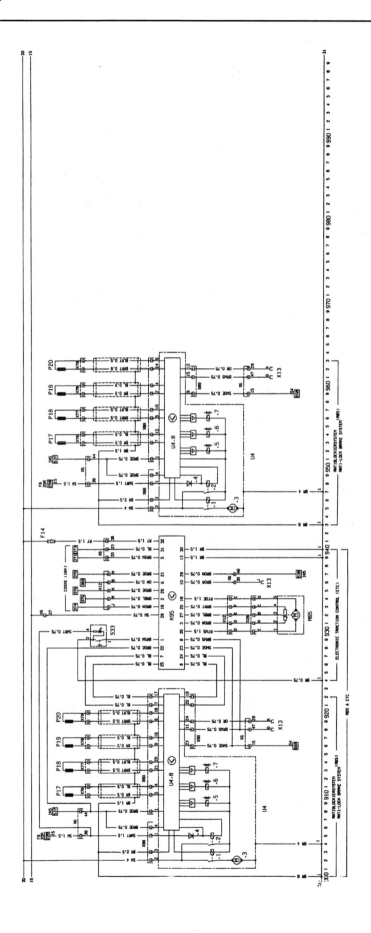

Wiring diagram for models with 30 fuses in fusebox (up to approximately February 1992) – continued

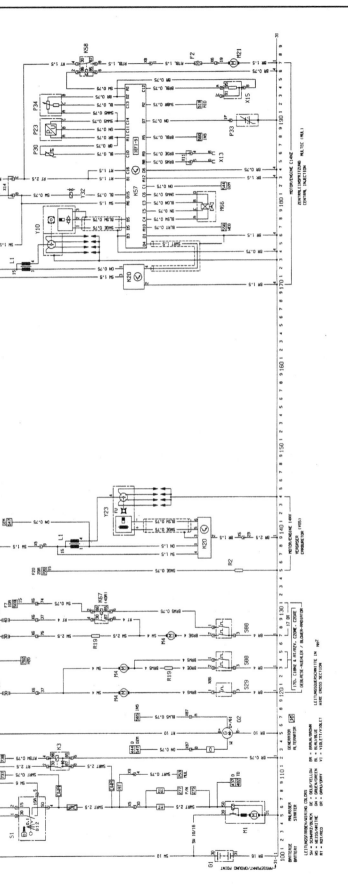

Wiring diagram for models with 28 fuses in fusebox (from approximately March 1992)

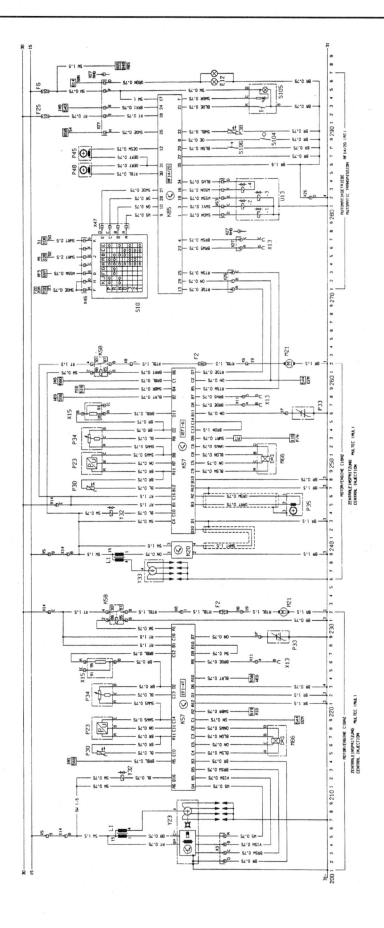

Wiring diagram for models with 28 fuses in fusebox (from approximately March 1992) – continued

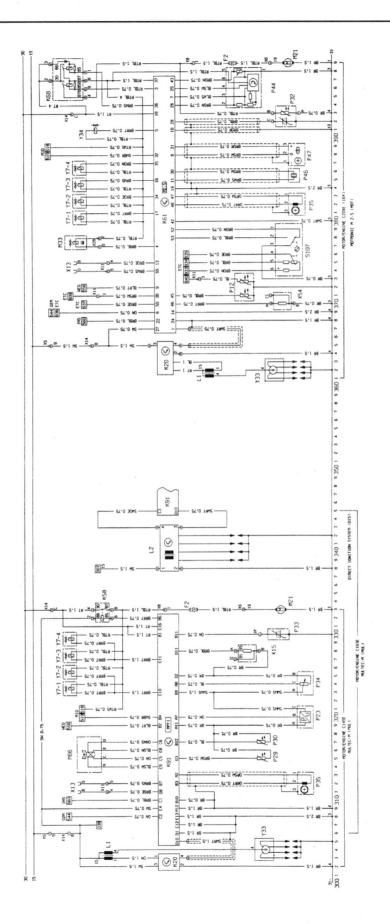

Wiring diagram for models with 28 fuses in fusebox (from approximately March 1992) – continued

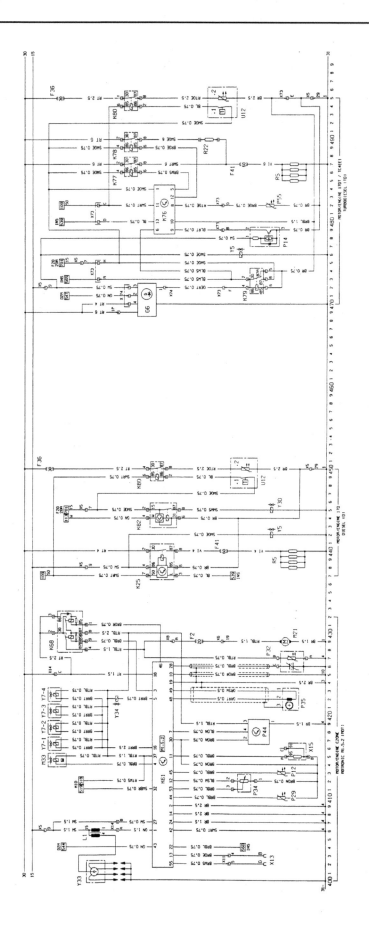

Wiring diagram for models with 28 fuses in fusebox (from approximately March 1992) – continued

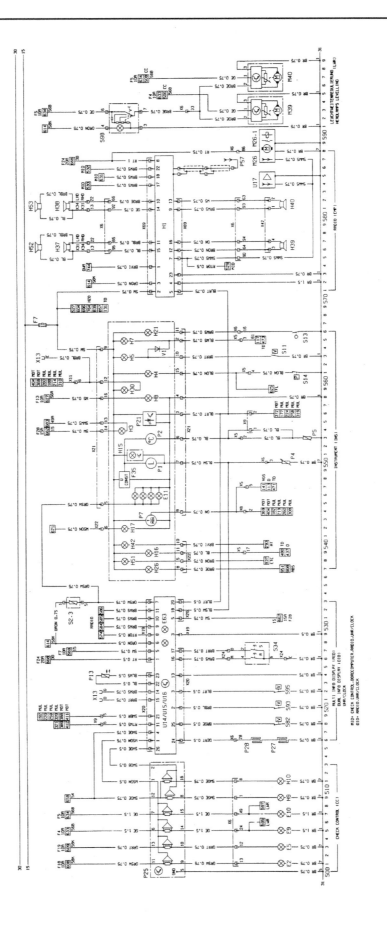

Wiring diagram for models with 28 fuses in fusebox (from approximately March 1992) – continued

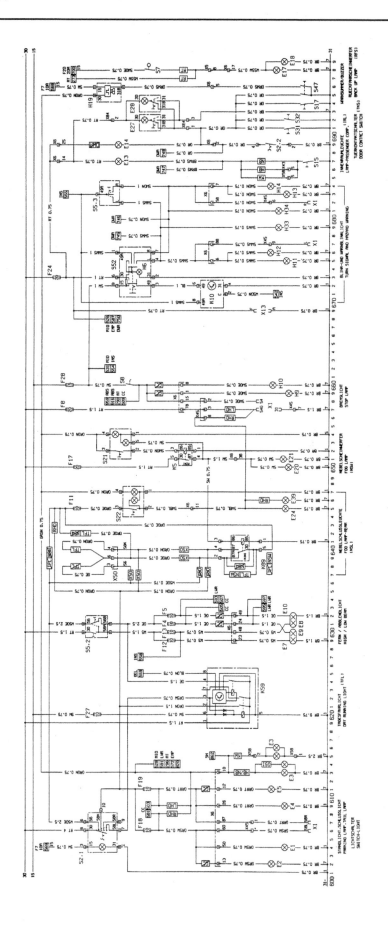

Wiring diagram for models with 28 fuses in fusebox (from approximately March 1992) – continued

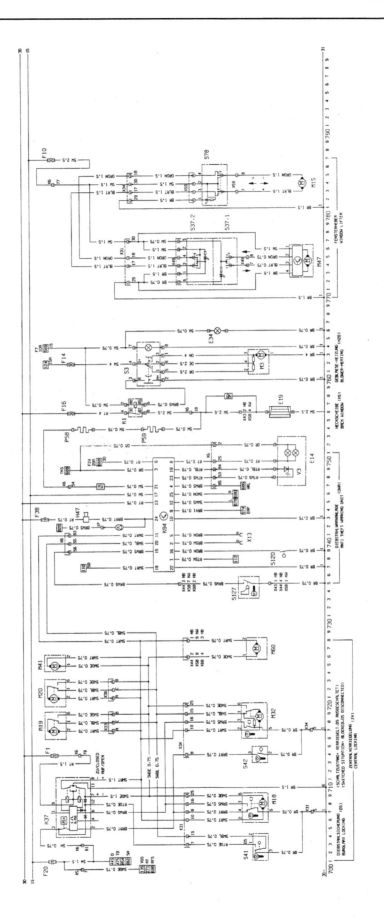

Wiring diagram for models with 28 fuses in fusebox (from approximately March 1992) – continued

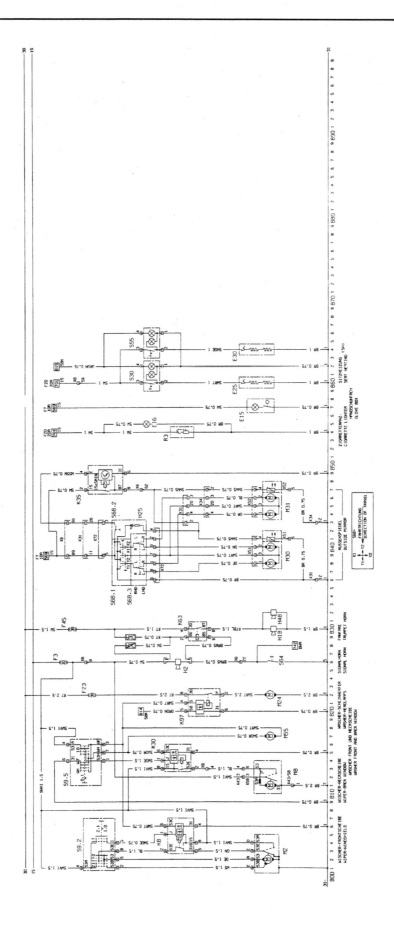

Wiring diagram for models with 28 fuses in fusebox (from approximately March 1992) – continued

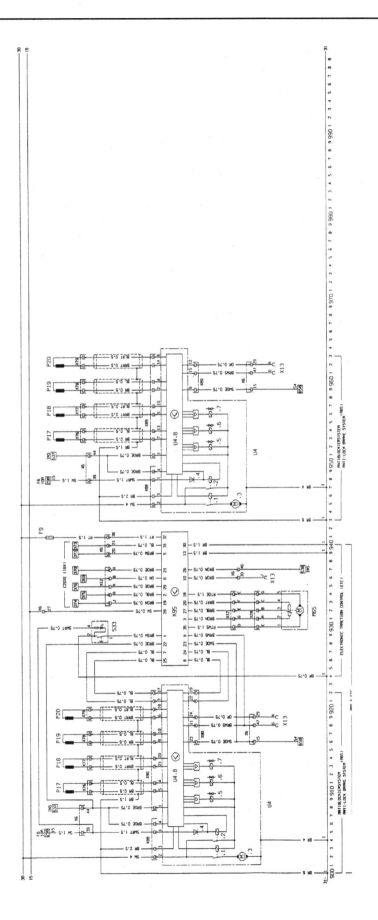

Wiring diagram for models with 28 fuses in fusebox (from approximately March 1992) – continued

Key to wiring diagram for 1994 to 1996 models

Not all items fitted to all model

No	Description	Track
E1	Sidelight, left	604
E2	Tail light, left	501, 602
E3	Number plate light	613 to 616
E4	Sidelight, right	609
E5	Tail light, right	503, 611
E7	Headlight main beam, left	629
E8	Headlight main beam, right	631
E9	Headlight dipped beam, left	505, 630
E10	Headlight dipped beam, right	507, 632
E11	Instrument lighting	546
E12	Automatic transmission selector illumination	296, 297
E13	Luggage compartment light	687
E14	Interior light	689
E15	Glovebox light	774
E16	Cigarette lighter illumination	773
E17	Reversing light, left	698
E18	Reversing light, right	699
E19	Heated rear window	756
E20	Foglight, front left	650
E21	Foglight, front right	651
E24	Foglight, rear left	645
E25	Seat heating, left	776
E27	Rear reading light, left	692
E28	Rear reading light, right	694
E30	Seat heating, right	780
E39	Foglight, rear right	646
E63	Display unit lights	528, 530
F1 to F28		
	Fuses in fusebox	Various
F35	Voltage stabiliser	548
F36	Fuel filter heating fuse (diesel, engine compartment)	450, 495
F38	Anti-theft alarm horn fuse	743
F41	Glow plug fuse ('maxi' type, engine compartment)	440, 487
F44	Hydraulic pump fuse	1102
F45	Horn fuse	832
G1	Battery	101
G2	Alternator	115
G6	Alternator (diesel)	469 to 472
H1	Radio/cassette	571 to 587
H2	Horn (single-tone)	828
H3	Direction indicator warning light	554
H4	Oil pressure warning light	561
H5	Brake fluid warning light	564
H6	Hazard flashers warning light	674
H7	Alternator/no-charge warning light	567
H8	Headlight main beam warning light	558
H9	Stop-light, left	509, 659
H10	Stop-light, right	511, 660
H11	Direction indicator light, front left	675
H12	Direction indicator light, rear left	676
H13	Direction indicator light, front right	683
H14	Direction indicator light, rear right	684
H15	Low fuel/fuel reserve warning light	551
H16	Glow plug warning light	539
H17	Trailer direction indicator warning light	542
H18	Horn (twin-tone)	832
H19	Headlights 'on' warning buzzer	695, 696
H22	Rear foglamp warning light	541
H23	Airbag warning lamp	536
H25	Heated mirror warning light	842
H26	ABS warning light	537
H30	Engine warning light	559
H33	Direction indicator side repeater light left	679
H34	Direction indicator side repeater light right	681
H37	Loudspeaker, front left	576, 577
H38	Loudspeaker, front right	581, 582
H39	Loudspeaker, rear left	576, 577

No	Description	Track
H40	Loudspeaker, rear right	581, 582
H42	Automatic transmission warning light	540
H46	Catalytic converter temperature warning light	542
H47	Anti-theft alarm horn	743
H48	Horn (twin-tone)	834
H51	Electronic traction control (ETC) warning light	538
H52	Tweeter, front left	576
H53	Tweeter, front right	581
K1	Heated rear window relay	756, 757
K3	Relay, starter (anti-theft warning unit, 70A)	111, 112
K5	Front foglight relay	651, 652
K6	Air conditioning relay	852, 853
K7	Air conditioning fan relay	862, 863
K8	Intermittent wiper relay (windscreen)	803 to 806
K10	Direction indicator flasher unit	670 to 672
K18	Horn (single-tone) - only with airbag	824, 825
K20	Ignition module/ignition coil	170 to 172, 239, 240, 360 to 364
K25	Glow time relay (70A)	437 to 440
K26	Radiator fan relay	882 to 884
K30	Intermittent wiper relay (tailgate)	813 to 815
K31	Airbag control unit	792 to 798
K35	Heated mirror relay	847 to 849
K37	Central door locking control unit	705 to 711
K51	Radiator fan relay, stage 1	129, 130, 887, 888
K52	Radiator fan relay	893 to 895
K57	Multec single-point control unit	175 to 194, 211 to 230, 242 to 261, 1008 to 1032
K58	Fuel pump relay (Multec single-point)	196, 197, 231, 232, 261, 262, 332, 333, 1036, 1037
K59	Day running light relay	619 to 625
K60	Compressor fan relay	874, 875
K61	Motronic control unit	366 to 396, 402 to 426
K63	Twin-tone horn relay	831, 832
K67	Radiator fan relay, stage 2	134, 135, 898, 899
K68	Fuel injection unit relay	393 to 397, 428 to 432, 1092 to 1096
K69	Simtec 56 control unit	1059 to 1095
K76	Glow time control unit	479 to 484
K77	Glow plug relay	486, 487
K79	Charging indicator relay	472 to 474
K80	Fuel filter heating relay (diesel)	449, 450, 494, 495
K82	Engine speed relay	444, 445
K85	Automatic transmission control unit	271 to 294
K88	Catalytic converter temperature control unit	454 to 456
K89	Rear foglight relay	639 to 641
K90	Compressor relay, AT	879, 880
K91	Multec multi-point control unit	306 to 332
K94	Anti-theft alarm control unit	737 to 749
K95	ETC system control unit	926 to 940
K97	Headlight washer delay relay	820 to 822
K100	Safety switch relay	1162 to 1164
K102	PBSL control unit	461 to 463
K104	Hydraulic pump relay	1101 to 1103
K105	Hydraulic pump relay	1107 to 1109
K106	Adjustment control relay	1117 to 1119
L1	Ignition coil	172, 205, 239, 406
L2	Ignition coil (DIS)	301 to 304, 359 to 363, 1001 to 1003, 1057 to 1060
M1	Starter motor	105, 106
M2	Windscreen wiper motor	801 to 804
M3	Heater fan motor	761 to 764
M4	Radiator cooling fan motor	120, 124, 129, 895
M8	Tailgate wiper motor	811 to 813
M10	Air conditioning fan motor	858 to 861
M11	Radiator fan motor	884
M14	Electric window motor, driver's door	1141
M15	Electric window motor, front passenger door	1146
M16	Electric window motor, rear left door	1151

Key to wiring diagram for 1994 to 1996 models

Not all items fitted to all model

No	Description	Track
M17	Electric window motor, rear right door	1156
M18	Central locking motor, driver's door	706 to 709
M19	Central locking motor, left rear door	717 to 719
M20	Central locking motor, right rear door	721 to 723
M21	Fuel pump	197, 232, 249 to 252, 333, 398, 429, 735, 1037, 1099
M24	Headlight washer pump	822
M26	Electric aerial motor	587 to 590
M26.1	Electric aerial motor relay	590
M30	Electric mirror (driver's side)	838 to 841
M31	Electric mirror (passenger side)	844 to 847
M32	Central locking motor, front passenger door	717 to 720
M33	Idle speed actuator/power unit	379, 380, 414, 415, 1071, 1072
M39	Headlight levelling motor, left	592 to 594
M40	Headlight levelling motor, right	596 to 598
M41	Central locking motor, fuel filler flap	725, 726
M47	Electric window motor, driver's door	973 to 976
M48	Electric window motor, passenger's door	985 to 988
M55	Windscreen/tailgate washer pump	817
M60	Central locking motor, boot lid/tailgate	726, 728
M64	Hydraulic pump motor	1105
M65	Throttle valve actuator (ETC system)	930 to 934
M66	Idle air stepper motor	178 to 181, 215 to 218, 314 to 317, 1015 to 1018
P1	Fuel gauge	550
P2	Coolant temperature gauge	553
P4	Fuel level sensor	550
P5	Coolant temperature sensor	553
P7	Tachometer	543
P12	Coolant temperature sensor	413
P13	Ambient air temperature sensor	531
P17	Wheel sensor, front left	910, 953
P18	Wheel sensor, front right	913, 956
P19	Wheel sensor, rear left	916, 959
P20	Wheel sensor, rear right	919, 962
P21	Distance sensor	555, 556
P23	MAP sensor	188 to 190, 217 to 219, 249 to 251, 319 to 321, 1020 to 1022
P25	Bulb test sensor	500 to 513
P27	Brake pad wear sensor, front left	515
P28	Brake pad wear sensor, front right	515
P29	Inlet manifold temperature sensor	315, 375, 410, 1068
P30	Coolant temperature sensor	186, 215, 247, 317, 376, 1018, 1069
P32	Exhaust gas oxygen sensor (heated)	393, 394, 426, 427, 1089 to 1092
P33	Exhaust gas oxygen sensor	190, 230, 256, 328, 1024
P34	Throttle potentiometer	191 to 193, 221 to 223, 252 to 254, 322 to 324, 377, 378, 411, 412, 1023 to 1025, 1071 to 1073
P35	Crankshaft impulse sensor	244 to 246, 311 to 313, 384 to 386, 420 to 422, 1007 to 1009, 1079 to 1082
P38	Automatic transmission fluid temperature sensor	286
P44	Air mass meter	396, 397, 417 to 419, 1094 to 1097
P45	Automatic transmission engine speed sensor	287, 288
P46	Knock sensor	381, 382, 1030, 1075, 1076
P47	Hall sensor (cylinder identification)	387 to 389, 1085 to 1087
P48	Automatic transmission distance sensor	285, 286
P50	Catalytic converter temperature sensor	455, 456
P57	Aerial	587
P58	Anti-theft alarm glass breakage sensor, rear left	754
P59	Anti-theft alarm glass breakage sensor, rear right	754
R3	Cigarette lighter	772
R5	Glow plugs	438, 440, 485 to 487
R19	Pre-resistor, radiator cooling fan motor	124, 129
S1	Ignition/starter switch	105, 106
S1.2	Key contact switch	572

No	Description	Track
S2	Light switch assembly	
S2.1	Light switch	604 to 607
S2.2	Interior light switch	689
S2.3	Instrument lighting dimmer	533
S3	Heater fan/heated rear window switch	760 to 765
S5	Direction indicator switch assembly	
S5.2	Headlight dipped beam switch	630, 631
S5.3	Direction indicator switch	682 to 684
S7	Reversing light switch	698
S8	Stop-light switch	660
S9	Wiper switch assembly	
S9.2	Intermittent wiper switch (windscreen)	801 to 804
S9.5	Tailgate wash/wipe switch	814 to 816
S10	Automatic transmission selector switch	271 to 277
S11	Brake fluid level switch	564
S13	Handbrake 'on' switch	565, 1119
S14	Oil pressure sender/switch	561
S15	Luggage compartment light switch	687
S17	Courtesy light switch, front passenger door	694
S20	Pressure switch assembly	
S20.1	Compressor low pressure switch	866
S20.2	Compressor high pressure switch	866
S20.3	Compressor high pressure switch	893
S21	Front foglight switch	652 to 654
S22	Rear foglight switch	645 to 647
S24	Air conditioning fan switch	857 to 861
S29	Coolant temperature switch	120, 888
S30	Seat heating switch, front left	776 to 778
S31	Courtesy light switch, left rear door	691
S32	Courtesy light switch, right rear door	692
S33	ETC system switch	929, 930
S34	Multi-information display switch	524, 525
S37	Electric window switch assembly (in driver's door)	
S37.1	Electric window switch, driver's window	974, 975, 1140, 1141
S37.2	Electric window switch, passenger window	972 to 977, 1145, 1146
S37.3	Electric window switch, rear left	1150, 1151
S37.4	Electric window switch, rear right	1155, 1156
S37.5	Safety switch	1159
S41	Anti-theft locking switch, driver's door	702 to 704
S42	Front passenger door locking switch	714
S47	Courtesy light switch, driver's door	695, 696
S52	Hazard warning light (hazard flashers) switch	671 to 676
S55	Seat heating switch, front right	780 to 782
S64	Horn switch	789, 828
S68	Electric mirror switch assembly	
S68.1	Electric mirror adjustment switch	836 to 840
S68.2	Electric mirror heating switch	842
S68.3	Electric mirror left/right selector switch	836 to 841
S78	Electric window switch assembly, passenger's door	985 to 988, 1144 to 1146
S79	Electric window switch assembly, rear left	1149 to 1151
S80	Electric window switch assembly, rear right	1149 to 1151
S82	Washer fluid level switch	517
S88	Coolant temperature switch	124 to 135
S93	Coolant level switch	519
S95	Engine oil level switch	521
S98	Headlight levelling switch	591 to 593
S101	Compressor switch	866
S104	Automatic transmission kickdown switch	288
S105	Automatic transmission 'Winter' switch	293 to 295
S106	Automatic transmission 'Economy'/'Sport' switch	290
S109	Revolution acceleration pressure switch	870
S114	Coolant temperature switch	482
S116	Stop lamp switch	663, 664
S120	Anti-theft alarm bonnet switch	739

Key to wiring diagram for 1994 to 1996 models

Not all items fitted to all model

No	Description	Track
S127	Boot lid/tailgate central locking switch	733
S128	Coolant temperature switch, compressor fan	898, 899
S132	Soft top switch	1111 to 1113
U4	ABS hydraulic unit	
U4.1	Pump motor relay	902, 903, 945, 946
U4.2	Solenoid valve relay	904, 905, 947, 948
U4.3	Pump motor	902, 945
U4.4	Diode	905, 948
U4.5	Solenoid valve, front left	909, 952
U4.6	Solenoid valve, front right	911, 954
U4.7	Solenoid valve, rear axle	913, 956
U4.8	ABS control unit	906 to 913, 949 to 963
U4.9	Solenoid valve plugs	952 to 956
U12	Heated fuel filter assembly	
U12.1	Temperature switch	449, 494
U12.2	Heating resistor	450, 495
U13	Automatic transmission solenoid valve block	
U13.1	Solenoid valve, shift 1	279
U13.2	Solenoid valve, shift 2	280
U13.3	Solenoid valve, lock-up control	281
U13.4	Solenoid valve, pressure control	282
U13.5	Sensor, ATF temperature	284
U14	Clock display unit	515 to 533
U15	Clock/radio display unit	515 to 533
U16	Clock/radio/computer display unit	515 to 533

No	Description	Track
U17	Aerial amplifier	584 to 585
U20	Contact unit assembly	789 to 794
U21	Airbag unit assembly, driver's side	792 to 794
U21.1	Airbag squib, driver's side	792 to 794
V3	Anti-theft alarm light/diode	671
V8	Compressor diode	877
V10	Adjustment control diode case	1112, 1113
V12	Diode (in wiring harness)	1119
V14	Knock signal filter	1031, 1032
V15	EGR amplifier	1031, 1032
X1	Trailer socket	606, 607
X2 to X98	Wiring connectors	Various
Y1	Air conditioning compressor clutch	879
Y5	Fuel solenoid valve	442, 477
Y7	Fuel injectors	323 to 330, 383 to 390, 416 to 423, 1080 to 1087
Y10	Distributor (HEI system)	174 to 179
Y18	EGR solenoid	1026 to 1029
Y23	Distributor (HEI system)	202 to 208
Y30	Cold start acceleration valve	445
Y32	Single-point fuel injector	181, 211, 244, 1012
Y33	Distributor (MHDI system)	237, 401
Y34	Fuel tank ventilation valve	377, 378, 422, 1010, 1074, 1075
Y47	PBSL lifting magnet	461

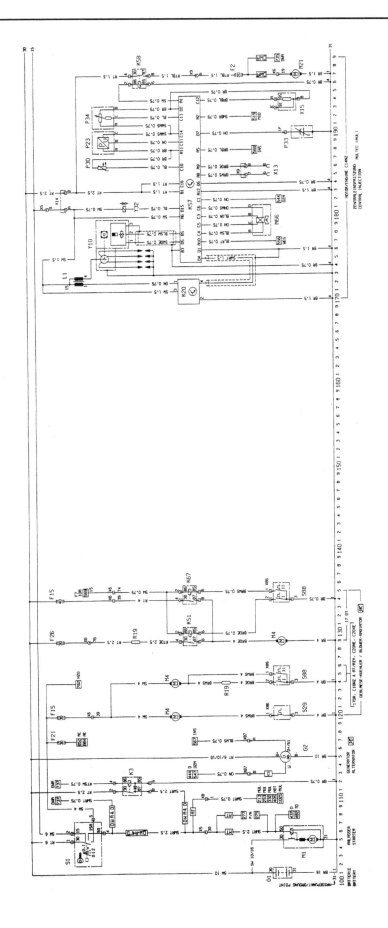

Wiring diagram for models from 1994 to 1996

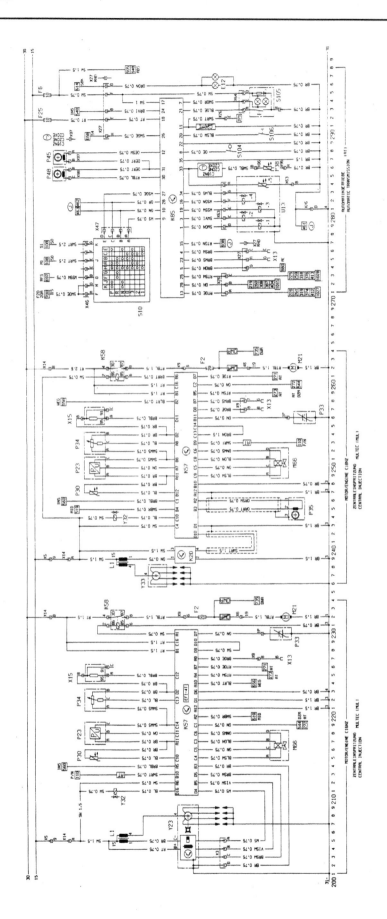

Wiring diagram for models from 1994 to 1996 (continued)

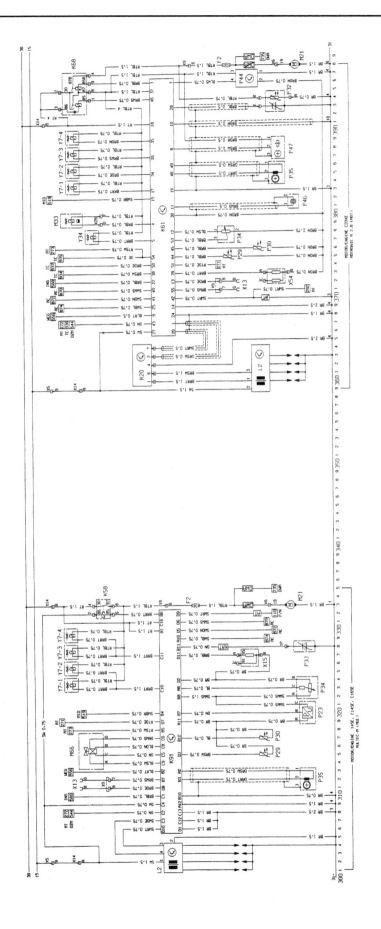

Wiring diagram for models from 1994 to 1996 (continued)

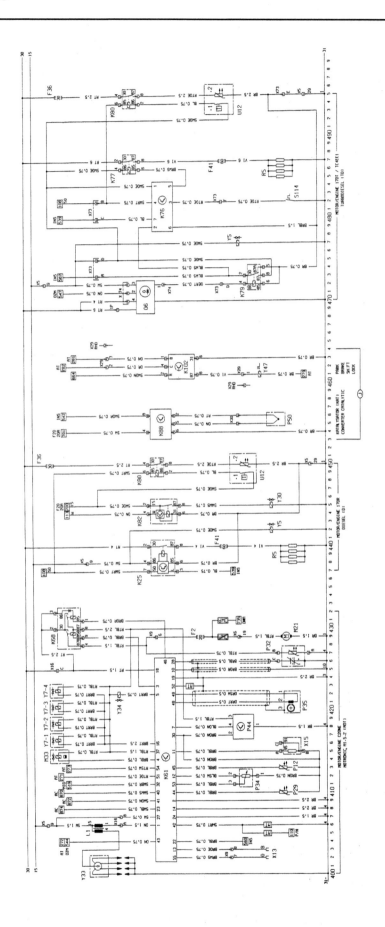

Wiring diagram for models from 1994 to 1996 (continued)

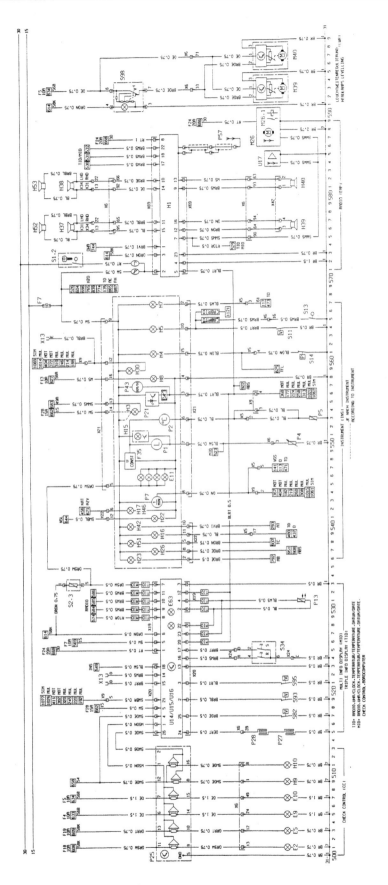

Wiring diagram for models from 1994 to 1996 (continued)

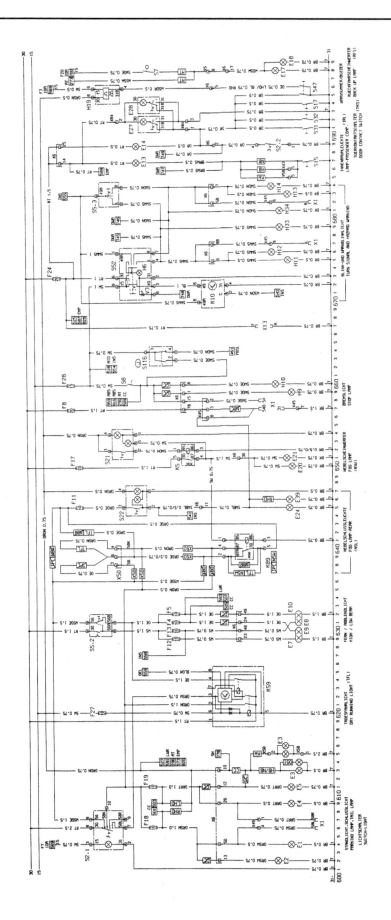

Wiring diagram for models from 1994 to 1996 (continued)

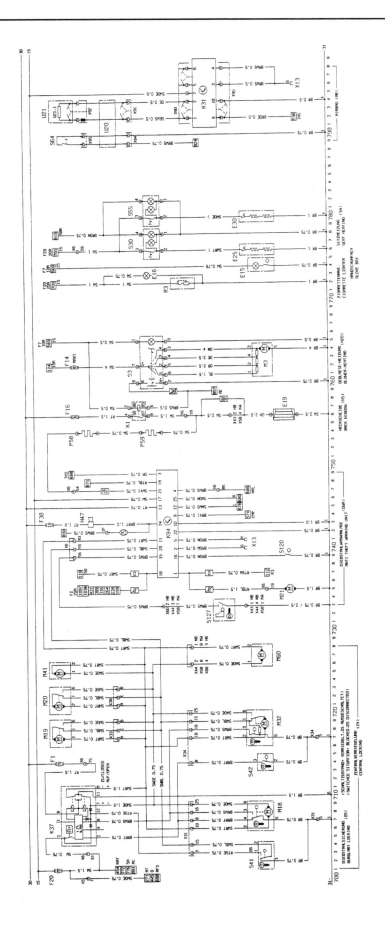

Wiring diagram for models from 1994 to 1996 (continued)

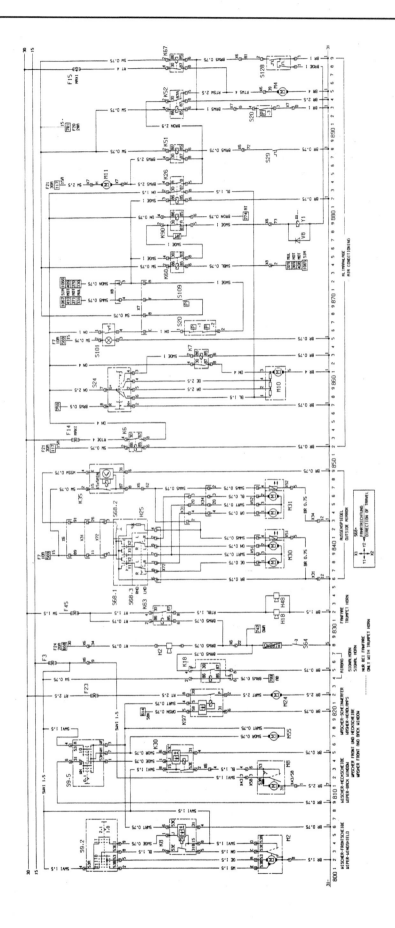

Wiring diagram for models from 1994 to 1996 (continued)

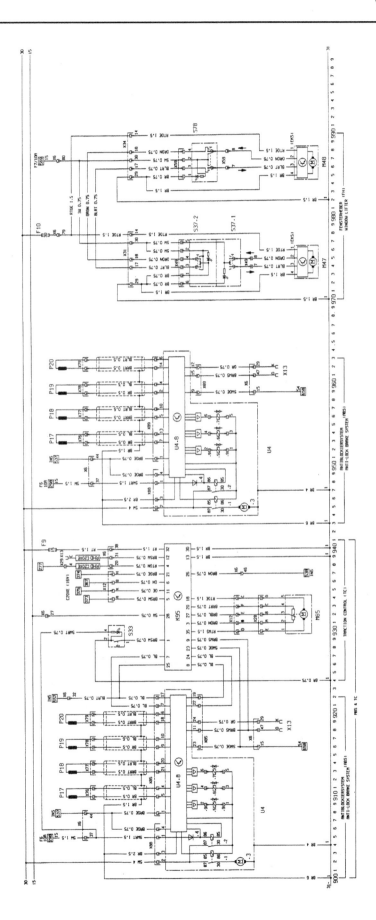

Wiring diagram for models from 1994 to 1996 (continued)

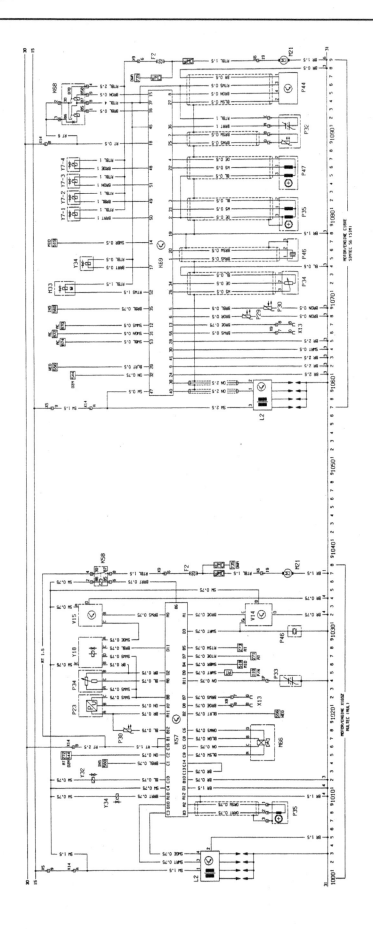

Wiring diagram for models from 1994 to 1996 (continued)

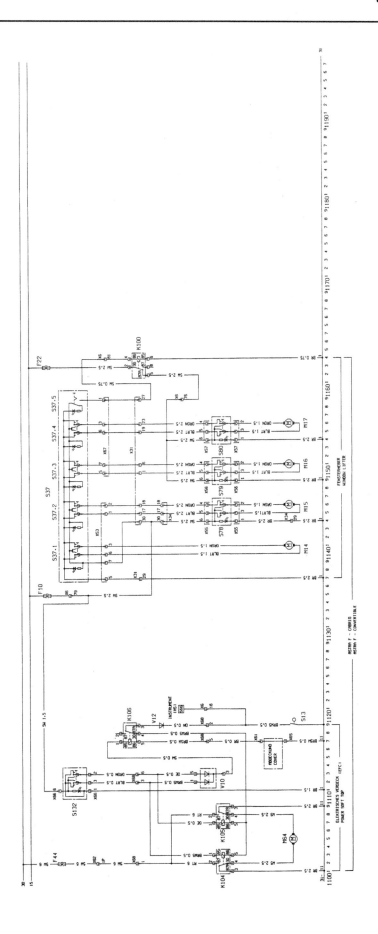

Wiring diagram for models from 1994 to 1996 (continued)

Key to wiring diagram for 1997-on models

Not all items fitted to all model

No	Description	Track
E1	Sidelight, left	602
E2	Tail light, left	501, 604
E3	Number plate light	613, 615, 616
E4	Sidelight, right	609
E5	Tail light, right	503, 611
E7	Headlight main beam, left	629
E8	Headlight main beam, right	631
E9	Headlight dipped beam, left	505, 630
E10	Headlight dipped beam, right	507, 632
E11	Instrument lighting	545 to 547
E12	Automatic transmission selector illumination	937, 938, 982, 983
E13	Luggage compartment light	685
E14	Interior light	407 to 411, 688, 750 to 752
E15	Glovebox light	777
E16	Cigarette lighter illumination	776
E17	Reversing light, left	698
E18	Reversing light, right	699
E19	Heated rear window	761
E20	Foglight, front left	650
E21	Foglight, front right	651
E24	Foglight, rear left	645
E25	Seat heating, left	780
E27	Rear reading light, left	691, 692
E28	Rear reading light, right	693, 694
E30	Seat heating, right	784
E39	Foglight, rear right	646
E63	Display unit lights	528, 530
F1 to F28	Fuses in fusebox	Various
F35	Voltage stabiliser	548
F36	Fuel filter heating fuse (diesel, engine compartment)	226, 498
F44	Hydraulic pump fuse	1102
F46	Fuse	392
F49	Secondary air induction fuse	1094, 1295, 1448
F54	Fuse	866
FV1	Fuse ('maxi' type)	184
FV2	Fuse ('maxi' type)	132
FV3	Fuse ('maxi' type)	143
FV4	Fuse ('maxi' type)	165
FV6	Fuse ('maxi' type)	171
FV7	Fuse ('maxi' type)	177
G1	Battery	101
G2	Alternator	115
H1	Radio/cassette	571, 591
H2	Horn (single-tone)	828
H3	Direction indicator warning light	554
H4	Oil pressure warning light	561
H5	Brake fluid warning light	564
H6	Hazard flashers warning light	672
H7	Alternator/no-charge warning light	567
H8	Headlight main beam warning light	558
H9	Stop-light, left	509, 659
H10	Stop-light, right	511, 660
H11	Direction indicator light, front left	673
H12	Direction indicator light, rear left	674
H13	Direction indicator light, front right	682
H14	Direction indicator light, rear right	681
H15	Low fuel/fuel reserve warning light	551
H16	Glow plug warning light	539
H17	Trailer direction indicator warning light	542
H18	Horn (twin-tone)	832
H19	Headlights 'on' warning buzzer	694 to 696
H22	Rear foglamp warning light	541
H23	Airbag warning lamp	536
H24	Alarm siren	753, 754
H25	Heated mirror warning light	842

No	Description	Track
H26	ABS warning light	537
H27	Safety checking warning buzzer	1169 to 1171
H28	Seat belt warning light	538
H30	Engine warning light	563
H33	Direction indicator side repeater light left	677
H34	Direction indicator side repeater light right	679
H37	Loudspeaker, front left	576, 577
H38	Loudspeaker, front right	581, 582
H39	Loudspeaker, rear left	576, 577
H40	Loudspeaker, rear right	581, 582
H42	Automatic transmission warning light	540
H46	Catalytic converter temperature warning light	542
H47	Anti-theft alarm horn	749
H48	Horn (twin-tone)	834
H52	Tweeter, front left	576, 577
H53	Tweeter, front right	581, 582
K1	Heated rear window relay	761, 762
K3	Relay, starter (anti-theft warning unit, 70A)	461, 462
K5	Front foglight relay	651, 652
K6	Air conditioning relay	852, 853
K8	Intermittent wiper relay (windscreen)	803 to 806
K10	Direction indicator flasher unit	668 to 670
K12	Secondary air induction relay	1093 to 1095, 1294 to 1296, 1447 to 1459
K18	Horn (single-tone) - only with airbag	824, 825
K20	Ignition module/ignition coil	239, 240, 1202 to 1204, 1560 to 1564
K25	Glow time relay (70A)	212 to 216
K26	Radiator fan relay	882 to 884
K30	Intermittent wiper relay (tailgate)	813 to 815
K31	Airbag control unit	792 to 798
K35	Heated mirror relay	847 to 849
K37	Central door locking control unit	705, 1305 to 1312
K43	Fuel injection relay	1286, 1287
K44	Fuel pump relay	1290, 1291
K51	Radiator fan relay, stage 1	428, 429, 887, 888
K52	Radiator fan relay	893 to 895
K57	Multec single-point control unit	242 to 261, 306 to 332, 1012 to 1031, 1050 to 1088, 1050 to 1088, 1207 to 1226, 1408 to 1443, 1408 to 1443, 1463 to 1496, 1507 to 1532
K58	Fuel pump relay (Multec single-point)	261, 262, 332, 333, 1032, 1033, 1088, 1089, 1228, 1229, 1443, 1444, 1495, 1496, 1535, 1536
K59	Day running light relay	635, 636
K60	Compressor fan relay	878, 879
K61	Motronic control unit	268 to 294, 369 to 393, 1566 to 1596
K63	Twin-tone horn relay	831, 832
K67	Radiator fan relay, stage 2	433, 434, 898, 899
K68	Fuel injection unit relay	293 to 297, 395 to 399, 1593 to 1597
K69	Simtec 56 control unit	1250 to 1290
K76	Glow time control unit	483, 484
K77	Glow plug relay	491, 492
K80	Fuel filter heating relay (diesel)	225, 226, 497, 498
K82	Engine speed relay	220, 221
K85	Automatic transmission control unit	901 to 935, 946 to 980
K88	Catalytic converter temperature control unit	1240 to 1242
K89	Rear foglight relay	639, 641
K94	Anti-theft alarm control unit	738 to 751
K97	Headlight washer delay relay	820 to 822
K100	Safety switch relay	1162 to 1164
K104	Hydraulic pump relay	1101 to 1103
K105	Hydraulic pump relay	1107 to 1109
K106	Adjustment control relay	1117 to 1119
K117	Immobiliser control unit	454 to 457, 470 to 474
L1	Ignition coil	239, 268, 373, 1006, 1204
L2	Ignition coil (DIS)	301 to 304, 1043 to 1046, 1248, 1402 to 1405, 1457 to 1460, 1501 to 1504, 1559 to 1563

Key to wiring diagram for 1997-on models

Not all items fitted to all model

No	Description	Track
M1	Starter motor	105, 106
M2	Windscreen wiper motor	801 to 804
M3	Heater fan motor	766 to 769, 895
M4	Radiator cooling fan motor	428
M8	Tailgate wiper motor	811 to 813
M10	Air conditioning fan motor	858 to 861
M11	Radiator fan motor	884
M13	Sunroof motor	1183
M14	Electric window motor, driver's door	1141
M15	Electric window motor, front passenger door	1146
M16	Electric window motor, rear left door	1151
M17	Electric window motor, rear right door	1156
M18	Central locking motor, driver's door	706 to 709, 1307 to 1310
M19	Central locking motor, left rear door	717 to 719, 1318 to 1320
M20	Central locking motor, right rear door	721 to 723, 1322 to 1324
M21	Fuel pump	262, 297, 333, 396, 1033, 1097, 1229, 1298, 1451, 1498, 1536, 1598
M24	Headlight washer pump	822
M26	Electric aerial motor	587 to 589
M26.1	Electric aerial motor relay	589
M27	Secondary air induction pump	1094, 1295, 1448
M30	Electric mirror (driver's side)	838 to 841
M31	Electric mirror (passenger side)	844 to 846
M32	Central locking motor, front passenger door	717 to 720, 1314 to 1317
M33	Idle speed actuator/power unit	279, 280, 381, 382, 1268, 1269, 1580, 1581
M39	Headlight levelling motor, left	992 to 994
M40	Headlight levelling motor, right	996 to 998
M41	Central locking motor, fuel filler flap	725, 726, 1326, 1327
M47	Electric window motor, driver's door	340 to 343, 1338 to 1341
M48	Electric window motor, passenger's door	351 to 354, 1347 to 1350
M49	Electric window motor, rear left	1355 to 1358
M50	Electric window motor, rear right	1363 to 1366
M55	Windscreen/tailgate washer pump	817
M60	Central locking motor, boot lid/tailgate	726 to 728, 1328, 1330
M64	Hydraulic pump motor	1102 to 1108
M66	Idle air stepper motor	250 to 253, 314 to 317, 1016 to 1019, 1071 to 1074, 1210 to 1213, 1415 to 1418, 1470 to 1473, 1514 to 1517
P1	Fuel gauge	550
P2	Coolant temperature gauge	553
P4	Fuel level sensor	550
P5	Coolant temperature sensor	553
P7	Tachometer	543
P12	Coolant temperature sensor	281, 380
P13	Ambient air temperature sensor	531
P17	Wheel sensor, front left	1386, 1387
P18	Wheel sensor, front right	1389, 1390
P19	Wheel sensor, rear left	1392, 1393
P20	Wheel sensor, rear right	1395, 1396
P21	Distance sensor	555, 556
P23	MAP sensor	249 to 251, 319 to 321, 1018 to 1020, 1066 to 1068, 1220 to 1222, 1424 to 1426, 1479 to 1481, 1519 to 1521
P25	Bulb test sensor	500 to 513
P27	Brake pad wear sensor, front left	515
P28	Brake pad wear sensor, front right	515
P29	Inlet manifold temperature sensor	283, 315, 316, 377, 1069, 1258, 1428, 1575
P30	Coolant temperature sensor	247, 317, 318, 1016, 1060, 1218, 1260, 1417, 1472, 1517, 1576
P32	Exhaust gas oxygen sensor (heated)	393, 394, 1280 to 1283, 1593, 1594
P33	Exhaust gas oxygen sensor	328, 1031, 1086, 1222, 1441, 1496, 1521
P34	Throttle potentiometer	252 to 254, 284, 285, 322 to 324, 378, 379, 1022 to 1024, 1062 to 1064, 1223 to 1225, 1262 to 1264, 1420 to 1422, 1475 to 1477, 1522 to 1524, 1577, 1578
P35	Crankshaft impulse sensor	246 to 248, 274 to 276, 311 to 313, 387 to 389, 1080 to 1082, 1271 to 1273, 1435 to 1437, 1490 to 1492, 1506 to 1508, 1584 to 1586
P38	Automatic transmission fluid temperature sensor	968
P44	Air mass meter	293 to 295, 384 to 386, 1285 to 1288, 1596, 1597
P45	Automatic transmission engine speed sensor	911, 912, 957, 958
P46	Knock sensor	290, 291, 1052, 1053, 1266 to 1268, 1429, 1430, 1484, 1485, 1528, 1581, 1582
P47	Hall sensor (cylinder identification)	1049, 1050, 1276 to 1278, 1407, 1408, 1587 to 1589
P48	Automatic transmission distance sensor	909, 910, 955, 956
P55	Engine temperature sensor	212
P57	Aerial	587
P58	Anti-theft alarm glass breakage sensor, rear left	757
P59	Anti-theft alarm glass breakage sensor, rear right	757
P60	Anti-theft alarm sensor	
R3	Cigarette lighter	775
R5	Glow plugs	216 to 218
R15	CO adjustment potentiometer	287, 288
R19	Pre-resistor, radiator cooling fan motor	423
S1	Ignition/starter switch	104 to 110
S2	Light switch assembly	
S2.1	Light switch	604 to 607
S2.2	Interior light switch	688
S2.3	Instrument lighting dimmer	533
S3	Heater fan/heated rear window switch	765 to 770
S5	Direction indicator switch assembly	
S5.2	Headlight dipped beam switch	630, 631
S5.3	Direction indicator switch	680 to 682
S7	Reversing light switch	698
S8	Stop-light switch	660
S9	Wiper switch assembly	
S9.2	Intermittent wiper switch (windscreen)	801 to 804
S9.5	Tailgate wash/wipe switch	814 to 816
S10	Automatic transmission selector switch	902 to 911, 947 to 956
S11	Brake fluid level switch	564
S13	Handbrake 'on' switch	565, 1119
S14	Oil pressure sender/switch	561
S15	Luggage compartment light switch	685
S17	Courtesy light switch, front passenger door	694
S20	Pressure switch assembly	866, 893
S20.1	Compressor low pressure switch	866, 893
S20.2	Compressor high pressure switch	866
S21	Front foglight switch	652, 654
S22	Rear foglight switch	645, 647
S29	Coolant temperature switch	419, 888
S30	Seat heating switch, driver	780
S31	Courtesy light switch, left rear door	691
S32	Courtesy light switch, right rear door	692
S34	Multi-information display switch	524
S35	Seat heating switch, passenger	784
S37	Electric window switch assembly (in driver's door)	1137 to 1161, 1337 to 1365
S37.1	Electric window switch, driver's window	341, 342, 1139 to 1141, 1339, 1340
S37.2	Electric window switch, passenger window	339, 344, 1145, 1146, 1348, 1349
S37.3	Electric window switch, rear left	1150, 1151, 1356, 1357

Key to wiring diagram for 1997-on models

Not all items fitted to all model

No	Description	Track
S37.4	Electric window switch, rear right	1155, 1156, 1364, 1365
S37.5	Safety switch	1159, 1360
S38	Electric window switch, passenger window	1351 to 1353
S39	Electric window switch, rear left	1359 to 1361
S40	Electric window switch, rear right	1367 to 1369
S41	Anti-theft locking switch, driver's door	702 to 704, 1302 to 1304
S42	Front passenger door locking switch	714, 1321
S47	Courtesy light switch, driver's door	695
S52	Hazard warning light (hazard flashers) switch	669 to 674
S57	Sunroof switch	1178 to 1183
S64	Horn switch	789, 828
S68	Electric mirror switch assembly	
S68.1	Electric mirror adjustment switch	836 to 841
S68.2	Electric mirror heating switch	836 to 841
S68.3	Electric mirror left/right selector switch	836 to 841
S78	Electric window switch assembly, passenger's door	351 to 354, 1144 to 1146
S79	Electric window switch assembly, rear left	1149 to 1151
S80	Electric window switch assembly, rear right	1154 to 1156
S82	Washer fluid level switch	517
S84	PBSL selector level unlock switch	940, 985
S85	PBSL parking position switch	942, 987
S88	Coolant temperature switch	423, 424
S89	Seatbelt switch	1171, 1236
S93	Coolant level switch	519
S95	Engine oil level switch	521
S98	Headlight levelling switch	991 to 993
S99	Electric window switch, driver's window	1336
S100	Electric window switch, passenger's window	1345
S101	Compressor switch	865, 866
S104	Automatic transmission kickdown switch	927, 972
S105	Automatic transmission 'Winter' switch	934 to 936, 979
S106	Automatic transmission 'Economy'/'Sport' switch	932, 977
S109	Revolution acceleration pressure switch	870
S114	Coolant temperature switch	483
S120	Anti-theft alarm bonnet switch	739
S127	Boot lid/tailgate central locking switch	733
S128	Coolant temperature switch, compressor fan	898, 899
S132	Soft top switch	1111 to 1113
U4	ABS hydraulic unit	1378 to 1396
U4.1	Pump motor relay	1378
U4.2	Solenoid valve relay	1380
U4.3	Pump motor	1378
U4.4	Diode	1381
U4.5	Solenoid valve, front left	1385
U4.6	Solenoid valve, front right	1387
U4.7	Solenoid valve, rear axle	1389
U4.8	ABS control unit	1382 to 1396

No	Description	Track
U4.9	Solenoid valve plugs	1385
U12	Heated fuel filter assembly	225, 226, 497, 498
U12.1	Temperature switch	225, 497
U12.2	Heating resistor	226, 498
U13	Automatic transmission solenoid valve block	974 to 918, 960 to 966
U13.1	Solenoid valve, shift 1	914, 961
U13.2	Solenoid valve, shift 2	915, 962
U13.3	Solenoid valve, lock-up control	916, 963
U13.4	Solenoid valve, pressure control	917, 964
U13.5	Solenoid valve, neutral control	960
U13.6	Sensor, ATF temperature	919, 966
U14	Clock display unit	515 to 533
U15	Clock/radio display unit	515 to 533
U16	Clock/radio/computer display unit	515 to 533
U17	Aerial amplifier	584, 585
U20	Contact unit assembly	789 to 794
U21	Airbag unit assembly, driver's side	792 to 794
U21.1	Airbag squib, driver's side	792 to 794
U22	Airbag unit assembly, passenger's side	796 to 798
U22.1	Airbag squib, passenger's side	796 to 798
U29	Phone/radio transformer	410, 411
V3	Anti-theft alarm light/diode	669
V8	Compressor diode	877
V10	Adjustment control diode case	1112, 1113
V12	Diode (in wiring harness)	1119
V14	Knock signal filter	1530, 1531
V15	EGR amplifier	1531 to 1533
X2 to X99	Wiring connectors	Various
Y1	Air conditioning compressor clutch	879
Y5	Fuel solenoid valve	219, 480
Y7	Fuel injectors	281 to 288, 323 to 330, 383 to 390, 1076 to 1083, 1276 to 1283, 1432 to 1439, 1432 to 1439, 1583 to 1590
Y10	Distributor (HEI system)	1206 to 1211
Y15	Secondary air induction solenoid valve	1091, 1293, 1294, 1445
Y18	EGR solenoid	1055 to 1057, 1270, 1271, 1412 to 1414, 1467 to 1469, 1527 to 1529
Y19	Change manifold solenoid valve	1274, 1275
Y21	PBSL lifting magnet	110
Y23	Distributor (HEI system)	1008 to 1010
Y30	Cold start acceleration valve	211
Y32	Single-point fuel injector	244, 1012, 1213, 1487, 1511
Y33	Distributor (MHDI system)	236 to 238, 265 to 267, 367 to 369
Y34	Fuel tank ventilation valve	389, 1086, 1272, 1273, 1441, 1493, 1509, 1578, 1579
Y47	PBSL lifting magnet	942, 987

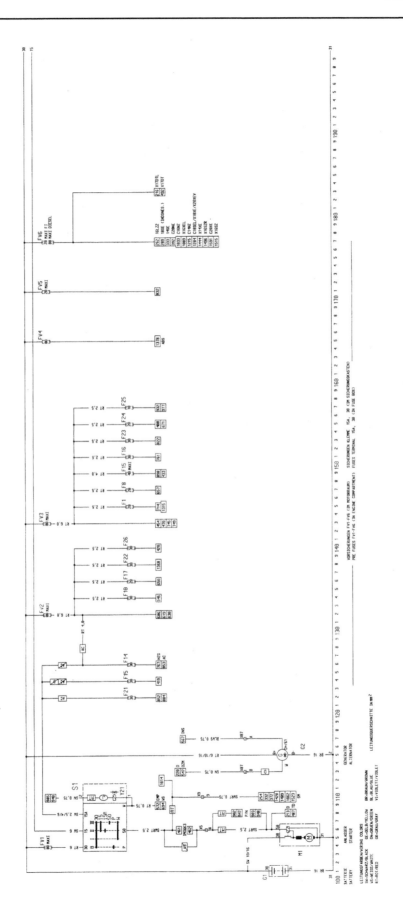

Wiring diagram for models from 1997-on

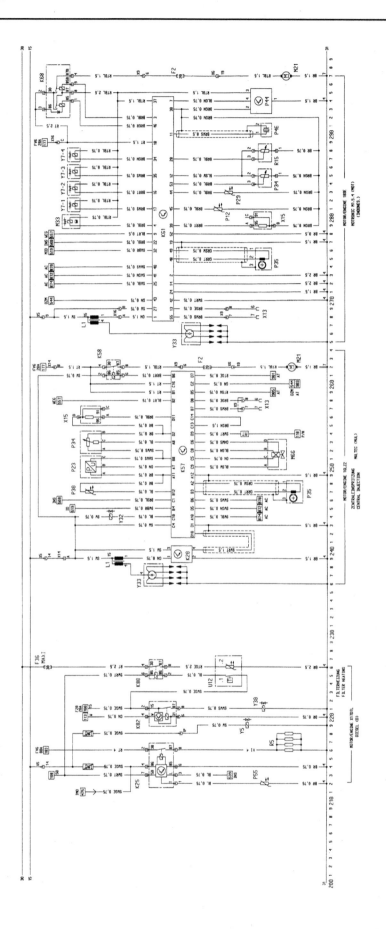

Wiring diagram for models from 1997-on (continued)

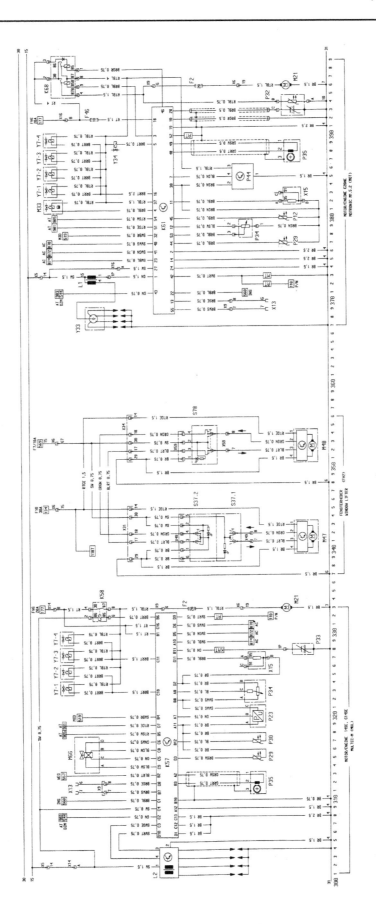

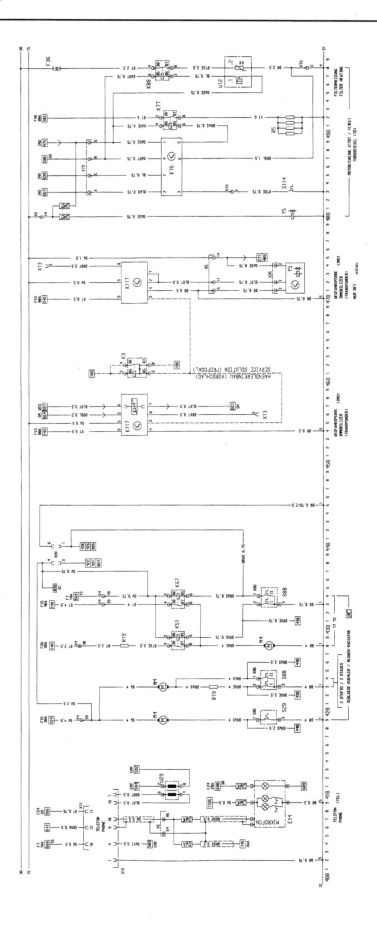

Wiring diagram for models from 1997-on (continued)

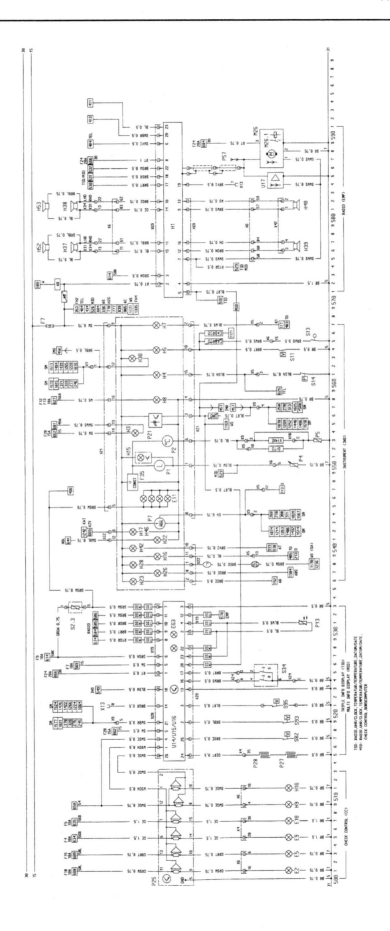

Wiring diagram for models from 1997-on (continued)

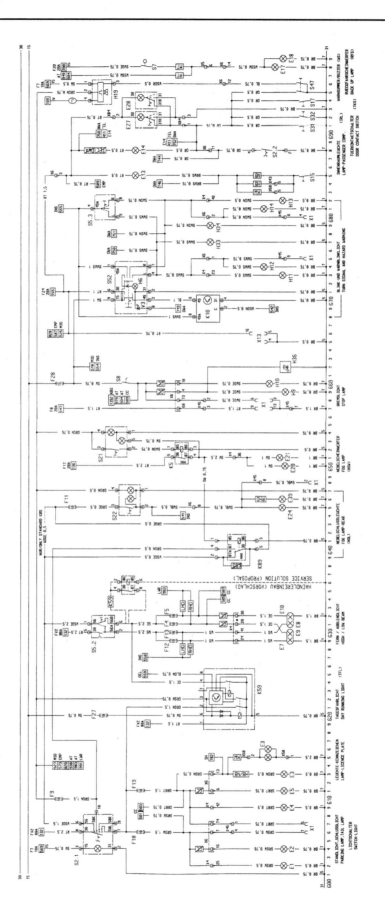

Wiring diagram for models from 1997-on (continued)

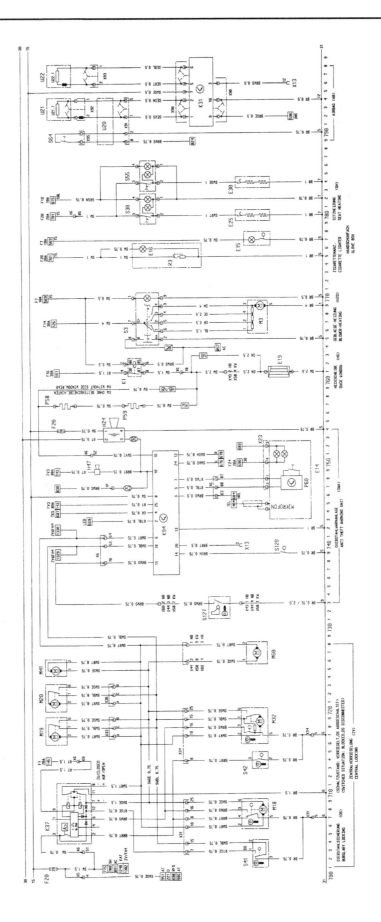

Wiring diagram for models from 1997-on (continued)

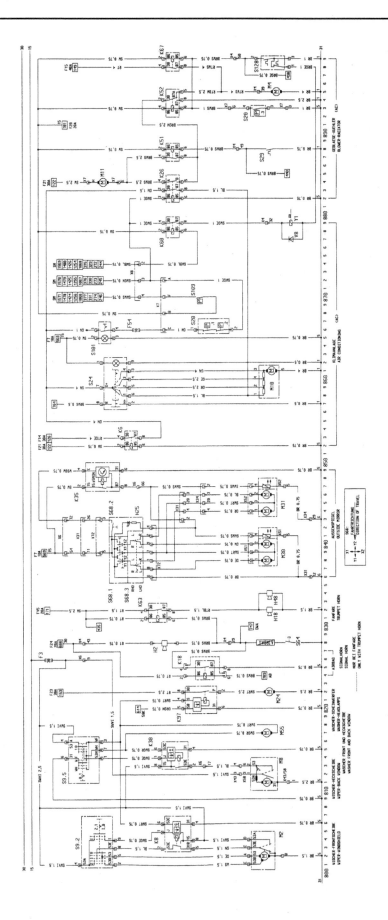

Wiring diagram for models from 1997-on (continued)

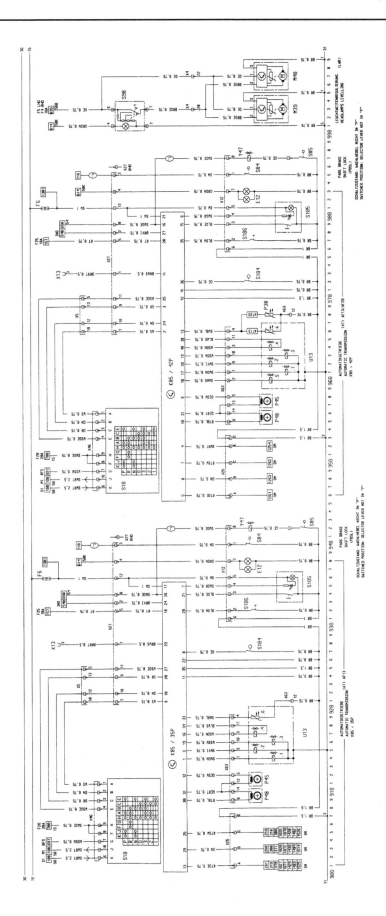

Wiring diagram for models from 1997-on (continued)

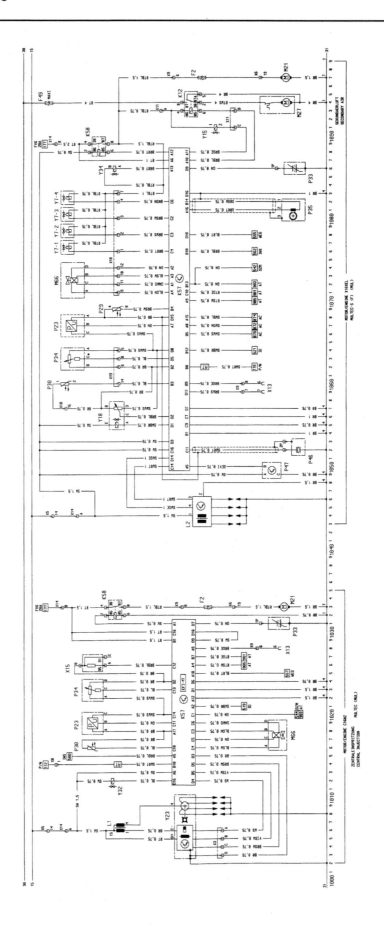

Wiring diagram for models from 1997-on (continued)

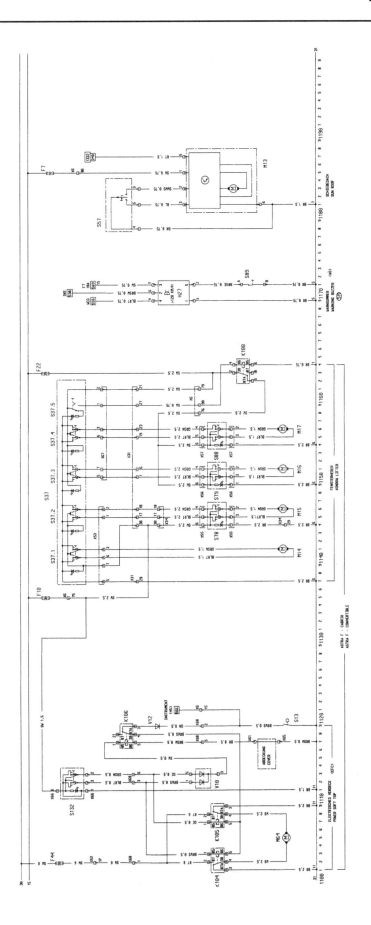

Wiring diagram for models from 1997-on (continued)

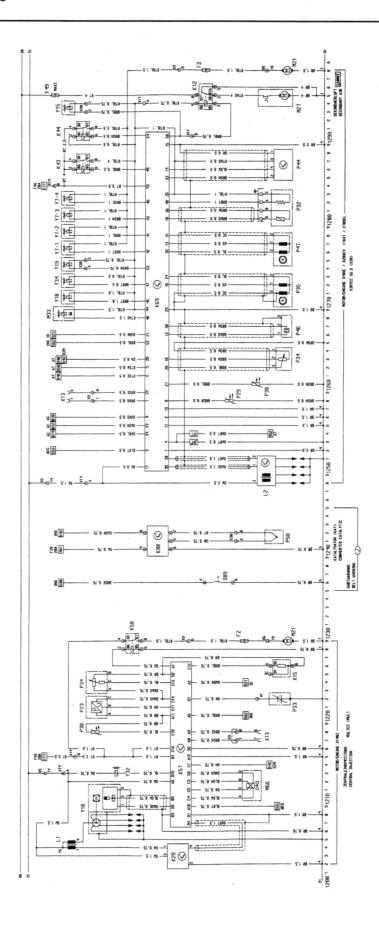

Wiring diagram for models from 1997-on (continued)

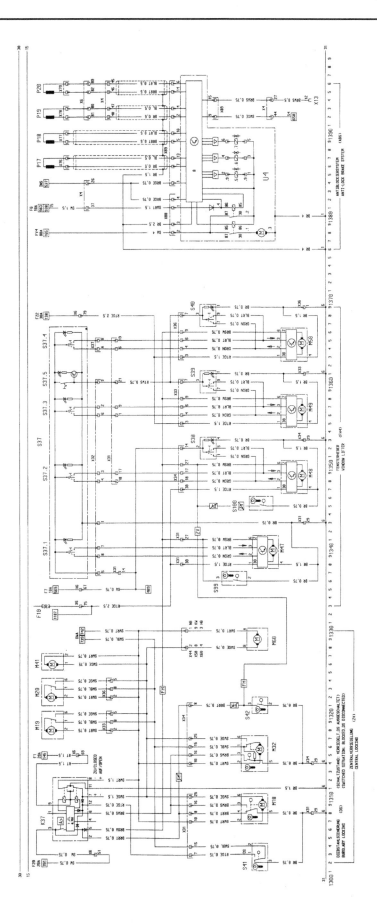

Wiring diagram for models from 1997-on (continued)

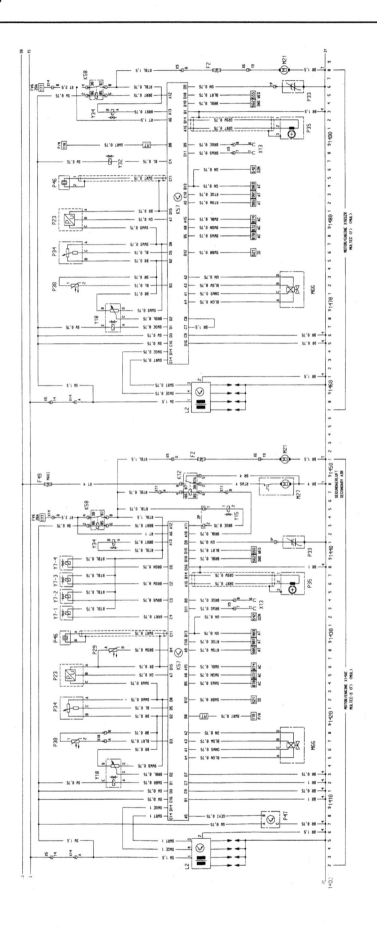

Wiring diagram for models from 1997-on (continued)

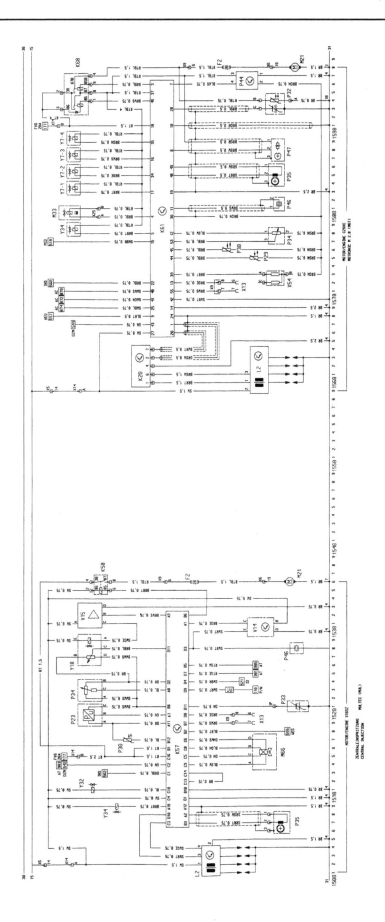

Dimensions and Weights

Note: *All figures and dimensions are approximate and may vary according to model. Refer to manufacturer's data for exact figures.*

Overall length

Saloon models	4239 mm
Hatchback models (except "GSi" models)	4051 mm
"GSi" models	4086 mm
Estate and Van models	4278 mm

Overall width

All models (excluding door mirrors)	1688 mm
All models (including door mirrors)	1795 mm

Overall height (unladen)

Saloon and Hatchback models	1410 mm
Estate models (without roof rails)	1475 mm
Estate models (with roof rails)	1525 mm
Van models (without roof rails)	1490 mm
Van models (with roof rails)	1540 mm

Wheelbase

All models	2517 mm

Turning circle

All models	9.8 metres

Ground clearance (minimum)

All models	130 mm

Weights

Kerb weight *

Saloon models	960 to 1090 kg
Hatchback models	930 to 1125 kg
Estate models	995 to 1127 kg
Van models	1030 to 1050 kg

* Exact kerb weights depend upon model and specification.

Maximum gross vehicle weight

All models	Refer to VIN plate

Maximum roof rack load

All models	100 kg

Maximum towing hitch downward load (noseweight)

All models	75 kg

Maximum towing weights

All models	Refer to dealer for latest recommendations

Length (distance)

Inches (in)	x 25.4	= Millimetres (mm)	x 0.0394	= Inches (in)
Feet (ft)	x 0.305	= Metres (m)	x 3.281	= Feet (ft)
Miles	x 1.609	= Kilometres (km)	x 0.621	= Miles

Volume (capacity)

Cubic inches (cu in; in³)	x 16.387	= Cubic centimetres (cc; cm³)	x 0.061	= Cubic inches (cu in; in³)
Imperial pints (Imp pt)	x 0.568	= Litres (l)	x 1.76	= Imperial pints (Imp pt)
Imperial quarts (Imp qt)	x 1.137	= Litres (l)	x 0.88	= Imperial quarts (Imp qt)
Imperial quarts (Imp qt)	x 1.201	= US quarts (US qt)	x 0.833	= Imperial quarts (Imp qt)
US quarts (US qt)	x 0.946	= Litres (l)	x 1.057	= US quarts (US qt)
Imperial gallons (Imp gal)	x 4.546	= Litres (l)	x 0.22	= Imperial gallons (Imp gal)
Imperial gallons (Imp gal)	x 1.201	= US gallons (US gal)	x 0.833	= Imperial gallons (Imp gal)
US gallons (US gal)	x 3.785	= Litres (l)	x 0.264	= US gallons (US gal)

Mass (weight)

Ounces (oz)	x 28.35	= Grams (g)	x 0.035	= Ounces (oz)
Pounds (lb)	x 0.454	= Kilograms (kg)	x 2.205	= Pounds (lb)

Force

Ounces-force (ozf; oz)	x 0.278	= Newtons (N)	x 3.6	= Ounces-force (ozf; oz)
Pounds-force (lbf; lb)	x 4.448	= Newtons (N)	x 0.225	= Pounds-force (lbf; lb)
Newtons (N)	x 0.1	= Kilograms-force (kgf; kg)	x 9.81	= Newtons (N)

Pressure

Pounds-force per square inch (psi; lbf/in²; lb/in²)	x 0.070	= Kilograms-force per square centimetre (kgf/cm²; kg/cm²)	x 14.223	= Pounds-force per square inch (psi; lbf/in²; lb/in²)
Pounds-force per square inch (psi; lbf/in²; lb/in²)	x 0.068	= Atmospheres (atm)	x 14.696	= Pounds-force per square inch (psi; lbf/in²; lb/in²)
Pounds-force per square inch (psi; lbf/in²; lb/in²)	x 0.069	= Bars	x 14.5	= Pounds-force per square inch (psi; lbf/in²; lb/in²)
Pounds-force per square inch (psi; lbf/in²; lb/in²)	x 6.895	= Kilopascals (kPa)	x 0.145	= Pounds-force per square inch (psi; lbf/in²; lb/in²)
Kilopascals (kPa)	x 0.01	= Kilograms-force per square centimetre (kgf/cm²; kg/cm²)	x 98.1	= Kilopascals (kPa)
Millibar (mbar)	x 100	= Pascals (Pa)	x 0.01	= Millibar (mbar)
Millibar (mbar)	x 0.0145	= Pounds-force per square inch (psi; lbf/in²; lb/in²)	x 68.947	= Millibar (mbar)
Millibar (mbar)	x 0.75	= Millimetres of mercury (mmHg)	x 1.333	= Millibar (mbar)
Millibar (mbar)	x 0.401	= Inches of water (inH$_2$O)	x 2.491	= Millibar (mbar)
Millimetres of mercury (mmHg)	x 0.535	= Inches of water (inH$_2$O)	x 1.868	= Millimetres of mercury (mmHg)
Inches of water (inH$_2$O)	x 0.036	= Pounds-force per square inch (psi; lbf/in²; lb/in²)	x 27.68	= Inches of water (inH$_2$O)

Torque (moment of force)

Pounds-force inches (lbf in; lb in)	x 1.152	= Kilograms-force centimetre (kgf cm; kg cm)	x 0.868	= Pounds-force inches (lbf in; lb in)
Pounds-force inches (lbf in; lb in)	x 0.113	= Newton metres (Nm)	x 8.85	= Pounds-force inches (lbf in; lb in)
Pounds-force inches (lbf in; lb in)	x 0.083	= Pounds-force feet (lbf ft; lb ft)	x 12	= Pounds-force inches (lbf in; lb in)
Pounds-force feet (lbf ft; lb ft)	x 0.138	= Kilograms-force metres (kgf m; kg m)	x 7.233	= Pounds-force feet (lbf ft; lb ft)
Pounds-force feet (lbf ft; lb ft)	x 1.356	= Newton metres (Nm)	x 0.738	= Pounds-force feet (lbf ft; lb ft)
Newton metres (Nm)	x 0.102	= Kilograms-force metres (kgf m; kg m)	x 9.804	= Newton metres (Nm)

Power

Horsepower (hp)	x 745.7	= Watts (W)	x 0.0013	= Horsepower (hp)

Velocity (speed)

Miles per hour (miles/hr; mph)	x 1.609	= Kilometres per hour (km/hr; kph)	x 0.621	= Miles per hour (miles/hr; mph)

Fuel consumption*

Miles per gallon, Imperial (mpg)	x 0.354	= Kilometres per litre (km/l)	x 2.825	= Miles per gallon, Imperial (mpg)
Miles per gallon, US (mpg)	x 0.425	= Kilometres per litre (km/l)	x 2.352	= Miles per gallon, US (mpg)

Temperature

Degrees Fahrenheit = (°C x 1.8) + 32   Degrees Celsius (Degrees Centigrade; °C) = (°F - 32) x 0.56

It is common practice to convert from miles per gallon (mpg) to litres/100 kilometres (l/100km), where mpg x l/100 km = 282

Spare parts are available from many sources, including maker's appointed garages, accessory shops, and motor factors. To be sure of obtaining the correct parts, it will sometimes be necessary to quote the vehicle identification number. If possible, it can also be useful to take the old parts along for positive identification. Items such as starter motors and alternators may be available under a service exchange scheme - any parts returned should be clean.

Our advice regarding spare parts is as follows.

Officially appointed garages

This is the best source of parts which are peculiar to your car, and which are not otherwise generally available (eg, badges, interior trim, certain body panels, etc). It is also the only place at which you should buy parts if the vehicle is still under warranty.

Accessory shops

These are very good places to buy materials and components needed for the maintenance of your car (oil, air and fuel filters, light bulbs, drivebelts, greases, brake pads, touch-up paint, etc). Components of this nature sold by a reputable shop are usually of the same standard as those used by the car manufacturer.

Besides components, these shops also sell tools and general accessories, usually have convenient opening hours, charge lower prices, and can often be found close to home. Some accessory shops have parts counters where components needed for almost any repair job can be purchased or ordered.

Motor factors

Good factors will stock all the more important components which wear out comparatively quickly, and can sometimes supply individual components needed for the overhaul of a larger assembly (eg, brake seals and hydraulic parts, bearing shells, pistons, valves). They may also handle work such as cylinder block reboring, crankshaft regrinding, etc.

Tyre and exhaust specialists

These outlets may be independent, or members of a local or national chain. They frequently offer competitive prices when compared with a main dealer or local garage, but it will pay to obtain several quotes before making a decision. When researching prices, also ask what "extras" may be added - for instance fitting a new valve and balancing the wheel are both commonly charged on top of the price of a new tyre.

Other sources

Beware of parts or materials obtained from market stalls, car boot sales or similar outlets. Such items are not invariably sub-standard, but there is little chance of compensation if they do prove unsatisfactory. in the case of safety-critical components such as brake pads, there is the risk not only of financial loss, but also of an accident causing injury or death.

Second-hand components or assemblies obtained from a car breaker can be a good buy in some circumstances, but this sort of purchase is best made by the experienced DIY mechanic.

Vehicle identification

Modifications are a continuing and unpublicised process in vehicle manufacture, quite apart from major model changes. Spare parts manuals and lists are compiled upon a numerical basis, the individual vehicle identification numbers being essential to correct identification of the component concerned.

When ordering spare parts, always give as much information as possible. Quote the car model, year of manufacture and registration, chassis and engine numbers as appropriate.

The *vehicle identification plate* is riveted on top of the front body panel and includes the *Vehicle Identification Number* (VIN), vehicle weight information and paint and trim colour codes **(see illustration)**.

The *Vehicle Identification Number (VIN)* is given on the vehicle identification plate and is also stamped into the body floor panel between the driver's seat and the door sill panel; lift the flap in the carpet to see it **(see illustration)**.

The *engine number* is stamped on a horizontal flat located on the exhaust manifold side of the cylinder block, at the distributor/DIS module end.

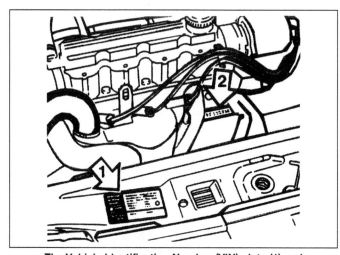

The Vehicle Identification Number (VIN) plate (1) and engine number (2) locations

The VIN is stamped on the floor next to the driver's seat

Whenever servicing, repair or overhaul work is carried out on the car or its components, observe the following procedures and instructions. This will assist in carrying out the operation efficiently and to a professional standard of workmanship.

Joint mating faces and gaskets

When separating components at their mating faces, never insert screwdrivers or similar implements into the joint between the faces in order to prise them apart. This can cause severe damage which results in oil leaks, coolant leaks, etc upon reassembly. Separation is usually achieved by tapping along the joint with a soft-faced hammer in order to break the seal. However, note that this method may not be suitable where dowels are used for component location.

Where a gasket is used between the mating faces of two components, a new one must be fitted on reassembly; fit it dry unless otherwise stated in the repair procedure. Make sure that the mating faces are clean and dry, with all traces of old gasket removed. When cleaning a joint face, use a tool which is unlikely to score or damage the face, and remove any burrs or nicks with an oilstone or fine file.

Make sure that tapped holes are cleaned with a pipe cleaner, and keep them free of jointing compound, if this is being used, unless specifically instructed otherwise.

Ensure that all orifices, channels or pipes are clear, and blow through them, preferably using compressed air.

Oil seals

Oil seals can be removed by levering them out with a wide flat-bladed screwdriver or similar implement. Alternatively, a number of self-tapping screws may be screwed into the seal, and these used as a purchase for pliers or some similar device in order to pull the seal free.

Whenever an oil seal is removed from its working location, either individually or as part of an assembly, it should be renewed.

The very fine sealing lip of the seal is easily damaged, and will not seal if the surface it contacts is not completely clean and free from scratches, nicks or grooves. If the original sealing surface of the component cannot be restored, and the manufacturer has not made provision for slight relocation of the seal relative to the sealing surface, the component should be renewed.

Protect the lips of the seal from any surface which may damage them in the course of fitting. Use tape or a conical sleeve where possible. Lubricate the seal lips with oil before fitting and, on dual-lipped seals, fill the space between the lips with grease.

Unless otherwise stated, oil seals must be fitted with their sealing lips toward the lubricant to be sealed.

Use a tubular drift or block of wood of the appropriate size to install the seal and, if the seal housing is shouldered, drive the seal down to the shoulder. If the seal housing is unshouldered, the seal should be fitted with its face flush with the housing top face (unless otherwise instructed).

Screw threads and fastenings

Seized nuts, bolts and screws are quite a common occurrence where corrosion has set in, and the use of penetrating oil or releasing fluid will often overcome this problem if the offending item is soaked for a while before attempting to release it. The use of an impact driver may also provide a means of releasing such stubborn fastening devices, when used in conjunction with the appropriate screwdriver bit or socket. If none of these methods works, it may be necessary to resort to the careful application of heat, or the use of a hacksaw or nut splitter device.

Studs are usually removed by locking two nuts together on the threaded part, and then using a spanner on the lower nut to unscrew the stud. Studs or bolts which have broken off below the surface of the component in which they are mounted can sometimes be removed using a stud extractor. Always ensure that a blind tapped hole is completely free from oil, grease, water or other fluid before installing the bolt or stud. Failure to do this could cause the housing to crack due to the hydraulic action of the bolt or stud as it is screwed in.

When tightening a castellated nut to accept a split pin, tighten the nut to the specified torque, where applicable, and then tighten further to the next split pin hole. Never slacken the nut to align the split pin hole, unless stated in the repair procedure.

When checking or retightening a nut or bolt to a specified torque setting, slacken the nut or bolt by a quarter of a turn, and then retighten to the specified setting. However, this should not be attempted where angular tightening has been used.

For some screw fastenings, notably cylinder head bolts or nuts, torque wrench settings are no longer specified for the latter stages of tightening, "angle-tightening" being called up instead. Typically, a fairly low torque wrench setting will be applied to the bolts/nuts in the correct sequence, followed by one or more stages of tightening through specified angles.

Locknuts, locktabs and washers

Any fastening which will rotate against a component or housing during tightening should always have a washer between it and the relevant component or housing.

Spring or split washers should always be renewed when they are used to lock a critical component such as a big-end bearing retaining bolt or nut. Locktabs which are folded over to retain a nut or bolt should always be renewed.

Self-locking nuts can be re-used in non-critical areas, providing resistance can be felt when the locking portion passes over the bolt or stud thread. However, it should be noted that self-locking stiffnuts tend to lose their effectiveness after long periods of use, and should then be renewed as a matter of course.

Split pins must always be replaced with new ones of the correct size for the hole.

When thread-locking compound is found on the threads of a fastener which is to be re-used, it should be cleaned off with a wire brush and solvent, and fresh compound applied on reassembly.

Special tools

Some repair procedures in this manual entail the use of special tools such as a press, two or three-legged pullers, spring compressors, etc. Wherever possible, suitable readily-available alternatives to the manufacturer's special tools are described, and are shown in use. In some instances, where no alternative is possible, it has been necessary to resort to the use of a manufacturer's tool, and this has been done for reasons of safety as well as the efficient completion of the repair operation. Unless you are highly-skilled and have a thorough understanding of the procedures described, never attempt to bypass the use of any special tool when the procedure described specifies its use. Not only is there a very great risk of personal injury, but expensive damage could be caused to the components involved.

Environmental considerations

When disposing of used engine oil, brake fluid, antifreeze, etc, give due consideration to any detrimental environmental effects. Do not, for instance, pour any of the above liquids down drains into the general sewage system, or onto the ground to soak away. Many local council refuse tips provide a facility for waste oil disposal, as do some garages. If none of these facilities are available, consult your local Environmental Health Department, or the National Rivers Authority, for further advice.

With the universal tightening-up of legislation regarding the emission of environmentally-harmful substances from motor vehicles, most vehicles have tamperproof devices fitted to the main adjustment points of the fuel system. These devices are primarily designed to prevent unqualified persons from adjusting the fuel/air mixture, with the chance of a consequent increase in toxic emissions. If such devices are found during servicing or overhaul, they should, wherever possible, be renewed or refitted in accordance with the manufacturer's requirements or current legislation.

Note: It is antisocial and illegal to dump oil down the drain. To find the location of your local oil recycling bank, call this number free.

The jack supplied with the vehicle tool kit should only be used for changing roadwheels. When carrying out any other kind of work, raise the vehicle using a hydraulic jack, and always supplement the jack with axle stands positioned under the vehicle jacking points.

When jacking up the vehicle with a trolley jack, position the jack head under one of the relevant jacking points (note that the jacking points for use with a hydraulic jack are different to those for use with the vehicle jack). **Do not** jack the vehicle under the sump or any of the steering or suspension components. Supplement the jack using axle stands. The jacking points and axle stand positions are shown in the accompanying illustrations **(see illustrations)**.

⚠ *Warning: Never work under, around, or near a raised car, unless it is adequately supported in at least two places.*

Front jacking point for hydraulic jack or axle stands

Rear jacking point for hydraulic jack or axle stands

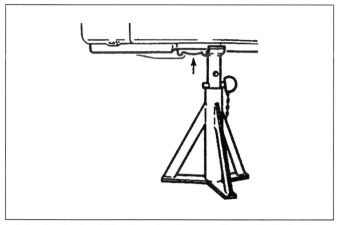

Axle stands should be placed under, or adjacent to the jacking point (arrowed)

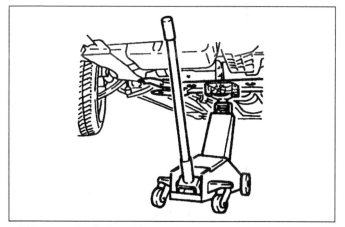

Using a trolley jack and block of wood under the centre of the front subframe

Disconnecting the battery

The radio/cassette unit fitted as standard equipment by Vauxhall/Opel is equipped with a built-in security code, to deter thieves. If the power source to the unit is cut, the anti-theft system will activate. Even if the power source is immediately reconnected, the radio/cassette unit will not function until the correct security code has been entered. Therefore, if you do not know the correct security code for the radio/cassette unit, **do not** disconnect the battery negative terminal of the battery, or remove the radio/cassette unit from the vehicle.

Refer to the Audio handbook supplied in the owners handbook pack, for further details of how to use the code.

If you should loose or forget the code, seek the advice of your Vauxhall/Opel dealer. On presentation of proof of ownership, a Vauxhall/Opel dealer will be able to unlock the unit and provide you with a new security code. Devices known as "memory-savers" (or "code-savers") can be used to avoid some of the above problems. Precise details vary according to the device used. Typically, it is plugged into the cigarette lighter, and is connected by its own wires to a spare battery; the vehicle's own battery is then dis-connected from the electrical system, leaving the "memory-saver" to pass sufficient current to maintain audio unit security codes and any other memory values, and also to run permanently-live circuits such as the clock.

⚠ *Warning: Some of these devices allow a considerable amount of current to pass, which can mean that many of the vehicle's systems are still operational when the main battery is disconnected. If a "memory-saver" is used, ensure that the circuit concerned is actually "dead" before carrying out any work on it!*

Introduction

A selection of good tools is a fundamental requirement for anyone contemplating the maintenance and repair of a motor vehicle. For the owner who does not possess any, their purchase will prove a considerable expense, offsetting some of the savings made by doing-it-yourself. However, provided that the tools purchased meet the relevant national safety standards and are of good quality, they will last for many years and prove an extremely worthwhile investment.

To help the average owner to decide which tools are needed to carry out the various tasks detailed in this manual, we have compiled three lists of tools under the following headings: *Maintenance and minor repair*, *Repair and overhaul*, and *Special*. Newcomers to practical mechanics should start off with the *Maintenance and minor repair* tool kit, and confine themselves to the simpler jobs around the vehicle. Then, as confidence and experience grow, more difficult tasks can be undertaken, with extra tools being purchased as, and when, they are needed. In this way, a *Maintenance and minor repair* tool kit can be built up into a *Repair and overhaul* tool kit over a considerable period of time, without any major cash outlays. The experienced do-it-yourselfer will have a tool kit good enough for most repair and overhaul procedures, and will add tools from the *Special* category when it is felt that the expense is justified by the amount of use to which these tools will be put.

Maintenance and minor repair tool kit

The tools given in this list should be considered as a minimum requirement if routine maintenance, servicing and minor repair operations are to be undertaken. We recommend the purchase of combination spanners (ring one end, open-ended the other); although more expensive than open-ended ones, they do give the advantages of both types of spanner.

- [ ] *Combination spanners:*
  Metric - 8 to 19 mm inclusive
- [ ] *Adjustable spanner - 35 mm jaw (approx.)*
- [ ] *Spark plug spanner (with rubber insert) - petrol models*
- [ ] *Spark plug gap adjustment tool - petrol models*
- [ ] *Set of feeler gauges*
- [ ] *Brake bleed nipple spanner*
- [ ] *Screwdrivers:*
  Flat blade - 100 mm long x 6 mm dia
  Cross blade - 100 mm long x 6 mm dia
  Torx - various sizes (not all vehicles)
- [ ] *Combination pliers*
- [ ] *Hacksaw (junior)*
- [ ] *Tyre pump*
- [ ] *Tyre pressure gauge*
- [ ] *Oil can*
- [ ] *Oil filter removal tool*
- [ ] *Fine emery cloth*
- [ ] *Wire brush (small)*
- [ ] *Funnel (medium size)*
- [ ] *Sump drain plug key (not all vehicles)*

Repair and overhaul tool kit

These tools are virtually essential for anyone undertaking any major repairs to a motor vehicle, and are additional to those given in the *Maintenance and minor repair* list. Included in this list is a comprehensive set of sockets. Although these are expensive, they will be found invaluable as they are so versatile - particularly if various drives are included in the set. We recommend the half-inch square-drive type, as this can be used with most proprietary torque wrenches.

The tools in this list will sometimes need to be supplemented by tools from the *Special* list:

- [ ] *Sockets (or box spanners) to cover range in previous list (including Torx sockets)*
- [ ] *Reversible ratchet drive (for use with sockets)*
- [ ] *Extension piece, 250 mm (for use with sockets)*
- [ ] *Universal joint (for use with sockets)*
- [ ] *Flexible handle or sliding T "breaker bar" (for use with sockets)*
- [ ] *Torque wrench (for use with sockets)*
- [ ] *Self-locking grips*
- [ ] *Ball pein hammer*
- [ ] *Soft-faced mallet (plastic or rubber)*
- [ ] *Screwdrivers:*
  Flat blade - long & sturdy, short (chubby), and narrow (electrician's) types
  Cross blade - long & sturdy, and short (chubby) types
- [ ] *Pliers:*
  Long-nosed
  Side cutters (electrician's)
  Circlip (internal and external)
- [ ] *Cold chisel - 25 mm*
- [ ] *Scriber*
- [ ] *Scraper*
- [ ] *Centre-punch*
- [ ] *Pin punch*
- [ ] *Hacksaw*
- [ ] *Brake hose clamp*
- [ ] *Brake/clutch bleeding kit*
- [ ] *Selection of twist drills*
- [ ] *Steel rule/straight-edge*
- [ ] *Allen keys (inc. splined/Torx type)*
- [ ] *Selection of files*
- [ ] *Wire brush*
- [ ] *Axle stands*
- [ ] *Jack (strong trolley or hydraulic type)*
- [ ] *Light with extension lead*
- [ ] *Universal electrical multi-meter*

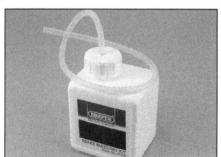

Sockets and reversible ratchet drive

Brake bleeding kit

Torx key, socket and bit

Hose clamp

Angular-tightening gauge

Special tools

The tools in this list are those which are not used regularly, are expensive to buy, or which need to be used in accordance with their manufacturers' instructions. Unless relatively difficult mechanical jobs are undertaken frequently, it will not be economic to buy many of these tools. Where this is the case, you could consider clubbing together with friends (or joining a motorists' club) to make a joint purchase, or borrowing the tools against a deposit from a local garage or tool hire specialist. It is worth noting that many of the larger DIY superstores now carry a large range of special tools for hire at modest rates.

The following list contains only those tools and instruments freely available to the public, and not those special tools produced by the vehicle manufacturer specifically for its dealer network. You will find occasional references to these manufacturers' special tools in the text of this manual. Generally, an alternative method of doing the job without the vehicle manufacturers' special tool is given. However, sometimes there is no alternative to using them. Where this is the case and the relevant tool cannot be bought or borrowed, you will have to entrust the work to a dealer.

- ☐ Angular-tightening gauge
- ☐ Valve spring compressor
- ☐ Valve grinding tool
- ☐ Piston ring compressor
- ☐ Piston ring removal/installation tool
- ☐ Cylinder bore hone
- ☐ Balljoint separator
- ☐ Coil spring compressors (where applicable)
- ☐ Two/three-legged hub and bearing puller
- ☐ Impact screwdriver
- ☐ Micrometer and/or vernier calipers
- ☐ Dial gauge
- ☐ Stroboscopic timing light
- ☐ Dwell angle meter/tachometer
- ☐ Fault code reader
- ☐ Cylinder compression gauge
- ☐ Hand-operated vacuum pump and gauge
- ☐ Clutch plate alignment set
- ☐ Brake shoe steady spring cup removal tool
- ☐ Bush and bearing removal/installation set
- ☐ Stud extractors
- ☐ Tap and die set
- ☐ Lifting tackle
- ☐ Trolley jack

Buying tools

Reputable motor accessory shops and superstores often offer excellent quality tools at discount prices, so it pays to shop around.

Remember, you don't have to buy the most expensive items on the shelf, but it is always advisable to steer clear of the very cheap tools. Beware of 'bargains' offered on market stalls or at car boot sales. There are plenty of good tools around at reasonable prices, but always aim to purchase items which meet the relevant national safety standards. If in doubt, ask the proprietor or manager of the shop for advice before making a purchase.

Care and maintenance of tools

Having purchased a reasonable tool kit, it is necessary to keep the tools in a clean and serviceable condition. After use, always wipe off any dirt, grease and metal particles using a clean, dry cloth, before putting the tools away. Never leave them lying around after they have been used. A simple tool rack on the garage or workshop wall for items such as screwdrivers and pliers is a good idea. Store all normal spanners and sockets in a metal box. Any measuring instruments, gauges, meters, etc, must be carefully stored where they cannot be damaged or become rusty.

Take a little care when tools are used. Hammer heads inevitably become marked, and screwdrivers lose the keen edge on their blades from time to time. A little timely attention with emery cloth or a file will soon restore items like this to a good finish.

Working facilities

Not to be forgotten when discussing tools is the workshop itself. If anything more than routine maintenance is to be carried out, a suitable working area becomes essential.

It is appreciated that many an owner-mechanic is forced by circumstances to remove an engine or similar item without the benefit of a garage or workshop. Having done this, any repairs should always be done under the cover of a roof.

Wherever possible, any dismantling should be done on a clean, flat workbench or table at a suitable working height.

Any workbench needs a vice; one with a jaw opening of 100 mm is suitable for most jobs. As mentioned previously, some clean dry storage space is also required for tools, as well as for any lubricants, cleaning fluids, touch-up paints etc, which become necessary.

Another item which may be required, and which has a much more general usage, is an electric drill with a chuck capacity of at least 8 mm. This, together with a good range of twist drills, is virtually essential for fitting accessories.

Last, but not least, always keep a supply of old newspapers and clean, lint-free rags available, and try to keep any working area as clean as possible.

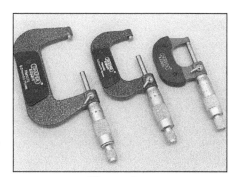
Micrometers

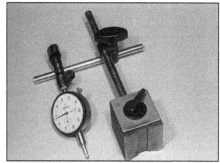
Dial test indicator ("dial gauge")

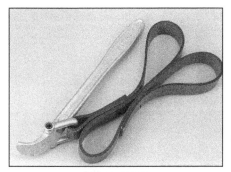
Strap wrench

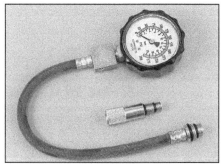
Compression tester

Fault code reader

This is a guide to getting your vehicle through the MOT test. Obviously it will not be possible to examine the vehicle to the same standard as the professional MOT tester. However, working through the following checks will enable you to identify any problem areas before submitting the vehicle for the test.

Where a testable component is in borderline condition, the tester has discretion in deciding whether to pass or fail it. The basis of such discretion is whether the tester would be happy for a close relative or friend to use the vehicle with the component in that condition. If the vehicle presented is clean and evidently well cared for, the tester may be more inclined to pass a borderline component than if the vehicle is scruffy and apparently neglected.

It has only been possible to summarise the test requirements here, based on the regulations in force at the time of printing. Test standards are becoming increasingly stringent, although there are some exemptions for older vehicles.

An assistant will be needed to help carry out some of these checks.

The checks have been sub-divided into four categories, as follows:

1 Checks carried out **FROM THE DRIVER'S SEAT**

2 Checks carried out **WITH THE VEHICLE ON THE GROUND**

3 Checks carried out **WITH THE VEHICLE RAISED AND THE WHEELS FREE TO TURN**

4 Checks carried out on **YOUR VEHICLE'S EXHAUST EMISSION SYSTEM**

---

1 Checks carried out **FROM THE DRIVER'S SEAT**

Handbrake

☐ Test the operation of the handbrake. Excessive travel (too many clicks) indicates incorrect brake or cable adjustment.

☐ Check that the handbrake cannot be released by tapping the lever sideways. Check the security of the lever mountings.

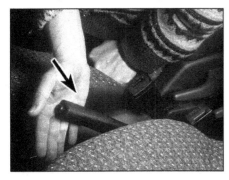

Footbrake

☐ Depress the brake pedal and check that it does not creep down to the floor, indicating a master cylinder fault. Release the pedal, wait a few seconds, then depress it again. If the pedal travels nearly to the floor before firm resistance is felt, brake adjustment or repair is necessary. If the pedal feels spongy, there is air in the hydraulic system which must be removed by bleeding.

☐ Check that the brake pedal is secure and in good condition. Check also for signs of fluid leaks on the pedal, floor or carpets, which would indicate failed seals in the brake master cylinder.

☐ Check the servo unit (when applicable) by operating the brake pedal several times, then keeping the pedal depressed and starting the engine. As the engine starts, the pedal will move down slightly. If not, the vacuum hose or the servo itself may be faulty.

Steering wheel and column

☐ Examine the steering wheel for fractures or looseness of the hub, spokes or rim.

☐ Move the steering wheel from side to side and then up and down. Check that the steering wheel is not loose on the column, indicating wear or a loose retaining nut. Continue moving the steering wheel as before, but also turn it slightly from left to right.

☐ Check that the steering wheel is not loose on the column, and that there is no abnormal

movement of the steering wheel, indicating wear in the column support bearings or couplings.

Windscreen, mirrors and sunvisor

☐ The windscreen must be free of cracks or other significant damage within the driver's field of view. (Small stone chips are acceptable.) Rear view mirrors must be secure, intact, and capable of being adjusted.

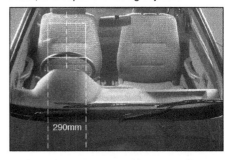

290mm

☐ The driver's sunvisor must be capable of being stored in the "up" position.

Seat belts and seats

Note: *The following checks are applicable to all seat belts, front and rear.*

☐ Examine the webbing of all the belts (including rear belts if fitted) for cuts, serious fraying or deterioration. Fasten and unfasten each belt to check the buckles. If applicable, check the retracting mechanism. Check the security of all seat belt mountings accessible from inside the vehicle.

☐ Seat belts with pre-tensioners, once activated, have a "flag" or similar showing on the seat belt stalk. This, in itself, is not a reason for test failure.

☐ The front seats themselves must be securely attached and the backrests must lock in the upright position.

Doors

☐ Both front doors must be able to be opened and closed from outside and inside, and must latch securely when closed.

2 Checks carried out WITH THE VEHICLE ON THE GROUND

Vehicle identification

☐ Number plates must be in good condition, secure and legible, with letters and numbers correctly spaced – spacing at (A) should be at least twice that at (B).

☐ The VIN plate and/or homologation plate must be legible.

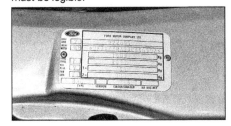

Electrical equipment

☐ Switch on the ignition and check the operation of the horn.

☐ Check the windscreen washers and wipers, examining the wiper blades; renew damaged or perished blades. Also check the operation of the stop-lights.

☐ Check the operation of the sidelights and number plate lights. The lenses and reflectors must be secure, clean and undamaged.

☐ Check the operation and alignment of the headlights. The headlight reflectors must not be tarnished and the lenses must be undamaged.

☐ Switch on the ignition and check the operation of the direction indicators (including the instrument panel tell-tale) and the hazard warning lights. Operation of the sidelights and stop-lights must not affect the indicators - if it does, the cause is usually a bad earth at the rear light cluster.

☐ Check the operation of the rear foglight(s), including the warning light on the instrument panel or in the switch.

☐ The ABS warning light must illuminate in accordance with the manufacturers' design. For most vehicles, the ABS warning light should illuminate when the ignition is switched on, and (if the system is operating properly) extinguish after a few seconds. Refer to the owner's handbook.

Footbrake

☐ Examine the master cylinder, brake pipes and servo unit for leaks, loose mountings, corrosion or other damage.

☐ The fluid reservoir must be secure and the fluid level must be between the upper (A) and lower (B) markings.

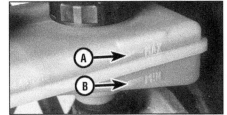

☐ Inspect both front brake flexible hoses for cracks or deterioration of the rubber. Turn the steering from lock to lock, and ensure that the hoses do not contact the wheel, tyre, or any part of the steering or suspension mechanism. With the brake pedal firmly depressed, check the hoses for bulges or leaks under pressure.

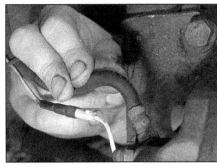

Steering and suspension

☐ Have your assistant turn the steering wheel from side to side slightly, up to the point where the steering gear just begins to transmit this movement to the roadwheels. Check for excessive free play between the steering wheel and the steering gear, indicating wear or insecurity of the steering column joints, the column-to-steering gear coupling, or the steering gear itself.

☐ Have your assistant turn the steering wheel more vigorously in each direction, so that the roadwheels just begin to turn. As this is done, examine all the steering joints, linkages, fittings and attachments. Renew any component that shows signs of wear or damage. On vehicles with power steering, check the security and condition of the steering pump, drivebelt and hoses.

☐ Check that the vehicle is standing level, and at approximately the correct ride height.

Shock absorbers

☐ Depress each corner of the vehicle in turn, then release it. The vehicle should rise and then settle in its normal position. If the vehicle continues to rise and fall, the shock absorber is defective. A shock absorber which has seized will also cause the vehicle to fail.

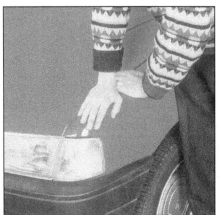

Exhaust system

☐ Start the engine. With your assistant holding a rag over the tailpipe, check the entire system for leaks. Repair or renew leaking sections.

3 Checks carried out
WITH THE VEHICLE RAISED AND THE WHEELS FREE TO TURN

Jack up the front and rear of the vehicle, and securely support it on axle stands. Position the stands clear of the suspension assemblies. Ensure that the wheels are clear of the ground and that the steering can be turned from lock to lock.

Steering mechanism

☐ Have your assistant turn the steering from lock to lock. Check that the steering turns smoothly, and that no part of the steering mechanism, including a wheel or tyre, fouls any brake hose or pipe or any part of the body structure.
☐ Examine the steering rack rubber gaiters for damage or insecurity of the retaining clips. If power steering is fitted, check for signs of damage or leakage of the fluid hoses, pipes or connections. Also check for excessive stiffness or binding of the steering, a missing split pin or locking device, or severe corrosion of the body structure within 30 cm of any steering component attachment point.

Front and rear suspension and wheel bearings

☐ Starting at the front right-hand side, grasp the roadwheel at the 3 o'clock and 9 o'clock positions and rock gently but firmly. Check for free play or insecurity at the wheel bearings, suspension balljoints, or suspension mountings, pivots and attachments.
☐ Now grasp the wheel at the 12 o'clock and 6 o'clock positions and repeat the previous inspection. Spin the wheel, and check for roughness or tightness of the front wheel bearing.

☐ If excess free play is suspected at a component pivot point, this can be confirmed by using a large screwdriver or similar tool and levering between the mounting and the component attachment. This will confirm whether the wear is in the pivot bush, its retaining bolt, or in the mounting itself (the bolt holes can often become elongated).

☐ Carry out all the above checks at the other front wheel, and then at both rear wheels.

Springs and shock absorbers

☐ Examine the suspension struts (when applicable) for serious fluid leakage, corrosion, or damage to the casing. Also check the security of the mounting points.
☐ If coil springs are fitted, check that the spring ends locate in their seats, and that the spring is not corroded, cracked or broken.
☐ If leaf springs are fitted, check that all leaves are intact, that the axle is securely attached to each spring, and that there is no deterioration of the spring eye mountings, bushes, and shackles.

☐ The same general checks apply to vehicles fitted with other suspension types, such as torsion bars, hydraulic displacer units, etc. Ensure that all mountings and attachments are secure, that there are no signs of excessive wear, corrosion or damage, and (on hydraulic types) that there are no fluid leaks or damaged pipes.
☐ Inspect the shock absorbers for signs of serious fluid leakage. Check for wear of the mounting bushes or attachments, or damage to the body of the unit.

Driveshafts
(fwd vehicles only)

☐ Rotate each front wheel in turn and inspect the constant velocity joint gaiters for splits or damage. Also check that each driveshaft is straight and undamaged.

Braking system

☐ If possible without dismantling, check brake pad wear and disc condition. Ensure that the friction lining material has not worn excessively, (A) and that the discs are not fractured, pitted, scored or badly worn (B).

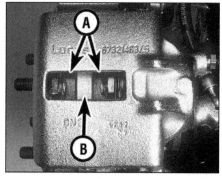

☐ Examine all the rigid brake pipes underneath the vehicle, and the flexible hose(s) at the rear. Look for corrosion, chafing or insecurity of the pipes, and for signs of bulging under pressure, chafing, splits or deterioration of the flexible hoses.
☐ Look for signs of fluid leaks at the brake calipers or on the brake backplates. Repair or renew leaking components.
☐ Slowly spin each wheel, while your assistant depresses and releases the footbrake. Ensure that each brake is operating and does not bind when the pedal is released.

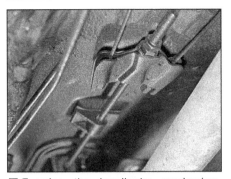

☐ Examine the handbrake mechanism, checking for frayed or broken cables, excessive corrosion, or wear or insecurity of the linkage. Check that the mechanism works on each relevant wheel, and releases fully, without binding.

☐ It is not possible to test brake efficiency without special equipment, but a road test can be carried out later to check that the vehicle pulls up in a straight line.

Fuel and exhaust systems

☐ Inspect the fuel tank (including the filler cap), fuel pipes, hoses and unions. All components must be secure and free from leaks.

☐ Examine the exhaust system over its entire length, checking for any damaged, broken or missing mountings, security of the retaining clamps and rust or corrosion.

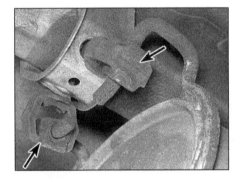

Wheels and tyres

☐ Examine the sidewalls and tread area of each tyre in turn. Check for cuts, tears, lumps, bulges, separation of the tread, and exposure of the ply or cord due to wear or damage. Check that the tyre bead is correctly seated on the wheel rim, that the valve is sound and properly seated, and that the wheel is not distorted or damaged.

☐ Check that the tyres are of the correct size for the vehicle, that they are of the same size and type on each axle, and that the pressures are correct.

☐ Check the tyre tread depth. The legal minimum at the time of writing is 1.6 mm over at least three-quarters of the tread width. Abnormal tread wear may indicate incorrect front wheel alignment.

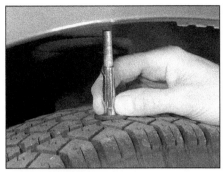

Body corrosion

☐ Check the condition of the entire vehicle structure for signs of corrosion in load-bearing areas. (These include chassis box sections, side sills, cross-members, pillars, and all suspension, steering, braking system and seat belt mountings and anchorages.) Any corrosion which has seriously reduced the thickness of a load-bearing area is likely to cause the vehicle to fail. In this case professional repairs are likely to be needed.

☐ Damage or corrosion which causes sharp or otherwise dangerous edges to be exposed will also cause the vehicle to fail.

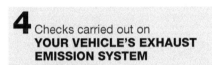

4 Checks carried out on YOUR VEHICLE'S EXHAUST EMISSION SYSTEM

Petrol models

☐ Have the engine at normal operating temperature, and make sure that it is in good tune (ignition system in good order, air filter element clean, etc).

☐ Before any measurements are carried out, raise the engine speed to around 2500 rpm, and hold it at this speed for 20 seconds. Allow the engine speed to return to idle, and watch for smoke emissions from the exhaust tailpipe. If the idle speed is obviously much too high, or if dense blue or clearly-visible black smoke comes from the tailpipe for more than 5 seconds, the vehicle will fail. As a rule of thumb, blue smoke signifies oil being burnt (engine wear) while black smoke signifies unburnt fuel (dirty air cleaner element, or other carburettor or fuel system fault).

☐ An exhaust gas analyser capable of measuring carbon monoxide (CO) and hydrocarbons (HC) is now needed. If such an instrument cannot be hired or borrowed, a local garage may agree to perform the check for a small fee.

CO emissions (mixture)

☐ At the time of writing, for vehicles first used between 1st August 1975 and 31st July 1986 (P to C registration), the CO level must not exceed 4.5% by volume. For vehicles first used between 1st August 1986 and 31st July 1992 (D to J registration), the CO level must not exceed 3.5% by volume. Vehicles first used after 1st August 1992 (K registration) must conform to the manufacturer's specification. The MOT tester has access to a DOT database or emissions handbook, which lists the CO and HC limits for each make and model of vehicle. The CO level is measured with the engine at idle speed, and at "fast idle". The following limits are given as a general guide:

At idle speed -
CO level no more than 0.5%
At "fast idle" (2500 to 3000 rpm) -
CO level no more than 0.3%
(Minimum oil temperature 60°C)

☐ If the CO level cannot be reduced far enough to pass the test (and the fuel and ignition systems are otherwise in good condition) then the carburettor is badly worn, or there is some problem in the fuel injection system or catalytic converter (as applicable).

HC emissions

☐ With the CO within limits, HC emissions for vehicles first used between 1st August 1975 and 31st July 1992 (P to J registration) must not exceed 1200 ppm. Vehicles first used after 1st August 1992 (K registration) must conform to the manufacturer's specification. The MOT tester has access to a DOT database or emissions handbook, which lists the CO and HC limits for each make and model of vehicle. The HC level is measured with the engine at "fast idle". The following is given as a general guide:

At "fast idle" (2500 to 3000 rpm) -
HC level no more than 200 ppm
(Minimum oil temperature 60°C)

☐ Excessive HC emissions are caused by incomplete combustion, the causes of which can include oil being burnt, mechanical wear and ignition/fuel system malfunction.

Diesel models

☐ The only emission test applicable to Diesel engines is the measuring of exhaust smoke density. The test involves accelerating the engine several times to its maximum unloaded speed.

Note: *It is of the utmost importance that the engine timing belt is in good condition before the test is carried out.*

☐ The limits for Diesel engine exhaust smoke, introduced in September 1995 are:

Vehicles first used before 1st August 1979:
Exempt from metered smoke testing, but must not emit "dense blue or clearly visible black smoke for a period of more than 5 seconds at idle" or "dense blue or clearly visible black smoke during acceleration which would obscure the view of other road users".
Non-turbocharged vehicles first used after 1st August 1979: 2.5m⁻¹
Turbocharged vehicles first used after 1st August 1979: 3.0m⁻¹

☐ Excessive smoke can be caused by a dirty air cleaner element. Otherwise, professional advice may be needed to find the cause.

Engine

☐ Engine fails to rotate when attempting to start
☐ Engine rotates, but will not start
☐ Engine difficult to start when cold
☐ Engine difficult to start when hot
☐ Engine starts, but stops immediately
☐ Starter motor noisy or excessively-rough in engagement
☐ Engine idles erratically
☐ Engine misfires at idle speed
☐ Engine misfires throughout the driving speed range
☐ Engine hesitates on acceleration
☐ Engine runs-on after switching off
☐ Engine stalls
☐ Engine lacks power
☐ Engine backfires
☐ Oil pressure warning light illuminated with engine running
☐ Engine noises

Cooling system

☐ Overheating
☐ Overcooling
☐ External coolant leakage
☐ Internal coolant leakage
☐ Corrosion

Fuel and exhaust systems

☐ Excessive fuel consumption
☐ Fuel leakage and/or fuel odour
☐ Excessive noise or fumes from exhaust system

Clutch

☐ Pedal travels to floor - no pressure or very little resistance
☐ Clutch fails to disengage (unable to select gears).
☐ Clutch slips (engine speed increases, with no increase in vehicle speed).
☐ Judder as clutch is engaged
☐ Noise when depressing or releasing clutch pedal

Manual transmission

☐ Noisy in neutral with engine running
☐ Noisy in one particular gear
☐ Difficulty engaging gears
☐ Jumps out of gear
☐ Vibration
☐ Lubricant leaks

Automatic transmission

☐ Fluid leakage
☐ Transmission fluid brown, or has burned smell
☐ General gear selection problems
☐ Transmission will not downshift (kickdown) with accelerator pedal fully depressed
☐ Engine will not start in any gear, or starts in gears other than Park or Neutral
☐ Transmission slips, shifts roughly, is noisy, or has no drive in forward or reverse gears

Driveshafts

☐ Vibration when accelerating or decelerating
☐ Clicking or knocking noise on turns (at slow speed on full-lock)

Braking system

☐ Vehicle pulls to one side under braking
☐ Noise (grinding or high-pitched squeal) when brakes applied
☐ Excessive brake pedal travel
☐ Brake pedal feels spongy when depressed
☐ Excessive brake pedal effort required to stop vehicle
☐ Judder felt through brake pedal or steering wheel when braking
☐ Brakes binding
☐ Rear wheels locking under normal braking

Suspension and steering

☐ Vehicle pulls to one side
☐ Wheel wobble and vibration
☐ Excessive pitching and/or rolling around corners, or during braking
☐ Wandering or general instability
☐ Excessively-stiff steering
☐ Excessive play in steering
☐ Lack of power assistance
☐ Tyre wear excessive

Electrical system

☐ Battery will not hold a charge for more than a few days
☐ Ignition/no-charge warning light remains illuminated with engine running
☐ Ignition/no-charge warning light fails to come on
☐ Lights inoperative
☐ Instrument readings inaccurate or erratic
☐ Horn inoperative, or unsatisfactory in operation
☐ Windscreen wipers inoperative, or unsatisfactory in operation
☐ Windscreen washers inoperative, or unsatisfactory in operation
☐ Electric windows inoperative, or unsatisfactory in operation
☐ Central locking system inoperative, or unsatisfactory in operation

Introduction

The vehicle owner who does his or her own maintenance according to the recommended service schedules should not have to use this section of the manual very often. Modern component reliability is such that, provided those items subject to wear or deterioration are inspected or renewed at the specified intervals, sudden failure is comparatively rare. Faults do not usually just happen as a result of sudden failure, but develop over a period of time. Major mechanical failures in particular are usually preceded by characteristic symptoms over hundreds or even thousands of miles. Those components that do occasionally fail without warning are often small and easily carried in the vehicle.

With any fault-finding, the first step is to decide where to begin investigations. Sometimes this is obvious, but on other occasions, a little detective work will be necessary. The owner who makes half a dozen haphazard adjustments or replacements may be successful in curing a fault (or its symptoms). However, will be none the wiser if the fault recurs, and ultimately may have spent more time and money than was necessary. A calm and logical approach will be found to be more satisfactory in the long run. Always take into account any warning signs or abnormalities that may have been noticed in the period preceding the fault - power loss, high or low gauge readings, unusual smells,

etc. - and remember that failure of components such as fuses or spark plugs may only be pointers to some underlying fault.

The pages that follow provide an easy-reference guide to the more common problems that may occur during the operation of the vehicle. These problems and their possible causes are grouped under headings denoting various components or systems, such as Engine, Cooling system, etc. The Chapter and/or Section that deals with the problem is also shown in brackets. Whatever the fault, certain basic principles apply. These are as follows:

Verify the fault. This is simply a matter of being sure that you know what the symptoms are before starting work. This is particularly important if you are investigating a fault for someone else, who may not have described it very accurately.

Do not overlook the obvious. For example, if the vehicle will not start, is there petrol in the tank? (Do not take anyone else's word on this particular point, and do not trust the fuel gauge either!) If an electrical fault is indicated, look for loose or broken wires before digging out the test gear.

Cure the disease, not the symptom. Substituting a flat battery with a fully charged one will get you off the hard shoulder, but if the underlying cause is not attended to, the new battery will go the same way. Similarly, changing oil-fouled spark plugs for a new set will get you moving again, but remember that the reason for the fouling (if it was not simply an incorrect grade of plug) will have to be established and corrected.

Do not take anything for granted. Particularly, do not forget that a "new" component may itself be defective (especially if it's been rattling around in the boot for months). Also do not leave components out of a fault diagnosis sequence just because they are new or recently fitted. When you do finally diagnose a difficult fault, you will probably realise that all the evidence was there from the start.

Engine

Engine fails to rotate when attempting to start
☐ Battery terminal connections loose or corroded ("*Weekly checks*").
☐ Battery discharged or faulty (Chapter 5A).
☐ Broken, loose or disconnected wiring in the starting circuit (Chapter 5A).
☐ Defective starter solenoid or switch (Chapter 5A).
☐ Defective starter motor (Chapter 5A).
☐ Starter pinion or flywheel ring gear teeth loose or broken (Chapters 2A, 2B and 5A).
☐ Engine earth strap broken or disconnected (Chapter 5A).

Engine rotates, but will not start
☐ Fuel tank empty.
☐ Battery discharged (engine rotates slowly) (Chapter 5A).
☐ Battery terminal connections loose or corroded ("*Weekly checks*").
☐ Ignition components damp or damaged (Chapters 1 and 5B).
☐ Broken, loose or disconnected wiring in the ignition circuit (Chapters 1 and 5B).
☐ Worn, faulty or incorrectly gapped spark plugs (Chapter 1).
☐ Choke mechanism incorrectly adjusted, worn or sticking - carburettor models (Chapter 4A).
☐ Faulty fuel cut-off solenoid - carburettor models (Chapter 4A).
☐ Fuel injection system fault - fuel-injected models (Chapter 4B).
☐ Major mechanical failure (e.g. camshaft drive), (Chapter 2).

Engine difficult to start when cold
☐ Battery discharged (Chapter 5A).
☐ Battery terminal connections loose or corroded ("*Weekly checks*").
☐ Worn, faulty or incorrectly gapped spark plugs (Chapter 1).
☐ Choke mechanism incorrectly adjusted, worn or sticking - carburettor models (Chapter 4A).
☐ Fuel injection system fault - fuel-injected models (Chapter 4B).
☐ Other ignition system fault (Chapters 1 and 5B).
☐ Low cylinder compressions (Chapter 2A or 2B).

Engine difficult to start when hot
☐ Air filter element dirty or clogged (Chapter 1).
☐ Choke mechanism incorrectly adjusted, worn or sticking - carburettor models (Chapter 4A).
☐ Fuel injection system fault - fuel-injected models (Chapter 4B).
☐ Low cylinder compressions (Chapter 2A or 2B).

Engine starts, but stops immediately
☐ Loose or faulty electrical connections in the ignition circuit (Chapters 1 and 5B).
☐ Vacuum leak at the carburettor/throttle body or inlet manifold (Chapter 4A or 4B).
☐ Blocked carburettor jet(s) or internal passages - carburettor models (Chapter 4A).
☐ Blocked injector/fuel injection system fault - fuel-injected models (Chapter 4B).

Starter motor noisy or excessively rough in engagement
☐ Starter pinion or flywheel ring gear teeth loose or broken (Chapters 2A, 2B and 5A).
☐ Starter motor mounting bolts loose or missing (Chapter 5A).
☐ Starter motor internal components worn or damaged (Chapter 5A).

Engine idles erratically
☐ Air filter element clogged (Chapter 1).
☐ Vacuum leak at the carburettor/throttle body, inlet manifold or associated hoses (Chapter 4A or 4B).
☐ Worn, faulty or incorrectly gapped spark plugs (Chapter 1).
☐ Uneven or low cylinder compressions (Chapter 2A or 2B).
☐ Camshaft lobes worn (Chapter 2A or 2B).
☐ Timing belt incorrectly tensioned (Chapter 2A or 2B).
☐ Blocked carburettor jet(s) or internal passages - carburettor models (Chapter 4A).
☐ Blocked injector/fuel injection system fault - fuel-injected models (Chapter 4B).

Engine misfires at idle speed
☐ Worn, faulty or incorrectly gapped spark plugs (Chapter 1).
☐ Faulty spark plug HT leads (Chapter 1).
☐ Vacuum leak at the carburettor/throttle body, inlet manifold or associated hoses (Chapter 4A or 4B).
☐ Blocked carburettor jet(s) or internal passages - carburettor models (Chapter 4A).
☐ Blocked injector/fuel injection system fault - fuel-injected models (Chapter 4B).
☐ Distributor cap cracked or tracking internally (where applicable), (Chapter 1).
☐ Uneven or low cylinder compressions (Chapter 2A or 2B).
☐ Disconnected, leaking, or perished crankcase ventilation hoses (Chapter 4C).

Engine misfires throughout the driving speed range
☐ Fuel filter choked (Chapter 1).
☐ Fuel pump faulty, or delivery pressure low (Chapter 4A or 4B).
☐ Fuel tank vent blocked, or fuel pipes restricted (Chapter 4A or 4B).
☐ Vacuum leak at the carburettor/throttle body, inlet manifold or associated hoses (Chapter 4A or 4B).
☐ Worn, faulty or incorrectly gapped spark plugs (Chapter 1).
☐ Faulty spark plug HT leads (Chapter 1).
☐ Distributor cap cracked or tracking internally (where applicable), (Chapter 1).
☐ Faulty ignition coil (Chapter 5B).
☐ Uneven or low cylinder compressions (Chapter 2A or 2B).
☐ Blocked carburettor jet(s) or internal passages - carburettor models (Chapter 4A).
☐ Blocked injector/fuel injection system fault - fuel-injected models (Chapter 4B).

Engine (continued)

Engine hesitates on acceleration

- ☐ Worn, faulty or incorrectly gapped spark plugs (Chapter 1).
- ☐ Vacuum leak at the carburettor/throttle body, inlet manifold or associated hoses (Chapter 4A or 4B).
- ☐ Blocked carburettor jet(s) or internal passages - carburettor models (Chapter 4A).
- ☐ Blocked injector/fuel injection system fault - fuel-injected models (Chapter 4B).

Engine runs-on after switching off

- ☐ Excessive carbon build-up in engine (Chapter 2).
- ☐ High engine operating temperature (Chapter 3).
- ☐ Faulty fuel cut-off solenoid - carburettor models (Chapter 4A).
- ☐ Fuel injection system fault - fuel-injected models (Chapter 4B).

Engine stalls

- ☐ Vacuum leak at the carburettor/throttle body, inlet manifold or associated hoses (Chapter 4A or 4B).
- ☐ Fuel filter choked (Chapter 1).
- ☐ Fuel pump faulty, or delivery pressure low (Chapter 4A or 4B).
- ☐ Fuel tank vent blocked, or fuel pipes restricted (Chapter 4A or 4B).
- ☐ Blocked carburettor jet(s) or internal passages - carburettor models (Chapter 4A).
- ☐ Blocked injector/fuel injection system fault - fuel-injected models (Chapter 4B).

Engine lacks power

- ☐ Timing belt incorrectly fitted or tensioned (Chapter 2A or 2B).
- ☐ Fuel filter choked (Chapter 1).
- ☐ Fuel pump faulty, or delivery pressure low (Chapter 4A or 4B).
- ☐ Uneven or low cylinder compressions (Chapter 2A or 2B).
- ☐ Worn, faulty or incorrectly gapped spark plugs (Chapter 1).
- ☐ Vacuum leak at the carburettor/throttle body, inlet manifold or associated hoses (Chapter 4A or 4B).
- ☐ Blocked carburettor jet(s) or internal passages - carburettor models (Chapter 4A).
- ☐ Blocked injector/fuel injection system fault - fuel-injected models (Chapter 4B).
- ☐ Brakes binding (Chapters 1 and 9).
- ☐ Clutch slipping (Chapter 6).

Engine backfires

- ☐ Timing belt incorrectly fitted or tensioned (Chapter 2A or 2B).
- ☐ Vacuum leak at the carburettor/throttle body, inlet manifold or associated hoses (Chapter 4A or 4B).
- ☐ Blocked carburettor jet(s) or internal passages - carburettor models (Chapter 4A).
- ☐ Blocked injector/fuel injection system fault - fuel-injected models (Chapter 4B).

Oil pressure warning light illuminated with engine running

- ☐ Low oil level, or incorrect oil grade ("Weekly checks").
- ☐ Faulty oil pressure warning light switch (Chapter 5A).
- ☐ Worn engine bearings and/or oil pump (Chapter 2).
- ☐ High engine operating temperature (Chapter 3).
- ☐ Oil pressure relief valve defective (Chapter 2A or 2B).
- ☐ Oil pick-up strainer clogged (Chapter 2A or 2B).

Engine noises

Pre-ignition (pinking) or knocking during acceleration or under load

- ☐ Ignition timing incorrect/ignition system fault (Chapters 1 and 5B).
- ☐ Incorrect grade of spark plug (Chapter 1).
- ☐ Incorrect grade of fuel (Chapter 1).
- ☐ Vacuum leak at the carburettor/throttle body, inlet manifold or associated hoses (Chapter 4A or 4B).
- ☐ Excessive carbon build-up in engine (Chapter 2).
- ☐ Blocked carburettor jet(s) or internal passages - carburettor models (Chapter 4A).
- ☐ Blocked injector/fuel injection system fault - fuel-injected models (Chapter 4B).

Whistling or wheezing noises

- ☐ Leaking inlet manifold or carburettor/throttle body gasket (Chapter 4A or 4B).
- ☐ Leaking exhaust manifold gasket or pipe-to-manifold joint (Chapter 4C).
- ☐ Leaking vacuum hose (Chapters 4A, 4B, 4C, 5B, 9 and 12).
- ☐ Blowing cylinder head gasket (Chapter 2A or 2B).

Tapping or rattling noises

- ☐ Worn valve gear or camshaft (Chapter 2A or 2B).
- ☐ Ancillary component fault (coolant pump, alternator, etc.) (Chapters 3, 5A, etc.).

Knocking or thumping noises

- ☐ Worn big-end bearings (regular heavy knocking, perhaps less under load), (Chapter 2A or 2B).
- ☐ Worn main bearings (rumbling and knocking, perhaps worsening under load), (Chapter 2A or 2B).
- ☐ Piston slap (most noticeable when cold), (Chapter 2A or 2B).
- ☐ Ancillary component fault (coolant pump, alternator, etc.) (Chapters 3, 5A, etc.).

Cooling system

Overheating

- ☐ Insufficient coolant in system ("Weekly checks").
- ☐ Thermostat faulty (Chapter 3).
- ☐ Radiator core blocked, or grille restricted (Chapter 3).
- ☐ Electric cooling fan or thermoswitch faulty (Chapter 3).
- ☐ Pressure cap faulty (Chapter 3).
- ☐ Ignition timing incorrect/ignition system fault (Chapters 1 and 5B).
- ☐ Inaccurate temperature gauge sender unit (Chapter 3).
- ☐ Airlock in cooling system (Chapter 1).

Overcooling

- ☐ Thermostat faulty (Chapter 3).
- ☐ Inaccurate temperature gauge sender unit (Chapter 3).

Internal coolant leakage

- ☐ Leaking cylinder head gasket (Chapter 2A or 2B).
- ☐ Cracked cylinder head or cylinder bore (Chapter 2A or 2B).

External coolant leakage

- ☐ Deteriorated or damaged hoses or hose clips (Chapter 1).
- ☐ Radiator core or heater matrix leaking (Chapter 3).
- ☐ Pressure cap faulty (Chapter 3).
- ☐ Water pump seal leaking (Chapter 3).
- ☐ Boiling due to overheating (Chapter 3).
- ☐ Core plug leaking (Chapter 2).

Corrosion

- ☐ Infrequent draining and flushing (Chapter 1).
- ☐ Incorrect coolant mixture or inappropriate coolant type ("Lubricants and fluids" and Chapter 1).

Fuel and exhaust systems

Excessive fuel consumption

- ☐ Air filter element dirty or clogged (Chapter 1).
- ☐ Choke cable incorrectly adjusted, or choke sticking - carburettor models (Chapter 4A).
- ☐ Fuel injection system fault - fuel injected models (Chapter 4B).
- ☐ Ignition timing incorrect/ignition system fault (Chapters 1 and 5B).
- ☐ Tyres under-inflated ("Weekly checks").

Fuel leakage and/or fuel odour

- ☐ Damaged or corroded fuel tank, pipes or connections (Chapter 4A or 4B).
- ☐ Carburettor float chamber flooding (float height incorrect) - carburettor models (Chapter 4A).

Excessive noise or fumes from exhaust system

- ☐ Leaking exhaust system or manifold joints (Chapters 1, 4A and 4B).
- ☐ Leaking, corroded or damaged silencers or pipe (Chapters 1, 4A and 4B).
- ☐ Broken mountings causing body or suspension contact (Chapter 1).

Clutch

Pedal travels to floor - no pressure or very little resistance

- ☐ Broken clutch cable (Chapter 6).
- ☐ Incorrect clutch cable adjustment (Chapter 6).
- ☐ Broken clutch release bearing or fork (Chapter 6).
- ☐ Broken diaphragm spring in clutch pressure plate (Chapter 6).

Noise when depressing or releasing clutch pedal

- ☐ Worn clutch release bearing (Chapter 6).
- ☐ Worn or dry clutch pedal bushes (Chapter 6).
- ☐ Faulty pressure plate assembly (Chapter 6).
- ☐ Pressure plate diaphragm spring broken (Chapter 6).
- ☐ Broken clutch disc cushioning springs (Chapter 6).

Clutch slips (engine speed increases, with no increase in vehicle speed).

- ☐ Incorrect clutch cable adjustment (Chapter 6).
- ☐ Clutch disc linings excessively worn (Chapter 6).
- ☐ Clutch disc linings contaminated with oil or grease (Chapter 6).
- ☐ Faulty pressure plate or weak diaphragm spring (Chapter 6).

Clutch fails to disengage (unable to select gears).

- ☐ Incorrect clutch cable adjustment (Chapter 6).
- ☐ Clutch disc sticking on transmission input shaft splines (Chapter 6).
- ☐ Clutch disc sticking to flywheel or pressure plate (Chapter 6).
- ☐ Faulty pressure plate assembly (Chapter 6).
- ☐ Clutch release mechanism worn or incorrectly assembled (Chapter 6).

Judder as clutch is engaged

- ☐ Clutch disc linings contaminated with oil or grease (Chapter 6).
- ☐ Clutch disc linings excessively worn (Chapter 6).
- ☐ Clutch cable sticking or frayed (Chapter 6).
- ☐ Faulty or distorted pressure plate or diaphragm spring (Chapter 6).
- ☐ Worn or loose engine or transmission mountings (Chapter 2A or 2B).
- ☐ Clutch disc hub or transmission input shaft splines worn (Chapter 6).

Manual transmission

Noisy in neutral with engine running

- ☐ Input shaft bearings worn (noise apparent with clutch pedal released, but not when depressed), (Chapter 7A).*
- ☐ Clutch release bearing worn (noise apparent with clutch pedal depressed, possibly less when released), (Chapter 6).

Noisy in one particular gear

- ☐ Worn, damaged or chipped gear teeth (Chapter 7A).*

Difficulty engaging gears

- ☐ Clutch fault (Chapter 6).
- ☐ Worn or damaged gear linkage (Chapter 7A).
- ☐ Incorrectly adjusted gear linkage (Chapter 7A).
- ☐ Worn synchroniser units (Chapter 7A).*

Vibration

- ☐ Lack of oil (Chapter 1).
- ☐ Worn bearings (Chapter 7A).*

Jumps out of gear

- ☐ Worn or damaged gear linkage (Chapter 7A).
- ☐ Incorrectly adjusted gear linkage (Chapter 7A).
- ☐ Worn synchroniser units (Chapter 7A).*
- ☐ Worn selector forks (Chapter 7A).*

Lubricant leaks

- ☐ Leaking differential output oil seal (Chapter 7A).
- ☐ Leaking housing joint (Chapter 7A).*
- ☐ Leaking input shaft oil seal (Chapter 7A).*

Although the corrective action necessary to remedy the symptoms described is beyond the scope of the home mechanic, the above information should be helpful in isolating the cause of the condition. This should enable the owner can communicate clearly with a professional mechanic.

Automatic transmission

Note: *Due to the complexity of the automatic transmission, it is difficult for the home mechanic to properly diagnose and service this unit. For problems other than the following, the vehicle should be taken to a dealer service department or automatic transmission specialist. Do not be too hasty in removing the transmission if a fault is suspected, as most of the testing is carried out with the unit still fitted.*

Fluid leakage

☐ Automatic transmission fluid is usually dark in colour. Fluid leaks should not be confused with engine oil, which can easily be blown onto the transmission by airflow.
☐ To determine the source of a leak, first remove all built-up dirt and grime from the transmission housing and surrounding areas using a degreasing agent, or by steam-cleaning. Drive the vehicle at low speed, so airflow will not blow the leak far from its source. Raise and support the vehicle, and determine where the leak is coming from. The following are common areas of leakage:
a) *Fluid pan or "sump" (Chapter 1 and 7B).*
b) *Dipstick tube (Chapter 1 and 7B).*
c) *Transmission-to-fluid cooler pipes/unions (Chapter 7B).*

Transmission fluid brown, or has burned smell

☐ Transmission fluid level low, or fluid in need of renewal (Chapter 1).

Transmission will not downshift (kickdown) with accelerator pedal fully depressed

☐ Low transmission fluid level (Chapter 1).
☐ Incorrect selector cable adjustment (Chapter 7B).

Engine will not start in any gear, or starts in gears other than Park or Neutral

☐ Incorrect starter/inhibitor switch adjustment (Chapter 7B).
☐ Incorrect selector cable adjustment (Chapter 7B).

General gear selection problems

☐ Chapter 7B deals with checking and adjusting the selector cable on automatic transmissions. The following are common problems that may be caused by a poorly adjusted cable:

a) *Engine starting in gears other than Park or Neutral.*
b) *Indicator panel indicating a gear other than the one actually being used.*
c) *Vehicle moves when in Park or Neutral.*
d) *Poor gear shift quality or erratic gear changes.*

☐ Refer to Chapter 7B for the selector cable adjustment procedure.

Transmission slips, shifts roughly, is noisy, or has no drive in forward or reverse gears

☐ There are many probable causes for the above problems, but the home mechanic should be concerned with only one possibility - fluid level. Before taking the vehicle to a dealer or transmission specialist, check the fluid level and condition of the fluid as described in Chapter 1. Correct the fluid level as necessary, or change the fluid and filter if needed. If the problem persists, professional help will be necessary.

Driveshafts

Clicking or knocking noise on turns (at slow speed on full-lock)

☐ Lack of constant velocity joint lubricant, possibly due to damaged gaiter (Chapter 8).
☐ Worn outer constant velocity joint (Chapter 8).

Vibration when accelerating or decelerating

☐ Worn inner constant velocity joint (Chapter 8).
☐ Bent or distorted driveshaft (Chapter 8).

Braking system

Note: *Before assuming that a brake problem exists, make sure that the tyres are in good condition and correctly inflated, that the front wheel alignment is correct, and that the vehicle is not loaded with weight in an unequal manner. Apart from checking the condition of all pipe and hose connections, any faults occurring on the anti-lock braking system should be referred to a Peugeot dealer for diagnosis.*

Vehicle pulls to one side under braking

☐ Worn, defective, damaged or contaminated brake pads/shoes on one side (Chapters 1 and 9).
☐ Seized or partially seized front brake caliper/wheel cylinder piston (Chapters 1 and 9).
☐ A mixture of brake pad/shoe lining materials fitted between sides (Chapters 1 and 9).
☐ Brake caliper or backplate mounting bolts loose (Chapter 9).
☐ Worn or damaged steering or suspension components (Chapters 1 and 10).

Noise (grinding or high-pitched squeal) when brakes applied

☐ Brake pad or shoe friction lining material worn down to metal backing (Chapters 1 and 9).
☐ Excessive corrosion of brake disc or drum. This may be apparent after the vehicle has been standing for some time (Chapters 1 and 9).
☐ Foreign object (stone chipping, etc.) trapped between brake disc and shield (Chapters 1 and 9).

Excessive brake pedal travel

☐ Inoperative rear brake self-adjust mechanism - drum brakes (Chapters 1 and 9).
☐ Faulty master cylinder (Chapter 9).
☐ Air in hydraulic system (Chapters 1 and 9).
☐ Faulty vacuum servo unit (Chapter 9).

Brake pedal feels spongy when depressed

☐ Air in hydraulic system (Chapters 1 and 9).
☐ Deteriorated flexible rubber brake hoses (Chapters 1 and 9).
☐ Master cylinder mounting nuts loose (Chapter 9).
☐ Faulty master cylinder (Chapter 9).

Excessive brake pedal effort required to stop vehicle

☐ Faulty vacuum servo unit (Chapter 9).
☐ Disconnected, damaged or insecure brake servo vacuum hose (Chapter 9).
☐ Primary or secondary hydraulic circuit failure (Chapter 9).
☐ Seized brake caliper or wheel cylinder piston(s) (Chapter 9).
☐ Brake pads or brake shoes incorrectly fitted (Chapters 1 and 9).
☐ Incorrect grade of brake pads or brake shoes fitted (Chapters 1 and 9).
☐ Brake pads or brake shoe linings contaminated (Chapters 1 and 9).

Braking system (continued)

Judder felt through brake pedal or steering wheel when braking

- ☐ Excessive run-out or distortion of discs/drums (Chapters 1 and 9).
- ☐ Brake pad or brake shoe linings worn (Chapters 1 and 9).
- ☐ Brake caliper or brake backplate mounting bolts loose (Chapter 9).
- ☐ Wear in suspension or steering components or mountings (Chapters 1 and 10).

Brakes binding

- ☐ Seized brake caliper or wheel cylinder piston(s) (Chapter 9).
- ☐ Incorrectly adjusted handbrake mechanism (Chapter 9).
- ☐ Faulty master cylinder (Chapter 9).

Rear wheels locking under normal braking

- ☐ Rear brake shoe linings contaminated (Chapters 1 and 9).
- ☐ Faulty brake pressure regulator (Chapter 9).

Suspension and steering

Note: *Before diagnosing suspension or steering faults, be sure that the trouble is not due to incorrect tyre pressures, mixtures of tyre types, or binding brakes.*

Vehicle pulls to one side

- ☐ Defective tyre (*"Weekly checks"*).
- ☐ Excessive wear in suspension or steering components (Chapters 1 and 10).
- ☐ Incorrect front wheel alignment (Chapter 10).
- ☐ Accident damage to steering or suspension components (Chapter 1).

Excessive pitching and/or rolling around corners, or during braking

- ☐ Defective shock absorbers (Chapters 1 and 10).
- ☐ Broken or weak spring and/or suspension component (Chapters 1 and 10).
- ☐ Worn or damaged anti-roll bar or mountings (Chapter 10).

Wandering or general instability

- ☐ Incorrect front wheel alignment (Chapter 10).
- ☐ Worn steering or suspension joints, bushes or components (Chapters 1 and 10).
- ☐ Roadwheels out of balance (Chapters 1 and 10).
- ☐ Faulty or damaged tyre (*"Weekly checks"*).
- ☐ Wheel bolts loose (Chapters 1 and 10).
- ☐ Defective shock absorbers (Chapters 1 and 10).

Excessively stiff steering

- ☐ Lack of steering gear lubricant (Chapter 10).
- ☐ Seized track rod end balljoint or suspension balljoint (Chapters 1 and 10).
- ☐ Broken or incorrectly adjusted auxiliary drivebelt - power steering (Chapter 1).
- ☐ Incorrect front wheel alignment (Chapter 10).
- ☐ Steering rack or column bent or damaged (Chapter 10).

Wheel wobble and vibration

- ☐ Front roadwheels out of balance (vibration felt mainly through the steering wheel), (Chapters 1 and 10).
- ☐ Rear roadwheels out of balance (vibration felt throughout the vehicle), (Chapters 1 and 10).
- ☐ Roadwheels damaged or distorted (Chapters 1 and 10).
- ☐ Faulty or damaged tyre (*"Weekly checks"*).
- ☐ Worn steering or suspension joints, bushes or components (Chapters 1 and 10).
- ☐ Wheel bolts loose (Chapters 1 and 10).

Excessive play in steering

- ☐ Worn steering column intermediate shaft universal joint (Chapter 10).
- ☐ Worn steering track rod end balljoints (Chapters 1 and 10).
- ☐ Worn rack-and-pinion steering gear (Chapter 10).
- ☐ Worn steering or suspension joints, bushes or components (Chapters 1 and 10).

Lack of power assistance

- ☐ Broken or incorrectly adjusted auxiliary drivebelt (Chapter 1).
- ☐ Incorrect power steering fluid level (*"Weekly checks"*).
- ☐ Restriction in power steering fluid hoses (Chapter 1).
- ☐ Faulty power steering pump (Chapter 10).
- ☐ Faulty rack-and-pinion steering gear (Chapter 10).

Tyre wear excessive

Tyres worn on inside or outside edges

- ☐ Tyres under-inflated (wear on both edges), (*"Weekly checks"*).
- ☐ Incorrect camber or castor angles (wear on one edge only), (Chapter 10).
- ☐ Worn steering or suspension joints, bushes or components (Chapters 1 and 10).
- ☐ Excessively hard cornering.
- ☐ Accident damage.

Tyre treads exhibit feathered edges

- ☐ Incorrect toe setting (Chapter 10).

Tyres worn in centre of tread

- ☐ Tyres over-inflated (*"Weekly checks"*).

Tyres worn on inside and outside edges

- ☐ Tyres under-inflated (*"Weekly checks"*).

Tyres worn unevenly

- ☐ Tyres/wheels out of balance (Chapter 1).
- ☐ Excessive wheel or tyre run-out (Chapter 1).
- ☐ Worn shock absorbers (Chapters 1 and 10).
- ☐ Faulty tyre (*"Weekly checks"*).

Electrical system

Note: *For problems associated with the starting system, refer to the faults listed under "Engine" earlier in this Section.*

Battery won't hold a charge for more than a few days

☐ Battery defective internally (Chapter 5A).
☐ Battery terminal connections loose or corroded ("*Weekly checks*").
☐ Auxiliary drivebelt worn or incorrectly adjusted (Chapter 1).
☐ Alternator not charging at correct output (Chapter 5A).
☐ Alternator or voltage regulator faulty (Chapter 5A).
☐ Short-circuit causing continual battery drain (Chapters 5A and 12).

Ignition/no-charge warning light remains illuminated with engine running

☐ Auxiliary drivebelt broken, worn, or incorrectly adjusted (Chapter 1).
☐ Alternator brushes worn, sticking, or dirty (Chapter 5A).
☐ Alternator brush springs weak or broken (Chapter 5A).
☐ Internal fault in alternator or voltage regulator (Chapter 5A).
☐ Broken, disconnected, or loose wiring in charging circuit (Chapter 5A).

Ignition/no-charge warning light fails to come on

☐ Warning light bulb blown (Chapter 12).
☐ Broken, disconnected, or loose wiring in light circuit (Chapter 12).
☐ Alternator faulty (Chapter 5A).

Lights inoperative

☐ Bulb blown (Chapter 12).
☐ Corrosion of bulb or bulbholder contacts (Chapter 12).
☐ Blown fuse (Chapter 12).
☐ Faulty relay (Chapter 12).
☐ Broken, loose, or disconnected wiring (Chapter 12).
☐ Faulty switch (Chapter 12).

Instrument readings inaccurate or erratic

Instrument readings increase with engine speed

☐ Faulty voltage regulator (Chapter 12).

Fuel or temperature gauges give no reading

☐ Faulty gauge sender unit (Chapters 3, 4A or 4B).
☐ Wiring open-circuit (Chapter 12).
☐ Faulty gauge (Chapter 12).

Fuel or temperature gauges give continuous maximum reading

☐ Faulty gauge sender unit (Chapters 3, 4A or 4B).
☐ Wiring short-circuit (Chapter 12).
☐ Faulty gauge (Chapter 12).

Horn inoperative, or unsatisfactory in operation

Horn operates all the time

☐ Horn push either earthed or stuck down (Chapter 12).
☐ Horn cable-to-horn push earthed (Chapter 12).

Horn fails to operate

☐ Blown fuse (Chapter 12).
☐ Cable and/or connections loose, broken or disconnected (Chapter 12).
☐ Faulty horn (Chapter 12).

Horn emits intermittent or unsatisfactory sound

☐ Cable connections loose (Chapter 12).
☐ Horn mountings loose (Chapter 12).
☐ Faulty horn (Chapter 12).

Windscreen/tailgate wipers inoperative, or unsatisfactory in operation

Wipers fail to operate, or operate very slowly

☐ Wiper blades stuck to screen, or linkage seized or binding (Chapters 1 and 12).
☐ Blown fuse (Chapter 12).
☐ Cable and/or connections loose, broken or disconnected (Chapter 12).
☐ Faulty relay (Chapter 12).
☐ Faulty wiper motor (Chapter 12).

Wiper blades sweep over too large or too small an area of the glass

☐ Wiper arms incorrectly positioned on spindles (Chapter 1).
☐ Excessive wear of wiper linkage (Chapter 12).
☐ Wiper motor or linkage mountings loose or insecure (Chapter 12).

Wiper blades fail to clean the glass effectively

☐ Wiper blade rubbers worn or perished (Chapter 1).
☐ Wiper arm tension springs broken, or arm pivots seized (Chapter 12).
☐ Insufficient windscreen washer additive to adequately remove road film (Chapter 1).

Windscreen/tailgate washers inoperative, or unsatisfactory in operation

One or more washer jets inoperative

☐ Blocked washer jet (Chapter 1).
☐ Disconnected, kinked or restricted fluid hose (Chapter 12).
☐ Insufficient fluid in washer reservoir (Chapter 1).

Washer pump fails to operate

☐ Broken or disconnected wiring or connections (Chapter 12).
☐ Blown fuse (Chapter 12).
☐ Faulty washer switch (Chapter 12).
☐ Faulty washer pump (Chapter 12).

Washer pump runs for some time before fluid is emitted from jets

☐ Faulty one-way valve in fluid supply hose (Chapter 12).

Electric windows inoperative, or unsatisfactory in operation

Window glass will only move in one direction

☐ Faulty switch (Chapter 12).

Window glass slow to move

☐ Regulator seized or damaged, or in need of lubrication (Chapter 11).
☐ Door internal components or trim fouling regulator (Chapter 11).
☐ Faulty motor (Chapter 12).

Window glass fails to move

☐ Blown fuse (Chapter 12).
☐ Faulty relay (Chapter 12).
☐ Broken or disconnected wiring or connections (Chapter 12).
☐ Faulty motor (Chapter 12).

Central locking system inoperative, or unsatisfactory in operation

Complete system failure

☐ Blown fuse (Chapter 12).
☐ Faulty relay (Chapter 12).
☐ Broken or disconnected wiring or connections (Chapter 12).
☐ Faulty control module (Chapter 12).

Latch locks but will not unlock, or unlocks but will not lock

☐ Faulty master switch (Chapter 12).
☐ Broken or disconnected latch operating rods or levers (Chapter 11).
☐ Faulty relay (Chapter 12).
☐ Faulty control module (Chapter 12).

One solenoid/motor fails to operate

☐ Broken or disconnected wiring or connections (Chapter 12).
☐ Faulty solenoid/motor (Chapter 12).
☐ Broken, binding or disconnected latch operating rods or levers (Chapter 11).
☐ Fault in door latch (Chapter 11).

A

ABS (Anti-lock brake system) A system, usually electronically controlled, that senses incipient wheel lockup during braking and relieves hydraulic pressure at wheels that are about to skid.

Air bag An inflatable bag hidden in the steering wheel (driver's side) or the dash or glovebox (passenger side). In a head-on collision, the bags inflate, preventing the driver and front passenger from being thrown forward into the steering wheel or windscreen.

Air cleaner A metal or plastic housing, containing a filter element, which removes dust and dirt from the air being drawn into the engine.

Air filter element The actual filter in an air cleaner system, usually manufactured from pleated paper and requiring renewal at regular intervals.

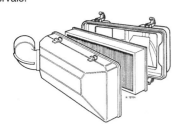

Air filter

Allen key A hexagonal wrench which fits into a recessed hexagonal hole.

Alligator clip A long-nosed spring-loaded metal clip with meshing teeth. Used to make temporary electrical connections.

Alternator A component in the electrical system which converts mechanical energy from a drivebelt into electrical energy to charge the battery and to operate the starting system, ignition system and electrical accessories.

Ampere (amp) A unit of measurement for the flow of electric current. One amp is the amount of current produced by one volt acting through a resistance of one ohm.

Anaerobic sealer A substance used to prevent bolts and screws from loosening. Anaerobic means that it does not require oxygen for activation. The Loctite brand is widely used.

Antifreeze A substance (usually ethylene glycol) mixed with water, and added to a vehicle's cooling system, to prevent freezing of the coolant in winter. Antifreeze also contains chemicals to inhibit corrosion and the formation of rust and other deposits that would tend to clog the radiator and coolant passages and reduce cooling efficiency.

Anti-seize compound A coating that reduces the risk of seizing on fasteners that are subjected to high temperatures, such as exhaust manifold bolts and nuts.

Asbestos A natural fibrous mineral with great heat resistance, commonly used in the composition of brake friction materials.

Asbestos is a health hazard and the dust created by brake systems should never be inhaled or ingested.

Axle A shaft on which a wheel revolves, or which revolves with a wheel. Also, a solid beam that connects the two wheels at one end of the vehicle. An axle which also transmits power to the wheels is known as a live axle.

Axleshaft A single rotating shaft, on either side of the differential, which delivers power from the final drive assembly to the drive wheels. Also called a driveshaft or a halfshaft.

B

Ball bearing An anti-friction bearing consisting of a hardened inner and outer race with hardened steel balls between two races.

Bearing The curved surface on a shaft or in a bore, or the part assembled into either, that permits relative motion between them with minimum wear and friction.

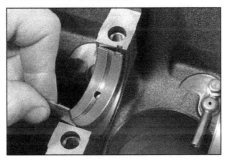

Bearing

Big-end bearing The bearing in the end of the connecting rod that's attached to the crankshaft.

Bleed nipple A valve on a brake wheel cylinder, caliper or other hydraulic component that is opened to purge the hydraulic system of air. Also called a bleed screw.

Brake bleeding Procedure for removing air from lines of a hydraulic brake system.

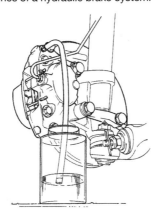

Brake bleeding

Brake disc The component of a disc brake that rotates with the wheels.

Brake drum The component of a drum brake that rotates with the wheels.

Brake linings The friction material which contacts the brake disc or drum to retard the vehicle's speed. The linings are bonded or riveted to the brake pads or shoes.

Brake pads The replaceable friction pads that pinch the brake disc when the brakes are applied. Brake pads consist of a friction material bonded or riveted to a rigid backing plate.

Brake shoe The crescent-shaped carrier to which the brake linings are mounted and which forces the lining against the rotating drum during braking.

Braking systems For more information on braking systems, consult the *Haynes Automotive Brake Manual*.

Breaker bar A long socket wrench handle providing greater leverage.

Bulkhead The insulated partition between the engine and the passenger compartment.

C

Caliper The non-rotating part of a disc-brake assembly that straddles the disc and carries the brake pads. The caliper also contains the hydraulic components that cause the pads to pinch the disc when the brakes are applied. A caliper is also a measuring tool that can be set to measure inside or outside dimensions of an object.

Camshaft A rotating shaft on which a series of cam lobes operate the valve mechanisms. The camshaft may be driven by gears, by sprockets and chain or by sprockets and a belt.

Canister A container in an evaporative emission control system; contains activated charcoal granules to trap vapours from the fuel system.

Canister

Carburettor A device which mixes fuel with air in the proper proportions to provide a desired power output from a spark ignition internal combustion engine.

Castellated Resembling the parapets along the top of a castle wall. For example, a castellated balljoint stud nut.

Castor In wheel alignment, the backward or forward tilt of the steering axis. Castor is positive when the steering axis is inclined rearward at the top.

Catalytic converter A silencer-like device in the exhaust system which converts certain pollutants in the exhaust gases into less harmful substances.

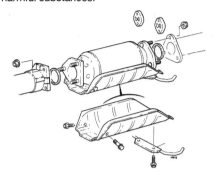

Catalytic converter

Circlip A ring-shaped clip used to prevent endwise movement of cylindrical parts and shafts. An internal circlip is installed in a groove in a housing; an external circlip fits into a groove on the outside of a cylindrical piece such as a shaft.

Clearance The amount of space between two parts. For example, between a piston and a cylinder, between a bearing and a journal, etc.

Coil spring A spiral of elastic steel found in various sizes throughout a vehicle, for example as a springing medium in the suspension and in the valve train.

Compression Reduction in volume, and increase in pressure and temperature, of a gas, caused by squeezing it into a smaller space.

Compression ratio The relationship between cylinder volume when the piston is at top dead centre and cylinder volume when the piston is at bottom dead centre.

Constant velocity (CV) joint A type of universal joint that cancels out vibrations caused by driving power being transmitted through an angle.

Core plug A disc or cup-shaped metal device inserted in a hole in a casting through which core was removed when the casting was formed. Also known as a freeze plug or expansion plug.

Crankcase The lower part of the engine block in which the crankshaft rotates.

Crankshaft The main rotating member, or shaft, running the length of the crankcase, with offset "throws" to which the connecting rods are attached.

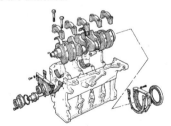

Crankshaft assembly

Crocodile clip See Alligator clip

D

Diagnostic code Code numbers obtained by accessing the diagnostic mode of an engine management computer. This code can be used to determine the area in the system where a malfunction may be located.

Disc brake A brake design incorporating a rotating disc onto which brake pads are squeezed. The resulting friction converts the energy of a moving vehicle into heat.

Double-overhead cam (DOHC) An engine that uses two overhead camshafts, usually one for the intake valves and one for the exhaust valves.

Drivebelt(s) The belt(s) used to drive accessories such as the alternator, water pump, power steering pump, air conditioning compressor, etc. off the crankshaft pulley.

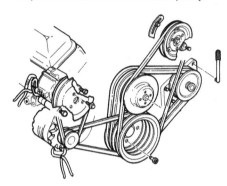

Accessory drivebelts

Driveshaft Any shaft used to transmit motion. Commonly used when referring to the axleshafts on a front wheel drive vehicle.

Drum brake A type of brake using a drum-shaped metal cylinder attached to the inner surface of the wheel. When the brake pedal is pressed, curved brake shoes with friction linings press against the inside of the drum to slow or stop the vehicle.

E

EGR valve A valve used to introduce exhaust gases into the intake air stream.

Electronic control unit (ECU) A computer which controls (for instance) ignition and fuel injection systems, or an anti-lock braking system. For more information refer to the *Haynes Automotive Electrical and Electronic Systems Manual*.

Electronic Fuel Injection (EFI) A computer controlled fuel system that distributes fuel through an injector located in each intake port of the engine.

Emergency brake A braking system, independent of the main hydraulic system, that can be used to slow or stop the vehicle if the primary brakes fail, or to hold the vehicle stationary even though the brake pedal isn't depressed. It usually consists of a hand lever that actuates either front or rear brakes mechanically through a series of cables and linkages. Also known as a handbrake or parking brake.

Endfloat The amount of lengthwise movement between two parts. As applied to a crankshaft, the distance that the crankshaft can move forward and back in the cylinder block.

Engine management system (EMS) A computer controlled system which manages the fuel injection and the ignition systems in an integrated fashion.

Exhaust manifold A part with several passages through which exhaust gases leave the engine combustion chambers and enter the exhaust pipe.

F

Fan clutch A viscous (fluid) drive coupling device which permits variable engine fan speeds in relation to engine speeds.

Feeler blade A thin strip or blade of hardened steel, ground to an exact thickness, used to check or measure clearances between parts.

Feeler blade

Firing order The order in which the engine cylinders fire, or deliver their power strokes, beginning with the number one cylinder.

Flywheel A heavy spinning wheel in which energy is absorbed and stored by means of momentum. On cars, the flywheel is attached to the crankshaft to smooth out firing impulses.

Free play The amount of travel before any action takes place. The "looseness" in a linkage, or an assembly of parts, between the initial application of force and actual movement. For example, the distance the brake pedal moves before the pistons in the master cylinder are actuated.

Fuse An electrical device which protects a circuit against accidental overload. The typical fuse contains a soft piece of metal which is calibrated to melt at a predetermined current flow (expressed as amps) and break the circuit.

Fusible link A circuit protection device consisting of a conductor surrounded by heat-resistant insulation. The conductor is smaller than the wire it protects, so it acts as the weakest link in the circuit. Unlike a blown fuse, a failed fusible link must frequently be cut from the wire for replacement.

G

Gap The distance the spark must travel in jumping from the centre electrode to the side electrode in a spark plug. Also refers to the spacing between the points in a contact breaker assembly in a conventional points-type ignition, or to the distance between the reluctor or rotor and the pickup coil in an electronic ignition.

Adjusting spark plug gap

Gasket Any thin, soft material - usually cork, cardboard, asbestos or soft metal - installed between two metal surfaces to ensure a good seal. For instance, the cylinder head gasket seals the joint between the block and the cylinder head.

Gasket

Gauge An instrument panel display used to monitor engine conditions. A gauge with a movable pointer on a dial or a fixed scale is an analogue gauge. A gauge with a numerical readout is called a digital gauge.

H

Halfshaft A rotating shaft that transmits power from the final drive unit to a drive wheel, usually when referring to a live rear axle.

Harmonic balancer A device designed to reduce torsion or twisting vibration in the crankshaft. May be incorporated in the crankshaft pulley. Also known as a vibration damper.

Hone An abrasive tool for correcting small irregularities or differences in diameter in an engine cylinder, brake cylinder, etc.

Hydraulic tappet A tappet that utilises hydraulic pressure from the engine's lubrication system to maintain zero clearance (constant contact with both camshaft and valve stem). Automatically adjusts to variation in valve stem length. Hydraulic tappets also reduce valve noise.

I

Ignition timing The moment at which the spark plug fires, usually expressed in the number of crankshaft degrees before the piston reaches the top of its stroke.

Inlet manifold A tube or housing with passages through which flows the air-fuel mixture (carburettor vehicles and vehicles with throttle body injection) or air only (port fuel-injected vehicles) to the port openings in the cylinder head.

J

Jump start Starting the engine of a vehicle with a discharged or weak battery by attaching jump leads from the weak battery to a charged or helper battery.

L

Load Sensing Proportioning Valve (LSPV) A brake hydraulic system control valve that works like a proportioning valve, but also takes into consideration the amount of weight carried by the rear axle.

Locknut A nut used to lock an adjustment nut, or other threaded component, in place. For example, a locknut is employed to keep the adjusting nut on the rocker arm in position.

Lockwasher A form of washer designed to prevent an attaching nut from working loose.

M

MacPherson strut A type of front suspension system devised by Earle MacPherson at Ford of England. In its original form, a simple lateral link with the anti-roll bar creates the lower control arm. A long strut - an integral coil spring and shock absorber - is mounted between the body and the steering knuckle. Many modern so-called MacPherson strut systems use a conventional lower A-arm and don't rely on the anti-roll bar for location.

Multimeter An electrical test instrument with the capability to measure voltage, current and resistance.

N

NOx Oxides of Nitrogen. A common toxic pollutant emitted by petrol and diesel engines at higher temperatures.

O

Ohm The unit of electrical resistance. One volt applied to a resistance of one ohm will produce a current of one amp.

Ohmmeter An instrument for measuring electrical resistance.

O-ring A type of sealing ring made of a special rubber-like material; in use, the O-ring is compressed into a groove to provide the sealing action.

Overhead cam (ohc) engine An engine with the camshaft(s) located on top of the cylinder head(s).

Overhead valve (ohv) engine An engine with the valves located in the cylinder head, but with the camshaft located in the engine block.

Oxygen sensor A device installed in the engine exhaust manifold, which senses the oxygen content in the exhaust and converts this information into an electric current. Also called a Lambda sensor.

P

Phillips screw A type of screw head having a cross instead of a slot for a corresponding type of screwdriver.

Plastigage A thin strip of plastic thread, available in different sizes, used for measuring clearances. For example, a strip of Plastigage is laid across a bearing journal. The parts are assembled and dismantled; the width of the crushed strip indicates the clearance between journal and bearing.

Plastigage

Propeller shaft The long hollow tube with universal joints at both ends that carries power from the transmission to the differential on front-engined rear wheel drive vehicles.

Proportioning valve A hydraulic control valve which limits the amount of pressure to the rear brakes during panic stops to prevent wheel lock-up.

R

Rack-and-pinion steering A steering system with a pinion gear on the end of the steering shaft that mates with a rack (think of a geared wheel opened up and laid flat). When the steering wheel is turned, the pinion turns, moving the rack to the left or right. This movement is transmitted through the track rods to the steering arms at the wheels.

Radiator A liquid-to-air heat transfer device designed to reduce the temperature of the coolant in an internal combustion engine cooling system.

Refrigerant Any substance used as a heat transfer agent in an air-conditioning system. R-12 has been the principle refrigerant for many years; recently, however, manufacturers have begun using R-134a, a non-CFC substance that is considered less harmful to the ozone in the upper atmosphere.

Rocker arm A lever arm that rocks on a shaft or pivots on a stud. In an overhead valve engine, the rocker arm converts the upward movement of the pushrod into a downward movement to open a valve.

Rotor In a distributor, the rotating device inside the cap that connects the centre electrode and the outer terminals as it turns, distributing the high voltage from the coil secondary winding to the proper spark plug. Also, that part of an alternator which rotates inside the stator. Also, the rotating assembly of a turbocharger, including the compressor wheel, shaft and turbine wheel.

Runout The amount of wobble (in-and-out movement) of a gear or wheel as it's rotated. The amount a shaft rotates "out-of-true." The out-of-round condition of a rotating part.

S

Sealant A liquid or paste used to prevent leakage at a joint. Sometimes used in conjunction with a gasket.

Sealed beam lamp An older headlight design which integrates the reflector, lens and filaments into a hermetically-sealed one-piece unit. When a filament burns out or the lens cracks, the entire unit is simply replaced.

Serpentine drivebelt A single, long, wide accessory drivebelt that's used on some newer vehicles to drive all the accessories, instead of a series of smaller, shorter belts. Serpentine drivebelts are usually tensioned by an automatic tensioner.

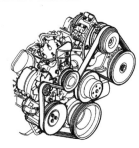

Serpentine drivebelt

Shim Thin spacer, commonly used to adjust the clearance or relative positions between two parts. For example, shims inserted into or under bucket tappets control valve clearances. Clearance is adjusted by changing the thickness of the shim.

Slide hammer A special puller that screws into or hooks onto a component such as a shaft or bearing; a heavy sliding handle on the shaft bottoms against the end of the shaft to knock the component free.

Sprocket A tooth or projection on the periphery of a wheel, shaped to engage with a chain or drivebelt. Commonly used to refer to the sprocket wheel itself.

Starter inhibitor switch On vehicles with an automatic transmission, a switch that prevents starting if the vehicle is not in Neutral or Park.

Strut See MacPherson strut.

T

Tappet A cylindrical component which transmits motion from the cam to the valve stem, either directly or via a pushrod and rocker arm. Also called a cam follower.

Thermostat A heat-controlled valve that regulates the flow of coolant between the cylinder block and the radiator, so maintaining optimum engine operating temperature. A thermostat is also used in some air cleaners in which the temperature is regulated.

Thrust bearing The bearing in the clutch assembly that is moved in to the release levers by clutch pedal action to disengage the clutch. Also referred to as a release bearing.

Timing belt A toothed belt which drives the camshaft. Serious engine damage may result if it breaks in service.

Timing chain A chain which drives the camshaft.

Toe-in The amount the front wheels are closer together at the front than at the rear. On rear wheel drive vehicles, a slight amount of toe-in is usually specified to keep the front wheels running parallel on the road by offsetting other forces that tend to spread the wheels apart.

Toe-out The amount the front wheels are closer together at the rear than at the front. On front wheel drive vehicles, a slight amount of toe-out is usually specified.

Tools For full information on choosing and using tools, refer to the *Haynes Automotive Tools Manual*.

Tracer A stripe of a second colour applied to a wire insulator to distinguish that wire from another one with the same colour insulator.

Tune-up A process of accurate and careful adjustments and parts replacement to obtain the best possible engine performance.

Turbocharger A centrifugal device, driven by exhaust gases, that pressurises the intake air. Normally used to increase the power output from a given engine displacement, but can also be used primarily to reduce exhaust emissions (as on VW's "Umwelt" Diesel engine).

U

Universal joint or U-joint A double-pivoted connection for transmitting power from a driving to a driven shaft through an angle. A U-joint consists of two Y-shaped yokes and a cross-shaped member called the spider.

V

Valve A device through which the flow of liquid, gas, vacuum, or loose material in bulk may be started, stopped, or regulated by a movable part that opens, shuts, or partially obstructs one or more ports or passageways. A valve is also the movable part of such a device.

Valve clearance The clearance between the valve tip (the end of the valve stem) and the rocker arm or tappet. The valve clearance is measured when the valve is closed.

Vernier caliper A precision measuring instrument that measures inside and outside dimensions. Not quite as accurate as a micrometer, but more convenient.

Viscosity The thickness of a liquid or its resistance to flow.

Volt A unit for expressing electrical "pressure" in a circuit. One volt that will produce a current of one ampere through a resistance of one ohm.

W

Welding Various processes used to join metal items by heating the areas to be joined to a molten state and fusing them together. For more information refer to the *Haynes Automotive Welding Manual*.

Wiring diagram A drawing portraying the components and wires in a vehicle's electrical system, using standardised symbols. For more information refer to the *Haynes Automotive Electrical and Electronic Systems Manual*.

Note : *References throughout this index are in the form - " **Chapter number** " • " **Page number** "*

Preserving Our Motoring Heritage

< *The Model J Duesenberg Derham Tourster. Only eight of these magnificent cars were ever built – this is the only example to be found outside the United States of America*

Almost every car you've ever loved, loathed or desired is gathered under one roof at the Haynes Motor Museum. Over 300 immaculately presented cars and motorbikes represent every aspect of our motoring heritage, from elegant reminders of bygone days, such as the superb Model J Duesenberg to curiosities like the bug-eyed BMW Isetta. There are also many old friends and flames. Perhaps you remember the 1959 Ford Popular that you did your courting in? The magnificent 'Red Collection' is a spectacle of classic sports cars including AC, Alfa Romeo, Austin Healey, Ferrari, Lamborghini, Maserati, MG, Riley, Porsche and Triumph.

A Perfect Day Out

Each and every vehicle at the Haynes Motor Museum has played its part in the history and culture of Motoring. Today, they make a wonderful spectacle and a great day out for all the family. Bring the kids, bring Mum and Dad, but above all bring your camera to capture those golden memories for ever. You will also find an impressive array of motoring memorabilia, a comfortable 70 seat video cinema and one of the most extensive transport book shops in Britain. The Pit Stop Cafe serves everything from a cup of tea to wholesome, home-made meals or, if you prefer, you can enjoy the large picnic area nestled in the beautiful rural surroundings of Somerset.

> *John Haynes O.B.E., Founder and Chairman of the museum at the wheel of a Haynes Light 12.*

< *Graham Hill's Lola Cosworth Formula 1 car next to a 1934 Riley Sports.*

The Museum is situated on the A359 Yeovil to Frome road at Sparkford, just off the A303 in Somerset. It is about 40 miles south of Bristol, and 25 minutes drive from the M5 intersection at Taunton.
Open 9.30am - 5.30pm (10.00am - 4.00pm Winter) 7 days a week, *except Christmas Day, Boxing Day and New Years Day*
Special rates available for schools, coach parties and outings Charitable Trust No. 292048